Market!

W9-AKX-420

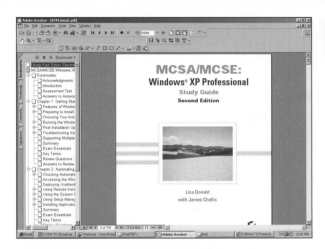

Search through the complete book in PDF!

- Access the entire *MCSA/MCSE: Windows XP Professional Study Guide*, Second Edition, complete with figures and tables, in electronic format.

- Search the *MCSA/MCSE: Windows XP Professional Study Guide*, Second Edition, chapters to find information on any topic in seconds.

- Look up any Key Term, along with other general terms, in the Glossary.

Use the Electronic Flashcards for PCs or Palm devices to jog your memory and prep last-minute for the exam!

- Reinforce your understanding of key concepts with these hardcore flashcard-style questions.

- Download the Flashcards to your Palm device, and go on the road. Now you can study anywhere, any time.

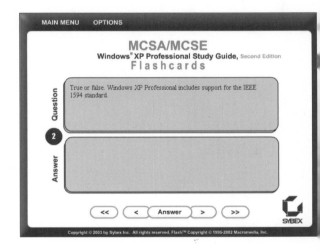

Prepare for Microsoft's tough simulation questions with the WinSim XP program!

- Use the simulators to guide you through real-world tasks step-by-step, or watch the movies to see the "invisible hand" perform the tasks for you.

MCSA/MCSE:
Windows XP Professional
Study Guide
Second Edition

MCSA/MCSE:
Windows® XP Professional
Study Guide
Second Edition

Lisa Donald

with James Chellis

San Francisco • London

Associate Publisher: Neil Edde
Acquisitions and Developmental Editor: Jeff Kellum
Production Editor: Lori Newman
Technical Editor: Warren Wyrostek
Copyeditor: Suzanne Goraj
Compositor: Interactive Composition Corporation
Graphic Illustrator: Interactive Composition Corporation
CD Coordinator: Dan Mummert
CD Technician: Kevin Ly
Proofreaders: Emily Hsuan, Darcey Maurer, Laurie O'Connell, Nancy Riddiough, Monique van den Berg
Indexer: Jack Lewis
Book Designer: Bill Gibson
Cover Designer: Archer Design
Cover Photographer: Colin Paterson, PhotoDisc

Library of Congress Card Number: 2003101650

ISBN: 0-7821-4241-9

SYBEX

To Our Valued Readers:

Thank you for looking to Sybex for your Microsoft certification exam prep needs. We at Sybex are proud of the reputation we've established for providing certification candidates with the practical knowledge and skills needed to succeed in the highly competitive IT marketplace.

With its release of Windows Server 2003, and the revised MCSA and MCSE tracks, Microsoft has raised the bar for IT certifications yet again. The new programs better reflect the skill set demanded of IT administrators in today's marketplace and offers candidates a clearer structure for acquiring the skills necessary to advance their careers.

Sybex is proud to have helped thousands of Microsoft certification candidates prepare for their exams over the years, and we are excited about the opportunity to continue to provide computer and networking professionals with the skills they'll need to succeed in the highly competitive IT industry.

The authors and editors have worked hard to ensure that the Study Guide you hold in your hand is comprehensive, in-depth, and pedagogically sound. We're confident that this book will exceed the demanding standards of the certification marketplace and help you, the Microsoft certification candidate, succeed in your endeavors.

As always, your feedback is important to us. Please send comments, questions, or suggestions to support@sybex.com. At Sybex we're continually striving to meet the needs of individuals preparing for IT certification exams.

Good luck in pursuit of your Microsoft certification!

Neil Edde
Associate Publisher—Certification
Sybex, Inc.

Software License Agreement: Terms and Conditions

For Katie, my sunshine

Acknowledgments

Writing a book is a team effort. The following people made it possible.

Huge thanks go out to Suzanne Goraj, who worked as the editor for this book; she put in countless hours, was highly detail oriented, and did a tremendous job. Lori Newman, the production editor, somehow managed to keep this project on track, which was not always an easy task, while at the same time always being wonderful to work with. Warren Wyrostek worked as the technical editor. He did a great job of keeping me honest and minimizing any errors within the book.

Thanks to James Chellis for allowing me to work on the MCSE series. Neil Edde, the associate publisher for this series, has nurtured the MCSE series since the early days. Jeff Kellum, the acquisitions and developmental editor, helped get the book going in the early stages.

Any errors missed by the editor and technical editors were caught by the book's proofreaders: Emily Hsuan, Darcey Maurer, Laurie O'Connell, Nancy Riddiough, and Monique van den Berg. Interactive Composition Corporation developed the artwork from my drawings and worked as the electronic publishing specialist. Dan Mummert and Kevin Ly managed and created content for the accompanying CD. Tanner Clayton and Matthew Sheltz helped create the CD exercises and test engine and were highly appreciated when the crunch time came. Without the great work of the team, this book would not have been possible.

On the local front, I'd like to thank my family and friends for their support. As always, Kevin and Katie for just being themselves. Thanks to my mom and dad for their emotional support. And finally Dietrich, who is always as adventure.

Contents at a Glance

Contents

Table of Exercises

Introduction

Microsoft's Microsoft Certified Systems Administrator (MCSA) and Microsoft Certified Systems Engineer (MCSE) tracks for Windows 2000 and Windows Server 2003 are the premier certifications for computer industry professionals. Covering the core technologies around which Microsoft's future will be built, these programs are powerful credentials for career advancement.

This book has been developed to give you the critical skills and knowledge you need to prepare for one of the core requirements of both the MCSA and MCSE certifications, in either the Windows 2000 or the new Windows Server 2003 tracks: *Installing, Configuring, and Administering Microsoft Windows XP Professional* (Exam 70-270).

The Microsoft Certified Professional Program

Since the inception of its certification program, Microsoft has certified almost 1.5 million people. As the computer network industry increases in both size and complexity, this number is sure to grow—and the need for *proven* ability will also increase. Companies rely on certifications to verify the skills of prospective employees and contractors.

Microsoft has developed its Microsoft Certified Professional (MCP) program to give you credentials that verify your ability to work with Microsoft products effectively and professionally. Obtaining your MCP certification requires that you pass any one Microsoft certification exam. Several levels of certification are available based on specific suites of exams. Depending on your areas of interest or experience, you can obtain any of the following MCP credentials:

Microsoft Certified System Administrator (MCSA) on Windows 2000 or Windows Server 2003 The MCSA certification is the latest certification track from Microsoft. This certification targets system and network administrators with roughly 6 to 12 months of desktop and network administration experience. The MCSA can be considered the entry-level certification. You must take and pass a total of four exams to obtain your MCSA. Or, if you are an MCSA on Windows 2000, you can take one Upgrade exam to obtain your MCSA on Windows Server 2003.

Microsoft Certified System Engineer (MCSE) on Windows 2000 or Windows Server 2003 This certification track is designed for network and systems administrators, network and systems analysts, and technical consultants who work with Microsoft Windows 2000 Professional and Server and/or Windows XP and Server 2003 software. You must take and pass seven exams to obtain your MCSE. Or, if you are an MCSE on Windows 2000, you can take two Upgrade exams to obtain your MCSE on Windows Server 2003.

MCSE versus MCSA

In an effort to provide those just starting off in the IT world a chance to prove their skills, Microsoft introduced its Microsoft Certified System Administrator (MCSA) program.

Targeted at those with less than a year's experience, the MCSA program focuses primarily on the administration portion of an IT professional's duties. Therefore, the Windows 2000, XP, and Server 2003 exams can be used for both the MCSA and MCSE programs.

Of course, it should be any MCSA's goal to eventually obtain his or her MCSE. However, don't assume that, because the MCSA has to take two exams that also satisfy an MCSE requirement, the two programs are similar. An MCSE must also know how to design a network. Beyond these two exams, the remaining MCSE required exams require the candidate to have much more hands-on experience.

Microsoft Certified Application Developer (MCAD) This track is designed for application developers and technical consultants who primarily use Microsoft development tools. Currently, you can take exams on Visual Basic .NET or Visual C# .NET. You must take and pass three exams to obtain your MCAD.

Microsoft Certified Solution Developer (MCSD) This track is designed for software engineers and developers and technical consultants who primarily use Microsoft development tools. Currently, you can take exams on Visual Basic .NET and Visual C# .NET. You must take and pass five exams to obtain your MCSD.

Microsoft Certified Database Administrator (MCDBA) This track is designed for database administrators, developers, and analysts who work with Microsoft SQL Server. As of this printing, you can take exams on either SQL Server 7 or SQL Server 2000. You must take and pass four exams to achieve MCDBA status.

Microsoft Certified Trainer (MCT) The MCT track is designed for any IT professional who develops and teaches Microsoft-approved courses. To become an MCT, you must first obtain your MCSE, MCSD, or MCDBA, then you must take a class at one of the Certified Technical Training Centers. You will also be required to prove your instructional ability. You can do this in various ways: by taking a skills-building or train-the-trainer class, by achieving certification as a trainer from any of several vendors, or by becoming a Certified Technical Trainer through CompTIA. Last of all, you will need to complete an MCT application.

How Do You Become Certified on Windows 2000 or Windows Server 2003?

Attaining an MCSA or MCSE certification has always been a challenge. In the past, students have been able to acquire detailed exam information—even most of the exam questions—from online "brain dumps" and third-party "cram" books or software products. For the new MCSE exams, this is simply not the case.

Microsoft has taken strong steps to protect the security and integrity of its certification tracks. Now prospective candidates must complete a course of study that develops detailed knowledge about a wide range of topics. It supplies them with the true skills needed, derived from working with Windows 2000, XP, Server 2003, and related software products.

The Windows 2000 and Server 2003 certification programs are heavily weighted toward hands-on skills and experience. Microsoft has stated that "nearly half of the core required exams' content demands that the candidate have troubleshooting skills acquired through hands-on experience and working knowledge."

Fortunately, if you are willing to dedicate the time and effort to learn Windows 2000, XP, and Server 2003, you can prepare yourself well for the exams by using the proper tools. By working through this book, you can successfully meet the exam requirements to pass the Windows XP Professional exam.

This book is part of a complete series of MCSA and MCSE Study Guides, published by Sybex Inc., that together cover the core MCSA and MCSE operating system requirements, as well as the Design requirements needed to complete your MCSE track. Please visit the Sybex web site at www.sybex.com for complete program and product details.

MCSA Exam Requirements

Candidates for MCSA certification on Windows 2000 or Windows Server 2003 must pass four exams.

 For a more detailed description of the Microsoft certification programs, including a list of all the exams, visit Microsoft's Training and Certification Web site at www.microsoft.com/traincert.

Windows 2000

For Windows 2000, you must take one of the following client operating system exams:

- Installing, Configuring, and Administering Microsoft Windows 2000 Professional (70-210)
- Installing, Configuring, and Administering Microsoft Windows XP Professional (70-270)

plus the following networking operating system exams:

- Installing, Configuring, and Administering Microsoft Windows 2000 Server (70-215)
- Managing a Microsoft Windows 2000 Network Environment (70-218)

plus one of a number of electives, including:

- Implementing and Supporting Microsoft Systems Management Server 2.0 (70-086)
- Implementing and Administering Security in a Microsoft Windows 2000 Network (20-214)
- Implementing and Administering a Microsoft Windows 2000 Network Infrastructure (70-216)
- Installing, Configuring, and Administering Microsoft Exchange 2000 Server (20-224)
- Installing, Configuring, and Administering Microsoft Internet Security and Acceleration (ISA) Server 2000, Enterprise Edition (70-227)

- Installing, Configuring, and Administering Microsoft SQL Server 2000 Enterprise Edition (70-228)
- Supporting and Maintaining a Microsoft Windows NT Server 4.0 Network (70-244)
- CompTIA's A+ and Network+ exams
- CompTIA's A+ and Server+ exams

Windows Server 2003

For Windows Server 2003, you must take one of the following client operating system exams:

- Installing, Configuring, and Administering Microsoft Windows 2000 Professional (70-210)
- Installing, Configuring, and Administering Microsoft Windows XP Professional (70-270)

plus the following networking operating system exams:

- Managing and Maintaining a Microsoft Windows Server 2003 Environment (70-290)
- Implementing, Managing, and Maintaining a Microsoft Windows Server 2003 Network Infrastructure (70-291)

plus one of a number of electives, including:

- Implementing and Supporting Microsoft Systems Management Server 2.0 (70-086)
- Installing, Configuring, and Administering Microsoft Internet Security and Acceleration (ISA) Server 2000, Enterprise Edition (70-227)
- Installing, Configuring, and Administering Microsoft SQL Server 2000 Enterprise Edition (70-228)
- CompTIA's A+ and Network+ exams
- CompTIA's A+ and Server+ exams

Also, if you are an MCSA on Windows 2000, you can take one Upgrade exam: Managing and Maintaining a Microsoft Windows Server 2003 Environment for an MCSA Certified on Windows 2000 (70-292).

MCSE Exam Requirements

Candidates for MCSE certification on Windows 2000 or Server 2003 must pass seven exams, including one client operating system exam, three networking operating system exams, one design exam, and two electives.

NOTE For a more detailed description of the Microsoft certification programs, visit Microsoft's Training and Certification Web site at www.microsoft.com/traincert.

Windows 2000

For Windows 2000, you must take one of the following client operating system exams:

- Installing, Configuring, and Administering Microsoft Windows 2000 Professional (70-210)
- Installing, Configuring, and Administering Microsoft Windows XP Professional (70-270)

plus the following networking operating system exams:

- Installing, Configuring, and Administering Microsoft Windows 2000 Server (70-215)
- Implementing and Administering a Microsoft Windows 2000 Network Infrastructure (70-216)
- Implementing and Administering a Microsoft Windows 2000 Directory Services Infrastructure (70-217)

plus one of the following Design exams:

- Designing a Microsoft Windows 2000 Directory Services Infrastructure (70-219)
- Designing Security for a Microsoft Windows 2000 Network (70-220)
- Designing a Microsoft Windows 2000 Network Infrastructure (70-221)
- Designing Highly Available Web Solutions with Microsoft Windows 2000 Server Technologies (70-226)

plus two of any of a number of electives, including:

- Implementing and Supporting Microsoft Systems Management Server 2.0 (70-086)
- Implementing and Administering Security in a Microsoft Windows 2000 Network (70-214)
- Managing a Microsoft Windows 2000 Network Environment (70-218)
- Migrating from Microsoft Windows NT 4.0 to Microsoft Windows 2000 (70-222)
- Installing, Configuring, and Administering Microsoft Exchange 2000 Server (70-224)
- Installing, Configuring, and Administering Microsoft Internet Security and Acceleration (ISA) Server 2000, Enterprise Edition (70-227)
- Installing, Configuring, and Administering Microsoft SQL Server 2000 Enterprise Edition (70-228)
- Designing and Implementing Databases with Microsoft SQL Server 2000 Enterprise Edition (70-229)
- Supporting and Maintaining a Microsoft Windows NT Server 4.0 Network (70-244)
- Any Design exam not taken as a requirement

Windows Server 2003

For Windows Server 2003, you must take one of the following client operating system exams:

- Installing, Configuring, and Administering Microsoft Windows 2000 Professional (70-210)
- Installing, Configuring, and Administering Microsoft Windows XP Professional (70-270)

plus the following networking operating system exams:

- Managing and Maintaining a Microsoft Windows Server 2003 Environment (70-290)
- Implementing, Managing, and Maintaining a Microsoft Windows Server 2003 Network Infrastructure (70-291)

- Planning and Maintaining a Microsoft Windows Server 2003 Network Infrastructure (70-293)
- Planning, Implementing, and Maintaining a Microsoft Windows Server 2003 Active Directory Infrastructure (70-294)

plus one of the following Design exams:

- Designing a Microsoft Windows Server 2003 Active Directory and Network Infrastructure (70-297)
- Designing Security for a Microsoft Windows Server 2003 Network 2000 Server Technologies (70-298)

plus one of a number of electives, including:

- Implementing and Supporting Microsoft Systems Management Server 2.0 (70-086)
- Installing, Configuring, and Administering Microsoft Internet Security and Acceleration (ISA) Server 2000, Enterprise Edition (70-227)
- Installing, Configuring, and Administering Microsoft SQL Server 2000 Enterprise Edition (70-228)
- Designing and Implementing Databases with Microsoft SQL Server 2000 Enterprise Edition (70-229)
- The Design exam not taken as a requirement

Also, if you are an MCSE on Windows 2000, you can take two Upgrade exams: Managing and Maintaining a Microsoft Windows Server 2003 Environment for an MCSA Certified on Windows 2000 and Planning, Implementing, and Maintaining a Microsoft Windows Server 2003 Environment for an MCSE Certified on Windows 2000.

Windows 2000 and Windows 2003 Certification

Microsoft recently announced that they will distinguish between Windows 2000 and Windows Server 2003 certifications. Those who have their MCSA or MCSE certification in Windows 2000 will be referred to as "certified on Windows 2000." When Microsoft releases the exams for Windows Server 2003 (expected in the Summer/Fall of 2003) those who obtained their MCSA or MCSE in the Windows Server 2003 will be referred to as "certified on Windows Server 2003."

If you are certified in Windows 2000, you can take either one Upgrade exam (for MCSA) or two Upgrade exams (for MCSE) to obtain your certification on Windows 2003.

Microsoft also introduced a more clear distinction between the MCSA and MCSE certifications, by more sharply focusing each certification. In the new Windows 2003 track, the objectives covered by the MCSA exams relate primarily to administrative tasks. The exams that relate specifically to the MCSE, however, deal mostly with design-level concepts. So, MCSA job tasks are considered to be more "hands-on", while the MCSE job tasks involve more strategic concerns of design and planning.

The *Installing, Configuring, and Administering Microsoft Windows XP Professional* Exam

The Windows XP Professional exam covers concepts and skills related to installing, configuring, and managing Windows XP Professional computers. It emphasizes the following elements of Windows XP Professional support:

- Installing Windows XP Professional
- Implementing and administering resources
- Implementing, managing, and troubleshooting hardware devices and drivers
- Monitoring and optimizing system performance and reliability
- Configuring and troubleshooting the Desktop environment
- Implementing, managing, and troubleshooting network protocols and services
- Implementing, monitoring, and troubleshooting security

This exam is quite specific regarding Windows XP Professional requirements and operational settings, and it can be particular about how administrative tasks are performed within the operating system. It also focuses on fundamental concepts of Windows XP Professional's operation. Careful study of this book, along with hands-on experience, will help you prepare for this exam.

Microsoft provides exam objectives to give you a general overview of possible areas of coverage on the Microsoft exams. Keep in mind, however, that exam objectives are subject to change at any time without prior notice and at Microsoft's sole discretion. Please visit Microsoft's Training and Certification Web site (www.microsoft.com/traincert) for the most current listing of exam objectives.

Types of Exam Questions

In an effort to both refine the testing process and protect the quality of its certifications, Microsoft has focused its Windows 2000, XP, and Server 2003 exams on real experience and hands-on proficiency. There is a greater emphasis on your past working environments and responsibilities, and less emphasis on how well you can memorize. In fact, Microsoft says an MCSE candidate should have at least one year of hands-on experience.

Microsoft will accomplish its goal of protecting the exams' integrity by regularly adding and removing exam questions, limiting the number of questions that any individual sees in a beta exam, limiting the number of questions delivered to an individual by using adaptive testing, and adding new exam elements.

Exam questions may be in a variety of formats: Depending on which exam you take, you'll see multiple-choice questions, as well as select-and-place and prioritize-a-list questions. Simulations and case study–based formats are included as well. You may also find yourself taking what's called an *adaptive format exam*. Let's take a look at the types of exam questions and examine the adaptive testing technique, so you'll be prepared for all of the possibilities.

With the release of Windows 2000, Microsoft has stopped providing a detailed score breakdown. This is mostly because of the various and complex question formats. Previously, each question focused on one objective. The Windows 2000, XP, and Server 2003 exams, however, contain questions that may be tied to one or more objectives from one or more objective sets. Therefore, grading by objective is almost impossible. Also, Microsoft no longer offers a score. Now you will only be told if you pass or fail.

MULTIPLE-CHOICE QUESTIONS

Multiple-choice questions come in two main forms. One is a straightforward question followed by several possible answers, of which one or more is correct. The other type of multiple-choice question is more complex and based on a specific scenario. The scenario may focus on several areas or objectives.

SELECT-AND-PLACE QUESTIONS

Select-and-place exam questions involve graphical elements that you must manipulate to successfully answer the question. For example, you might see a diagram of a computer network, as shown in the following graphic taken from the select-and-place demo downloaded from Microsoft's Web site.

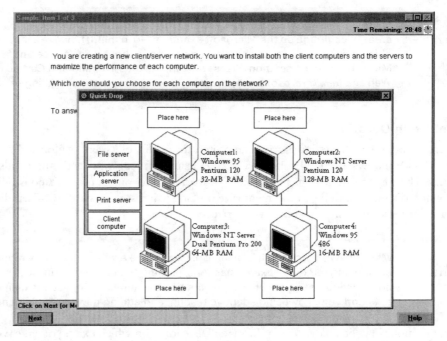

A typical diagram will show computers and other components next to boxes that contain the text "Place here." The labels for the boxes represent various computer roles on a network, such as a print server and a file server. Based on information given for each computer, you are asked to select each label and place it in the correct box. You need to place *all* of the labels correctly. No credit is given for the question if you correctly label only some of the boxes.

In another select-and-place problem you might be asked to put a series of steps in order, by dragging items from boxes on the left to boxes on the right, and placing them in the correct order. One other type requires that you drag an item from the left and place it under an item in a column on the right.

For more information on the various exam question types, go to www.microsoft .com/traincert/mcpexams/policies/innovations.asp.

SIMULATIONS

Simulations are the kinds of questions that most closely represent actual situations and test the skills you use while working with Microsoft software interfaces. These exam questions include a mock interface on which you are asked to perform certain actions according to a given scenario. The simulated interfaces look nearly identical to what you see in the actual product, as shown in this example:

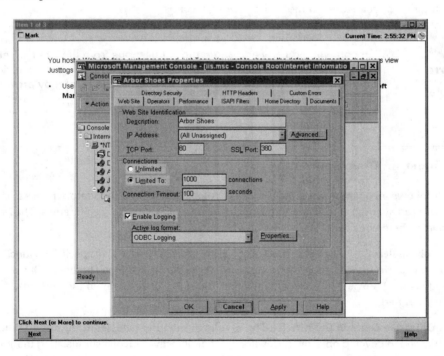

Because of the number of possible errors that can be made on simulations, be sure to consider the following recommendations from Microsoft:

- Do not change any simulation settings that don't pertain to the solution directly.
- When related information has not been provided, assume that the default settings are used.

- Make sure that your entries are spelled correctly.
- Close all the simulation application windows after completing the set of tasks in the simulation.

The best way to prepare for simulation questions is to spend time working with the graphical interface of the product on which you will be tested.

We recommend that you study with the WinSim XP product, which is included on the CD that accompanies this Study Guide. By completing the exercises in this Study Guide and working with the WinSim XP software, you will greatly improve your level of preparation for simulation questions.

CASE STUDY–BASED QUESTIONS

Case study–based questions first appeared in the MCSD program. These questions present a scenario with a range of requirements. Based on the information provided, you answer a series of multiple-choice and select-and-place questions. The interface for case study–based questions has a number of tabs, each of which contains information about the scenario. At present, this type of question appears only in most of the Design exams.

Microsoft will regularly add and remove questions from the exams. This is called *item seeding*. It is part of the effort to make it more difficult for individuals to merely memorize exam questions that were passed along by previous test-takers.

Exam Question Development

Microsoft follows an exam-development process consisting of eight mandatory phases. The process takes an average of seven months and involves more than 150 specific steps. The MCP exam development consists of the following phases:

Phase 1: Job Analysis Phase 1 is an analysis of all the tasks that make up a specific job function, based on tasks performed by people who are currently performing that job function. This phase also identifies the knowledge, skills, and abilities that relate specifically to the performance area being certified.

Phase 2: Objective Domain Definition The results of the job analysis phase provide the framework used to develop objectives. Development of objectives involves translating the job-function tasks into a comprehensive package of specific and measurable knowledge, skills, and abilities. The resulting list of objectives—the *objective domain*—is the basis for the development of both the certification exams and the training materials.

Phase 3: Blueprint Survey   The final objective domain is transformed into a blueprint survey in which contributors are asked to rate each objective. These contributors may be MCP candidates, appropriately skilled exam-development volunteers, or Microsoft employees. Based on the contributors' input, the objectives are prioritized and weighted. The actual exam items are written according to the prioritized objectives. Contributors are queried about how they spend their time on the job. If a contributor doesn't spend an adequate amount of time actually performing the specified job function, his or her data are eliminated from the analysis. The blueprint survey phase helps determine which objectives to measure, as well as the appropriate number and types of items to include on the exam.

Phase 4: Item Development   A pool of items is developed to measure the blueprinted objective domain. The number and types of items to be written are based on the results of the blueprint survey.

Phase 5: Alpha Review and Item Revision   During this phase, a panel of technical and job-function experts reviews each item for technical accuracy. The panel then answers each item and reaches a consensus on all technical issues. Once the items have been verified as being technically accurate, they are edited to ensure that they are expressed in the clearest language possible.

Phase 6: Beta Exam   The reviewed and edited items are collected into beta exams. Based on the responses of all beta participants, Microsoft performs a statistical analysis to verify the validity of the exam items and to determine which items will be used in the certification exam. Once the analysis has been completed, the items are distributed into multiple parallel forms, or *versions*, of the final certification exam.

Phase 7: Item Selection and Cut-Score Setting   The results of the beta exams are analyzed to determine which items will be included in the certification exam. This determination is based on many factors, including item difficulty and relevance. During this phase, a panel of job-function experts determines the *cut score* (minimum passing score) for the exams. The cut score differs from exam to exam because it is based on an item-by-item determination of the percentage of candidates who answered the item correctly and who would be expected to answer the item correctly.

Phase 8: Live Exam   In the final phase, the exams are given to candidates. MCP exams are administered by Prometric and Virtual University Enterprises (VUE).

Tips for Taking the Windows XP Professional Exam

Here are some general tips for achieving success on your certification exam:

- Arrive early at the exam center so that you can relax and review your study materials. During this final review, you can look over tables and lists of exam-related information.

- Read the questions carefully. Don't be tempted to jump to an early conclusion. Make sure you know *exactly* what the question is asking.

- Answer all questions. Remember that the adaptive format does *not* allow you to return to a question. Be very careful before entering your answer. Because your exam may be shortened by correct answers (and lengthened by incorrect answers), there is no advantage to rushing through questions.

- On simulations, do not change settings that are not directly related to the question. Also, assume default settings if the question does not specify or imply which settings are used.

- For questions you're not sure about, use a process of elimination to get rid of the obviously incorrect answers first. This improves your odds of selecting the correct answer when you need to make an educated guess.

Exam Registration

You may take the Microsoft exams at any of more than 1000 Authorized Prometric Testing Centers (APTCs) and VUE Testing Centers around the world. For the location of a testing center near you, call Prometric at 800-755-EXAM (755-3926), or call VUE at 888-837-8616. Outside the United States and Canada, contact your local Prometric or VUE registration center.

Find out the number of the exam you want to take, and then register with the Prometric or VUE registration center nearest to you. At this point, you will be asked for advance payment for the exam. The exams are $125 each and you must take them within one year of payment. You can schedule exams up to six weeks in advance or as late as one working day prior to the date of the exam. You can cancel or reschedule your exam if you contact the center at least two working days prior to the exam. Same-day registration is available in some locations, subject to space availability. Where same-day registration is available, you must register a minimum of two hours before test time.

You may also register for your exams online at www.prometric.com or www.vue.com.

When you schedule the exam, you will be provided with instructions regarding appointment and cancellation procedures, ID requirements, and information about the testing center location. In addition, you will receive a registration and payment confirmation letter from Prometric or VUE.

Microsoft requires certification candidates to accept the terms of a Non-Disclosure Agreement before taking certification exams.

Is This Book for You?

If you want to acquire a solid foundation in Windows XP Professional, and your goal is to prepare for the exam by learning how to use and manage the new operating system, this book is for you. You'll find clear explanations of the fundamental concepts you need to grasp, and plenty of help to achieve the high level of professional competency you need to succeed in your chosen field.

If you want to become certified as an MCSE or MCSA, this book is definitely for you. However, if you just want to attempt to pass the exam without really understanding Windows XP, this Study Guide is *not* for you. It is written for people who want to acquire hands-on skills and in-depth knowledge of Windows XP.

What's in the Book?

What makes a Sybex Study Guide the book of choice for over 100,000 MCPs? We took into account not only what you need to know to pass the exam, but what you need to know to take what you've learned and apply it in the real world. Each book contains the following:

Objective-by-objective coverage of the topics you need to know   Each chapter lists the objectives covered in that chapter.

> The topics covered in this Study Guide map directly to Microsoft's official exam objectives. Each exam objective is covered completely.

Assessment Test   Directly following this introduction is an Assessment Test that you should take. It is designed to help you determine how much you already know about Windows XP. Each question is tied to a topic discussed in the book. Using the results of the Assessment Test, you can figure out the areas where you need to focus your study. Of course, we do recommend you read the entire book.

Exam Essentials   To highlight what you learn, you'll find a list of Exam Essentials at the end of each chapter. The Exam Essentials section briefly highlights the topics that need your particular attention as you prepare for the exam.

Key Terms and Glossary   Throughout each chapter, you will be introduced to important terms and concepts that you will need to know for the exam. These terms appear in italic within the chapters, and a list of the Key Terms appears just after the Exam Essentials. At the end of the book, a detailed Glossary gives definitions for these terms, as well as other general terms you should know.

Review questions, complete with detailed explanations   Each chapter is followed by a set of Review Questions that test what you learned in the chapter. The questions are written with the exam in mind, meaning that they are designed to have the same look and feel as what you'll see on the exam. Question types are just like the exam, including multiple choice, exhibits, and select-and-place.

Hands-on exercises   In each chapter, you'll find exercises designed to give you the important hands-on experience that is critical for your exam preparation. The exercises support the topics of the chapter, and they walk you through the steps necessary to perform a particular function.

Real World Scenarios   Because reading a book isn't enough for you to learn how to apply these topics in your everyday duties, we have provided Real World Scenarios in special sidebars. These explain when and why a particular solution would make sense, in a working environment you'd actually encounter.

Interactive CD   Every Sybex Study Guide comes with a CD complete with additional questions, flashcards for use with an interactive device, a Windows simulation program, and the book in electronic format. Details are in the following section.

What's on the CD?

With this new member of our best-selling MCSE Study Guide series, we are including quite an array of training resources. The CD offers numerous simulations, bonus exams, and flashcards to help you study for the exam. We have also included the complete contents of the Study Guide in electronic form. The CD's resources are described here:

The Sybex E-book for Windows XP Professional   Many people like the convenience of being able to carry their whole Study Guide on a CD. They also like being able to search the text via computer to find specific information quickly and easily. For these reasons, the entire contents of this Study Guide are supplied on the CD, in PDF. We've also included Adobe Acrobat Reader, which provides the interface for the PDF contents as well as the search capabilities.

WinSim XP   We developed the WinSim XP product to allow you to experience the multimedia and interactive operation of working with Windows XP Professional. WinSim XP provides both audio/video files and hands-on experience with key features of Windows XP Professional. Built around the Study Guide's exercises, WinSim XP will help you attain the knowledge and hands-on skills you must have in order to understand Windows XP Professional (and pass the exam). Here is a sample screen from WinSim XP:

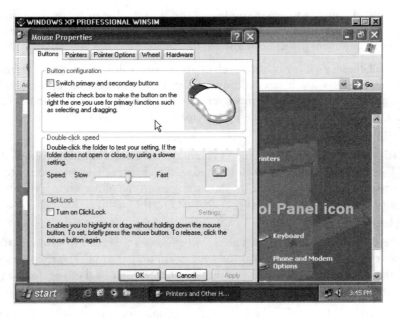

The Sybex MCSE Test Engine   This is a collection of multiple-choice questions that will help you prepare for your exam. There are four sets of questions:

- Two bonus exams designed to simulate the actual live exam.
- All the questions from the Study Guide, presented in a test engine for your review. You can review questions by chapter or by objective, or you can take a random test.
- The Assessment Test.

Here is a sample screen from the Sybex MCSE Test Engine:

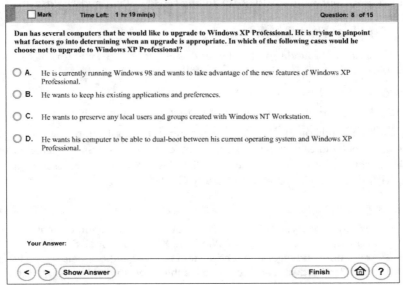

Sybex MCSE Flashcards for PCs and Handheld Devices   The "flashcard" style of question offers an effective way to quickly and efficiently test your understanding of the fundamental concepts covered in the exam. The Sybex MCSE Flashcards set consists of more than 150 questions presented in a special engine developed specifically for this Study Guide series. Here's what the Sybex MCSE Flashcards interface looks like:

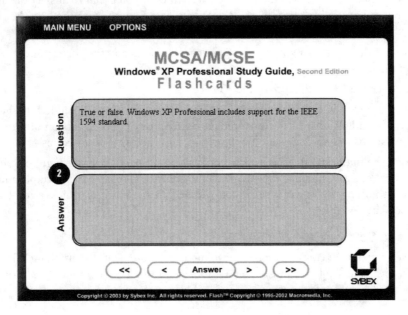

Because of the high demand for a product that will run on handheld devices, we have also developed, in conjunction with Land-J Technologies, a version of the flashcard questions that you can take with you on your Palm OS PDA (including the PalmPilot and Handspring's Visor).

How Do You Use This Book?

This book provides a solid foundation for the serious effort of preparing for the exam. To best benefit from this book, you may wish to use the following study method:

1. Take the Assessment Test to identify your weak areas.
2. Study each chapter carefully. Do your best to fully understand the information.
3. Complete all the hands-on exercises in the chapter, referring back to the text as necessary so that you understand each step you take. If you don't have access to a lab environment in which you can complete the exercises, install and work with the exercises available in the WinSim XP software included with this Study Guide.

> To do the exercises in this book, your hardware should meet the minimum hardware requirements for Windows XP Professional. See Chapter 1 for the minimum and recommended system requirements, or below for a list of recommended hardware and software we think you should have in your home lab.

4. Read over the Real World Scenarios to improve your understanding of how to use what you learn in the book.
5. Study the Exam Essentials and Key Terms to make sure you are familiar with the areas you need to focus on.
6. Answer the review questions at the end of each chapter. If you prefer to answer the questions in a timed and graded format, install the Sybex Test Engine from the book's CD and answer the chapter questions there instead of in the book.
7. Take note of the questions you did not understand, and study the corresponding sections of the book again.
8. Go back over the Exam Essentials and Key Terms.
9. Go through the Study Guide's other training resources, which are included on the book's CD. These include WinSim XP, electronic flashcards, the electronic version of the chapter review questions (try taking them by objective), and the two bonus exams.

To learn all the material covered in this book, you will need to study regularly and with discipline. Try to set aside the same time every day to study, and select a comfortable and quiet place in which to do it. If you work hard, you will be surprised at how quickly you learn this material. Good luck!

Hardware and Software Requirements

You should verify that your computer meets the minimum requirements for installing Windows XP Professional as listed in Table 1.1 in Chapter 1. We suggest that your computer meets or exceeds the recommended requirements for a more enjoyable experience.

The exercises in this book assume that your computer is configured in a specific manner. Your computer should have at least a 3GB drive that is configured with the minimum space requirements and partitions. Other exercises in this book assume that your computer is configured as follows:

- 2GB (about 2000MB) C: primary partition with the FAT file system
- 500MB D: extended partition with the FAT file system
- 500MB of free space

Of course, you can allocate more space to your partitions if it is available.

The first exercise in the book assumes that you are performing a clean installation and not an upgrade. Your partitions should be created and formatted as previously specified.

Contacts and Resources

To find out more about Microsoft Education and Certification materials and programs, to register with Prometric or VUE, or to obtain other useful certification information and additional study resources, check the following resources:

Microsoft Training and Certification Home Page

www.microsoft.com/traincert

This Web site provides information about the MCP program and exams. You can also order the latest Microsoft Roadmap to Education and Certification.

Microsoft TechNet Technical Information Network

www.microsoft.com/technet

800-344-2121

Use this Web site or phone number to contact support professionals and system administrators. Outside the United States and Canada, contact your local Microsoft subsidiary for information.

PalmPilot Training Product Development: Land-J

www.land-j.com

407-359-2217

Land-J Technologies is a consulting and programming business currently specializing in application development for the 3Com PalmPilot Personal Digital Assistant. Land-J developed the Palm version of the EdgeTests, which is included on the CD that accompanies this Study Guide.

Prometric

www.prometric.com

800-755-3936

Contact Prometric to register to take an MCP exam at any of more than 800 Prometric Testing Centers around the world.

Virtual University Enterprises (VUE)

www.vue.com

888-837-8616

Contact the VUE registration center to register to take an MCP exam at one of the VUE Testing Centers.

MCP Magazine Online

www.mcpmag.com

Microsoft Certified Professional Magazine is a well-respected publication that focuses on Windows certification. This site hosts chats and discussion forums, and tracks news related to the MCSE program. Some of the services cost a fee, but they are well worth it.

Windows & .NET Magazine

www.windows2000mag.com

You can subscribe to this magazine or read free articles at the Web site. The study resource provides general information on Windows 2000, XP, and .NET Server.

Cramsession on Brainbuzz.com

cramsession.brainbuzz.com

Cramsession is an online community focusing on all IT certification programs. In addition to discussion boards and job locators, you can download one of several free cram sessions, which are nice supplements to any study approach you take.

Assessment Test

1. What extension is applied by default to custom consoles that are created for the MMC?

   A. .mmc

   B. .msc

   C. .con

   D. .mcn

2. You want to create roaming profiles for users in the Sales department. They frequently log on at computers in a central area. The profiles should be configured as mandatory and roaming profiles. Which users are able to manage mandatory profiles on Windows XP Professional computers?

   A. The user who uses the profile

   B. Server Operators

   C. Power Users

   D. Administrators

3. You want to monitor the CPU, memory, and disk usage on your computer to ensure that there are no bottlenecks. Which MMC snap-in would you load to access System Monitor?

   A. System Monitor

   B. Performance Monitor

   C. ActiveX Control

   D. Performance Logs and Alerts

4. If you wanted only users with valid usernames and passwords to have access to a specific resource, to which of the following groups would you assign permissions?

   A. Domain Users

   B. Users

   C. Everyone

   D. Authenticated Users

5. You want to install several computers through unattended installation. Which of the following options cannot be configured as a part of an answer file?

   A. Display settings

   B. Network settings

   C. Time zone

   D. Screen saver

6. Which of the following print permissions are applied to the members of the Power Users group by default on shared Windows XP Professional printers? (Choose all that apply.)

   A. No permissions are granted automatically.

   B. Print.

   C. Manage Printers.

   D. Manage Documents.

7. You have a user with limited vision. Which accessibility utility is used to read aloud screen text, such as the text in dialog boxes, menus, and buttons?

   A. Read-Aloud

   B. Orator

   C. Dialog Manager

   D. Narrator

8. You have just purchased a new computer that has Windows XP Professional preinstalled. You want to migrate existing users from your previous computer that was running Windows 2000 Professional. Which two files would you use to manage this process through the User State Migration Tool?

   A. usmt.exe

   B. ScanState.exe

   C. LoadState.exe

   D. xpMigrate.exe

9. You have scheduled a specific program that is required by the Accounting department to run as a scheduled task every day. When you log on as administrator, you can run the task, but when the scheduled task is supposed to run, it does not run properly. You have already verified that the Task Scheduler task is running. What else should you check?

   A. Verify that the task has been configured to run in unattended mode.

   B. Make sure the user who is scheduled to run the task has the appropriate permissions.

   C. Make sure that the time is properly synchronized on the computer.

   D. Verify that the Process Manager task is running.

10. What utility is used to set processor affinity if you have multiple processors installed on your Windows XP Professional computer?

   A. Control Panel, Processors

   B. System Monitor

   C. System Manager

   D. Task Manager

11. You have a user, Jan, who travels between Germany and the U.S. Jan wants to use a German interface for Windows XP Professional when in Germany, and an English interface for Windows XP Professional when in the U.S. Jan has a multilingual version of XP Professional. Where do you configure which language is used by the user interface?

A. Control Panel, Regional Options

B. Control Panel, Locale Settings

C. `Langsetup.exe`

D. `Muisetup.exe`

12. Susan is a member of the Sales and Managers groups. The Managers group has been allowed the Full Control permission to the `D:\DATA` folder. The Sales group has been allowed the Read & Execute permission to `D:\DATA` but has been denied the Full Control permission. What are Susan's effective rights?

A. Full Control

B. Read & Execute

C. Read

D. No permissions

13. You have an older network card that has a Windows XP driver available. Which utility can you use to install a non–Plug and Play network adapter in a Windows XP Professional computer?

A. Control Panel (Classic view), Network icon

B. Control Panel (Classic view), Network and Dial-up Connections icon

C. Control Panel (Classic view), Network Adapters icon

D. Control Panel (Classic view), Add Hardware icon

14. You want Linda to be able to create users and groups on your Windows XP Professional computer. Linda says she is not able to create new users after she logs on. When you change Linda's group memberships, which groups can you make her a member of to allow her the necessary permissions for creating new users? (Choose two answers.)

A. Admins

B. Administrators

C. Power Users

D. Server Operators

15. You have a user who has configured his Windows XP Professional computer to automatically store his password. You want to ensure that when he attaches to the network he is providing a valid password, and not using a stored password. Which of the following security options should you configure?

A. In Security Policy Options, configure Do Not Allow Use of Cached Credentials.

B. In Security Policy Options, configure Do Not Allow Stored User Names and Passwords to Save Passwords or Credentials for Network Authentication.

C. In the Local Users and Groups utility, configure Tools, Security to disallow the use of cached credentials.

D. In the Device Manager, configure Tools, Security to disallow the use of cached credentials.

16. Which separator page file would you use if you want to set up a separator page on a Windows XP Professional computer and you're using a PostScript print device that does not support dual-mode printing?

A. `pcl.sep`

B. `pscript.sep`

C. `sysprint.sep`

D. `sysprintj.sep`

17. Which option would you use if you wanted to access network files from your laptop while traveling and then have the file resynchronize with the network when you reattach the laptop to the network?

A. Synchronized folders

B. Managed folders

C. Roaming folders

D. Offline files and folders

18. You have a DNS server that contains corrupt information. You fix the problem with the DNS server, but one of your users is complaining that they are still unable to access Internet resources. You verify that everything works on another computer on the same subnet. Which command can you use to fix the problem?

A. `IPCONFIG /flush`

B. `IPCONFIG /flushdns`

C. `PING /flush`

D. `GROPE /flushdns`

19. What information must be configured on a VPN client so that it can access a VPN server? (Choose two answers.)

   A. IP address

   B. MAC address

   C. Domain name

   D. Connection address

20. Which of the following statements is true regarding the creation of a group?

   A. Only members of the Administrators group can create users on a Windows XP Professional computer.

   B. Group names can be up to 64 characters.

   C. Group names can contain spaces.

   D. Group names can be the same as usernames, but not the same as other group names on the computer.

21. You need to expand the disk space on your Windows XP Professional computer. You are considering using spanned volumes. Which of the following statements is/are true concerning spanned volumes? (Choose all that apply.)

   A. Spanned volumes can contain space from 2 to 32 physical drives.

   B. Spanned volumes can contain space from 2 to 24 physical drives.

   C. Spanned volumes can be formatted as FAT16, FAT32, or NTFS partitions.

   D. Spanned volumes can be formatted only as NTFS partitions.

22. Which of the following user rights is required to install computers through RIS? (Choose two answers.)

   A. Join a Computer to the Domain.

   B. Remotely Install Windows XP.

   C. Log On as a Batch Job.

   D. Authorize the RIS Server.

23. You have a third-party disk driver that is not on the Windows XP Professional CD. You need to be able to load this driver to successfully install Windows XP Professional. What process should you take during installation?

   A. Right before the installation goes to search for a suitable disk driver, press F6 when prompted to supply a third-party disk driver.

   B. Before the installation begins, create a folder called `\Windows\Drivers` and copy the third-party driver there.

   C. Before the installation begins, create a folder called `\Windows\OEM\$Drivers$` and copy the third-party driver there.

   D. When the installation prompts for additional drivers, press the Insert button and supply the third-party disk driver.

24. How do you start the Windows XP Recovery Console if you cannot start your Windows XP Professional operating system?

    A. Use the Windows XP Professional CD.

    B. Start it through WINNT32 /RC.

    C. Press F8 during the boot sequence.

    D. Boot with the Windows XP boot disk, then type `WINNT /CMDCONS`.

25. Which of the following will prevent a Windows XP Professional upgrade from successfully installing? (Choose all that apply.)

    A. A drive that was compressed with DoubleSpace

    B. A drive that was compressed with DriveSpace

    C. A computer that has only 64MB of RAM

    D. A computer that has only a Pentium 233MHz processor

26. You have a remote user who would like to be able to send print jobs to a network printer from an Internet connection using a URL. Which of the following protocols allows Windows XP to support this option?

    A. IPP

    B. RPP

    C. MPP

    D. IIP

27. How do you access advanced startup options in Windows XP during the boot process?

    A. Press the spacebar.

    B. Press F6.

    C. Press F8.

    D. Press F10.

28. You installed Windows XP Professional on 10 computers in the Sales department. After 30 days, the computers stopped working and will no longer boot to Windows XP Professional. What is the most likely problem?

    A. The computers have not had product activation completed, and need to be activated.

    B. You have a virus and need to run the latest virus scanning and cleanup software.

    C. The computers have not yet run Windows Update, and need to be updated before they can be used.

    D. The Windows XP Professional installations have become corrupt and need to be reinstalled.

29. Which utility is used to upgrade a FAT16 or FAT32 partition to NTFS?

    A. UPFS

    B. UPGRADE

    C. Disk Manager

    D. CONVERT

30. You want to be able to track which users are accessing the `C:\PAYROLL` folder, and whether the access requests are successful. Which of the following audit policy options allows you to track events related to file and print object access?

    A. File and Object Access

    B. Audit Object Access

    C. Audit File and Print Access

    D. Audit All File and Print Events

Answers to Assessment Test

1. **B.** When you create a custom console for the MMC, the `.msc` filename extension is automatically applied. See Chapter 4 for more information.

2. **D.** Only members of the Administrators group can manage mandatory profiles. See Chapter 6 for more information.

3. **C.** Select ActiveX Control in the Add/Remove Snap-in dialog box (Console ➤ Add/Remove Snap-in). Then, from the Insert ActiveX Control dialog box, select System Monitor Control to access the System Monitor utility. See Chapter 13 for more information.

4. **D.** You would assign permissions to the Authenticated Users group if you wanted only users with valid usernames and passwords to access a specific resource. See Chapter 6 for more information.

5. **D.** You can't configure user preference items, such as screen saver options, in an answer file. See Chapter 2 for more information.

6. **B, C, D.** By default, the Power Users group is allowed Print, Manage Printers, and Manage Documents permissions. See Chapter 11 for more information.

7. **D.** The Narrator utility uses a sound output device to read on-screen text. See Chapter 5 for more information.

8. **B, C.** Windows XP Professional ships with a utility called the User State Migration Tool (USMT) that is used by administrators to migrate users from one computer to another via a command-line utility. The USMT consists of two executable files, `ScanState.exe` and `LoadState.exe`. See Chapter 3 for more information.

9. **B.** If you are using Task Scheduler and your jobs are not running properly, make sure that the Task Scheduler service is running and is configured to start automatically. You should also ensure that the user who configured to run the scheduled task has sufficient permissions to run the task. See Chapter 14 for more information.

10. **D.** You can set processor affinity for Windows XP processes through the Task Manager utility. Processor affinity is the ability to assign a processor to a dedicated process (program). This feature is only available when multiple processors are installed. See Chapter 4 for more information.

11. **D.** If you have a multilingual copy of Windows XP Professional installed, and different multilanguage files installed for each language you wish to use, you can set the default user interface (UI) language, or add/remove UI languages through the `Muisetup.exe` file. See Chapter 5 for more information.

12. **B.** Susan is not allowed the Full Control permission because it was explicitly denied through her membership in the Sales group. She is allowed the Read & Execute permission. See Chapter 9 for more information.

13. D. In Windows XP, you add hardware through the Add Hardware option in Control Panel (Classic view). You can manage existing network adapters through Network and Dial-up Connections. See Chapter 10 for more information.

14. B, C. On Windows XP Professional computers, members of the Administrators and Power Users groups are able to create new users. See Chapter 6 for more information.

15. B. If you do not want users to be able to log on to a Windows XP domain, in Security Policy Options, configure Do Not Allow Stored User Names and Passwords to Save Passwords or Credentials for Network Authentication. See Chapter 7 for more information.

16. C. You would use the `sysprint.sep` separator page if you have a PostScript print device that does not support dual-mode printing. If you want to use separator pages on a print device that does support dual-mode printing, you would use the `pcl.sep` separator page. See Chapter 11 for more information.

17. D. You would use offline files and folders to take data offline and then resynchronize data when you reattach the laptop to the network. See Chapter 9 for more information.

18. B. The `IPCONFIG /flushdns` command is used to purge the DNS Resolver cache. The `IPCONFIG` command displays a computer's IP configuration. See Chapter 10 for more information.

19. A, C. When you configure a VPN connection, you see the Destination Address dialog box. There you must specify the IP address or host domain name of the computer to which you'll connect. See Chapter 12 for more information.

20. C. Administrators and members of the Power Users local groups can create new groups. Group names can contain up to 256 characters and can contain spaces. Group names must be unique to the computer, different from all the other usernames and group names that have been specified on that computer. See Chapter 6 for more information.

21. A, C. You can create a spanned volume from free space that exists on a minimum of 2 to a maximum of 32 physical drives. When the spanned volume is initially created, it can be formatted with FAT16, FAT32, or NTFS. If you extend a volume that already contains data, however, the partition must be NTFS. See Chapter 8 for more information.

22. A, C. To install an image through RIS, the user who is installing the RIS client must have the Join a Computer to the Domain user right and the Logon as a Batch Job right. See Chapter 2 for more information.

23. A. When you insert the Windows XP Professional CD to start the installation, the Setup program will start automatically. If you need to install a third-party disk driver, you would use F6 during this process when prompted. See Chapter 1 for more information.

24. A. Start the Recovery Console through the Windows XP Professional CD, or by installing the Recovery Console using the `WINNT32/ CMDCONS` command prior to failure. See Chapter 14 for more information.

25. A, B.   You can upgrade a computer that only has 64MB of RAM or a Pentium 233MHz processor, but you can't upgrade drives that have DoubleSpace or DriveSpace installed. See Chapter 3 for more information.

26. A.   The Internet Printing Protocol (IPP) allows users to print to a URL. See Chapter 12 for more information.

27. C.   During the boot process, you are prompted to press F8 to access the Advanced Options menu. See Chapter 14 for more information.

28. A.   Unless you have a corporate license for Windows XP Professional, you will need to perform post-installation activation. This can be done online or through a telephone call. After Windows XP is installed, you will be prompted to activate the product. There is a 30-day grace period where you will be able to use the operating system without activation. After the grace period expires, you will not be able to successfully log onto the computer without activation if you restart or log out of the computer. See Chapter 1 for more information.

29. D.   The CONVERT utility is used to convert a FAT16 or FAT32 partition to NTFS. See Chapter 8 for more information.

30. B.   Though all four options seem plausible, only the Audit Object Access option actually exists. Audit Object Access is used to enable auditing of access to files, folders, and printers. Once you enable auditing of object access, you must enable file auditing through NTFS security, or enable print auditing through printer security. See Chapter 7 for more information.

Chapter

1

Getting Started with Windows XP Professional

MICROSOFT EXAM OBJECTIVES COVERED IN THIS CHAPTER:

- ✓ Perform and troubleshoot an attended installation of Windows XP Professional.
- ✓ Perform post-installation updates and product activation.
- ✓ Troubleshoot failed installations.

Windows XP Professional combines the features of Windows 2000 Professional, Windows 98, and Windows Me. The main benefits of using Windows XP Professional include its reliability, performance, security, ease of use, support for remote users, networking and communication support, management and deployment capabilities, and help and support features.

After you decide that Windows XP Professional is the operating system for you, your next step is to install it. This process is fairly easy if you have prepared for the installation, know what the requirements are, and have met the prerequisites for a successful installation.

Preparing for an installation involves making sure that your hardware meets the minimum requirements and that Windows XP Professional supports your hardware. When you install Windows XP Professional, you should also decide whether you are upgrading or installing a clean copy on your computer. An upgrade preserves existing settings; a clean install puts a fresh copy of the operating system on your computer. Installation preparation also involves making choices about your system's configuration, such as selecting a file system and a disk-partitioning scheme.

Once you've completed all the planning, you are ready to install Windows XP Professional. This is a straightforward process that is highly automated and user friendly.

To complete the Windows XP Professional installation, you will need to activate the product through Product Activation. This process is used to reduce software piracy. After Windows XP Professional is installed, you can keep the operating system up to date with post-installation updates.

When you install Windows XP, you should also consider whether the computer will be used for dual-boot or multi-boot purposes. Dual-booting or multi-booting allows you to have your computer boot with operating systems other than Windows XP Professional.

The first section of this chapter covers the new features of Windows XP Professional. Then you will learn how to prepare for Windows XP Professional installation, perform the installation, and troubleshoot any installation problems.

Features of Windows XP Professional

Windows XP Professional includes the following features as enhancements to the Windows 2000, Windows 98, and Windows Me operating systems:

- Increased reliability
- Performance enhancements
- Better security

- Greater ease of use
- Better support for remote users
- Improved networking and communication support
- Better management and deployment tools
- Help and support features

These features are covered in detail in the following sections.

Increased Reliability

The reliability features that are included with Windows XP Professional include the following:

Architecture that incorporates previous Windows technologies   Windows XP Professional was developed on the 32-bit architecture used by Windows 2000. By also including technologies integrated with Windows 98 and Windows Me, Windows XP is able to leverage the benefits and stability of existing technology while adding additional enhancements.

Enhanced device driver verification   Device drivers have been known to cause system problems in previous operating systems. Windows 2000 included a device driver verification mechanism that is expanded in Windows XP. With Windows XP, device drivers are tested more thoroughly, which provides you with greater system stability.

Decreased need to reboot with configuration changes   In Windows 2000, Windows 98, and Windows Me, installing new hardware, software, or services typically requires you to restart the computer. The need to restart the computer has been reduced in Windows XP, which means greater uptime.

Better code protection   Better code protection means that the critical kernel data structures used by Windows XP are read-only, so they can't be corrupted by drivers or other applications.

Windows File Protection   Windows XP introduces a feature called Windows File Protection, which keeps core system files from being replaced by application installations. If an application does overwrite a critical file, then Windows File Protection will restore the correct version of the file.

Better Windows Installer   The Windows Installer is a new service that is used to manage applications by helping users install, configure, update, and uninstall applications properly.

Enhanced software restriction policies   Software restriction policies are used to control software and its ability to be executed. Through software restriction policies, administrators can now identify the software that is running and control specific software's ability to execute. This is useful for virus prevention.

Performance Enhancements

Performance features included with Windows XP include the following:

Preemptive multitasking architecture   With preemptive multitasking, a user can run multiple tasks simultaneously with good system response time.

Scalable memory and processor support   Scalable memory and processor support means that Windows XP Professional can support up to 4GB of memory and two symmetric processors.

Better Security

Windows XP uses the following security features:

Encrypting File System for multiple user access support   Encrypting File System (EFS) provides a high level of security by encrypting files. With Windows XP, you can encrypt a file and allow multiple permitted users to access the encrypted file. In Windows 2000 Professional, only the owner of an encrypted file could access the file through EFS.

IP Security   IP Security (IPSec) protects files that are transferred through IP to Virtual Private Networks (VPNs) over the Internet.

Support for Kerberos   Kerberos is an industry-standard authentication protocol. This provides a fast logon with a high level of security.

Support for smart cards   Smart cards are used to combine software security with hardware security. Windows XP supports standard logons with smart keys as well as also supporting smart cards used with terminal server sessions, which are hosted on Windows Server 2003 servers.

Greater Ease of Use

The features that make Windows XP easy to use include the following:

Improved user interface   Windows XP updates the user interface by consolidating and simplifying common tasks. Users or administrators can select whether they will use the classic Windows 2000 Professional interface or the updated Windows XP interface with the click of a button.

Adaptive user environment features   The adaptive user environment uses a redesigned Start menu to show the most frequently used applications first. Also, when you open multiple files in the same application (for example, multiple files in Word), the open windows (represented in the Taskbar as buttons) are consolidated into a single Taskbar button. The purpose of these features is to reduce desktop clutter. These features are set through Group Policy.

Support for rich media features   Rich media is used to support digital media activities through Windows Media Player for XP. Some of the support included with Windows XP includes the ability to create custom CDs easily and quickly, view DVD movies, have easy access to over 3,000 Internet radio stations, and have the best possible audio and video quality over the network.

Context-Sensitive Task Menus   When a file is selected in Windows Explorer, a Context-Sensitive Task Menu is displayed that lists the type of tasks that are appropriate for the selected file type.

Integrated support for CD-RW devices in Windows Explorer   Windows Explorer now includes support for CD-R and CD-RW drives. This allows you to burn CDs as easily as copying data to a floppy without having to use third-party software.

Ease of publishing content to the Web   Information can be easily published to the Web or to the company's intranet via any Web service that uses the WebDAV protocol.

Support for DualView   DualView allows a single desktop to display two monitors that are connected via a single video adapter. For example, a laptop user can connect an external monitor and see video on the LCD adapter and the external monitor. This functionality is also included on some high-end video adapters used with desktop computers.

Enhanced troubleshooting support   Better troubleshooters help users and administrators configure, optimize, and troubleshoot Windows XP, which reduces support and help desk calls.

Better Support for Remote Users

Windows XP provides additional support for remote users that includes the following:

Remote Desktop support   Remote Desktop Protocol (RDP) support allows a user to access data and applications that are installed on their desktop computer from any other computer on the network that runs Windows 95 or later through a virtual session.

Credential Manager   You use Credential Manager as a secure store for user and password information for users who are not always connected to a domain or who require access to resources in domains that do not have trust relationships defined. This allows the user to input usernames and passwords once, and then subsequent access requests are transparently processed by the Credential Manager.

Offline File and Folder support   Offline File and Folder support is used to allow offline access to network files even when a user is not connected to a network. When the computer is reconnected to the network, the offline files are automatically resynchronized with the network through the Synchronization Manager. Windows XP includes support for encrypting offline files.

ClearType technology   ClearType technology is a new display technology for LCD screens that triples the horizontal resolution through software technology. This allows users to see clearer displays.

Offline viewing for Web pages   You can view web pages and graphics offline while disconnected from the Web through new features of Windows XP.

Better power management   Better power management monitors CPU state so the amount of power that is used can be dynamically managed. Windows XP also predicts remaining battery power more accurately. Power management can also be set for all users on a computer or by individual user preference. Windows XP uses the features of Advanced Configuration and Power Interface (ACPI).

Hot docking support   Hot docking support allows users to switch a laptop computer between a docked and undocked state without having to change hardware configuration or reboot the computer.

Wireless network support   Wireless network support allows users to move between wireless networks while providing secure access and performance improvements.

Improved Networking and Communication Support

Windows XP has made several improvements to networking and communication support. The new features include the following:

Windows Messenger service integration   Windows Messenger is used for online conferencing and collaboration by allowing you to communicate with coworkers, customers, family, and friends in real time. Windows Messenger allows you to transfer text, audio, and video. You can also easily see which of your contacts are currently online.

Internet Connection Firewall support   Windows XP includes Internet Connection Firewall support that is used to protect the home user or small business from common Internet attacks by setting up secure Internet connections.

Improved Network Setup Wizard   An improved Network Setup Wizard makes it easy to configure common network configuration tasks such as sharing files, printers, and Internet connections and to configure the Internet Connection Firewall.

Support for Internet Connection Sharing   Internet Connection Sharing (ICS) is used to allow multiple users to connect to the Internet via a single dial-up or broadband connection. ICS provides network address translation, addressing, and name resolution service for the shared connection.

Better peer-to-peer networking support   With better peer-to-peer networking support, Windows XP easily interoperates with earlier versions of Windows that use peer-to-peer networking.

Better Management and Deployment Tools

Windows XP Professional includes a wide range of management and deployment tools, which include the following:

Better application compatibility   Applications that have run with older versions of Windows that do not run on Windows 2000 Professional are now more likely to be supported by Windows XP Professional. Windows XP includes hundreds of application fixes, and new fixes will continue to be added through the Windows Update service.

User State Migration Tool   With the User State Migration Tool, administrators can migrate user accounts and users' settings from an older computer to a new Windows XP Professional computer.

Dynamic Update   When you install Windows XP Professional, the Setup process will check with Dynamic Update to ensure that you are installing the most recent files.

Ability to update Windows XP automatically   After Windows XP Professional is installed, if you are connected to the Internet and choose to use Windows Update, the most critical system and security downloads will be downloaded to your computer as a background process. You can choose which updates will be installed.

Ability to update application and device drivers automatically   Windows Update will also allow you to apply application compatibility updates and new drivers from the Windows Update website. The user or the administrator can manage how Windows Update is implemented.

Support for the latest hardware standards   Windows XP Professional supports the latest hardware standards, including UDF 2.01, which is the latest DVD standard. There is also support for formatting DVDs with the FAT32 file system. Support is also included for Infrared Data Association (IrDA), IEEE 1394, and Universal Serial Bus (USB).

Unattended installation   Unattended installation support allows an administrator to create scripts for unattended installations. With Windows XP Professional unattended installation support, security is better than with Windows 2000 Professional because passwords can now be encrypted within the answer files.

Internet Explorer 6 Administration Kit   Administrators can use the Internet Explorer 6 Administration Kit to customize the deployment of Internet Explorer 6.

Multilingual support   Multilingual support is used to support the creation and editing of multilingual documents in a localized version of Windows XP Professional. Windows XP Professional also comes with a Multilingual User Interface, which allows users to change the user interface to support different languages.

Safe Mode startup options   Safe Mode startup options allow you to start the operating system at a basic level, which is useful for troubleshooting operating systems when system problems occur.

Expanded Group Policy   Windows XP Professional uses an expanded Group Policy that includes hundreds of new policies. Group policies are used to manage settings, security, and management options for groups of users.

Resultant Set of Policy   With the Resultant Set of Policy (RSoP), administrators can see the effect of Group Policy on a targeted computer or user before the policies are implemented.

Microsoft Management Console   Microsoft Management Console (MMC) uses a centralized console for administration.

Help and Support Features

The help and support features that are included with Windows XP Professional include the following:

Better help and support services   Windows XP Professional now includes the Help and Support Center, which provides help and support services. Features of the Help and Support Center include the ability to query for help (including help from the Internet) and tools such as My Computer Information and System Restore.

Remote access capability through Remote Assistance   Remote Assistance allows an administrator to take remote control of a user's computer so that troubleshooting can be done remotely.

Recovery Console for repairing operating system errors   The Recovery Console is used to repair operating system errors at the command-line prompt if Windows XP Professional will not boot. Through Recovery Console, you can start and stop services, read and write to the local drive, format drives, and perform other administrative tasks.

Ability to roll back device drivers for recovery purposes   When you update a device driver in Windows XP Professional, the operating system maintains the previously installed driver, which can then be rolled back if the new driver has problems.

Preparing to Install Windows XP Professional

Windows XP Professional is easy to install. But this doesn't mean you don't need to prepare for the installation process. Before you begin the installation, you should know what is required for a successful installation and have all of the pieces of information you'll need to supply during the installation process. In preparing for the installation, you should make sure you have the following information:

- The hardware requirements for Windows XP Professional

- How to use the Hardware Compatibility List (HCL) to determine whether your hardware is supported by Windows XP Professional

- Verification that your computer's BIOS is compatible with Windows XP Professional

- Whether the devices in your computer have Windows XP drivers

- The difference between a clean install and an upgrade

- The installation options suitable for your system, including which disk-partitioning scheme and file system you should select for Windows XP Professional to use

The following sections describe the preparation that is required prior to installing Windows XP Professional.

Hardware Requirements

To install Windows XP Professional successfully, your system must meet certain hardware requirements. Table 1.1 lists the minimum requirements for an *x*86-based computer, as well as the more realistic recommended requirements.

The standard Windows XP Professional operating system is based on the Intel *x*86-based processor architecture, which uses a 32-bit operating system. Windows XP 64-bit edition is the first 64-bit client operating system to be released by Microsoft. The 64-bit version of Windows XP requires a computer with an Itanium processor, and is designed to take advantage of performance offered by the 64-bit processor. The hardware requirements for Windows XP 64-bit edition are different from the hardware requirements of a standard version of Windows XP Professional.

TABLE 1.1   Hardware Requirements (Non-Network Installation)

Component	Minimum Requirement	Recommended Requirement
Processor	Intel Pentium (or compatible) 233MHz or higher	Intel Pentium II (or compatible) 300MHz or higher
Memory	64MB	128MB

TABLE 1.1   Hardware Requirements (Non-Network Installation) *(continued)*

Component	Minimum Requirement	Recommended Requirement
Disk space	1.5GB of free disk space	2GB or more of free disk space
Network	None	Network card and any other hardware required by your network topology if you want to connect to a network or if you will install over the network
Display	Video adapter and monitor with VGA resolution	Video adapter and monitor with SVGA resolution or higher
Peripheral devices	Keyboard, mouse, or other pointing device	Keyboard, mouse, or other pointing device
Removable storage	CD-ROM or DVD-ROM drive if installing from CD	12x or faster CD-ROM or DVD-ROM

The minimum requirements specify the minimum hardware required before you should even consider installing Windows XP Professional. These requirements assume that you are installing only the operating system and not running any special services or applications. For example, you may be able to get by with the minimum requirements if you are just installing the operating system to learn the basics of the software.

The recommended requirements are what Microsoft suggests to achieve what would be considered "acceptable performance" for the most common configurations. Since computer technology and the standard for acceptable performance are constantly changing, the recommendations are somewhat subjective. However, the recommended hardware requirements are based on the standards at the time that Windows XP Professional was released.

The hardware requirements listed in Table 1.1 were those specified at the time this book was published. Check Microsoft's website at www.microsoft.com/windowsxp/pro/evaluation/sysreqs.asp for the most current information.

 Real World Scenario

Deciding on Minimum Hardware Requirements

The company you work for has decided that everyone will have their own laptop running Windows XP Professional. You need to decide on the new computers' specifications for processor, memory, and disk space.

The first step is to determine which applications will be used. Typically, most users will work with an e-mail program, a word processor, a spreadsheet, presentation software, and maybe a drawing or graphics program. Under these demands, a low-end Pentium processor and 64MB of RAM will make for a very slow-running machine with a real likelihood of memory errors. So for this usage, you can assume that the minimum baseline configuration would be a Pentium III processor with 128MB of RAM.

Based on your choice of baseline configuration, you should then fit a test computer with the applications that will be used on it, and test the configuration in a lab environment simulating normal use. This will give you an idea whether the RAM and processor calculations you have made for your environment are going to provide suitable response.

Today's disk drives have become capable of much larger capacity, while dropping drastically in price. So for disk space, the rule of thumb is to buy whatever is the current standard. Hard drives are currently shipping in the GB range, which is sufficient for most users. If users plan to store substantial graphics or video files, you may need to consider buying larger-than-standard drives.

Also consider what the business requirements will be over the next 12 to 18 months. If you will be implementing applications that are memory or processor intensive, you may want to spec out the computers initially with hardware sufficient to support upcoming needs, to avoid costly upgrades in the near future.

Depending on the installation method you choose, other devices may be required, as follows:

- If you are installing Windows XP Professional from the CD, you should have at least a 12x CD-ROM drive.
- If you choose to install Windows XP Professional from the network, you need a network connection and a server with the distribution files.

 Windows XP Professional supports computers with one or two processors.

Measurement Units Used in Hardware Specifications

Computer processors are typically rated by speed. The speed of the processor, or *central processing unit (CPU)*, is rated by the number of clock cycles that can be performed in one second. This measurement is typically expressed in *megahertz (MHz)*. One MHz is one million cycles per second.

Hard disks are commonly rated by capacity. The following measurements are used for disk space and memory capacity:

1*MB (megabyte)* = 1024KB (kilobytes)

1*GB (gigabyte)* = 1024MB

1*TB (terabyte)* = 1024GB

1*PB (petabyte)* = 1024TB

1*EB (exabyte)* = 1024PB

The Hardware Compatibility List (HCL)

Along with meeting the minimum requirements, your hardware should appear on the *Hardware Compatibility List (HCL)*. The HCL is an extensive list of computers and peripheral hardware that have been tested with the Windows XP Professional operating system.

The Windows XP Professional operating system requires control of the hardware for stability, efficiency, and security. The hardware and supported drivers on the HCL have been put through rigorous tests to ensure their compatibility with Windows XP Professional. Microsoft guarantees that the items on the list meet the requirements for Windows XP and do not have any incompatibilities that could affect the stability of the operating system.

If you call Microsoft for support, the first thing a Microsoft support engineer will ask about is your configuration. If you have any hardware that is not on the HCL, you won't be able to get support from Microsoft.

To determine if your computer and peripherals are on the HCL, check the most up-to-date list at www.microsoft.com/hcl.

BIOS Compatibility

Before you install Windows XP Professional, you should verify that your computer has the most current BIOS (Basic Input/Output System). This is especially important if your current BIOS does not include support for Advanced Configuration and Power Interface (ACPI) functionality. Check the computer's vendor for the latest BIOS version information.

Driver Requirements

To successfully install Windows XP Professional, you must have the critical device drivers for your computer, such as the hard drive device driver. The Windows XP Professional CD comes with an extensive list of drivers. If your computer's device drivers are not on the CD, you should check the device manufacturer's website. If the device driver can't be found on the manufacturer's website, and there is no other compatible driver, you are out of luck. Windows XP will not recognize devices that don't have XP drivers.

If you are upgrading from Windows 98 or Windows Me, the device drivers will not migrate at all. These versions of Windows used virtual device drives (VxDs) and these drivers are not compatible with Windows XP Professional.

Clean Install or Upgrade?

Once you've determined that your hardware not only meets the minimum requirements but also is on the HCL, you need to decide whether you want to do a *clean install* or an *upgrade*.

The only operating systems that can be upgraded to Windows XP Professional are Windows 98, Windows Me, Windows NT 4 Workstation, and Windows 2000 Professional.

 For Windows 98 and Me, you need to get the updated drivers first.

Any other operating system cannot be upgraded, but it may be able to coexist with Windows XP in a dual-boot environment.

 Dual-booting is covered in the "Supporting Multiple-Boot Options" section later in this chapter.

If you don't have an operating system that can be upgraded, or if you want to keep your previous operating system intact, you need to perform a clean install. A clean install puts the Windows XP Professional operating system into a new folder and uses its default settings the first time the operating system is loaded.

 The process for a clean installation is described in the "Running the Windows XP Professional Installation Process" section later in this chapter.

Installation Options

You will need to make many choices during the Windows XP Professional installation process. Following are some of the options that you will configure:

- How your hard disk space will be partitioned
- The file system your partitions will use
- Whether the computer will be a part of a workgroup or a domain
- The language and locale for the computer's settings

Before you start the installation, you should know which choices you will select. The following sections describe the options and considerations for picking the best ones for your installation.

Partitioning of Disk Space

Disk partitioning is the act of taking the physical hard drive and creating logical partitions. A *logical drive* is how space is allocated to the drive's primary and logical partitions. For example, if you have a 5GB hard drive, you might partition it into two logical drives: a C: drive, which might be 2GB, and a D: drive, which might be 3GB.

The following are some of the major considerations for disk partitioning:

- The amount of space required
- The location of the system and boot partition
- Any special disk configurations you will use
- The utility you will use to set up the partitions

These considerations are covered in detail in the following sections.

Partition Size

One important consideration in your disk-partitioning scheme is determining the partition size. You need to consider the amount of space taken up by your operating system, the applications that will be installed, and the amount of stored data. It is also important to consider the amount of space required in the future.

Just for Windows XP, Microsoft recommends that you allocate at least 2GB of disk space. This allows room for the operating system files and for future growth in terms of upgrades and installation files that are placed with the operating system files.

The System and Boot Partitions

When you install Windows XP, files will be stored in two locations: the system partition and the boot partition.

The *system partition* contains the files needed to boot the Windows XP Professional operating system. The System Partition contains the Master Boot Record (MBR) and boot sector of the active drive partition. It is often the first physical hard drive in the computer and normally contains the necessary files to boot the computer. The files stored on the system partition do not take any significant disk space. By default, the system partition uses the computer's active partition, which is usually the C: drive.

The *boot partition* contains the files that are the Windows XP operating system files. By default, the Windows operating system files are located in a folder named Windows. You can, however, specify the location of this folder during the installation process. Microsoft recommends that the boot partition be at least 2GB.

Special Disk Configurations

Windows XP Professional supports several disk configurations. Options include simple, spanned, and striped volumes. These configuration options are covered in detail in Chapter 8, "Managing Disks."

 Windows 2000 Server and Windows Server 2003 also include options for mirrored and RAID 5 volumes.

Disk Partition Configuration Utilities

If you are partitioning your disk prior to installation, you can use several utilities, such as the DOS or Windows FDISK program or a third-party utility like PowerQuest's Partition Magic. You might want to create only the first partition where Windows XP Professional will be installed. You can then use the Disk Management utility in Windows XP to create any other partitions you need. The Windows XP Disk Management utility is covered in Chapter 8.

You can get more information about FDISK and other disk utilities from your DOS or Windows documentation. Also, basic DOS functions are covered in *MCSA/MCSE .NET JumpStart: Computer and Network Basics* by Lisa Donald (Sybex, 2003).

File System Selection

Another factor that determines your disk-partitioning scheme is the type of file system you use. Windows XP Professional supports three file systems:

- *File Allocation Table (FAT16)*
- *FAT32*
- *New Technology File System (NTFS)*

The following sections briefly describe these three file systems.

See Chapter 8 for more details about the features of FAT, FAT32, and NTFS.

FAT16

FAT16 (originally just FAT) is the 16-bit file system widely used by DOS and Windows 3.*x*. FAT16 tracks where files are stored on a disk using a file allocation table and a directory entry table. The disadvantages of FAT16 are that it only supports partitions up to 2GB and it does not offer the security features of NTFS. The advantage of FAT is that it is backward compatible, which is important if the computer will be dual-booted with another operating system, such as DOS, Unix, Linux, OS/2, or Windows 3.1. Almost all PC operating systems read FAT16 partitions.

FAT32

FAT32 is the 32-bit version of FAT, which was first introduced in 1996 with Windows 95, with OEM (original equipment manufacturer) Service Release 2 (OSR2). With FAT32, disk partitions can be as large as 2TB (terabytes). It has more fault-tolerance features than FAT16, and also improves disk-space usage by reducing the size of clusters. However, it lacks several of the features offered by NTFS for a Windows XP or Windows 2000 system, such as local security, file encryption, disk quotas, and compression.

If you choose to use FAT, Windows XP Professional will automatically format the partition with FAT16 if the partition is less than 2GB. If the partition is over 2GB, it will be automatically partitioned as FAT32.

Windows NT 4 and earlier releases of NT do not support FAT32 partitions.

NTFS

NTFS is a file system designed to provide additional features for Windows NT, Windows 2000, Windows XP, and Windows Server 2003 computers. Some of the features NTFS offers include the following:

- The ability to set local security on files and folders.
- The option to compress data. This feature reduces disk-storage requirements.
- The flexibility to assign disk quotas. Disk quotas are used to limit the amount of disk space a user can use.
- The option to encrypt files. Encryption offers an additional level of security.

Unless you are planning on dual-booting your computer to an operating system other than Windows NT, Windows 2000, or another instance of Windows XP, Microsoft recommends using NTFS.

Membership in a Domain or Workgroup

One Windows XP Professional installation choice is whether your computer will be installed as a part of a *workgroup* or as part of a *domain*.

You should install as part of a workgroup if you are part of a small, decentralized network or if you are running Windows XP on a computer that is not part of a network. To join a workgroup, you simply choose that workgroup.

Domains are part of larger, centrally administered networks. You should install as part of a domain if any Windows 2000 and Server 2003 servers on your network are configured as domain controllers with the Microsoft Active Directory installed. There are two ways to join a domain. You can preauthorize a computer before installation, through the Active Directory Users and Computers utility. The second way is done during the Windows XP Professional installation, when you specify an Administrator name and password (or other user who has rights to add computers to the domain). To successfully join a domain, a domain controller for the domain and a DNS server must be available to authenticate the request to join the domain.

If you want a user to be able to add computers to the domain without giving them administrative rights, you can grant them the "Add workstations to the domain" user right. User rights are covered in greater detail in Chapter 7, "Managing Security."

Language and Locale

Language and locale settings are used to determine the language the computer will use. Windows XP supports many languages for the operating system interface and utilities.

Locale settings are used to configure the locality for items such as numbers, currencies, times, and dates. An example of a locality is that English for United States specifies a short date as *mm/dd/yyyy* (month/day/year), and English for South Africa specifies a short date as *yyyy/mm/dd* (year/month/day).

Choosing Your Installation Method

You can install Windows XP Professional either from the bootable CD or through a network installation using files that have been copied to a network share point. If your computer can't boot to a CD, you can start the installation with the WINNT or WINNT32 command-line utilities, dependant on the current operating system you are using, once the computer has started and the CD-drive is accessible.

The Windows XP Professional CD is a bootable CD. To start the installation, you simply reboot your computer and boot to the CD. The installation process will begin automatically.

     We discuss how to install Windows XP in more detail in the next section.

If you are installing Windows XP Professional from the network, you need a *distribution server* and a computer with a network connection. A distribution server is a server that has the Windows XP Professional distribution files copied to a shared folder. The files in this folder must include the \I386 folder from the Windows XP Professional distribution CD. The following steps are used to install Windows XP Professional over the network:

1. Boot the target computer.
2. Attach to the distribution server and access the share that has the \I386 folder shared.
3. Launch WINNT or WINNT32 (depending on the computer's current operating system).
4. Complete the Windows XP Professional installation.

     You can also install Windows XP Professional through an unattended process, which is covered in detail in Chapter 2, "Automating the Windows XP Installation."

Running the Windows XP Professional Installation Process

This section describes how to run the Windows XP Professional installation process. As explained in the previous section, you can run the installation from the CD or over a network. The only difference in the installation procedure is your starting point: from your CD-ROM drive or from a network share. The steps in the following sections assume that the disk drive is clean and that you are starting the installation using the Windows XP Professional CD.

There are four main steps in the Windows XP Professional installation process:

- Collecting information

- Preparing installation
- Installing Windows
- Finalizing installation

Each of these steps is covered in detail in the following sections.

The following sections give the details of the installation process to show how the process works. But you should not actually install Windows XP Professional until you reach Exercise 1.1. In that exercise, you'll set up your computer to complete the rest of the exercises in this book.

Collecting Information

When you boot to the Windows XP Professional CD, the Setup program will automatically start the Windows XP installation. In this stage of the installation, you start the installation program, choose the partition where Windows XP Professional will be installed, and then copy files.

The following steps are involved in running the Setup program:

1. Insert the Windows XP Professional CD in your computer and restart the computer. Boot the computer to the CD-ROM.

2. The Setup program will start automatically. If you need to install a third-party disk driver, you would use F6 during this when prompted. For automatic recovery, you would press F2 when prompted.

3. The Welcome to Setup dialog box will appear. You can press Enter to install Windows XP Professional, R to repair a Windows XP installation, or F3 to quit the Setup program.

4. The Windows XP Licensing Agreement will appear. Press F8 to accept the agreement—or ESC to not accept the agreement, at which time the installation process will be terminated.

5. The Windows XP Professional Setup dialog box will appear. This will list all existing partitions and unpartitioned disk space on your computer. From this screen you can add or delete partitions and select the partition where Windows XP Professional will be installed. If you create a new partition, you will have the option to format the drive through the Setup program.

6. The Setup files will then be automatically copied to the selected partition.

7. Remove the Windows XP Professional CD and restart your computer.

After the file copying is complete, the computer automatically reboots.

If Windows XP does not recognize your hard drive controller or hard drive because it uses a driver that is not on the XP Professional CD, you will need to provide the driver during the Setup phase.

Preparing Installation

During the Preparing Installation phase, all the files required by the Setup program will be copied to the hard drive. This process will take several minutes and will display a tutorial of helpful Windows XP information.

Installing Windows XP Professional

Once your computer finishes with the file copying and reboots, you will be in the Installing Windows phase of the installation. This first part of the installation is automated and shows you how long the installation has remaining in minutes and what is currently being installed, and gives you interesting reading material while the installation process is running.

During this process you may see your screen flicker as the video driver is detected.

During the installation process, Setup will gather information about your locale, name, and product key as follows (click Next after completing each dialog box):

1. The Regional Settings dialog box appears. From this dialog box, you choose your locale and keyboard settings. Locale settings are used to configure international options for numbers, currencies, times, and dates. Keyboard settings allow you to configure your keyboard to support different local characters or keyboard layouts. For example, you can choose Danish or United States–Dvorak through this option.

2. In the Personalize Your Software dialog box, you fill in the Name and Organization boxes. This information is used to personalize your operating system software and the applications that you install. If you install Windows XP Professional in a workgroup, the Name entry here is used for the initial user.

3. The Product Key dialog box appears. In the boxes at the bottom of this dialog box, you type in the 25-character product key, which can be found on the back of your Windows XP CD case.

4. The Computer Name and Administrator Password dialog box appears. Here, you specify a name that will uniquely identify your computer on the network. Your computer name can be up to 15 characters. The Setup Wizard suggests a name, but you can change it to another name. Through this dialog box, you also type and confirm the Administrator password. An account called Administrator will automatically be created as a part of the installation process.

Be sure that the computer name is a unique name within your network. If you are part of a corporate network, you should also verify that the computer name follows the naming convention specified by your Information Services (IS) department.

5. If you have a Plug and Play modem installed, you will see the Modem Dialing Information dialog box. Here, you specify your country/region, your area code (or city code), whether you dial a number to get an outside line, and whether the telephone system uses tone dialing or pulse dialing.

6. The Date and Time Settings dialog box appears. In this dialog box, you specify date and time settings and the time zone in which your computer is located. You can also configure the computer to automatically adjust for daylight savings time.

7. The Network Settings dialog box appears. This dialog box is used to specify how you want to connect to other computers, networks, and the Internet. You have two choices:

   • Typical Settings installs network connections for Client for Microsoft Networks, as well as File and Print Sharing for Microsoft Networks. It also installs the TCP/IP protocol with an automatically assigned address.

   • Custom Settings allows you to customize your network settings. You can choose whether you want to use Client for Microsoft Networks, File and Print Sharing for Microsoft Networks, and the TCP/IP protocol. You should use the custom settings if you need to specify particular network settings, such as a specific IP address and subnet mask (rather than using an automatically assigned address).

8. In the next dialog box, Workgroup or Computer Domain, specify whether your computer will be installed as part of a local workgroup or as part of a domain. (See the "Membership in a Domain or Workgroup" section earlier in this chapter for details about these choices.)

9. The computer will perform some final tasks, including installing Start menu items, registering components, saving settings, and removing any temporary files. This will take several minutes.

10. The Display Settings dialog box will appear, stating that Windows will automatically adjust the resolution of your screen. The Monitor Settings dialog box will then ask you to verify the settings.

Finalizing Installation

Once your computer finishes with the installation, you will be asked to set up your computer. The options that will be configured include the following:

• Specifying how the computer will connect to the Internet. You can select Telephone Modem, Digital Subscriber Line (DSL) or cable modem, or Local Area Network (LAN).

• Activating Windows, which can be done over the Internet, or you can specify that you want to be reminded every few days.

• Deciding whether or not you want to set up Internet access at the present time.

• Providing the name(s) of the user(s) that will use the computer.

When you are done, the primary user will be logged on and you will see the new Windows XP Professional interface.

Setting Up Your Computer for Hands-On Exercises

Before beginning Exercise 1.1, verify that your computer meets the requirements for installing Windows XP Professional as listed in Table 1.1. Exercise 1.1 assumes that you are not currently running a previous version of Windows that will be upgraded.

The exercises in this book assume that your computer is configured in a specific manner. Your computer should have at least a 3GB drive that is configured with the minimum space requirements and partitions. Other exercises in this book assume that your computer is configured as follows:

- 2GB (about 2000MB) C: primary partition with the FAT file system

- 500MB D: extended partition with the FAT file system

- 500MB of free space

Of course, you can allocate more space to your partitions if it is available.

You are probably wondering why we are not using any NTFS partitions. The reason is that you will convert a FAT partition to NTFS and use the features of NTFS in Chapter 8. You will also use the features of NTFS in Chapter 9, "Accessing Files and Folders." You are probably also wondering about the free space requirement. You need free space because you will create partitions in Chapter 8. If no free space exists, you won't be able to complete that exercise.

Exercise 1.1 assumes that you are performing a clean installation and not an upgrade. Your partitions should be created and formatted as previously specified.

As noted earlier in this chapter, you can set up your partitions through the DOS or Windows FDISK utility or a third-party program. For example, if you have a Windows 98 computer, you can use it to create a Windows 98 boot disk. Set up the Windows 98 boot disk with FDISK and FORMAT from the Windows folder on the Windows 98 computer. Then you will be able to boot your computer and see your CD-ROM drive.

You should make a complete backup of your computer before repartitioning your disk or installing new operating systems. All data will be lost during this process!

In Exercise 1.1, you will be installing Windows XP Professional on your system.

EXERCISE 1.1

Installing Windows XP Professional

In this exercise, you will install Windows XP Professional.

Information Collection

1. Boot your computer with the Windows XP CD inserted into your CD-ROM drive.

2. The Welcome to Setup screen appears. Press Enter to set up Windows XP Professional.

3. The License Agreement dialog box appears. Scroll down to the bottom of the page. Press F8 to agree to the license terms if you wish to continue.

4. In the next dialog box, specify the C: partition as the one you want to use to set up Windows XP Professional. Then press Enter.

5. In the next dialog box, choose to leave the current file system intact (no changes). Press Enter to continue. The file copying will take a few minutes to complete.

Installing Windows

6. The Installing Windows phase of installation will begin. You will see a series of informational screens as the system does some background installation tasks.

7. The Regional and Language Options dialog box will appear. Verify that the settings are correct, and click the Next button.

8. In the Personalize Your Software dialog box, type your name and organization. Click the Next button.

9. In the Product Key dialog box, type the 25-character product key (this key can be found on a sticker on the installation folder). Click the Next button.

10. The Computer Name and Administrator Password dialog box appears. Type in the computer name. You can also specify an Administrator password (since this computer will be used for practice, you can leave the Password field blank if you want to). Click the Next button.

11. If you have a Plug and Play modem installed, the Modem Dialing Information dialog box appears. Specify the settings for your environment and click the Next button.

12. The Date and Time Settings dialog box appears. Verify that all of the settings are correct, and click the Next button.

13. After the Networking component files are copied (which takes a few minutes), the Network Settings dialog box appears. Confirm that the Typical Settings button is selected. Then click the Next button.

14. In the Workgroup and Computer Domain dialog box, confirm that the option No, This Computer Is Not on a Network, or Is on a Network without a Domain, is selected to indicate that you don't want to put the computer in a domain. In this dialog box, you can accept the default workgroup name, WORKGROUP, or you can specify a unique workgroup name. Since this is a practice computer, the workgroup name is not important. Click the Next button. The Setup components are installed, which takes several minutes.

15. The Display Settings dialog box will appear. Click the OK button to have your screen resolution automatically adjusted.

EXERCISE 1.1 *(continued)*

16. The Monitor Settings dialog box will appear. If you can see the video properly, click the OK button.

Finalizing Installation

17. The Welcome to Microsoft Windows dialog box will appear. Click the Next button to continue.

18. The system will check to see if you are connected to the Internet. You will see the How Will This Computer Connect to the Internet? dialog box. Specify your connectivity method and click the Next button. Depending on the option you select, you will be directed through a series of dialog boxes. If you do not want to connect to the Internet, click the Skip button.

19. The Ready to Activate Windows? dialog box will appear. Select your option for activation and click the Next button.

20. The Who Will Use This Computer? dialog box will appear. Type in your name and click the Next button.

21. The Thank You dialog box will appear. Click the Finish button.

Windows XP Professional is now installed, and you should be logged on to the new Windows XP interface.

Post-Installation Updates and Product Activation

Once you are done with the Windows XP Professional installation, you can keep your operating system up-to-date through post-installation updates. Product activation is Microsoft's way of reducing software piracy.

Unless you have a corporate license for Windows XP Professional, you will need to perform post-installation activation. This can be done online or through a telephone call. After Windows XP is installed, you will be prompted to activate the product. There is a 30-day grace period when you will be able to use the operating system without activation. After the grace period expires, you will not be able to successfully log on to the computer without activation if you restart or log out of the computer. When the grace period runs out, the Product Activation Wizard will automatically start; it will walk you through the activation process.

Post-Installation Updates

You can perform post-installation updates of Windows XP Professional through Windows Update. Windows Update is a utility that connects to Microsoft's website and checks to ensure that you have the most up-to-date version of XP Professional files. To access Windows Update, confirm that your computer is connected to the Internet and access Start ➤ Help and Support. From the Help and Support dialog box, select Windows Update. Your computer will be scanned, and a list of suggested downloads will be customized and listed for you to select from. Some of the common update categories include:

- Critical updates and Service Packs
- Windows XP updates
- Drivers

Windows Service Packs

Service Packs are updates to the Windows XP operating system that include bug fixes and product enhancements. Some of the options that might be included in Service Packs are security fixes or updated versions of software, such as Internet Explorer.

You can download Service Packs from Microsoft.com or you can pay for a CD of the Service Pack to be mailed to you. Before you install a Service Pack, you should read the Release Note that is provided for each Service Pack on Microsoft's website.

Troubleshooting Installation Problems

The Windows XP installation process is designed to be as simple as possible. The chances for installation errors are greatly minimized through the use of wizards and the step-by-step process. However, it is possible that errors may occur.

In the following sections, you will more about:

- Identifying and resolving common installation problems
- Troubleshooting installation problems that relate to the `Boot.ini` file
- Installing non-supported hard drives
- Troubleshooting installation errors using installation log files

Identifying Common Installation Problems

As most of you are aware, most installations seldom go off without a hitch. Table 1.2 lists some possible installation errors you might encounter.

TABLE 1.2   Common Installation Problems

Problem	Description
Media errors	Media errors are caused by defective or damaged CDs. To check the CD, put it into another computer and see if you can read it. Also check your CD for scratches or dirt—it may just need to be cleaned.

TABLE 1.2   Common Installation Problems *(continued)*

Problem	Description
Insufficient disk space	Windows XP needs at least 2GB of free space for the installation program to run properly. If the Setup program cannot verify that this space exists, the program will not let you continue.
Not enough memory	Make sure that your computer has the minimum amount of memory required by Windows XP Professional (64MB). Having insufficient memory may cause the installation to fail or blue-screen errors to occur after installation.
Not enough processing power	Make sure that your computer has the minimum processing power required by Windows XP Professional (Pentium 233MHz). Having insufficient processing power may cause the installation to fail or blue-screen errors to occur after installation.
Hardware that is not on the HCL	If your hardware is not on the HCL, Windows XP may not recognize the hardware, or the device may not work properly.
Hardware with no driver support	Windows XP will not recognize hardware without driver support.
Hardware that is not configured properly	If your hardware is Plug and Play–compatible, Windows should configure it automatically. If your hardware is not Plug and Play–compatible, you will need to manually configure the hardware per the manufacturer's instructions.
Incorrect CD key	Without a valid CD key, the installation will not go past the Product Key dialog box. Make sure that you have not typed in an incorrect key (check your Windows XP installation folder for this key).
Failure to access TCP/IP network resources	If you install Windows XP with typical settings, the computer is configured as a DHCP client. If there is no DHCP server to provide IP configuration information, the client will still generate an auto-configured IP address, but be unable to access network resources through TCP/IP if the other network clients are using DHCP addresses.
Failure to connect to a domain controller when joining a domain	Make sure that you have specified the correct domain name. If your domain name is correct, verify that your network settings have been set properly and that a domain controller and DNS server are available. If you still can't join a domain, install the computer in a workgroup, then join the domain after installation.

Troubleshooting Installation Errors with the *Boot.ini* File

If the text-based portion of the installation completes successfully, but the GUI-based portion of the installation fails, the error may be caused by a device driver that is failing to load properly. If you suspect that this is causing the installation error, you can edit a file called Boot.ini to list the drivers that are being loaded during the boot process. The Boot.ini file is located in the root of the system partition.

In order to cause the device drivers to be listed during the boot process, you need to edit the Boot.ini file to include the /sos switch, as shown:

```
[operating systems]
multi(0)disk(0)rdisk(0)partition(1)\WINDOWS = "Microsoft
    Windows XP Professional" /sos
```

You can learn more about editing the Boot.ini file in Chapter 14, "Performing System Recovery Functions."

Installing Non-Supported Hard Drives

If your computer is using a hard disk that does not have a driver included on the Windows XP Professional CD, you will receive an error message stating that the hard drive cannot be found. You should verify that the hard drive is properly connected and functional. You will need to obtain a disk driver from the manufacturer for Windows XP, then specify that you are using a manufacturer-supplied driver (by pressing the F6 key when prompted) during the text-mode portion of the installation process.

Troubleshooting with Installation Log Files

When you install Windows XP Professional, several log files are created by the Setup program. You can view these logs to check for any problems during the installation process. Two log files are particularly useful for troubleshooting:

- The action log includes all of the actions that were performed during the setup process and a description of each action. These actions are listed in chronological order. The action log is stored as *Windir*\setupact.log.

- The error log includes any errors that occurred during the installation. For each error, there is a description and an indication of the severity of the error. This error log is stored as *Windir*\setuperr.log.

In Exercise 1.2, you will view the Windows XP setup logs to determine whether there were any problems with your Windows XP installation.

EXERCISE 1.2

Troubleshooting Failed Installations with Setup Logs

In this exercise, you will view the installation with setup logs, which could be helpful in troubleshooting failed installations.

1. Select Start ➢ All Programs ➢ Accessories ➢ Windows Explorer.

2. In Windows Explorer, click My Computer, click Local Disk (C:), and click Windows.

3. Since this is the first time you have opened the Windows folder, click the Contents of This Folder option.

4. In the Windows folder, click the setupact file to view your action log in Notepad. When you are finished viewing this file, close Notepad.

5. Double-click the setuperr file to view your error file in Notepad. If no errors occurred during installation, this file will be empty. When you are finished viewing this file, close Notepad.

6. Close Windows Explorer.

Supporting Multiple-Boot Options

You may want to install Windows XP Professional but still be able to run other operating systems. *Dual-booting* or *multi-booting* allows your computer to boot multiple operating systems. Your computer will be automatically configured for dual-booting if there was a supported operating system on your computer prior to the Windows XP Professional installation (and you didn't upgrade from that operating system).

One reason for dual-booting is to test various systems. If you have a limited number of computers in your test lab, and you want to be able to test multiple configurations, you dual-boot. For example, you might configure one computer to multi-boot with Windows NT 4 Workstation, Windows NT 4 Server configured as a Primary Domain Controller (PDC), Windows 2000 Professional, and Windows XP Professional.

Another reason to set up dual-booting is for software backward compatibility. For example, you may have an application that works with Windows 98 but not under Windows XP Professional. If you want to use Windows XP but still access your legacy application, you can configure a dual-boot.

Here are some keys to successful dual-boot configurations:

- Make sure you have plenty of disk space. It's a good idea to put each operating system on a separate partition, although this is not required.

- Put the simplest operating systems on first. If you want to support dual-booting with DOS and Windows XP Professional, DOS must be installed first. If you install Windows XP Professional first, you cannot install DOS without ruining your Windows XP configuration. This requirement also applies to Windows 9x and Windows 2000.

- Never, ever, upgrade to Windows XP dynamic disks. Dynamic disks are seen only by Windows 2000 and Windows XP, and are not recognized by any other operating system, including Windows NT.

- Do not convert your file system to NTFS if you are planning a dual-boot with any operating system except Windows NT, Windows 2000, or Windows XP. These operating systems are the only ones that recognize NTFS.

- If you will dual-boot with Windows NT, you must turn off disk compression, or Windows XP will not be able to read the drive properly.

 If you are planning on dual-booting with Windows NT 4, you should upgrade it to NT 4 Service Pack 4 (or higher), which provides NTFS version 5 support.

Once you have installed each operating system, you can choose the operating system that you will boot to during the boot process. You will see a boot selection screen that asks you to choose which operating system you want to boot.

Summary

In this chapter, you learned how to install Windows XP Professional. We covered the following topics:

- The design goals of Windows XP Professional, which include taking the best features of Windows 98, Windows Me, and Windows 2000 Professional, providing a wide range of support for hardware, making the operating system easy to use, and lowering the cost of ownership.

- Installation preparation, which begins with making sure that your computer meets the minimum system requirements and that all of your hardware is on the Hardware Compatibility List (HCL). Then you need to decide whether you will perform a clean install or an upgrade. Finally, you should plan which options you will select during installation. Options include methods of partitioning your disk space, selecting a file system, whether the computer will be installed as part of a workgroup or a domain, and your language and locale settings.

- The methods you can use for installation, which include using the distribution files on the Windows XP Professional CD or using files that have been copied to a network share point.

- How to install Windows XP Professional, which proceeds in four main installation phases: information collection, installation preparation, Windows installation, and installation finalization.

- The post-installation update and product activation feature. Post-installation updates are used to ensure that you have the latest files. Product activation is used to complete the Windows XP licensing process.

- How to troubleshoot installation problems. Common errors are caused by media problems, lack of disk space or memory, and hardware problems. Other common errors include an improperly configured `Boot.ini` file or using non-supported hard drives. You can view Setup log files to check for problems that occurred during the installation.

- Information about supporting dual-boot or multi-boot environments. Dual-booting and multi-booting allow you to boot to a choice of two or more operating systems.

Exam Essentials

Be able to tell if a computer meets minimum hardware requirements for Windows XP Professional.   Windows XP has minimum hardware requirements that must be met. In addition, the hardware must be on the HCL, and Windows XP drivers must be available for all devices.

Understand the different methods that can be used for Windows XP Professional installation. Be able to specify the steps and setup involved in installing Windows XP through options such as local CD and through network installation.

Understand the reasons why a Windows XP installation would fail.   You should be able to list common reasons for failure of a Windows XP Professional installation and be able to offer possible fixes or solutions.

Specify what is required to support multiple-boot configurations.   If you plan to install Windows XP Professional on the same computer that is running other operating systems, be able to specify what must be configured to support dual- or multiple-boot configurations.

Key Terms

Before you take the exam, be certain you are familiar with the following terms:

`Boot.ini`	File Allocation Table (FAT16)
boot partition	logical drive
central processing unit (CPU)	megahertz (MHz)
clean installation	New Technology File System (NTFS)
disk partitioning	system partition
distribution server	upgrade
domain	workgroup

Review Questions

1. James is the network administrator for a large corporation. He is in charge of compatibility testing and needs to test his corporation's standard applications on the Windows XP Professional operating system. He has decided to install Windows XP on a test computer in the lab. He can choose among several computers. When making his selection, what is the minimum processor required for an Intel-based computer to install and run Windows XP Professional?

    A. A Pentium with a 133MHz or better processor

    B. A Pentium with a 233MHz or better processor

    C. A Pentium II with a 166MHz or better processor

    D. A Pentium III with a 333MHz or better processor

2. Martina has a Windows NT 4 Workstation installed on her home desktop computer. This computer is running some applications that require the use of her sound card; however, her sound card does not have a Windows XP–compatible driver. Martina is planning on replacing the sound card at some point, and she has purchased an upgrade to Windows XP Professional. She decides to install Windows XP Professional on her desktop computer in a dual-boot configuration. She has an extra 4GB partition that can be used. What is the minimum free disk space required to install Windows XP Professional on the extra partition?

    A. 500MB

    B. 650MB

    C. 1GB

    D. 1.5GB

3. Dionne is purchasing 12 new computers for the training room. She needs to make sure that the computers will support Windows XP Professional. What is the name of the list that shows the computers and peripheral hardware that have been extensively tested with the Windows XP Professional operating system?

    A. The Windows Compatibility List

    B. The XP Compatibility List

    C. The Microsoft Compatibility List

    D. The Hardware Compatibility List

4. You are the network administrator for a small company. You have recently purchased 20 brand-new computers that came with no operating system but are configured with the latest hardware. Each computer has a SCSI controller and an 80GB SCSI hard drive. When you purchased the computers, they came with a minimal operating system so that the CD drive would read CDs and a CD that contained all of the Windows XP drivers for the devices in the computer. You put the Windows XP Professional CD in the CD drive and start the installation. During the Setup phase, Windows XP reports that no disk device is available. Which of the following actions should you take?

    A. Install a full version of Windows 98 on the computer, and then try to upgrade to Windows XP Professional.

    B. Verify that the BIOS for the SCSI controller is enabled.

    C. During the Setup phase, when the disk is being detected, provide the Windows XP device drivers that are on the manufacturer's CD.

    D. Replace the SCSI drive with a drive that has a driver on the Windows XP Professional CD.

5. Mike is the network administrator for a medium-sized company. All of the computers that are installed must be a part of the Active Directory and installed in SJ.MASTERMCSE.COM. The computers should be installed into the Active Directory during initial installation. When Mike installs the computers, he has no problem adding them to the domain. Mike has asked Steve, a contract worker, to assist with installations. When Steve attempts to add computers to the domain, he is denied access. What are the minimum rights that Steve needs to be assigned so that he can also add computers to the domain during installation?

    A. Steve needs to be made a member of the Domain Admins group.

    B. Steve needs to be made a member of the Power Users group.

    C. Steve needs to be made a member of the Server Operators group.

    D. Steve needs to be granted the user right to add workstations to the domain.

6. You are the network administrator of a large corporation. Your company issues a laptop to each user. The laptops are brand new. You verify that you can access the hard drive with the operating system that came installed with the laptops. However, when you attempt to install Windows XP Professional, you keep getting an error that the hard drive cannot be accessed. You restart the installation and get the same error. What action should you take?

    A. Go into the system BIOS and verify that the UDMA for the hard drive is enabled.

    B. Go into the system BIOS and verify that the APM for the hard drive is disabled.

    C. Reserve an IRQ for the hard drive in the system BIOS.

    D. Get an XP driver from the hard drive manufacturer and install the disk driver during the text-mode portion of the installation when prompted.

7. You are the network administrator of a large corporation. Currently your network runs a mixture of Windows 98, Windows Me, and Windows 2000 Professional computers. You are considering adopting a corporate standard that all new computers will be installed with Windows XP Professional. Part of the reason you want to adopt Windows XP Professional is that you have had problems with users updating applications, then having major operating system problems because the application has overwritten core operating system files. Which of the following Windows XP features is used to protect core operating system files so that they are not overwritten improperly by application files?

A. Windows File Protection

B. Windows File Manager

C. Kernel Mode File Protection

D. Ring 0 Manager

8. Sean has four computers in the test lab. He wants to install Windows XP Professional. The configurations for each of his computers are listed in the exhibit below. Place a mark on the computer that does *not* meet the minimum requirements for Windows XP Professional.

	Computer A	Computer B	Computer C	Computer D
Processor	PII/266	PIII/450	PII/166	Pentium/233
Memory	64MB	64MB	32MB	64MB
Free Disk Space	2GB	750GB	650GB	2GB

9. James is installing a Windows XP Professional computer in the `Sales.ABCCorp.com` domain. Select and place the servers that must be available on the network to support the addition of James's computer to the domain.

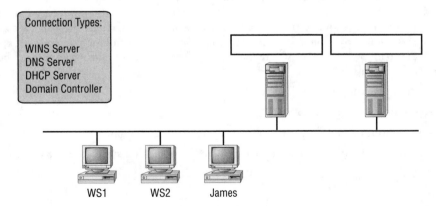

Connection Types:

WINS Server
DNS Server
DHCP Server
Domain Controller

WS1   WS2   James

10. Your computer is configured with two hard drives. You have decided to configure logical drive C: on disk 0, and logical drive D: on disk 1. You want to run Windows 98 for backward compatibility with some applications that will not run under Windows XP. However, you also want to run Windows XP Professional to take advantage of the Windows XP features. On drive D:, you want to store files that should have a high level of security. You will install Windows 98 on drive C: and Windows XP Professional on drive D:. How should the drives on this computer be configured?

   A. Configure both logical drives as FAT32.

   B. Configure both logical drives with NTFS.

   C. Configure logical drive C: as FAT32 and logical drive D: as NTFS.

   D. Configure logical drive C: as NTFS and logical drive D: as FAT32.

11. You are the network administrator of a large corporation. You manage a computer lab that is used for compatibility testing. Many of the computers are configured to support dual-booting of operating systems. One of the racks of computers is configured to dual-boot between Windows NT 4 Workstation and Windows XP Professional. Which of the following statements reflects proper configuration for these computers?

   A. You should turn off disk compression on the Windows NT 4 Workstation configuration.

   B. You should enable dynamic disks on the Windows XP Professional configuration.

   C. You should install both operating systems into the same *Windir* directory so you can access applications under both operating systems.

   D. You should edit the Registry on the Windows XP computer for HKEY_LOCAL_ MACHINE\DualBoot to a value of 1 so you can access applications under both operating systems.

12. You are the network administrator of a small company. You have decided to install Windows XP Professional on all of the company's computers. Because of your company's high security needs, your network is not connected to the Internet. After you installed Windows XP Professional, you did not perform the post-installation activation because you did not have an Internet connection and have not had time to call the Microsoft Clearing House to properly complete post-installation activation. After the grace period for post-installation activation expires, which of the following actions will require you to activate the computer before it can be used? (Choose all that apply.)

   A. Putting the computer in sleep mode.

   B. Restarting the computer.

   C. Logging out of the computer and attempting to log on again.

   D. You are automatically required to activate the operating system before any further actions can be taken.

13. Catherine is the network administrator for a large company. She needs to install Windows XP Professional on 25 computers that, for security purposes, do not have CD-ROM drives installed. Each of the computers has a valid network connection and is able to connect to a server called DIST. Catherine decides to use the network installation method to install Windows XP Professional on these computers. What folder must be copied from the Windows XP Professional CD to the network share that has been created in the DIST server?

    A. \OEM

    B. \I386

    C. \Intel

    D. \$WINI386

14. Eammon is the network administrator for a small company. His company recently purchased three new computers that need to have Windows XP Professional installed on them. When Eammon attempted to install the first computer with Windows XP Professional, the text-mode portion of the installation process completed. When the GUI-portion of the installation process started, the computer stopped responding. Eammon suspects that the problem is due to a device driver failing to load properly. Which of the following steps should he take?

    A. Modify the `Boot.ini` file to include the `/sos` switch.

    B. Modify the `Boot.ini` file to include the `/fastdetect` switch.

    C. Modify the `Boot.ini` file to include the `/report` switch.

    D. Modify the `Boot.ini` file to include the `/error` switch.

15. You are the network administrator for your company. You are attempting to install Windows XP Professional on a computer in the lab, but the installation process keeps failing halfway through. During the process of troubleshooting the Windows XP Professional installation, you decide to verify all of the actions that were taken during the Setup phase. Where can you find a log file that will tell you this information?

    A. *Windir*\verify.log

    B. \Logfiles\verify.log

    C. *Windir*\setupact.log

    D. \Logfiles\setup.log

Answers to Review Questions

1. B. The processor must be a Pentium 233MHz or better. You can verify the current requirements for Windows XP Professional at http://www.microsoft.com/windowsxp/pro/evaluation/sysreqs.asp.

2. D. You must have a minimum of a 2GB drive with at least 1.5GB of free space to install Windows XP Professional. You can verify the current requirements for Windows XP Professional at http://www.microsoft.com/windowsxp/pro/evaluation/sysreqs.asp.

3. D. The Hardware Compatibility List (HCL) shows the computers and components that have been tested to work with Windows XP Professional. When selecting hardware, you should always check for HCL compatibility.

4. C. If you have a disk device that does not have a driver on the Windows XP Professional CD, and the manufacturer provides a Windows XP Professional driver, you can load the alternate driver during the Setup phase of Windows XP Professional installation.

5. D. The minimum right needed to add computers to the domain is the granting of the "Add workstations to the domain" user right. Administrators and Server Operators can also add computers to the domain, but also grants the user additional rights.

6. D. You will need to obtain a disk driver from the manufacturer for Windows XP, then specify that you are using a manufacturer-supplied driver (by pressing the F6 key when prompted) during the text-mode portion of the installation process.

7. A. Windows File Protection is a new feature of Windows XP Professional that prevents core operating system files from being overwritten by application files.

8. C. You should have placed a mark on Computer C. Computers A, B, and D meet the minimum requirements of a Pentium 233MHz or higher processor, 64MB of memory, and at least 1.5GB of free disk space. Computer C does not.

9. You must have a domain controller and a DNS server running in your domain to add a computer to the domain. These services are also required for the Active Directory.

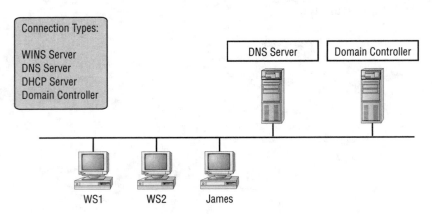

10. C.   You should configure logical drive C: as FAT32 because Windows 98 will not read NTFS partitions. Logical drive D: should be configured as NTFS because you want to implement local security.

11. A.   You should turn off disk compression before you dual-boot. Windows XP Professional does not support the disk compression that was used by Windows NT 4 Workstation. There is no way to configure the operating systems to recognize applications under both platforms.

12. B, C.   Once the grace period for product activation expires, you will not be able to access the operating system if you log out of the computer or restart the computer.

13. B.   You must copy the \I386 folder and share the folder to install Windows XP Professional over a network. You should verify that all subfolders of the \I386 folder are copied as well.

14. A.   If the text-based portion of the installation completes successfully, but the GUI-based portion of the installation fails, the error may be caused by a device driver that is failing to load properly. If you suspect that this is causing the installation error, you can edit a file called Boot.ini to list the drivers that are being loaded during the boot process. The Boot.ini file is located in the root of the system partition. In order to cause the device drivers to be listed during the boot process, you need to edit the Boot.ini file to include the /sos switch.

15. C.   You can find the log file that details Setup actions in *Windir*\\setupact.log. This log can be useful in identifying installation errors.

Chapter

2

Automating the Windows XP Installation

MICROSOFT EXAM OBJECTIVES COVERED IN THIS CHAPTER:

✓ **Perform and troubleshoot an unattended installation of Windows XP Professional.**

- Install Windows XP Professional by using Remote Installation Services (RIS).
- Install Windows XP Professional by using the System Preparation Tool.
- Create unattended answer files by using Setup Manager to automate the installation of Windows XP Professional.

✓ **Manage applications by using Windows Installer packages.**

You can automate the installation of Windows XP Professional in several ways: by using unattended installation, by using Remote Installation Services (RIS) to remotely deploy unattended installations (which requires a Windows 2000 Server or Windows Server 2003), or by using the System Preparation Tool for disk imaging. To help customize all three options for automating remote installations, you can also use answer files. Answer files are used with automated installations to provide answers to the questions that are normally asked during the installation process. After you've installed Windows XP Professional, you can also automate the installation of applications by using Windows Installer packages.

This chapter begins with an overview of the three automated deployment options. Then you will learn how to access the Windows XP Professional Deployment Tools. Next, it details the use of unattended installation, RIS, how the System Preparation Tool is used to create disk images for automated installation, and how to use Setup Manager to create unattended answer files. Finally, you will learn how to automate application installation through the use of Windows Installer packages.

Choosing Automated Deployment Options

If you need to install Windows XP Professional on multiple computers, you could manually install the operating system on each computer, as described in Chapter 1, "Getting Started with Windows XP Professional." However, automatic deployment will make your job easier, more efficient, and more cost effective if you have a large number of client computers to install. Windows XP Professional comes with several utilities that can be used for deploying and automating the Windows XP Professional installation. By offering multiple utilities with different functionality, administrators have increased flexibility in determining how to best deploy Windows XP Professional within a large corporate environment.

The following sections contain overviews of the automated deployment options, which will help you choose which solution is best for your requirements and environment. Each utility will then be covered in more detail throughout the chapter. The three options for automated deployment of Windows XP Professional are:

- Unattended installation, or unattended setup, which uses the Winnt32 and Winnt command-line utilities and options to automate the Windows XP Professional installation

- Remote Installation Services (RIS), which requires Windows 2000 Server or Windows Server 2003 for deployment

- System Preparation Tool (`Sysprep.exe`), which is used to create and deploy disk imaging or cloning

At the end of this section, you will see a table that summarizes the features and requirements of each installation deployment option.

 Windows XP Professional can also be deployed through Systems Management Server (SMS), which is beyond the scope of this book. You can learn more about SMS on the Microsoft website at http://www.microsoft.com.

An Overview of Unattended Installation

Unattended installation is a practical method of automatic deployment when you have a large number of clients to install and the computers require different hardware and software configurations. Unattended installations require the use of the *Winnt* or *Winnt32* command-line utilities in conjunction with an answer file called *Unattend.txt* to provide configuration information during the unattended installation process. With an unattended installation, you use a distribution server to install Windows XP Professional on a target computer. You can also use a Windows XP Professional CD with an answer file on a floppy disk.

Unattended installations also allow you to create custom installations, which are modifications of standard Windows XP Professional installations. Custom installations can be used to support custom hardware and software installations. This requires that additional setup files be added to the distribution folder and additional configuration of the answer files be done. In addition to providing standard Windows XP configuration information, the answer files can be used to provide installation instructions for applications, additional language support, service packs, and device drivers.

The *distribution server* contains the Windows XP Professional operating system files and possibly an answer file to respond to installation configuration queries. The target computer must be able to connect to the distribution server over the network. After the distribution server and target computers are connected, you can initiate the installation process. Figure 2.1 illustrates the unattended installation process.

FIGURE 2.1 Unattended installation with distribution server and a target computer

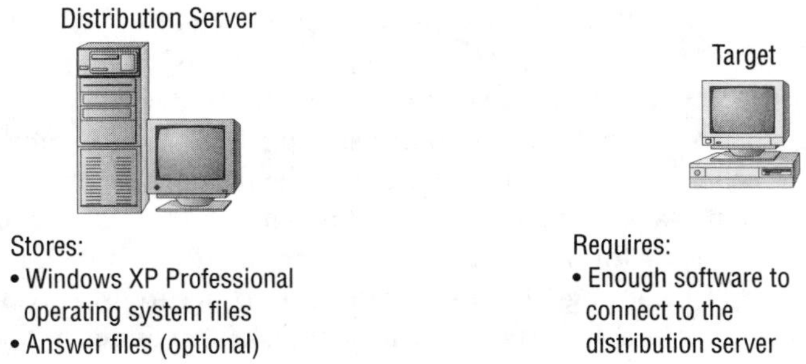

Distribution Server

Target

Stores:
- Windows XP Professional operating system files
- Answer files (optional)

Requires:
- Enough software to connect to the distribution server

Using and configuring unattended installations is covered in detail in the "Deploying Unattended Installations" section of this chapter.

Advantages of Unattended Installation

The advantages of using unattended installations as a method for automating Windows XP Professional installations include:

- Save time and money because users do not have to interactively respond to each installation query.
- Can be configured to provide automated query response, while still selectively allowing users to provide specified input during installations.
- Can be used to install clean copies of Windows XP Professional or upgrade an existing operating system (providing it is on the list of permitted operating systems) to Windows XP Professional.
- Can be expanded to include installation instructions for applications, additional language support, service packs, and device drivers.
- The physical media for Windows XP Professional does not need to be distributed to all computers that will be installed.

Disadvantages of Unattended Installation

The disadvantages of using unattended installations as a method for automating Windows XP Professional installations include:

- Requires more initial setup than a standard installation of Windows XP Professional.
- Someone must have access to each client computer, and must initiate the unattended installation process.
- Does not allow you to use reference computer images to automate the installation of specific configurations and applications.

An Overview of Remote Installation

Remote Installation Services (RIS) was introduced in Windows 2000 Server and is also supported by Windows Server 2003. It allows you to remotely install Windows XP Professional.

A RIS server installs Windows XP Professional on RIS clients, as illustrated in Figure 2.2. The RIS server must have the RIS server software installed and configured. RIS clients are computers that have a *Pre-boot eXecution Environment (PXE)* network adapter or use a RIS boot disk. PXE is a technology that is used to boot to the network when no operating system or network configuration has been installed and configured on a client computer. The RIS boot disk is a PXE ROM emulator for network adapters that don't have a PXE boot ROM or for a PC that doesn't support booting from the network. In order to use a RIS boot disk, the network adapter must be PCI-compliant. The RIS boot disk is generated with the *Remote Boot Floppy Generator* (rbfg.exe) utility.

FIGURE 2.2   Remote Installation Services (RIS) uses a RIS server and RIS clients.

RIS Server

RIS Client

Stores:
• RIS server software
• Windows XP Professional,
  CD-based, or RIPrep images
• Answer files (optional)

Requires:
• PXE-based boot ROM, or
• RIS boot disk with a network adapter that
  supports PXE, or
• Net PC computer

The RIS clients access RIS servers through Dynamic Host Configuration Protocol (DHCP) to remotely install the operating system from the RIS server. The network must have a DHCP server, a Domain Name System (DNS) server, and Active Directory to connect to the RIS server. No other client software is required to connect to the RIS server. Remote installation is a good choice for automatic deployment when you need to deploy to large numbers of computers and your clients are PXE compliant.

The RIS server can be configured with either of two types of images:

- A CD-based image that contains only the Windows XP Professional operating system. You can create answer files for CD-based images to respond to the Setup program's configuration prompts.

- A Remote Installation Preparation (RIPrep) image that can contain the Windows XP operating system and applications. This type of image is based on a preconfigured computer.

RIS installation is discussed in the "Using Remote Installation Services (RIS)" section later in this chapter.

Advantages of RIS

The advantages of using RIS as a method for automating Windows XP Professional installations include:

- Windows XP Professional installations can be standardized across a group or organization.

- The physical media for Windows XP Professional does not need to be distributed to all computers that will be installed.

- Uses a technology called Single Instance Store (SIS) to reduce duplicate distribution files, even if you store multiple distribution configurations. This greatly reduces storage requirements for distribution servers.

- End-user installation deployment can be controlled through the Group Policy utility. For example, you can configure what choices a user can access or are automatically specified through the end-user Setup Wizard.

Disadvantages of RIS

The disadvantages of using RIS as a method for automating Windows XP Professional installations include:

- Can only be used if your network is running Windows 2000 Server or Windows Server 2003 with Active Directory installed.

- The clients that use RIS must have a PXE-compliant network adapter or have a remote boot disk that can be used with a PCI-compliant network adapter.

- RIS images can be created only from the C: partition of a hard disk.

- RIS can be used only for clean installations and can't be used to upgrade a previous version of Windows.

An Overview of the System Preparation Tool and Disk Imaging

The System Preparation Tool (Sysprep.exe) is used to prepare a computer for disk imaging, which can be done with a third-party image software or with disk-duplicator hardware. *Disk imaging* (also sometimes called disk cloning or disk duplication) is the process of creating a *reference computer* for the automated deployment. The reference, or source, computer has Windows XP Professional installed and is configured with the settings and applications that should be installed on the target computers. An image is then created that can be transferred to other computers, thus installing the operating system, settings, and applications that were defined on the reference computer.

Using the System Preparation Tool and disk imaging is a good choice for automatic deployment when you have the hardware that supports disk imaging and you have a large number of computers with similar configuration requirements. For example, education centers that reinstall the same software every week might use this technology.

To perform an unattended install, the System Preparation Tool prepares the reference computer by stripping away the *security identifier (SID)*, which is used to uniquely identify each computer on the network. The System Preparation Tool also detects any Plug and Play devices that are installed and can adjust dynamically for any computers that have different hardware installed.

If you are using disk-duplicator hardware, you create a reference computer, then use the System Preparation Tool to create the image. You would then remove the drive that has the disk image and insert it into a special piece of hardware, called a disk duplicator, to copy the image. The copied disks are inserted into the target computers. After you add the hard drive that contains the disk image to the target computers, you can complete the installation from those computers. Figure 2.3 illustrates the disk-imaging process. You can also copy disk images by using special third-party software.

When the client computer starts an installation using a disk image, a Mini-Setup Wizard will execute. You can customize what is displayed on the Windows Welcome screen and the options that are displayed through the Mini-Setup Wizard process, which query for information such as username or time zone selection. You can also create fully automated deployments with disk imaging through the use of answer files.

FIGURE 2.3   Disk imaging with disk-duplicator hardware

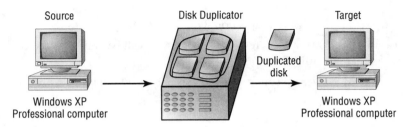

Source   Disk Duplicator   Target

Duplicated disk

Windows XP
Professional computer   Windows XP
Professional computer

You can also configure disk imaging so that the drive is not removed. The reference computer is booted to an image boot disk. The image is labeled and uploaded to a remote server. When the image is required, you boot the computer with the image boot disk and download the selected image from a menu.

The process for using the System Preparation Tool to create disk images is covered in detail in the "Using the System Preparation Tool to Create Disk Images" section later in this chapter.

Advantages of the System Preparation Tool

The advantages of using the System Preparation Tool as a method for automating Windows XP Professional installations include:

- For large numbers of computers with similar hardware, it greatly reduces deployment time by copying the operating system, applications, and Desktop settings from a reference computer to multiple cloned computers.

- Using disk imaging facilitates the standardization of Desktops, administrative policies, and restrictions throughout an organization.

- Reference images can be copied across a network connection or through CDs that are physically distributed to client computers.

- By default, it does not perform full Plug and Play re-detection, which means that the Plug and Play process that is run at the destination computer is greatly reduced (therefore, is faster) compared to the standard Plug and Play detection process.

Disadvantages of the System Preparation Tool

The disadvantages of using the System Preparation Tool as a method for automating Windows XP Professional installations include:

- You must use either third-party imaging software or hardware disk-duplicator devices.

- The Hardware Abstraction Layer (HAL) must be the same on the reference and target computers.

- Will not detect any hardware that is non–Plug and Play compliant.

- If you use a CD to distribute the reference image, you will be limited to the capacity of the CD (approximately 650MB).

- Can only be used for clean installations and can't be used to upgrade a previous version of Windows.

Summary of Windows XP Professional Deployment Options

Table 2.1 summarizes the installation options for Windows XP Professional and notes the required client hardware, server requirements, and whether the option supports clean install or upgrade.

TABLE 2.1   Summary of Windows XP Professional Installation Options

Attended Installation	Unattended Installation	RIS	System Preparation Tool
Required Client Hardware			
PC that meets Windows XP Professional requirements	PC that meets Windows XP Professional requirements, access to the network	PC that meets the Windows XP Professional requirements that is PXE-compliant or uses a remote boot disk with a PCI-compliant network adapter	Reference computer with Windows XP installed and configured, PC that meets the Windows XP Professional requirements, third-party disk imaging software or hardware disk-duplicator device
Required Server Hardware and Services			
None	None with CD; if using network installation, distribution server with \I386 folder	Windows 2000 Server or Windows Server 2003 to act as a RIS server with image files, Active Directory, DNS server, and DHCP server	None
Clean Install or Upgrade Only			
Clean install or upgrade	Clean install or upgrade	Clean install only	Clean install only

Table 2.2 summarizes the unattended installation tools and files that are used with automated installations of Windows XP Professional, the associated installation method, and a description of each tool.

TABLE 2.2   Summary of Windows XP Professional Unattended Deployment Utilities

Tool or File	Automated Installation Option	Description
Winnt32.exe or Winnt.exe	Unattended installation	Program used to initiate the unattended installation process
Unattend.txt	Unattended installation	Answer file used to customize installation queries
Setupmgr.exe	Unattended installation RIS (Remote Installation Services) Sysprep (Disk Duplication)	Setup Manager utility, used to create and modify answer files and distribution folders
Risetup.exe	RIS	Remote Installation Services Wizard, used to create and configure a CD-based Windows XP Professional image to be used by the RIS server
Riprep.exe	RIS	Remote Installation Preparation Tool, used to prepare a pre-installed and configured Windows XP Professional computer for disk imaging and then to replicate the disk image to a RIS server
Rbfg.exe	RIS	Remote Boot File Generator utility, used with RIS to create RIS boot disks
Sysprep.exe	Sysprep (Disk Duplication)	System Preparation Tool, prepares a source reference computer that will be used in conjunction with disk duplication through third-party software or hardware disk-duplication devices

Accessing the Windows XP Professional Deployment Tools

The Windows XP Professional installation utilities and resources relating to automated deployment are located in a variety of locations. Table 2.3 provides a quick reference for each utility or resource and its location.

TABLE 2.3   Location of Windows XP Professional Deployment Utilities and Resources

Utility	Location
Winnt32.exe or Winnt.exe	Windows XP Professional distribution CD, \I386 folder
Sysprep.exe	Windows XP Professional distribution CD, \Support\Tools; Sysprep.exe must be extracted from the Deploy.cab file
Setupmgr.exe	Windows XP Professional distribution CD, \Support\Tools; Setupmgr.exe must be extracted from the Deploy.cab file
RIS Server	Included with Windows 2000 Server and Windows Server 2003
Risetup.exe	RIS Server
Riprep.exe	RIS Server
Rbfg.exe	*RIS_Server*\Reminst\Admin\I386\Rbfg.exe

In Exercise 2.1, you will extract the Windows XP Deployment Tools.

EXERCISE 2.1

Extracting the Windows XP Deployment Tools

1.   Log onto your Windows XP computer as Administrator.

2.   Use Windows Explorer to create a folder named Deployment Tools on the root folder of your C: drive.

3.   Insert the Windows XP Professional CD. Using Windows Explorer, copy the \Support\Tools\Deploy file (the .cab extension is hidden by default) to the C:\Deployment Tools folder.

4.   Double-click the Deploy.cab file to display its contents.

5.   In Windows Explorer, select Edit ➢ Select All. Then select File ➢ Extract.

6.   The Select a Destination dialog box appears. Select My Computer, Local Disk (C:), and then Deployment Tools. Click the Extract button to extract the files to the specified folder.

7.   Verify that the Deployment Tools were extracted to C:\Deployment Tools. There should be 11 items (including the Deploy.cab file).

Deploying Unattended Installations

You can deploy Windows XP Professional installations or upgrades through the Window XP Professional distribution CD or a distribution server that has a network share of the \I386 folder. Using a CD can be advantageous if the computer you are installing Windows XP on is not connected to the network or is connected via a low-bandwidth network. It is also typically faster to install Windows XP Professional from CD than to use a network connection. The drawback to using a CD for unattended installation is that the answer file (winnt.sif) must be located on a floppy disk.

Unattended installations rely on command-line switches used with the Winnt32 or Winnt command-line utilities, along with answer files, to deploy Windows XP Professional. Answer files are text files that contain the settings that are typically supplied by the installer during attended installations of Windows XP Professional. Answer files can also contain instructions for how programs and applications should be run.

 You will learn more about answer files in the section "Using Setup Manager to Create Answer Files" later in this chapter.

You run Winnt32 to install or upgrade to Windows XP Professional from computers that are running Windows 98, Windows Me, Windows NT 4 Workstation, Windows 2000 Professional, or Windows XP Home Edition. You would run Winnt from all other operating systems.

Typically, when you run Winnt32 or winnt in unattended mode, you use the following syntax.

Winnt32 /unattend:answerfile

The Winnt32 command-line utility has a wide range of switches that can be applied, many of which are used with unattended installations. Each Winnt32 switch is described in Table 2.4.

TABLE 2.4   Winnt32 Command-Line Switches and Descriptions

Winnt32 Switch	Description
/checkupgradeonly	Does not install or upgrade to Windows XP Professional. Used to check the current operating system for upgrade compatibility with the hardware and software that is currently installed and will be upgraded to Windows XP Professional.
/cmd:command line	Allows you to specify that a command should be executed before the GUI mode of setup is complete. This option is typically used with cmdlines.txt to specify what applications should be installed on the computer before the Setup phase of Windows XP Professional is complete.
/cmdcons	Used to support the Recovery Console for repair of failed installations.

TABLE 2.4 Winnt32 Command-Line Switches and Descriptions *(continued)*

Winnt32 Switch	Description
/copydir:*folder name*	Used to create customized subfolders that can be used with the Windows XP Professional installation. For example, if your computer contains hardware that does not have drivers on the Windows XP distribution CD, you can create a custom folder called \Custom Drivers that contains the custom driver files.
/copysource:*folder name*	Used to create a temporary subfolder for Windows XP Professional files to be used during the installation process. Once the installation process is complete, the folders created with this process are deleted. If you use the \copydir option, the folder is not deleted.
/debug:[*level*] [*filename*]	Used to create debugging files, which are used in troubleshooting. Level specifies the amount of detail that will be included in the log file, and file name specifies the filename that will be created.
/dudisable	Used to prevent dynamic update from running during the installation process.
/duprepare:*pathname*	Used to prepare a network share that will be used to provide dynamic update files to clients installing Windows XP Professional.
/dushare:*pathname*	Specifies the installation share to be used with dynamic update files that have been downloaded from the Windows Update website. The dynamic updates are then accessed from a network connection, rather than an Internet connection, during the installation process.
/m:*folder name*	Used with Setup to specify that replacement files should be copied from the specified location. If the files are not present, then Setup will use the default location.
/makelocalsource	Copies the installation files to a local hard disk. Used if the CD will not be available for the entire installation process.
/noreboot	Normally, when the file copy phase of Winnt32 is complete, the computer restarts. This option specifies that the computer should not restart so that you can execute another command prior to the restart.
/s:*sourcepath*	By default, the installation process looks for the Windows XP Professional installation files in the current folder. This option allows you to specify the source location for the Windows XP Professional installation files. You can use this option to specify up to eight sources, which allows you to simultaneously copy files from multiple servers.

TABLE 2.4 Winnt32 Command-Line Switches and Descriptions *(continued)*

Winnt32 Switch	Description
/syspart:*drive letter*	Used to copy the Setup startup files to a hard disk and mark the disk as active for installation into another computer. When you start the computer that the disk has been moved to, Setup will automatically start at the next phase. This option must be used with the /tempdrive option, and both the /syspart and the /tempdrive options must specify the same partition on the secondary hard disk.
/tempdrive:*drive letter*	Specifies the location that will be used to store the temporary files for Windows XP Professional and the installation partition for Windows XP Professional. This option must be used with the /syspart option.
/udf:*ID, UDB file*	Used by the Setup program to specify how a Uniqueness Database file (UDB) will be used to modify an answer file. UDF settings override any conflicting settings specified through an answer file.
/unattend	Used to upgrade a previous version of Windows using unattended installation. This option automatically uses Windows Update and preserves all user settings from the previous installation. When this option is specified, an upgrade requires no user intervention.
/unattend:*seconds* :*answerfile*	Specifies that you will be using an unattended installation for Windows XP Professional. The seconds variable specifies the number of seconds that Windows will wait between finishing the file copy and restarting the computer. The answer file variable points to the custom answer file you will use for installation.

Using Remote Installation Services (RIS)

You can remotely install Windows XP Professional through RIS. A variety of installation options are available through the *Windows XP Client Installation Wizard (CIW)*. For RIS installation, you need a RIS server that stores the Windows XP Professional operating system files in a shared image folder, and clients that can access the RIS server. Depending on the type of image you will distribute, you may also want to configure answer files so that users need not respond to any Windows XP Professional installation prompts. (Answer files are described in the "Using Setup Manager to Create Answer Files" section of this chapter.)

Following are some of the advantages of using RIS for automated installation:

- You can remotely install Windows XP Professional.

- The procedure simplifies management of the server image by allowing you to access Windows XP distribution files and use Plug and Play hardware detection during the installation process.
- You can quickly recover the operating system in the event of a computer failure.

Windows XP security is retained when you restart the destination computer. Here are the basic steps of the RIS process:

1. The RIS client initiates a special boot process through the PXE network adapter (and the computer's BIOS configured for a network boot), or through a special RIS boot disk. On a PXE client, the client presses F12 to start the PXE boot process, and to indicate that they want to perform a RIS installation.

2. The client computer sends out a DHCP discovery packet that requests an IP address for the client and the IP address of a RIS server (running Windows 2000 Server or Windows Server 2003). Within the discovery packet, the client also sends its Globally Unique Identifier (GUID). The GUID is a unique 32-bit address that is used to identify the computer account as an object within the Active Directory.

3. If the DHCP server and the RIS server are on the same computer, the information requested in the discovery packet is returned. If the DHCP server and the RIS server are on separate networks, the DHCP server will return the client information for IP configuration. Then the client will send out another broadcast to contact the RIS server.

4. The client contacts the RIS server using the Boot Information Negotiation Layer (BINL) protocol. The RIS server contacts Active Directory to see if the client is a "known client" and whether it has already been authorized (also called pre-staged) through Active Directory. The authorization process is discussed later in this section.

5. If the client is authorized to access the RIS server, BINL provides to the client the location of the RIS server and the name of the *bootstrap image* (enough software to get the client to the correct RIS server).

6. The RIS client accesses the bootstrap image via the Trivial File Transfer Protocol (TFTP), and the Windows XP Client Installation Wizard (CIW) is started.

7. The RIS client is prompted for a username and password that can be used to log onto the Windows 2000 or Windows 2003 domain that contains the RIS server.

8. Depending on the user or group credentials, the user sees a menu offering the operating systems (images) that can be installed. The user sees only the options for the installs determined by the parameters defined on the RIS server.

The following sections describe how to set up the RIS server and the RIS clients, and how to install Windows XP Professional through RIS.

RIS Client Options

RIS offers several client installation options. This allows administrators to customize remote installations based on organizational needs. When the client accesses the Windows XP Client Installation Wizard (CIW), they see the installation options that have been defined by the administrator. Remote installation options include the following:

Automatically setting up the computer   When you automatically set up the computer, the user sees a screen indicating which operating system will be installed but is not prompted for any configuration settings. If only one operating system is offered, the user does not even have to make any selections and the entire installation process is automatic.

Customizing the setup of the computer   If you configure RIS to support customizing the setup of the computer, then Administrators who install computers within the enterprise can override the RIS settings to specify the name and location of the computer being installed within Active Directory.

Restarting a previous setup attempt   The option to restart a previous setup attempt is used when a remote installation fails prior to completion. The operating system installation will restart when this option is selected from the CIW.

Performing maintenance or troubleshooting   The maintenance and troubleshooting option provides access to third-party troubleshooting and maintenance tools. Examples of tasks that can be completed through this option include updating flash BIOS and using PC diagnostic tools.

Preparing the RIS Server

The RIS server is used to manage and distribute the Windows XP Professional operating system to RIS client computers. As explained earlier in this chapter, RIS servers can distribute CD-based images (created with the `Risetup.exe` utility) or images created from a reference Windows XP computer, called *RIPrep images* (created with the `Riprep.exe` utility). A CD-based image contains the operating system installation files taken directly from the Windows XP Professional CD and can be customized for specific computers through the use of answer files. RIPrep images are based on a pre-configured computer and can contain applications as well as the operating system. `RIPrep.exe` is used to deploy these images to target computers.

The RIS server is configured to specify how client computers will be installed and configured. The Administrator can configure the following options for client computers:

- Define the operating system installation options that will be presented to the user. Based on access permissions from Access Control Lists (ACLs), Administrators can define several installation options, and then allow specific users to select an option based on their specific permissions.

- Define an automatic client-computer naming format, which bases the computer name on a custom naming format. For example, the computer names might be a combination of location and username.

- Specify the default Active Directory location for client computers that are installed through remote installation.

- Pre-stage client computers through Active Directory so that only authorized computers can access the RIS server. This option requires a specified computer name, a default Active Directory location, and identification of RIS servers and the RIS clients they will service.

- Authorize RIS servers so that unauthorized RIS servers can't offer RIS services to clients.

- Create and modify the RIS answer file.

The following steps for preparing the RIS server are discussed in the sections coming up:

1. Make sure that the server meets the requirements for running RIS.
2. Install RIS.
3. Configure and start RIS, using either a CD-based image or a RIPrep image.
4. Authorize the RIS server through DHCP Manager.
5. Grant users who will perform RIS installations the user right to create computer accounts.
6. Grant users who will perform the RIS installation the Log On as a Batch Job user right.
7. Configure the RIS server to respond to client computers (if this was not configured when RIS was installed).
8. Configure RIS template files (if you wish to customize installation options for different computers or groups).

 There is a hands-on exercise to create a RIS server in *MCSE: Windows 2000 Server Study Guide*, 2nd edition, by Lisa Donald with James Chellis (Sybex, 2001)

Meeting the RIS Server Requirements

For RIS to work, the computer acting as the RIS server must be a Windows 2000 Server or Windows Server 2003 domain controller or member server. The server on which you will install RIS must meet the hardware requirements for RIS and be able to access the required network services.

Hardware Requirements

The RIS server must meet the following hardware requirements:

- Pentium 133MHz or higher minimum processor and a minimum of 128MB of memory for Windows 2000 Server or Windows Server 2003.
- At least two disk partitions, one for the operating system and one for RIS images. The partition that will hold the RIS images should be at least 2GB and formatted as NTFS.
- A network adapter installed.

 If you are deploying Windows XP Professional RIPrep images from Windows 2000 RIS servers, the Remote Installation Preparation Tool Update must be installed. You can access this update on the Microsoft website.

Network Services

The following network services must be running on the RIS server or be accessible to the RIS server from another network server:

- TCP/IP, installed and configured.
- A Dynamic Host Configuration Protocol (DHCP) server, which is used to assign DHCP addresses to RIS clients. (Make sure that your DHCP scope has enough addresses to accommodate all the RIS clients that will need IP addresses.)

- A Domain Name System (DNS) server, which is used to locate the Active Directory controller.
- Active Directory, which is used to locate RIS servers and RIS clients, as well as to authorize RIS clients and manage RIS configuration settings and client installation options.

Installing the RIS Server

You add the RIS server components through the Add/Remove Programs icon in Control Panel. To install the components on a RIS server running Windows 2000 Server, take the following steps:

1. Select Start ➢ Programs ➢ Administrative Tools ➢ Configure Your Server.
2. The Windows 2000 Configure Your Server dialog box appears. Click the Advanced option in the panel on the left, and select Optional Components.
3. Click the Start the Windows Components Wizard option.
4. When the wizard starts, select the Remote Installation Services option and click the Next button.
5. The Insert Disk dialog box prompts you to insert the Windows 2000 Server CD so that the proper files can be copied. Insert the CD and click the OK button.
6. After the process is complete, you'll see the Completing the Windows Components Wizard dialog box. Click the Finish button.
7. When you see the System Settings Change dialog box, click the Yes button to restart your computer.

As part of the RIS installation, the following services are loaded on the server (these services are required for the RIS server to function properly):

BINL   The *Boot Information Negotiation Layer (BINL)* protocol is used to respond to client requests for DHCP and the CIW.

SIS   The *Single Instance Store (SIS)* manages duplicate copies of images by replacing duplicate images with a link to the original files. The main purpose of this service is to reduce disk space that is used.

SIS Groveler   The *SIS Groveler service* scans the SIS volume for files that are identical. If identical files are found, this service creates a link to the duplicate files instead of storing duplicate files.

TFTP   The *Trivial File Transfer Protocol (TFTP)* is a UDP-based file transfer protocol that is used to download the CIW from the RIS server to the RIS clients.

Configuring and Starting RIS with a CD-Based Image

After you have the RIS server components installed on the RIS server, you can use the Risetup utility to configure the RIS installation. This utility performs the following actions:

- Locates an NTFS partition that will be used to store the remote image(s)
- Creates the directory structure that will be used for the remote images
- Copies all the files that are required to install Windows XP Professional
- Copies the Client Installation Wizard files and screens
- Configures the Remote Installation Service

- Starts the services that are required by RIS, which include BINL, TFTP, and the SIS Groveler service

- Creates a share named Reminist that provides the share for the root of the RIS directory structure

- Creates the appropriate IntelliMirror management *Service Control Point (SCP)* object that is used within Active Directory to support RIS

- Creates the SIS common store directory and the related files that are required to support SIS on the RIS server

With RIS installed, you can configure the RIS server through the following steps:

1. Select Start ➤ Run, type **Risetup** in the Run dialog box, and click the OK button.

2. When the Remote Installation Services Setup Wizard starts, click the Next button to continue.

3. The Remote Installation Folder Location dialog box appears next. The remote installation folder must be on an NTFS version 3.0 (or later) partition and must not reside on the same partition as the system or boot partition. Specify the path of the remote installation folder and click the Next button.

4. Next up is the Initial Settings dialog box. Here you configure client support during server configuration. You can specify that the server should respond to client computers requesting service, and that the server should not respond to unknown client computers. You can select one or both options, or leave them both unchecked and configure client support later. Make your selection(s) and click the Next button.

5. In the Installation Source Files Location dialog box that appears next, specify the location of the Windows XP Professional distribution files and click the Next button.

6. In the Windows Installation Image Folder Name dialog box, specify the name of the folder to be used for the Windows XP Professional distribution files and click the Next button.

7. The Friendly Description and Help Text dialog box appears next. Here you specify a friendly name and help text to help users select the Windows installation image. Enter a name and text, and click Next to continue.

8. The Review Settings dialog box appears next, where you confirm your installation choices. If all of the settings are correct, click the Finish button.

9. The installation files will be copied, which can take several minutes. When the process is complete, click the Done button.

Configuring and Starting RIS with a RIPrep Image

The *Remote Installation Preparation Tool* (`Riprep.exe`) is used to prepare a pre-installed and configured Windows XP Professional computer for disk imaging and then to replicate the disk image to a RIS server. In addition to containing the Windows XP operating system, the disk image can include applications and customized configuration settings. In order to use a RIPrep image, the reference computer must have Windows XP Professional and all of the applications that will be imaged located on the C: drive prior to running the `RIPrep` utility.

The HAL for the imaged computer and the target computers must match. For example, you could not apply an ACPI-based HAL on a non-ACPI-based computer. For other hardware differences, the RIPrep wizard will use Plug and Play capabilities to detect any hardware differences between the source and destination computers.

You would take the following steps to create a RIS image:

1. Install the Windows XP Professional operating system and any applications that will be used for the RIPrep image on a reference computer.

2. From the reference computer, attach to the RIS server and run `Riprep.exe`. This will start the Remote Installation Preparation Wizard.

3. You will be prompted to specify the name of the RIS Server, the folder location that will store the RIPrep image, and a description for the RIPrep image.

4. The image preparation process will begin and the image will be copied to the RIS server.

Authorizing the RIS Server through DHCP Manager

For a RIS server to respond to client requests, the DHCP server must be authorized through the Active Directory. By authorizing DHCP servers, you ensure that rogue DHCP servers do not assign client IP addresses.

 You'll learn more about DHCP in Chapter 10, "Managing Network Connections."

To authorize the DHCP server on Windows 2000 Server, take the following steps:

1. Select Start ➢ Programs ➢ Administrative Tools ➢ DHCP.

2. In the left pane of the DHCP window, right-click your DHCP server. From the pop-up menu, select Authorize, as shown in Figure 2.4.

FIGURE 2.4   Authorizing a DHCP server

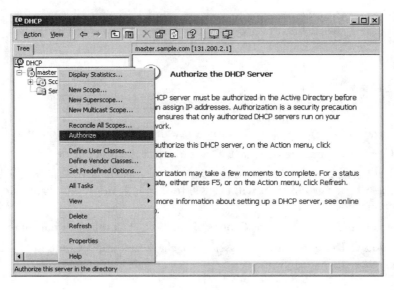

3. Close the DHCP console.

    To authorize a RIS server, use this same process.

Granting the User Right to Create Computer Accounts

To install an image using RIS, users must have the user right to create a computer account in the Active Directory. You can specify that users can create accounts anywhere in the domain, or that users can create computer accounts only in specific organizational units.

   To grant the user right to create computer accounts, take the following steps on a Windows 2000 Server:

1. Select Start ➢ Programs ➢ Administrative Tools ➢ Active Directory Users and Computers.

2. The Active Directory Users and Computers window appears, as shown in Figure 2.5. Right-click the domain or organizational unit where you want to allow users to create computer accounts and select Delegate Control from the pop-up menu.

FIGURE 2.5   The Active Directory Users and Computers window

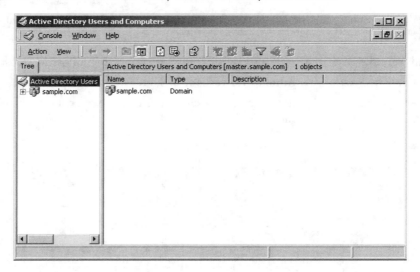

3. The Delegation of Control Wizard starts. Click the Next button to continue.

4. In the Users or Groups dialog box (Figure 2.6), click the Add button.

5. The Select Users, Computers, or Groups dialog box appears next, as shown in Figure 2.7. Select the users or groups that will use RIS to install Windows XP Professional, click the Add button, and click OK.

6. When you return to the Users or Groups dialog box, click the Next button to continue.

7. In the Tasks to Delegate dialog box, select the check box Join a Computer to the Domain and then click the Next button.

FIGURE 2.6   The Users or Groups dialog box

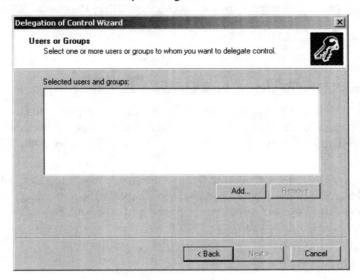

FIGURE 2.7   The Select Users, Computers, or Groups dialog box

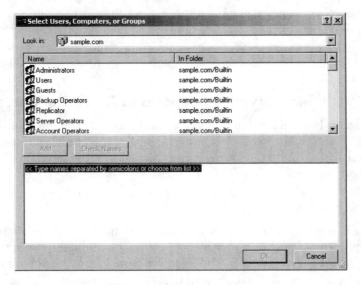

8. In the Completing the Delegation of Control dialog box, verify that all the configuration options are correct and click the Finish button.

9. Close the Active Directory Users and Computers window.

Active Directory is covered in detail in *MCSE: Windows 2000 Directory Services Administration Study Guide,* 2nd ed., by Anil Desai with James Chellis (Sybex, 2001).

Granting the User Right to Log On as a Batch Job

The user account that will perform the remote installation must have the user right that allows logging on as a batch job. By default, the Administrators group does not have this user right. To assign the Log On as a Batch Job user right on a Windows 2000 Server, take the following steps:

1. Log on as Administrator and add the Group Policy snap-in to the MMC administrator console. (The MMC and snap-ins are covered in Chapter 4, "Configuring the Windows XP Environment." Adding the Group Policy snap-in and assigning user rights are covered in Chapter 7, "Managing Security.")

2. Select Local Computer Policy ➢ Computer Configuration ➢ Windows Settings ➢ Security Settings ➢ Local Policies ➢ User Rights Assignment.

3. Double-click the Log On as a Batch Job user right.

4. The Local Security Policy Setting dialog box appears. Click the Add button.

5. The Select Users or Groups dialog box appears. Click the user or group to which you want to assign this permission, click the Add button, and then click the OK button.

6. You will return to the Local Security Policy Setting dialog box. Click the OK button.

Configuring the RIS Server to Respond to Client Requests

The RIS server must be configured to respond to client requests. You can configure the server response as a part of the RIS server installation or do it later, after the RIS server is installed and ready for client requests. Take the following steps to configure the RIS server on a Windows 2000 Server to respond to client requests:

1. Select Start ➢ Programs ➢ Administrative Tools ➢ Active Directory Users and Computers.

2. The Active Directory Users and Computers window appears. Expand your domain and select Computers or Domain Controllers to access the computer that acts as your RIS server. Right-click the RIS server, and select Properties from the pop-up menu.

3. In the computer's Properties dialog box, select the Remote Install tab to see the dialog box shown in Figure 2.8.

4. Check the Respond to Client Computers Requesting Service check box. Click the OK button.

5. Close the Active Directory Users and Computers window.

FIGURE 2.8   The Remote Install tab of the computer's Properties dialog box

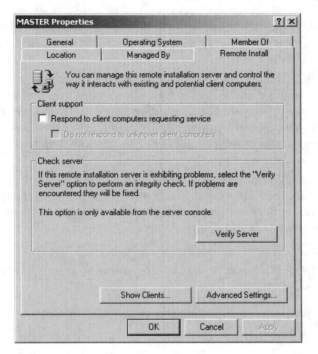

Using RIS Template Files

RIS template files are used to specify the installation parameters for your client computers. When you use the Risetup utility, a standard template called Ristndrd.sif is automatically created, which acts as the answer file. You can have as many template files as you need to perform custom installations for different computers, or for groups that require custom configurations such as Sales and Marketing. Template files must have a .sif filename extension. The Ristndrd.sif template can also be configured with the description that will be displayed during the CIW when the user is presented with a menu or operating system images to select from.

Preparing the RIS Client

The RIS client is the computer on which Windows XP Professional will be installed. RIS clients rely on a technology called PXE (Pre-boot eXecution Environment), which allows the client computer to remotely boot and connect to a RIS server.

To act as a RIS client, the computer must meet all the hardware requirements for Windows XP Professional (see Chapter 1) and have a network adapter installed. In addition, the RIS client must support one of the following configurations:

- Use a PXE-based boot ROM (a boot ROM is a special chip that uses read-only memory) with a BIOS that supports starting the computer with the PXE-based boot ROM (as opposed to booting from the hard disk).

- Follow the *Net PC/PC 98* standard for PCs, which uses industry-standard components for the computer. This includes processor, memory, hard disk, video, audio, and an integrated network adapter and modem, in a locked case with limited expansion capabilities. The primary advantages of Net PCs are that they are less expensive to purchase and to manage.

- Have a network adapter that supports PXE and that can be used with a RIS boot disk. The only network adapters that can be used with RIS boot disks are the network adapters that are displayed when running the RBFG.exe utility. If your network adapter is not on the list, ensure that you have the most current RBFG.exe utility, since Microsoft makes updates and adds drivers to this utility periodically. You can obtain updates through Windows Update or Service Packs.

If the client computer does not have a network adapter that contains a PXE-based boot ROM, then you can use a RIS boot disk to simulate the PXE startup process. The PXE-based boot disk is used to provide network connectivity to the RIS server. In order to use a RIS boot disk, the client computer must use a PCI-compliant network adapter.

 WARNING   If your client uses PCMCIA or ISA network adapters, there is no support to use RIS boot disks.

To create a RIS boot disk, take the following steps:

1. On a Windows XP Professional computer that is connected to the same network as the RIS server, select Start ➢ Run. In the Run dialog box, type the following command and click the OK button:

   \\RIS_Server\Reminst\Admin\I386\Rbfg.exe

2. The Windows XP Remote File Generator dialog box appears. Insert a blank floppy disk in your computer, select the appropriate destination drive, select the installed network card from the Adapter List, and click the Create Disk button. The network adapter must be on the list of those shown when running the RBFG.exe utility. When the disk is made, it will support any and all of these network adapters.

3. You see a message verifying that the boot floppy was created and asking whether you want to create another disk. You can click Yes and repeat the procedure to create another boot disk, or click No. After you are finished creating RIS boot disks, click the Close button.

Installing Windows XP Professional through RIS

After the RIS server has been installed and configured, you can install Windows XP Professional on a RIS client that uses either a PXE-compliant network card or a RIS boot disk with a network card that supports PXE.

To install Windows XP Professional on the RIS client, take the following steps:

1. Start the computer. When prompted, press F12 for a network service boot.

2. The Client Installation Wizard starts. Press Enter to continue.

3. The Windows XP Logon dialog box appears. Specify the domain to which you will log on, and enter a valid domain username and password.

4. A menu appears with the options Automatic Setup, Custom Setup, Restart a Previous Setup Attempt, and Maintenance and Troubleshooting. Select Automatic Setup.

If you have only one RIS image, it will automatically be installed. If you have multiple RIS images, the user will see a menu of RIS images. After you select a RIS image, the remote installation process will start. What happens next depends on the image type and whether you have configured answer files.

Using the System Preparation Tool to Create Disk Images

You can use disk images to install Windows XP Professional on several computers that have the same configuration. Also, if a computer is having technical difficulties, you can use a disk image to quickly restore it to a baseline configuration.

To create a disk image, you install Windows XP Professional on the source computer with the configuration that you want to copy. The source computer's configuration should also include any applications that should be installed.

Once you have your source computer configured, you use the System Preparation Tool (Sysprep.exe) to prepare the disk image for disk duplication. After you've created the disk image, you can copy the image to destination computers through third-party software or through hardware disk duplication.

Preparing for Disk Duplication

To use a disk image, the source and target computers must meet the following requirements:

-   Both the source and destination computers must be able to use the same hard-drive controller driver.

-   Both the source and destination computers must have the same HAL (Hardware Abstraction Layer). For example, both use an ACPI HAL. If the source computer is ACPI-compatible and the target computer is non-ACPI-compatible, Windows XP Professional will not load properly.

-   The size of the installation partition must be as large as the smallest space the image program will install the image to.

-   Plug and Play devices on the source and destination computers do not need to match, as long as the drivers for the Plug and Play devices are available.

Using the System Preparation Tool

The System Preparation Tool (Sysprep.exe) is included on the Windows XP Professional CD in the \Support\Tools folder, in the Deploy.cab file. When you run this utility on the source computer, it strips out information from the master copy that must be unique for each computer, such as the security ID (SID).

After you install the copied image on the target computer, a Mini-Setup Wizard runs. This Wizard automatically creates a unique computer SID and then prompts the user for computer-specific information, such as the product ID, regional settings, and network configuration. The required information can also be supplied through an automated installation script.

Table 2.5 defines the command switches that you can use to customize the System Preparation Tool's (Sysprep.exe) operation.

TABLE 2.5   System Preparation Command-Line Switches

Switch	Description
-quiet	Runs the installation with no user interaction
-pnp	Forces Setup to run Plug and Play detection of hardware
-reboot	Restarts the target computer after the System Preparation Tool completes
-noreboot	Specifies that the computer should be shut down without a reboot.
-clean	Specifies that critical devices should be cleaned out.
-nosidgen	Doesn't create a SID on the destination computer (used with disk cloning)
-activated	Prevents Windows Product Activation from resetting
-factory	Allows you to add additional drivers and applications to the image after the computer has restarted
-reseal	Reseals an image and prepares the computer for delivery after modifications have been made to an image using the factory mode
-bmsd	Used to build a list of all available mass storage devices in sysprep.inf.
-forceshutdown	If you have used the -reseal switch, prepares the operating system as specified, then immediately shuts down the computer without any user intervention
-mini	Specifies that you want to run the Mini-Setup Wizard on the next restart of the computer

After you run the System Preparation Tool on a computer, you need to run the Mini-Setup Wizard. Then run the Setup Manager to create an answer file that will answer the Mini-Setup Wizard's questions when the computer (the imaged computer or the original computer that has had the System Preparation Tool run on it) is restarted.

In the following sections you will learn how to create a disk image and how to copy and install from a disk image.

Creating a Disk Image

To run the System Preparation Tool and create a disk image, take the following steps:

1. Install Windows XP Professional on a source computer. The computer should have a similar hardware configuration to the destination computer(s). You should not join a domain, and the Administrator password should be left blank. (See Chapter 1 for instructions on installing Windows XP Professional.)

2. Log onto the source computer as Administrator and, if desired, install and configure any applications, files (such as newer versions of Plug and Play drivers), or custom settings (for example, a custom Desktop) that will be applied to the target computer(s).

3. Verify that your image meets the specified configuration criteria and that all applications are properly installed and working. Extract the `Deploy.cab` file from the Windows XP Professional CD. (See Exercise 2.1 for instructions on extracting this file.)

4. Select Start ➢ Run and click the Browse button in the Run dialog box. Select Local Drive (C:), then Deployment Tools; double-click `Sysprep` and click the OK button.

5. The Windows System Preparation Tool dialog box appears, as shown in Figure 2.9. This dialog box warns you that the execution of this program will modify some of the computer's security parameters. Click the OK button.

FIGURE 2.9   The Windows System Preparation Tool dialog box

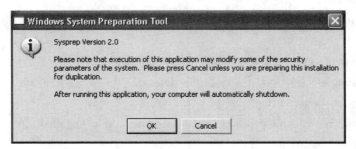

6. You will be prompted to turn off your computer.

7. You may now boot up with third-party imaging software and create an image of the computer to deploy to other computers.

In Exercise 2.2, you will use the System Preparation Tool to prepare the computer for disk imaging. This exercise assumes that you have completed Exercise 2.1.

EXERCISE 2.2

Using the System Preparation Tool

1. Log onto the source computer as Administrator and, if desired, install and configure any applications that should also be installed on the target computer.

2. Select Start ➢ Run and click the Browse button. Select Local Drive (C:), Deployment Tools. Double-click Sysprep and click the OK button.

3. In the Windows System Preparation Tool dialog box, click the OK button.

4. The System Preparation Tool dialog box will appear. Click the Reseal button.

5. The Windows System Preparation Tool dialog box will ask you to confirm the current settings. If you will not be using Disk Imaging, click the Cancel button and close the Windows System Preparation Tools dialog box.

Copying and Installing from a Disk Image

After you've run the System Preparation Tool on the source computer, you can copy the image and then install it on the target computer.

If you are using special hardware (a disk duplicator) to duplicate the disk image, shut down the source computer and remove the disk. Copy the disk and install the copied disk into the target computer. If you are using special software, copy the disk image per the software vendor's instructions.

After the image is copied, turn on the destination computer. The Mini-Setup Wizard runs and prompts you as follows (if you have not configured an answer file):

- Accept the End User License Agreement.

- Specify regional settings.

- Enter a name and organization.

- Specify your product key.

- Specify the computer name and Administrator password.

- Specify dialing information (if a modem is detected).

- Specify date and time settings.

- Specify which networking protocols and services should be installed.

- Join a workgroup or a domain.

 If you have created an answer file for use with disk images, as described in the section "Using Setup Manager to Create Answer Files" later in this chapter, the installation will run without requiring any user input.

In Exercise 2.3, you will use the stripped image that was created in Exercise 2.2 to simulate the process of continuing an installation from a disk image.

EXERCISE 2.3

Installing Windows XP Professional from a Disk Image

1. Turn on your computer. The Windows XP Setup Wizard will start. Click the Next button to continue (this will happen automatically if you don't click the Next button after about 10 seconds).

2. In the License Agreement dialog box, click the I Accept This Agreement option and click the Next button.

3. In the Regional Settings dialog box, click Next to accept the default settings and continue.

4. In the Personalize Your Software dialog box, enter your name and organization. Then click the Next button.

5. In the Your Product Key dialog box, type the 25-character product key and click the Next button.

6. In the Computer Name and Administrator Password dialog box, specify the computer name and an Administrator password (if desired). Then click the Next button.

7. If you have a modem installed, the Modem Dialing Information dialog box appears. Specify your dialing configuration and click the Next button.

8. In the Date and Time Settings dialog box, specify the date, time, and time zone. Then click the Next button.

9. In the Network Settings dialog box, verify that Typical Settings is selected and click the Next button.

10. In the Workgroup or Computer Domain dialog box, verify that the No, This Computer Is Not on a Network, or Is on a Network without a Domain Controller option is selected and click the Next button.

11. When the Completing the Windows XP Setup Wizard dialog box appears, click the Finish button.

12. When the computer restarts, start Windows XP Professional.

13. When the Network Identification Wizard starts, click the Next button.

14. In the Users of This Computer dialog box, select the Users Must Enter a User Name and Password to Use This Computer option and click the Next button.

15. When the Completing the Network Identification Wizard dialog box appears, click the Finish button.

16. Log onto the computer as Administrator.

Using Setup Manager to Create Answer Files

Answer files are automated installation scripts used to answer the questions that appear during a normal Windows XP Professional installation. You can use answer files with Windows XP unattended installations, the System Preparation Tool (disk images), or RIS installations. Setting up answer files allows you to easily deploy Windows XP Professional to computers that may not be configured in the same manner, with little or no user intervention.

You create answer files through the *Setup Manager* (`Setupmgr`) utility. There are several advantages to using Setup Manager to create answer files:

- You can easily create answer files through a graphical interface, which reduces syntax errors.

- It simplifies the addition of user-specific or computer-specific configuration information.

- You can include application setup scripts within the answer file.

- The utility creates the distribution folder and allows you to populate the distribution folder by adding files, programs, and applications that will be used along with the installation files.

In the following sections, you will learn about options that can be configured through Setup Manager, how to create answer files with Setup Manager, answer file format, and how to manually edit answer files.

Options That Can Be Configured through Setup Manager

The Setup Manager can be used to configure a wide variety of installation options. The following list defines what can be configured through Setup Manager and gives a short description of each parameter:

Set user interaction   Sets the level of user interaction that will be used during the setup process. This can be fully automated, or the user can supply configuration information for the items you specify.

Set default username   Specifies the username and organization that will be defined for the computer.

Define computer names   Configures multiple usernames during the setup process. In this case, Setup Manager will generate a Uniqueness Database File (UDF), which maps unique names and settings to specific computers.

Set an administrator password   Encrypts the Administrator password that has been defined within the answer file, or allows you to prompt the user on the first logon to specify an Administrator password.

Display settings   Configures the display for color depth, screen area, and the refresh frequency display settings that should be applied.

Configure network settings   Specifies any custom network settings you want to be applied. You can also configure the computer to be added to a domain or workgroup, and if you join a domain, automatically create an account within the domain for the computer.

Set time zone and regional options   Specifies the appropriate time zone to be configured for the target computer. Regional options include language settings such as how time and date are displayed.

Set Internet Explorer settings   Configures the basic settings that will be applied to Internet connections.

Set telephony settings   Configures telephony properties—for example, area codes and dialing rules.

Add Cmdlines.txt file   Adds applications during the GUI-mode phase of Windows XP Professional installation.

Create an installation folder   Uses the default installation folder (Windows) to generate or set a custom folder during the setup process.

Install printers   Sets up and configures printers as a part of the automated deployment process.

Add command to the Run Once   Installs whatever command or applications you specify the first time a user logs onto the computer.

Run command at the end of setup   Runs a command at the end of the setup process, but before a user logs onto the computer the first time.

Copy additional files   Copies additional files to the user Desktop.

Create a distribution folder   Creates a Windows distribution folder on a network share that contains the Windows XP Professional source files or any additional files (such as device drivers) you want to add.

Creating Answer Files with Setup Manager

After you have extracted the Windows XP Deployment Tools from the Windows XP Professional CD, you can run the Setup Manager utility to create a new answer file, create an answer file that duplicates the current computer's configuration, or edit existing answer files.

The following steps describe how to create a new installation script. In this example, the instructions are for creating an answer file for a RIS installation. This answer file provides default answers, uses the default display configuration, configures typical network settings, and does not edit any additional options.

1. Select Start ➢ Run and click the Browse button in the Run dialog box. Double-click the Deployment Tools folder, double-click the Setupmgr program, and then click the OK button.

2. The Windows Setup Manager Wizard starts. Click the Next button.

3. The New or Existing Answer File dialog box appears, as shown in Figure 2.10. This dialog box provides choices for creating a new answer file or modifying an existing answer file. Select the option Create a New Answer File and click the Next button.

FIGURE 2.10   The New or Existing Answer File dialog box

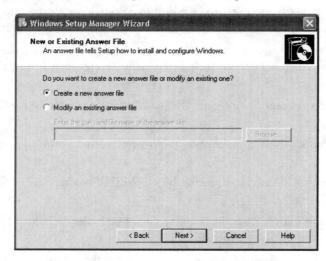

4. The Product to Install dialog box appears, as shown in Figure 2.11. You can choose Windows Unattended Installation, Sysprep Install, or Remote Installation Services. Select Remote Installation Services and click the Next button.

FIGURE 2.11   The Product to Install dialog box

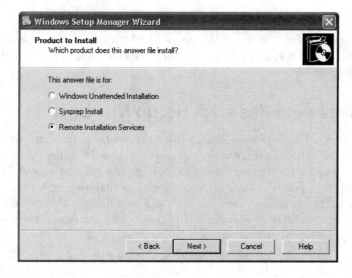

5. The User Interaction Level dialog box appears, as shown in Figure 2.12. This dialog box offers the following options:

- Provide Defaults allows you to configure default answers that will be displayed. The user is prompted to review the default answer and can change the answer if desired.

- Fully Automated uses all the answers in the answer file and will not prompt the user for any interaction.

- Hide Pages lets you hide the wizard page from the user, if you have supplied all of the answers on the Windows Setup Wizard page.

- Read Only allows the user to see the Setup Wizard display page, but not to make any changes to it (this option is used if the Setup Wizard display page is shown to the user).

- GUI Attended allows only the text-mode portion of the Windows Setup program to be automated.

Select the Provide Defaults option and click the Next button to continue.

FIGURE 2.12   The User Interaction Level dialog box

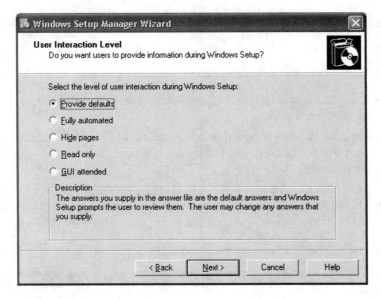

6. Next, from the Display Settings dialog box (Figure 2.13), you can configure the following settings:

- For the Colors option, set the display color to the Windows default, 16 colors, 256 colors, high color (16 bit), high color (24 bit), or high color (32 bit).

- The Screen Area option allows you to set the screen area to the Windows default, or to one of the following: 640×480, 800×600, 1024×768, 1280×1024, or 1600×1200.

- The Refresh Frequency option (the number of times the screen is updated) allows you to set the refresh frequency to the Windows default or to 60Hz, 70Hz, 72Hz, 75Hz, or 85Hz.

- The Custom button displays a dialog box in which you can further customize display settings for the color, screen area, and refresh frequency.

For this example, click Next to accept the default configuration and continue.

FIGURE 2.13 The Display Settings dialog box

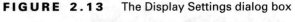

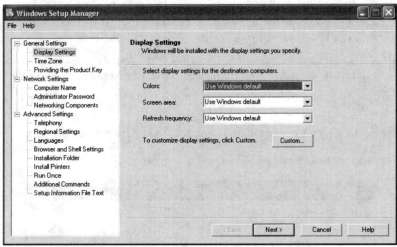

7. The Time Zone dialog box appears. Select your computer's time zone from the drop-down list and click the Next button.

8. The Providing the Product Key dialog box appears. Type in the product key for the computer that will be installed. Each computer will need its own license key. When you are done, click the Next button.

9. The Computer Name dialog box will appear as shown in Figure 2.14. You can let a computer name be automatically generated or you can choose to specify the destination computer name. In this example, we will specify a computer name and click the Next button.

FIGURE 2.14 The Computer Name dialog box

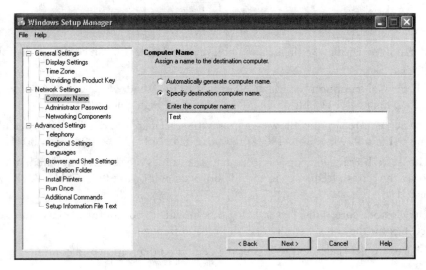

10. Next is the Administrator Password dialog box. You can choose to prompt the user for a password, or you can specify the Administrator password. You can also specify that when the computer starts, the Administrator will automatically be logged on. Enter and confirm an Administrator password. Then click the Next button.

11. In the Network Settings dialog box, you can choose from Typical Settings, which installs TCP/IP, enables DHCP, and installs Client for Microsoft Networks; or Custom Settings, which allows you to customize the computer's network settings. Select the Typical Settings option and click the Next button.

12. The Advanced Settings dialog box options appear. These additional settings allow you to configure the following options:

   - Telephony settings
   - Regional settings
   - Languages
   - Browser and shell settings
   - Installation folder
   - Install printers
   - A command that will run once the first time a user logs on
   - Additional commands that should be run at the end of unattended setup

13. The Setup Information File Text dialog box appears, as shown in Figure 2.15. This dialog box allows you to give the answer file a descriptive name and help text. Enter the name in the Description String text box, and the help text in the Help String text box. Click Finish to continue.

FIGURE 2.15   The Setup Information File Text dialog box

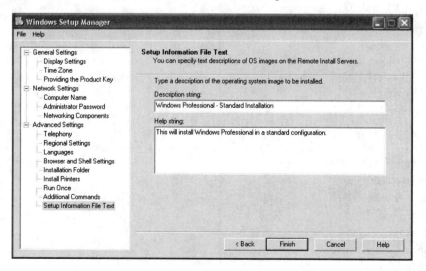

14. The Setup Manager dialog box appears. Specify the path and file name you want to use to save your answer file, then click the OK button.

15. When you see the Completing Setup Manager dialog box, click the Finish button.

> An answer file can be used to provide automated answers for a CD-based installation. Simply create a new answer file named winnt.sif and copy it to a floppy. Insert the Windows XP Professional CD and set the BIOS to boot from CD. As the installation begins, Windows XP will look for winnt.sif and use it as the answer file.

Manually Editing Unattended Answer Files

In addition to creating answer files through Setup Manager, you can edit or create your answer files through a text editor program. Answer files consist of section headers, parameters, and values for the parameters. You do not have to specify every option through your answer file if the option is not required by the installation. Following is a sample answer file, Unattended.txt.

```
;SetupMgrTag
[Data]
    AutoPartition=1
    MsDosInitiated="0"
    UnattendedInstall="Yes"

[Unattended]
    UnattendMode=ProvideDefault
    OemPreinstall=Yes
    TargetPath=\WINNT

[GuiUnattended]
    AdminPassword=abc
    OEMSkipRegional=1
    TimeZone=4

[UserData]
    FullName="Test User "
    OrgName="ABC Corp"
    ComputerName=SJ-UserTest

[TapiLocation]
    CountryCode=1
    AreaCode=408
```

```
[SetupMgr]
    DistFolder=C:\winXPdist
    DistShare=winXPdist

[Identification]
    JoinDomain=SJ-CORP
    DomainAdmin=administrator
    DomainAdminPassword=test

[Networking]
    InstallDefaultComponents=Yes
```

The Setup Manager utility allows you to configure answer files through a GUI interface. However, it has limitations on what can be configured, and many additional options can be configured by manually editing the answer files in a text editor (such as Notepad). In the following sections, you will learn how to configure settings for the following options:

- Mass storage devices
- Plug and Play devices
- HALs
- Passwords
- Language, regional, and time zone settings
- Display settings
- NTFS conversion
- Application installation
- Windows product activation
- Dynamic updates
- Driver signing

Mass Storage Devices

If you have a mass storage device on the remote computer and it is recognized and supported by Windows XP, you need not specify anything in the answer file for mass storage devices. However, if the device has a driver that is not shipped with the Windows XP Professional CD, possibly because the device is brand new, you can configure the device under the [MassStorageDrivers] section of the answer file.

Here are the steps to configure mass storage devices:

1. The distribution folder that contains the remote image files (all the files that will be used by the remote installation) must have a folder that was manually created called \$OEM$. Within the \$OEM$ folder, create a folder called Textmode and copy into it the Windows XP mass storage device driver that was provided by the device manufacturer. The driver files should include files with extensions of *.sys, *.dll, *.inf, and *.cat, and the

Txtsetup.oem file. If you specified additional Plug and Play drivers in the [PnPdrvrs] section heading, you would also copy the Plug and Play driver files to the \OEM folder.

2. Within your answer file, create a [MassStorageDrivers] section. The parameters and values to be set within the Txtsetup.oem file should be provided by the manufacturer of the mass storage device.

3. Within your answer file, create a section named [OEMBootFiles] that includes a list of all of the driver files that are in the \OEM\Textmode folder. For example, a device named driver might be configured as follows:

```
[OEMBootFiles]
    driver.sys
    driver.dll
    driver.inf
    Txtsetup.oem
```

4. In the [Unattended] section, include OemPreinstall=Yes.

Plug and Play Devices

If you have a Plug and Play device that does not have a driver included on the Windows XP Professional CD, you can add the driver to the unattended installation as follows:

1. Within the \$OEM$\$1 subfolder, create a folder that will be used to store the Plug and Play drivers—for example, \$OEM$\$1\PnPdrivers. You may even want to create subdirectories for specific devices, such as \$OEM$\$1\PnPdrivers\Modems.

2. In the answer file, edit the [Unattended] section heading to reflect the location of your Plug and Play drivers. For example, if you installed your Plug and Play modem in \$OEM$\$1\PnPdrivers\Modems and your sound card in \$OEM$\$1\PnPdrivers\SoundCards, your answer file would have the following line:

```
[Unattended]
    OEMPnPDriversPath=PnPdrivers\Modems;
    PnPdrivers\SoundCards
```

If the drivers you are installing are not digitally signed, you will have to configure the driver-signing policy within the [Unattended] section of the answer file as DriverSigningPolicy=Ignore. Use unsigned drivers with caution, as they have not been tested by Microsoft and could cause operating system instability. Unsigned drivers are covered in greater detail in Chapter 4, "Configuring the Windows XP Environment."

HALs

If you want to use alternate HALs, follow these steps:

1. Create a folder called \OEM\Textmode (or verify that one exists).

2. Copy any files that are provided by the HAL vendor into the Textmode folder.

3. Edit the [Unattended] section of the answer file based on the instructions from the HAL manufacturer.

Passwords

If you are upgrading a Windows 98 or Windows Me computer to Windows XP Professional, you can customize the answer file to set passwords for the user accounts. You can also opt to force users to change their passwords during the first logon.

Table 2.6 explains the options that can be configured for passwords.

TABLE 2.6   Password Options for Answer Files

Answer File Section	Key	Usage	Example
[Win9xUpg]	DefaultPassword	Sets a password to whatever you specify, for all computers that are upgraded from Windows 98 or Windows Me to Windows XP Professional	DefaultPassword= *password*
[Win9xUpg]	ForcePassword	Forces all users who have upgraded from Windows 98 or Windows Me to change their password the first time they log on	ForcePassword-Change=Yes
[Win9xUpg]	UserPassword	Forces specific users to change their passwords on their local accounts when they log onto Windows XP Professional for the first time after upgrading from Windows 98 or Windows Me	UserPassword=*user, password,user,password*
[GuiUnattended]	AdminPassword	Sets the local Administrator password	AdminPassword= *password*

Language, Regional, and Time Zone Settings

The [RegionalSettings] section heading is used to set language and regional settings. Time zone settings are in the [GUIUnattended] section under the TimeZone option.

To set regional settings for answer files, you must copy the appropriate language files to the computer's hard disk. This can be accomplished by using the /copysource:*lang* switch with Winnt32, or the /rx:*lang* switch with Winnt. Table 2.7 lists the options that can be set for the [RegionalSettings] section.

TABLE 2.7   Regional Setting Options for Answer Files

Option	Description
InputLocale	Specifies the input locale and the keyboard layout for the computer
Language	Specifies the language and locale that will be used by the computer
LanguageGroup	Specifies default settings for the SystemLocale, InputLocale, and UserLocale keys
SystemLocale	Allows localized applications to run and to display menus and dialog boxes in the language selected
UserLocale	Controls settings for numbers, time, and currency

To set the time zone, you edit the [GuiUnattended] section of the answer file as follows:

```
[GuiUnattended]
    TimeZone=TimeZone
```

Display Settings

The [Display] section of the answer file is normally used to customize the display settings for portable computers. You should verify that you know what the proper settings are before you set this option. Table 2.8 lists the options that can be set in this section of the answer file.

TABLE 2.8   Display Setting Options for Answer Files

Option	Description
BitsPerPel	Specifies the number of valid bits per pixel for the graphics device
Vrefresh	Sets the refresh rate for the graphics device that will be used
Xresolution	Specifies the horizontal resolution for the graphics device that will be used
Yresolution	Specifies the vertical resolution for the graphics device that will be used

NTFS Conversion

You can configure the answer file to automatically convert FAT16 or FAT32 partitions during the installation. To convert the drives, you add the following entry:

[Unattended]
    FileSystem=ConvertNTFS

Application Installation

You can install applications through unattended installations in a variety of ways. Following are some of the options you can choose:

- Use the Cmdlines.txt file to add applications during the GUI portion of setup.
- Within the answer file, configure the [GuiRunOnce] section to install an application the first time a user logs on.
- Create a batch file.
- Use the Windows Installer (discussed in the last section of this chapter).
- Use the Sysdiff tool to install applications that do not have automated installation routines. To use the Sysdiff method, install Windows XP Professional on a reference computer and take a snapshot of the base configuration. Then add your applications and take another snapshot of the reference computer with the differences. The difference file (difference between first snapshot and second snapshot) can then be applied to computers that are being installed through unattended installations.

Windows Product Activation

Windows XP Professional includes a new feature called Windows Product Activation, which is used to prevent software piracy. You can create an entry within the answer file that supplies a unique product key for each computer that will be deployed within a mass deployment. To set Windows Product Activation, you must create a separate answer file for each computer, and use the value ProductKey under the [UserData] section of each specific user file. Under the [Unattended] section of the answer file, the Autoactivate=Yes parameter can be used to automate product activation.

Dynamic Updates

Dynamic updates are used to provide reliability and compatibility improvements to Windows XP Professional after the operating system CD has been released. You can apply dynamic updates to automated installations through Dynamic Update Packages. Dynamic Update Packages can be downloaded from the Microsoft website. You apply dynamic updates through the [Unattended] section of the answer file under Dushare=*path to update share* key and value.

Driver Signing

When drivers are applied to Windows XP Professional, they are checked to see if the driver has been digitally verified and signed. Drivers that are signed by Microsoft have passed extensive testing and are verified to be non-harmful to your system. Driver signing options can be set to Ignore, Warn, or Require. To set driver signing within an answer file, you use the [Unattended] section and the DriverSigningPolicy key.

Installing Applications with Windows Installer Packages

With Windows XP, you can easily distribute new applications through *Windows Installer packages*, which are special application distribution files. To use Windows Installer packages, you must have a Windows Server 2003 configured as a domain controller (so that Active Directory is running).

Windows Installer packages work with applications that are one of the following file types:

- *Microsoft Installer (MSI)* format files, which are usually provided by the software vendor. They support components such as on-demand installation of features as they are accessed by users.

- Repackaged applications (MSI files) that do not include the native Windows Installer packages. Repackaged applications are used to provide users with applications that can be cleanly installed, are easily deployed, and can perform self-diagnosis and repair.

- ZAP files, which are used if you do not have MSI files. ZAP files are used to install applications using their native Setup program.

 If your application includes a modification tool, you can create customized application installations that include specific features of the application through the use of modification (.mst) files.

Windows Installer packages work as *published applications* or *assigned applications*. When you publish an application, users can choose to install the application through the Control Panel Add or Remove Programs icon, or can choose not to install it. When you assign an application to users or computers, the package is automatically installed when the user selects the application on the Start ➢ All Programs menu or via document invocation (by the document extension, which means if a user clicks on a file with a specified extension and does not have the associated application installed, it will be automatically installed for them).

The primary steps for using Windows Installer packages to distribute applications are as follows, and are discussed in the sections coming up:

1. Copy the MSI application to a network share.
2. Create a Group Policy Object (GPO) for the application.
3. Filter the GPO so only authorized users can access the application.
4. Add the package to the GPO.
5. If it is a published application, install it through the Control Panel Add or Remove Programs icon.

Copying the MSI Application to a Share

As noted earlier, Windows Installer works with MSI applications. Applications that use the MSI standard will include a file with an `.msi` extension on the application's distribution media. Create a network share that will be used to store the application, and copy the `.msi` file to the network share. For example, suppose Windows 2000 Server Administrative Tools is the sample application that you want to distribute. You would copy the application file named `Adminpak.msi` from the Windows 2000 Server CD `\I386` folder to the `D:\Packages\AdminTools` folder on the Windows 2000 Server domain controller.

Creating a Group Policy Object

Your next step in preparing an application for distribution is to create a Group Policy Object (GPO) on a Windows 2000 Server domain controller. To create a GPO on a Windows 2000 Server, take the following steps:

1. Select Start ➤ Programs ➤ Administrative Tools ➤ Active Directory Users and Computers.

2. Right-click your domain name and select Properties from the pop-up menu. Click the Group Policy tab.

3. In the Group Policy tab (Figure 2.16), click the New button.

FIGURE 2.16   The Group Policy tab of the domain Properties dialog box

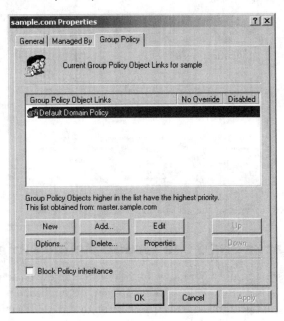

4. A new Group Policy Object will be created. Specify the new GPO name (for this example, type AdminTools).

Filtering the Group Policy Object

After you've created the GPO, you must filter it so that only authorized users will be able to install the application. To filter a GPO on a Windows 2000 Server, take the following steps:

1. In the Group Policy tab of the domain Properties dialog box (see Figure 2.16), highlight the Group Policy Object (AdminTools) you created and click the Properties button.

2. The GPO's Properties dialog box appears. Click the Security tab (see Figure 2.17).

    ▪ Remove permissions from all groups except Domain Admins and SYSTEM, by highlighting the group and clicking the Remove button.

    ▪ For the Domain Admins group, click the Allow boxes to set these permissions: Read, Write, Create All Child Objects, Delete All Child Objects, and Apply Group Policy.

FIGURE 2.17   The Security tab of the GPO's Properties dialog box, with default settings

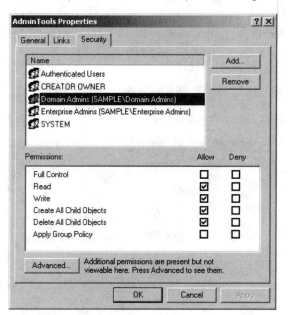

3. Click the OK button to close the GPO's Properties dialog box.

Adding the Package to the Group Policy Object

The next step in preparing to use a Windows Installer is to add the package (MSI) to the GPO you created for it. You can configure the package so that it is published or assigned to a user or a computer. Published applications are advertised through the Add/Remove Programs utility. Assigned applications are advertised through the Programs menu.

If you are configuring the package for a user, you add the package to the User Configuration\ Software Settings\Software installation. If the package is for a computer, you add it to the

`Computer Configuration\Software Settings\Software` installation. In this example, the application will be published for users. To publish an application on a Windows 2000 Server, take the following steps:

1. In the Group Policy tab of the domain Properties dialog box (see Figure 2.16), highlight the Group Policy Object (AdminTools) and click the Edit button.

2. The Group Policy window appears, as shown in Figure 2.18. Expand User Configuration, then Software Settings.

FIGURE 2.18   The Group Policy window

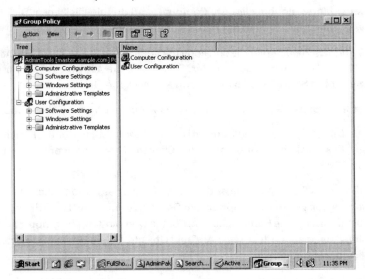

3. Right-click Software Installation and select New ➢ Package. Specify the location of the software package and click the Open button.

4. The Deploy Software dialog box appears next, as shown in Figure 2.19. Here, you'll specify the deployment method. The options are Published, Assigned, and Advanced Published or Assigned. For this example, select Published and click the OK button.

FIGURE 2.19   Specifying the deployment method

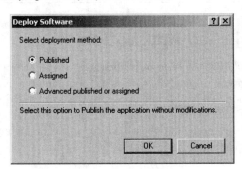

If you have access to a Windows 2000 domain controller, you can complete the steps in Exercise 2.4, which shows you how to publish an application. You will also need to have access to the Windows 2000 Server CD.

EXERCISE 2.4

Publishing an Application with Windows Installer

1. Select Start ➢ Programs ➢ Accessories ➢ Windows Explorer.

2. In Windows Explorer, double-click My Computer and double-click Local Disk (C:). Select File ➢ New ➢ Folder and type in the name **AdminTools**.

3. Insert the Windows 2000 Server CD and copy the application file named I386\Adminpak.msi from the CD to the C:\AdminTools folder. Right-click the AdminTools folder and select Sharing. Select the Share This Folder option and click the OK button.

4. Select Start ➢ Programs ➢ Administrative Tools ➢ Active Directory Users and Computers.

5. In the Active Directory Users and Computers window, right-click your domain name and select Properties. Click the Group Policy tab. Click the New button and enter the name **AdminTools**.

6. Highlight the AdminTools package and click the Properties button. Click the Security tab. Remove permissions from all groups except Domain Admins and SYSTEM by highlighting each group and clicking the Remove button. For the Domain Admins group, check the Allow boxes to allow the Read, Write, Create All Child Objects, Delete All Child Objects, and Apply Group Policy permissions. Click the OK button.

7. Highlight the AdminTools package and click the Edit button. Expand User Configuration, then Software Settings. Right-click Software Installation and select New ➢ Package.

8. Specify the network location (based on your computer name and the share name) of the software package and click the Open button.

9. In the Deploy Software dialog box, specify the deployment method Published, then click the OK button.

Installing a Published Application

After the application (package) has been published, users who have permission to access the application can install it on a Windows XP Professional computer that is a part of the same domain that contains the application. The published application is available through the Add/Remove Programs icon in Control Panel. In the Add/Remove Programs utility, click the Add New Programs option, and you will see the published application listed in the dialog box. Select the application and click the Add button to install it.

Real World Scenario

Publishing Software Applications

Your company uses a variety of applications. You only want to install the applications on computers where a particular application will actually be used, so that you can manage your costs for software licensing. However, you don't want the IT staff running around constantly installing applications all over the enterprise.

You decide to use Windows Installer packages to automatically install applications when users try to access files with filename extensions matching applications associated with Windows Installer packages. The first application you installed was ABC.MSI version 1.0. When the new version, ABC.MSI 2.0, became available, you added the upgraded software to the list of published applications. However, users are complaining that when they invoke ABC files, the older version of the software is being installed.

To correct this problem, you need to edit the order of software listed within the GPO so that the newer version of ABC.MSI is listed before the older version of the software. You should also configure the upgrade to be mandatory so that all of your users will be using the same version of the software.

If you completed Exercise 2.4, you can follow the steps in Exercise 2.5 to install the published application.

EXERCISE 2.5

Installing a Published Application

1. Log onto a Windows XP Professional computer that is a part of the domain that contains the published application. Log on as a user who has permission to access the application.

2. Select Start ➤ Control Panel. Double-click the Add/Remove Programs icon, then click the Add New Programs option.

3. The published application (AdminTools) is listed in the dialog box. To install the application, highlight it and click the Add button.

Summary

In this chapter, you learned how to install Windows XP Professional through automated installation. We covered the following topics:

- An overview of the three common methods for automated installation: unattended installations, remote installation (RIS), and using the System Preparation Tool and disk imaging

- Using the `Winnt` and `Winnt32` command-line utilities with command-line switches to perform unattended installations
- How to use RIS, including installing and configuring the RIS server as well as the requirements for the RIS clients
- Creating disk images using the System Preparation Tool (`Sysprep.exe`)
- Using unattended answer files to automatically respond to the queries that are generated during a normal installation process
- Installing applications through Windows Installer packages

Exam Essentials

Know the difference between unattended installation methods.   Understand the various options available for unattended installations of Windows XP Professional and when it is appropriate to use each installation method.

Understand how to use unattended installation for Windows XP Professional deployment. Know when it is appropriate to use unattended installations for Windows XP Professional deployment and the command-line switches that are associated with the `Winnt` and `Winnt32` commands. Know when you would use the `Winnt` command or the `Winnt32` command.

Understand the features and uses of RIS.   Know when it is appropriate to use RIS to manage unattended installations. Be able to list the requirements for setting up RIS servers and RIS clients. Be able to complete an unattended installation using RIS.

Be able to use disk images for unattended installations.   Know how to perform unattended installations of Windows XP Professional using the System Preparation Tool and disk images.

Know how to use Setup Manager to create answer files.   Understand how to access and use Setup Manager to create answer files. Be able to edit the answer files and know the basic options that can be configured for answer files.

Be able to install applications using Windows Installer packages.   Know the requirements for installing applications using Windows Installer packages, and understand how to successfully deploy those packages.

Key Terms

Before you take the exam, be certain you are familiar with the following terms:

answer files   Boot Information Negotiation Layer (BINL)

assigned applications   bootstrap image disk imaging

distribution server

Microsoft Installer (MSI)

Net PC/PC 98

Pre-boot eXecution Environment (PXE)

published applications

reference computer

Remote Boot Floppy Generator (RBFG)

Remote Installation Preparation Tool (RIPrep)

Remote Installation Services (RIS)

RIPrep images

security identifier (SID)

Service Control Point (SCP)

Setup Manager

Single Instance Store (SIS)

SIS Groveler service

Trivial File Transfer Protocol (TFTP)

`Unattend.txt`

unattended installation

Windows Installer packages

Windows XP Client Installation Wizard (CIW)

`Winnt`

`Winnt32`

Review Questions

1. You are the network administrator of a large corporation. Your company has decided to use RIS to install 100 client computers. You have set up the RIS server and now want to test a single RIS client to make sure that the installation will go smoothly. In the following diagram, select and place the servers that need to be on the network to support the RIS installation.

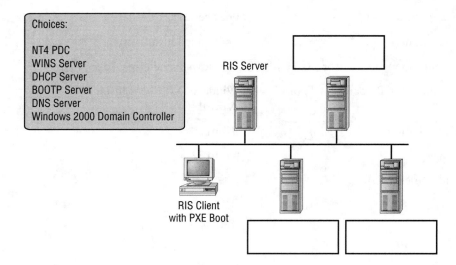

Choices:

NT4 PDC
WINS Server
DHCP Server
BOOTP Server
DNS Server
Windows 2000 Domain Controller

RIS Server

RIS Client
with PXE Boot

2. You are the network manager of a Fortune 500 company. The Sales group you support is moving into a new building and as a part of the move you are creating a deployment plan to install Windows XP Professional computers for 300 computers. All of the computers meet or exceed the minimum requirements for Windows XP Professional, and have hardware that is on the Hardware Compatibility List (HCL). Half of the clients are PXE compliant, and the other half are not. The computers that are not PXE compliant are listed on the HCL and have PCI-network adapters, which can work with a RIS boot disk. What command should you run to create a RIS boot disk?

   A. RBFG

   B. PXEBOOT

   C. RIPREP

   D. RISBOOT

3. You are the network administrator for Widgets R Us. You are in charge of developing a plan to install 200 Windows XP Professional computers in your company's data center. You decide to use RIS. You are using a Windows 2000 Server domain, and have verified that your network meets the requirements for using RIS services. What command should you use to configure the RIS server?

    A. RIPREP

    B. RISCONFIG

    C. RISETUP

    D. The RIS icon in Control Panel

4. Your company has a variety of client computers that are running Windows 98. You want to upgrade these machines to Windows XP using RIS. What requirement must be met on a client computer to upgrade to Windows XP Professional from a RIS server?

    A. The computer must use a PXE-based boot ROM.

    B. The computer must use a RIPrep-based boot ROM.

    C. The computer must use a RIS boot disk with any network adapter that supports RIPrep.

    D. There is no option to upgrade with RIS.

5. You have 75 computers that you need to install through RIS. Most of the computers have similar hardware. You are creating an Unattend.txt file that will be used in conjunction with unattended installations. The computers on which Windows XP Professional will be installed currently have FAT32 partitions. You want to convert the partitions to NTFS during the unattended installation. Which of the following options should you use in the file?

    A. [Unattended]
        FileSystem=ConvertNTFS

    B. [FileSystem]
        FileSystem=ConvertNTFS

    C. [Unattended]
        FileSystem=NTFS

    D. [FileSystem]
        FileSystem=NTFS

6. Curtis is the network manager for a large company. He has been tasked with creating a deployment plan to automate installations for 100 computers that need to have Windows XP Professional installed. Curtis wants to use RIS for the installations. In order to fully automate the installations, he needs to create an answer file. He does not want to create the answer files with a text editor. What other program can he use to create unattended answer files via a GUI interface?

    A. UAF

    B. Answer Manager

    C. Setup Manager

    D. System Preparation Tool

7. Mike recently published a software upgrade of the ABC.MSI program through Windows Installer packages using a Group Policy Object. When users invoke documents associated with this application, they are still installing the older version of the application. What does Mike need to do to ensure that the latest version of the software is installed on all of the client computers? (Choose all that apply.)

    A. Specify that the upgrade is mandatory.

    B. Configure the newer version of the application with high priority.

    C. Make sure that the newest version of the application is listed at the top of the GPO.

    D. Configure the newest version of the application with a .zap extension.

8. Bob is using RIS to install 100 clients that are identically configured. The first 65 computers are installed with no problems. When he tries to install the other 35, he receives an error and the installation process will not begin. Which of the following would cause this failure?

    A. The RIS server has been authorized to serve only 65 clients.

    B. The WINS server is no longer available.

    C. The DHCP server does not have enough IP addresses to allocate to the RIS clients.

    D. The network bandwidth has become saturated.

9. Mike wants to use Windows Installer packages to install the ABC.MSI application. Which of the following services must be running on the network to support the use of Windows Installer packages?

    A. DHCP

    B. WINS

    C. Installer

    D. Active Directory

10. You run a training department that needs the same software installed from scratch on the training computers each week. You decide to use third-party software to deploy disk images. Which Windows XP utility can you use in conjunction with third-party imaging software to create these disk images?

    A. UAF

    B. Answer Manager

    C. Setup Manager

    D. System Preparation Tool

11. You are trying to decide whether you want to use RIS as a method of installing Windows XP Professional within your company. Which of the following options is *not* an advantage of using a RIS automated installation?

    A. The Windows XP security is retained when you restart the computer.

    B. Plug and Play hardware detection is used during the installation process.

    C. Unique information is stripped out of the installation image so that it can be copied to other computers.

    D. You can quickly recover the operating system in the event of a system failure.

12. You are the network manager of the XYZ Corporation. You are in charge of developing an automated deployment strategy for rolling out new Windows XP Professional computers. You want to install a RIS server, and are evaluating whether an existing server can be used as a RIS server for Windows XP Professional deployment. Which of the following is *not* a requirement for configuring the RIS server?

   A. The remote installation folder must be NTFS version 3.0 or later.

   B. The remote installation folder must reside on the system partition.

   C. You need to configure the RIS server through the `Risetup` command.

   D. The DHCP server must be authorized through the Active Directory.

13. You are using RIS to install 20 Windows XP Professional computers. When the clients attempt to use RIS, they are not able to complete the unattended installation. You suspect that the RIS server has not been configured to respond to client requests. Which one of the following utilities would you use to configure the RIS server to respond to client requests?

   A. Active Directory, Users and Computers

   B. Active Directory, Users and Groups

   C. RIS Manager

   D. RISMAN

14. You want to install a group of 25 computers using disk images created through the System Preparation Tool. Your plan is to clone a reference computer and then copy the clone to all the machines. You do not want to create a SID on the destination computer when you use the image. Which `Sysprep` command-line switch should you use to set this up?

   A. `-nosid`

   B. `-nosidgen`

   C. `skipsid`

   D. `-quiet`

15. You are attempting to install an application through the Microsoft Installer program. You realize that the application you want to install does not have Microsoft Installer files. What type of files can you use with this application to install it through Windows Installer packages?

   A. ZAW files

   B. ZIP files

   C. ZAP files

   D. MSI files

Answers to Review Questions

1. DNS, DHCP, and the Active Directory must be properly configured and running for RIS services to work. The RIS server must also be installed and configured.

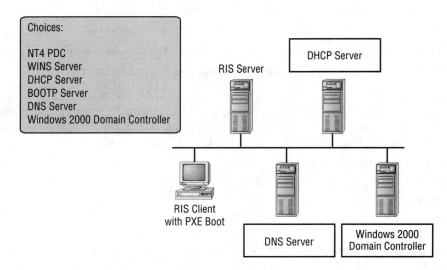

2. A. You can create a RIS boot disk from any Windows XP computer by attaching to *RIS_Server*\REMINST\ADMIN\i386 and running the Rbfg.exe command. The computer that uses the RIS boot disk must be PCI-compliant and must be listed through the Remote Boot File Generator utility.

3. C. The RISETUP command is used to configure the RIS server. The RIS server must meet minimum requirements and be configured with a CD-based image or a disk image. There are several other configuration options that need to be set on the RIS server.

4. D. If you are using RIS you can't upgrade from a previous operating system, you can only install a fresh copy of Windows XP Professional. Unattended installations can be used to support automated upgrades.

5. A. You can configure the answer file to automatically convert FAT16 or FAT32 partitions during the installation. To convert the drives, you add the following entry to the UNATTENDED.TXT:

    [Unattended]
        FileSystem=ConvertNTFS

6. C. Setup Manager (Setupmgr) is used to create unattended answer files. It uses a GUI-based interface to set up and configure the most common options that are used within an answer file.

7. A, C. If you want to require all users to use the most updated software, you should configure the upgrade as mandatory. The newest version of the software should be listed at the top of the GPO.

8. C. To access the RIS server, the RIS clients must be able to access the DHCP server. Each RIS client will use an IP address from the DHCP server's scope, so you should ensure that the DHCP server has enough addresses to accommodate all of the RIS clients.

9. D. You must have Active Directory installed to use Windows Installer packages. You must also have the Windows Server that will support the Windows Installer packages properly configured.

10. D. Once you have a reference computer installed, you can use the System Preparation Tool to prepare the computer to be used with disk imaging. Disk imaging also requires third-party software or hardware disk-duplicating devices. The image can then be transferred to the destination computer(s).

11. C. Unique information is stripped out of the installation image when you use the System Preparation Tool to create a disk image—for example, the unique SID that is applied to every computer. Unique information is then generated when the target computer is installed.

12. B. When you configure your RIS server, the remote installation folder can't be on the system partition. RIS servers must have a minimum of two partitions.

13. A. You enable RIS servers to respond to client requests through the Active Directory Users and Computers utility. In the Remote Install tab of the RIS server Properties dialog box, enable the option Respond to Client Computers Requesting Service.

14. B. The -nosidgen switch prevents SID generation. The Sysprep command can be used with a variety of switches. You can see a complete list by typing **sysprep /?** from a command-line prompt.

15. C. ZAP files are used if you don't have MSI files. ZAP files are used to install applications using their native setup programs.

Chapter

3

Upgrading to Windows XP Professional

MICROSOFT EXAM OBJECTIVES COVERED IN THIS CHAPTER:

✓ **Upgrade from a previous version of Windows to Windows XP Professional.**

- Prepare a computer to meet upgrade requirements.
- Migrate existing user environments to a new installation.

Before you attempt to upgrade Windows XP Professional, you need to understand the difference between an upgrade and a clean installation. If your previous operating system can be upgraded to Windows XP Professional and you want to retain your system settings, then you choose to perform an upgrade. If your operating system does not support a Windows XP upgrade or if you want to start from scratch, then you choose to perform a clean installation. Client upgrade paths and requirements are used to determine whether your operating system can be upgraded to Windows XP Professional. To upgrade, you must be running Windows 98, Windows Me, Windows NT 4 Workstation, or Windows 2000 Professional, and your hardware must meet the minimum requirements. This chapter covers the requirements for upgrading to Windows XP Professional.

You should also consider possible upgrade problems or known issues. This is especially important if you are upgrading from Windows 98 or Windows Me, because the upgrading process is not as smooth as it is when you are starting from a Windows NT 4 Workstation or Windows 2000 Professional system. An example of an upgrade issue is lack of support in Windows XP for applications or utilities that use virtual device drivers. You'll find a discussion of these issues in this chapter.

You should perform several tasks to prepare your computer before you start the upgrade process. This chapter provides an upgrade checklist to help you plan your upgrade strategy. The checklist includes items such as deleting any unnecessary files or applications and taking an inventory of your computer's configuration.

Finally, after you've made your preparations, you are ready for the big moment. You will learn about all of the steps involved in the Windows XP upgrade process. You will also learn how to migrate user data and files and settings, which is useful when you buy a new computer with Windows XP Professional already installed, and you want to transfer user data or files and settings from an existing computer. Finally, you will learn about basic troubleshooting techniques in the event that you have upgrade problems.

Deciding Whether to Upgrade

An upgrade allows you to preserve existing settings. A clean installation places Windows XP in a new folder. After a fresh install, you need to reinstall all of your applications and reset your preferences.

You should perform an upgrade if the following conditions are true:

- You are running Windows 98, Windows Me, Windows NT 4 Workstation, or Windows 2000 Professional.

- You want to keep your existing applications and preferences.
- You want to preserve any local users and groups you've created under Windows NT 4 Workstation or Windows 2000 Professional.
- You want to upgrade your current operating system with the Windows XP operating system.

You should perform a clean install if any of the following conditions are true:

- There is no operating system currently installed.
- You have an operating system installed that does not support an upgrade to Windows XP (such as DOS Windows 3.*x*, or Windows 95).
- You want to start from scratch, without keeping any existing preferences.
- You want to be able to dual-boot between Windows XP and your previous operating system.

 Performing a clean install and dual-booting are covered in detail in Chapter 1, "Getting Started with Windows XP Professional."

Preparing to Upgrade to Windows XP Professional

Like any other major change to your computer, upgrading to Windows XP Professional requires some preparation.

Getting ready to upgrade to Windows XP Professional involves the following steps:

- Make sure that your system meets the operating system and hardware requirements.
- Consider upgrade issues, particularly if you're upgrading from Windows 98 or Me.
- Use an upgrade checklist to plan for the upgrade.

These preparations are discussed in detail in the following sections.

Client Upgrade Paths and Requirements

To upgrade to Windows XP Professional, you must follow a particular path. Only the following operating systems can be directly upgraded to Windows XP Professional:

- Windows 98 (all releases)
- Windows Me
- Windows NT 4 Workstation (requires Service Pack 5 or higher)
- Windows 2000 Professional

There is no supported direct upgrade path for Windows 3.*x*, Windows 95, Windows NT 3.51, or any version of NT 4 Server or Windows 2000 Server.

The hardware requirements for upgrading are the same as those for a clean installation. To upgrade to Windows XP Professional, your computer hardware must meet the following requirements:

- Pentium 233MHz or higher processor (300MHz or higher is recommended)
- 64MB of RAM (128MB or higher memory is recommended)
- 1.5GB of available hard disk space (2GB or more is recommended)
- VGA or better resolution monitor (SVGA is recommended)

It is also possible to upgrade the Windows XP Home Edition to Windows XP Professional Edition.

Along with meeting these requirements, your hardware should be listed on the Hardware Compatibility List (HCL). See Chapter 1 for more information about the HCL.

Upgrade Considerations for Windows NT 4 Workstation and Windows 2000 Professional

If you are upgrading from Windows NT 4 Workstation, you should first verify that you have Service Pack 5 or higher installed. Windows NT and Windows 2000 applications use common attributes and are highly compatible with Windows XP Professional applications. This means that almost all Windows NT and Windows 2000 applications should run with Windows XP. However, there are a few exceptions to this statement, which include the following:

- Applications that use file-system filters, such as antivirus software, may not be compatible.
- Custom power-management tools are not supported.
- Custom Plug and Play solutions are not supported.
- Before upgrading to Windows XP, you should remove any virus scanners, network services, or other client software.

Upgrade Considerations for Windows 98 and Windows Me

The upgrade to Windows XP Professional from Windows NT 4 Workstation or Windows 2000 Professional is a smoother process than it is from Windows 98 and Windows Me. This is because the Windows NT 4 Workstation and Windows 2000 Professional structures have more in common with Windows XP's than the Windows 98 and Windows Me structures do. Therefore, upgrading from Windows 98 or Windows Me requires more planning and testing than upgrading from Windows NT 4 Workstation or Windows 2000 Professional.

Hardware Compatibility Issues

If you are upgrading from Windows 98 or Windows Me, you need to ensure that you have Windows XP device drivers for your hardware. The device drivers that were used with Windows 98 and Windows Me are not compatible because they use an older technology, virtual device drivers (VxDs).

If you have a video driver without an XP-compatible driver, the Windows XP upgrade will install the Standard VGA driver, which will display the video in 640×480 mode with 256 colors. Once you get the XP driver for your video, you can install it and adjust video properties accordingly.

Application Compatibility Issues

Not all applications that were written for Windows 98 and Windows Me will work with Windows XP Professional. After the upgrade, if you have application problems, you can address the problems as follows:

- If the applications are compatible with Windows XP, reinstall the application after the upgrade is complete.
- If the application uses Dynamic Link Libraries (DLLs), and there are migration DLLs for the application, apply the migration DLLs.
- Use the Application Compatibility Program, Apcompat.exe, which is found in the \Support \Tools folder (in a compressed file called Support.cab, which can be compressed with the Extract utility) on the Windows XP Professional distribution CD. The Application Compatibility Program is designed to overcome the most common application compatibility issues that occur when you are upgrading to Windows XP Professional. The Application Compatibility Program does the following tasks:
  - Attempts to fix any conflicts that are determined to exist between Windows XP Professional and the application.
  - Identifies any memory management conflicts.
  - Checks the \Temp folder to try to identify any incompatibilities.
  - Determines whether Windows XP Professional has enough free disk space to support the application.
  - Stores any application compatibility settings that are identified.
- If applications were written for earlier versions of Windows, but are incompatible with Windows XP, use the Program Compatibility Wizard, from Start ➤ All Programs ➤ Accessories ➤ Program Compatibility Wizard. This utility is covered in greater detail in the "Troubleshooting XP Professional Upgrades" section at the end of this chapter.
- Upgrade your application to a Windows XP–compliant version.

Compatibility Problems and the Check Upgrade Only Option

To assist you in the upgrade process, the Windows XP Setup program provides a Check Upgrade Only mode, which generates compatibility reports and stores them in a central location. You can then analyze these reports to determine whether your hardware or software applications will port properly from Windows 98 or Windows Me to Windows XP Professional.

You can generate the Windows XP compatibility report by running `Winnt32 /checkupgrade-only`, which will launch the Windows XP Setup program, but will only run enough of the Setup procedure to generate the compatibility report. This utility can be found on the Windows XP Professional CD under the \I386 folder.

The *Upgrade Report* will contain the following information:

- Microsoft MS-DOS configuration, including `AUTOEXEC.BAT` and `CONFIG.SYS` files; these files verify whether any of the entries in the configuration files show hardware or software being used that is incompatible with Windows XP Professional.

- List of Plug and Play hardware, including hardware that may not be supported by Windows XP without the use of additional files.

- Software that is incompatible with Windows XP, which might require you to apply upgrade packs to the software to provide Windows XP Professional compatibility. *Upgrade packs* are used to replace files and settings that are incompatible with Windows XP Professional with files and settings that are compatible with Windows XP Professional.

- Software that will need to be reinstalled, including a list of upgrade packs that are recommended in conjunction with the upgrade.

If the Check Upgrade Only utility identifies an application as being incompatible with Windows XP Professional, you should uninstall the incompatible application before you upgrade to Windows XP Professional.

Unsupported Options

Although Windows 98 and Windows Me can be upgraded to Windows XP Professional, you should be aware that the following options are not supported through the upgrade process:

Applications that use file-system filters   This includes third-party antivirus software and disk-quota management software. These types of file-system filters won't work under Windows XP. You should contact vendors who use file-system filters for upgraded software supported by Windows XP Professional. One example of an error you might see is a Master Boot Record (MBR) error when Windows XP reboots during the upgrade. In this case, you should verify that the virus checker is disabled.

Any custom power-management solutions or tools   Custom power-management solutions are no longer used, because these features are added through Windows XP Advanced Configuration and Power Interface (ACPI). You should remove any custom power-management solutions or tools prior to running the upgrade process. (ACPI is covered in Chapter 4, "Configuring the Windows XP Environment.")

Any custom Plug and Play solutions   Custom Plug and Play solutions are no longer used, because Windows XP has a full set of Plug and Play features. You should remove any custom Plug and Play solutions before starting the upgrade process.

Third-party applications for Windows 98 and Windows Me that support compressed drives, disk defragmenters, and disk utilities   These are not supported by Windows XP because it offers native support for disk compression and disk defragmentation (which are discussed in Chapter 8, "Managing Disks"). If you want to use third-party utilities, contact the vendor to get an upgrade of your application that has been written specifically for Windows XP. If the application can't be upgraded to a Windows XP–specific version, you should remove the utility prior to running the upgrade process.

WARNING   If you are upgrading from Windows 98 or Windows Me to Windows XP Professional, then you should not convert to the NTFS file system during the upgrade process. If you upgrade to NTFS, you will not be able to uninstall the upgrade if it fails and revert back to your previous operating system.

 Real World Scenario

Handling Upgrade Failure

Imagine that, although you thought you had prepared for the upgrade to Windows XP Professional from Windows 98, something has gone wrong and now you can't access the network driver, which has no compatible XP driver, and one of your critical applications is no longer running. You are in a panic and just want to go back to your Windows 98 operating system!

Because the upgrade from Windows 98 or Windows Me to Windows XP Professional is less compatible than the upgrade from Windows NT 4 Workstation or Windows 2000 Professional, Microsoft includes the option of rolling back to Windows 98 or Windows Me if you encounter upgrade problems. Uninstall files are automatically created, and to uninstall Windows XP and return to Windows 98 or Windows Me, you simply access Control Panel and select the Uninstall Windows XP option in Add or Remove Program Tools. If you cannot start the GUI interface, you can uninstall XP manually by using the osuninst.exe command from the C:\windows\system32 folder. Note that this option will not work if you have converted the drives to NTFS, and are trying to revert back to Windows 98 or Windows Me since these operating systems do not support NTFS file systems.

An Upgrade Checklist

Once you have made the decision to upgrade, you should develop a plan of attack. The following upgrade checklist (valid for upgrading from Windows 98 or Windows Me, Windows NT 4

Workstation, and Windows 2000 Professional) will help you plan and implement a successful upgrade strategy.

- Verify that your computer meets the minimum hardware requirements for Windows XP Professional. Be sure that all of your hardware is on the HCL.

- Run the Windows XP Upgrade Advisor tool from the Microsoft Web site, which also includes documentation on using the utility, to audit the current configuration and status of your computer. It will generate a report of any known hardware or software compatibility issues based on your configuration. You should resolve any reported issues before you upgrade to Windows XP Professional.

- Back up your data and configuration files. Before you make any major changes to your computer's configuration, you should back up your data and configuration files and then verify that you can successfully restore your backup. Chances are if you have a valid backup, you won't have any problems. Chances are if you *don't* have a valid backup, you will have problems.

- Delete any unnecessary files or applications, and clean up any program groups or program items you don't use. Theoretically, you want to delete all the junk on your computer before you upgrade. Think of this as the spring-cleaning step.

- Verify that there are no existing problems with your drive prior to the upgrade. Perform a disk scan, a current virus scan, and defragmentation. These, too, are spring-cleaning chores. This step just prepares your drive for the upgrade.

- Uncompress any partitions that have been compressed with DriveSpace or DoubleSpace. You cannot upgrade partitions that are currently compressed.

- Once you verify that your computer and components are on the HCL, make sure that you have the Windows XP drivers for the hardware. You can verify this with the hardware manufacturer.

- Make sure that your BIOS (Basic Input/Output System) is current. Windows XP requires that your computer has the most current BIOS. If it does not, the computer may not be able to use advanced power-management features or device-configuration features. In addition, your computer may cease to function during or after the upgrade. Use caution when performing BIOS updates, as installing the incorrect BIOS can cause your computer to fail to boot.

- Take an inventory of your current configuration. This inventory should include documentation of your current network configuration, the applications that are installed, the hardware items and their configuration, the services that are running, and any profile and policy settings.

- Perform the upgrade. In this step, you upgrade from your previous operating system to Windows XP Professional.

- Verify your configuration. After Windows XP Professional has been installed, use the inventory to compare and test each element that was previously inventoried prior to the upgrade to verify that the upgrade was successful.

Real World Scenario

Handling an Upgrade Application Failure

You have a laptop that is running Windows NT 4 Workstation. You upgrade the laptop to Windows XP Professional and add it to a Windows XP Organizational Unit that has default security applied. Your laptop uses an application called XYZ.EXE, which worked perfectly under NT 4. After the upgrade, however, you find that you can no longer run XYZ.EXE and you suspect that the problem is related to the security settings.

In this case, Windows XP provides a template called Compatws.inf, which can be used within the Security Templates utility. (The Security Templates utility is discussed in detail in *MCSE: Windows 2000 Server Study Guide*, 2nd edition, by Lisa Donald with James Chellis, Sybex, 2001.) By default, the Windows XP permissions are fairly restrictive, which can cause older applications to fail because they were not designed to run under the Windows XP operating system. The Compatws.inf file corrects this problem by loosening the default permissions so that older applications are more likely to run successfully. However, this configuration is not considered a secure one as the default security settings that are applied to Windows XP Professional by default. It is recommended that you use an updated application that supports Windows 2000, Windows XP Professional, or Windows Server 2003 when available, since they are designed to use higher security settings by default.

The Contingency Plan

Before you upgrade, you should have a contingency plan in place. Your plan should assume the worst-case scenario. For example, what happens if you upgrade and the computer doesn't work anymore? It is possible that, after checking your upgrade list and verifying that everything should work, your attempt at the actual upgrade may not work. If this happens, you may want to return your computer to the original, working configuration.

Indeed, I have made these plans, created my backups (two, just in case), verified my backups, and then had a failed upgrade anyway—only to discover that I had no clue where to find my original operating system CD. A day later, with the missing CD located, I was able to get up and running again. My problem was an older BIOS, and the manufacturer of my computer did not have an updated BIOS.

Performing the Windows XP Upgrade

As you would expect, the process of upgrading to Windows XP is much simpler than performing a clean installation (as we did in Chapter 1). You pick the system from which you are upgrading, and then follow the Setup Wizard's instructions to provide the information the Setup program needs. The final steps in the upgrade process are automatic. Exercise 3.1 gives the steps used in the Windows XP Professional upgrade process.

To set up your computer to be used for the exercises in this book, in Chapter 1 you installed Windows XP Professional from scratch. You would follow the steps in Exercise 3.1 if you were upgrading from your current operating system, and you had not yet performed the clean install procedure outlined in Exercise 1.2.

EXERCISE 3.1

Upgrading to Windows XP Professional

1. Insert the Windows XP Professional CD into your CD-ROM drive. If Autoplay is enabled, you will see the Welcome to Microsoft Windows XP dialog box.

2. Before you perform an upgrade, click the Check System Compatibility option, then the Check My System Automatically option to ensure that your computer can be upgraded to Windows XP Professional.

3. The Get Updated Setup Files dialog box will appear. Make your selection based on your Internet connectivity, and click the Next button.

4. The Report System Compatibility screen will list all problems. Ideally this dialog box will say Windows XP Upgrade Check Found No Incompatibilities or Problems. Click the Finish button to continue. Click the Back button to return to the main Windows XP installation screen.

5. Click the Install Windows XP button.

6. The Welcome to Windows Setup dialog box will appear. Select Upgrade Installation Type and click the Next button.

7. In the License Agreement dialog box, click the option to accept the agreement, and click the Next button.

8. In the Product Key dialog box, type in your 25-character product key. Then click the Next button.

9. The Setup program will run automatically and the computer will reboot again.

10. The Display Setting dialog box will appear. Click the OK button to have Windows automatically adjust your screen resolution.

11. Click the OK button in the Monitor Settings dialog box if the screen resolution is correct.

12. Windows XP Professional will now start and guide you through some last configuration options based on the upgraded configuration.

When the process is complete, Windows XP Professional will be installed on your computer. At this point, it's a good idea to verify that everything was upgraded properly. Using the inventory you made before upgrading (see the "An Upgrade Checklist" section earlier in the chapter), to test and verify that your hardware and software have made it through the transition and are working properly.

Migrating User Data

Windows XP Professional ships with a utility called the *User State Migration Tool (USMT)* that is used by administrators to migrate users from one computer to another via command-line utilities.

In the following sections you will learn more about the User State Migration Tool, requirements for the User State Migration Tool, and how the User State Migration tool is used.

Overview of User State Migration Tool

The USMT consists of two executable files, ScanState.exe and LoadState.exe. These files are located on the Windows XP Professional distribution CD under the \valueadd\Msft\Usmt folder. In addition, there are four migration rule information files: Migapp.inf, Migsys.inf, Miguser.inf, and Sysfiles.inf. The purpose of these files is as follows:

- ScanState.exe collects user data and settings information based on the configuration of the Migapp.inf, Migsys.inf, Miguser.inf, and Sysfiles.inf files.

- LoadState.exe then deposits the information that is collected from the source computer to a computer running a fresh copy of Windows XP Professional.

 This process cannot be run on a computer that has been upgraded to Windows XP Professional.

The information that is migrated includes the following:
- Internet Explorer settings
- Outlook Express settings and store
- Outlook settings and store
- Dial-up connections
- Phone and modem options
- Accessibility
- Classic Desktop
- Screen saver selection
- Fonts
- Folder options
- Taskbar settings

- Mouse and keyboard settings
- Sounds settings
- Regional options
- Office settings
- Network drives and printers
- Desktop folder
- My Documents folder
- My Pictures folder
- Favorites folder
- Cookies folder
- Common Office file types

Requirements for the User State Migration Tool

In order to use the User State Migration Tool, minimum requirements need to be met for the source computer, the intermediate store device, and the destination computer.

The source computer requirements are as follows:

- The source computer must be running one of the following operating systems: Windows 95, Windows 98, Windows Me, Windows NT 4 Workstation, or Windows 2000 Professional.
- The source computer must have access to the intermediate store, which holds the configuration information until it is transferred to the destination computer. Examples of intermediates store devices are tape drive or CD-RW device. The intermediate store that is used must have sufficient free storage to save all of the information that will be transferred.

The destination computer requirements are as follows:

- The destination computer must be running Windows XP Professional.
- The destination computer must have access to the intermediate store.
- The destination computer must have sufficient disk space to accommodate the user state data that is being transferred.

Using the User State Migration Tool

In its simplest form, the User State Migration Tool is used in the following manner:

1. ScanState.exe is run on the source computer, and the user state data is copied to an intermediate store. The intermediate store (for example, a CD-RW) must be large enough to accommodate the data that will be transferred. Scanstate would commonly be executed as a shortcut sent to the user that they will deploy in the evening or through a scheduled script.

2. The target computer is installed with a fresh copy of Windows XP Professional.

3. LoadState.exe is run on the target computer, and the intermediate store is accessed to restore the user settings.

Migrating Files and Settings

Windows XP Professional ships with a utility called the *File and Settings Transfer Wizard* that is used by administrators to migrate files and settings from one computer to another computer. This option is used when you purchase a new computer with Windows XP Professional already installed, and you want to migrate files and settings from an existing computer that is running a previous version of Windows.

The settings that can be transferred include:

- Personalized settings for Internet Explorer
- Personalized settings for Microsoft Outlook Express
- Desktop settings
- Display settings
- Dial-up connection settings

The File and Settings Transfer Wizard works through the following process:

1. On the source computer that contains the files and settings to be transferred, you access the Transfer and File Settings Wizard on the Windows XP Professional CD, from the \Support\Tools folder through Windows Explorer. Double-click the `Fastwiz.exe` command to start the wizard. The wizard will walk you through the process of selecting the files and settings that will be transferred and the media that will be used for storing the files and settings.

2. Files and settings will be copied to an intermediate storage device—for example, tape or CD-RW.

3. The target Windows XP Professional computer uses Start ➤ All Programs ➤ Accessories ➤ System Tools ➤ File and Settings Transfer Wizard to start the transfer to their computer. The wizard will walk them through the process of locating the files and settings that are to be transferred.

Troubleshooting XP Professional Upgrades

Some of the problems you might encounter when upgrading to Windows XP Professional include:

- Incompatible drivers for hardware
- Incompatible software applications

If you are unable to resolve these issues, you may need to reverse the Windows XP upgrade. We will look at these two issues, as well as how to reverse the upgrade, in the following sections.

Incompatible Hardware Drivers

When you upgrade from a previous operating system to Windows XP Professional, you need to ensure that you have Windows XP drivers for all of your hardware. For instance, assume you are running Windows NT 4 Workstation and have your video set for high resolution, and then you upgrade to Windows XP Professional. Your video is now set to display settings of 640×480 and 16 colors. When you try to change the video settings, you realize that you can't and that the default video driver has been loaded. This is a common error and will cause most applications to fail. To fix this problem, you will need to install a video driver that is XP Professional–compatible. You should check the video manufacturer's website for the most up-to-date drivers.

Incompatible Software Applications

You may have legacy applications that will not run under Windows XP Professional. Microsoft provides a Program Compatibility Wizard to help address this issue. You should not use this wizard if the application makes kernel-level calls or if the application is Windows XP compatible. To use the wizard, you would take the following steps:

1. Select Start ➤ All Programs ➤ Accessories ➤ Program Compatibility Wizard.
2. You will see a caution statement that this wizard should not be used for older virus detection, backup, or system programs that may make kernel-level execution calls. Click the Next button.
3. Locate the program that requires the compatibility settings. Choose from the options that appear on your screen and click the Next button:
    -   Select from a list of programs (Windows XP will detect all currently installed programs and provide you with a list).
    -   Use the program in the CD-ROM drive.
    -   Locate the program manually.
4. The next option allows you to select the compatibility for the application. Choose from the options that appear on your screen and click the Next button:
    -   Microsoft Windows 95
    -   Microsoft Windows NT 4.0 (Service Pack 5)
    -   Microsoft Windows 98/ Windows Me
    -   Microsoft Windows 2000
    -   Do not apply a compatibility mode
5. The next option will allow you to configure the display settings for the program. Choose from the options that appear on your screen and click the Next button:
    -   256 colors
    -   640×480 screen resolution
    -   Disable visual themes

6.   You will then be asked to confirm your selections and a test will be performed to verify that the display settings work with your application.

 The most common applications that require you to change video settings are older educational software programs and games.

Reversing a Windows XP Professional Upgrade

If you upgrade to Windows XP Professional, and decide that you want to revert to the previously used operating system, you can. Access the Add or Remove Programs option through Control Panel and choose to remove Windows XP Professional Installation. This will restore the previous operating system. You would use this option if you upgraded to Windows XP Professional and realized that you did not have Windows XP Professional drivers for critical hardware or the applications you use are not compatible with Windows XP Professional. The only exception to this process is if you have upgraded from Windows 98 or Windows Me and during the upgrade process you converted your file system to NTFS. Since Windows 98 and Windows Me do not support NTFS, you will not be able to successfully uninstall Windows XP Professional and revert to the previous operating system.

Summary

In this chapter, you learned how to upgrade to Windows XP Professional. We covered the following topics:

- Guidelines for when you should upgrade and when you should install a fresh copy of Windows XP Professional

- The client upgrade paths that can upgrade to Windows XP Professional and the minimum hardware requirements to perform an upgrade

- Upgrade considerations and potential problems with the Windows XP Professional upgrade process

- An upgrade checklist with steps to help ensure a successful upgrade

- All of the steps in the Windows XP Professional upgrade process

- How to migrate user data from one computer to another using the User State Migration Tool and how to migrate files and settings from one computer to another using the File and Settings Transfer Wizard

- How to troubleshoot and resolve common upgrade errors

Exam Essentials

Be able to list the requirements for a Windows XP Professional upgrade.   Know the requirements for upgrading a computer to Windows XP Professional, including what operating systems can be upgraded, what the hardware requirements are, and the steps for completing an upgrade.

Know all the possible issues that may arise during a Windows XP Professional upgrade.   Be aware of possible upgrade problems. This includes application compatibility, and the fact that other system configurations may work with Windows 98 or Windows Me but will be incompatible with Windows XP Professional.

Understand how to migrate users from one computer to another computer.   Know how to use the User State Migration Tool.

Key Terms

Before you take the exam, be certain you are familiar with the following terms:

File and Settings Transfer Wizard	Upgrade Report
upgrade packs	User State Migration Tool (USMT)

Review Questions

1.   Gabriella is the network administrator for her company. The network currently consists of a variety of operating systems, which include Windows 95, Windows 98, Windows Me, NT 3.51 Workstation, NT 4 Workstation, and Windows 2000 Professional. Gabriella would like to create as standardized an environment as possible and upgrade as many of the office computers to Windows XP Professional as possible. Assuming the computers meet the minimum requirements for Windows XP Professional, which of the following operating systems can be directly upgraded? (Choose all that apply.)

   A. Windows 95

   B. Windows 98

   C. Windows Me

   D. Windows NT 3.51 Workstation

   E. Windows NT 4 Workstation

   F. Windows 2000 Professional

2.   You are the system administrator for your company. One of your users, Tom, wants to upgrade his Windows 98 computer to Windows XP Professional. You upgrade the computer, and when you restart, you notice that his display is set to 640×480 mode and is only displaying 256 colors. When you go to display properties to the computer, there is no option to reset the display properties to the settings Tom used prior to the upgrade. What action should you take?

   A. Use the driver rollback feature in Windows XP to roll the video driver back to the video's Windows 98 driver.

   B. Within the Registry, set `Hkey_Local_Computer\Video\Compatibility\W98` to 1.

   C. Within the Registry, set `Hkey_Local_Computer\Video\Compatibility\W98` to 0.

   D. Install the Windows XP version driver for the video adapter and then configure settings per users' preference.

3.   Steven is the application specialist for the IT group in your company. A user named Mike calls Steven and reports that after his computer was upgraded from Windows 98 to Windows XP Professional, he could no longer properly access one of his critical applications. Steven suspects that there is a compatibility issue between the Windows 98 application and Windows XP Professional. He decides to run the Windows XP Compatibility Tool. What program does he use to launch this tool?

   A. `APCOMPAT`

   B. `WIN9XCOMP`

   C. `BACKCOMP`

   D. `WINNT32 /COMP`

4. Corrine is the network administrator of her company's network. One of the users, Gary, has asked Corrine to upgrade his Windows 98 computer to Windows XP Professional. Corrine verified that Gary's computer had sufficient hardware to be upgraded. After the upgrade, Gary could no longer access two critical applications that used to run under Windows 98. Corrine unsuccessfully attempted to eliminate the compatibility problems. Gary needs to return to a productive state as soon as possible, and just wants Windows 98 back on his computer. Which of the following actions would uninstall Windows XP Professional? (Choose two answers.)

    A. Reinstall Windows 98 and restore the data from the last backup she made prior to installation.

    B. In Control Panel, select the Uninstall Windows XP option in Add/Remove Program Tools.

    C. Set the Registry for `Hkey_Local_Computer\Upgrade\Rollback` to 1 and restart the computer.

    D. From C:\Windows\System32, run `osuninst.exe`.

5. Serena is the network administrator of the Funky Widgets Corporation. She is in the process of evaluating which computers are good candidates for upgrade to Windows XP Professional. Part of her upgrade checklist involves whether the current operating system can be upgraded. The other part of the checklist involves whether the current hardware is sufficient. What is the minimum amount of memory required so that a computer can be upgraded to Windows XP Professional?

    A. 32MB

    B. 64MB

    C. 128MB

    D. 256MB

6. Cindy is the network administrator for the Funky Monkey Corporation. She has decided to upgrade the marketing department's computers from Windows 98 to Windows XP Professional. During the upgrade of the first computer, the Windows XP Professional upgrade fails and reports that the MBR is missing or corrupt. Prior to installation she ran a virus check with the latest virus checking software, so she knows that she does not have an MBR virus. She boots the computer with a bootable floppy and verifies that all of the system boot files are still present. She next verifies that she can still successfully boot to Windows 98. What is the next step Cindy should take to complete the upgrade process?

    A. Verify that the virus checker has been disabled.

    B. Boot to the Windows Recovery Console and replace the system and boot files from the last backup.

    C. From C:\Windows\System32, run the `FIXMBR` command.

    D. From C:\Windows\System32, run the `MBRUPDATE` command.

7. You are the network administrator for a medium-sized company. Your company uses an application called WidgetManagement that was originally designed to run with Windows NT 4 Workstation. The computers were initially installed with Windows XP Professional and then had the WidgetManagement application installed, can run the application with no problem. The computers that ran Windows NT 4 Workstation and ran the WidgetManagement application were also able to run the application successfully. After the computers that were running Windows NT 4 Workstation have been upgraded to Windows XP Professional, users are reporting that they are having problems running the application. You suspect that the problem with the application is due to new security settings applied by Windows XP Professional. Which of the following security templates should be applied to the upgraded computers?

    A. `Basicws.inf`

    B. `Compatws.inf`

    C. `Upgradews.inf`

    D. `Sectemp.inf`

8. Dan has several computers that he would like to upgrade to Windows XP Professional. He is trying to pinpoint what factors go into determining when an upgrade is appropriate. In which of the following cases would he choose *not* to upgrade to Windows XP Professional?

    A. He is currently running Windows 98 and wants to take advantage of the new features of Windows XP Professional.

    B. He wants to keep his existing applications and preferences.

    C. He wants to preserve any local users and groups created with Windows NT Workstation.

    D. He wants his computer to be able to dual-boot between his current operating system and Windows XP Professional.

9. You are the network administrator for a Fortune 500 company. You upgrade a user's computer from Windows 98 to Windows XP Professional. After you complete the upgrade, you realize that the user has a digital camera that they use that does not have a Windows XP Professional driver. You also realize that the user is running several legacy applications that are not working properly with Windows XP Professional. The user needs to be able to access the digital camera and the legacy applications to perform their job. What is the fastest course of action to restore the user's computer to the pre-upgrade condition?

    A. Use a third-party application that contains the image of the computer that was taken prior to the upgrade.

    B. Run Install/Remove from the Windows XP Professional CD.

    C. Use the Add or Remove Programs option and select Remove the Windows XP Professional Installation option.

    D. Run Setup/uninstall from the Windows XP Professional CD.

10. You are the network administrator for a Fortune 500 company. One of your users asks you to upgrade their computer from Windows 98 to Windows XP Professional. After the upgrade, you verify that all of the computer's devices are functioning properly and have the correct Windows XP drivers installed. The next step you take is verifying that all of the applications work. When you go to test the applications, everything works properly except for one application. It was originally designed to work with Windows 98, and when you attempt to run it with Windows XP Professional, the display is garbled and the application window is not properly displayed. You contact the manufacturer of the application and discover that there is no Windows XP–compliant version. What course of action should you take?

    A. Adjust the screen settings for the computer to a lower resolution.

    B. Set the screen's refresh rate to a lower value that is compatible with the legacy application.

    C. Use the Program Compatibility Wizard to configure the legacy applications display settings.

    D. In the Monitor Settings, click the Advanced button, and click Compatibility Settings enabled for Legacy Applications.

11. Otto is the network manager of a small company. Several of the users have asked to have their computers upgraded to Windows XP Professional. One of the users, Jennifer, wants to upgrade her computer from Windows NT 3.51 Workstation to Windows XP Professional. Which of the following options should Otto use?

    A. Run `WINNT`.

    B. Run `WINNT32`.

    C. Run `Upgrade`.

    D. First, upgrade to Windows NT 4 Workstation or Windows 2000 Professional, then upgrade to Windows XP Professional.

12. You are the network administrator for a medium-sized company. Your company recently purchased 20 new Windows XP computers for the accounting department. Previously, the accounting department was using older computers, running Windows 2000 Professional. The accounting department users are asking to have their Windows 2000 Professional settings transferred to their new computers. Which of the following options should you use?

    A. Connect the computers to the network whose user state data needs to be migrated, and run the `XPMIGRATE` command-line utility.

    B. Connect the computers to the network whose user state data needs to be migrated, and run the `XPTRANSFER` command-line utility.

    C. Create a GPO for Migration and apply it to the new Windows XP computers.

    D. Use the `ScanState` and `LoadState` command line utilities to collect and migrate user state data.

13. Kaitlin is the network administrator for the Crazy Widgets Corporation. Currently all of the computers in the sales department run Windows Me. Kaitlin would like to upgrade the sales computers to Windows XP with the fewest possible problems. As part of the planning process, she decides to check for compatibility problems prior to the upgrade. Which of the following options should Kaitlin use?

   A. WINNT32 with /Checkupgradeonly

   B. WINNT32 with /Upgrdrpt

   C. WINNT32 with /Upgradecomp

   D. WINNT32 with /Chkcomp

14. Kevin is in charge of managing a migration of user state data from existing Windows 2000 Professional computers to recently purchased Windows XP Professional computers. Which of the following items can be transferred through the User State Migration Tool? (Choose all that apply.)

   A. Internet Explorer settings

   B. Folder options

   C. Cookies folder

   D. My Documents folder

15. You have Windows Me installed in your C:\Windows folder. You install Windows XP Professional to the C:\Windows.xp folder. What is the result of this configuration?

   A. You have upgraded to Windows XP Professional and will be able to dual-boot to Windows Me.

   B. You have upgraded to Windows XP Professional and won't be able to access your Windows Me operating system.

   C. You have configured your computer to dual-boot and will be able to access the Windows Me settings, since both installation folders are on the same partition.

   D. You have configured your computer to dual-boot. When you boot to Windows XP Professional, you won't be able to access the Windows Me settings because the operating system files are in different installation folders.

Answers to Review Questions

1. B, C, E, F. You can upgrade to Windows XP Professional from Windows 98, Windows Me, Windows NT 4 Workstation, and Windows 2000 Professional. If you want to upgrade from Windows 95 or Windows NT 3.51 Workstation, you must first upgrade to an operating system in the supported upgrade list.

2. D. If you upgrade to Windows XP and no compatible video driver is found during the upgrade, Windows XP will default to a standard VGA driver. After the upgrade, simply install the Windows XP compatible driver, and adjust settings as desired.

3. A. Not all applications written for Windows 98 or Windows Me will work properly with Windows XP Professional. To use the Compatibility Tool, you use the APCOMPAT command-line utility. This utility can be used to set compatible application settings for older applications.

4. B, D. Because the upgrade from Windows 98 or Windows Me to Windows XP Professional is less compatible than the upgrade from Windows NT 4 Workstation or Windows 2000 Professional, Microsoft includes the option of rolling back to Windows 98 or Windows Me if you encounter upgrade problems. Uninstall files are automatically created, and to uninstall Windows XP and return to Windows 98 or Windows Me, you simply access Control Panel and select the Uninstall Windows XP option in Add or Remove Program Tools. If you are unable to start the GUI interface, you can uninstall XP manually by using the osuninst.exe command from the C:\windows\system32 folder.

5. B. The memory requirements for an installation and an upgrade are the same. Your computer must have a minimum of 64MB of memory to install or upgrade to Windows XP Professional. 128MB of memory is recommended.

6. A. Windows XP does not support applications that use file-system filters such as third-party antivirus software and disk-quota management software. These features should be disabled prior to upgrading to Windows XP Professional.

7. B. Windows XP provides a template called Compatws.inf, which can be used within the Security Templates utility. By default, the Windows XP permissions are fairly restrictive, which can cause older applications to fail because they were not designed to run under the Windows XP environment. The Compatws.inf file corrects this problem by loosening the default permissions so that older applications are more likely to run successfully. However, this environment is not considered a secure one, and an updated application that supports Windows XP should be used when available.

8. D. If Dan wants his computer to dual-boot, he should install a clean copy of Windows XP Professional instead of upgrading to Windows XP Professional. He should install the non–Windows XP Professional operating system(s) first, then install Windows XP Professional.

9. C. If you upgrade to Windows XP Professional, and decide that you want to revert to the previously used operating system, you can. Access the Add or Remove Programs option through Control Panel and choose to remove Windows XP Professional Installation. This will restore the previous operating system. You would use this option if you upgraded to Windows XP Professional and realized that you did not have Windows XP Professional drivers for critical hardware or the applications you use are not compatible with Windows XP Professional.

10. C. It is possible that you may have legacy applications that will not run under Windows XP Professional. Microsoft provides a Program Compatibility Wizard to help address this issue. You should not use this wizard if the application makes kernel-level calls or if the application is Windows XP–compatible.

11. D. There is no direct upgrade path from Windows NT 3.51 Workstation to Windows XP Professional. To upgrade from Windows NT 3.51, Otto must first upgrade to Windows NT 4 Workstation or Windows 2000 Professional.

12. D. The User State Migration Tool consists of two executable files, `ScanState.exe` and `LoadState.exe`. `ScanState.exe` collects user data and settings information based on the configuration of the `Migapp.inf`, `Migsys.inf`, `Miguser.inf`, and `Sysfiles.inf` files. `LoadState.exe` then deposits the information that is collected on the source computer to a computer running a fresh copy of Windows XP Professional. This process cannot be run on a computer that has been upgraded to Windows XP Professional.

13. A. To test a computer for compatibility issues without actually performing an upgrade, use the `WINNT32` command with the `/Checkupgradeonly` switch. Any incompatibilities will then be reported prior to the upgrade.

14. A, B, C, D. The User State Migration Tool will migrate Internet Explorer settings, Outlook Express settings and store, Outlook settings and store, dial-up connections, phone and modem options, accessibility, classic Desktop, screen saver selection, fonts, folder options, taskbar settings, mouse and keyboard settings, sounds settings, regional options, Office settings, network drives and printers, Desktop folder, My Documents folder, My Pictures folder, Favorites folder, Cookies folder, and Common Office file types.

15. D. If you put the installation files in separate folders, you will create a computer that dual-boots. There will be no sharing of configuration information from Windows Me to Windows XP Professional when the computer is booted to the Windows XP Professional operating system.

Chapter

4

Configuring the Windows XP Environment

MICROSOFT EXAM OBJECTIVES COVERED IN THIS CHAPTER:

✓ **Implement, manage, and troubleshoot disk devices.**

- Install, configure, and manage DVD and CD-ROM devices.
- Monitor and configure removable media, such as tape devices.

✓ **Implement, manage, and troubleshoot display devices.**

- Configure multiple-display support.
- Install, configure, and troubleshoot a video adapter.

✓ **Configure Advanced Configuration Power Interface (ACPI).**

✓ **Implement, manage, and troubleshoot input and output (I/O) devices.**

- Monitor, configure, and troubleshoot I/O devices, such as printers, scanners, multimedia devices, mouse, keyboard, and smart card reader.
- Monitor, configure, and troubleshoot multimedia hardware, such as cameras.
- Install, configure, and manage Infrared Data Association (IrDA) devices.
- Install, configure, and manage wireless devices.
- Install, configure, and manage USB devices.
- Install, configure, and manage hand held devices.

✓ **Manage and troubleshoot drivers and driver signing.**

✓ **Monitor and configure multiprocessor computers.**

✓ **Manage, monitor, and optimize system performance for mobile users.**

After you've installed Windows XP Professional, you will need to install and configure your hardware. The easiest hardware devices to install are those that follow the Plug and Play standard. However, it's not that difficult to install non–Plug and Play hardware through the Add/Remove Hardware utility in Control Panel.

To configure your hardware, you generally use the Computer Management utility or Control Panel. You can also create custom administrative consoles through the Microsoft Management Console (MMC).

In this chapter, you will examine the process of configuring the Windows XP environment, beginning with an overview of the main configuration utilities. Then you will learn how to update drivers and manage driver signing. Next, you will see how to configure many different types of hardware, including disk devices, display devices, mobile computer hardware, I/O devices, imaging devices, and multiple processors. Finally, you will learn how to configure and manage Windows XP services and multiple hardware profiles.

New Device and Hardware Support for Windows XP

If you are familiar with Windows 2000 configuration, then Windows XP configuration will be very similar. For those readers who are familiar with Windows 2000 configuration, this chapter begins with the difference between Windows XP configuration support and Windows 2000 configuration support.

Windows XP includes new device and hardware support for the following options:

- Windows Image Acquisition architecture (WIA)

- Better support for digital audio and video

- Improved Dualview multi-monitor support

These options are covered in greater detail in the following sections.

Windows Image Acquisition Architecture

Windows Image Acquisition (WIA) is designed to manage images between the image capture device (such as digital cameras or image scanners) and the computer's software applications.

This allows still images to be easily transferred and edited. There is also support for Microsoft DirectShow webcams and digital video camcorders so you can capture frames from video streams.

Connecting WIA Devices

You can connect capture devices to Windows XP Professional with WIA technology through the following:

- IEEE 1394
- Universal Serial Bus (USB)
- Small Computer System Interface (SCSI)

If you connect your image device through a standard COM port (serial or parallel port) or through infrared, then support would be based on existing standards.

Components of WIA

WIA is made up of several software components. They include the following:

- Scanner and Camera Wizard
- Extensions to the Windows Explorer User Interface (UI)
- WIA applications
- Imaging Class Installer
- WIA scripting interface
- Common system dialog devices
- Device objects
- WIA Device Manager

Each component is covered in greater detail in the following subsections.

Scanner and Camera Wizard

The Scanner and Camera Wizard is used to retrieve images from WIA-enabled devices. The wizard allows you to preview and view picture properties. The wizard is launched for the following activities:

- Connect events, which occur when a Plug and Play image device that uses the WIA standard is connected
- Scan events, which are activated when WIA-enabled scanners are used
- Media-insertion events, which are triggered by inserting flash memory cards or CD-ROMs, which contain image files

You can configure your computer so that it will use another imaging application instead of the Scanner and Camera Wizard for image management.

Extensions to the Windows Explorer User Interface (UI)

When you install a WIA device, it will automatically appear as an icon in My Computer. When you open the WIA device in My Computer, you will see thumbnail pictures of all the pictures stored on the WIA device. Other extensions include the following:

- Option to e-mail pictures
- Option to order prints from the Internet
- Support for posting pictures to a website
- Ability to save pictures to CD-RW media

WIA Applications

Windows XP Professional supports two classes of WIA applications, those for editing images and those for authoring documents.

Imaging Class Installer

The Imaging Class Installer is the component of Windows XP that allows Plug and Play support for WIA devices.

WIA Scripting Interface

The WIA scripting interface is used to support the development of WIA applications through scripting languages such as Microsoft Visual Basic.

Common System Dialog Devices

The common system dialog devices are used to view pictures and their properties, scan pictures, edit pictures, and select WIA devices and device properties. These objects are viewed through the UI as dialog boxes. The common system dialog objects include the following:

- Scanner common dialog object
- Still camera common dialog object
- Video camera common dialog object
- Device selection common dialog object

Device Objects

When a WIA device is installed and its associated driver is loaded, a device object is started by the operating system. The device objects that are created include the following:

- WIA mini driver
- WIA generic flatbed scanner
- WIA generic digital still camera, which is based on the Public Transfer Protocol (PTP)
- WIA generic video camera object

WIA Device Manager

The WIA Device Manager establishes communication between WIA devices and imaging applications.

Support for Digital Audio and Video

Windows 2000 and Windows Me include support for digital audio and video. Windows XP extends the support for digital audio and video through the following options:

- Multichannel audio output and playback support, which, if your speakers are configured in a multichannel configuration, sets each speaker's volume individually
- Acoustic Echo Cancellation (AEC), which is a technology that reduces echo and feedback from an input channel such as a USM microphone
- Global Effects (GFX), which is used to support USB audio devices such as USB array microphones

Dualview Multi-Monitor Support

Multi-monitor support is available with Windows 98, Windows 2000, and Windows Me. Windows XP expands this support with Dualview, which is used to support mobile computers.

Dualview support is used to allow mobile computers to use multiple display outputs, such as a laptop's built-in display and an external monitor, at the same time. Each display can then be configured to display independent applications or data.

Windows XP Management Utilities

Windows XP Professional includes several utilities for managing various aspects of the operating system configuration. In this section, you will learn about the Microsoft Management Console and the Registry Editor.

Microsoft Management Console

The *Microsoft Management Console (MMC)* is the console framework for management applications. The MMC provides a common environment for *snap-ins*, which are administrative tools developed by Microsoft or third-party vendors. The MMC offers many benefits, including the following:

- The MMC is highly customizable—you add only the snap-ins you need.
- Snap-ins use a standard, intuitive interface, so they are easier to use than previous versions of administrative utilities.
- MMC consoles can be saved and shared with other administrators.
- You can configure permissions so that the MMC runs in authoring mode, which an administrator can manage, or in user mode, which limits what users can access.
- Most snap-ins can be used for remote computer management.

As shown in Figure 4.1, the MMC console contains two panes: a console tree on the left and a details pane on the right. The console tree lists the hierarchical structure of all snap-ins that have been loaded into the console. The details pane contains a list of properties or other items that are part of the snap-in that is highlighted in the console tree.

FIGURE 4.1   The MMC console tree and details pane

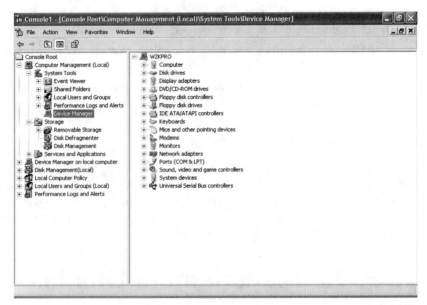

On a Windows XP Professional computer, there is no item created for the MMC by default. To open the console, select Start ➢ Run and type MMC in the Run dialog box. When you first open the MMC, it contains only the Console Root folder, as shown in Figure 4.2. The MMC does not have any default administrative functionality. It is simply a framework used to organize administrative tools through the addition of snap-in utilities.

FIGURE 4.2   The opening MMC window

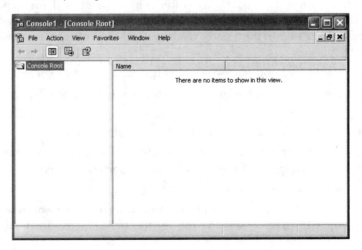

Configuring MMC Modes

You can configure the MMC to run in author mode, for full access to the MMC functions, or in one of three user modes, which have more limited access to the MMC functions. To set a console mode, select File ➢ Options to open the Options dialog box. In this dialog box, you can select from the console modes listed in Table 4.1.

TABLE 4.1 MMC Console Modes

Console Mode	Description
Author mode	Allows use of all the MMC functions.
User mode—full access	Allows users full access to window management commands, but they cannot add or remove snap-ins.
User mode—limited access, multiple window	Allows users to create new windows, but they can access only the areas of the console tree that were visible when the console was last saved.
User mode—limited access, single window	Allows users to access only the areas of the console tree that were visible when the console was last saved, and they cannot create new windows.

Adding Snap-Ins

To add snap-ins to the MMC console and save it, take the following steps:

1. From the main console window, select File ➢ Add/Remove Snap-In to open the Add/Remove Snap-In dialog box.

2. Click the Add button to open the Add Standalone Snap-In dialog box.

3. Highlight the snap-in you wish to add, and click the Add button.

4. If prompted, specify whether the snap-in will be used to manage the local computer or a remote computer. Then click the Finish button.

5. Repeat steps 3 and 4 to add each snap-in you want to include in your console.

6. When you are finished adding snap-ins, click the Close button.

7. Click the OK button to return to the main console screen.

8. After you have added snap-ins to create a console, you can save it by selecting File ➢ Save As and entering a name for your console. You can save the console to a variety of locations, including a program group or the Desktop. By default, custom consoles have an .msc extension.

In exercises in later chapters, you will add MMC snap-ins to create different custom consoles and save them in various locations. This will give you an idea of the flexibility of the MMC and how you can set up custom consoles for your administrative tasks.

Registry Editor

The *Registry* is a database used by the operating system to store configuration information. The *Registry Editor* program is used to edit the Registry. This utility is designed for advanced configuration of the system. Normally, when you make changes to your configuration, you use other utilities, such as Control Panel.

Only experienced administrators should use the Registry Editor. It is intended for making configuration changes that can only be made directly through the Registry. For example, you might edit the Registry to specify an alternate location for a print spool folder. Improper changes to the Registry can cause the computer to fail to boot. Use the Registry Editor with extreme caution.

Windows XP uses the REGEDIT program as the primary utility for Registry editing in Windows XP. It supports full editing of the Registry. To use REGEDIT, select Start ➢ Run and type **REGEDIT** in the Run dialog box.

The REGEDIT program that is included with Windows XP Professional includes full search capabilities and full Registry support. You can still use the REGEDT32 from the Run command, but it will redirect you to the REGEDIT command.

The Registry is organized in a hierarchical tree format of keys and subkeys that represent logical areas of computer configuration. By default, when you open the Registry Editor, you see five Registry key listings, as shown in Figure 4.3 and described in Table 4.2.

FIGURE 4.3 The Registry Editor Window

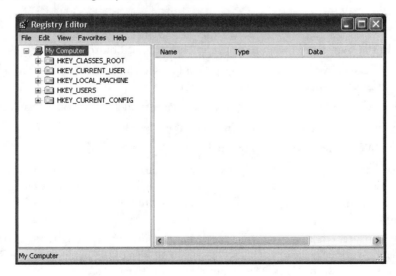

TABLE 4.2   Registry Keys

Registry Key	Description
HKEY_CURRENT_USER	Configuration information for the user who is currently logged on to the computer. This key is a subkey of the HKEY_USERS key.
HKEY_USERS	Configuration information for all users of the computer.
HKEY_LOCAL_MACHINE	Computer hardware configuration information. This computer configuration is used regardless of the user who is logged in.
HKEY_CLASSES_ROOT	Configuration information used by Windows Explorer to properly associate file types with applications.
HKEY_CURRENT_CONFIG	Configuration of the hardware profile that is used during system startup.

Installing Hardware

If you buy new hardware, it will probably be Plug and Play. If you use older, non–Plug and Play hardware, you will most likely need to configure the hardware to be properly recognized by the operating system.

Installing Plug and Play Devices

Plug and Play technology uses a combination of hardware and software that allows the operating system to automatically recognize and configure new hardware without any user intervention. Windows XP Plug and Play support includes the following features:

- Automatic and dynamic recognition of hardware that is installed
- Automatic resource allocation (or reallocation, if necessary)
- Determination of the correct driver that needs to be loaded for hardware support
- Support for interaction with the Plug and Play system
- Support for power management features

Installing Non–Plug and Play Devices

Legacy or older hardware is also supported by Windows XP Professional. When you install this type of hardware, you need to configure it just as you did before Plug and Play technology was introduced.

First, you need to configure the hardware device's resources manually on the device or through a software configuration program. Hardware resources include the device's interrupt request (IRQ), I/O port address, memory address, and Direct Memory Access (DMA) settings. Before you configure the resources for the new device, determine which resources are available. You can view a listing of the currently allocated resources in the Device Manager utility, as follows:

1. From the Start menu, right-click My Computer and select Manage. In the Computer Management window, select System Tools and then Device Manager.

2. Select View ➤ Resources by Connection.

3. Device Manager displays a list of the current resources. Click a resource, then the Resources tab to see all of the allocated resources of that type. Figure 4.4 shows an example of an IRQ listing in Device Manager.

FIGURE 4.4 Viewing resource allocation in Device Manager

Through View ➤ Resources by Type, you see a listing for Direct Memory Access (DMA), Input/Output (I/O), Interrupt Request (IRQ), and Memory. By expanding each resource type, you will see all devices that have been assigned resources within the category. This view is useful when you are determining what resources are in use, and what resources are available.

After you've configured the hardware resources, you can use the Add Hardware icon in Control Panel (Classic View) to add the new device to Windows XP Professional and install the device driver. If the device is not listed, you will need a manufacturer-provided driver. Insert the disk that contains the driver and click the Have Disk button in Add/Remove Hardware.

You can also access Device Manager by right-clicking My Computer in the Start menu, and then selecting the Properties ➤ Hardware tab ➤ Device Manager button. Windows XP Professional often offers many alternatives for completing the same task. Throughout this book, you will be presented with some of the different options for completing the same tasks.

Managing Device Drivers

A *device driver* is software that allows a specific piece of hardware to communicate with the Windows XP operating system. Most of the devices on the Microsoft Hardware Compatibility List (HCL) have drivers that are included on the Windows XP Professional distribution CD. Managing device drivers involves updating them when necessary and deciding how to handle drivers that may not have been properly tested.

Updating Drivers

Device manufacturers periodically update device drivers to add functionality or enhance driver performance. The updated drivers are typically posted on the manufacturer's website.

Exercise 4.1 takes you through the steps to update a device driver. To complete this exercise, you need to have an updated driver for one of your hardware devices.

EXERCISE 4.1

Updating a Device Driver

1. Select Start, then right-click My Computer and select Manage from the pop-up menu.

2. The Computer Management window opens. Select System Tools, then Device Manager.

3. The right side of the window lists all the devices that are installed on your computer. Right-click the device whose driver you want to update.

4. Select Update Driver from the pop-up menu. The Hardware Update Wizard will start. Click the Next button.

5. In the Welcome to the Hardware Update Wizard dialog box, you can choose to have the wizard search for a suitable driver and install the software automatically, which is recommended, or you can have the wizard install the driver from a list or specific location. This exercise assumes you will be installing your new driver from an installation CD or floppy disk that came with the device and that you are using. In this case, select the Install from a list or specific location (Advanced) option. Make sure the installation CD or floppy is inserted, and click the Next button.

6. The files will be installed for your driver. Then you will see the Completing the Upgrade Device Driver Wizard dialog box. Click the Finish button to close this dialog box.

7. You may see a dialog box indicating that you must restart your computer before the change can be successfully implemented. If necessary, restart your computer.

Windows XP Professional offers a new feature called Roll Back Driver. This option can be used to roll back to a previously installed driver in the event that the new driver is installed and is faulty. To roll back a driver, restart the computer in Safe Mode and select Roll Back Driver through the device's properties in Device Manager. Roll Back Driver is covered in greater detail in Chapter 14, "Performing System Recovery Functions."

Managing Driver Signing

In the past, poorly written device drivers have caused problems in Windows operating systems. Microsoft is now promoting a mechanism called *driver signing* as a way of ensuring that drivers are properly tested before they are released to the public.

Through the Driver Signing Options dialog box, you can specify how Windows XP Professional will respond if you choose to install an unsigned driver. To access this dialog box, from the Start menu, right-click My Computer, select Properties from the pop-up menu, and click the Hardware tab in the System Properties dialog box. This tab has Add Hardware Wizard, Device Manager, and Hardware Profiles options, as shown in Figure 4.5. Clicking the Driver Signing button in the Device Manager section opens the Driver Signing Options dialog box, as shown in Figure 4.6.

FIGURE 4.5   The Hardware tab of the System Properties dialog box

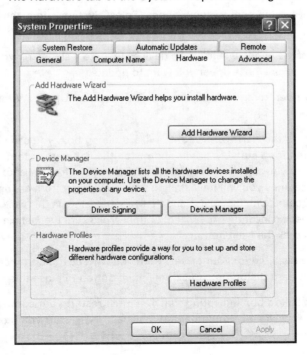

FIGURE 4.6   Driver signing options

In the Driver Signing Options dialog box, you can select from three options for file system verification:

- The Ignore option has Windows XP install all of the files, whether or not they are signed. You will not see any type of message about driver signing.

- The Warn option has Windows XP display a warning message before installing an unsigned file. You can then choose to continue with the installation or cancel it. This is the default setting.

- The Block option has Windows XP prevent the installation of any unsigned file. You will see an error message when you attempt to install the unsigned driver, and you will not be able to continue.

By default, when you apply driver settings, they are only applied to the user who is currently logged on. If you check the Make This Action the System Default option, the settings that you apply will be used by all users who log on to the computer.

You can run a utility called SigVerif from a command line. This utility will check all of your files for current verification status, and then display a list of all drivers that have not been digitally signed. The log file created (sigverif.txt) is accessed by clicking the Advanced button within the SigVerif dialog box.

In Exercise 4.2, you will check the system's setting for driver signing.

EXERCISE 4.2

Managing Driver Signing

1. Select Start, then right-click My Computer and select Properties.

2. In the System Properties dialog box, click the Hardware tab, then click the Driver Signing button.

3. In the Driver Signing Options dialog box, verify that the Warn radio button is selected and the Make This Action the System Default check box is checked.

4. Click the OK button to close the dialog box.

Managing Disk Devices

You can manage disk devices through the Device Manager utility. The following sections describe how to manage CD-ROM, *DVD*, and removable media devices. Managing disks is covered in Chapter 8, "Managing Disks."

> You install DVD and CD-ROMs as you would any Plug and Play or non–Plug and Play device. Installing Plug and Play and non–Plug and Play devices was discussed previously in this chapter in the "Installing Hardware" section.

Managing DVD and CD-ROM Devices

DVDs and CD-ROMs are listed together under DVD/CD-ROM Drives in Device Manager. Double-click DVD/CD-ROM Drives, then double-click the device you wish to manage. This brings up the device Properties dialog box, which has five tabs:

General   Lists the device type, manufacturer, and location. It also shows the device status, which indicates whether the device is working properly. If the device is not working properly, you can click the Troubleshoot button at the lower right of the dialog box to get some help with resolving the problem.

Properties   Allows you to set options such as volume and playback settings.

DVD Region   Plays regionally encoded DVDs for a maximum of five regional changes.

Volumes   Is used to display CD properties such as disk, type, status, partition style, capacity, unallocated space, and reserved space.

Driver   Shows information about the currently loaded driver, as well as buttons that allow you to see driver details, uninstall the driver, roll back the driver, or update the driver. (See the "Updating Drivers" section earlier in the chapter for details on updating a driver.)

Right-clicking DVD/CD-ROM Drives in Device Manager allows you the option of updating the driver, disabling the device, uninstalling the device, scanning for hardware changes, or viewing the properties of the device.

In Exercise 4.3, you will manage disk devices.

EXERCISE 4.3

Managing Disk Devices

1. Select Start, then right-click My Computer and select Manage. In Computer Management, select System Tools, then Device Manager.

2. Double-click DVD/CD-ROM Drives, then double-click the DVD or CD-ROM device you wish to manage.

3. In the General tab of the device Properties dialog box, verify that your device is working properly. If the device is not working properly, click the Troubleshoot button. The Troubleshooter Wizard will ask you a series of questions and attempt to help you resolve the problem.

4. Click the Properties tab, and configure the options to suit your personal preferences.

5. Click the Driver tab. Note the information about the currently loaded driver.

6. Click the OK button to save your settings and close the dialog box.

Managing Removable Media

Removable media are devices such as tape devices and Zip drives. Like DVD and CD-ROM devices, removable media can also be managed through Device Manager.

Removable media are listed under Disk Drives in Device Manager. Double-click Disk Drives, and then double-click the removable media device you wish to manage. This brings up the device Properties dialog box. The General and Driver tabs are similar to those for CD-ROM and DVD devices, as described in the preceding section. The Disk Properties tab contains options for the specific removable media device.

 In order to access removable media, the user needs to be a member of the Backup Operators group. The Backup Operators group is covered in Chapter 6, "Managing Users and Groups."

Managing Display Devices

A *video adapter* is the device that outputs the display to your monitor. You install a video adapter in the same way that you install other hardware. If it is a Plug and Play device, all you need to do is shut down your computer, add the video adapter, and turn on your computer. Windows XP Professional will automatically recognize the new device.

You can configure several options for your video adapters, and if you have multiple monitors with their own video adapters, you can configure multiple-display support. The following sections describe video adapter configuration, and how to configure your computer to support multiple monitors.

You install video adapters as you would any Plug and Play or non–Plug and Play device. Installing Plug and Play and non–Plug and Play devices was discussed earlier in the chapter in the "Installing Hardware" section.

Configuring Video Adapters

The options for video adapters are on the Settings tab of the Display Properties dialog box, as shown in Figure 4.7. To access this dialog box, select Control Panel ➤ Appearance and Themes ➤ Display, then select the Settings tab. Alternately, you could right-click an empty area on your Desktop and select Properties from the pop-up menu, then select the Setting tab.

FIGURE 4.7 The Settings tab of the Display Properties dialog box

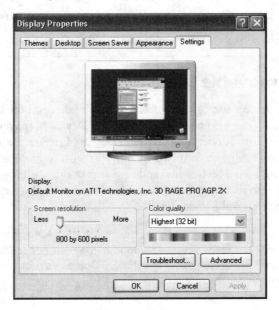

The Color Quality option in the Settings tab sets the color quality, for example to 32-bit quality or 16-bit quality, for your video adapter. The Screen Resolution option allows you to set the resolution for your video adapter.

The other tabs in the Display Properties dialog box allow you to customize the appearance of your Desktop. These options are discussed in Chapter 5, "Managing the Windows XP Professional Desktop."

To configure advanced settings for your video adapter, click the Advanced button in the lower-right corner of the Settings tab. This brings up the Properties dialog box for the monitor, as shown in Figure 4.8. There are five tabs with options for your video adapter and monitor.

FIGURE 4.8   The Properties dialog box for a display monitor

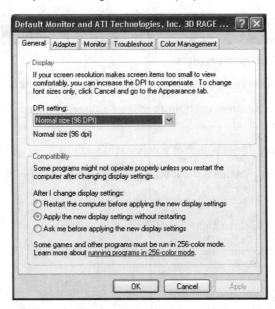

General   Allows you to configure the font size for the display. You can also specify what action Windows XP will take after you change your display settings.

Adapter   Allows you to view and configure the properties of your video adapter.

Monitor   Allows you to view and configure the properties of your monitor, including the refresh frequency (how often the screen is redrawn).

A lower refresh frequency setting can cause your screen to flicker. Setting the refresh frequency too high can damage some hardware.

Troubleshoot   Allows you to configure how Windows XP uses your graphics hardware. For example, you can configure hardware acceleration settings.

Color Management   Allows you to select color profiles (the colors that are displayed on your monitor).

In Exercise 4.4, you will view the properties of your video adapter.

 Normally, the video adapter is configured for typical use. Be careful if you change these settings, because improper settings may cause your display to be unreadable. In Chapter 14, "Performing System Recovery Functions," you learn how to modify the Boot.ini file to start Windows XP Professional using a standard VGA driver, which allows standard video access. Then, you will be able to load and configure the correct, specific video adapter settings for your specific hardware.

EXERCISE 4.4

Viewing Video Adapter Settings

1. Right-click an empty area on the Desktop, choose Properties, and select the Settings tab.

2. Click the Advanced button at the bottom of the Settings tab. Make a note of your current settings in the General tab.

3. Click the Adapter tab. Make a note of your current settings.

4. Click the Monitor tab. Make a note of your current settings.

5. Click the Troubleshoot tab. Make a note of your current settings.

6. Click the OK button to close the monitor Properties dialog box.

7. Click the OK button to close the Display Properties dialog box.

Setting the Video's Resolution, Color Selection, and Refresh Rate

Depending on your video adapter, you can configure a monitor's resolution, color selection, and refresh rate. *Resolution* specifies how densely packed the pixels are. The more pixels, or dots per inch (dpi), the clearer the image. The SVGA (super video graphics adapter) standard is 1024×768, but high-end models can display higher resolution; for example, 1600×1200. The *color* selection specifies how many colors are supported by your video adapter; for example, the monitor may be displaying 16 colors or 256 colors. *Refresh rate* indicates how many times per second the screen is refreshed (redrawn). To avoid flickering, this rate should be set to at least 72Hz.

Certain applications require specific configurations based on graphics used. If you run across an application that requires a specific resolution, color selection, or refresh rate, or if a user makes a request based on personal preferences, you can easily determine what options are supported by the video adapter. In Control Panel, select Appearance and Themes ➢ Display ➢ Settings ➢ Advanced ➢ Adapter ➢ List All Modes.

Using Multiple-Display Support

Windows XP Professional allows you to extend your Desktop across a maximum of 10 monitors. This means you can spread your applications across multiple monitors.

To set up multiple-display support, you must have a video adapter installed for each monitor, and you must use either Peripheral Connection Interface (PCI) or Accelerated Graphics Port (AGP) video adapter cards. To use the video adapter that is built into the system board for multiple-display support, the chip set must use the PCI or AGP standard.

If your computer has the video adapter built into the system board, you should install Windows XP Professional before you install the second video adapter. This is because Windows XP will disable the video adapter that is built into the system board if it detects a second video adapter. When you add a second video adapter after Windows XP is installed, it will automatically become the primary video adapter.

In Exercise 4.5, you will configure multiple-display support.

EXERCISE 4.5

Configuring Multiple-Display Support

1. Turn off your computer and install the PCI or AGP adapters. Plug your monitors into the video adapters and turn on your computer. Assuming that the adapters are Plug and Play, Windows XP will automatically recognize your new adapters and load the correct drivers.

2. Open the Display Properties dialog box (right-click an empty area on your Desktop and select Properties) and click the Settings tab. You should see an icon for each of the monitors.

3. Click the number of the monitor that will act as your additional display. Then select the Extend My Windows Desktop onto This Monitor check box. Repeat this step for each additional monitor you wish to configure.

   You can arrange the order in which the displays are arranged by dragging and dropping the monitor icons in the Settings tab of the Display Properties dialog box.

4. When you are finished configuring the monitors, click OK to close the dialog box.

Troubleshooting Multiple-Display Support

If you are having problems with multiple-display support, use the following troubleshooting guidelines:

The Extend My Windows Desktop onto This Monitor option isn't available.   If the Settings tab of the Display Properties dialog box doesn't give you the option Extend My Windows Desktop onto This Monitor, confirm that your secondary adapter is supported for multiple-display support. Confirm that you have the most current drivers (that are XP compliant and support dual-mode capabilities) loaded. Confirm that Windows XP is able to detect the secondary video adapter. Try selecting the secondary adapter rather than the primary adapter in the Display Properties dialog box.

No output appears on the secondary display.   Confirm that your secondary adapter is supported for multiple-display support, especially if you are using the built-in motherboard video adapter. Confirm that the correct video driver has been installed for the secondary display. Restart the computer to see if the secondary video driver is initialized. Check the status of the video adapter in Device Manager. Try switching the order of the video adapters in the computer's slots. See if the system will recognize the device as the primary display.

An application is not properly displayed.   Disable the secondary display to determine if the problem is specific to multiple-display support. Run the application on the primary display. If you are running MS-DOS applications, try running the application in full-screen mode. For Windows applications, try running the application in a maximized window.

Managing Mobile Computer Hardware

Windows XP Professional includes several features that are particularly useful for laptop computers. For example, through Power Options in Control Panel (found in the Performance and Maintenance section), you can set power schemes and enable power management features with Windows XP. You will also learn how to manage card services for mobile computers.

Power Management

In this section you will learn about improvements to power management, how to manage power states, how to manage power options, and how to troubleshoot power management.

Improvements to Power Management

Windows XP builds upon the power management features that were introduced with Windows 2000 with the following enhancements:

- Better boot and resume capabilities, so that startup and shutdown processes occur more quickly

- Better power efficiency

- Wake-on support, which allows a computer to respond to wake-up events such as telephone calls or network requests

- Power management policies that can be set for individual devices

- Power management features for applications that are designed to be used with power management; for example, presentation applications can be configured so that the monitor does not go to sleep when that application is running

Managing Power States

In Windows XP, the *Advanced Configuration Power Interface (ACPI)* specifies six different levels of power states:

- Complete shutdown of PC
- Hibernation
- Standby (three levels)
- Fully active PC

The similarity between hibernation and standby is that they both allow you to avoid shutting down your computer to save power. The key difference is in your computer's state of shutdown.

Hibernation falls short of a complete shutdown of the computer. With hibernation, the computer saves all of your Desktop state as well as any open files. To use the computer again, press the power button. The computer starts more quickly than from a complete shutdown because it does not have to go through the complete startup process. You will have to again log on to the computer. You will also notice that all the documents that were open when the computer went into hibernation are still available. With hibernation you can easily resume work where you left off. You can configure your computer to hibernate through Power Options, or by entering Start ➢ Shut Down and then selecting Hibernate from the drop-down menu. This option will appear only if hibernation has been enabled through Power Options.

Standby does not save data automatically as hibernation does. With standby you can access your computer more quickly than a computer that is in hibernation, usually through a mouse click or keystroke, and the desktop appears as it was prior to the standby. The response time depends on the level of your computer's standby state. On an ACPI-compliant computer, there are three levels of standby, each level putting the computer into a deeper sleep. The first level turns off power to the monitor and hard drives. The second level turns off power to the CPU and cache. The third level supplies power to RAM only and preserves the Desktop in memory. You will see an option to configure standby only on Windows XP computers in which a battery has been detected. You can configure your computer for standby through Power Options, or through Start ➢ Shut Down and then selecting Standby from the drop-down menu. This option will appear only if standby has been enabled through Power Options.

 Put your computer in standby mode if you will be away for a few minutes. Use hibernation mode if you will be away for a more extended period of time.

To determine whether Windows XP is running in ACPI mode:

1. Click Start ➢ Control Panel ➢ Performance and Maintenance.
2. Double-click Administrative Tools, and click Computer Management.
3. Click Device Manager, then click System Devices.

If Microsoft ACPI-Compliant System is listed under System Devices, then the computer is operating in ACPI mode. During Windows XP Setup, ACPI is installed only on systems that have an ACPI-compatible BIOS.

You may be able to upgrade your computer's BIOS to make it ACPI capable. Check with your computer's manufacturer for upgrade information.

Managing Power Options

You configure power options through the Power Options Properties dialog box, as shown in Figure 4.9. To access this dialog box, access Control Panel ➤ Performance and Maintenance ➤ Power Options. On a laptop, this dialog box has five tabs: Power Schemes, Alarms, Power Meter, Advanced, and Hibernate. If your computer is a stand-alone PC, you will see a tab for UPS, Uninterruptible Power Supply, which is used to provide an alternate power source in the event that your computer loses regular power. The Power Options for laptop computers are described in the following sections.

FIGURE 4.9   The Power Options Properties dialog box

Configuring Power Schemes

The Power Schemes tab (see Figure 4.9) helps you select the most appropriate power scheme for your computer. Power schemes control automatic turn-off of the monitor and hard disks, based on a specified period of inactivity. This feature allows you to conserve your laptop's battery when the computer isn't being used. From the drop-down list, you can select one of the preconfigured power schemes listed in Table 4.3. Alternatively, you can create a custom power scheme by clicking the Save As button, giving the power scheme a new name, and choosing power scheme options.

TABLE 4.3   Windows XP Power Schemes

Power Scheme	Turn Off Monitor	Turn Off Hard Disks
Home/Office Desk	After 20 minutes	Never
Portable/Laptop	After 15 minutes	After 30 minutes
Presentation	Never	Never
Always On	After 20 minutes	Never
Minimal Power Management	After 15 minutes	Never
Max Battery	After 15 minutes	Never

Configuring Alarms

The Alarms tab of Power Options Properties (shown in Figure 4.10) is used to specify Low Battery Alarm and Critical Battery Alarm. With Low Battery Alarm and Critical Battery Alarm, you can specify that notification, action (such as hibernation), or run program events be triggered when the power level reaches a specified threshold.

FIGURE 4.10   Alarms tab of Power Options Properties

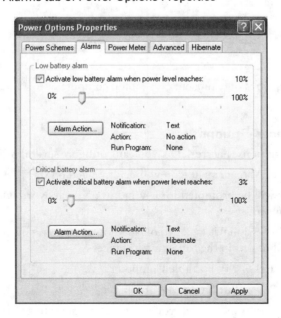

This tab is only present on a laptop computer with a battery installed.

Configuring Power Meter Options

The Power Meter tab (shown in Figure 4.11) is used to show you what your current power source is, either AC power or battery. You can also see what percentage the battery is charged to.

FIGURE 4.11   Power Meter tab of Power Options Properties

 This tab is only present on a laptop computer.

Configuring Advanced Options

Among the advanced options (Figure 4.12), you can configure several power options, including

- Whether the Power Management icon will be displayed on the Taskbar.
- Whether the user will be prompted for a Windows XP password when the computer resumes from standby.

   If Windows XP Professional is installed on a laptop computer, you will also see options for managing power buttons in the following instances:

- When I Close the Lid of My Portable Computer
- When I Press the Power Button on My Computer

In these instances you can specify that you want the computer to go on standby or power-off mode. With the When I Close the Lid of My Portable Computer, you also have the additional option of doing nothing.

FIGURE 4.12   Advanced tab of Power Options Properties

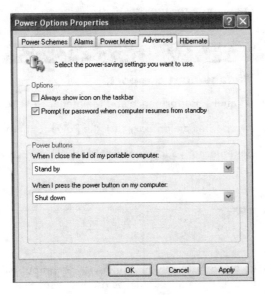

Configuring Hibernation

Hibernation for a computer means that anything stored in memory is also stored on your hard disk. This ensures that when your computer is shut down, you do not lose any of the information that is stored in memory. When you take your computer out of hibernation, it returns to its previous state.

To configure your computer to hibernate, use the Hibernate tab of the Power Options Properties dialog box, as shown in Figure 4.13. Simply select the Enable Hibernation check box.

FIGURE 4.13   The Hibernate tab of Power Options Properties

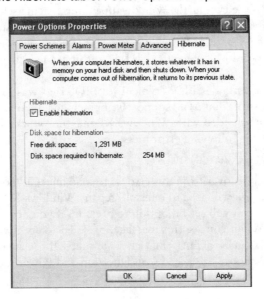

If you have a laptop running Windows XP Professional, you can complete the steps in Exercise 4.6 to configure the laptop to support ACPI.

EXERCISE 4.6

Configuring Power Management Support

1. Select Start ➢ Control Panel ➢ Performance and Maintenance ➢ Power Options icon.

2. In the Power Options Properties dialog box, click the Power Schemes tab.

3. Configure the Power Schemes for your computer based on your personal preferences, and click OK.

4. Close Control Panel.

 If you are using ACPI on your Windows XP computer and your BIOS does not support ACPI, you may experience problems such as the computer's inability to shut down. In this case you should upgrade your computer with a BIOS that supports ACPI, or you can disable ACPI support on the computer.

Troubleshooting Power Management Issues

Windows XP (and all versions of Windows NT, 2000, and Server 2003) rely on a *Hardware Abstraction Layer (HAL)* to provide hardware-independent code for specific hardware platforms. By using portable code to act between the Windows operating system and platform-specific hardware, the code that is used within the Windows operating system itself it platform independent.

If you have a computer that does not have an ACPI-enabled BIOS installed, a legacy hardware abstraction layer will be installed. This can also occur if you upgrade to Windows XP from a previous version of Windows, since the HAL is not upgraded during a normal upgrade process.

If your computer has an older BIOS, typically a BIOS that was manufactured prior to January 1, 1999, it is possible that ACPI support is not included. If you then upgrade your BIOS, the HAL that is currently loaded with Windows XP may not work. When you restart your computer, you may see the following error message:

`"STOP: 0x000000079HAL_MISMATCH."`

The only way you can recover from this error is to load an ACPI-compliant HAL. To force an upgrade of the HAL, you will need to reinstall (repair) Windows XP. During the text-mode portion of the upgrade, you will see an option to press F6 if you need to install a third-party SCSI or RAID driver. When you see this message, press F5 to specify the installation of an alternate HAL. You will see a list of HALs that can be installed. If you are using a standard PC with one processor, you will choose Advanced Configuration and Power Interface (ACPI) PC.

Real World Scenario

Managing Power Consumption with Laptops

You have users with laptops configured with network and modem cards. When the users are attached to the network or at home, they work off of an external power source, but when they travel, especially on long flights, they find that they go through their battery power fairly quickly. You want to manage the power consumption as much as possible.

With laptop computers, you can conserve power by disabling devices that are not in use, such as network cards, modems, or other external devices. To customize hardware profiles, create the profile by right-clicking My Computer, and then select Properties, then the Hardware tab. Click the Hardware Profiles option and copy an existing profile to create a new one. When you restart the computer, you will have the option of selecting the hardware profile you want to use. Make the changes you want, such as disabling devices that won't be used, and they will automatically be saved with the profile you logged in with. If you no longer have a need for multiple profiles, you can delete the alternate profile, and with only one selection, you will no longer see a hardware profiles selection screen during the computer startup process.

Managing Card Services

To add devices to a laptop computer, you use special credit card–sized devices called *PCMCIA* (Personal Computer Memory Card International Association) Cards, or more simply, PC Cards. PC Cards have three different standards:

Type I cards   Can be up to 3.3 mm thick. These cards are primarily used for adding memory to a computer.

Type II cards   Can be up to 5.5 mm thick. These cards are typically used for modem and network cards.

Type III cards   Can be up to 10.5 mm thick. These cards are typically used for portable disk drives.

Windows XP Professional allows you to exchange PC Cards on-the-fly (called hot swapping). However, you should make sure that your laptop supports hot-swap technology before you try to remove a card from or add a card to a running computer.

As with any Plug and Play device, when you add a PC Card to a Windows XP Professional computer, the card will be recognized automatically. You can view and manage PC Cards through Device Manager.

Managing I/O Devices

Your input/output (I/O) devices are the ones that allow you to get information into and out of your computer. Examples of I/O devices are keyboards, mice, printers, and scanners. Your devices may be connected to your computer by standard cabling, or they may use wireless technology (such as IrDA or RF) or be connected through a USB port.

The following subsections describe how to manage your keyboard, mouse, wireless devices, and USB devices. Scanners are covered in the next section. You will learn how to install and configure printers in Chapter 11, "Managing Printing."

Configuring the Keyboard

Most of the time you leave the keyboard settings at default values. However, if needed you can configure advanced keyboard options.

You can configure keyboard options through the Keyboard Properties dialog box, shown in Figure 4.14. To access this dialog box, open Control Panel, then Printers and Other Hardware, and then select the Keyboard icon.

You must have a keyboard attached to your computer before you can install Windows XP Professional.

FIGURE 4.14   The Keyboard Properties dialog box

This dialog box has two tabs with options that control your keyboard's behavior:

- The Speed tab lets you configure how quickly characters are repeated when you hold down a key. You can also specify the cursor blink rate.

- The Hardware tab specifies the device settings for your keyboard.

Configuring the Mouse

You can configure your mouse through the Mouse Properties dialog box, shown in Figure 4.15. To access this dialog box, open Control Panel, then Printers and Other Hardware, and then select the Mouse option.

FIGURE 4.15   The Mouse Properties dialog box

The Mouse Properties dialog box has five tabs with options that control your mouse's behavior:

Buttons   Allows you to configure the mouse properties for right-handed or left-handed use. You can also configure the speed that is used to indicate a double-click. The ClickLock option is used to highlight and drag a selection without holding down the mouse button while the object is being moved. ClickLock is not enabled by default.

Pointers   Lets you select a pre-defined pointer scheme that is used by your mouse, for example Dinosaur (system scheme) that uses dinosaur themed pointers. You can also create custom pointer schemes.

Pointer Options   Lets you specify how fast your mouse pointer moves. You can also configure the snap-to-default feature, which automatically moves the pointer to a default button in a dialog box when new dialog boxes are opened. Visibility options are used to configure if pointer trails are displayed, if the pointer is hidden while typing, and whether the location of the pointer is shown when the CTRL key is pressed.

Wheel   Is used to configure wheel scrolling.

Hardware   Specifies the device settings for your mouse.

In Exercise 4.7, you will configure your keyboard and mouse I/O devices.

Configuring I/O Devices

1. Select Start ➤ Control Panel ➤ Printers and Other Hardware ➤ Keyboard icon.

2. In the Speed tab, set the Repeat Delay and Repeat Rate options based on your personal preferences. Also adjust the Cursor Blink Rate if you want to change it. Click the OK button.

3. In Control Panel, Printers and Other Hardware, click the Mouse icon.

4. In the Pointers Options tab, set the Motion and Snap-To options as you prefer. Click the OK button.

5. Close Control Panel.

Configuring Wireless Devices

Wireless devices use wireless transmission rather than transmitting over cable. Following are two of the technologies used for wireless transmission:

- Infrared Data Association (IrDA), which is a standard for transmitting data through infrared light waves

- RF (Radio Frequency), which is a standard for transmitting data through radio waves

Common examples of wireless devices include keyboards, mice, and network cards. You should follow the vendor's instructions to install wireless devices. Wireless devices are configured in the same manner as other devices on your computer. For example, you can set options for a wireless keyboard through the Keyboard Properties dialog box.

Managing USB Devices

Universal Serial Bus (USB) is an external bus standard that allows you to connect USB devices through a USB port. USB supports transfer rates up to 12Mbps. A single USB port can support up to 127 devices. Examples of USB devices include modems, printers, and keyboards.

Configuring USB Devices

If your computer supports USB, and USB is enabled in the BIOS, you will see Universal Serial Bus Controller listed in Device Manager. Double-click your USB controller to see the dialog box shown in Figure 4.16.

FIGURE 4.16   The USB controller Properties dialog box

The USB controller Properties dialog box has four tabs with options and information for your USB adapter:

General   Lists the device type, manufacturer, and location. It also shows the device status, which indicates whether the device is working properly. If the device is not working properly, you can click the Troubleshoot button in the lower-right area of the dialog box.

Advanced   Allows you to configure how much of the bandwidth each device that is connected to the USB adapter can use.

Driver   Shows driver properties and lets you uninstall or update the driver.

Resources   Shows all of the resources that are used by the USB adapter.

After the USB adapter is configured, you can attach USB devices to the adapter in a daisy-chain configuration.

Troubleshooting USB

Some of the errors you may encounter with USB and the associated fixes are as follows:

- You may have malfunctioning or incorrectly configured USB hardware. If you suspect that this is the case, and you have another computer running USB, you should try and run the USB hardware on the alternate computer. You should also check the status of the device in Device Manager. To support USB, the computer must have an IRQ assigned for the root USB controller in the computer's BIOS.

- You may have mismatched cabling. USB supports two standards, high-speed and low-speed. Make sure the cables are the proper type for your configuration.

- Make sure your BIOS and firmware is up-to-date. If the BIOS or firmware is not compatible with USB, you may see multiple instances of your device in Device Manager with no associated drivers for the multiple instances.

- The root hub may be improperly configured. USB controllers require that an IRQ be assigned in the computer's BIOS. If the controller is not properly configured, you will see the root hub displayed in Device Manager with a yellow exclamation point.

- If you are using a USB bus-powered hub, the device attached to the hub may require more power than the hub can provide. In this case you should use a self-powered USB hub. You can determine if the hub is the problem by removing the hub and directly attaching the device to the computer's USB. You can also troubleshoot this error by attaching the device to a self-powered USB hub and seeing if it works.

If your computer has a built-in USB device and does not detect the device through Device Manager, confirm that the USB is enabled in the computer's BIOS and that the BIOS supports USB devices.

Managing Imaging Devices

A scanner is a device that can read text or graphics that are on paper and translate the information to digital data that the computer can understand. Digital cameras take pictures in a digital format that can be read by the computer.

After you install a scanner or digital camera on a Windows XP Professional computer, you can manage the device through the Scanners and Cameras Properties dialog box. You access this dialog box by selecting the Scanners and Cameras icon in Control Panel from the Printers and Other Hardware option.

The Scanners and Cameras Properties dialog box lists the devices that are recognized by your computer. You can click the Add an Imaging Device option to add a scanner or camera, the Remove button to remove the selected device, or the Troubleshoot button to run a Troubleshooter Wizard. Clicking the Properties button displays a dialog box with additional options.

The scanner or camera Properties dialog box has three tabs with options and information about the device:

General   Lists the manufacturer, description, port, and status of the device. It also contains a button that you can click to test the scanner or camera.

Events   Allows you to associate an event with an application. For example, you can specify that when you scan a document, it should be automatically linked to the imaging program, and the imaging program will start and display the document you just scanned.

Color Management   Allows you to associate a color profile with the scanner or camera.

If you have a scanner or digital camera installed on your computer, you can complete the steps in Exercise 4.8 to view and configure its properties.

Managing and Monitoring Imaging Devices

1. Select Start ➢ Control Panel ➢ Printers and Other Hardware, and click the Scanners and Cameras icon.

2. In the Scanners and Cameras Properties dialog box, click the Properties button.

3. In the General tab of the scanner or camera Properties dialog box, click the Test Scanner or Camera button to make sure the device is working properly.

4. Click the Events tab. Set any associations based on your computer's configuration and your personal preferences.

5. Click the Color Management tab. If desired, associate a color profile with the scanner or camera.

6. Click the OK button to close the scanner or camera Properties dialog box.

7. Click the OK button to close the Scanners and Cameras Properties dialog box.

8. Close Control Panel.

Managing Processors

Normally, multiple processors are associated with servers. However, Windows XP Professional can support up to two processors. If your computer is capable of supporting multiple processors, you should follow the computer manufacturer's instructions for installing the second processor. This usually involves updating the processor's driver to a driver that supports multiple processors through the Upgrade Device Driver Wizard.

Once you install a second processor, you can monitor the processors through the System Monitor utility. You can verify that multiple processors are recognized by the operating system, as well as configure multiple processors, through the Task Manager utility. Chapter 13 discusses the System Monitor and Task Manager utilities in detail.

To configure multiple processors, you can associate each processor with specific processes that are running on the computer. This is called *processor affinity*. Once you have two processors installed on your computer, you can set processor affinity. You'll do this in Exercise 4.9.

Configuring Multiple Processors

1. Press Ctrl+Alt+Del and click the Task Manager button.

2. In the Task Manager dialog box, click the Processes tab.

3.   In the Processes tab, right-click the `explorer.exe` process and select Processor Affinity.

4.   In the Processor Affinity dialog box, check the CPU 1 check box and click the OK button.

5.   Close the Task Manager utility.

Configuring Fax Support

Windows XP Professional allows you to add and configure fax support. To add fax support, you must have a device connected to your computer that can send and receive faxes. The most common example of a fax device is a fax modem.

You configure fax support through the Printers and Faxes option in Control Panel and start the Fax Service through the Computer Management utility, as described in the following sections.

Setting Fax Properties

To configure fax support and set fax properties, take the following steps. Select Start ➢ Control Panel ➢ Printers and Other Hardware, right-click the Fax icon, and select Properties. You will see the Fax Properties dialog box, as shown in Figure 4.17.

FIGURE 4.17   The General tab of Fax Properties

The Fax Properties dialog box has seven tabs with options and information for your fax support:

General   Enables you to name your fax device, define a location and include any comments for the device, and see the features of the device.

Sharing   Allows you to specify whether the fax device is shared for network use.

Security   Is used to specify what rights different users and groups have to the fax device. These rights are similar to print rights.

Fax Security   Is used to set special permissions specific to the fax device.

Devices   Allows you to enable your computer to send and receive faxes.

Tracking   Enables you to select fax devices to monitor, set up notification options for fax events, and configure the Fax Monitor to open when faxes are sent or received.

Archives   Is used to configure a folder where incoming or successfully sent faxes can be saved.

 You can also configure the Fax Queue, Fax Service Management, My Faxes, and Send Cover Page Fax options through the Fax Service Management utility. To access this utility, select Start ➢ All Programs ➢ Accessories ➢ Communications ➢ Fax ➢ Fax Console.

Starting the Fax Service

After you configure fax support, you need to start the Fax Service in Windows Professional. To start the service, take the following steps:

1. Right-click My Computer from the Start menu and select Manage from the pop-up menu.

2. Expand Services and Applications, then Services.

3. Double-click Fax Service and click the Start button.

4. Select Automatic as the Startup Type and click the OK button.

5. Close the Computer Management window.

Starting and configuring Windows XP Professional services is discussed in more detail in the next section.

 Real World Scenario

Setting Up Send and Receive Fax Support

Your boss asks you to configure fax support on a computer for a user in the sales department. After you configure the fax support, the user complains that the computer will send faxes but not receive faxes.

To correct the situation so that the computer can receive faxes, you will need to do two things. First, verify that a fax printer has been created through Control Panel, Printers and Other Hardware, (click the Fax icon, then Advanced Options, then Add a Fax Printer). Second, verify that the Fax Service Management is configured to receive faxes. By default, the fax service is configured to send faxes but not receive faxes. If this default setting is your user's problem, access the Fax Properties Advanced Properties tab, select Fax Service Management Console, then Devices, and expand Devices. If the computer is *not* configured to receive, double-click your fax device. This brings up a dialog box in which you can specify that the fax should also receive faxes.

If you are having trouble with your fax device, use the Troubleshooter Wizard available through the Device Manager utility, as described for sound cards in the next section.

Troubleshooting Devices

When Device Manager does not properly recognize a device, it reports the problem by displaying an exclamation point icon next to the device. To troubleshoot a device that is not working properly, double-click the device to open its Properties dialog box.

If a device connected to your computer doesn't appear in Device Manager, you can get some hints on troubleshooting through the Troubleshooter Wizard. As an example, if your sound card is not working properly and is not listed in Device Manager, you can use the Troubleshooter Wizard, as shown in Exercise 4.10.

EXERCISE 4.10

Using the Troubleshooter Wizard

1. Select Start, then right-click My Computer and select Manage. In Computer Management, select System Tools, then Device Manager.

2. In Device Manager, double-click Computer and double-click Advanced Configuration and Power Interface (ACPI) PC.

3. The Advanced Configuration and Power Interface (ACPI) PC Properties dialog box appears. Click the Troubleshoot button.

4. The Help and Support Center window opens, with the Hardware Troubleshooter displayed. Verify that I'm Having a Problem with My Hardware Device is selected.

5. Select the option Yes, My Hardware Is on the HCL and then click Next.

6. In this case we'll assume that the problem was a bad driver and that using the roll-back option fixed the error. Click the Yes, This Solves the Problem option and click Next.

7. Close the Help and Support Center window.

Managing Windows XP Services

A service is a program, routine, or process that performs a specific function within the Windows XP operating system. You can manage services through the Services window (Figure 4.18), which can be accessed in a variety of ways. If you go through the Computer Management utility, right-click My Computer, select Manage, expand Services and Applications, and then expand Services. You can also go through Administrative Tools, or set up Services as an MMC snap-in.

FIGURE 4.18   The Services window

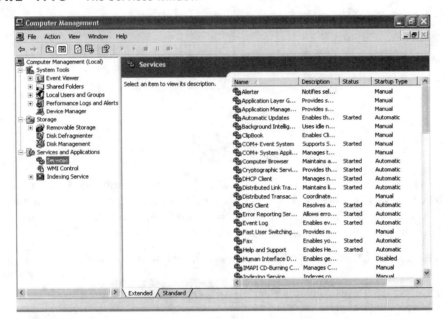

For each service, the Services window lists the name, a short description, the startup type, and the logon account that is used to start the service. To configure the properties of a service, double-click it to open its Properties dialog box, shown in Figure 4.19. This dialog box contains four tabs of options for services: General, Log On, Recovery, and Dependencies.

General   Allows you to view and configure the following options:

- The service display name
- A description of the service
- The path to the service executable
- The startup type, which can be automatic, manual, or disabled
- The current service status
- Startup parameters that can be applied when the service is started

In addition, the buttons across the lower part of the dialog box allow you change the service status to start, stop, pause, or resume the service.

FIGURE 4.19 · Service Properties dialog box

Log On   The Log On tab, shown in Figure 4.20, allows you to configure the logon account that will be used to start the service. Choose the local system account or specify another logon account. At the bottom, you can select hardware profiles with which to associate the service. For each hardware profile, you can set the service as enabled or disabled.

FIGURE 4.20   The Log On tab of the service Properties dialog box

Recovery   The Recovery tab, shown in Figure 4.21, allows you to designate what action will be taken if the service fails to load. For the first, second, and subsequent failures, you can select from the following actions:

- Take No Action
- Restart the Service
- Run a Program
- Reboot the Computer

If you choose to Run a Program, specify it along with any command-line parameters. If you choose to Reboot the Computer, you can configure a message that will be sent to users who are connected to the computer before it is restarted.

FIGURE 4.21   The Recovery tab of the service Properties dialog box

Dependencies   The Dependencies tab, shown in Figure 4.22, lists any services that must be running in order for the specified service to start. If a service fails to start, you can use this information to examine the dependencies and then make sure each one is running. In the bottom panel, you can verify whether any other services depend on this service before you decide to stop.

FIGURE 4.22   The Dependencies tab of the service Properties dialog box

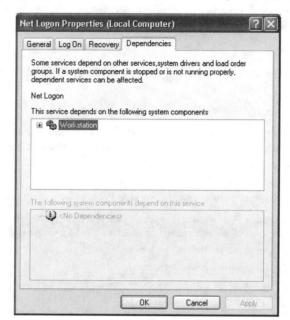

Managing Multiple Hardware Profiles

A *hardware profile* contains all of the settings for a computer. When you install a desktop computer, a profile called Profile1 is automatically created. If you install a laptop computer, the profile will be called Docked or Undocked by default. If the computer has been upgraded, the profile might be called Original Configuration (Current). Any time you make configuration changes to your computer, the changes are automatically saved in the hardware profile.

If your computer uses multiple configuration settings—for example, a laptop that uses different devices at different locations—you can create multiple hardware profiles for the different configurations the computer uses. If you have only one hardware profile, it is loaded by default when the computer starts. If you have multiple hardware profiles, you are prompted to select the hardware profile you want to use when the computer is started. You are able to specify what profile is used by default.

To create alternate hardware profiles, you would take the following steps:

1. Select Start ➢ Control Panel ➢ Performance and Maintenance ➢ System.

2. From the Hardware tab, select the Hardware Profiles button.

3. From the Hardware Profiles dialog box, shown in Figure 4.23, click the Copy button to create a new profile.

FIGURE 4.23   Hardware Profiles dialog box

4. In the Copy Profile dialog box, specify a name for the new profile and click the OK button.

5. Restart Windows XP Professional, and select the new profile when prompted during the startup process.

6. Make any changes needed to the hardware profile. For example, if you have a laptop computer and you want to conserve power for unused devices with this profile, access Device Manager and disable the devices that will not be used.

7. Any changes you make to the profile will be saved automatically when the computer is shut down.

If you are no longer using multiple hardware profiles, you should delete the unused profile so the user will not be prompted to select a hardware profile during the Windows XP Professional startup process.

Summary

In this chapter, you learned about configuring the Windows XP Professional environment. We covered the following topics:

▪ New enhancements to Windows XP Professional configuration and support

▪ Utilities used to manage configuration, which include the Microsoft Management Console (MMC) and the Registry Editor

- Installing hardware, including Plug and Play and non–Plug and Play devices
- Managing device drivers, including how to update drivers and set options for driver signing
- Managing disk devices, including CD-ROM devices, DVD devices, and removable media
- Managing display devices, including video adapters and multiple displays
- Managing mobile computer hardware, including how to set power options and configure card services
- Managing I/O devices, including keyboards, mice, wireless devices, and USB devices
- Managing imaging devices, including scanners and digital cameras
- Managing processors, including how to set processor affinity in a multiple-processor computer
- Configuring fax support and starting the Fax Service
- Using the Windows XP Troubleshooter Wizard to troubleshoot problems with devices
- Managing Windows XP Professional services
- Managing multiple hardware profiles

Exam Essentials

Understand how to install new hardware on your computer.   Be able to successfully install hardware that is Plug and Play compatible, as well as hardware that is not Plug and Play compatible.

Manage and update device drivers.   Be able to successfully upgrade device drivers. Understand and be able to configure your computer to use different levels of driver signing.

Manage display devices.   Understand how to configure your computer with a single monitor or multiple monitors. Be able to list the requirements for installing and configuring multiple monitors.

Support mobile computers through power management features.   Understand the features that are available through ACPI and be able to configure a laptop computer to use these features.

Know the configuration requirements to support multiple processors.   Windows XP Professional can support up to two processors. Be able to specify what options must be configured when upgrading to the second processor.

Key Terms

Before you take the exam, be certain you are familiar with the following terms:

Advanced Configuration Power Interface (ACPI)	Plug and Play
device driver	processor affinity
Digital Video Disk (DVD)	REGEDIT
driver signing	Registry
Hardware Abstraction Layer (HAL)	Registry Editor
hardware profile	snap-ins
hibernation	Standby
Microsoft Management Console (MMC)	Universal Serial Bus (USB)
Personal Computer Memory Card International Association (PCMCIA)	video adapter

Review Questions

1. You are the system administrator for a large company. All of the users in the sales department use laptop computers. The laptop computers are configured with a combined modem and network card. When the sales users work out of the office or at home, they are typically using an external power source. When they are traveling, especially on long plane rides, they want to conserve as much battery power as possible. Which of the following actions should you take to minimize battery use?

   A. Create two hardware profiles and disable the modem and network card in the profile that will be used when traveling.

   B. Configure a power scheme for Max Battery and have users use that profile when traveling.

   C. Configure the users' laptops to use hibernation features.

   D. Configure Advanced features in Power Options to disable external devices when in battery mode.

2. The system administrator of the XYZ network wants to edit the Registry, including setting security on the Registry keys. What primary utility that supports full editing of the Windows XP Registry should the system administrator use?

   A. REGEDIT

   B. REDIT

   C. REGEDIT32

   D. REGEDITOR

3. Jim has an XYZ-manufactured modem installed in his computer. The XYZ Corporation released a new driver for the modem. Jim is slightly worried that the driver may not have been fully tested and may cause his computer to work improperly. What is the process that Microsoft uses with Windows XP to ensure that the drivers you install on your computer are properly tested and verified?

   A. Driver confirmation

   B. Driver optimization

   C. Driver signing

   D. Driver verification

4. Tracey is the network administrator for a large company. One of her users wants to set up a dual monitor work area for her Windows XP computer. Which of the following statements are true regarding configuration of multiple displays? (Choose all that apply.)

   A. You need a special cable that allows you to connect two monitors to a video adapter.

   B. You must install an adapter for each monitor that you will configure.

   C. You must use PCI or AGP adapters.

   D. Windows XP allows you to extend your Desktop across up to eight monitors.

5. You are the network administrator for a large company. Most of the users use laptop computers without docking stations. One of the users, Anne, reports that when she closes her laptop, she has to restart it, but when John closes his laptop and reopens it, he is in standby mode and only has to log on again. What do you need to do to Anne's computer so that she can also be in standby mode when she closes and opens her laptop?

   A. Configure the Power Scheme tab in Power Options Properties for Portable/Laptop.

   B. Configure the Power Scheme tab in Power Options Properties for Max Battery.

   C. Configure Advanced Power Options to Standby When I Close the Lid of My Portable Computer.

   D. Configure the Hibernate tab to enable Hibernation When I Close the Lid of My Portable Computer.

6. You are the network administrator for a small company. One of your users, Todd, has a new device that connects to his computer through either the serial port or the USB port. He attempts to connect the device to the USB port through a USB root hub, but the device is not recognized. You verify that all of the hardware is on the Hardware Compatibility List for Windows XP Professional and that you have the latest drivers. No other devices will connect to the USB root hub, and they also don't work. You verify that the USB root hub and USB device will work on another computer, which is running Windows 2000 and has USB configured. What is the next course of action you should take?

   A. Verify that an IRQ has been assigned to the USB controller in the computer's BIOS.

   B. Configure the Registry setting for `HKEY_LOCAL_COMPUTER\HARDWARE_DEVICES\USB` to 0.

   C. Configure the Registry setting for `HKEY_LOCAL_COMPUTER\HARDWARE_DEVICES\USB` to 1.

   D. Downgrade the drivers to Windows 2000 drivers and see if the device will work.

7. Tina is dissatisfied with the configuration of her keyboard and mouse. She wants to reset the keyboard speed and the mouse pointer rate. Which utility should she use to configure the keyboard and mouse properties?

   A. Control Panel

   B. Computer Management

   C. Microsoft Management Console

   D. Registry Editor

8. Cam is trying to install a network card that is not Plug and Play compatible. When she restarts the computer, the card is not recognized. She has a Windows XP driver for the device and wants to manually configure the network card. Which utility should she use to install the network card?

   A. Device Manager

   B. Computer Manager

   C. Control Panel (Classic View), Add or Remove Hardware icon

   D. MMC

9. Elena is using a laptop computer that uses ACPI. She wants to see what percentage of the battery power is still available. She also wants to know if hibernation has been configured. Which of the following utilities should she use?

   A. Device Manager

   B. Computer Manager

   C. Control Panel, Power Management

   D. MMC

10. Fred does not have a separate fax machine and wants to be able to use the fax support included in Windows XP in conjunction with his modem. Which utility should he use to configure fax support in Windows XP?

    A. Device Manager

    B. Computer Manager

    C. Control Panel, Printers and Other Hardware

    D. MMC

11. Jason has a computer that can support two processors. Currently his computer is configured with a single processor, but he is planning on adding a second processor. Which of the following steps would you need to take in Windows XP Professional so that the second processor will be recognized when it is installed?

    A. Update the driver to support multiple processors.

    B. Through Device Manager, access the computer's properties and enable the Allow Multiple Processors option.

    C. Through Control Panel, access System Properties, open the Advanced tab, and enable the Allow Multiple Processors option.

    D. Do nothing; this is enabled by default.

12. Jose has inherited a Windows XP laptop from work; it was originally licensed to Bill Gates. He wants to change that name to Jose Gonzales. He wants to change the value of this specification within the Registry but doesn't know the name of the key that is used to set the license name. What command should Jose use to change the licensing information through the Registry?

    A. REGEDIT

    B. REDIT

    C. REGEDIT32

    D. EDTREG32

13. You have a user, Bob, who needs to install a new digital camera on his laptop. Originally when the computer was installed, the default setting for driver signing options was Block—Never Install Unsigned Driver Software. The driver for the digital camera is not signed, but you know that the driver is okay to load. You log in as the Administrator for the laptop and change the driver signing to Warn—Prompt Me Each Time to Choose an Action. When Bob logs on to install the digital camera, he is still unable to install the new driver. What course of action should you take?

    A. In the `Boot.ini` file for the computer, add the `/Fastdetect` switch.

    B. In the driver signing options, make sure you selected the Make This Action the System Default check box.

    C. Verify that the local security setting for the computer is not configured for Prevent Users from Installing New Drivers.

    D. Verify that the Registry setting `HKEY_LOCAL_COMPUTER\Drivers\Edit` is not set to 0.

14. You are the administrator for a Fortune 500 company. You have a group of computers that were running Windows 2000 Professional and have been upgraded to Windows XP Professional. One of the users complains that none of them are able to take advantage of the ACPI features of Windows XP Professional. When you investigate the problem, you realize that the computers are all using an outdated BIOS that is not ACPI compliant. You contact the computer manufacturer and obtain the latest flash BIOS for the computers. The BIOS is fully Windows XP compliant. You successfully update the BIOS on the first computer. When you restart the computer, Windows XP will not load, and you see the following error message:

STOP: 0x000000079HAL_MISMATCH

What course of action should you take?

    A. In the computers BIOS settings, enable ACPI power management support.

    B. Use the Recovery Console to replace the `HAL.DLL` file with `ACPIHAL.DLL`, then restart the computer.

    C. Use the Recovery Console to replace the `APMHAL.DLL` file with `ACPIHAL.DLL`, then restart the computer.

    D. Reinstall Windows XP Professional with the Repair option and update the HAL during the installation process.

15. You have configured your computer for multiple-display support. Everything works properly when you run Windows applications. However, you do not see your MS-DOS application properly displayed. What can you do?

    A. Try running the application in full-screen mode.

    B. Restart the computer and see if the secondary video adapter is initialized.

    C. Increase the screen area on both displays to 1024 × 768.

    D. Set the colors to 256 Colors.

Answers to Review Questions

1. A. You can conserve power for laptops by creating multiple hardware profiles and, through Device Manager, disabling devices that are not used when the laptop is not connected to an external power source.

2. A. In Windows XP, you can edit the Registry with REGEDIT or REGEDT32 (using the Run command). You should always use extreme caution when editing the Registry, as improper configurations can cause the computer to fail to boot.

3. C. Microsoft uses driver signing to verify that drivers have been properly tested before they are installed on a Windows XP computer. By default, you will see a warning message when you try to install a driver that has not been signed.

4. B, C. If you want to configure multiple displays in Windows XP, you need a PCI or an AGP video adapter for each monitor that will be connected. Windows XP allows you to extend your Desktop across up to 10 monitors.

5. C. Power buttons can be configured through the Advanced tab of Power Options Properties so that when you close the lid of the portable computer, either nothing happens, the computer goes into standby mode, or the computer is powered off.

6. A. The root hub may be improperly configured. USB controllers require that an IRQ be assigned in the computer's BIOS. If the controller is not properly configured, you will see the root hub displayed in Device Manager with a yellow exclamation point.

7. A. You configure keyboard and mouse properties through their respective icons in Control Panel.

8. C. The Add or Remove Hardware icon in Control Panel (Classic View) starts the Add or Remove Hardware Wizard to install hardware that is not Plug and Play compatible. You need to verify that any other devices do not already use the configuration settings that you select for resource use.

9. C. On a laptop computer, Control Panel ➤ Performance and Maintenance ➤ Power Options icon is used to configure options such as power schemes, alarms, and power meters. These options maximize battery life based on user requirements.

10. C. You configure fax support in Windows XP through the Printers and Other Hardware option in Control Panel.

11. A. When you upgrade your computer from a single processor to a multiple-processor configuration, you must update the processor's driver to support this configuration.

12. A. In Windows XP, you can edit the Registry with REGEDIT or REGEDT32 (through the Run command). You should always use extreme caution when editing the Registry, as improper configurations can cause the computer to fail to boot.

13. B. By default, when you apply driver settings, they are only applied to the user who is currently logged on. If you check the Apply Setting As System Default option, the settings that you apply will be used by all users who log on to the computer.

14. D.   The only way you can recover from this error is to load an ACPI-compliant HAL. To force an upgrade of the HAL, you will need to re-install (repair) Windows XP. During the text-mode portion of the upgrade, you will see an option to press F6 if you need to install a third-party SCSI or RAID driver. When you see this message, press F5 to specify the installation of an alternate HAL. You will see a list of HALs that can be installed. If you are using a standard PC with one processor, you will choose Advanced Configuration and Power Interface (ACPI) PC.

15. A.   If you are running an MS-DOS application with multiple-display support and you do not see the application properly, try running the application in full-screen mode. If the problem is occurring with a Windows application, try running the application in a maximized window. You could also try disabling the secondary display to determine whether the problem was specific to multiple-display support.

Chapter

5

Managing the Windows XP Professional Desktop

MICROSOFT EXAM OBJECTIVES COVERED IN THIS CHAPTER:

✓ **Configure support for multiple languages or multiple locations.**

- Enable multiple-language support.
- Configure multiple-language support for users.
- Configure local settings.
- Configure Windows XP Professional for multiple locations.

✓ **Configure and manage user profiles and desktop settings.**

Windows XP Professional offers many options for configuring the Desktop to suit personal preferences. These options include customizing the Taskbar and Start menu, creating shortcuts, and setting display properties.

Windows XP Professional also includes support for multiple languages and regional settings. The support that comes with localized versions of Windows XP Professional allows users to view, edit, and print multilingual documents, which are documents that are written in almost any language. You can also specify locale settings for the Desktop to customize items such as the date format and currency for your geographical location.

Accessibility options are used to support users with limited sight, hearing, or mobility. You can configure the Desktop and use Windows XP Professional utilities to provide a higher degree of accessibility.

This chapter describes how to manage Desktop settings, multilanguage support, and accessibility options.

Managing Desktop Settings

Windows XP Professional can be viewed using the Windows XP theme, the Windows Classic theme (the interface from Windows 2000 Professional), or any customized theme you would like to use. The Windows XP Professional *Desktop*, shown in Figure 5.1, appears after a user has logged on to a Windows XP Professional computer. Users can configure their Desktops to suit their personal preferences and to work more efficiently.

FIGURE 5.1   The Windows XP Desktop

If you have installed Windows XP Professional from a clean install, you will notice that the desktop is clean, with all the options for managing the computer grouped under the Start option.

The items listed in Table 5.1 lists the common options that appear on the Start menu.

TABLE 5.1   Default Desktop Items

Item	Description
Internet (*Internet Explorer*)	The built-in web browser. When used with an Internet connection, Internet Explorer (IE) provides an interface for accessing the Internet or a local intranet.
E-mail (Outlook Express)	Starts the default e-mail application, Outlook Express.
MSN Explorer	Allows you to connect to the Internet by using the MSN Internet Service.
Windows Media Player	Used to play multimedia files.
Windows Movie Maker	Used to view and edit video files.
Files and Settings Transfer Wizard	Used to transfer files and settings from an old computer to a new computer that came with Windows XP Professional pre-installed.
Tour Windows XP	Provides an online tutorial of Windows XP.
My Documents	By default, stores the documents that are created. Each user has a unique My Documents folder, so even if a computer is shared, each user will have unique personal folders.
My Recent Documents	Lists the documents you have recently accessed.
My Pictures	Shows any pictures that are in the My Pictures folder.
My Music	Shows any music that is in the My Music folder.
My Computer	Allows you to centrally manage your computer's files, hard drives, and devices with removable storage. Also allows you to manage system tasks, other places (such as My Network Places), and to view details about your computer.
Control Panel	Allows you to configure your computer.

TABLE 5.1 Default Desktop Items *(continued)*

Item	Description
Printers and Faxes	Used to connect, create, or manage printer and fax resources.
Help and Support	Used to access Windows XP Help and Support resources.
Search	Searches for pictures, music, video, documents, files and folders, computers, or people (in your address book).
Run	Used to run a program or application.
Log Off	Logs the current user out.
Turn Off Computer	Shuts down the computer.

 If you use any kind of remote management tools, you may want to rename the My Computer icon to the actual computer's name. This allows you to easily identify which computer is being accessed.

To switch between the Windows XP Professional theme and the Windows 2000 Classic theme, right-click an area of open space on the Desktop and select Properties. In the Display Properties dialog box, on the Themes tab, you can then select the Theme you want to use from the Theme pull-down menu.

You can configure the Desktop by customizing the Taskbar and Start menu, adding shortcuts, and setting display properties. These configurations are described in the following sections.

The Desktop also includes the *Recycle Bin* in the lower right-hand corner. The Recycle Bin is a special folder that holds the files and folders that have been deleted, assuming that your hard drive has enough free space to hold the deleted files. If the hard drive is running out of disk space, the files that were deleted first will be copied over first. Files can be retrieved or cleared (for permanent deletion) from the Recycle Bin.

Customizing the Taskbar and Start Menu

Users can customize the *Taskbar* and *Start menu* through the Taskbar and Start Menu Properties dialog box, shown in Figure 5.2. The easiest way to access this dialog box is to right-click a blank area in the Taskbar and choose Properties from the pop-up menu.

The Taskbar and Start Menu Properties dialog box has two tabs, Taskbar and Start Menu, containing the options described in the following sections.

FIGURE 5.2   The Taskbar tab of the Taskbar and Start Menu Properties dialog box

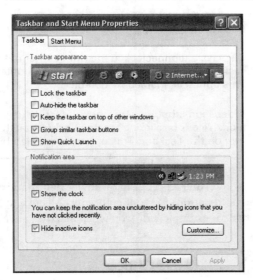

Configuring Taskbar Properties

Through the Taskbar tab of the Taskbar and Start Menu Properties dialog box (shown in Figure 5.2), you can specify Taskbar and Start menu features such as whether the Taskbar is always visible and whether the clock is shown on the Start menu. Table 5.2 lists the properties on the Taskbar tab.

TABLE 5.2   Taskbar Properties

Property	Description
Lock the taskbar	Locks the Taskbar into the current position so it cannot be moved around the desktop and the size of the Taskbar. This option is enabled by default.
Auto-hide the taskbar	Hides the Taskbar. This option is disabled by default. When it is enabled, you show the Taskbar by clicking the area of the screen where the Taskbar appears.
Keep the taskbar on top of other windows	Keeps the Taskbar visible, even if you open full-screen applications. This option is enabled by default.
Group similar taskbar buttons	Keeps all Taskbar buttons for the same program in the same location. Also specifies that if you have many applications open and the Taskbar becomes crowded, all the buttons for a single application should be collapsed into a single button. This option is enabled by default.
Show Quick Launch	Shows the Quick Launch icon on the Taskbar. Quick Launch is used to get back to the Windows desktop with a single click. This option is enabled by default.

TABLE 5.2   Taskbar Properties *(continued)*

Property	Description
Show the clock	Displays a digital clock in the right corner of the Taskbar. By right-clicking the clock, you can adjust the computer's date and time. This option is enabled by default.
Hide inactive icons	Hides icons that have not been recently used. You can access the hidden icons by clicking the double arrow on the left side of the system tray on the Taskbar. This option is enabled by default.

The Customize button, shown on Figure 5.2 in the lower right-hand corner of the dialog box, is used to list the icons and notifications for your computer. All current items are listed, and you can define each item's status; for example hide icon when inactive, always hide icon, and always show icon.

Configuring Start Menu Properties

The Start Menu tab of the Taskbar and Start Menu Properties dialog box allows you to customize your Start menu. By selecting Start menu, you edit the Windows XP Professional theme and by selecting Classic Start menu, you edit the standard Windows 2000 theme.

You can add or remove items from the Start menu, remove records of recently accessed items, and specify which options are displayed by clicking the Customize button for the theme you want to use. Figure 5.3 shows the options for customizing the Start menu for the Windows XP Professional theme.

FIGURE 5.3   Customize Start Menu dialog box

The Customize Start Menu dialog box shows two tabs, General and Advanced. The General tab allows you to set basic preferences and the Advanced tab allows you to set Start menu settings. We'll look at each in the following sections.

General Options for Start Menu Customization

The General options for Start menu customization allow you to configure the following:

- Whether you will use large icons or small icons
- The number of shortcuts that will be created for the programs you use most frequently
- The Internet and e-mail applications that will be shown on the Start menu

Advanced Options for Start Menu Customization

The Start Menu Settings section of the Advanced tab allows you to configure various Start menu advanced configuration features (listed in Table 5.3).

TABLE 5.3   The Start Menu Advanced Settings

Setting	Description
Open submenus when I pause on them with my mouse	If a Start menu item contains submenus, they will automatically open if you point to the main Start menu item.
Highlight newly installed programs	If this option is selected, then programs that are newly installed will be highlighted in a different color in the All Programs list.
Start Menu Items	Allows you to configure which items appear in the Start menu and which items can be accessed as quick links.
Recent Documents	Specifies whether most recently used documents will be displayed.

In Exercise 5.1, you will check your current Taskbar and Start menu configuration and then set general and advanced Taskbar and Start Menu properties.

EXERCISE 5.1

Configuring Taskbar and Start Menu Options

1. Select Start ➢ All Programs. Note the size of the icons in the Start menu. Notice that there is no Programs menu item for Administrative Tools or Windows Explorer.

2. Right-click an empty space on the Taskbar and choose Properties.

3. Click the Start Menu tab. Verify that the Start menu button is selected and click the Customize button.

EXERCISE 5.1 *(continued)*

4.   In the Start Menu Items section of the Advanced tab, scroll down to System Administrative Tools and click the Display on the All Programs menu, then click the OK button twice.

5.   Select Start ➢ All Programs and note that the All Programs menu lists Administrative Tools.

6.   Edit the Taskbar and Start Menu properties as you like, or return them to their default settings.

Using Shortcuts

Shortcuts are links to items that are accessible from your computer or network. You can use a shortcut to quickly access a file, program, folder, printer, or computer from your Desktop. Shortcuts can exist in various locations, including on the Desktop, on the Start menu, and within folders.

To create a shortcut from Windows Explorer, just right-click the item for which you want to create a shortcut and select Create Shortcut from the pop-up menu. Then you can click the shortcut and drag it to where you want it to appear.

In Exercise 5.2, you will create a shortcut and place it on the Desktop.

EXERCISE 5.2

Creating a Shortcut

1.   Select Start ➢ All Programs ➢ Accessories ➢ Windows Explorer to start Windows Explorer.

2.   Expand My Computer, then Local Disk, then Windows, then System32. On the right side of the screen, click Show the contents of this folder.

3.   On the right side of the screen, scroll down until you see calc. Right-click calc and select Create Shortcut. You see an icon labeled Shortcut to calc.exe.

4.   Click the Shortcut to calc icon and drag it to the Desktop (you may need to minimize Windows Explorer first). When you are done, close Windows Explorer.

Setting Display Properties

The options in the Display Properties dialog box, shown in Figure 5.4, allow you to customize the appearance of your Desktop. You can access this dialog box by right-clicking an empty area on the Desktop and selecting Properties from the pop-up menu. Alternatively, you can select Start ➢ Control Panel ➢ Appearance and Themes ➢ Display.

FIGURE 5.4   The Display Properties dialog box

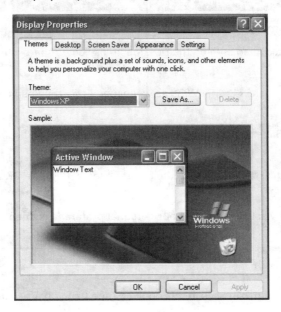

The Display Properties dialog box has five tabs with options that control various aspects of your display:

Themes tab   This allows you to customize the background used by your Desktop, including the sounds, icons, and other Desktop elements that personalize your Desktop.

Desktop tab   This lets you pick your Desktop background, which uses a picture or an HTML document as wallpaper.

Screen Saver tab   This lets you select a screen saver that will start after the system has been idle for a specified amount of time. You can also specify a password that must be used to reaccess the system after it has been idle. When the idle time has been reached, the computer will be locked, and the password of the user who is currently logged on must be entered to access the computer. You can also adjust monitor power settings.

Appearance tab   This lets you choose which Windows interface, buttons, color scheme, and font size will be used for the Desktop.

The Settings tab is used to configure display properties, which are not related to user preferences. Configuring the display is covered in Chapter 4, "Configuring the Windows XP Environment."

In Exercise 5.3, you will configure display options.

EXERCISE 5.3

Configuring Display Options

1. Right-click an unoccupied area on the Desktop and select Properties to open the Display Properties dialog box.

2. In the Desktop tab, select Prairie Wind as wallpaper. From the Position drop-down list, select Stretch.

3. Click the Screen Saver tab, select the Starfield screen saver, and specify a wait of five minutes.

4. Click the Appearance tab, then select the Silver Scheme. Click the OK button to see your new display settings.

5. Change the display settings to suit your personal preferences, then close the Display Properties dialog box.

All of the exercises in this book assume that you are using the Windows XP theme.

Through the Mouse and Keyboard icons in Control Panel, you can specify your personal preferences for mouse and keyboard settings. Mouse and keyboard properties are covered in Chapter 4.

Configuring Personal Preferences

The most common configuration change made by users is to configure their Desktop. This lets them use the computer more efficiently, and the customization makes them more comfortable with it.

To help users work more efficiently with their computers, you should determine what applications or files are frequently and commonly used, and verify that shortcuts or Start menu items are added for those elements. You can also remove shortcuts or Start menu items for elements that are used seldom or not at all, helping to make the work area less cluttered and confusing.

Less-experienced users will feel more comfortable with their computer if they have a Desktop personalized to their preferences. This might include their choice of Desktop theme, for example Windows XP or Windows Classic themes, and screen saver.

Managing Multiple Languages and Regional Settings

In addition to configuring your desktop, you can also configure the language and regional settings that are used on your computer desktop. Windows XP Professional supports multiple languages through the use of multilanguage technology. Multilanguage technology is designed to meet the following needs:

- Provide support for multilingual editing of documents
- Provide support for various language interfaces in your environment
- Allow users who speak various languages to share the same computer

In the following sections, you will learn about multilingual technology, what options are available for Windows XP Professional multilingual support, and how to enable and configure multilingual support.

Using Multilingual Technology

Windows XP Professional supports user options to view, edit, and process documents in a variety of different languages. These options are provided through Unicode support, National Language Support API, Multilingual API, Resource Files, and Multilingual developer support. Each is dicussed here:

Unicode   This is an international standard that allows character support for the common characters used in the world's most common languages.

National Language Support API   This is used to provide information for locale, character mapping, and keyboard layout. *Locale settings* are used to set local information such as date and time format, currency format, and country names. Character mapping arranges the mapping of local character encodings to Unicode. Keyboard layout settings include character typing information and sorting information.

Multilingual API   This is used to set up applications to support keyboard input and fonts from various language versions of applications. For example, Japanese users will see vertical text, and Arabic users will see right-to-left ligatures. This technology allows users to create mixed-language documents.

Resource files   These are files in which Windows XP Professional stores all language-specific information, such as text for help files and dialog boxes. They are separate from the operating system files. System code can thus be shared by all language versions of Windows XP Professional, which allows modular support for different languages.

Multilingual developer support   This is a special set of APIs that enables developers to create generic code and then provide support for multiple languages.

Choosing Windows XP Multiple-Language Support

Multilanguage support consists of two technologies:

- Multilingual editing and viewing, which support multiple languages while a user is viewing, editing, and printing documents

- Multilanguage user interfaces, which allow the Windows XP Professional user interface to be presented in different languages

Depending on the level of language support required by your environment, you may use either a localized version of Window XP Professional or the Multilanguage Version of Windows XP Professional. The following sections describe these versions and how to configure multilanguage support.

Using Localized Windows XP

Microsoft provides localized editions of Windows XP Professional. For example, users in the United States will most likely use the English version, and users in Japan will most likely use the Japanese version. Localized versions of Windows XP Professional include fully localized user interfaces for the language that was selected. In addition, localized versions allow users to view, edit, and print documents in more than 60 different languages. However, localized versions do not support multilanguage user interfaces.

Using Windows XP Multilanguage Version

Windows XP Multilanguage Version provides user interfaces in several different languages. This version is useful in multinational corporations where users speak several languages and must share computers. It is also appropriate when administrators want to deploy a single version of Windows XP Professional worldwide. You can manage multiple users who share a single computer and speak different languages through user profiles (covered in Chapter 6, "Managing Users and Groups") or through group policies (covered in Chapter 7, "Managing Security").

Two sets of files are necessary to support Windows XP Multilanguage Version:

- Language groups, which contain the fonts and files required to process and display the specific languages

- Windows XP Professional Multilanguage Version files, which contain the language content required by the user interface and help files

When you install Windows XP Multilanguage Version, you select the initial language that will be installed on the computer. For each language that you wish to use, you must also have the appropriate language group installed. For example, if you want to use the Japanese user interface, you must also install the Japanese language group. If you want to install other language support after installation, you can install and remove Windows XP Multilanguage Version files and language groups through Date, Time, Language and Regional Options in Control Panel. Each instance of Multilanguage Version files will use approximately 45MB of disk space. You can set the default user interface (UI) language, or add/remove UI languages through the Muisetup.exe file.

Windows XP Multilanguage Version is not available through retail stores. You order this version of Windows XP Professional through Microsoft Volume Licensing Programs. For more information about the Multilanguage Version, go to www.microsoft.com/licensing.

 Real World Scenario

MUI Setup and Upgrade

Let's say one of your users had a Multilanguage support setup on their computer running Windows 2000 Professional. After the computer was upgraded to Windows XP Professional, the only language that was available was English. It turns out that the CD used to upgrade to Windows XP Professional was a localized version of XP Professional for English.

To recover the ability to support multiple language UIs, use the Muisetup.exe program from a Multilanguage Version of Windows XP Professional, and add the support for the additional languages you require. Current information on the Muisetup.exe program can be found at www.microsoft.com/globaldev/faqs/muixpsp1.asp.

Enabling and Configuring Multilingual Support

On a localized version of Windows XP Professional, you enable and configure multilingual editing and viewing through Start ➢ Control Panel ➢ Date, Time, Language and Regional Options ➢ Regional Options. This allows access to the Regional and Language Options dialog box, shown in Figure 5.5.

FIGURE 5.5 The Regional and Language Options dialog box

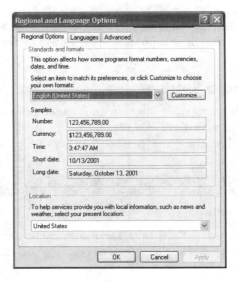

Through Regional and Language Options you can configure Regional Options, Languages, and Advanced Settings. We will look at each of these in the following sections.

Configuring Regional Options

For localized Windows XP Professional as well as the Multilanguage Version, you can also configure locale settings for numbers, currency, time, and date formats, and for input locales (which allows you to select the input language you will use). Like multilingual support, these settings are made through the Regional Options dialog box. Simply select the locale (location) for the regional settings that you want to use from the drop-down list at the top of the dialog box in the Standards and format section.

In the list box at the bottom of the Regional Options dialog box under the Location section, check the language settings that you wish to support on the computer. After you click OK, you may be prompted to insert the Windows XP Professional CD to copy the distribution files required for multiple-language support. Then you will need to restart your computer for the new changes to take effect. After the restart, you will notice a new icon on the Taskbar that shows the current locale and keyboard inputs that are being used. You can switch to another supported language by clicking this icon and selecting the locale input you wish to use.

Configuring Languages

The Languages tab is used to provide supplemental language support. The options that can be configured include the following:

- Install Files for Complex Script and Right-to-Left Languages (Including Thai), which is used to support languages such as Arabic, Armenian, Georgian, Hebrew, Indic languages, Thai, and Vietnamese.

- Install Files for East Asian Languages, which is used to support Chinese, Japanese, and Korean languages.

You should only install these options if you will use them. The option to install East Asian language support requires 230MB of disk space.

Configuring Advanced Settings

The Advanced settings tab allows you to support languages for non-Unicode programs. This enables non-Unicode programs to display menus and dialog boxes in the users' native language.

In Exercise 5.4, you will configure the locale settings on your computer.

EXERCISE 5.4

Configuring Locale Settings

1. Select Start ➤ Control Panel ➤ Date, Time, Language, and Regional Options ➤ Regional and Language Options. On the Regional Options tab, note your current locale.

EXERCISE 5.4 *(continued)*

2. One by one, click the Regional Options, Languages, and Advanced tabs and note the configurations in each tab.

3. Click the Regional Options tab, and select the Danish locale (location) from the drop-down list at the top of the dialog box in the Standards and formats section. Then click the Apply button.

4. In the Number, Currency, Time, and Date fields, note the changed configurations.

5. Return to the General tab, reset your locale to the original configuration, and click the Apply button.

 Real World Scenario

Supporting Multilingual Environments

Your company has an office in Tokyo. Computers are shared by users there who require both English and Japanese language support, for document management as well as the UI. Your CIO has asked you to set up a system that lets users in the Tokyo office use Windows XP Professional in any language.

To do this, you must use Windows XP Multilanguage Version. Each computer user can select the preferred UI and specify locale information. This is stored as part of the user's profile. When you log on as a specific user, you see the linguistic and locale information that has been configured.

Configuring Accessibility Features

Windows XP Professional allows you to configure the desktop so those users with limited accessibility can use the Windows XP Professional desktop more easily. Through its accessibility options and accessibility utilities, Windows XP Professional supports users with limited sight, hearing, or mobility. The following sections describe how to use these accessibility features.

Setting Accessibility Options

Through *Accessibility Options* in Control Panel, you can configure keyboard, sound, display, mouse, and general properties of Windows XP Professional for users with special needs. To access the Accessibility Options dialog box (see Figure 5.6), select Control Panel ➢ Accessibility Options, and then click the Accessibility Options icon.

FIGURE 5.6   The Accessibility Options dialog box

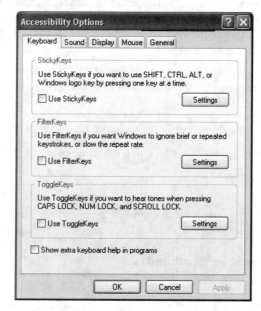

The Accessibility Options dialog box has five tabs with options to configure special behavior for your computer:

Keyboard tab   This contains settings for using StickyKeys, FilterKeys, and ToggleKeys. StickyKeys allows the Shift, Ctrl, Alt, or Windows logo key to be used in conjunction with another key by pressing the keys separately rather than simultaneously. FilterKeys ignores brief or repeated keystrokes and slows the repeat rate. ToggleKeys makes a noise whenever you press the Caps Lock, Num Lock, or Scroll Lock key. At the bottom of the screen, you can select the Show Extra Keyboard Help in Programs option, which specifies that programs display extra help about using the program, if that functionality has been added with the Help feature.

Sound tab   This allows you to specify whether you want to use SoundSentry, which generates a visual warning whenever the computer makes a sound, and ShowSounds, which displays captions for speech and sounds on your computer.

Display tab   This contains high-contrast settings for Windows colors and fonts. The default setting for high-contrast scheme is High Contrast Black (Large). In the bottom half of the screen you can set cursor options, which sets the speed at which the cursor blinks and the width of the cursor.

Mouse tab   This lets you enable use of MouseKeys, which allows you to control the mouse pointer through the keyboard.

General tab   This contains several maintenance and administrative options. You can choose to automatically turn off accessibility features after these features have been idle for a specified amount of time, and to use notification features to notify you when accessibility features are turned on or off. You can also configure SerialKey devices to provide alternative access to keyboard and mouse features. Administrative options allow you to apply accessibility options to the logon Desktop and to defaults for new users.

Using Accessibility Utilities

Windows XP Professional provides several accessibility utilities, including the Accessibility Wizard, Magnifier, Narrator, On-Screen Keyboard, and Utility Manager. Each of these options is covered in more detail in the following sections.

The Accessibility Wizard

The *Accessibility Wizard* configures a computer based on the user's vision, hearing, and mobility needs. Through the Accessibility Wizard, the user selects the text size that is the easiest to read. The wizard also collects input to determine whether the user has vision, hearing, or mobility challenges.

Through the Accessibility Wizard, you can also configure the option "I want to set administrative options." This lets you configure accessibility options for all of a computer's new user accounts or for only the current user profile. You can also create an .acw file (Accessibility Wizard Settings) that can then be copied to another user's profile folder. This can be on the same computer or a different one; it allows the new user to have the same accessibility configuration. The Accessibility Wizard is accessed through Start ➢ All Programs ➢ Accessories ➢ Accessibility ➢ Accessibility Wizard.

The Magnifier Utility

The *Magnifier utility* creates a separate window to magnify a portion of your screen, as shown in Figure 5.7. This option is useful for users who have poor vision. To access Magnifier, select Start ➢ All Programs ➢ Accessories ➢ Accessibility ➢ Magnifier.

FIGURE 5.7 The Magnifier utility

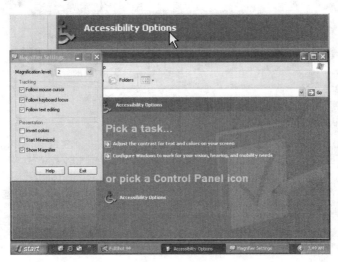

The Narrator Utility

The *Narrator utility* can read aloud on-screen text, dialog boxes, menus, and buttons. This utility requires that you have some type of sound output device installed and configured. To access Narrator, select Start ➤ All Programs ➤ Accessories ➤ Accessibility ➤ Narrator. This brings up the dialog box shown in Figure 5.8.

FIGURE 5.8 The Narrator dialog box

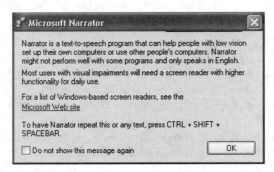

The On-Screen Keyboard

The *On-Screen Keyboard* displays a keyboard on the screen, as shown in Figure 5.9. Users can use the On-Screen Keyboard keys through a mouse or another input device as an alternative to the keys on the regular keyboard. To access the On-Screen Keyboard, select Start ➤ All Programs ➤ Accessories ➤ Accessibility ➤ On-Screen Keyboard.

FIGURE 5.9 The On-Screen Keyboard

The Utility Manager

The *Utility Manager* allows you to start and stop the Windows XP Professional accessibility utilities. You can also specify whether these utilities are automatically started when Windows XP Professional starts or when the Utility Manager is started. To access the Utility Manager, select Start ➤ All Programs ➤ Accessories ➤ Accessibility ➤ Utility Manager. Figure 5.10 shows the Utility Manager.

FIGURE 5.10   The Utility Manager

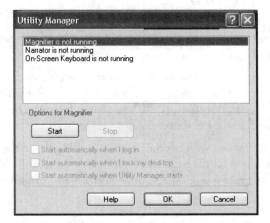

In Exercise 5.5, you will use the Windows XP Professional accessibility features.

EXERCISE 5.5

Using Accessibility Features

1. Select Start ➤ All Programs ➤ Accessories ➤ Accessibility ➤ Magnifier.

2. Experiment with the Magnifier utility. When you are finished, click the Exit button in the Magnifier Settings dialog box.

3. Select Start ➤ All Programs ➤ Accessories ➤ Accessibility ➤ On-Screen Keyboard.

4. Select Start ➤ All Programs ➤ Accessories ➤ Notepad to open Notepad.

5. Create a text document using the On-Screen Keyboard. When you are finished, close the Notepad document without saving it.

6. Close the On-Screen Keyboard.

Summary

In this chapter, you learned about managing the Windows XP Professional Desktop. We covered the following topics:

- Managing Desktop settings, which include customizing the Taskbar and Start menu, using shortcuts, and setting display properties

- Managing multiple languages and regional settings, which include enabling and configuring multilingual support and choosing locale settings

- Configuring accessibility options and using accessibility utilities

Exam Essentials

Be able to configure desktop settings.   Understand how to customize and configure the Windows XP desktop settings.

Configure the computer for multiple language support.   Be able to define the language features that are available in various versions of Windows XP Professional. Know how to configure locale information and support multiple-language requirements for document processing and the user interface on a single computer.

Set accessibility options for users with special needs.   Be able to list the accessibility options and their capabilities. Know how to use the Accessibility Wizard and Utility Manager, and be able to specify the administrative tasks that can be performed through each utility.

Key Terms

Before taking the exam, you should be familiar with the following terms:

Accessibility Options	Narrator utility
Accessibility Wizard	On-Screen Keyboard
Desktop	Recycle Bin
Internet Explorer	Regional Options
locale settings	shortcut
Magnifier utility	Start menu
My Computer	Taskbar
My Documents	Utility Manager

Review Questions

1. You are the network administrator of a large network. Your company recently hired three employees who need to use Windows XP Professional's accessibility features. All of the users need the same configuration. You want to configure these options on one computer and copy them to the other computers. Which utility do you use to create the accessibility file and what extension should the file have?

   A. Accessibility Wizard, `.acw` file

   B. Accessibility Wizard, `.acc` file

   C. Utility Manager, `.acw` file

   D. Utility Manager, `.acc` file

2. You are the network administrator for a medium-sized company. You support any user desktop issues. Dan is using Windows XP Professional on his laptop computer. Programs he frequently uses are not on the Taskbar or Start menu, and programs he has never used are still listed from the manufacturer's initial install. Which of the following options should Dan use to configure the Taskbar and Start menu in Windows XP Professional?

   A. Right-click an empty space on the Taskbar and choose Properties from the pop-up menu.

   B. Select Control Panel ➢ Menu Settings.

   C. Right-click My Computer and choose Manage from the pop-up menu.

   D. Right-click My Computer and choose Properties from the pop-up menu.

3. You are the network administrator for a multinational company. Tran, a user in San Jose, California, is the account manager for all accounts in Vietnam. Tran needs to be able to create and view files in Vietnamese. What support needs to be configured on her computer?

   A. You need to enable supplemental language support for complex script for right-to-left languages (including Thai).

   B. You need to enable supplemental language support to install files for East Asian languages.

   C. You need to install language support for non-Unicode programs.

   D. You need to set Regional Options for Vietnam.

4. Barbara has a laptop that is using the Windows XP Professional localized version for English. She is spending the summer in Mexico City and wants to configure the user interface so that it is displayed in Spanish. How should she configure her computer?

   A. Configure Regional Options to add Spanish language support.

   B. Through Control Panel, Add/Remove Software icon, add Spanish language support.

   C. Configure Regional Options to add Spanish language support, then set the locale settings for Mexico.

   D. None of the above.

5. You are the network administrator of a large corporation. One of your users, Bob, has impaired vision and is having trouble reading documents on his Windows XP laptop. Which accessibility utility can Bob use to enlarge a portion of the screen for better visibility?

    A. Enlarger

    B. Expander

    C. Magnifier

    D. Microscope

6. You are supporting Windows XP Professional computers used by a variety of employees from several countries. When they visit your location, each employee would like their desktop to appear as it would in their native country. Which of the following locale options can you configure for these users through Windows XP Professional? (Choose all that apply.)

    A. The format of the date displayed on the computer

    B. The language that is used to display the UI

    C. The currency symbol used by default on the computer

    D. The format of the time displayed on the computer

7. You work on the help desk for a large company. One of your users calls you and reports that they just accidentally deleted their C:\Documents\Timesheet.xls file. What is the easiest way to recover this file?

    A. In Folder Options, click the Show Deleted Files option.

    B. In Folder Options, click the Undo Deleted Files option.

    C. Click the Recycle Bin icon on the Desktop and restore the deleted file.

    D. Restore the file from your most recent tape backup.

8. You are the administrator of a multinational corporation. One of your users, Francine, travels between France and the United States on a regular basis. Previously, Francine had a Multilanguage Version of Windows 2000 Professional installed on her computer, so she used a French version of Windows while in France and an English version of Windows while in the United States. Francine recently upgraded her computer to Windows XP Professional and is now reporting that she can access only the English version of the Windows interface. What action should you take?

    A. Add French support in Regional Options and Settings.

    B. Rerun the upgrade with a Multilanguage Version of Windows XP Professional.

    C. Run Muisetup.exe from a Multilanguage Version of Windows XP and add French support.

    D. Run Langsupp.exe from a Multilanguage Version of Windows XP and add French support.

9. Jeff has a new display adapter and monitor. He wants to set display properties for his Desktop. Which of the following options are *not* set through the Display Properties dialog box?

    A. Desktop background

    B. Screen saver

    C. Special visual effects for your Desktop

    D. Contrast and brightness of the monitor

10. You sit in a busy area of the office. Sometimes, you forget to log off or lock the computer when you leave your desk. How can you configure your computer so that it will become password protected if it is idle for more than 10 minutes?

    A. Through Control Panel, Logon/Logoff icon

    B. Through Display Properties, Screen Saver tab

    C. Through Control Panel, Security icon

    D. Through Local Users and Groups, Security properties

11. Brett is using a laptop computer that has Windows XP Multilanguage Version installed. The computer is configured for English and Spanish, with English as the default language. Brett has been assigned to work in Mexico City for a year and now wants his default user interface to be in Spanish. Through which file can you edit the default language interface?

    A. `Muisetup.exe`

    B. `MLsetup.exe`

    C. `Langsetup.exe`

    D. `Muiconfig.exe`

12. You are planning to install Windows XP Multilanguage Version in your environment. Maria has requested that you install user interfaces on her computer for Russian, Polish, and English. When determining the resources required for this configuration, how much disk space should be allocated for each language?

    A. 10MB

    B. 20MB

    C. 45MB

    D. 85MB

13. Cindy has just installed Windows XP Professional on her home computer. The Windows XP version she is using is a localized English version. Cindy would also like to be able to use Simplified Chinese to create documents to send to her friends in Taiwan. How can she configure the computer to support Simplified Chinese language settings?

    A. Through Control Panel ➤ Date, Time, Language and Regional Options ➤ Language icon

    B. Through Control Panel ➤ Date, Time, Language and Regional Options ➤ Regional Options icon

    C. Through Control Panel ➤ Date, Time, Language and Regional Options ➤ Multilanguage Support icon

    D. Only by upgrading to Windows XP Multilanguage Version

14. Ken configured his computer with the accessibility options StickyKeys and ToggleKeys. Everything was working properly. Then Ken went to a meeting. When he returned after 30 minutes, his accessibility options were no longer working. What is most likely the problem?

   A. The accessibility options are configured to be automatically reset if the computer remains idle for a specified amount of time.

   B. Ken needs to log on again to enable the accessibility features.

   C. Ken needs to restart his computer to enable the accessibility features.

   D. The accessibility settings have become corrupt and need to be reset.

15. Meredith is a user with limited mobility. She wants to use an alternative pointing device instead of a regular mouse pointer. You install the device and load the appropriate driver. What additional step should you take?

   A. Configure SerialKey Devices through Accessibility Options.

   B. Configure Disable Serial Devices through Accessibility Options.

   C. Configure Alternative Serial Devices through Accessibility Options.

   D. Configure ParallelKey Devices through Accessibility Options.

Answers to Review Questions

1. **A.** You can copy a user's accessibility settings by using the administrative options in the Accessibility Wizard. After you create the desired configuration, you can save it as an `.acw` file, which can then be copied to the target user's profile folder.

2. **A.** The easiest way to configure the Taskbar and Start menu properties is by right-clicking an open area of the Taskbar and choosing Properties. There is no Menu Settings option in Control Panel.

3. **A.** The option to install files for complex script for right-to-left languages (including Thai) is used to support languages such as Arabic, Armenian, Georgian, Hebrew, Indic languages, Thai, and Vietnamese.

4. **D.** Localized versions of Windows XP Professional do not support multilanguage user interfaces. Localized versions support only the ability to view, edit, and print documents in other languages. Language support for the UI is provided in Windows XP Multilanguage Version.

5. **C.** The Magnifier utility creates a separate window that magnifies the portion of the screen that is being used. None of the other choices exists in Windows XP Professional.

6. **A, C, D.** Locale settings are used to configure regional settings for numbers, currency, time, date, and input locales.

7. **C.** The easiest way to recover a deleted file is to restore it from the Recycle Bin. The Recycle Bin holds all of the files and folders that have been deleted, as long as there is space on the disk. From this utility, you can retrieve or permanently delete files.

8. **C.** If you upgrade a Windows 2000 Multilanguage computer with a Localized version of Windows XP, you will lose your Multilanguage User Interface support. To correct this issue, run `Muisetup.exe` from a Multilanguage version of Windows XP Professional.

9. **D.** Through the Display Properties dialog box, you can set your Desktop background, the screen saver to be used by your computer, and any special visual effects for your Desktop. Contrast and brightness of the monitor are typically set through the monitor's controls.

10. **B.** The Screen Saver tab of the Display Properties dialog box allows you to select a screen saver that will start after the computer has been idle for a specified amount of time. You can configure the screen saver to require the user's password in order to resume the computer's normal function. When the password is invoked, the computer will be locked. To access the locked computer, you must enter the password of the user who is currently logged on.

11. **A.** You can edit the default user language interface or add or remove user interface languages through the `Muisetup.exe` file.

12. **C.** Each instance of Multilanguage Version files will use approximately 45MB of disk space.

13. B. Localized versions of Windows XP Professional include fully localized user interfaces for the language that was selected. In addition, localized versions include the ability to view, edit, and print documents in more than 60 different languages. On a localized version of Windows XP Professional, you enable and configure multilingual editing and viewing through the Regional Options icon in Control Panel.

14. A. Through the Accessibility Options icon of Control Panel, you can control how long the accessibility options will be active if the computer is idle. A setting on the General tab allows you to turn off accessibility options if the computer has been idle for a specified number of minutes. You should check this setting if working accessibility options unexpectedly become disabled.

15. A. In the General tab of the Accessibility Options dialog box, you can select the Support SerialKey Devices option to allow alternative access to keyboard and mouse features.

Chapter

6

Managing Users and Groups

MICROSOFT EXAM OBJECTIVES COVERED IN THIS CHAPTER:

✓ Configure, manage, and troubleshoot local user and group accounts.

 ▪ Configure, manage, and troubleshoot account settings.

✓ Configure and manage user profiles and desktop settings.

One of the most fundamental tasks in network management is the creation of user and group accounts. Without a user account, a user cannot log on to a computer, server, or network. Group accounts are used to ease network administration by grouping users who have similar permission requirements together.

When users log on, they supply a username and password. Then their user accounts are validated by a security mechanism. In Windows XP Professional, users can log on to a computer locally, or they can log on through Active Directory.

When you first create users, you assign them usernames, passwords, and password settings. After a user is created, you can change these settings and select other options for that user through the *User* Properties dialog box.

Groups are an important part of network management. Many administrators are able to accomplish the majority of their management tasks through the use of groups; they rarely assign permissions to individual users. Windows XP Professional includes built-in local groups, such as Administrators and Backup Operators. These groups already have all the permissions needed to accomplish specific tasks. Windows XP Professional also uses default special groups, which are managed by the system. Users become members of special groups based on their requirements for computer and network access.

You create and manage local groups through the Local Users and Groups utility. Through this utility, you can add groups, change group membership, rename groups, and delete groups.

In this chapter, you will learn about user management at the local level, including creating user accounts and managing user properties. Then you will learn how to create and manage local groups.

Overview of Windows XP User Accounts

When you install Windows XP Professional, several user accounts are created automatically. You can then create new user accounts. On Windows XP Professional computers, you can create local user accounts. If your network has a Windows Server 2003 or Windows 2000 Server domain controller, your network can have domain user accounts, as well.

In the following sections, you will learn about the default user accounts that are created by Windows XP Professional and the difference between local and domain user accounts.

Built-in Accounts

By default, a computer that is installed with Windows XP Professional in a workgroup has five user accounts:

Administrator   The *Administrator account* is a special account that has full control over the computer. You provide a password for this account during Windows XP Professional installation. The Administrator account can perform all tasks, such as creating users and groups, managing the file system, and setting up printing.

Guest   The *Guest account* allows users to access the computer even if they do not have a unique username and password. Because of the inherent security risks associated with this type of user, the Guest account is disabled by default. When this account is enabled, it is usually given very limited privileges.

Initial user   The *initial user* account uses the name of the registered user. This account is created only if the computer is installed as a member of a workgroup, rather than as part of a domain. By default, the initial user is a member of the Administrators group.

HelpAssistant (new for Windows XP)   The *HelpAssistant* account is used in conjunction with the Remote Desktop Help Assistance feature. This feature is covered in Chapter 14, "Performing System Recovery Functions."

Support_*xxxxxx* (new for Windows XP)   Microsoft uses the *Support_xxxxxx* account for the Help and Support Service. This account is disabled by default.

By default, the name Administrator is given to the account with full control over the computer. You can increase the computer's security by renaming the Administrator account and then creating an account named Administrator without any permissions. This way, even if a hacker is able to log on as Administrator, they won't be able to access any system resources.

Local and Domain User Accounts

Windows XP supports two kinds of users: local users and domain users. A computer that is running Windows XP Professional has the ability to store its own user accounts database. The users stored at the local computer are known as *local user accounts*.

The *Active Directory* is a directory service that is available with the Windows Server 2003 and Windows 2000 Server platforms. It stores information in a central database that allows users to have a single user account for the network. The users stored in the Active Directory's central database are called *domain user accounts*.

If you use local user accounts, they must be configured on each computer that the user needs access to within the network. For this reason, domain user accounts are commonly used to manage users on large networks.

On Windows XP Professional computers and Windows Server 2003 and Windows 2000 Server member servers (a member server has a local accounts database and does not store the

Active Directory), you create local users through the Local Users and Groups utility, as described in the "Working with User Accounts" section later in the chapter. On Windows Server 2003 and Windows 2000 Server domain controllers, you manage users with the Microsoft Active Directory Users and Computers utility.

Active Directory is covered in detail in *MCSE: Windows 2000 Directory Services Administration Study Guide*, 2nd edition, by Anil Desai with James Chellis (Sybex, 2001).

Logging On and Logging Off

Users must log on to a Windows XP Professional computer before they can use that computer. When you create user accounts, you set up the computer to accept the logon information provided by the user. You can log on locally to an XP Professional computer, or you can log on to a domain. When you install the computer, you specify that it will be a part of a workgroup, which implies a local logon, or that the computer will be a part of a domain, which implies a domain logon.

When users are ready to stop working on a Windows XP Professional computer, they should log off. Logging off is accomplished through the Windows Security dialog box.

In the following sections you will learn about local user authentication and how a user logs out of a Windows XP Professional computer.

Local User Logon Authentication

Depending on whether you are logging into a computer locally or are logging into a domain, Windows XP Professional uses two different logon procedures. When you log on to a Windows XP Professional computer locally, you must present a valid username and password (ones that exist within the local accounts database). As part of a successful *authentication*, the following steps take place:

1. At system startup, the user is prompted to click their username from a list of users who have been created locally. This is significantly different from the Ctrl+Alt+Del logon sequence that was used by Windows NT and Windows 2000. The Ctrl+Alt+Del sequence is still used when you log on to a domain environment. You can also configure this logon sequence as an option in a local environment.

2. The local computer compares the user's logon credentials with the information in the local security database.

3. If the information presented matches the account database, an *access token* is created. Access tokens are used to identify the user and the groups of which that user is a member.

Access tokens are created only when you log on. If you change group memberships, you need to log off and log on again to update the access token.

Figure 6.1 illustrates the three main steps in the logon process.

FIGURE 6.1   The logon process

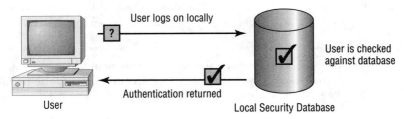

User logs on locally

User is checked
against database

Authentication returned

User

Local Security Database

Other actions that take place as part of the logon process include the following:

- The system reads the part of the Registry that contains user configuration information.

- The user's profile is loaded. (User profiles are discussed in the "Setting Up User Profiles, Logon Scripts, and Home Folders" section later in this chapter.)

- Any policies that have been assigned to the user through a user or group policy are enforced. (Policies for users are discussed later in Chapter 7, "Managing Security.")

- Any logon scripts that have been assigned are executed. (Assigning logon scripts to users is discussed in the "Setting Up User Profiles, Logon Scripts, and Home Folders" section.)

- Persistent network and printer connections are restored. (Network connections are discussed in Chapter 10, "Managing Network Connections," and printer connections are covered in Chapter 11, "Managing Printing.")

Through the logon process, you can control what resources a user can access by assigning permissions. Permissions are granted to either users or groups. Permissions also determine what actions a user can perform on a computer. In Chapter 9, "Accessing Files and Folders," you will learn more about assigning resource permissions.

Logging Off Windows XP Professional

To log off of Windows XP Professional, you click Start ➢ Logoff. If Windows XP is installed as a stand alone computer and is using the new logon interface where the users are listed on the logon screen, pressing Ctrl+Alt+Del, as you did in Windows NT or Windows 2000, will not bring up the Windows Security dialog box; instead, you will access the Task Manager utility (which does not have an option for logoff). The Windows Security dialog box includes options for Shut Down and Log Off. If you are using the classic Windows logon option, which presents you with a dialog box for entering your username and password, and when you press Ctrl+Alt+Del, you will be presented with the Windows Security dialog box.

Working with User Accounts

To set up and manage users, you use the *Local Users and Groups* utility. With Local Users and Groups, you can create, disable, delete, and rename user accounts, as well as change user passwords.

 The procedures for many basic user management tasks—such as creating, disabling, deleting, and renaming user accounts—are the same for both Windows XP Professional and Windows 2000 Server and Windows Server 2003.

Using the Local Users and Groups Utility

The first step in working with Windows XP Professional user accounts is to access the Local Users and Groups utility. There are two common methods for accessing this utility:

- You can load Local Users and Groups as a Microsoft Management Console (MMC) snap-in. (See Chapter 4, "Configuring the Windows XP Environment," for details on the MMC and the purpose of snap-ins.)

- You can access the Local Users and Groups utility through the Computer Management utility.

    In Exercise 6.1, you will use both methods for accessing the Local Users and Groups utility.

EXERCISE 6.1

Accessing the Local Users and Groups Utility

In this exercise, you will first add the Local Users and Groups snap-in to the MMC. Next, you will add a shortcut to your Desktop that will take you to the MMC. Finally, you will use the other access technique of opening the Local Users and Groups utility from the Computer Management utility.

Adding the Local Users and Groups Snap-in to the MMC

1.   Select Start ➢ Run. In the Run dialog box, type **MMC** and press Enter.

2.   Select File ➢ Add/Remove Snap-in.

3.   In the Add/Remove Snap-in dialog box, click the Add button.

4.   In the Add Standalone Snap-in dialog box, select Local Users and Groups and click the Add button.

5.   In the Choose Target Machine dialog box, click the Finish button to accept the default selection of Local Computer.

6.   Click the Close button in the Add Standalone Snap-in dialog box. Then click the OK button in the Add/Remove Snap-in dialog box.

EXERCISE 6.1 *(continued)*

7. In the MMC window, expand the Local Users and Groups folder to see the Users and Groups folders.

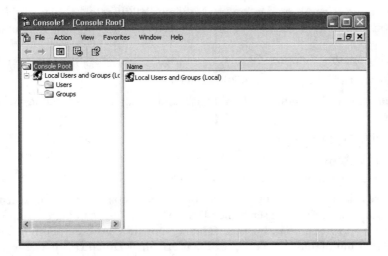

Adding the MMC to Your Desktop

8. Select File ➢ Save. Click the folder with the Up arrow icon until you are at the root of the computer.

9. Select the Desktop option and specify **Admin Console** as the filename. The default extension is .msc. Click the Save button.

Accessing Local Users and Groups through Computer Management

10. Select Start, then right-click My Computer and select Manage.

11. In the Computer Management window, expand the System Tools folder and then the Local Users and Groups folder.

If your computer doesn't have the MMC configured, the quickest way to access the Local Users and Groups utility is through the Computer Management utility.

Creating New Users

To create users on a Windows XP Professional computer, you must be logged on as a user with permissions to create a new user, or you must be a member of the Administrators group or

Power Users group. In the following sections, you will learn about username rules and conventions and usernames and security identifiers in more detail.

Username Rules and Conventions

The only real requirement for creating a new user is that you must provide a valid username. "Valid" means that the name must follow the Windows XP rules for usernames. However, it's also a good idea to have your own rules for usernames, which form your naming convention.

The following are the Windows XP rules for usernames:

- A username must be between 1 and 20 characters.

- The username must be unique to all other user and group names stored on the specified computer.

- The username cannot contain the following characters:

    * / \ [ ] : ; | = , + * ? < > "

- A username cannot consist exclusively of periods or spaces.

Keeping these rules in mind, you should choose a naming convention (a consistent naming format). For example, consider a user named Kevin Donald. One naming convention might use the last name and first initial, for the username DonaldK. Another naming convention might use the first initial and last name, for the username KDonald. Other user-naming conventions are based on the naming convention defined for e-mail names, so that the logon name and e-mail name match. You should also provide a mechanism that would accommodate duplicate names. For example, if you had a user named Kevin Donald and a user named Kate Donald, you might use a middle initial for usernames, such as KLDonald and KMDonald.

Naming conventions should also be applied to objects such as groups, printers, and computers.

Usernames and Security Identifiers

When you create a new user, a *security identifier (SID)* is automatically created on the computer for the user account. The username is a property of the SID. For example, a user SID might look like this:

S-1-5-21-823518204-746137067-120266-629-500

It's apparent that using SIDs for user identification would make administration a nightmare. Fortunately, for your administrative tasks, you see and use the username instead of the SID.

SIDs have several advantages. Because Windows XP Professional uses the SID as the user object, you can easily rename a user while still retaining all the properties of that user. SIDs also ensure that if you delete and re-create a user account with the same username, the new user account will not have any of the properties of the old account, because it is based on a new, unique SID. Renaming and deleting user accounts is discussed later in this chapter in the "Renaming User Accounts" and "Deleting User Accounts" sections.

Make sure that your users know that usernames are not case sensitive, but passwords are.

In Exercise 6.2, you will use the New User dialog box to create several new local user accounts. We will put these user accounts to work in subsequent exercises in this chapter. Table 6.1 describes all the options available in the New User dialog box.

TABLE 6.1   User Account Options Available in the New User Dialog Box

Option	Description
User name	Defines the username for the new account. Choose a name that is consistent with your naming convention (e.g., WSmith). This is the only required field. Usernames are not case sensitive.
Full name	Allows you to provide more detailed name information. This is typically the user's first and last name (e.g., Wendy Smith). By default, this field contains the same name as the User Name field.
Description	Typically used to specify a title and/or location (e.g., Sales-Texas) for the account, but it can be used to provide any additional information about the user.
Password	Assigns the initial password for the user. For security purposes, avoid using readily available information about the user. Passwords can be up to 14 characters and are case sensitive.
Confirm password	Confirms that you typed the password the same way two times to verify that you entered the password correctly.
User must change password at next logon	If enabled, forces the user to change the password the first time they log on. This is done to increase security. By default, this option is selected.
User cannot change password	If enabled, prevents a user from changing their password. It is useful for accounts such as Guest and accounts that are shared by more than one user. By default, this option is not selected.
Password never expires	If enabled, specifies that the password will never expire, even if a password policy has been specified. For example, you might enable this option if this is a service account and you do not want the administrative overhead of managing password changes. By default, this option is not selected.
Account is disabled	If enabled, specifies that this account cannot be used for logon purposes. For example, you might select this option for template accounts or if an account is not currently being used. It helps keep inactive accounts from posing security threats. By default, this option is not selected.

Before you start this exercise, make sure that you are logged on as a user with permissions to create new users and have already added the Local Users and Groups snap-in to the MMC (see Exercise 6.1).

Creating New Local Users

1. Open the Admin Console MMC shortcut that was created in Exercise 6.1 and expand the Local Users and Groups snap-in.

2. Highlight the Users folder and select Action ➤ New User. The New User dialog box appears.

3. In the User Name text box, type **Cam**.

4. In the Full Name text box, type **Cam Presely**.

5. In the Description text box, type **Sales Vice President**.

6. Leave the Password and Confirm Password text boxes empty and accept the defaults for the check boxes. Make sure you uncheck the User Must Change Password at Next Logon option. Click the Create button to add the user.

7. Use the New User dialog box to create six more users, filling out the fields as follows:

    Name: **Kevin**; Full Name: **Kevin Jones**; Description: **Sales-Florida**; Password: (blank)

    Name: **Terry**; Full Name: **Terry Belle**; Description: **Marketing**; Password: (blank)

    Name: **Ron**; Full Name: **Ron Klein**; Description: **PR**; Password: **superman**

EXERCISE 6.2 *(continued)*

Name: **Wendy**; Full Name: **Wendy Smith**; Description: **Sales-Texas**; Password: **supergirl**

Name: **Emily**; Full Name: **Emily Buras**; Description: **President**; Password: **Peach** (with a capital "P").

Name: **Michael**; Full Name: **Michael Phillips**; Description: **Tech Support**; Password: **apple**

8. After you've finished creating all of the users, click the Close button to exit the New User dialog box.

You can also create users through the command-line utility NET USER. For more information about this command, type **NET USER /?** from a command prompt.

Disabling User Accounts

When a user account is no longer needed, the account should be disabled or deleted. After you've disabled an account, you can later enable it again to restore it with all of its associated user properties. An account that is deleted, however, can never be recovered.

User accounts that are not in use pose a security threat because an intruder could access your network though an inactive account. For example, after inheriting a network, I ran a network security diagnostic and noticed several accounts for users who no longer worked for the company. These accounts had Administrative rights, including dial-in permissions. This was a very risky situation, and the accounts were deleted on the spot.

You might disable an account because a user will not be using it for a period of time, perhaps because that employee is going on vacation or taking a leave of absence. Another reason to disable an account is that you're planning to put another user in that same function. For example, suppose that Rick, the engineering manager, quits. If you disable his account, when your company hires a new engineering manager, you can simply rename Rick's user account (to the username for the new manager) and enable that account. This ensures that the user who takes over Rick's position will have all the same user properties and own all the same resources.

Disabling accounts also provides a security mechanism for special situations. For example, if your company were laying off a group of people, a security measure would be to disable their accounts at the same time the layoff notices were given out. This prevents those users from inflicting any damage to the company's files on their way out. (Yes, this does seem cold-hearted, and other employees are bound to fear for their jobs any time the servers go down and they aren't able to log on, but it does serve the purpose.)

In Exercise 6.3, you will disable a user account. Before you follow this exercise, you should have already created new users (see Exercise 6.2).

EXERCISE 6.3

Disabling a User

1. Open the Admin Console MMC shortcut that was created in Exercise 6.1 and expand the Local Users and Groups snap-in.

2. Open the Users folder. Double-click user Kevin to open his Properties dialog box.

3. In the General tab, check the Account Is Disabled box. Click the OK button.

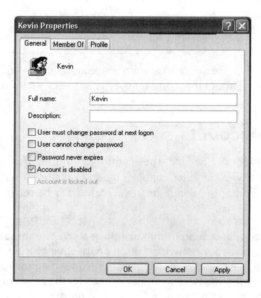

4. Log off as Administrator and attempt to log on as Kevin. This should fail, since the account is now disabled.

5. Log on as Administrator.

 You can also access a user's Properties dialog box by highlighting the user, right-clicking (clicking the secondary mouse button, and selecting Properties).

Deleting User Accounts

As noted in the preceding section, you should delete a user account if you are sure that the account will never be needed again.

To delete a user, open the Local Users and Groups utility, highlight the user account you wish to delete, and click Action to bring up the menu shown in Figure 6.2. Then select Delete.

FIGURE 6.2   Deleting a user account

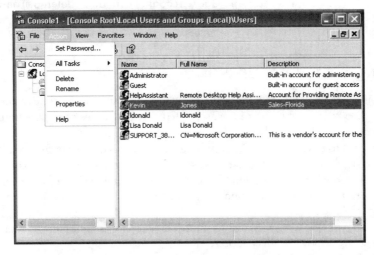

Because user deletion is a permanent action, you will see the dialog box shown in Figure 6.3, asking you to confirm that you really wish to delete the account. After you click the Yes button here, you will not be able to re-create or re-access the account (unless you restore your local user accounts database from a backup).

FIGURE 6.3   Confirming user deletion

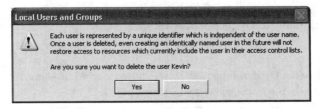

In Exercise 6.4, you will delete a user account. This exercise assumes that you have completed the previous exercises in this chapter.

EXERCISE 6.4

Deleting a User

1. Open the Admin Console MMC shortcut that was created in Exercise 6.1 and expand the Local Users and Groups snap-in.

2. Expand the Users folder and single-click on user Kevin to select his user account.

3. Select Action ➢ Delete. The dialog box for confirming user deletion appears.

4. Click the Yes button to confirm that you wish to delete this user.

The Administrator and Guest accounts cannot be deleted. The *initial user* account can be deleted.

Renaming User Accounts

Once an account has been created, you can rename the account at any time. Renaming a user account allows the user to retain all of the associated user properties of the previous username. As noted earlier in the chapter, the name is a property of the SID.

You might want to rename a user account because the user's name has changed (for example, the user got married) or because the name was spelled incorrectly. Also, as explained in the "Disabling User Accounts" section, you can rename an existing user's account for a new user, such as someone hired to take an ex-employee's position, when you want the new user to have the same properties.

In Exercise 6.5, you will rename a user account. This exercise assumes that you have completed all of the previous exercises in this chapter.

EXERCISE 6.5

Renaming a User

1. Open the Admin Console MMC shortcut that was created in Exercise 6.1 and expand the Local Users and Groups snap-in.

2. Open the Users folder and highlight user Terry.

3. Select Action ➢ Rename.

4. Type in the username **Taralyn** and press Enter. Notice that the Full Name retained the original property of Terry in the Local Users and Groups utility.

Renaming a user does not change any "hard-coded" names, such as the user's home folder. If you want to change these names as well, you need to modify them manually, for example through Windows Explorer.

Changing a User's Password

What should you do if a user forgot her password and can't log on? You can't just open a dialog box and see her old password. However, as the Administrator, you can change the user's password, and then she can use the new one.

In Exercise 6.6, you will change a user's password. This exercise assumes that you have completed all of the previous exercises in this chapter.

EXERCISE 6.6

Changing a User's Password

1. Open the Admin Console MMC shortcut that was created in Exercise 6.1 and expand the Local Users and Groups snap-in.

2. Open the Users folder and highlight user Ron.

3. Select Action ➤ Set Password. The Set Password dialog box appears.

4. A warning appears indicating risks involved in changing the password. Select Proceed.

5. Type in the new password and then confirm the password. Click the OK button.

Managing User Properties

For more control over user accounts, you can configure user properties. Through the user Properties dialog box, you can change the original password options, add the users to existing groups, and specify user profile information.

To open a user's Properties dialog box, access the Local Users and Groups utility, open the Users folder, and double-click the user account. The user Properties dialog box has tabs for the three main categories of properties: General, Member Of, and Profile.

The General tab (shown in Exercise 6.3 earlier in the chapter) contains the information that you supplied when you set up the new user account, including any Full Name and Description information, the password options you selected, and whether the account is disabled. (See "Creating New Users" earlier in this chapter.) If you want to modify any of these properties after you've created the user, simply open the user Properties dialog box and make the changes on the General tab.

The Member Of tab is used to manage the user's membership in groups. The Profile tab lets you set properties to customize the user's environment. These properties are discussed in detail in the following sections.

Managing User Group Membership

The Member Of tab of the user Properties dialog box displays all the groups that the user belongs to, as shown in Figure 6.4. From this tab, you can add the user to an existing group or remove that user from a group. To add a user to a group, click the Add button and select the group that the user should belong to. If you want to remove the user from a group, highlight the group and click the Remove button.

FIGURE 6.4   The Member Of tab of the user Properties dialog box

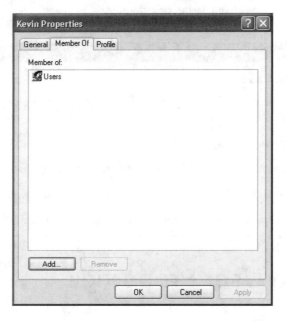

 Groups are used to logically organize users who have similar resource access requirements. Managing groups is much easier than managing individual users.

The steps used to add a user to an existing group are shown in Exercise 6.7. This exercise assumes that you have completed all of the previous exercises in this chapter.

EXERCISE 6.7

Adding a User to a Group

1. Open the Admin Console MMC shortcut that was created in Exercise 6.1 and expand the Local Users and Groups snap-in.

2. Open the Users folder and double-click user Wendy. The Wendy Properties dialog box appears.

3. Select the Member Of tab and click the Add button. The Select Groups dialog box appears.

4. Under Enter the object names to select option, type in **Power Users** and click the OK button.

5. Click the OK button to close the Wendy Properties dialog box.

Setting Up User Profiles, Logon Scripts, and Home Folders

The Profile tab of the user Properties dialog box, shown in Figure 6.5, allows you to customize the user's environment. Here, you can specify the following items for the user:

- User profile path
- Logon script
- Home folder

The following sections describe how these properties work and when you might want to use them.

FIGURE 6.5   The Profile tab of the user Properties dialog box

Setting a Profile Path

User profiles contain information about the Windows XP environment for a specific user. For example, profile settings include the Desktop arrangement, program groups, and screen colors that users see when they log on.

Each time you log on to a Windows XP Professional computer, the system checks to see if you have a *local user profile* in the Documents and Settings folder, which was created on the boot partition when you installed Windows XP Professional.

If your computer was upgraded from Windows NT 4 Workstation to Windows XP Professional, the default location for user profiles is \WINNT\Profiles\ *UserName*. If you install Windows XP Professional from scratch, or upgrade from Windows 2000 Professional, the default location for user profiles is *systemdrive*:\Documents and Settings*UserName*.

The first time users log on, they receive a default user profile. A folder that matches the user's logon name is created for the user in the Documents and Settings folder. The user profile folder that is created holds a file called NTUSER.DAT, as well as subfolders that contain directory links to the user's Desktop items.

In Exercise 6.8, you will create new users and set up local user profiles.

EXERCISE 6.8

Using Local Profiles

1. Using the Local Users and Groups utility, create two new users: **Liz** and **Tracy**. Deselect the User Must Change Password at Next Logon option for each user.

2. Select Start ➢ All Programs ➢ Accessories ➢ Windows Explorer. Expand My Computer, then Local Disk (C:), then Documents and Settings. Notice that the Documents and Settings folder does not contain user profile folders for the new users.

3. Log off as Administrator and log on as Liz.

4. Right-click an open area on the Desktop and select Properties. In the Display Properties dialog box, click the Appearance tab. Select the color scheme Olive Green, click the Apply button, and then click the OK button.

5. Right-click an open area on the Desktop and select New ➢ Shortcut. In the Create Shortcut dialog box, type **CALC**. Accept CALC as the name for the shortcut and click the Finish button.

6. Log off as Liz and log on as Tracy. Notice that user Tracy sees the Desktop configuration stored in the default user profile.

7. Log off as Tracy and log on as Liz. Notice that Liz sees the Desktop configuration you set up in steps 3, 4, and 5.

8. Log off as Liz and log on as Administrator. Select Start ➢ All Programs ➢ Accessories ➢ Windows Explorer. Expand My Computer, then Local Disk (C:), then Documents and Settings. Notice that this folder now contains user profile folders for Liz and Tracy.

If you need to reapply the default user profile for a user, you can delete the user's profile through the System icon in Control Panel ➢ Performance and Maintenance ➢ Advanced Tab ➢ User Profile ➢ Settings button.

The drawback of local user profiles is that they are available only on the computer where they were created. For example, suppose all of your Windows XP Professional computers are a part of a domain and you use only local user profiles. User Rick logs on at Computer A and creates a customized user profile. When he logs on to Computer B for the first time, he will receive the default user profile rather than the customized user profile he created on Computer A.

For users to access their user profile from any computer they log on to, you need to use roaming profiles; however, these require the use of a network server and can't be stored on a local Windows XP Professional computer.

> As noted, each user's unique settings are stored in the *systemdrive*:\Documents and Settings*UserName* folder. Settings that are common to all users are stored in the *systemdrive*:\Documents and Settings\All Users folder. If multiple users share a computer, and you don't want any user to affect other users' settings, you should remove permissions for each individual user who accesses the computer from the *systemdrive*:\Documents and Settings\All Users folder.

In the next sections, you will learn about how roaming profiles and mandatory profiles can be used. In order to have a roaming profile or a mandatory profile, your computer must be a part of a network with server access.

Roaming Profiles

A *roaming profile* is stored on a network server and allows users to access their user profile, regardless of the client computer to which they're logged on. Roaming profiles provide a consistent Desktop for users who move around, no matter which computer they access. Even if the server that stores the roaming profile is unavailable, the user can still log on using a local profile.

> Normally you would configure roaming profiles for users who are part of an Active Directory domain. In this case, you would use the Active Directory Users and Computers utility to specify the location of a user's roaming profile.

If you are using roaming profiles, the contents of the user's *systemdrive*:\Documents and Settings *UserName* folder will be copied to the local computer each time the roaming profile is accessed. If you have stored large files in any subfolders of your user profile folder, you may notice a significant delay when accessing your profile remotely as opposed to locally. If this problem occurs, you can reduce the amount of time the roaming profile takes to load by moving the subfolder to another location, such as the user's home directory, or you can use Group Policy Objects within the Active Directory to specify that specific folders should be excluded when the roaming profile is loaded.

Using Mandatory Profiles

A *mandatory profile* is a profile that can't be modified by the user. Only members of the Administrators group can manage mandatory profiles. You might consider creating mandatory profiles for users who should maintain consistent Desktops. For example, suppose that you have a group of 20 salespeople who know enough about system configuration to make changes, but not enough to fix any problems they create. For ease of support, you could use mandatory profiles. This way, all of the salespeople will always have the same profile and will not be able to change their profiles.

You can create mandatory profiles for a single user or a group of users. The mandatory profile is stored in a file named NTUSER.MAN. A user with a mandatory profile can set different Desktop preferences while logged on, but those settings will not be saved when the user logs off.

Only roaming profiles can be used as mandatory profiles. Mandatory profiles do not work for local user profiles.

Copying User Profiles

Within your company you have a user, Sharon, who logs in with two different user accounts. One account is a regular user account, and the other is an Administrator account used for administration tasks only.

When Sharon established all her Desktop preferences and installed the computer's applications, they were installed with the Administrator account. Now when she logs in with the regular user account, she can't access the Desktop and profile settings that were created for her as an administrative user.

To solve this problem, you can copy a local user profile from one user to another (for example from Sharon's administrative account to her regular user account) through Control Panel ➢ Performance and Maintenance ➢ System, Advanced tab, User Profiles Settings button. When you copy a user profile, the following items are copied: Favorites, Cookies, My Documents, Start menu items, and other unique user Registry settings.

Using Logon Scripts

Logon scripts are files that run every time a user logs on to the network. They are usually batch files, but they can be any type of executable file.

You might use logon scripts to set up drive mappings or to run a specific executable file each time a user logs on to the computer. For example, you could run an inventory management file that collects information about the computer's configuration and sends that data to a central management database. Logon scripts are also useful for compatibility with non–Windows XP clients that want to log on but still maintain consistent settings with their native operating system.

To run a logon script for a user, enter the script name in the Logon Script text box in the Profile tab of the user Properties dialog box.

Logon scripts are not commonly used in Windows Server 2003 or Windows 2000 Server network environments. Windows XP Professional automates much of the user's configuration. This isn't the case in (for example) older NetWare environments, when administrators use logon scripts to configure the users' environment.

Setting Up Home Folders

Users normally store their personal files and information in a private folder called a *home folder*. In the Profile tab of the user Properties dialog box, you can specify the location of a home folder as a local folder or a network folder.

To specify a local path folder, choose the Local Path option and type the path in the text box next to that option. To specify a network path for a folder, choose the Connect option and specify a network path using a Universal Naming Convention (UNC) path. A UNC consists of the computer name and the share that has been created on the computer. In this case, a network folder should already be created and shared. For example, if you wanted to connect to a folder called \Users\Wendy (that had been shared as Users from the \Users folder) on a server called SALES, you'd choose the Connect option and select a drive letter that would be mapped to the home directory, and then type \\SALES\Users\Wendy in the To box.

> If the home folder that you are specifying does not exist, Windows XP will attempt to create the folder for you. You can also use the variable **%username%** in place of a specific user's name.

In Exercise 6.9, you will assign a home folder to a user. This exercise assumes that you have completed all of the previous exercises in this chapter.

EXERCISE 6.9

Assigning a Home Folder to a User

1. Open the Admin Console MMC shortcut that was created in Exercise 6.1 and expand the Local Users and Groups snap-in.

2. Open the Users folder and double-click user Wendy. The Wendy Properties dialog box appears.

3. Select the Profile tab and click the Local Path radio button to select it.

4. Specify the home folder path by typing **C:\Users\Wendy** in the text box for the Local Path option. Then click the OK button.

5. Use Windows Explorer to verify that this folder was created.

 Real World Scenario

Using Home Folders

You are the administrator for a 100-user network. One of your primary responsibilities is to make sure that all data is backed up daily. This has become difficult because daily backup of each user's local hard drive is impractical. You have also had problems with employees deleting important corporate information as they are leaving the company.

After examining the contents of a typical user's local drive, you realize that most of the local disk space is taken by the operating system and the user's stored applications. This information does not change and does not need to be backed up. What you are primarily concerned with is backing up the user's data.

To more effectively manage this data and accommodate the necessary backup, you should create home folders for each user, stored on a network share. This allows the data to be backed up daily, to be readily accessible should a local computer fail, and to be easily retrieved if the user leaves the company.

Here are the steps to create a home folder that resides on the network. Decide which server will store the users' home folders, create a directory structure that will store the home folders efficiently (for example, C:\HOME), and create a single share to the home folder. Then use NTFS and share permissions to ensure that only the specified user has permissions to their home folder. Setting permissions is covered in Chapter 9. After you create the share and assign permissions, you can specify the location of the home folder through the Profile tab of user Properties dialog box.

Troubleshooting User Accounts Authentication

When a user attempts to log on through Windows XP Professional and is unable to be authenticated, you will need to track down the reason for the problem. The following sections offer some suggestions that can help you troubleshoot logon authentication errors for local and domain user accounts.

Troubleshooting Local User Account Authentication

If a local user is having trouble logging on, the problem may be with the username, the password, or the user account itself. The following are some common causes of local logon errors:

Incorrect username   You can verify that the username is correct by checking the Local Users and Groups utility. Verify that the name was spelled correctly.

Incorrect password   Remember that passwords are case sensitive. Is the Caps Lock key on? If you see any messages relating to an expired password or locked-out account, the reason for the problem is obvious. If necessary, you can assign a new password through the Local Users and Groups utility.

Prohibitive user rights   Does the user have permission to log on locally at the computer? By default, the Log On Locally user right is granted to the Users group, so all users can log on to Windows XP Professional computers. However, if this user right was modified, you will see an error message stating that the local policy of this computer does not allow interactive logon. The terms *interactive logon* and *local logon* are synonymous and mean that the user is logging on at the computer where the user account is stored on the computer's local database.

A disabled or deleted account   You can verify whether an account has been disabled or deleted by checking the account properties through the Local Users and Groups utility.

A domain account logon at the local computer   If a computer is a part of a domain, the logon dialog box has options for logging on to the domain or to the local computer. Make sure that the user has chosen the correct option.

Domain User Accounts Authentication

Troubleshooting a logon problem for a user with a domain account involves checking the same areas as you do for local account logon problems, as well as a few others.

The following are some common causes of domain logon errors:

Incorrect username   You can verify that the username is correct by checking the Microsoft Active Directory Users and Computers utility to verify that the name was spelled correctly.

Incorrect password   As with local accounts, check that the password was entered in the proper case (and the Caps Lock key isn't on), the password hasn't expired, and the account has not been locked out. If the password still doesn't work, you can assign a new password through the Microsoft Active Directory Users and Computers utility.

Prohibitive user rights   Does the user have permission to log on locally at the computer? This assumes that the user is attempting to log on to the domain controller. Regular users do not have permission to log on locally at the domain controller. The assumption is that users will log on to the domain from network workstations. If the user has a legitimate reason to log on locally at the domain controller, that user should be assigned the Log On Locally user right.

A disabled or deleted account   You can verify whether an account has been disabled or deleted by checking the account properties through the Microsoft Active Directory Users and Computers utility.

A local account logon at a domain computer   Is the user trying to log on with a local user account name instead of a domain account? Make sure that the user has selected to log on to a domain in the Logon dialog box.

The computer is not part of the domain   Is the user sitting at a computer that is a part of the domain to which the user is trying to log on? If the Windows XP Professional computer is not a part of the domain that contains the user account or does not have a trust relationship defined with the domain that contains the user account, the user will not be able to log on.

Unavailable domain controller, DNS Server, or Global Catalog   Is the domain controller available to authenticate the user's request? If the domain controller is down for some reason, the user will not be able to log on until it comes back up (unless the user logs on using a local user account). A DNS Server and the Global Catalog for Active Directory are also required.

Use of the Microsoft Active Directory Users and Computers utility is covered in *MCSE: Windows 2000 Directory Services Administration Study Guide*, 2nd edition, by Anil Desai with James Chellis (Sybex, 2001).

In Exercise 6.10, you will propose solutions to user authentication problems.

EXERCISE 6.10

Troubleshooting User Authentication

1. In this section, we will start by changing settings so the computer will use the classic logon process, instead of presenting the user accounts on the Welcome screen. To enable the classic Windows logon process, select Start ➢ Control Panel ➢ User Accounts. In the User Accounts dialog box, under Pick a Task, select Change the way users log on or off. In the Select logon and logoff options dialog box, uncheck the Use the Welcome screen option, then the Apply Options button.

2. Close all open windows and logoff as Administrator.

3. Log on as user Emily with the password **peach** (all lowercase). You should see a message indicating that the system could not log you on. The problem is that Emily's password is Peach, and passwords are case sensitive.

4. Log on as user Bryan with the password **apple**. You should see the same error message that you saw in step 1. The problem is that the user Bryan does not exist.

5. Log on as Administrator. From the Start menu, right-click My Computer and select Manage. Double-click Local Users and Groups.

6. Right-click Users and select New User. Create a user named **Gus**. Type in and confirm the password **abcde**. Deselect the User Must Change Password at Next Logon option and check the Account Is Disabled option.

7. Log off as Administrator and log on as Gus with no password. You will see a message indicating that the system could not log you on because the username or password was incorrect.

8. Log on as Gus with the password **abcde**. You will see a different message indicating that your account has been disabled.

9. Log on as Administrator.

Creating and Managing Groups

Groups are an important part of network management. Many administrators are able to accomplish the majority of their management tasks through the use of groups; they rarely assign permissions to individual users. Windows XP Professional includes built-in local groups, such as Administrators and Backup Operators. These groups already have all the permissions needed to accomplish specific tasks. Windows XP Professional also uses default special groups, which are managed by the system. Users become members of special groups based on their requirements for computer and network access.

You create and manage local groups through the Local Users and Groups utility. Through this utility, you can add groups, change group membership, rename groups, and delete groups.

Local group policies allow you to set computer configuration and user configuration options that apply to every user of the computer. Group policies are typically used with Active Directory and are applied as Group Policy Objects (GPOs). Local group policies may be useful for computers that are not part of a network or in networks that don't have a domain controller. Although group policies are not represented in an official test objective, the topic is covered on the exam; you should understand how group policies work. In this chapter, you will learn about all the built-in groups. Then you will learn how to create and manage groups. The final sections in this chapter cover local group policies and GPOs within Active Directory.

Using Built-in Groups

On a Windows XP Professional computer, default local groups have already been created and assigned all necessary permissions to accomplish basic tasks. In addition, there are built-in special groups that the Windows XP system handles automatically. These groups are described in the following sections.

Windows XP Professional, Windows 2000 Server, and Windows Server 2003 operating systems that are installed as member servers have the same default groups.

Default Local Groups

A *local group* is a group that is stored on the local computer's accounts database. These are the groups you can add users to and can manage directly on a Windows XP Professional computer. By default, the following local groups are created on Windows XP Professional computers:

- Administrators
- Backup Operators
- Guests
- Network Configuration Operators (new for Windows XP)
- Power Users
- Remote Desktop Users (new for Windows XP)
- Replicator
- Users
- HelpServicesGroup (new for Windows XP)

The following sections briefly describe each group, its default permissions, and the users assigned to the group by default.

 If possible, you should add users to the built-in local groups rather than creating new groups from scratch. This simplifies administration because the built-in groups already have the appropriate permissions. All you need to do is add the users that you want to be members of the group.

The Administrators Group

The *Administrators group* has full permissions and privileges. Its members can grant themselves any permissions they do not have by default, to manage all the objects on the computer. (Objects include the file system, printers, and account management.) By default, the Administrator and *initial user* account are members of the Administrators local group.

 Assign users to the Administrators group with caution since they will have full permissions to manage the computer.

Members of the Administrators group can perform the following tasks:

- Install the operating system.
- Install and configure hardware device drivers.
- Install system services.
- Install service packs, hot fixes, and Windows updates.
- Upgrade the operating system.
- Repair the operating system.
- Install applications that modify the Windows system files.
- Configure password policies.
- Configure audit policies.
- Manage security logs.
- Create administrative shares.
- Create administrative accounts.
- Modify groups and accounts that have been created by other users.
- Remotely access the Registry.
- Stop or start any service.
- Configure services.
- Increase and manage disk quotas.
- Increase and manage execution priorities.

- Remotely shut down the system.
- Assign and manage user rights.
- Reenable locked-out and disabled accounts.
- Manage disk properties, including formatting hard drives.
- Modify systemwide environment variables.
- Access any data on the computer.
- Back up and restore all data.

The Backup Operators Group

Members of the *Backup Operators group* have permissions to back up and restore the file system, even if the file system is NTFS and they have not been assigned permissions to access the file system. However, the members of Backup Operators can access the file system only through the Backup utility. To access the file system directly, Backup Operators must have explicit permissions assigned. There are no default members of the Backup Operators local group.

The Guests Group

The *Guests group* has limited access to the computer. This group is provided so that you can allow people who are not regular users to access specific network resources. As a general rule, most administrators do not allow Guest access because it poses a potential security risk. By default, the Guest user account is a member of the Guests local group.

The Network Configuration Operators Group

Members of the *Network Configuration Operators group* have some administrative rights to manage the computer's network configuration, for example editing the computers TCP/IP settings.

The Power Users Group

The *Power Users group* has fewer rights than the Administrators group, but more rights than the Users group. There are no default members of the Power Users local group.

WARNING Assign users to the Power Users group with caution, since they have administrative rights for managing users and groups that they have created, managing shares, managing printers, and managing services.

Members of the Power Users group can perform the following tasks:

- Create local users and groups.
- Modify the users and groups they have created.
- Create and delete network shares (except administrative shares).
- Create, manage, and delete local printers.
- Modify the system clock.

220   Chapter 6 · Managing Users and Groups

- Stop or start services (except services that are configured to start automatically).
- Modify power options.
- Install programs or applications that do not make modifications to the operating system files or install any system services.
- Modify the program files directory.

 Members of the Power Users group cannot access any NTFS resources that they have not been given explicit permissions to use.

The Remote Desktop Users Group

The *Remote Desktop Users group* allows members of the group to log on remotely for the purpose of using the Remote Desktop service.

The Replicator Group

The *Replicator group* is intended to support directory replication, which is a feature used by domain servers. Only domain users who will start the replication service should be assigned to this group. The Replicator local group has no default members.

The Users Group

The *Users group* is intended for end users who should have very limited system access. If you have installed a fresh copy of Windows XP Professional, the default settings for the Users group prohibit its members from compromising the operating system or program files. By default, all users who have been created on the computer, except Guest, are members of the Users local group.

 An efficient function for the Users group is to allow users to run but not modify installed applications. Users should not be allowed general access to the file system.

The HelpServicesGroup Group

The *HelpServicesGroup group* has special permissions needed to support the computer through Microsoft Help Services.

Special Groups

Special groups are used by the system. Membership in these groups is automatic if certain criteria are met. You cannot manage special groups through the Local Users and Groups utility. Table 6.2 describes the special groups that are built into Windows XP Professional.

TABLE 6.2 Special Groups in Windows XP Professional

Group	Description
Creator Owner	The account that created or took ownership of the object. This is typically a user account. Each object (files, folders, printers, and print jobs) has an owner. Members of the Creator Owner group have special permissions to resources. For example, if you are a regular user who has submitted 12 print jobs to a printer, you can manipulate your print jobs as Creator Owner, but you can't manage any print jobs submitted by other users.
Creator	The group that created or took ownership of the object (rather than an individual user). When a regular user creates an object or takes ownership of an object, the username becomes the Creator Owner. When a member of the Administrators group creates or takes ownership of an object, the group Administrators becomes the *Creator group.*
Everyone	The group that includes anyone who could possibly access the computer. The Everyone group includes all users who have been defined on the computer (including Guest), plus (if your computer is a part of a domain) all users within the domain. If the domain has trust relationships with other domains, all users in the trusted domains are part of the Everyone group as well. The exception to automatic group membership with the Everyone group is that members of the Anonymous Logon group are no longer a part of the Everyone group. This is a new option in Windows XP Professional; previous versions of Windows did not exclude any group from the Everyone group.
Interactive	The group that includes all users who use the computer's resources locally. Local users belong to the Interactive group.
Network	The group that includes users who access the computer's resources over a network connection. Network users belong to the Network group.
Authenticated Users	The group that includes users who access the Windows XP Professional operating system through a valid username and password. Users who can log on belong to the Authenticated Users group.
Anonymous Logon	The group that includes users who access the computer through anonymous logons. When users gain access through special accounts created for anonymous access to Windows XP Professional services, they become members of the Anonymous Logon group.
Batch	The group that includes users who log on as a user account that is only used to run a batch job. Batch job accounts are members of the Batch group.
Dialup	The group that includes users who log on to the network from a dial-up connection. Dial-up users are members of the Dialup group. (Dial-up connections are covered in Chapter 12, "Dial-Up Networking and Internet Connectivity.")

TABLE 6.2   Special Groups in Windows XP Professional *(continued)*

Group	Description
Service	The group that includes users who log on as a user account that is only used to run a service. You can configure the use of user accounts for logon through the Services program (discussed in Chapter 4), and these accounts become members of the Service group.
System	When the system accesses specific functions as a user, that process becomes a member of the System group.
Terminal Server User	The group that includes users who log on through Terminal Services. These users become members of the Terminal Server User group.

Working with Groups

Groups are used to logically organize users with similar rights requirements. Groups simplify administration because you can manage a few groups rather than many user accounts. For the same reason, groups simplify troubleshooting. Users can belong to as many groups as needed, so it's not difficult to put users into groups that make sense for your organization.

For example, suppose Jane is hired as a data analyst, to join the four other data analysts who work for your company. You sit down with Jane and create an account for her, assigning her the network permissions for the access you think she needs. Later, however, you find that the four other data analysts (who have similar job functions) sometimes have network access Jane doesn't have, and sometimes she has access they don't have. This is happening because all their permissions were assigned individually, and months apart. To avoid such problems and reduce your administrative workload, you can assign all the company's data analysts to a group and then assign the appropriate permissions to that group. Then, as data analysts join or leave the department, you can simply add them to or remove them from the group.

You can create new groups for your users, and you can use the Windows XP Professional default local built-in groups that were described in the previous section. In both cases, your planning should include checking to see if an existing local group meets your requirements before you decide to create a new group. For example, if all the users need to access a particular application, it makes sense to use the default Users group rather than creating a new group and adding all the users to that group.

To work with groups, you use the Local Users and Groups utility. The procedures for many basic group-management tasks—creating, deleting, and renaming groups—are the same for both Windows XP Professional and Windows Server 2003 if it is configured as a member server.

Creating Groups

To create a group, you must be logged on as a member of the Administrators group or the Power Users group. The Administrators group has full permissions to manage users and groups. The members of the Power Users group can manage only the users and groups that they create.

As you do in your choices for usernames, keep your naming conventions in mind when assigning names to groups. When you create a local group, consider the following guidelines:

- The group name should be descriptive (for example, Accounting Data Users).

- The group name must be unique to the computer, different from all other group names and usernames that exist on that computer.

- Group names can be up to 256 characters. It is best to use alphanumeric characters for ease of administration. The backslash (\\) character is not allowed.

Creating groups is similar to creating users, and it is a fairly easy process. After you've added the Local Users and Groups snap-in to the MMC, expand it to see the Users and Groups folders. Right-click the Groups folder and select New Group from the pop-up menu. This brings up the New Group dialog box, shown in Figure 6.6.

FIGURE 6.6 The New Group dialog box

The only required entry in the New Group dialog box is the group name. If appropriate, you can enter a description for the group, and you can add (or remove) group members. When you're ready to create the new group, click the Create button.

In Exercise 6.11, you will create two new local groups.

EXERCISE 6.11

Creating Local Groups

1. Open the Admin Console MMC shortcut that was created in Exercise 6.1 and expand the Local Users and Groups snap-in.

2. Right-click the Groups folder and select New Group.

3. In the New Group dialog box, type **Data Users** in the Group Name text box. Click the Create button.

4. In the New Group dialog box, type **Application Users** in the Group Name text box. Click the Create button.

Managing Group Membership

After you've created a group, you can add members to it. As mentioned earlier, you can put the same user in multiple groups. You can easily add and remove users through a group's Properties dialog box, shown in Figure 6.7. To access this dialog box from the Groups folder in the Local Users and Groups utility, double-click the group you want to manage.

FIGURE 6.7 A group Properties dialog box

From the group's Properties dialog box, you can change the group's description and add or remove group members. When you click the Add button to add members, the Select Users dialog box appears (Figure 6.8). Here, you enter the object names of the users you want to add. You can use the Check Names button to validate the users against the database. Select the user accounts you wish to add and click the Add button. Click the OK button to add the selected users to the group. (Although the special groups that were covered earlier in the chapter are listed in this dialog box, you cannot manage the membership of these special groups.)

To remove a member from the group, select the member in the Members list of the Properties dialog box and click the Remove button.

FIGURE 6.8   The Select Users dialog box

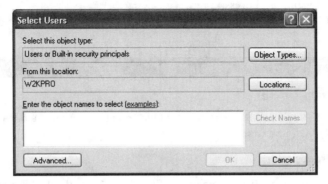

In Exercise 6.12, you will create new user accounts and then add these users to one of the groups you created in Exercise 6.11.

EXERCISE 6.12

Adding Users to a Local Group

1. Open the Admin Console MMC shortcut that was created in Exercise 6.1 and expand the Local Users and Groups snap-in.

2. Create two new users: **Bent** and **Claire**. Deselect the User Must Change Password at Next Logon option for each user.

3. Expand the Groups folder.

4. Double-click the Data Users group (created in Exercise 6.11).

5. In the Data Users Properties dialog box, click the Add button.

6. In the Select Users dialog box, type in the username **Bent**, then click the OK button. Click the Add button and type in the username **Claire**, then click the OK button.

7. In the Data Users Properties dialog box, you will see that the users have all been added to the group. Click OK to close the group Properties dialog box.

Renaming Groups

Windows XP Professional provides an easy mechanism for changing a group's name (this capability was not offered in any versions of Windows NT, although it was offered in Windows 2000). For example, you might want to rename a group because its current name does not conform to existing naming conventions.

As happens when you rename a user account, a renamed group keeps all of its properties, including its members and permissions.

To rename a group, right-click the group and choose Rename from the pop-up menu. Enter a new name for the group and press Enter.

In Exercise 6.13, you will rename one of the groups you created in Exercise 6.11.

EXERCISE 6.13

Renaming a Local Group

1. Open the Admin Console MMC shortcut that was created in Exercise 6.1 and expand the Local Users and Groups snap-in.

2. Expand the Groups folder.

3. Right-click the Data Users group (created in Exercise 6.11) and select Rename.

4. Rename the group to **App Users** and press Enter.

Deleting Groups

If you are sure that you will never again want to use a particular group, you can delete it. Once a group is deleted, you lose all permissions assignments that have been specified for the group.

To delete a group, right-click the group and choose Delete from the pop-up menu. You will see a warning that once a group is deleted, it is gone for good. Click the Yes button if you're sure you want to delete the group.

   If you delete a group and give another group the same name, the new group won't be created with the same properties as the deleted group.

In Exercise 6.14, you will delete the group that you created in Exercise 6.11 and renamed in Exercise 6.13.

EXERCISE 6.14

Deleting a Local Group

1. Open the Admin Console MMC shortcut that was created in Exercise 6.1 and expand the Local Users and Groups snap-in.

2. Expand the Groups folder.

3. Right-click the App Users group and choose Delete.

4. In the dialog box that appears, click Yes to confirm that you want to delete the group.

Summary

In this chapter, you learned about user management features in Windows XP Professional. We covered the following topics:

- The types of accounts supported by Windows XP Professional. You can set up local user accounts and domain user accounts.

- The user logon and logoff processes. To log on to a Windows XP Professional computer, the user must supply a username and password, with which the system authenticates the user. The Log Off option is in the Windows Security dialog box.

- The procedures for creating and managing user accounts. You create user accounts and manage them through the Local Users and Groups utility.

- What user properties are and how they can be configured for user accounts. The General tab of User Properties allows you specify logon, password, and whether an account is disabled. Through the Member Of tab of the user Properties dialog box, you can add users to groups or remove them from group membership. Through the Profile tab, you can set a profile path, logon script, and home folder for the user.

- Troubleshooting user logon and authentication problems. Some of the problems you may encounter are incorrect usernames or passwords, prohibitive user rights, and disabled or deleted accounts.

- The Windows XP Professional built-in groups, which include default local groups such as Administrators and Power Users, and default special groups such as Everyone and Network. You can manage the default local groups, but the special groups are managed by the system.

- The procedure for creating groups. You create groups through the Local Users and Groups utility.

- The procedure for adding users to groups and removing users from groups. You perform these tasks through the group's Properties dialog box.

- Renaming and deleting groups. Both of these tasks are performed by right-clicking the group in the Groups folder of the Local Users and Groups utility, and selecting the appropriate option from the pop-up menu.

Exam Essentials

Create and manage user accounts.   When creating user accounts, be aware of the requirements for doing so. Know how to rename and delete user accounts. Be able to manage all user properties.

Configure and manage local user authentication.   Understand the options that can be configured to manage local user authentication and when these options would be used to create a more secure environment. Be able to specify where local user authentication options are configured.

Set up a security configuration based on network requirements.   Define the options that can be configured for secure network environments. Know where to configure each option.

Be able to manage local groups.   Know the local groups that are created on Windows XP Professional computers by default, and understand what rights each group has. Know how to create and manage new groups.

Key Terms

Before you take the exam, be certain you are familiar with the following terms:

access token	local user accounts
Administrator account	local user profile
Administrators group	Local Users and Groups
Authentication	logon scripts
Backup Operators group	mandatory profile
Creator group	Network Configuration Operators group
domain user accounts	Power Users group
Guest account	Remote Desktop Users group
Guests group	Replicator group
HelpAssistant	roaming profile
HelpServices group	security identifier (SID)
home folder	special groups
interactive logon	Support_xxxxxxx
local group	user profiles
local logon	Users group

Review Questions

1. You are the network administrator for a medium-sized company. A user, John, has created a local profile on his Windows XP computer that now contains some corrupted settings. You want to look at his profiles folder and delete the corrupted information. His computer was initially installed with Windows XP Professional. Where are user profiles stored by default on this computer?

    A. \WINNT\Profiles*username*

    B. *systemdrive*:\Documents and Settings*username*

    C. \WINNT\User Profiles*username*

    D. *systemdrive*:\User Profiles*username*

2. You are the system administrator for the Psychic Buds network. One of your users, Bill, uses two different Windows XP computers. He wants to be able to use his user profile from either computer. Which of the following steps would you need to take to specify that a user profile is available over the network for a Windows XP client?

    A. In Control Panel, in the User Profiles tab of the System Properties dialog box, specify that the profile is a roaming profile.

    B. Rename the user profile to `NTUSER.NET`.

    C. Use Windows Explorer to copy the user profile to a network share.

    D. In the Local Users and Groups utility, in the Profile tab of the user Properties dialog box, specify a UNC path for the roaming profile.

3. Rob is the network administrator of a large company. The company requires that all Sales users use a profile that has been specified by the IT department as the corporate standard. Rob has been having problems because users in the Sales group are changing their profiles so that they are no longer using the corporate defined standard. Which of the following steps should Rob take to create a mandatory profile in Windows XP Professional? (Choose all that apply.)

    A. In Control Panel, in the User Profiles tab of the System Properties dialog box, specify that the profile is a mandatory profile.

    B. Rename the user profile to `NTUSER.MAN`.

    C. Copy the profile to a network share using the User Profiles tab of the System Properties dialog box in Control Panel.

    D. In the Local Users and Groups utility, in the Profile tab of the user Properties dialog box, specify a UNC path for the roaming profile.

4. Sean works in the IT unit, where all of the Windows XP Professional computers have been configured in a workgroup called IT. You want him to be able to create users and groups on the Windows XP Professional computers within the workgroup, but not to manage properties of users and groups that he did not create. To which of the following groups should you add Sean on each Windows XP Professional computer he will manage?

   A. Administrators

   B. Power Users

   C. Server Operators

   D. Power Operators

5. Rick has been added to the Administrators group, but you suspect that he is abusing his administrative privileges. All he really needs permission for is creating and managing local user accounts. You do not want Rick to be able to look at any NTFS folders or files to which he has not explicitly been granted access. To which group should you add Rick so that he can do his job but will have the minimum level of administrative rights?

   A. Administrators

   B. Power Users

   C. Account Operators

   D. Server Operators

6. You are logged on as John, who is a member of the Power Users group. When John accesses the Printers folder, he does not see an Add Printer option. What is the most likely reason for this?

   A. There are no Plug and Play printers attached to the computer.

   B. There are no LPT ports defined in the computer's BIOS.

   C. In the group policy settings, addition of printers is disabled.

   D. Members of the Power Users group do not have permissions to create new printers.

7. Cam has just installed Windows XP Professional. No changes have been made to the default user accounts. She is trying to determine if any of the default account assignments poses a security threat. Which of the following statements are true regarding the built-in accounts? (Choose all that apply.)

   A. By default, the Administrator account cannot be deleted.

   B. By default, the Guest account can be deleted.

   C. By default, the Administrator account is enabled.

   D. By default, the Guest account is enabled.

8. You are the network administrator of a small network. None of the users' local computers' data is backed up for recovery purposes. Only data that is stored on the network servers is backed up on a daily basis. One of your users, Dionne, needs to have her critical data backed up daily. She decides to create a home folder that will be used in conjunction with offline folders. Which option should she select within the Profile tab of User Properties to create a home folder that was located on a network path?

    A. Connect

    B. Local path

    C. Network path

    D. Connect path

9. You are the network administrator for a medium-sized company. Rick was the head of HR and recently resigned. John has been hired to replace Rick and has been given Rick's laptop. You want John to have access to all of the resources that Rick had access to. What is the easiest way to manage the transition?

    A. Rename Rick's account to John.

    B. Copy Rick's account and call the copied account John.

    C. Go into the Registry and do a search and replace to replace all of Rick's entries to John's name.

    D. Take ownership of all of Rick's resources and assign John Full Control to the resources.

10. You are the system administrator for a large network. One of your remote users, Brett, needs to make sure that his files are backed up on a daily basis. You install a tape backup drive on Brett's laptop. You make Brett a member of the Backup Operators group for his computer. Which of the following statements about the Backup Operators group is true?

    A. By default, only Administrators and Power Users can be members of the Backup Operators group.

    B. Backup Operators do not require any additional permissions to NTFS file systems to back up and restore the file system.

    C. Backup Operators have full access to the NTFS file system.

    D. Backup Operators can modify any services that relate to system backup.

11. If you log on as user Brad to a Windows XP Professional computer that contains the user account Brad, which of the following groups will you belong to by default? (Choose all that apply.)

    A. Users

    B. Authenticated Users

    C. Everyone

    D. Interactive

12. When Kalea logs on to the Windows XP Professional computer XPSales1, she sees her normal Desktop. When Kalea logs on to the Windows XP Professional computer XPSales2, she does not see her normal Desktop. What is the most likely cause?

    A. A roaming user profile is not configured for Kalea.

    B. Kalea does not have permissions to access her user profile from XPSales2.

    C. Kalea has a mandatory profile configured in XPSales2.

    D. The computer at which Kalea is logging on is a Windows NT 4 computer.

13. You want to allow Sarah to create and manage the mandatory profiles that are used by the sales department. Which of the following group memberships would allow her to manage mandatory user profiles?

    A. The user to whom the profile is assigned

    B. The Administrators group

    C. The Power Users group

    D. The Server Operators group

14. Nicky and Jaime share the same Windows XP Professional computer. Nicky has configured a Desktop that Jaime would like to use. How can you configure Jaime's user profile so that it will initially match Nicky's settings?

    A. Copy the NTUSER.DAT file from Nicky's folder to Jaime's folder.

    B. Configure a roaming profile that will be used by both users.

    C. Copy Nicky's user profile to Jaime's folder in the Documents and Settings folder (using Control Panel ≻ Performance and Maintenance ≻ System and selecting the User Profiles tab). Configure the profile so that Jaime is permitted to use the copied profile.

    D. Copy Nicky's user profile to Jaime's folder in the Profiles folder using Control Panel ≻ Performance and Maintenance ≻ System ≻ User Profiles tab.

15. Christine wants to connect her home folder to a shared folder that exists in the workgroup SALES, on a computer called DATA, and on a share called Users. Christine has full access to this folder and share. She also wants to use a variable for her username when she specifies the path to the network folder. Which of the following options should Christine use?

    A. In the Profiles tab of Christine's User Properties, she should click the Connect button and specify the path as **\\SALES\DATA\Users\%logonname%**.

    B. In the Profiles tab of Christine's User Properties, she should click the Connect button and specify the path as **\\SALES\DATA\Users\%username%**.

    C. In the Profiles tab of Christine's User Properties, she should click the Connect button and specify the path as **\\DATA\Users\%logonname%**.

    D. In the Profiles tab of Christine's User Properties, she should click the Connect button and specify the path as **\\DATA\Users\%username%**.

Answers to Review Questions

1. B.   The default location for user profiles is the *systemdrive*:\Documents and Settings*username* folder in Windows XP and Windows 2000. In Windows NT 4, the default location for user profiles was \WINNT\Profiles.

2. D.   After you create the profile that will be used as the roaming profile, you create a folder and share on the network location where the roaming profile will be stored. You use Control Panel ➤ Performance and Maintenance ➤ System ➤ User Profiles tab to copy the local profile to the network share. Finally, you specify that the user is using a roaming profile by configuring the user's properties through the Local Users and Groups utility. In the Profile tab, you specify a UNC path for the roaming profile.

3. B, C, D.   Creating a mandatory profile involves three main steps. First, rename the user profile from NTUSER.DAT to NTUSER.MAN. Second, copy the profile to a network share using Control Panel ➤ Performance and Maintenance ➤ System ➤ User Profiles tab. Third, in the Local Users and Groups utility, access the properties of the user who will be assigned the roaming profile, and specify the location of the mandatory profile. This path must be a UNC path for the mandatory profile to work.

4. B.   Members of the Power Users group can create users and groups, but they can manage only the users and groups they themselves have created. Administrators can manage all users and groups. The Server Operators group exists only on Windows 2000 and Windows 2003 domain controllers. The Power Operators group does not exist by default on Windows XP computers.

5. B.   The members of the Power Users group have the rights to create and then manage the local users and groups that they have created, without being able to look at NTFS folders and files that they have not been given access to. Account Operators and Server Operators are not built-in groups on Windows XP Professional computers.

6. C.   Members of the Power Users group can create new printers. The most likely reason John doesn't have the Add Printer option is that the option to add new printers has been disabled in the group policy settings. You do not need a Plug and Play printer attached to the computer, nor do you need to have LPT ports configured to create a printer.

7. A, C.   By default, the Administrator and Guest accounts cannot be deleted, although they can both be renamed. The Administrator account is enabled by default, but the Guest account is disabled by default for security reasons. It is strongly recommended that you use a complex password for the Administrator account during the system installation.

8. A.   All of the options seem plausible, but the only option that appears on the Profile tab of the user Properties dialog box is Connect.

9. A.   The easiest way to manage this transition is to simply rename Rick's account to John. John will automatically have all of the rights and permissions to any resource that Rick had access to.

10. B.   There are no default members of the Backup Operators group. Members of this group have access to the file system during the backup process, but they do not have normal file access. Backup Operators group members have no special permissions to modify system services.

11. A, B, C, D.   By default, all users who exist on a Windows XP Professional computer are added to the computer's Users group. Users who log on with a valid username and password automatically become a member of the Authenticated Users special group. By default, anyone who can use the computer becomes a member of the special group Everyone. Since Brad works at the computer where his user account actually resides, he automatically becomes a member of the special group Interactive.

12. A.   By default, profiles are only configured to be used locally. In this case, it is likely that no roaming profile has been configured for Kalea.

13. B.   Only members of the Administrators group can create and assign mandatory user profiles.

14. C.   You can copy Nicky's user profile so that Jaime can use it initially by copying Nicky's user profile to Jaime's folder in the Document and Settings folder. You can perform this copy operation through Control Panel ➤ Performance and Maintenance ➤ System ➤ User Profiles tab.

15. D.   To connect to a shared network folder for a user's home folder, you must use the UNC path to the share. In this case, Christine would specify \\DATA\Users. The variable that can be used is %username%.

Chapter

7

Managing Security

MICROSOFT EXAM OBJECTIVES COVERED IN THIS CHAPTER:

✓ **Configure, manage, and troubleshoot a security configuration and local security policy.**

✓ **Configure, manage, and troubleshoot local user and group accounts.**

  - Configure, manage, and troubleshoot auditing.

  - Configure, manage, and troubleshoot account policy.

  - Configure, manage, and troubleshoot user and group rights.

  - Troubleshoot cache credentials.

Windows XP Professional offers a wide variety of security options. If the Windows XP Professional computer is a part of a Windows 2000 or Windows 2003 domain, then security can be applied through a group policy within Active Directory. If the Windows XP Professional computer is not a part of a Window 2000 or Windows 2003 domain, then you use Local Group Policy Objects to manage local security. In the first part of the chapter, you will learn about the different environments that Windows XP Professional can be installed in and the utilities that are used to manage security.

Policies are used to help manage user accounts. Account policies are used to control the logon environment for the computer, such as password and logon restrictions. Local policies specify what users can do once they log on, and include auditing, user rights, and security options.

Security can be managed and analyzed through the Security Configuration and Analysis tool or the `Secedit` command-line utility.

Options for Managing Security Configurations

The tools that are used to manage Windows XP Professional computer security configurations are dependent on whether the Windows XP Professional computer is a part of a Windows 2000 or Windows 2003 domain environment.

If the Windows XP Professional client is not a part of a Windows 2000 or Windows 2003 domain—for example, if the computer is installed as a stand-alone computer or part of a Windows workgroup, Windows NT 4 domain, Unix network, or NetWare network—then you apply security settings through *Local Group Policy Objects (LGPOs)*. LGPOs are a set of security configuration settings that are applied to users and computers. LGPOs are created and stored on the Windows XP Professional computer.

If your Windows XP Professional computer is a part of a Windows 2000 Server or Windows Server 2003 domain, both of which use the services of *Active Directory*, then you typically manage and configure security through *Group Policy Objects (GPOs)*. Group Policy is an MMC snap-in that is used to define security (called group policies) for users, groups, and computers via the Active Directory. Windows XP Professional computers that are a part of a Windows 2000 or Windows 2003 domain still have an LGPO, and the LGPO can be used in conjunction with the Active Directory group policies.

This book focuses on understanding and applying LGPOs. Usage of Group Policy Objects is covered in greater detail in *MCSE: Windows 2000 Server Study Guide*, 2nd edition, by Lisa Donald with James Chellis (Sybex, 2001).

The settings that can be applied through the Group Policy utility within Active Directory are more comprehensive than the settings that can be applied through LGPOs. By default, the LGPO is stored in *systemroot*\System32\GroupPolicy. Table 7.1 lists all of the options that can be set for GPOs within the Active Directory and which of those options can be applied through LGPOs.

TABLE 7.1   Group Policy and LGPO Setting Options

Group Policy Setting	Available for LGPO?
Software installation	No
Scripts	Yes
Security settings	Yes
Administrative templates	Yes
Folder redirection	No
RIS options	No
Internet Explorer configuration management	No

Group Policy Objects and Active Directory

Most Windows XP Professional computers reside within Windows 2000 domains or Windows 2003 domains. Typically, GPOs are applied through the Active Directory, as this is much easier to globally manage than applying LGPOs at local levels. To help you understand how GPOs and LGPOs work together, this section will first overview the Active Directory and then show you how GPOs and LGPOs are applied based on predefined inheritance rules.

Active Directory Overview

Within Active Directory, you have several levels of hierarchical structure. A typical structure will consist of domains and Organizational Units. Other levels exist within Active Directory, but this overview focuses on domains and *Organizational Units (OUs)* in the context of using GPOs.

The domain is the main unit of organization within Active Directory. Within a domain are many domain objects (including users, groups, and GPOs). Each domain object can have security applied that specifies who can access the object and the level of access they have.

Within a domain, you can further subdivide and organize domain objects through the use of Organizational Units. This is one of the key differences between Windows NT 3.51 and Windows NT 4 domains, and Windows 2000 Server and Windows Server 2003 domains. The NT domains were not able to store information hierarchically. Windows 2000 Server and Windows Server 2003 domains, through the use of OUs, allow you to store objects hierarchically, typically based on function or geography.

For example, assume that your company is called ABCCORP. You have locations in New York, San Jose, and Belfast. You might create a domain called ABCCORP.COM with OUs called NY, SJ, and Belfast. In a very large corporation, you might also organize the OUs based on function. For example, the domain could be ABCCORP.COM and the OUs might be SALES, ACCT, and TECHSUPP. Based on the size and security needs of your organization, you might also have OUs nested within OUs. As a general rule, however, you will want to keep your Active Directory structure as simple as possible.

GPO Inheritance

When GPOs are created within Active Directory, there is a specific order of inheritance. That is, the policies are applied in a specific order within the hierarchical structure of Active Directory. When a user logs onto Active Directory, depending on where within the hierarchy GPOs have been applied, the order of application is as follows:

1. Local computer
2. Site (group of domains)
3. Domain
4. OU

What this means is that the local policy is, by default, applied first when a user logs on. Then the site policies are applied, and if the site policy contains settings that the local policy doesn't have, they are added to the local policy. If there are any conflicts, the site policy overrides the local policy. Then the domain policies are defined. Again, if the domain policy contains additional settings, they are incorporated. When settings conflict, the domain policy overrides the site policy. Next, the OU policies are applied. Additional settings are incorporated; for conflicts, the OU policy overrides the domain policy. If conflicts occur between computer and user policy settings, the computer policy setting is applied.

The following options are available for overriding the default behavior of GPO execution:

No Override   The No Override option is used to specify that child containers can't override the policy settings of higher-level GPOs. In this case, the order of precedence would be that site settings override domain settings, and domain settings override OU settings. The No Override option would be used if you wanted to set corporate-wide policies without allowing administrators of lower-level containers to override your settings. This option can be set per-container, as needed.

Block Inheritance The Block Inheritance option is used to allow the child container to block GPO inheritance from parent containers. This option would be used if you did not want to inherit GPO settings from parent containers and wanted only the GPO you had set for your container to be applied.

If a conflict exists between the No Override and the Block Inheritance settings, then the No Override option would be applied.

Using the Group Policy Result Tool

When a user logs on to a computer or domain, a resulting set of policies to be applied is generated based on the LGPO, site GPO, domain GPO, and OU GPO. The overlapping nature of group policies can make it difficult to determine what group policies will actually be applied to a computer or user.

To help determine what policies will actually be applied, Windows XP includes a tool called the Windows XP Operating System *Group Policy Result Tool*. This tool is accessed through the GPResult.exe command-line utility. The GPResult.exe command displays the resulting set of policies that were enforced on the computer and the specified user during the logon process, as shown in Figure 7.1.

FIGURE 7.1   Results from GPResult utility

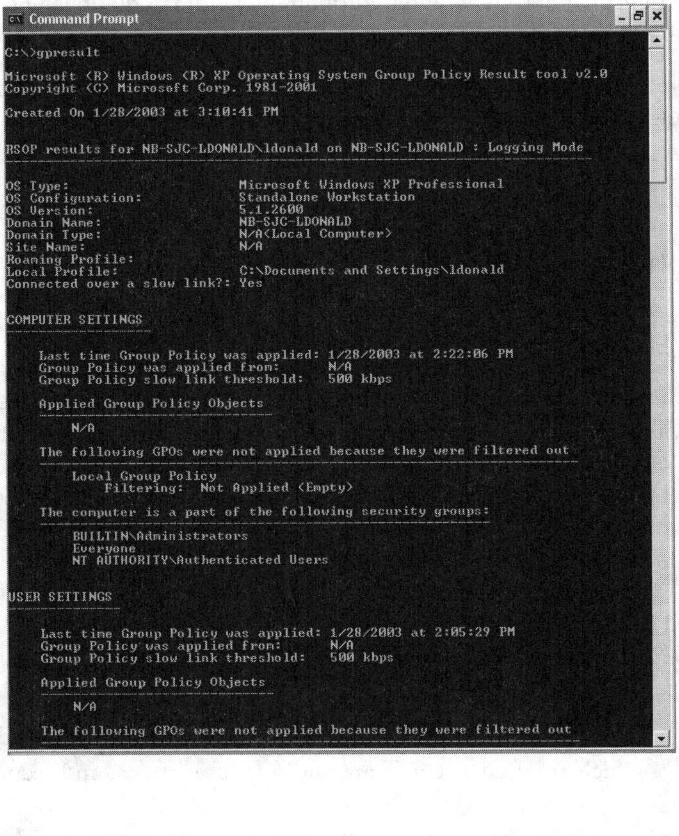

You can use this utility by accessing a command prompt and typing `GPResult`. This will display the Resultant Set of Policy (RSOP) for the computer and user who is currently logged in. Several options can be used with this command. Use `GPResult /?` to get verbose help on each command switch option.

 Real World Scenario

Applying GPOs

You manage a network that consists of 500 computers all running Windows XP Professional. You are already using Active Directory and have logically defined your OUs based on function. One OU, called Sales, has 50 users. Your task is to configure the Sales computers so they all have a consistent desktop that can't be modified. You also need to add the new Sales Management software to each computer.

It would take days for you to manually configure each computer with a local group policy and then add the software. In this case, GPOs are a real benefit. As the Administrator of the Sales OU, you can create a single GPO that will be applied to all users of the container. You can specify the desktop settings and publish any applications that you want to install. Next time the Sales users log on, the group policies will be applied, and the users' Registries will be updated to reflect the changes. In addition, through the automated publishing applications, it can be configured to be automatically loaded on each of the Sales users' computers.

By using GPOs, you can add new software, configure computers, and accomplish other tasks from your computer that would normally require you to physically visit each machine.

Applying LGPOs

When you use an LGPO on a Windows XP Professional computer, there is only one Group Policy Object, which applies to all of the computer's users. Policies that have been linked though Active Directory will take precedence over any established local group policies. Local group policies are typically applied to computers that are not part of a network or are in a network that does not have a domain controller, and thus do not use Active Directory.

You apply an LGPO to a Windows XP Professional computer through the *Local Computer Policy snap-in* within the MMC. On a Windows XP Professional computer, the *Local Group Policy snap-in* will be displayed within the MMC as Local Computer Policy, as shown in Figure 7.2.

Through local group policies, you can set a wide range of security options. At the top levels, they are managed as Computer Configuration and User Configuration. The following sections describe in detail how to apply security settings through local group policy. The two main areas of security configuration are:

- Account policies, which are used to configure password and account lockout features

- Local policies, which are used to configure auditing, user rights, and security options

FIGURE 7.2   Accessing the Account Policies folders

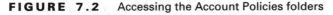
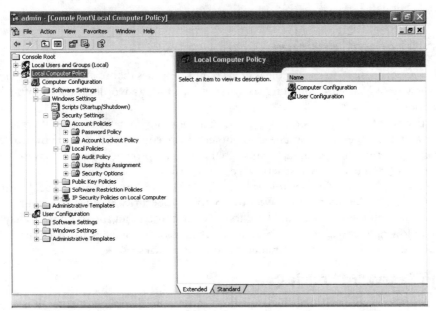

 You can also access the account policies and local policies by opening the Control Panel and selecting Performance and Maintenance ➢ Administrative Tools ➢ Local Security Policy.

In Exercise 7.1, you will see how to add the Local Group Policy snap-in to the MMC.

EXERCISE 7.1

Adding the Local Computer Policy Snap-In to the MMC

1. Open the Admin Console MMC shortcut that was created in Exercise 6.1 and expand the Local Users and Groups snap-in.

2. From the main menu, select File ➢ Add/Remove Snap-in.

3. In the Add/Remove Snap-in dialog box, click the Add button.

4. Highlight the Group Policy option and click the Add button.

5. The Group Policy Object specifies Local Computer by default. Click the Finish button.

6. Click the Close button.

7. In the Add/Remove Snap-in dialog box, click the OK button. Leave the Admin Console open, as it will be used for the other exercises in this chapter.

You'll take a look at both the account policies and local policies in more detail in the following sections.

Using Account Policies

Account policies are used to specify the user account properties that relate to the logon process. They allow you to configure computer security settings for passwords and account lockout specifications.

If security is not an issue—perhaps because you are using your Windows XP Professional computer at home—then you don't need to bother with account policies. If, on the other hand, security is important—for example, because your computer provides access to payroll information—then you should set very restrictive account policies.

To access the Account Policies folder from the MMC, follow this path: Local Computer Policy ➢ Computer Configuration ➢ Windows Settings ➢ Security Settings ➢ Account Policies. You will look at all these folders and how to use them throughout the rest of this chapter.

In the following sections you will learn about the password policies and account lockout policies that define how security is applied to account policies.

Setting Password Policies

Password policies ensure that security requirements are enforced on the computer. It is important to understand that the password policy is set on a per-computer basis; it cannot be configured for specific users. Figure 7.3 shows the password policies, which are described in Table 7.2.

FIGURE 7.3   The password policies

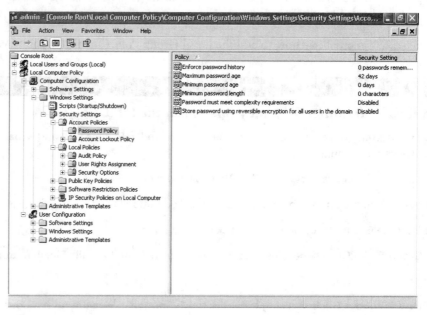

TABLE 7.2   Password Policy Options

Policy	Description	Default	Minimum	Maximum
Enforce Password History	Keeps track of user's password history	Remember 0 passwords	Same as default	Remember 24 passwords
Maximum Password Age	Determines maximum number of days user can keep valid password	Keep password for 42 days	Keep password for 1 day	Keep password for up to 999 days
Minimum Password Age	Specifies how long password must be kept before it can be changed	0 days (password can be changed immediately)	Same as default	999 days
Minimum Password Length	Specifies minimum number of characters password must contain	0 characters (no password required)	Same as default	14 characters
Password Must Meet Complexity Requirements	Allows you to install password filter	Disabled		
Store Password Using Reversible Encryption for All Users in the Domain	Specifies higher level of encryption for stored user passwords	Disabled		

The password policies in Table 7.2 are used as follows:

Enforce Password History   Prevents users from using the same password. Users must create a new password when their password expires or is changed.

Maximum Password Age   Forces users to change their password after the maximum password age is exceeded.

Minimum Password Age   Prevents users from changing their password several times in rapid succession in order to defeat the purpose of the Enforce Password History policy.

Minimum Password Length   Ensures that users create a password and specifies the length requirement for that password. If this option isn't set, users are not required to create a password at all.

Password Must Meet the Complexity Requirements of the Installed Password Filters Prevents users from using as passwords items found in a dictionary of common names.

Store Password Using Reversible Encryption for All Users in the Domain Provides a higher level of security for user passwords. This is required for SPAP authentication, which is used with remote access.

In Exercise 7.2, you will configure password policies for your computer. This exercise assumes that you have added the Local Computer Policy snap-in to the MMC (see Exercise 7.1).

EXERCISE 7.2

Setting Password Policies

1. Open the Admin Console MMC shortcut that was configured in Exercise 7.1 and expand the Local Computer Policy Snap-in.

2. Expand the folders as follows: Computer Configuration ➢ Windows Settings ➢ Security Settings ➢ Account Policies ➢ Password Policy.

3. Open the Enforce Password History policy. On the Local Security Setting tab, specify that **5** passwords will be remembered. Click the OK button.

4. Open the Maximum Password Age policy. On the Local Security Setting tab, specify that the password expires in **60** days. Click the OK button.

Setting Account Lockout Policies

The *account lockout policies* are used to specify how many invalid logon attempts should be tolerated. You configure the account lockout policies so that after *x* number of unsuccessful logon attempts within *y* number of minutes, the account will be locked for a specified amount of time or until the Administrator unlocks the account.

 Account lockout policies are similar to a bank's arrangements for ATM access code security. You have a certain number of chances to enter the correct PIN. That way, anyone who steals your card can't just keep guessing your access code until they get it right. Typically, after three unsuccessful attempts, the ATM takes the card. Then you need to request a new card from the bank.

Figure 7.4 shows the account lockout policies, which are described in Table 7.3.

FIGURE 7.4   The account lockout policies

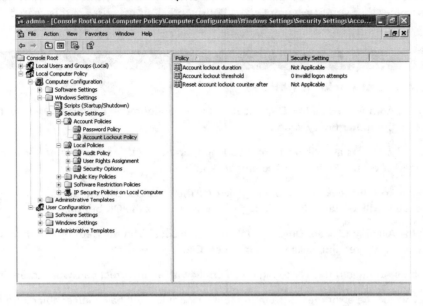

TABLE 7.3   Account Lockout Policy Options

Policy	Description	Default	Minimum	Maximum	Suggested
Account Lockout Duration	Specifies how long account will remain locked if Account Lockout Threshold is exceeded	0; but if Account Lockout Threshold is enabled, 30 minutes	Same as default	99,999 minutes	5 minutes
Account Lockout Threshold	Specifies number of invalid attempts allowed before account is locked out	0 (disabled, account will not be locked out)	Same as default	999 attempts	5 attempts
Reset Account Lockout Counter After	Specifies how long counter will remember unsuccessful logon attempts	0; but if Account Lockout Threshold is enabled, 5 minutes	Same as default	99,999 minutes	5 minutes

In Exercise 7.3, you will configure account lockout policies and test their effects. This exercise assumes that you have completed all of the previous exercises in this chapter.

EXERCISE 7.3

Setting Account Lockout Policies

1. Open the Admin Console MMC shortcut that was configured in Exercise 7.1 and expand the Local Computer Policy snap-in.

2. Expand the folders as follows: Computer Configuration ➤ Windows Settings ➤ Security Settings ➤ Account Policies ➤ Account Lockout Policy.

3. Open the Account Lockout Threshold policy. On the Local Security Setting tab, specify that the account will lock after **3** invalid logon attempts. Click the OK button.

4. Open the Account Lockout Duration policy. On the Local Security Setting tab, specify that the account will remain locked for **5** minutes. Click the OK button.

5. Log off as Administrator. Try to log on as Emily with an incorrect password three times.

6. After you see the error message stating that account lockout has been enabled, log on as Administrator.

7. To unlock Emily's account, open the Local Users and Groups snap-in in the MMC, expand the Users folder, and double-click user Emily.

8. In the General tab of Emily's Properties dialog box, click to remove the check from the Account Is Locked Out check box. Then click OK.

Using Local Policies

As you learned in the preceding section, account policies are used to control logon procedures. When you want to control what a user or group can do *after* logging on, you use *local policies*. With local policies, you can implement auditing, specify user rights, and set security options.

To use local policies, first add the Local Computer Policy snap-in to the MMC (see Exercise 7.1). Then, from the MMC, follow this path of folders to access the Local Policies folders: Local Computer Policy ➤ Computer Configuration ➤ Windows Settings ➤ Security Settings ➤ Local Policies. Figure 7.5 shows the three Local Policies folders: Audit Policy, User Rights Assignment, and Security Options. You will look at each of those in the following sections.

Setting Audit Policies

Audit policies can be implemented to track success or failure of specified user actions. You audit events that pertain to user management through the audit policies. By tracking certain events, you can create a history of specific tasks, such as user creation and successful or unsuccessful logon attempts. You can also identify security violations that arise when users attempt to access system management tasks for which they do not have permission.

FIGURE 7.5   Accessing the Local Policies folders

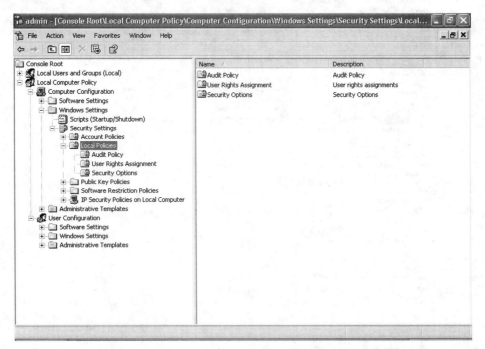

> **WARNING**   Users who try to go to areas for which they do not have permission usually fall into two categories: hackers and people who are just curious to see what they can get away with. Both are very dangerous.

When you define an audit policy, you can choose to audit success or failure of specific events. The success of an event means that the task was successfully accomplished. The failure of an event means that the task was not successfully accomplished.

By default, auditing is not enabled, and it must be manually configured. Once auditing has been configured, you can see the results of the audit through the Event Viewer utility, Security log. (The Event Viewer utility is covered in Chapter 14, "Performing System Recovery Functions.")

> **WARNING**   Auditing too many events can degrade system performance due to its high processing requirements. Auditing can also use excessive disk space to store the audit log. You should use this utility judiciously.

Figure 7.6 shows the audit policies, which are described in Table 7.4.

FIGURE 7.6 The audit policies

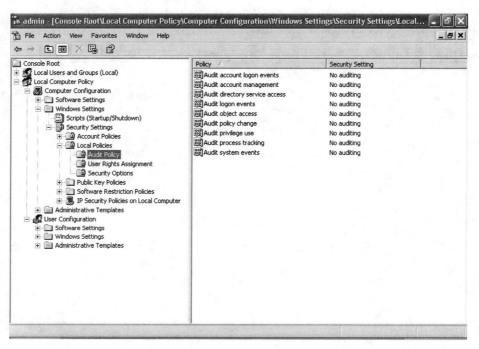

TABLE 7.4 Audit Policy Options

Policy	Description
Audit Account Logon Events	Tracks when a user logs on, logs off, or makes a network connection
Audit Account Management	Tracks user and group account creation, deletion, and management actions, such as password changes
Audit Directory Service Access	Tracks directory service accesses
Audit Logon Events	Audits events related to logon, such as running a logon script or accessing a roaming profile
Audit Object Access	Enables auditing of access to files, folders, and printers
Audit Policy Change	Tracks any changes to the audit policy

TABLE 7.4 Audit Policy Options *(continued)*

Policy	Description
Audit Privilege Use	Tracks any changes to who can or cannot define or see the results of auditing
Audit Process Tracking	Tracks events such as activating a program, accessing an object, and exiting a process
Audit System Events	Tracks system events such as shutting down or restarting the computer, as well as events that relate to the Security log in Event Viewer

After you set the Audit Object Access policy to enable auditing of object access, you must enable file auditing through NTFS security, or print auditing through printer security.

In Exercise 7.4, you will configure audit policies and view their results. This exercise assumes that you have completed all previous exercises in this chapter.

EXERCISE 7.4

Setting Audit Policies

1. Open the Admin Console MMC shortcut that was configured in Exercise 7.1 and expand the Local Computer Policy snap-in.

2. Expand the folders as follows: Computer Configuration ➤ Windows Settings ➤ Security Settings ➤ Local Policies ➤ Audit Policy.

3. Open the Audit Account Logon Events policy. In the Local Policy Setting field, specify Audit These Attempts. Check the boxes for Success and Failure. Click the OK button.

4. Open the Audit Account Management policy. On the Local Security Setting tab, specify Audit These Attempts. Check the boxes for Success and Failure. Click the OK button.

5. Log off as Administrator. Attempt to log back on as Administrator with an incorrect password. The logon should fail (because the password is incorrect).

6. Log on as Administrator with the correct password. Select Start ➤ Control Panel ➤ Performance and Maintenance ➤ Administrative Tools ➤ Event Viewer to open Event Viewer.

7. From Event Viewer, open the Security log. You should see the audited events listed in this log.

WARNING

You may want to limit the number of events that are audited. If you audit excessive events on a busy computer, the log file can grow very quickly. In the event that the log file becomes full, you can configure the computer to shut down through a security option policy, Audit: Shut Down System Immediately if Unable to Log Security Audits. If this option is triggered, the only user that will be able to log on to the computer will be the Administrator. If this option is not enabled and the log file becomes full, you will have the option of overwriting older log events. Setting security option policies is covered later in this chapter, in the section "Defining Security Options."

Assigning User Rights

The *user right policies* determine what rights a user or group has on the computer. User rights apply to the system. They are not the same as permissions, which apply to a specific object (permissions are discussed in Chapter 9, "Accessing Files and Folders").

An example of a user right is the Back Up Files and Directories right. This right allows a user to back up files and folders, even if the user does not have permissions that have been defined through NTFS file system permissions. The other user rights are similar because they deal with system access as opposed to resource access.

Figure 7.7 shows the user right policies, which are described in Table 7.5.

FIGURE 7.7 The user right policies

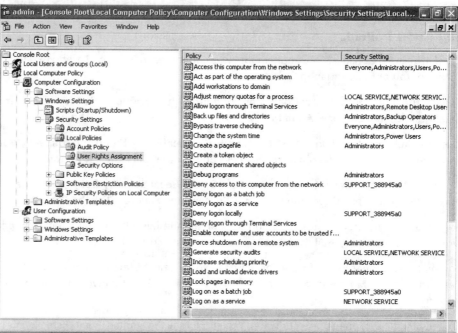

TABLE 7.5   User Rights Assignment Policy Options

Right	Description
Access This Computer from the Network	Allows a user to access the computer from the network.
Act as Part of the Operating System	Allows low-level authentication services to authenticate as any user.
Add Workstations to Domain	Allows a user to create a computer account on the domain.
Adjust Memory Quotas for a Process	Allows you to configure how much memory can be used by a specific process. This is a new user right for Windows XP Professional.
Allow Logon through Terminal Services	Gives a user permission to log on through Terminal Services. This is a new user right for Windows XP Professional.
Back Up Files and Directories	Allows a user to back up all files and directories, regardless of how the file and directory permissions have been set.
Bypass Traverse Checking	Allows a user to pass through and traverse the directory structure, even if that user does not have permissions to list the contents of the directory.
Change the System Time	Allows a user to change the internal time of the computer.
Create a Pagefile	Allows a user to create or change the size of a page file.
Create a Token Object	Allows a process to create a token if the process uses the NtCreateToken API.
Create Permanent Shared Objects	Allows a process to create directory objects through the Windows XP Object Manager.
Debug Programs	Allows a user to attach a debugging program to any process.
Deny Access to This Computer from the Network	Allows you to deny specific users or groups access to this computer from the network.
Deny Logon as a Batch Job	Allows you to prevent specific users or groups from logging on as a batch file.

TABLE 7.5 User Rights Assignment Policy Options *(continued)*

Right	Description
Deny Logon as a Service	Allows you to prevent specific users or groups from logging on as a service.
Deny Logon Locally	Allows you to deny specific users or groups access to the computer locally.
Deny Logon through Terminal Services	Specifies that a user is not able to log on through Terminal Services. This is a new user right for Windows XP Professional.
Enable Computer and User Accounts to Be Trusted for Delegation	Allows a user or group to set the Trusted for Delegation setting for a user or computer object.
Force Shutdown from a Remote System	Allows the system to be shut down by a user at a remote location on the network.
Generate Security Audits	Allows a user, group, or process to make entries in the Security log.
Increase Scheduling Priority	Specifies that a process can increase or decrease the priority that is assigned to another process.
Load and Unload Device Drivers	Allows a user to dynamically unload and load Plug and Play device drivers.
Lock Pages in Memory	With this user right, an account can create a process that only runs in physical RAM and is not paged.
Log On as a Batch Job	Allows a process to log on to the system and run a file that contains one or more operating system commands.
Log On as a Service	Allows a service to log on in order to run the specific service.
Log On Locally	Allows a user to log on at the computer where the user account has been defined.
Manage Auditing and Security Log	Allows a user to manage the Security log.
Modify Firmware Environment Variables	Allows a user or process to modify the system environment variables.

TABLE 7.5 User Rights Assignment Policy Options *(continued)*

Right	Description
Perform Volume Maintenance Tasks	Allows a user to perform volume maintenance tasks such as running Disk Cleanup and Disk Defragmenter. This is a new user right for Windows XP Professional.
Profile Single Process	Allows a user to monitor non-system processes through tools such as the Performance Logs and Alerts utility.
Profile System Performance	Allows a user to monitor system processes through tools such as the Performance Logs and Alerts utility.
Remove Computer from Docking Station	Allows a user to undock a laptop through the Windows XP user interface.
Replace a Process Level Token	Allows a process to replace the default token that is created by the subprocess with the token that the process specifies.
Restore Files and Directories	Allows a user to restore files and directories, regardless of file and directory permissions.
Shut Down the System	Allows a user to shut down the local Windows XP computer.
Synchronize Directory Service Data	Allows a user to synchronize data associated with a directory service.
Take Ownership of Files or Other Objects	Allows a user to take ownership of system objects.

In Exercise 7.5, you will apply a user right policy. This exercise assumes that you have completed all of the previous exercises in this chapter.

EXERCISE 7.5

Setting User Rights

1. Open the Admin Console MMC shortcut that was configured in Exercise 7.1 and expand the Local Computer Policy snap-in.

2. Expand folders as follows: Computer Configuration ➢ Windows Settings ➢ Security Settings ➢ Local Policies ➢ User Rights Assignment.

3. Open the Log On as a Service user right. The Local Security Policy Setting dialog box appears.

4. Click the Add User or Group button. The Select Users or Groups dialog box appears.

5. Click the Advanced button, then select Find Now.

6. Select user Emily. Click the Add button. Then click the OK button.

7. In the Local Security Setting dialog box, click the OK button.

Defining Security Options

Security option policies are used to configure security for the computer. Unlike user right policies, which are applied to a user or group, security option policies apply to the computer. Figure 7.8 shows the security option policies, which are described briefly in Table 7.6.

FIGURE 7.8   The security option policies

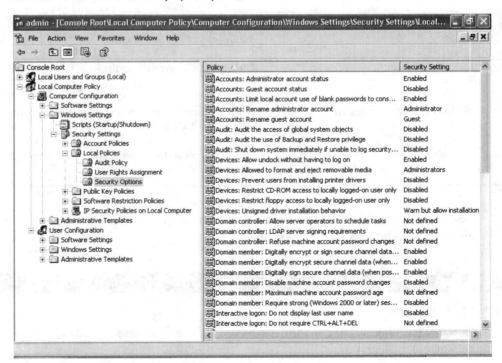

TABLE 7.6 Security Options

Option	Description	Default
Accounts: Administrator Account Status	Specifies whether the Administrator account is enabled or disabled under normal operation. Booting under Safe Mode, the Administrator account is enabled, regardless of this setting.	Enabled
Accounts: Guest Account Status	Determines whether the Guest account is enabled or disabled.	Disabled
Accounts: Limit Local Account Use of Blank Passwords to Console Logon Only	Means that if a user has a blank password, and this option is enabled, users can't use a blank password to log on from network logons. This setting does not apply to domain logon accounts.	Enabled
Accounts: Rename Administrator Account	Allows the Administrator account to be renamed.	Administrator account is named Administrator.
Accounts: Rename Guest Account	Allows the Guest account to be renamed.	Guest account is named Guest.
Audit: Audit the Access of Global System Objects	Allows access of global system objects to be audited.	Disabled
Audit: Audit the use of Backup and Restore privilege	Allows the use of backup and restore privileges to be audited.	Disabled
Audit: Shut Down System Immediately if Unable to Log Security Audits	Specifies that the system shuts down immediately if it is unable to log security audits.	Disabled
Devices: Allow Undock without Having to Log On	Allows a user to undock a laptop computer from a docking station by pushing the computer's eject button without first having to log on.	Enabled
Devices: Allowed to Format and Eject Removable Media	Specifies who can format and eject removable NTFS media.	Administrators

TABLE 7.6 Security Options *(continued)*

Option	Description	Default
Devices: Prevent Users from Installing Printer Drivers	If enabled, allows only Administrators and Power Users to install network print drivers.	Disabled on workstations and Enabled on servers
Devices: Restrict CD-ROM Access to Locally Logged-On User Only	Specifies whether the CD-ROM is accessible to local users and network users.	Disabled.
Devices: Restrict Floppy Access to Locally Logged-On User Only	Specifies whether the floppy drive is accessible to local users and network users.	Disabled
Devices: Unsigned Driver Installation Behavior	Controls the behavior of the unsigned driver installation.	Warn but allow installation
Domain Controller: Allow Server Operators to Schedule Tasks	Allows server operators to schedule specific tasks to occur at specific times or intervals. Only applies to tasks scheduled through the AT command and does not affect tasks scheduled through Task Scheduler.	Not defined
Domain Controller: LDAP server signing requirements	Specifies that the domain controller should use the Lightweight Directory Access Protocol for server signing.	Not defined
Domain Controller: Refuse Machine Account Password Changes	Specifies whether a domain controller will accept password changes for computer accounts.	Disabled
Domain Member: Digitally Encrypt or Sign Secure Channel Data (Always)	Specifies whether a secure channel must be created with the domain controller before secure channel traffic is generated.	Enabled
Domain Member: Digitally Encrypt Secure Channel Data (when Possible)	Specifies that if a secure channel can be created between the domain controller and the domain controller partner, it will be.	Enabled

T A B L E   7 . 6   Security Options *(continued)*

Option	Description	Default
Domain Member: Digitally Sign Secure Channel Data (when Possible)	Specifies that all secure channel traffic be signed if both domain controller partners who are transferring data are capable of signing secure data.	Enabled
Domain Member: Disable Machine Account Password Changes	Specifies whether a domain member must periodically change its computer account password as defined in the "Domain Member: Maximum Age for Machine Account Password" setting.	Disabled
Domain Member: Maximum Machine Account Password Age	Specifies the maximum age of a computer account password.	30 days
Domain Member: Require Strong (Windows 2000 or Later) Session Key	If enabled, the domain controller must encrypt data with a 128-bit session key; if not enabled, 64-bit session keys can be used.	Disabled
Interactive Logon: Do Not Display Last User Name	Prevents the last username in the logon screen from being displayed.	Disabled
Interactive Logon: Do Not Require Ctrl+Alt+Del	Allows the Ctrl+Alt+Delete requirement for logon to be disabled.	Not defined, but it is automatically used on stand-alone workstations, meaning users who log on to the workstation see a start screen with icons for all users who have been created on the computer
Interactive Logon: Message Text for Users Attempting to Log On	Displays message text for users trying to log on, usually configured for displaying legal text messages.	Text space is blank.
Interactive Logon: Message Title for Users Attempting to Log On	Displays a message title for users trying to log on.	Not defined

TABLE 7.6 Security Options *(continued)*

Option	Description	Default
Interactive Logon: Number of Previous Logon Attempts to Cache (in Case Domain Controller Is Not Available)	Specifies the number of previous logon attempts stored in the cache. This option is useful if a domain controller is not available.	10
Interactive Logon: Prompt User to Change Password before Expiration	Prompts the user to change the password before expiration.	14 days before password expiration
Interactive Logon: Require Domain Controller Authentication to Unlock	Specifies that a username and password be required to unlock a locked computer. When this is disabled, a user can unlock a computer with cached credentials. When this is enabled, a user can only unlock the computer using a domain controller for authentication.	Disabled
Interactive Logon: Smart Card Removal Behavior	Specifies what happens if a user who is logged on with a smart card removes the smart card.	No action
Microsoft Network Client: Digitally Sign Communications (Always)	Specifies that the server should always digitally sign client communication.	Disabled
Microsoft Network Client: Digitally Sign Client Communication (if Server Agrees)	Specifies that the server should digitally sign client communication when possible.	Enabled
Microsoft Network Client: Send Unencrypted Password to Connect to Third-Party SMB Servers	Allows third-party Server Message Block servers to use unencrypted passwords for authentication.	Disabled
Microsoft Network Client: Amount of Idle Time Required before Idle before Suspending Session	Allows sessions to be disconnected when they are idle.	15 minutes for servers and undefined for workstations
Microsoft Network Server: Digitally Sign Communications (Always)	Ensures that server communications will always be digitally signed.	Disabled

TABLE 7.6   Security Options *(continued)*

Option	Description	Default
Microsoft Network Server: Digitally Sign Communications (if Client Agrees)	Specifies that server communications should be signed when possible.	Disabled on workstations and Enabled on servers
Microsoft Network Server: Disconnect Clients when Logon Hours Expire	If a user logs on and then their logon hours expire, specifies whether an existing connection will remain connected or be disconnected.	Undefined
Network Access: Allow Anonymous SID/Name Translation	Specifies whether an anonymous user can request the security identifier (SID) attributes for another user.	Disabled on workstations and Enabled on servers
Network Access: Do Not Allow Anonymous Enumeration of SAM Accounts	If enabled, prevents an anonymous connection from enumerating Security Account Manager (SAM) accounts.	Enabled on workstations and Disabled on servers
Network Access: Do Not Allow Anonymous Enumeration of SAM Accounts and Shares	If enabled, prevents an anonymous connection from enumerating Security Account Manager (SAM) accounts and network shares.	Disabled
Network Access: Let Everyone Permission Apply to Anonymous Users	Specifies whether Everyone permissions will apply to anonymous users.	Disabled
Network Access: Named Pipes that Can Be Accessed Anonymously	Specifies which communication sessions will have anonymous access.	Defined
Network Access: Remotely Accessible Registry Paths	Determines which Registry paths will be accessible when the winreg key is accessed for remote Registry access.	Defined
Network Access: Shares that Can Be Accessed Anonymously	Specifies which network shares can be accessed by anonymous users.	Defined
Network Access: Sharing and Security Model for Local Accounts	Specifies how network models that use local accounts will be authenticated.	Guest only-local users authenticate as Guest

TABLE 7.6 Security Options *(continued)*

Option	Description	Default
Network Security: Do Not Store LAN Manager Hash Value on Next Password Change	Specifies whether LAN Manager will store hash values from password changes.	Disabled
Network Security: Force Logoff when Logon Hours Expire	Specifies whether a user with a current connection will be automatically logged off when their logon hours expire.	Disabled
Network Security: LAN Manager Authentication Level	Specifies the LAN Manager Authentication Level.	Send LAN Manager and NTLM (NT LAN Manager) responses
Network Security: LDAP Client Signing Requirements	Specifies the client signing requirements that will be enforced for LDAP clients.	Negotiate signing
Network Security: Minimum Session Security for NTLM SSP Based (Including Secure RPC) Clients	Specifies the minimum security standards for application-to-application client communications.	No minimum
Network Security: Minimum Session Security for NTLM SSP Based (Including Secure RPC) Servers	Specifies the minimum security standards for application-to-application server communications.	No minimum
Recovery Console: Allow Automatic Administrative Logon	Specifies that when the Recovery Console is loaded, Administrative logon should be automatic, as opposed to a manual process.	Disabled
Recovery Console: Allow Floppy Copy and Access to All Drives and Folders	Allows you to copy files from all drives and folders when the Recovery Console is loaded.	Disabled
Shutdown: Allow System to Be Shut Down without Having to Log On	Allows the user to shut down the system without logging on.	Enabled on workstations and Disabled on servers
Shutdown: Clear Virtual Memory Pagefile	Specifies whether the virtual memory pagefile will be cleared when the system is shut down.	Disabled

TABLE 7.6   Security Options *(continued)*

Option	Description	Default
System Cryptography: Use FIPS Compliant Algorithms for Encryption	Specifies which encryption algorithms should be supported for encrypting file data.	Disabled
System Objects: Default Owner for Objects Created by Members of the Administrators Group	Determines whether, when an object is created by a member of the Administrators group, the owner will be the Administrators group or user who created the object.	Object creator
System Objects: Require Case Insensitivity to Non-Windows Subsystems	By default, Windows XP does not specify case insensitivity for file subsystems. However, subsystems such as POSIX use case-sensitive file systems, so this option allows you to configure case sensitivity.	Enabled
System Objects: Strengthen Default Permissions of Internal System Objects (e.g. Symbolic Links)	Specifies the default discretionary access control list for objects.	Enabled

In Exercise 7.6, you will define some security option policies and see how they work. This exercise assumes that you have completed all of the previous exercises in this chapter.

EXERCISE 7.6

Defining Security Options

1. Open the Admin Console MMC shortcut that was configured in Exercise 7.1 and expand the Local Computer Policy snap-in.

2. Expand folders as follows: Computer Configuration ➢ Windows Settings ➢ Security Settings ➢ Local Policies ➢ Security Options.

3. Open the policy Interactive Logon: Message Text for Users Attempting to Log On. On the Local Policy Setting page, type **Welcome to all authorized users**. Click the OK button.

4. Open the policy Interactive Logon: Prompt User to Change Password before Expiration. On the Local Security Setting page, specify **3** days. Click the OK button.

5. Log off as Administrator and log on as Michael (with the password **apple**).

6. Log off as Michael and log on as Administrator.

Analyzing System Security

You can analyze your system security by comparing your current configuration to a predefined template or through a customized template based on your organization's needs. This is accomplished through the `Secedit.exe` command-line utility or the *Security Configuration and Analysis tool*, which is a GUI interface implemented as an MMC snap-in.

The `Secedit` command-line utility can be used to perform the following options:

- Analyze security
- Set security configuration options
- Export a database of existing security configurations
- Validate security settings based on predefined security templates

The Security Configuration and Analysis utility works by comparing your actual security configuration to a security template configured with your desired settings.

The following steps are involved in the security analysis process:

1. Using the Security Configuration and Analysis tool, specify a working security database that will be used during the security analysis.

2. Import a security template that can be used as a basis for how you would like your security to be configured.

3. Perform the security analysis. This will compare your configuration against the template that you specified in step 2.

4. Review the results of the security analysis, and resolve any discrepancies that have been identified through the security analysis results.

The Security Configuration and Analysis tool is accessed as an MMC snap-in. After you add this utility to the MMC, you can use it to run the security analysis process, as described in the following sections.

To add the Security Configuration and Analysis tool, follow these steps:

1. Open the Admin Console MMC shortcut that was configured in Exercise 7.1.

2. Select File ➢ Add/Remove Snap-in.

3. In the Add/Remove Snap-In dialog box, click the Add button. Highlight the Security Configuration and Analysis snap-in and click the Add button. Then click the Close button.

4. In the Add/Remove Snap-In dialog box, click the OK button.

Specifying a Security Database

The security database is used to store the results of your security analysis. To specify a security database, take the following steps:

1. In the MMC, right-click the Security Configuration and Analysis snap-in and select the Open Database option.

2. The Open Database dialog box appears. In the File Name text box, type the name of the database you will create. By default, this file will have a `.sdb` (for security database) extension. Then click the Open button.

3. The Import Template dialog box appears. Select the template that you want to import. You can select a predefined template through this dialog box. In the next section, you will learn how to create and use a customized template file. Make your selection and click the Open button.

Importing a Security Template

The next step in the security analysis process is to import a security template. The security template is used as a comparison tool. The Security Configuration and Analysis tool compares the security settings in the security template to your current security settings. You do not set security through the security template. Rather, the security template is where you organize all of your security attributes in a single location.

 As an administrator, you can define a base security template on a single Windows XP Professional computer and then export the security template to other Windows XP Professional computers in your network.

The template you use can be one of the predefined user templates, a predefined template you have customized for your own needs, or a template you have defined from scratch. In the following sections, you will learn about the default templates that are provided with Windows XP Professional and how the templates can be modified.

Creating a Security Template

By default, Windows XP Professional ships with a variety of predefined security templates. Each of the templates defines a standard set of security values based on the requirements of your environment. The template groups that are included by default are defined in Table 7.7.

TABLE 7.7   Default Security Templates

Template	Filename	Description
Default Security	Setup security.inf	Default security settings that are applied by default when a new computer is installed.
Compatible	Compatws.inf	Used for backward compatibility. This template relaxes the security used by Windows XP so applications that are not certified to work with Windows XP can still run. This template is typically associated with computers that have been upgraded and are having problems running applications that have run in the past.

TABLE 7.7 Default Security Templates *(continued)*

Template	Filename	Description
Secure	Secure*.inf	Implements recommended security settings for XP Professional in all security areas except for files, folders, and Registry keys.
High Secure	Hisec*.inf	Defines highly secure network communications for Windows XP computers. If you apply this security template, Windows XP computers can only communicate with other Windows 2000 Professional and Server, Windows XP (all versions), and Windows Server 2003 computers.
System Root Security	Rootsec.inf	Specifies that the new root permissions introduced with Windows XP be applied.

You create security templates through the Security Templates snap-in in the MMC. You can configure security templates with the items listed in Table 7.8.

TABLE 7.8 Security Template Configuration Options

Security Template Item	Description
Account Policies	Specifies configurations that should be used for password policies, account lockout policies, and Kerberos policies
Local Policies	Specifies configurations that should be used for audit policies, user rights assignments, and security options
Event Log	Allows you to set configuration settings that apply to Event Viewer log files
Restricted Groups	Allows you to administer local group memberships
Registry	Specifies security for local Registry keys
File System	Specifies security for the local file system
System	Sets security for system services and the startup mode that local system services will use

After you add the Security Templates snap-in to the MMC, you can open a sample security template and modify it, as follows:

1. In the MMC, expand the Security Templates snap-in and then expand the folder for *Windir*\Security\Templates.

2. Double-click the sample template that you want to edit. There are several sample templates, including `securews` (for secure workstation) and `compatws` (for workstations that need backward-compatibility settings).

3. Make any changes you want to the sample security template. Changes to the template are not applied to the local system by default. They are simply a specification for how you would like the system to be configured.

4. Once you have made all of the changes to the sample template, save the template by highlighting the sample template file, right-clicking, and selecting the Save As option from the pop-up menu. Specify a location and a filename for the new template. By default, the security template will be saved with an .inf extension in the *Windir*\Security\Templates folder.

Opening a Security Template

Once you have configured a security template, you can import it for use with the Security Configuration and Analysis tool, assuming that a security database has already been configured. To import a security template, in the MMC right-click the Security Configuration and Analysis tool and select the Import Template option from the pop-up menu. Then highlight the template file you wish to import and click the Open button.

Performing a Security Analysis

The next step is to perform a security analysis. To run the analysis, simply right-click the Security Configuration and Analysis tool and select the Analyze Computer Now option from the pop-up menu. You will see a Perform Analysis dialog box that allows you to specify the location and filename for the error log file path that will be created during the analysis. After this information is configured, click the OK button.

When the analysis is complete, you will be returned to the main MMC window. From there, you can review the results of the security analysis.

Reviewing the Security Analysis and Resolving Discrepancies

The results of the security analysis are stored in the Security Configuration and Analysis snap-in, under the configured security item. For example, to see the results for password policies, double-click the Security Configuration and Analysis snap-in, double-click Account Policies, and then double-click Password Policy, as shown in Figure 7.9.

FIGURE 7.9   Security Analysis Results dialog box

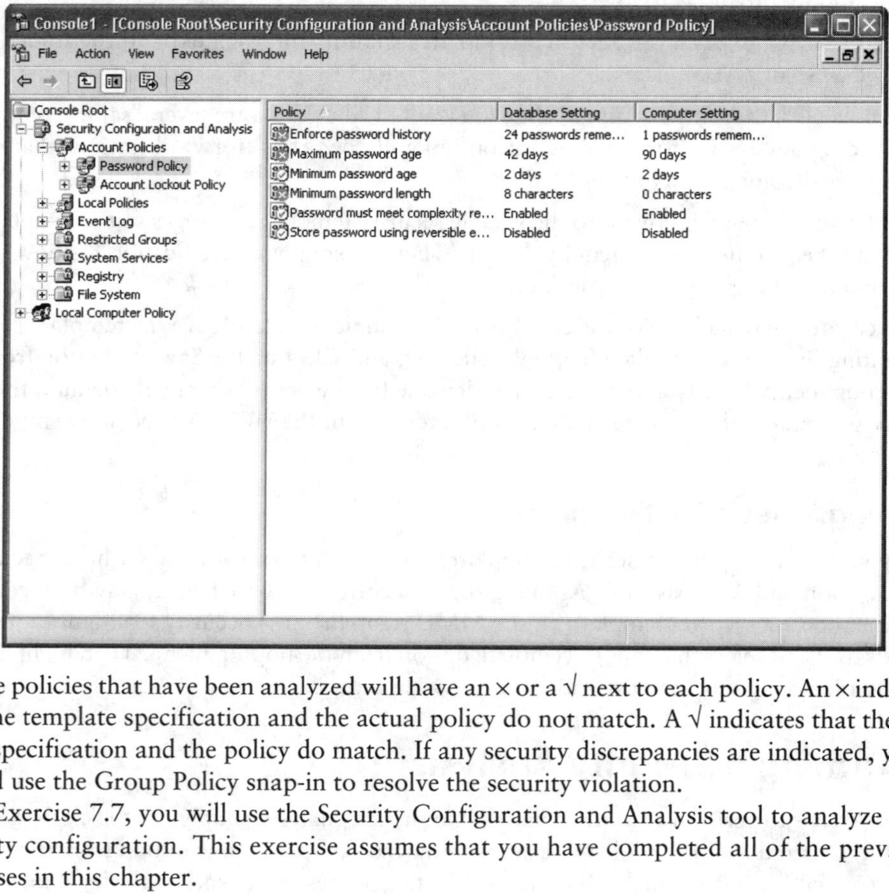

The policies that have been analyzed will have an × or a √ next to each policy. An × indicates that the template specification and the actual policy do not match. A √ indicates that the template specification and the policy do match. If any security discrepancies are indicated, you should use the Group Policy snap-in to resolve the security violation.

In Exercise 7.7, you will use the Security Configuration and Analysis tool to analyze your security configuration. This exercise assumes that you have completed all of the previous exercises in this chapter.

EXERCISE 7.7

Using the Security Configuration and Analysis Tool

In this exercise, you will specify a security database, create a security template, import the template, perform an analysis, and review the results.

Specifying the Security Database

1. In the MMC, right-click Security Configuration and Analysis and select Open Database.

2. In the Open Database dialog box, type **sampledb** in the File Name text box. Then click the Open button.

3. In the Import Template dialog box, select the template securews and click the Open button.

Creating the Security Template

4. In the MMC, select File ➢ Add/Remove Snap-in.

5. In the Add/Remove Snap-In dialog box, click the Add button. Highlight the Security Templates snap-in and click the Add button. Then click the Close button.

6. In the Add/Remove Snap-In dialog box, click the OK button.

7. Expand the Security Templates snap-in, then expand the `WINDOWS\Security\Templates` folder.

8. Double-click the `securews` file.

9. Select Account Policies, then Password Policy.

10. Edit the password policies as follows:

    ▪ Set the Enforce Password History option to **10** passwords remembered.

    ▪ Enable the Passwords Must Meet Complexity Requirements option.

    ▪ Set the Maximum Password Age option to **30** days.

11. Highlight the `securews` file, right-click, and select the Save As option.

12. In the Save As dialog box, place the file in the default folder and name the file **xptest.** Click the Save button.

Importing the Security Template

13. Highlight the Security Configuration and Analysis snap-in, right-click, and select the Import Template option.

14. In the Import Template dialog box, highlight the `xptest` file and click the Open button.

Performing and Reviewing the Security Analysis

15. Highlight the Security Configuration and Analysis snap-in, right-click, and select the Analyze Computer Now option.

16. In the Perform Analysis dialog box, accept the default error log file path and click the OK button.

17. When you return to the main MMC window, double-click the Security Configuration and Analysis snap-in.

18. Double-click Account Policies, and then double-click Password Policy. You will see the results of the analysis for each policy, indicated by an ✕ or a √ next to the policy.

Summary

In this chapter, you learned how to define security for Windows XP Professional. We covered the following topics:

- The difference between LGPOs, which are applied at the local level, and GPOs, which are applied through a Windows 2000 or Windows 2003 domain, and how they are applied.

- Account policies, which control the logon process. The two types of account policies are password and account lockout policies.

- Local policies, which control what a user can do at the computer. The three types of local policies are audit, user rights, and security options policies.

- How to manage security through the Security Configuration and Analysis tool.

- How to use the Group Policy Result Tool to analyze current configuration settings.

Exam Essentials

Understand how group policies are applied locally and through the Active Directory.   Know how group policies can be applied either locally through LGPOs or through the Active Directory with GPOs. Understand how group policy is applied through the order of inheritance. Be able to use the Group Policy Result Tool to view how group policy is currently configured for a specific computer.

Set up a security configuration based on network requirements.   Define the options that can be configured for secure network environments. Know where to configure each option.

Know how to set local group policies.   Understand the purpose of account policies and local policies. Understand the purpose and implementation of account policies for managing password policies and account lockout policies. Understand the purpose and implementation of local policies and how they can be applied to users and groups for audit policies, user rights assignments, and security options.

Know how to analyze security.   Be able to analyze security through the Security Configuration and Analysis tool. Understand the use of templates and the function of the default templates that are provided with Windows XP Professional.

Key Terms

Before you take the exam, be certain you are familiar with the following terms:

account lockout policies

account policies

Active Directory

audit policies

Group Policy Objects (GPOs)

Group Policy Result Tool

Local Computer Policy snap-in

Local Group Policy Objects (LGPOs)

Local Group Policy snap-in

local policies

organizational units (OUs)

password policies

Security Configuration and Analysis tool

security option policies

user right policies

Review Questions

1. Your network's security has been breached. You are trying to redefine security so that a user cannot repeatedly attempt user logon with different passwords. To accomplish this, which of the following items (in the Local Security Settings dialog box shown here) should you define?

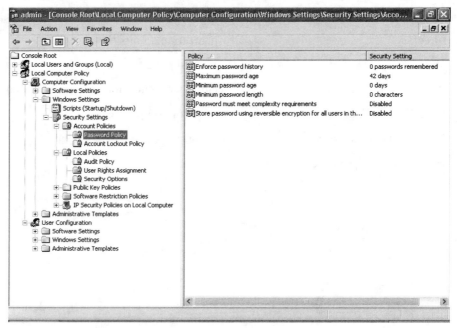

    A. Password policy

    B. Account lockout policy

    C. Audit policy

    D. Security options

2. You are the network administrator for a Fortune 500 company. The Accounting department has recently purchased a custom application for running financial models. To run properly, the application requires that you make some changes to the computer policy. You decide to deploy the changes through the Group Policy setting. You create an OU called Sales and apply the policy settings. When you log on as a member of the Sales OU and run the application, it is still not running properly. You suspect that the policy is not being applied properly because of a conflict somewhere with another Group Policy setting. What command should you run to see a listing of how the group policies have been applied to the computer and the user?

    A. `GPResult.exe`

    B. `GPOResult.exe`

    C. `GPAudit.exe`

    D. `GPInfo.exe`

3. You have a Windows XP Professional computer that is located in an unsecured area. You want to track usage of the computer by recording user logon and logoff events. To do this, which of the following auditing policies must be enabled?

   A. Audit Account Logon Events

   B. Audit Process Tracking

   C. Audit Logon Events

   D. Audit System Events

4. Bill is very good at troubleshooting hardware, installing new devices, and updating drivers. You want Bill to be able to add and remove hardware and install and update drivers on the Windows XP Professional computers in your network. What is the minimum assignment that will allow Bill to complete this task?

   A. Add Bill to the Administrators group.

   B. Add Bill to the Server Operators group.

   C. Add Bill to the Manage Devices group.

   D. Grant Bill the user right Load and Unload Device Drivers on each computer he will manage.

5. You are the network administrator of a small company. You have just decided to install the XYZ Virus Scanner application. The scanner runs as a service. You create a user account called VirScan that will be used to run the service. What user right must be granted for this account?

   A. Log On as a Batch Job

   B. Log On as a Service

   C. Process Service Requests

   D. Manage Services and Security

6. You are the system administrator for the ACME Corp. You have a computer that is shared by many users. You want to ensure that when users press Ctrl+Alt+Delete to log on, they do not see the name of the last user. What do you configure?

   A. Set the security option Clear User Settings When Users Log Off.

   B. Set the security option Do Not Display Last User Name in Logon Screen.

   C. Set the security option Prevent Users from Seeing Last User Name.

   D. Configure nothing; this is the default setting.

7. You are the network administrator of a medium-sized company. Due to recent security breaches, you have configured auditing so that you can track events such as account management tasks and system events. Where can you view the results of the audit?

   A. Audit Manager

   B. *Windir*\audit.log

   C. Event Viewer ➢ System log

   D. Event Viewer ➢ Security log

8. You have recently hired Al as an assistant for network administration. You have not decided how much responsibility you want Al to have. In the meantime, you want Al to be able to restore files on Windows XP Professional computers in your network, but you do not want Al to be able to run the backups. What is the minimum assignment that will allow Al to complete this task?

   A. Add Al to the Administrators group.

   B. Grant Al the Read right to the root of each volume he will back up.

   C. Add Al to the Backup Operators group.

   D. Grant Al the user right Restore Files and Directories.

9. You are the network administrator of a medium-sized company. Your company requires a fair degree of security and you have been tasked with defining and implementing a security policy. You have configured password policies so that users must change their passwords every 30 days. Which password policy would you implement if you want to prevent users from reusing passwords they have used recently?

   A. Passwords Must Be Advanced

   B. Enforce Password History

   C. Passwords Must Be Unique

   D. Passwords Must Meet the Complexity Requirements of the Installed Password Filters

10. **Prioritize-a-list:** As network administrator, you have configured GPOs for your local computers, domains, sites, and OUs. Your GPOs are not being applied as you had expected. You have not set any filter or inheritance settings. What is the default order of inheritance that will be applied to the GPOs?

    Local Computer

    Domain

    Site

    OU

11. A user in your San Jose domain is attempting to install an updated modem driver. They report that they can't get the driver to update properly. You log on to the user's computer with administrative rights to the San Jose domain and attempt to update the driver. When you check the driver through Device Manager, you notice that the old driver is still installed. In Control Panel, you open the System icon and see that driver signing is configured with Ignore for the driver signing verification. You suspect that the problem may be with the GPO's configuration. Which of the following actions should you take that will make the least impact on the GPO for Active Directory?

    A. Configure the domain GPO for the Warn file signature verification, and then attempt to update the driver.

    B. For the Sales domain, set the No Override option.

    C. For the Sales domain, set the Block Inheritance option.

    D. Configure the local computer for the Warn file signature verification, and then attempt to update the driver.

12. Your Active Directory structure consists of a domain called CCCUSA, which is a part of a site called CCCCORP. There is an OU called Sales, and each computer within Sales has a local policy set. You have configured all of the GPOs with the No Override option. Which of the following policies will be applied in the event of conflict?

   A. Domain

   B. Site

   C. OU

   D. Local computer

13. You are the network administrator for the Wacky Widgets Corporation. Your network requires a high level of security. You evaluate the `hisecws.inf` security template and determine that the settings this template uses will meet the needs of your network. Which of the following two options can be used to deploy the `hisecws.inf` security template?

   A. Security Configuration and Analysis tool

   B. `Secedit.exe`

   C. `RSOP.exe`

   D. Security Templates MMC snap-in

14. You are the administrator of a medium-sized network. Your company requires that custom security settings be applied to all Windows XP Professional computers within the network. You define all of the security settings that should be applied. Which of the following utilities can be used to create a template with your custom security settings that can then be used for security analysis?

   A. Security Configuration and Analysis tool

   B. `Secedit.exe`

   C. `RSOP.exe`

   D. Security Templates MMC snap-in

15. You are the network administrator for a medium-sized company. You recently upgraded 10 Windows NT 4 Workstation computers to Windows XP Professional. Some of the applications that worked properly under Windows NT 4 Workstation no longer work properly with Windows XP Professional. Which of the following security templates might correct the application compatibility issues?

   A. `security.inf`

   B. `application.inf`

   C. `rootsec.inf`

   D. `compatws.inf`

Answers to Review Questions

1. B. Account lockout policies, a subset of account policies, are used to specify options that prevent a user from attempting multiple failed logon attempts. If the Account Lockout Threshold value is exceeded, the account will be locked. The account can be reset based on a specified amount of time, or through Administrator intervention.

2. A. The System Group Policy Result Tool is accessed through the `GPResult.exe` command-line utility. The `GPResult.exe` command displays the resulting set of policies that were enforced on the computer and the specified user during the logon process.

3. A. Audit Account Logon Events is used to track when a user logs on, logs off, or makes a network connection. You can configure auditing for success or failure and audited events can be tracked through Event Viewer.

4. D. The Load and Unload Device Drivers user right allows a user to dynamically unload and load Plug and Play device drivers. You could allow a user to complete this task through Administrator or Power User group membership, but by assigning user rights, you can better control security access.

5. B. The Log On as a Service user right allows a service to log on in order to run the specific service. This user right can be assigned to users or groups.

6. B. The security option Do Not Display Last User Name is used to prevent the last username in the logon screen from being displayed in the logon dialog box. This option is commonly used in environments where computers are used publicly.

7. D. Once auditing has been configured, you can see the results of the audit through the Security log in the Event Viewer utility. In order to view the security logs, you must be a member of the Administrators group or have appropriate user rights to view or manage the audit logs.

8. D. The Restore Files and Directories user right allows a user to restore files and directories, regardless of file and directory permissions. Assigning this user right is an alternative to making a user a member of the Backup Operators group.

9. B. The Enforce Password History policy allows the system to keep track of a user's password history for up to 24 passwords. This prevents a user from using the same password over and over again.

10. Local Computer

    Site

    Domain

    OU

    By default, GPOs are applied in the order of local computer, site, domain, and OU. The policies will be combined unless conflicting settings are applied, in which case the last policy that is applied contains the effective setting.

11. A.   You should just configure a specific GPO so that the file signature verification is set to Warn as opposed to Block, which will refuse upgrading of the driver if it is unsigned without any user notification. The last GPO applied is the domain's, so you should edit the Sales domain's GPO for this arrangement.

12. B.   The No Override option is used to specify that child containers can't override the policy settings of higher-level GPOs. In this case, the order of precedence would be as follows: Site would override Domain, and Domain would override OU. The No Override option can be used if you want to set corporate-wide policies and do not want to give administrators of lower-level containers the capability to override your settings. This option can be set on a per-container basis as needed.

13. A, B.   The Security Configuration and Analysis tool and the `Secedit` command-line utility can be used to apply security templates. The Security Templates MMC snap-in is used to create and modify templates.

14. D.   By default, Windows XP Professional ships with a variety of predefined security templates. You create security templates through the Security Templates snap-in in the MMC.

15. D.   The `compatws.inf` template is used for backward compatibility. This template relaxes the security used by Windows XP so that applications that are not certified to work with Windows XP can still run. This template is typically associated with computers that have been upgraded and are having problems running applications that have run in the past.

Chapter

8

Managing Disks

MICROSOFT EXAM OBJECTIVES COVERED IN THIS CHAPTER:

✓ **Monitor, manage, and troubleshoot access to files and folders.**

  ▪ Configure, manage, and troubleshoot file compression.

  ▪ Optimize access to files and folders.

✓ **Configure and manage file systems.**

  ▪ Convert from one file system to another file system.

  ▪ Configure NTFS, FAT32, or FAT file systems.

✓ **Implement, manage, and troubleshoot disk devices.**

  ▪ Monitor and configure disks.

  ▪ Monitor, configure, and troubleshoot volumes.

✓ **Configure, manage, and troubleshoot Encrypting File System (EFS).**

When you install Windows XP Professional, you designate the initial configuration for your disks. Through Windows XP Professional's utilities and features, you can change that configuration and perform disk-management tasks.

For file system configuration, you can choose FAT, FAT32, or NTFS. You can also update a FAT or FAT32 partition to NTFS. This chapter covers the features of each file system and how to use the Convert utility to upgrade to NTFS.

Another factor in disk management is choosing the configuration for your physical drives. Windows XP supports basic storage and dynamic storage. When you install Windows XP Professional or upgrade from Windows NT Workstation 4, the drives are configured as basic storage. Dynamic storage is supported by Windows 2000 (all versions), Windows XP Professional, and Windows Server 2003 and allows you to create simple volumes, spanned volumes, and striped volumes.

Once you decide how your disks should be configured, you implement the disk configurations through the Disk Management utility. This utility helps you view and manage your physical disks and volumes. In this chapter, you will learn how to manage both types of storage and to upgrade from basic storage to dynamic storage.

The other disk-management features covered in this chapter are data compression, disk quotas, data encryption, disk defragmentation, disk cleanup, and disk error checking.

The procedures for many disk-management tasks are the same for both Windows XP Professional, Windows 2000 (all versions) and Windows Server 2003. The main difference is that Windows 2000 Server and Windows Server 2003 also support mirrored and RAID-5 volumes.

Configuring File Systems

Each partition (each *logical drive* that is created on your hard drive) you create under Windows XP Professional must have a file system associated with it.

When selecting a file system, you can select FAT (also referred to as FAT16), FAT32, or NTFS. You typically select file systems based on the feature you want to use and based on whether you will need to access the file system using other operating systems. If you have a FAT or FAT32 partition and want to update it to NTFS, you can use the Convert utility. The features of each file system and the procedure for converting file systems are covered in the following sections.

In this book, the terms FAT and FAT16 are used synonymously.

File System Selection

Your file system is used to store and retrieve the files stored on your hard drive. One of the most fundamental choices associated with file management is the choice of your file system's configuration. As explained in Chapter 1, "Getting Started with Windows XP Professional," Windows XP Professional supports the FAT16, FAT32, and NTFS file systems. You should choose FAT16 or FAT32 if you want to dual-boot your computer, because these file systems are backward compatible with other operating systems. Choose NTFS, however, if you want to take advantage of features such as local security, file compression, and file encryption.

Table 8.1 summarizes the capabilities of each file system, and they are described in more detail in the following sections.

TABLE 8.1   File System Capabilities

Feature	FAT16	FAT32	NTFS
Supporting operating systems	Most	Windows 95 OSR2, Windows 98, Windows Me, Windows 2000, Windows XP, and Windows Server 2003	Windows NT, Windows 2000, Windows XP, and Windows Server 2003
Long filename support	Yes	Yes	Yes
Efficient use of disk space	No	Yes	Yes
Compression support	No	No	Yes
Quota support	No	No	Yes
Encryption support	No	No	Yes
Support for local security	No	No	Yes
Support for network security	Yes	Yes	Yes
Maximum volume size	2GB	32GB	2TB

Windows XP Professional also supports *Compact Disk File System (CDFS)*.
However, CDFS cannot be managed. It is used only to mount and read CDs.

FAT16

FAT16 was first used with DOS (Disk Operating System) 3.0 in 1981. With FAT16, the directory-entry table keeps track of the location of the file's first block, the filename and extension, the date- and timestamps on the file, and any attributes associated with the file. FAT16 is similar in nature to a card catalog at a library—when the operating system needs a file, the FAT listing is consulted.

The main advantage of FAT16 is that almost all operating systems support this file system. This makes FAT16 a good choice if the computer will dual-boot with other operating systems (see Chapter 1 for more information about dual-booting). FAT16 is also a good choice for small partitions (FAT16 partitions can only be up to 2GB in size). Because FAT16 is a very simple file system, the overhead associated with storing files is much smaller than with NTFS. In addition, FAT16 partitions only support disk compression through utilities such as DRVSPACE, although this utility is not supported by Windows XP.

The problem with using FAT16 is that it was designed to be used as a single-user file system, and thus it does not support any kind of security. Prior to Windows 95, FAT16 did not support long filenames. Other file systems, such as NTFS, offer many more features, including local security, file compression, and encrypting capabilities.

FAT32

FAT32 is an updated version of FAT. FAT32 was first shipped with Windows 95 OSR2 (Operating System Release 2), and it currently ships with Windows 98. It is supported by Windows XP.

One of the main advantages of FAT32 is its support for smaller cluster sizes, which results in more efficient space allocation than was possible with FAT16. Files stored on a FAT32 partition can use 20 to 30 percent less disk space than files stored on a FAT16 partition. FAT32 supports drive sizes of up to 2TB, although if you create and format a FAT32 partition through Windows XP Professional, the FAT32 partition can only be up to 32GB. Because of the smaller cluster sizes, FAT32 can also load programs up to 50 percent faster than programs loaded from FAT16 partitions.

The main disadvantage of FAT32 is that it is not compatible with previous versions of Windows NT, including NT 4. It also offers no native support for disk compression.

NTFS

NTFS, which was first used with the NT operating system, now offers the highest level of service and features for Windows XP computers. NTFS partitions can be up to 2TB.

NTFS offers comprehensive folder- and file-level security. This allows you to set an additional level of security for users who access the files and folders locally or through the network. For example, two users who share the same Windows XP Professional computer can be assigned different NTFS permissions, so that one user has access to a folder but the other user is denied access to that folder.

NTFS also offers disk management features—such as compression, disk quotas, and encryption services—and data recovery features. The disk management features are covered later in this chapter. The data recovery features are covered in Chapter 14, "Performing System Recovery Functions."

The main drawback of using NTFS is that only the Windows NT, Windows 2000, Windows XP, and Windows Server 2003 operating systems recognize the NTFS file system. If your computer dual-boots with other operating systems, such as Windows 98, the NTFS partition will not be recognized.

You should also be aware that there are several different versions of NTFS. Windows 2000 (all versions) uses NTFS 3.0. Windows XP and Windows Server 2003 use NTFS 3.1. NTFS versions 3.0 and 3.1 use similar disk formats, so Windows 2000 computers can access NTFS 3.1 volumes and Windows XP computers can access NTFS 3.0 volumes. The features of NTFS 3.1 include:

- The ability to specify disk quotas on a per-volume basis. Quota levels are stored on NTFS volumes with three quota attributes: off, tracking, and enforced.

- When files are read or written to a disk, they can be automatically encrypted and decrypted.

- Reparse points that are used with mount points to redirect data as it is written or read from a folder to another volume or physical disk.

- Support for sparse files, which is used by programs that create large files, but only allocate disk space as needed.

 If you are upgrading Windows NT Workstation 4 to Windows XP Professional or will dual-boot Windows XP Professional with any version of Windows NT 4, you will need to apply Service Pack 4 or higher to the Windows NT 4 operating system. Windows NT 4 used a version of NTFS that is incompatible with Windows XP Professional. The Service Pack updates the `Ntfs.sys` file, which makes Windows NT 4 compatible with NTFS 3.1.

File System Conversion

In Windows XP, you can convert both FAT16 and FAT32 partitions to NTFS. File system conversion is the process of converting one file system to another without the loss of data. If you format a drive as another file system, as opposed to converting that drive, all the data on that drive will be lost.

To convert a partition, you use the *Convert* command-line utility. The syntax for the Convert command is as follows:

```
Convert [drive:] /fs:ntfs
```

For example, if you wanted to convert your D: drive to NTFS, you would type the following from a command prompt:

```
Convert D: /fs:ntfs
```

When the conversion process begins, it will attempt to lock the partition. If the partition cannot be locked—perhaps because the partition contains the Windows XP operating system files or the system's page file—the conversion will not take place until the computer is restarted.

You can use the /v switch with the Convert command. This switch specifies that you want to use verbose mode, and all messages will be displayed during the conversion process. You can also use the /NoSecurity switch, which specifies that all converted files and folders will have no security applied by default so they can be accessed by anyone.

In Exercise 8.1, you will convert your D: drive from FAT16 to NTFS.

EXERCISE 8.1

Converting a FAT16 Partition to NTFS

1. Copy some folders to the D: drive.

2. Select Start ➢ All Programs ➢ Accessories ➢ Command Prompt.

3. In the Command Prompt dialog box, type **Convert D: /fs:ntfs** and press Enter.

4. After the conversion process is complete, close the Command Prompt dialog box.

5. Verify that the folders you copied in step 1 still exist on the partition.

If you choose to convert a partition from FAT or FAT32 to NTFS, and the conversion has not yet taken place, you can cancel the conversion by editing the Registry with the REGEDIT command. The key that needs to be edited is HKEY_LOCAL_MACHINE\System\CurrentControlSet\Control\SessionManager. The value needs to be changed from autoconv \DosDevices\x: /FS:NTFS to autocheck autochk*.

Configuring Disk Storage

Windows XP Professional supports two types of disk storage: basic storage and dynamic storage. Basic storage is backward compatible with other operating systems and can be configured to support up to four partitions. Dynamic storage is supported by Windows 2000, Windows XP, and Windows Server 2003 and allows storage to be configured as volumes. The following sections describe the basic storage and dynamic storage configurations.

Basic Storage

Basic storage consists of primary and extended partitions. The first partition that is created on a hard drive is called a *primary partition*, and is usually represented as drive C:. Primary partitions use all of the space that is allocated to the partition and use a single drive letter to represent the partition. Each physical drive can have up to four partitions. You can set up four primary partitions, or you can have three primary partitions and one extended partition. With an *extended partition*, you can allocate the space however you like, and each sub-allocation of space is represented by a different drive letter. For example, a 500MB extended partition could have a 250MB D: partition and a 250MB E: partition.

At the highest level of disk organization, you have a physical hard drive. You cannot use space on the physical drive until you have logically partitioned the physical drive. A *partition* is a logical definition of hard drive space.

One of the advantages of using multiple partitions on a single physical hard drive is that each partition can have a different file system. For example, the C: drive might be FAT32 and the D: drive might be NTFS. Multiple partitions also make it easier to manage security requirements.

Laptop computers support only basic storage.

Dynamic Storage

Dynamic storage is a Windows XP feature that consists of a *dynamic disk* divided into dynamic *volumes*. Dynamic volumes cannot contain partitions or logical drives, and they are not accessible through DOS.

Dynamic storage supports three dynamic volume types: simple volumes, spanned volumes, and striped volumes. These are similar to disk configurations that were used with Windows NT Workstation 4. However, if you've upgraded from NT Workstation 4, you are using basic storage, and you can't add volume sets. Fortunately, you can upgrade from basic storage to dynamic storage, as explained in the "Upgrading a Basic Disk to a Dynamic Disk" section later in this chapter.

To set up dynamic storage, you create or upgrade a basic disk to a dynamic disk. Then you create dynamic volumes within the dynamic disk. You create dynamic storage with the Windows XP Disk Management utility, which is discussed after the descriptions of the dynamic volume types.

Simple Volumes

A *simple volume* contains space from a single dynamic drive. The space from the single drive can be contiguous or noncontiguous. Simple volumes are used when you have enough disk space on a single drive to hold your entire volume. Figure 8.1 illustrates two simple volumes on a physical disk.

FIGURE 8.1 Two simple volumes

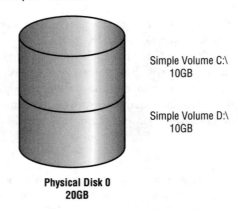

Simple Volume C:\
10GB

Simple Volume D:\
10GB

Physical Disk 0
20GB

Spanned Volumes

A *spanned volume* consists of disk space on two or more dynamic drives; up to 32 dynamic drives can be used in a spanned volume configuration. Spanned volume sets are used to dynamically increase the size of a dynamic volume. When you create spanned volumes, the data is written sequentially, filling space on one physical drive before writing to space on the next physical drive in the spanned volume set. Typically, administrators use spanned volumes when they are running out of disk space on a volume and want to dynamically extend the volume with space from another hard drive.

You do not need to allocate the same amount of space to the volume set on each physical drive. This means you could combine a 500MB partition on one physical drive with two 750MB partitions on other dynamic drives, as shown in Figure 8.2.

FIGURE 8.2 A spanned volume set

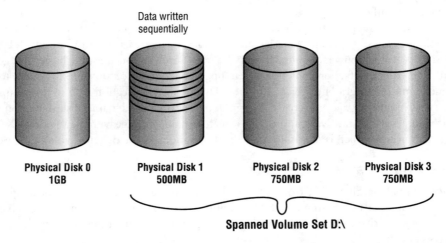

Data written
sequentially

Physical Disk 0   Physical Disk 1   Physical Disk 2   Physical Disk 3
1GB   500MB   750MB   750MB

Spanned Volume Set D:\

Because data is written sequentially, you do not see any performance enhancements with spanned volumes as you do with striped volumes (discussed next). The main disadvantage of spanned volumes is that if any drive in the spanned volume set fails, you lose access to all of the data in the spanned set.

Striped Volumes

A *striped volume* stores data in equal stripes between two or more (up to 32) dynamic drives, as illustrated in Figure 8.3. Since the data is written sequentially in the stripes, you can take advantage of multiple I/O performance and increase the speed at which data reads and writes take place. Typically, administrators use striped volumes when they want to combine the space of several physical drives into a single logical volume and increase disk performance.

FIGURE 8.3   A striped volume set

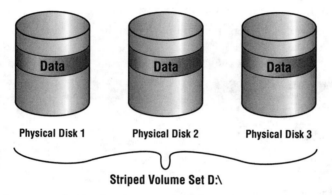

The main disadvantage of striped volumes is that if any drive in the striped volume set fails, you lose access to all of the data in the striped set.

 Mirrored volumes and RAID-5 volumes are fault-tolerant dynamic disk configurations. These options are available only with Windows 2000 Server and Windows Server 2003.

 If you created a multidisk volume—such as a spanned, mirrored, or striped set, or a striped set with parity—with Windows NT 4 or earlier, they are not supported by Windows XP Professional or Windows Server 2003.

Using the Disk Management Utility

The *Disk Management utility* is a graphical tool for managing disks and volumes within the Windows XP environment. In this section, you will learn how to access the Disk Management utility and use it to manage basic tasks, basic storage, and dynamic storage. You will also learn about troubleshooting disks through disk status codes.

To have full permissions to use the Disk Management utility, you must be logged on with Administrative privileges. To access the utility, right-click My Computer from the Start menu and select Manage, then in Computer Management, select Disk Management. You could also use Control Panel ➢ Performance and Maintenance ➢ Administrative Tools ➢ Computer Management. Expand the Storage folder to see the Disk Management utility. The Disk Management utility's opening window, shown in Figure 8.4, shows the following information:

- The volumes that are recognized by the computer
- The type of disk, either basic or dynamic
- The type of file system used by each partition
- The status of the partition and whether the partition contains the system or boot partition
- The capacity (amount of space) allocated to the partition
- The amount of free space remaining on the partition
- The amount of overhead associated with the partition

FIGURE 8.4   The Disk Management window

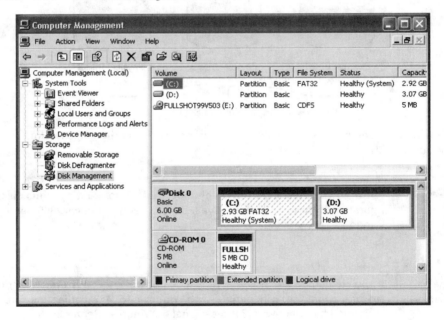

 You can also add Disk Management as a Microsoft Management Console (MMC) snap-in, as described in Chapter 4.

 Windows XP Professional includes a new command-line utility called Diskpart, which can be used as a command-line alternative to the Disk Management utility. You can view all of the options associated with the Diskpart utility by typing **Diskpart /?** from a command prompt.

Managing Basic Tasks

With the Disk Management utility, you can perform a variety of basic tasks. These tasks are discussed in the sections that follow:

- View disk properties.
- View volume and local disk properties.
- Add a new disk.
- Create partitions and volumes.
- Upgrade a basic disk to a dynamic disk.
- Change a drive letter and path.
- Delete partitions and volumes.

Viewing Disk Properties

To view the properties of a disk, right-click the disk number in the lower panel of the Disk Management main window (see Figure 8.4) and choose Properties from the pop-up menu. This brings up the Disk Properties dialog box. Click the Volumes tab to see the volumes associated with the disk, as shown in Figure 8.5, which contains the following disk properties:

- The disk number
- The type of disk (basic, dynamic, CD-ROM, removable, DVD, or unknown)
- The status of the disk (online or offline)
- The capacity of the disk
- The amount of unallocated space on the disk
- The logical volumes that have been defined on the physical drive

FIGURE 8.5 The Volumes tab of the Disk Properties dialog box

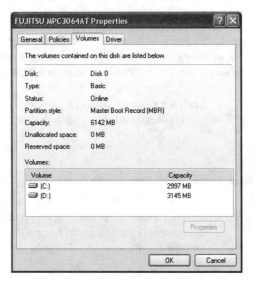

If you click on the General tab of Disk Properties, the hardware device type, the hardware vendor who produced the drive, the physical location of the drive, and the device status are displayed.

Viewing Volume and Local Disk Properties

On a dynamic disk, you manage volume properties. On a basic disk, you manage local disk properties. Volumes and local disks perform the same function, and the options discussed in the following sections apply to both. (The examples here are based on a dynamic disk using a simple volume. If you are using basic storage, you will view the local disk properties rather than the volume properties.)

To see the properties of a volume, right-click the volume in the upper panel of the Disk Management main window and choose Properties. This brings up the volume Properties dialog box. Volume properties are organized on six tabs: General, Tools, Hardware, Sharing, Security, and Quota. The Security and Quota tabs appear only for NTFS volumes. All these tabs are covered in detail in the following sections.

If the Security and Sharing tabs do not appear for your NTFS partition, and you are not a part of a domain, then Simple File Sharing is probably enabled, which will keep this option from appearing. To disable Simple File Sharing, from My Computer, select Tools, then Folder Options. In Advanced Settings on the View Tab, clear the box for Use Simple File Sharing (Recommended).

General

The information on the General tab of the volume Properties dialog box, as seen in Figure 8.6, gives you a general idea of how the volume is configured. This dialog box shows the label, type, file system, used and free space, and capacity of the volume. The label is shown in an editable text box, and you can change it if desired. The space allocated to the volume is shown in a graphical representation as well as in text form.

The label on a volume or local disk is for informational purposes only. For example, depending on its use, you might give a volume a label such as APPS or ACCTDB.

The Disk Cleanup button starts the Disk Cleanup utility, with which you can delete unnecessary files and free disk space. This utility is discussed later in this chapter in the "Using the Disk Cleanup Utility" section.

Tools

The Tools tab of the volume Properties dialog box, shown in Figure 8.7, provides access to three tools:

- Click the Check Now button to run the Check Disk utility to check the volume for errors. You would do this if you were experiencing problems accessing the volume, or if the volume had been open during a system restart that did not go through a proper shutdown sequence. This utility is covered in more detail in "Troubleshooting Disk Devices and Volumes" later in this chapter.

- Click the Defragment Now button to run the Disk Defragmenter utility. This utility defragments files on the volume by storing the files contiguously on the hard drive. Defragmentation is discussed later in this chapter, in the "Defragmenting Disks" section.
- Click the Backup Now button to run the Backup or Restore Wizard, which steps you through backing up the files on the volume. Backup procedures are covered in Chapter 14.

FIGURE 8.6 General properties for a volume

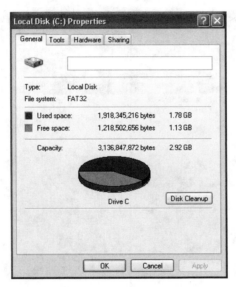

FIGURE 8.7 The Tools tab of the volume's Properties dialog box

Hardware

The Hardware tab of the volume Properties dialog box, shown in Figure 8.8, lists the hardware associated with the disk drives that are recognized by the Windows XP Professional operating system. The bottom half of the dialog box shows the properties of the device that is highlighted in the top half of the dialog box.

FIGURE 8.8   The Hardware tab of the volume Properties dialog box

For more details about a hardware item, highlight it and click the Properties button in the lower-right corner of the dialog box. This brings up a Properties dialog box for the item (for example, Figure 8.9). With luck, your Device Status field will report that "This device is working properly." If that's not the case, you can click the Troubleshoot button to get a troubleshooting wizard that will help you discover what the problem is.

Sharing

In the Sharing tab of the volume Properties dialog box, shown in Figure 8.10, you can specify whether or not the volume is shared. All volumes are shared by default. The share name is the drive letter followed by a $ (dollar sign). The $ indicates that the share is hidden. From this dialog box, you can set the user limit, permissions, and cacheing for the share. Sharing is covered in Chapter 9, "Accessing Files and Folders."

Security

The Security tab of the volume Properties dialog box, shown in Figure 8.11, appears only for NTFS volumes. The Security tab is used to set the NTFS permissions for the volume.

FIGURE 8.9   A disk drive's Properties dialog box accessed through the Hardware tab of the volume Properties dialog box

FIGURE 8.10   The Sharing tab of the volume Properties dialog box

FIGURE 8.11   The Security tab of the volume Properties dialog box

Notice that the default permissions allow the Everyone group Full Control permissions at the root of the volume. This could cause major security problems if any user decides to manipulate or delete the data within the volume. Managing NTFS security is covered in Chapter 9.

Quota

Like the Security tab, the Quota tab of the volume Properties dialog box appears only for an NTFS volume. Through this tab, you can limit the amount of space available to users within the volume. Quotas are covered in detail in the later section "Setting Disk Quotas."

Adding a New Disk

To increase the amount of disk storage you have, you can add a new disk. This is a fairly common task that you will need to perform as your application programs and files grow larger. How you add a disk depends on whether your computer supports hot swapping of drives. *Hot swapping* is the process of adding a new hard drive while the computer is turned on. Most computers do not support this capability.

If your computer supports hot swapping, the following list specifies configuration options:

Computer doesn't support hot swapping   If your computer does not support hot swapping, you must first shut down the computer before you add a new disk. Then add the drive according to the manufacturer's directions. When you're finished, restart the computer. You should find the new drive listed in the Disk Management utility.

Computer supports hot swapping   If your computer does support hot swapping, you don't need to turn off your computer first. Just add the drive according to the manufacturer's directions. Then open the Disk Management utility and select Action ➤ Rescan Disks. You should find the new drive listed in the Disk Management utility.

> You must be a member of the Administrators group in order to install a new drive.

Creating Partitions and Volumes

Once you add a new disk, the next step is to create a partition (on a basic disk) or a volume (on a dynamic disk). Partitions and volumes fill similar roles in storage of data on disks, and the processes for creating them are similar as well.

Creating a Volume

The Create Volume Wizard guides you through the process of creating a new volume, as follows:

1. In the Disk Management utility, right-click an area of free storage space and choose New Volume Logical Drive.

2. The Welcome to the New Partition Wizard dialog box appears. Click the Next button to continue.

3. The Select Volume Type dialog box appears, as shown in Figure 8.12. In this dialog box, select the type of volume you want to create: simple, spanned, or striped. Only the options supported by your computer's hardware configuration are available. Click the radio button for the type, and then click Next to continue.

FIGURE 8.12   The Select Volume Type dialog box

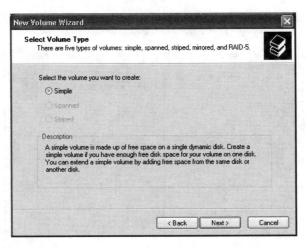

4. The Select Disks dialog box appears, as shown in Figure 8.13. Here, you select the disk and specify the maximum volume size, up to the amount of free disk space that is recognized. Choose the disk that you want the volume to be created on and click the Next button.

FIGURE 8.13   The Select Disks dialog box

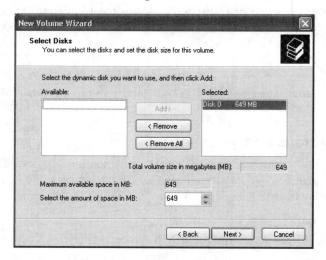

5. Next you see the Assign Drive Letter or Path page of the wizard, as shown in Figure 8.14. You can specify a drive letter, mount the volume as an empty folder, or choose not to assign a drive letter or drive path. If you choose to mount the volume as an empty folder, you can have an unlimited number of volumes, negating the drive-letter limitation. Make your selections, and click Next to continue.

If you choose not to assign a drive letter or path, users will not be able to access the volume.

FIGURE 8.14   The Assign Drive Letter or Path dialog box

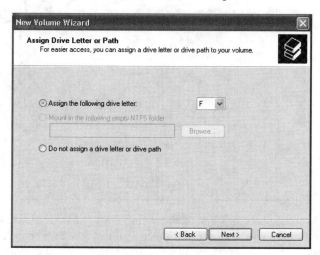

6. The Format Volume dialog box appears, as shown in Figure 8.15. This dialog box allows you to choose whether you will format the volume. If you choose to format the volume, you can format it as FAT, FAT32, or NTFS. You can also select the allocation block size, enter a volume label (for information only), specify a quick format, or choose to enable file and folder compression. After you've made your choices, click the Next button.

FIGURE 8.15   The Format Volume dialog box

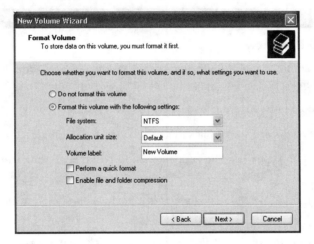

 Specifying a quick format is risky because this format does not scan the disk for bad sectors, which is done in a normal format operation.

7. The Completing the Create Volume Wizard dialog box appears next. Verify your selections. If you need to change any of them, click the Back button to reach the appropriate dialog box. When everything is correctly set, click the Finish button.

Creating a Partition

The steps to create a logical drive are similar to the steps for creating a volume, which were covered in the preceding section. When you right-click an area of free space in the Disk Management utility and select the Create Logical Drive option, the New Partition Wizard starts. This wizard displays a series of dialog boxes to guide you through the process of creating a partition:

- In the Select Partition Type dialog box, you select the type of partition you want to create: a primary partition, an extended partition, or a logical drive.

- In the Specify Partition Size dialog box, you specify the maximum partition size, up to the amount of free disk space that is recognized.

- In the Assign Drive Letter or Path dialog box, you assign a drive letter or a drive path. There is also an option to leave the drive letter or path unassigned; but if you enable this option, users will not be able to access the volume. (This "unassigned" option is only used when you have already allocated all 26-drive letters and is not often implemented.)

- The Format Partition dialog box lets you specify whether you want to format the partition. If you choose to format the partition, you can select the file system, allocation unit size, and volume label. You can also choose to perform a quick format and to enable file and folder compression.

In Exercise 8.2, you will create a partition from the free space that was left on your drive when you installed Windows XP Professional (in Exercise 1.1), as specified in Chapter 1.

EXERCISE 8.2

Creating a New Partition

1. Select Start ≻ Control Panel ≻ Performance and Maintenance ≻ Administrative Tools. Double-click Computer Management, then expand Storage, then Disk Management.

2. Right-click an area of free storage and select the New Partition option.

3. The New Partition Wizard starts. Click the Next button to continue.

4. The Select Partition Type dialog box appears. Choose Primary Partition and click the Next button.

5. The Specify Partition Size dialog box appears. Specify a partition size of 250MB and click the Next button.

6. The Assign Drive Letter or Path dialog box appears. Click Next to assign the default drive letter shown in this dialog box. If you are using the recommended configuration, C: and D: are assigned as drive letters, E: should be your CD-ROM drive, and the next available drive will be F:.

7. In the Format Partition dialog box, choose to format the drive as NTFS and leave the other settings at their default values. Click the Next button.

8. The Completing the New Partition Wizard dialog box appears. Click the Finish button.

Upgrading a Basic Disk to a Dynamic Disk

When you install Windows XP Professional or upgrade your computer from Windows NT 4 to Windows XP Professional, your drives are configured as basic disks. To take advantage of the features offered by Windows XP dynamic disks, you must upgrade your basic disks to dynamic disks.

Upgrading basic disks to dynamic disks is a one-way process as far as preserving data is concerned and a potentially dangerous operation. If you decide to revert to a basic disk, you will have to first delete all volumes associated with the drive; then, in the Disk Management utility, you can select Convert to Basic Disk. Before you do this upgrade (or make any major change to your drives or volumes), create a new backup of the drive or volume and verify that you can successfully restore the backup.

The following steps are involved in the disk-upgrade process:

1. In the Disk Management utility, right-click the disk you want to convert, and select the Upgrade to Dynamic Disk option.

2. In the Upgrade to Dynamic Disk dialog box, check the disk that you want to upgrade and click the OK button.

3. In the Disks to Convert dialog box, click the Convert button.

4. A confirmation dialog box warns you that you will no longer be able to boot previous versions of Windows from this disk. Click the Yes button to continue.

5. Another confirmation dialog box warns you that any file systems mounted on the disk will be dismounted. Click Yes to continue.

6. If you are upgrading the disk that contains the system or boot partition, an information dialog box tells you that a reboot is required to complete the upgrade. Click the OK button. Your computer will restart, and the disk-upgrade process is complete.

Changing the Drive Letter and Path

Suppose that you have drive C: assigned as your first partition and drive D: assigned as your CD drive. You add a new drive and partition it as a new volume. By default, the new partition is assigned as drive E:. If you want your logical drives to appear listed before the CD drive, you can use the Disk Management utility's Change Drive Letter and Path option to rearrange your drive letters.

When you need to reassign drive letters, right-click the volume for which you want to change the drive letter and choose Change Drive Letter and Paths. This brings up the dialog box shown in Figure 8.16. Click the Change button to access the Change Drive Letter or Path dialog box (Figure 8.17). Use the drop-down list next to the Assign the Following Drive Letter option to select the drive letter you want to assign to the volume.

FIGURE 8.16   The dialog box for changing a drive letter or path

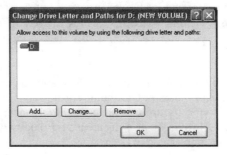

FIGURE 8.17   Editing the drive letter

In Exercise 8.3, you will edit the drive letter of the partition you created in Exercise 8.2.

EXERCISE 8.3

Editing a Drive Letter

1. Select Start ➤ Control Panel ➤ Performance and Maintenance ➤ Administrative Tools. Double-click Computer Management, then expand Storage, then Disk Management.

2. Right-click the drive you created in Exercise 8.2 and select Change Drive Letter and Path.

3. In the Change Drive Letter and Paths dialog box, click the Change button.

4. In the Change Drive Letter or Path dialog box, select a new drive letter and click the OK button.

5. In the dialog box that appears, click the Yes button to confirm that you want to change the drive letter.

Deleting Partitions and Volumes

You might delete a partition or volume if you wanted to reorganize your disk, or to make sure that data would not be accessed.

Once you delete a partition or volume, it is gone forever.

To delete a partition or volume, in the Disk Management window right-click the partition or volume and choose the Delete Volume (or Delete Partition) option. You will see a warning that all the data on the partition or volume will be lost. Click Yes to confirm that you want to delete the volume or partition.

The system volume, the boot volume, or any volume that contains the active paging (swap) file can't be deleted through the Disk Management utility. If you are trying to remove these partitions because you want to delete Windows XP Professional, you can use third-party disk management utilities, such as Partition Magic or Delpart.

Managing Basic Storage

The Disk Management utility offers limited support for managing basic storage. You can create, delete, and format partitions on basic drives. You also can delete volume sets and striped sets that were created under Windows NT. Most other disk-management tasks require that you upgrade your drive to dynamic disks. (The upgrade process was described in the earlier section, "Upgrading a Basic Disk to a Dynamic Disk.")

Managing Dynamic Storage

As noted earlier in this chapter, a dynamic disk can contain simple, spanned, or striped volumes. Through the Disk Management utility, you can create volumes of each type. You can also create an extended volume, which is the process of adding disk space to a single simple volume. The following sections describe these disk-management tasks.

Creating Simple, Spanned, and Striped Volumes

As explained earlier in "Creating Partitions and Volumes," you use the Create Volume Wizard to create a new volume. To start the wizard, in the Disk Management utility right-click an area of free space where you want to create the volume. Choose Create Volume. When the wizard displays the Select Volume Type dialog box, choose the type of volume you want to create.

When you choose to create a spanned volume, you are creating a new volume from scratch that includes space from two or more physical drives, up to a maximum of 32 drives. You can create spanned volumes that are formatted as FAT, FAT32, or NTFS.

When you choose to create a striped volume, you are creating a new volume that combines free space from two to 32 drives into a single logical partition. The free space on all drives must be equal in size. Data in the striped volume is written across all drives in 64KB stripes. (Data in spanned and extended volumes is written sequentially.)

Creating Extended Volumes

When you create an extended volume, you are taking a single, simple volume (maybe one that is almost out of disk space) and adding more disk space to it, using free space that exists on the same physical hard drive. When the volume is extended, it is seen as a single drive letter. To extend a volume, the simple volume must be formatted as NTFS. You cannot extend a system or boot partition.

An extended volume assumes that you are only using one physical drive. A spanned volume assumes that you are using two or more physical drives.

Here are the steps to create an extended volume:

1. In the Disk Management utility, right-click the volume you want to extend and choose Extend Volume.

2. The Extend Volume Wizard starts. Click the Next button.

3. The Select Disks dialog box appears, as shown in Figure 8.18. You can specify the maximum size of the extended volume. The maximum size you can specify is determined by the amount of free space that exists in all of the dynamic drives on your computer.

FIGURE 8.18 The Select Disks dialog box

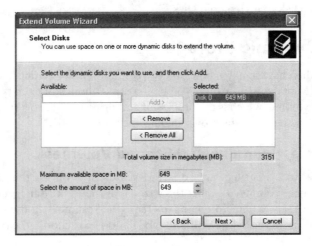

4. The Completing the Extend Volume Wizard dialog box appears. Click the Finish button.

WARNING Once a volume is extended, no portion of the volume can be deleted without losing data on the entire set.

🌐 Real World Scenario

You're Running Out of Disk Space

Martha, a user on your network, is running out of disk space. The situation needs to be corrected so she can be brought back up and running as quickly as possible. Martha has a 10GB drive (C:) that runs a customer database. She needs additional space added to the C: drive so the database will recognize the data, since it must be stored on a single drive letter. Martha's computer has a single IDE drive with nothing attached to the second IDE channel.

You have two basic options for managing space in these circumstances. One is to upgrade the disk to a larger disk, but this will necessitate reinstalling the OS and the applications, and restoring the user's data. The other choice is to add a temporary second drive and extend the volume. This will at least allow Martha to be up and running—but it should not be considered a permanent solution. If you do choose to extend the volume, and then either drive within the volume set fails, the user will lose access to both drives. When Martha's workload allows time for maintenance, you can replace the volume set with a single drive.

Troubleshooting Disk Management

The Disk Management utility can be used to troubleshoot disk errors through a set of status codes; however, if a disk will not initialize, no status code will be displayed. Disks will not initialize if there is not a valid disk signature.

Using Disk Management Status Codes

The main window of the Disk Management utility displays the status of disks and volumes. The following list contains the possible status codes and a description of each code; these are very useful in troubleshooting disk problems.

Online   Indicates that the disk is accessible and that it is functioning properly. This is the normal disk status.

Online (Errors)   Only used with dynamic disks. Indicates that I/O errors have been detected on the dynamic disk. One possible fix for this error is to right-click the disk and select Reactivate Disk to attempt to return the disk to Online status. This fix will work only if the I/O errors were temporary. You should immediately back up your data if you see this error and suspect that the I/O errors are not temporary.

Healthy   Specifies that the volume is accessible and functioning properly.

Healthy (At Risk)   Used to indicate that a dynamic volume is currently accessible, but I/O errors have been detected on the underlying dynamic disk. This option is usually associated with Online (Errors) for the underlying disk.

Offline or Missing   Only used with dynamic disks. Indicates that the disk is not accessible. This can occur if the disk is corrupt or the hardware has failed. If the error is not caused by hardware failure or major corruption, you may be able to re-access the disk by using the Reactivate Disk option to return the disk to Online status. If the disk was originally offline and then the status changed to Missing, it indicates that the disk has become corrupt, been powered down, or was disconnected.

Unreadable   This can occur on basic or dynamic disks. Indicates that the disk is inaccessible and might have encountered hardware errors, corruption, or I/O errors, or that the system disk configuration database is corrupt. This message may also appear when a disk is spinning up while the Disk Management utility is rescanning the disks on the computer.

Failed   Can be seen with basic or dynamic volumes. Specifies that the volume can't be started. This can occur because the disk is damaged or the file system is corrupt. If this message occurs with a basic volume, you should check the underlying disk hardware. If the error occurs on a dynamic volume, verify that the underlying disks are Online.

Unknown   Used with basic and dynamic volumes. Occurs if the boot sector for the volume becomes corrupt—for example, from a virus. This error can also occur if no disk signature is created for the volume.

Incomplete   Occurs when you move some, but not all, of the disks from a multidisk volume. If you do not complete the multivolume set, then the data will be inaccessible.

Foreign Can occur if you move a dynamic disk from one computer to another computer running Windows 2000 (any version) or Windows XP Professional. This error is caused because configuration data is unique to computers where the dynamic disk was created. You can correct this error by right-clicking the disk and selecting the option Import Foreign Disks. Any existing volume information will then be visible and accessible.

Troubleshooting Disks That Fail to Initialize

When you add a new disk to your computer in Windows XP Professional, the disk does not initially contain a disk signature, which is required for the disk to be recognized by Windows XP Professional. Disk signatures are at the end of the sector marker on the Master Boot Record (MBR) of the drive. When you install a new drive and run the Disk Management utility, a wizard starts and lists all new disks that have been detected. The disk signature is written through this process. If you cancel the wizard before the disk signature is written, you will see the disk status Not Initialized.

To initialize a disk, you right-click the disk you want to initialize and select the Initialize Disk option. If you are running a 32-bit edition of Windows XP Professional, you will write the disk signature to the MBR of the drive. If you are using Windows XP 64-bit edition, you can write the signature to the MBR or the GUID Partition Table (GPT).

Managing Data Compression

Data compression is the process of storing data in a form that takes less space than does uncompressed data. If you have ever "zipped" or "packed" a file, you have used data compression. With Windows XP, data compression is available only on NTFS partitions. You can manage data compression through Windows Explorer or the Compact command-line utility.

Files as well as folders in the NTFS file system can be either compressed or uncompressed. Files and folders are managed independently, which means that a compressed folder can contain uncompressed files, and an uncompressed folder can contain compressed files.

Access to compressed files by DOS or Windows applications is transparent. For example, if you access a compressed file through Microsoft Word, the file will be uncompressed automatically when it is opened, and then automatically compressed again when it is closed.

Data compression is available only on NTFS partitions. If you copy or move a compressed folder or file to a FAT partition (or a floppy disk), Windows XP will automatically uncompress the folder or file.

Windows XP Professional does not allow you to have a folder or file compressed and encrypted at the same time. A new feature with Windows Server 2003 is that it supports concurrent compression and encryption. Encryption is discussed in the "Managing Data Encryption with EFS" section later in this chapter.

In Exercise 8.4, you will compress and uncompress folders and files. This exercise assumes that you have completed Exercise 8.1.

EXERCISE 8.4

Compressing and Uncompressing Folders and Files

1. Select Start ➤ Run, then type **Explorer** and click OK.

2. In Windows Explorer, find and select My Computer, the Local Disk (D:), then a folder on the D: drive. The folder you select should contain files.

3. Right-click the folder and select Properties. In the General tab of the folder Properties dialog box, note the value listed for Size on Disk. Then click the Advanced button.

4. In the Advanced Attributes dialog box, check the Compress Contents to Save Disk Space option. Then click the OK button.

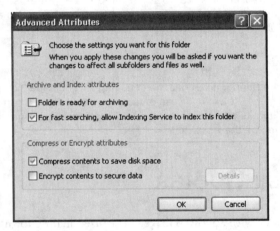

5. In the Confirm Attribute Changes dialog box, select the option to Apply Changes to This Folder, Subfolders and Files. (If this confirmation dialog box does not appear, you can display it by clicking the Apply button in the Properties dialog box.) Click the OK button to confirm your changes.

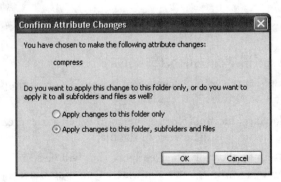

6. In the General tab of the folder Properties dialog box, note the value that now appears for Size on Disk. This size should have decreased because you compressed the folder.

To uncompress folders and files, repeat the steps of this exercise and uncheck the Compress Contents to Save Disk Space option in the Advanced Attributes dialog box.

You can specify that compressed files be displayed in a different color from the uncompressed files. To do so, in Windows Explorer, select Tools ➢ Folder Options ➢ Views. Under Files and Folders, check the Display Compressed Files and Folders with an Alternate Color option.

The command-line options for managing file and folder compression are Compact and Expand. You can access these commands from a command prompt. For more details on each command and associated options, type the command, followed by the /? switch.

Setting Disk Quotas

Suppose you have a server with an 18GB drive that is used mainly for users' home folders, and you start getting "out of disk space" error messages. On closer inspection, you find that a single user has taken up 10GB of space by storing multimedia files that she has downloaded from the Internet. This type of problem can be avoided through the use of disk quotas. *Disk quotas* are used to specify the amount of disk space a user is allowed on specific NTFS volumes. You can specify disk quotas for all users, or you can limit disk space on a per-user basis.

Before you administer disk quotas, keep in mind the following aspects of disk quota management:

- Disk quotas can be specified only for NTFS volumes.

- Disk quotas apply only at the volume level, even if the NTFS partitions reside on the same physical hard drive.

- Disk usage is calculated on file and folder ownership. When a user creates, copies, or takes ownership of a file, that user is the owner of the file.

- When a user installs an application, the free space that will be seen by the application is based on the disk quota availability, not on the actual amount of free space on the volume. The user also only sees the space available as defined by the quota limitation.

- The calculation of disk quota space used is based on actual file size. There is no mechanism to support or recognize file compression.

 Disk quotas are not applied to or enforced for the Administrator account or for members of the Administrators group.

The following sections describe how to set up and monitor disk quotas.

Configuring Disk Quotas

You configure disk quotas through the NTFS volume Properties dialog box (discussed in detail in the earlier section, "Managing Basic Tasks"). You learned that you can access the volume's Properties dialog box in the Disk Management utility by right-clicking the drive letter and selecting Properties from the pop-up menu. Another way to access this dialog box is from Windows Explorer—just right-click the drive letter in the Explorer listing and select Properties. In the volume's Properties dialog box, click the Quota tab to see the dialog box shown in Figure 8.19. When you open the Quota tab, you will see that disk quotas are disabled by default.

FIGURE 8.19 The Quota tab of the volume Properties dialog box

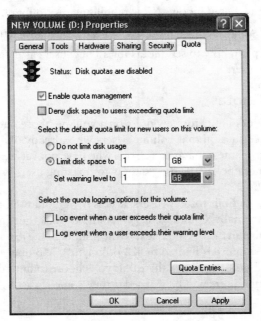

Table 8.2 describes the options that can be configured through the Quota tab.

TABLE 8.2 Disk Quota Configuration Options

Option	Description
Enable quota management	Specifies whether quota management is enabled for the volume.
Deny disk space to users exceeding the quota limit	Specifies that users who exceed their disk quota will not be able to override their disk allocation. Those users will receive "out of disk space" error messages.
Select the default quota limit for new users on this volume	Allows you to define quota limits for new users. Options include not limiting disk space, limiting disk space, and specifying warning levels.
Select the quota logging options for this volume	Specifies whether logged events that relate to quotas will be recorded. You can enable the logging of events for users exceeding quota limits or users exceeding warning limits.

Notice the traffic light icon in the upper-left corner of the Quota tab. It indicates the status of disk quotas, as follows:

- A red light means that disk quotas are disabled.
- A yellow light means that Windows XP is rebuilding disk quota information.
- A green light means that the disk quota system is enabled and active.

The next sections explain how to set quotas for all new users as default quotas, and how to set quotas for a specific user.

Setting Default Quotas

When you set default quota limits for new users on a volume, those quotas apply only to users who have not yet created files on that volume. Users who already own files or folders on the volume will be exempt from the quota policy. Users who have not yet created a file on the volume will be bound by the quota policy. (Setting quotas for existing users is covered in "Setting an Individual Quota," below.)

To set the default quota limit for new users, access the Quota tab of the volume Properties dialog box and check the Enable Quota Management box. Click the Limit Disk Space To radio button, and enter a number in the first box next to the option. In the drop-down list in the second box, specify whether disk space is limited by KB (kilobytes), MB (megabytes), GB (gigabytes), TB (terabytes), PB (petabytes), or EB (exabytes). If you choose to limit disk space, you can also set a warning level, so that users will be warned if they come close to reaching their limit.

If you want to apply disk quotas for all users, apply the quota when the volume is first created. That way, no users will have already created files on the volume, and thus, they will not be exempt from the quota limit.

In Exercise 8.5, you will set a default quota limit on your D: drive. This exercise assumes that you have completed Exercise 8.1.

EXERCISE 8.5

Applying Default Quota Limits

1. Use the Local Users and Groups utility to create two new users, **Shannon** and **Dana**. (See Chapter 6, "Managing Users and Groups," for details on creating user accounts.) Deselect the User Must Change Password at Next Logon option for each user.

2. Log off as Administrator and log on as Shannon. Drag and drop some folders to drive D:.

3. Log on as Administrator. Select Start ➤ Run, then type **Explorer**.

4. In Windows Explorer, expand My Computer. Right-click Local Disk (D:) and select Properties.

5. In the Local Disk Properties dialog box, select the Quota tab.

6. Check the Enable Quota Management check box.

7. Click the Limit Disk Space To radio button. Specify 5MB as the limit. Specify the Set Warning Level To value as 4MB.

8. Click the Apply button, then click the OK button.

9. Log off as Administrator and log on as Dana. Drag and drop folders that total more than 5MB to drive D:. You should see a warning when 4MB worth of files are copied and not be allowed to copy additional files after you reach the 5MB limit.

10. Log off as Dana and log on as Administrator.

Setting an Individual Quota

You can also set quotas for individual users. There are several reasons for setting quotas this way:

-   You can set restrictions on other users and at the same time allow a user who routinely updates your applications to have unlimited disk space.

-   You can set warnings at lower levels for a user who routinely exceeds disk space.

-   You can apply the quota to users who already had files on the volume before the quota was implemented and thus have been granted unlimited disk space.

To set an individual quota, click the Quota Entries button in the bottom-right corner of the Quota tab. This brings up the dialog box shown in Figure 8.20. To modify a user's quota, double-click that user. This brings up a dialog box similar to the one shown in Figure 8.21. Here, you can specify whether the user's disk space should be limited, and you can set the limit and the warning level.

FIGURE 8.20   The Quota Entries for volume dialog box

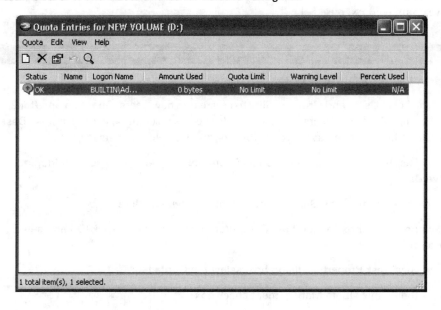

FIGURE 8.21   The quota settings for a user

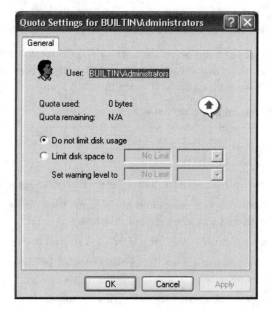

You can also modify the quotas of several users at once by pressing Ctrl while clicking to highlight several users and selecting Quota ➢ Properties.

In Exercise 8.6, you will configure the quotas for individual users. This exercise assumes that you have completed Exercise 8.5.

Applying Individual Quota Limits

1. Select Start ➤ Run and type **Explorer**.

2. In Windows Explorer, expand My Computer. Right-click Local Disk (D:) and select Properties.

3. In the Local Disk Properties dialog box, select the Quota tab. Then click the Quota Entries button.

4. Double-click user Dana to bring up his Quota Settings dialog box. Notice that Dana has limited disk space. Click the Do Not Limit Disk Usage radio button. Click the Apply button and then click the OK button.

Monitoring Disk Quotas

If you implement disk quotas, you will want to monitor the quotas on a regular basis. This allows you to check disk usage by all users who own files on the volume with those quotas applied.

It is especially important to monitor quotas if you have specified that disk space should be denied to users who exceeded their quota limit. Otherwise, some users may not be able to get their work done. For example, suppose that you have set a limit for all users on a specific volume. Your boss tries to save a file she has been working on all afternoon, but she gets an "out of disk space" error message because she has exceeded her disk quota. Although your intentions of setting up and using disk quotas were good, the boss is still cranky.

Disk quota monitoring is accomplished through the Quota Entries dialog box (see Figure 8.20), which appears when you click the Quota Entries button in the Quota tab of the volume Properties dialog box. The dialog box shows the following information:

- The status of the user's disk quota, represented as follows:
    - A green arrow in a dialog bubble means the status is OK.
    - An exclamation point in a yellow triangle means the warning threshold has been exceeded.
    - An exclamation point in a red circle means the user threshold has been exceeded.
- The name and logon name of the user who has stored files on the volume
- The amount of disk space consumed by the user on the volume
- The user's quota limit
- The user's warning level
- The percentage of disk space consumed by the user in relation to their disk quota

Managing Data Encryption with EFS

Data encryption is a way to increase data security. Encryption is the process of translating data into code that is not easily accessible. Once data has been encrypted, you must have a password or key to decrypt the data. Unencrypted data is known as *plain text*, and encrypted data is known as *cipher text*.

The *Encrypting File System (EFS)* is the Windows XP technology that is used to store encrypted files on NTFS partitions. Encrypted files add an extra layer of security to your file system. A user with the proper key can transparently access encrypted files. A user without the proper key is denied access. If the user who encrypted the files is unavailable, you can use the *data recovery agent (DRA)* to provide the proper key to decrypt folders or files.

In the following sections you will learn about the new features for EFS for Windows XP and Windows Server 2003, how to create and manage DRAs, how to recover encrypted files, how to share encrypted files, and how to use the Cipher utility.

New EFS Features in Windows XP and Windows Server 2003

The functionality of EFS has been improved in Windows XP Professional and Windows Server 2003. The enhanced and new features include:

- Automatically color codes encrypted files in green text, so you can easily identify files that have been encrypted
- Support so that offline folders can also be encrypted
- A shell user interface (UI) that is used to support encrypted files for multiple users
- Improved performance and reliability
- New security features that better protect EFS data
- Improved recovery policy

Encrypting and Decrypting Folders and Files

To use EFS, a user specifies that a folder or file on an NTFS partition should be encrypted. The encryption is transparent to that user, who has access to the file. However, when other users try to access the file, they will not be able to unencrypt the file—even if those users have Full Control NTFS permissions. Instead, they will receive an error message.

To encrypt a folder or a file, take the following steps:

1. Select Start ➢ Run and type **Explorer**.
2. In Windows Explorer, find and select the folder or file you wish to encrypt.
3. Right-click the folder or file and select Properties from the pop-up menu.
4. In the General tab of the folder or file Properties dialog box, click the Advanced button.

5. The Advanced Attributes dialog box appears. Check the Encrypt Contents to Secure Data check box. Then click the OK button.

6. The Confirm Attribute Changes dialog box appears. Specify whether you want to apply encryption only to this folder (Apply Changes to This Folder Only) or to the subfolders and files in the folder, as well (Apply Changes to This Folder, Subfolders and Files). Then click the OK button.

To decrypt folders and files, repeat these steps, but uncheck the Encrypt Contents to Secure Data option in the Advanced Attributes dialog box.

In Exercise 8.7, you will use EFS to encrypt a folder. This exercise assumes that you have completed Exercise 8.1.

EXERCISE 8.7

Using EFS to Manage Data Encryption

1. Use the Local Users and Groups utility to create the new user **Lauren**. (See Chapter 6 for details on creating user accounts.) Deselect the User Must Change Password at Next Logon option for this user.

2. Select Start ➤ Run and type **Explorer**.

3. In Windows Explorer, find and select a folder on the D: drive. The folder you select should contain files. Right-click the folder and select Properties.

4. In the General tab of the folder Properties dialog box, click the Advanced button.

5. In the Advanced Attributes dialog box, check the Encrypt Contents to Secure Data option. Then click the OK button.

6. In the Confirm Attribute Changes dialog box (if this dialog box does not appear, click the Apply button in the Properties dialog box to display it), select Apply Changes to This Folder, Subfolders and Files. Then click the OK button.

7. Log off as Administrator and log on as Lauren.

8. Open Windows Explorer and attempt to access one of the files in the folder you encrypted. You should receive an error message stating that the file is not accessible.

9. Log off as Lauren and log on as Administrator.

Managing EFS File Sharing

In Windows 2000 and Windows XP Professional, only one user can use or access a folder that has been encrypted. However, Windows XP Professional does allow you to support EFS file sharing at the file level (as opposed to the folder level). By implementing EFS file sharing, you provide an additional level of recovery in the event that the person who encrypted the files is unavailable.

To implement EFS file sharing, you would take the following steps:

1. Encrypt the file if it is not already encrypted (see previous section for instructions).

2. Through Windows Explorer, access the encrypted file's properties, as shown in Figure 8.22. At the bottom of the dialog box, click the Advanced button.

FIGURE 8.22 An encrypted file's Properties dialog box

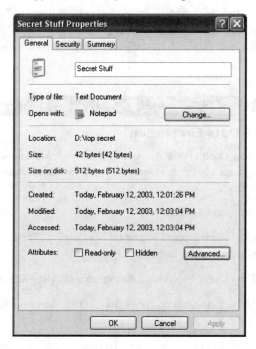

3. The Advanced Attributes dialog box will appear, as shown in Figure 8.23.

FIGURE 8.23 Advanced Attributes dialog box

4. In the Compress or Encrypt Attributes section of the Advanced Attributes dialog box, click the Details button, which brings up the Encryption Details dialog box shown in Figure 8.24.

FIGURE 8.24   Encryption Details dialog box

5. In the Encryption Details dialog box, click the Add button to add any additional users (provided they have a valid certificate for EFS in the Active Directory) who should have access to the encrypted file.

Using the DRA to Recover Encrypted Files

If the user who encrypted the folders or files is unavailable to decrypt the folders or files when they're needed, you can use the data recovery agent (DRA) to access the encrypted files. DRAs are implemented differently depending on the version of your operating system and the configuration of your computer.

- For Windows 2000 Professional and Windows 2000 Server computers, a DRA was mandatory, and EFS could not be used if a DRA was not in place. For Windows 2000 Professional computers that were installed as a part of the Active Directory, the domain Administrator user account is automatically assigned the role of the DRA. If the Windows 2000 Professional computer was not a part of the Active Directory, then the local Administrator user account is automatically assigned the role of DRA.

- For Windows XP Professional computers that are a part of a Windows 2000 or Windows 2003 Active Directory domain, the domain Administrator user account is automatically assigned the role of DRA.

- For Windows XP Professional computers that are installed as stand-alone computers or if the computer is a part of a workgroup, no default DRA is assigned.

You should use extreme caution when using EFS on a stand-alone Windows XP Professional computer. If the user who encrypts the files is unavailable, there is no default recovery process, and all access to the files will be lost.

Creating a DRA on a Stand-Alone Windows XP Professional Computer

If Windows XP Professional is installed as a stand-alone computer or on a computer that is part of a workgroup, then no DRA is created by default. To manually create a DRA, you use the Cipher command-line utility as follows:

Cipher /R:*filename*

The /R switch is used to generate two files, one with a .pfx extension and one with a .cer extension. The .pfx file is used for data recovery and the .cer file includes a self-signed EFS recovery agent certificate. The .cer file (self-signed public key certificate) can then be imported into the local security policy and the .pfx file (private key) can be stored in a secure location.

Once you have created the public and private keys to be used with EFS, you can specify the DRA through Local Security Policy, using the following steps:

1. Through Local Security Policy, which can be accessed through Administrative Tools or the Local Computer Policy MMC snap-in (see Exercise 7.1), expand Public Key Policies ➢ Encrypting File System, as shown in Figure 8.25.

FIGURE 8.25   Local Security Settings dialog box

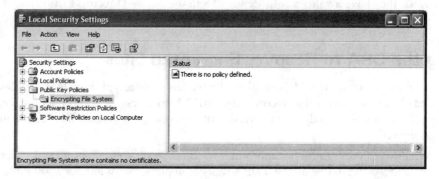

2. Right-click Encrypting File System and select Add Data Recovery Agent.
3. The Add Recovery Agent Wizard will start. Click the Next button to continue.
4. The Select Recovery Agents dialog box will appear as shown in Figure 8.26. Click the Browse Folders button to access the .cer file you created with the **Cipher /R:*filename*** command. Select the certificate and click the Next button.
5. The Completing the Add Recovery Agent Wizard dialog box will appear. Confirm the settings are correct and click the Finish button.

FIGURE 8.26   Add Recovery Agent dialog box

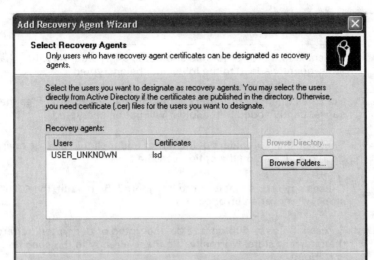

6.   You will see the Data Recovery Agent listed in the Local Security Settings dialog box, under Encrypting File System.

Recovering Encrypted Files

If DRA has the private key to the DRA certificate (that was created through `Cipher /R:filename`), the DRA can decrypt files in the same manner as the user who originally encrypted the file. Once the encrypted files are opened by a DRA, they are available as unencrypted files, and can be stored as either encrypted or unencrypted files.

In Windows 2000, encrypted files could be accessed by changing the password of the user who encrypted the files, and then logging in as that user. On a Windows XP Professional computer, if a user's local password is changed by an administrator or any method other than the local user changing their own password, all access to previously encrypted files will be blocked to the local user.

Using the *Cipher* Utility

Cipher is a command-line utility that can be used to encrypt files on NTFS volumes. The syntax for the `Cipher` command is as follows:

`Cipher /[command parameter] [filename]`

Table 8.3 lists the command parameters associated with the `Cipher` command.

TABLE 8.3   Cipher Command Parameters

Parameter	Description
/e	Specifies that files or folders should be encrypted. Any files that are subsequently added to the folder will be encrypted.
/d	Specifies that files or folders should be decrypted. Any files that are subsequently added to the folder will not be encrypted.
/s:dir	Specifies that subfolders of the target folder should also be encrypted or decrypted based on the option specified.
/I	Causes any errors that occur to be ignored. By default, the CIPHER utility stops whenever an error occurs.
/f	Forces all files and folders to be encrypted or decrypted, regardless of their current state. Normally, if a file is already in the specified state, it is skipped.
/q	Runs CIPHER in quiet mode and displays only the most important information.
/a	Specifies that you want the operation you are executing to be applied to all files and folders.
/h	By default, files with hidden or system attributes are omitted from display. This option specifies that hidden and system files should be displayed.
/r	Used to generate a recovery agent key and certificate for use with EFS.

In Exercise 8.8, you will use the CIPHER utility to encrypt files. This exercise assumes that you have completed Exercise 8.7.

EXERCISE 8.8

Using the CIPHER Utility

1. Select Start ➢ All Programs ➢ Accessories ➢ Command Prompt.

2. In the Command Prompt dialog box, type **D:** and press Enter to access the D: drive.

3. From the D:\> prompt, type **cipher**. You will see a list of folders and files and the state of encryption. The folder you encrypted in Exercise 8.7 should be indicated by an E.

4. Type **MD TEST** and press Enter to create a new folder named Test.

5. Type **cipher /e test** and press Enter. You will see a message verifying that the folder was encrypted.

Using the Disk Defragmenter Utility

Data is normally stored sequentially on the disk as space is available. *Fragmentation* naturally occurs as users create, delete, and modify files. The access of noncontiguous data is transparent to the user; however, when data is stored in this manner, the operating system must search through the disk to access all the pieces of a file. This slows down data access.

Disk defragmentation rearranges the existing files so they are stored contiguously, which optimizes access to those files. In Windows XP, you use the *Disk Defragmenter utility* to defragment your disk.

To access the Disk Defragmenter, select Start ➢ Control Panel ➢ Performance and Maintenance ➢ Administrative Tools ➢ Computer Management, then select Storage, Disk Defragmenter. The main Disk Defragmenter window (Figure 8.27) lists each volume, the file system used, capacity, free space, and the percentage of free space.

FIGURE 8.27 The main Disk Defragmenter window

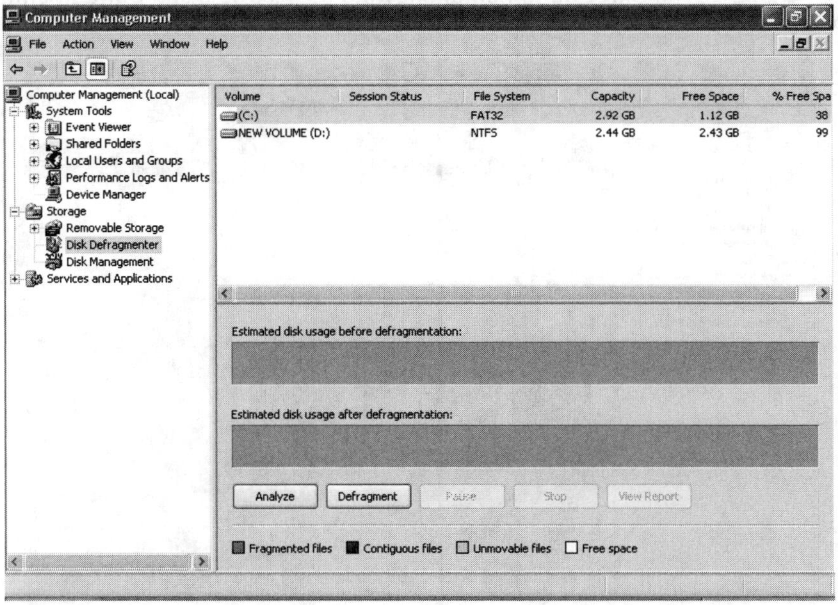

In addition to defragmenting disks, you can also use the Disk Defragmenter to analyze your disk and report on the current file arrangement. The processes of analyzing and defragmenting disks are covered in the following sections.

You can also defragment disks through the command-line utility, Defrag. This utility is new to Windows XP Professional. The disk needs to have at least 15 percent free space for Defrag to run properly. You can analyze the state of the disk by using Defrag *VolumeName* /a.

Analyzing Disks

To analyze a disk, open the Disk Defragmenter utility, select the drive to be analyzed, and click the Analyze button at the bottom-left of the window.

When you analyze a disk, the Disk Defragmenter utility checks for fragmented files, contiguous files, system files, and free space. The results of the analysis are shown in the Analysis display bar (see Figure 8.28). If you chose to defragment your disk, the defragmentation results would be listed in the bottom display bar. Though you can't see it in the figure, on your screen these bars are color-coded as follows:

Fragmented files	Red
Contiguous files	Blue
Unmovable files	Green
Free space	White

FIGURE 8.28   The Disk Defragmenter showing the Analysis and Defragmentation display bars

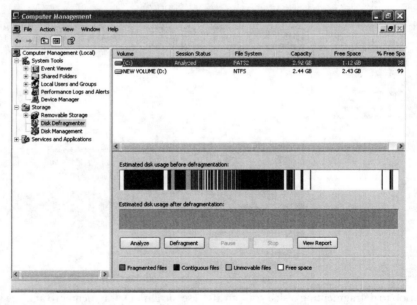

The Disk Defragmenter's analysis also produces a report, which is displayed when you click the View Report button. The report contains the following information:

- An indication of whether the volume needs defragmenting
- Volume information, including general volume statistics, volume fragmentation, file fragmentation, page file fragmentation, directory fragmentation, and master file table (MFT) fragmentation
- A list of the most fragmented files

Defragmenting Disks

To defragment a disk, open the Disk Defragmenter utility, select the drive to be defragmented, and click the Defragment button (to the right of the Analyze button at the bottom of the window). Defragmenting causes all files to be stored more efficiently in contiguous space. When defragmentation is complete, you can view a report of the defragmentation process.

You will use the Disk Defragmenter utility in Exercise 8.9 to analyze and defragment a disk.

<hr>

EXERCISE 8.9

Analyzing and Defragmenting Disks

1. Select Start ➤ Control Panel ➤ Performance and Maintenance ➤ Administrative Tools ➤ Computer Management, then expand Storage and select Disk Defragmenter.

2. Highlight the C: drive and click the Analyze button.

3. When the analysis is complete, click the View Report button to see the analysis report. Record the following information:

   a. Volume size: _____

   b. Cluster size: _____

   c. Used space: _____

   d. Free space: _____

   e. Volume fragmentation—Total fragmentation: _____

   f. Most fragmented file: _____

4. Click the Defragment button.

5. When the defragmentation process is complete, click the Close button.

<hr>

Using the Disk Cleanup Utility

The *Disk Cleanup utility* identifies areas of disk space that can be deleted to free hard disk space. Disk Cleanup works by identifying temporary files, Internet cache files, and unnecessary program files.

To access this utility, select Start ➤ Control Panel ➤ Performance and Maintenance ➤ Free Up Space on Your Hard Disk. You select the drive you want to clean up, and the Disk Cleanup utility then runs and calculates the amount of disk space you can free up.

In Exercise 8.10, you will use the Disk Cleanup utility.

EXERCISE 8.10

Using the Disk Cleanup Utility

1. Select Start ➤ Control Panel ➤ Performance and Maintenance ➤ Free Up Space on Your Hard Disk.

2. In the Select Drive dialog box, select the C: drive and click the OK button.

3. After the analysis is complete, you see the Disk Cleanup dialog box, listing files that are suggested for deletion and showing how much space will be gained by deleting those files. For this exercise, leave all the boxes checked and click the OK button.

4. When you are asked to confirm that you want to delete the files, click the Yes button. The Disk Cleanup utility deletes the files and automatically closes the Disk Cleanup dialog box.

Troubleshooting Disk Devices and Volumes

If you are having trouble with your disk devices or volumes, you can use the Windows XP *Check Disk utility*. This utility detects bad sectors, attempts to fix errors in the file system, and scans for and attempts to recover bad sectors.

File system errors can be caused by a corrupt file system or by hardware errors. If you have software errors, the Check Disk utility may help you find them. There is no way to fix hardware errors through software, however. If you have excessive hardware errors, you should replace your disk drive.

In Exercise 8.11, you will run the Check Disk utility.

EXERCISE 8.11

Using the Check Disk Utility

1. Select Start ➤ Control Panel ➤ Performance and Maintenance ➤ Administrative Tools.

2. Double-click Computer Management, then expand Storage and select Disk Management.

3. Right-click the D: drive and choose Properties.

4. Click the Tools tab, then click the Check Now button.

5. In the Check Disk dialog box, you can choose one or both of the options to automatically fix file system errors, and to scan for and attempt recovery of bad sectors. For this exercise, check both of the disk options check boxes. Then click the Start button.

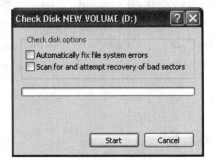

If the system cannot gain exclusive access to the partition, the disk will be checked the next time the system is restarted. You cannot gain exclusive access to partitions or volumes that contain the system or boot partition.

There are two command-line utilities associated with checking your disk: Chkntfs and Chkdsk. Chkntfs is used to display or specify whether automatic system checking is scheduled to be run with FAT, FAT32, or an NTFS volume when the system is started. Chkdsk is used to create and display a status report, which is based on the file system you are using.

Summary

In this chapter, you learned about disk management with Windows XP Professional. We covered the following topics:

- File system configuration, which can be FAT16, FAT32, or NTFS. You also learned how to convert a FAT or FAT32 partition to NTFS by using the Convert command-line utility.

- Disk storage configuration, which can be basic storage or dynamic storage. Dynamic storage is used to create simple volumes, spanned volumes, and striped volumes.

- Using the Disk Management utility to manage routine tasks, basic storage, and dynamic storage.

- Data compression, which is used to store files in a compressed format that uses less disk space.

- Disk quotas, which are used to limit the amount of disk space users can have on an NTFS partition.

- Data encryption, which is implemented through the Encrypting File System (EFS) and provides increased security for files and folders.

- Disk defragmentation, which is accomplished through the Disk Defragmenter utility and allows you to store files contiguously on your hard drive for improved access speeds.

- The Disk Cleanup utility, which is used to free disk space by removing unnecessary files.

- The Check Disk utility, which can be used to troubleshoot disk errors.

- Troubleshooting disks and volumes, which is used in the event of disk or volume errors or for maintenance.

Exam Essentials

Configure and manage file systems.   Understand the differences and features of the FAT16, FAT32, and NTFS file systems. Know how to configure options that are specific to the NTFS file system. Understand that you can convert a file system from FAT16 or FAT32 to NTFS, but that you can't convert from NTFS to anything else.

Be able to monitor and configure disks.   Use the Disk Management utility to configure disks for simple, spanned, or striped volumes. Be aware of the lack of fault tolerance in disk configurations used by Windows XP Professional. Be able to use Disk Management to monitor disks for physical drive and logical drive errors. Be able to use the Disk Cleanup utility and the Disk Defragmenter utility.

Know how to use disk compression.   Understand what types of files can benefit from disk compression and be able to configure and manage compressed folders and files.

Be able to use encryption to protect files.   Know when it is appropriate to use encryption. Be able to manage compression through Windows Explorer, as well as through the `CIPHER` command-line utility. Know how to recover encrypted files if the user who encrypted the files is unavailable.

Be able to troubleshoot disks and volumes.   Know what options and utilities can be used to troubleshoot disks and volumes and be able to repair disks and volumes that are not functioning properly.

Key Terms

Before you take the exam, be certain you're familiar with the following terms:

basic storage	dynamic storage
Check Disk utility	Encrypting File System (EFS)
`Cipher`	extended partition
cipher text	FAT16
Compact Disk File System (CDFS)	FAT32
`Convert`	fragmentation
data compression	hot swapping
data encryption	logical drive
Data Recovery Agent (DRA)	NTFS
Disk Cleanup utility	partition
disk defragmentation	primary partition
Disk Defragmenter utility	simple volume
Disk Management utility	spanned volume
disk quotas	striped volume
dynamic disk	volumes

Review Questions

1. Steve has installed Windows XP Professional on his computer. He has FAT16, FAT32, and NTFS partitions. In addition, he boots his computer to Windows NT 4 Workstation for testing an application he is writing, checking for compatibility with both operating systems. Which of the following file systems will be seen by both operating systems?

   A. FAT16 and FAT32

   B. FAT32 and NTFS

   C. FAT16 and NTFS

   D. All three file systems will be seen by both operating systems.

2. Jack has an NTFS partition on his Windows XP Professional computer. He wants to dual-boot to the Windows 98 operating system to access an application that is not supported by Windows XP. What command or utility should he use to convert his NTFS partition to FAT?

   A. Convert.

   B. Disk Administrator.

   C. Disk Manager.

   D. This operation is not supported.

3. Brad is the Payroll manager and stores critical files on his local drive for added security on his Windows XP Professional computer. He wants to ensure that he is using the disk configuration with the most fault tolerance and the highest level of consistent availability. Which of the following provisions should he use?

   A. Disk striping

   B. Spanned volumes

   C. Mirrored volumes

   D. A good backup scheme

4. Carrie is considering upgrading her basic disk to a dynamic disk on her Windows XP Professional computer. She asks you for help in understanding the function of dynamic disks. Which of the following statements is true of dynamic disks in Windows XP Professional? (Choose all that apply.)

   A. Dynamic disks can be recognized by Windows NT 4 or Windows XP.

   B. Dynamic disks are only supported by Windows 2000, Windows XP, and Windows Server 2003.

   C. Dynamic disks support features such as simple volumes, extended volumes, spanned volumes, and striped volumes.

   D. Dynamic disks support features such as simple volumes, extended volumes, spanned volumes, mirrored volumes, and striped volumes.

5. Linda is using Windows XP Professional on her laptop computer, and the C: partition is running out of space. You want to identify any areas of free space that can be reclaimed from temporary files. What utility should you use?

   A. Disk Cleanup

   B. Disk Manager

   C. Disk Administrator

   D. Disk Defragmenter

6. Greg is using Windows XP Professional to store video files. He doesn't access the files very often and wants to compress the files to utilize disk space. Which of the following options allows you to compress files in Windows XP Professional?

   A. COMPRESS.EXE

   B. Cipher.EXE

   C. PACKER.EXE

   D. Windows Explorer

7. Susan wants the highest level of security possible for her data. She stores the data on an NTFS partition and has applied NTFS permissions. Now she wants to encrypt the files through EFS (Encrypting File System). Which command-line utility can she use to manage data encryption?

   A. ENCRYPT

   B. Cipher

   C. CRYPTO

   D. EFS

8. You have compressed a 4MB file into 2MB. You are copying the file to another computer that has a FAT32 partition. How can you ensure that the file will remain compressed?

   A. When you copy the file, use the XCOPY command with the /Comp switch.

   B. When you copy the file, use the Windows Explorer utility and specify Keep Existing Attributes.

   C. On the destination folder, make sure that the folder's properties are configured to Compress Contents to Save Disk Space.

   D. You can't maintain disk compression on a non-NTFS partition.

9. Julie is trying to save a file that is 2MB in size, but she's getting an error message that the disk is out of space. When the administrator checks available disk space, he determines that more than 4GB of free disk space remain. What is the most likely cause of the space problem on this computer?

   A. The disk needs to be defragmented.

   B. Julie does not have the NTFS permissions she needs to access the folder where she is trying to save the file.

   C. Julie has exceeded her disk quota.

   D. The folder is encrypted and Julie does not have the key required to write to the folder.

10. Tom is the manager of Human Resources in your company. He is concerned that members of the Administrators group, who have implied access to all NTFS resources, will be able to easily view the contents of the sensitive personnel files. What is the highest level of security that can be applied to the payroll files?

    A. Apply NTFS permissions to the files.

    B. Encrypt the files with EFS.

    C. Secure the files with the `Secure.exe` command.

    D. Encrypt the files with HSP.

11. Scott frequently works with a large number of files. He is noticing that the larger the files get, the longer it takes to access them. He suspects that the problem is related to the files being spread over the disk. What utility can be used to store the files sequentially on the disk?

    A. Disk Cleanup

    B. Disk Manager

    C. Disk Administrator

    D. Disk Defragmenter

12. You are the network administrator for a small company. Your laptop dual-boots between Windows 98 and Windows XP. You currently have Windows 98 on drive C: and Windows XP on drive D:. You decide to convert the D: drive to NTFS so that you can apply additional security to some of the files. You use the `Convert` command-line utility to convert the D: drive. Before you reboot and convert the drive, you realize that data on the drive needs to be accessed from the Windows 98 operating system. How can you cancel the conversion process?

    A. Use `Convert D: /cancel`.

    B. Use `Convert D: /fs:FAT`.

    C. In Disk Administrator, select Tools ≻ Cancel Conversion for Drive C:.

    D. Edit the Registry setting for `HKEY_LOCAL_MACHINE\System\CurrentControlSet \Control\SessionManager` to `autocheck autochk *`.

13. Cindy is the payroll manager at your company. The day before the payroll is processed, Cindy is involved in a minor car accident and spends two days in the hospital. She has Windows XP Professional installed as a part of a workgroup and has encrypted the payroll files with EFS. All of the EFS settings for the computer are set to default values. How can these files be accessed in her absence?

    A. The Administrator user account can access the files by backing up the files, restoring the files on the computer where the recovery agent is located, and disabling the files' Encrypt the Contents to Secure Data option.

    B. The Administrator user account can access the files by using the `unencrypt` command-line utility.

    C. The Administrator user account can access the files by using the `encrypt -d` command-line utility.

    D. Unless a DRA has been configured, there will be no access to the files.

14. You have an extremely large database that needs to be stored on a single partition. Your boss asks you about the maximum capacity for an NTFS partition. What is the correct answer?

   A. 32GB

   B. 64GB

   C. 132GB

   D. 2TB

15. You have just added a new disk to your computer that supports hot swapping. Your computer now has two physical drives. When you look at Disk Management, you see the screen shown just below. What is the fastest way to allow Windows XP Professional to recognize the new disk?

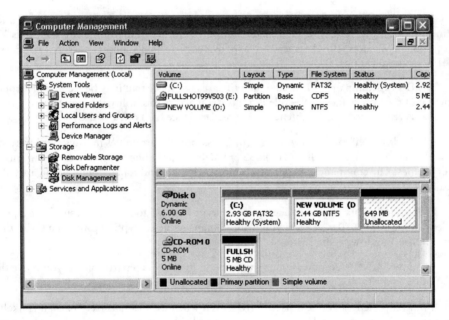

   A. Restart the computer.

   B. In Disk Manager, select Action ➤ Rescan Disk.

   C. In Disk Management, select Action ➤ Rescan Disk.

   D. In System Tools, select Update Disks.

Answers to Review Questions

1. C. Windows NT 4 does not recognize FAT32 partitions, so the only file systems that will be recognized by Windows NT 4 and Windows XP are the FAT16 and NTFS file systems. Windows XP Professional supports FAT16, FAT32, and the NTFS file systems.

2. D. You can convert from FAT16 or FAT32 to NTFS, but it is a one-way process if you want to preserve your data. You cannot convert from NTFS back to FAT16 or FAT32 without first deleting all existing partitions.

3. D. Windows XP Professional supports simple, spanned, and striped volumes. Mirrored volumes are available with Windows 2000 Server and Windows Server 2003. Brad should make sure he has a good backup for reliability.

4. B, C. Dynamic disks can only be accessed through Windows XP, Windows 2000, and Windows Server 2003/2000. There is no support for mirrored volumes in Windows XP Professional. Windows 2000 Server and Windows Server 2003 supports mirrored volumes and RAID-5 configurations.

5. A. The Disk Cleanup utility is used to identify areas of space that may be reclaimed through the deletion of temporary files or Recycle Bin files. You access this utility through Start ➤ Control Panel ➤ Performance and Maintenance ➤ Free Up Space on Your Hard Disk.

6. D. In Windows XP, one way you can compress files is through Windows Explorer. Windows XP has no programs called COMPRESS or PACKER. The Cipher program is used to encrypt or decrypt files. The command-line options for managing file and folder compression are COMPACT and EXPAND.

7. B. The Cipher utility is used to encrypt or decrypt files. Windows XP doesn't have a program called ENCRYPT, CRYPTO, or EFS. If you want to manage file encryption through a GUI utility, you can use Windows Explorer.

8. D. Windows XP data compression is supported only on NTFS partitions. If you move the file to a FAT32 partition, then it will be stored as uncompressed.

9. C. If Julie experiences "out of space" errors even when the disk has free space, it is likely that the disk has disk quotas applied and Julie has exceeded her quota limitation. The administrator can see if quotas have been applied through the Windows Explorer utility.

10. B. You can increase the level of security on folders and files on an NTFS partition by using Encrypting File System (EFS). Only a user who is configured as a DRA with the correct private key can access this data.

11. D. The Disk Defragmenter utility is used to rearrange files so that they are stored contiguously on the disk. This optimizes access to those files. You can also defragment disks through the command-line utility, Defrag.

12. D. The only way to cancel an NTFS conversion prior to reboot is to edit the Registry setting for HKEY_LOCAL_MACHINE\System\CurrentControlSet\Control\SessionManager to autocheck autochk *. Once the conversion has taken place, there is no unconversion process.

13. D.   By default, a Windows XP Professional computer that is installed as a stand-alone computer or a part of a workgroup, has no DRA automatically configured. You will not be able to access her files.

14. D.   You can have NTFS partitions that are up to 2TB in size. NTFS supports the largest partitions of any of the file systems supported by Windows XP Professional.

15. C.   If your computer supports hot swapping, all you need to do after you add a new disk is select Action ➢ Rescan Disk in the Disk Management utility. The disk will then be listed through the Disk Management utility and can be configured as needed.

Chapter
9

Accessing Files and Folders

MICROSOFT EXAM OBJECTIVES COVERED IN THIS CHAPTER:

✓ **Monitor, manage, and troubleshoot access to files and folders.**

- Control access to files and folders by using permissions.
- Optimize access to files and folders.

✓ **Manage and troubleshoot access to shared folders.**

- Create and remove shared folders.
- Control access to shared folders by using permissions.

✓ **Manage and troubleshoot access to and synchronization of offline files.**

Administrators must have basic file management skills, including the ability to create a well-defined, logically organized directory structure and maintain that structure. Windows XP Professional Folder Options dialog box allows you to configure many properties associated with files and folders, such as what you see when you access folders, file type associations, and the use of offline files and folders. Finally, you should know how to search for files and folders.

Local access defines what access a user has to local resources. You can limit local access by applying security for files and folders on NTFS partitions. You should know what NTFS permissions are and how they are applied.

A powerful feature of networking is the ability to allow network access to local folders. In Windows XP Professional, it is very easy to share folders. You can also apply security to shared folders in a manner that is similar to applying NTFS permissions. Once you share a folder, users with appropriate access rights can access the folders through a variety of methods.

To effectively manage both local and network resource access and to troubleshoot related problems, you should understand the resource-access process. Windows XP Professional uses access tokens, discretionary access control lists, and access control entries to handle resource access.

This chapter covers file and folder management tasks, beginning with the basics of planning and creating a directory structure.

File and Folder Management Basics

Before you perform tasks such as managing NTFS security and network shares, you need to understand how to perform basic file and folder management tasks. The first step in file and folder management is organizing your files and folders. After you have created the structure, you can manage folder options. Another common task is searching for files and folders. These tasks are covered in the following sections.

Organizing Files and Folders

When your files and folders are well organized, you can easily access the information that is stored on your computer. Organizing your files and folders is similar to storing your papers. If you don't have very many papers, the task is easy. The more papers you have, the more challenging the task becomes.

The key to organization is good planning. For example, you might decide to store all of your applications on your C: drive and all of your data on your D: drive. You might organize data by function or by type. Figure 9.1 shows an example of a directory structure that has been logically organized.

FIGURE 9.1 A sample directory structure

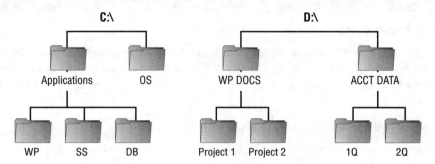

Once you plan your directory structure, you are ready to create the structure on your computer. This involves creating files and folders and may also require you to rename, delete, move, and copy files and folders. These tasks are described in the following sections.

Creating Files and Folders

You can create folders in several ways—through Windows Explorer, the DOS MD command, and My Computer. The examples in this chapter use Windows Explorer for folder management.

There are many ways to create files, too. The most common way is through applications, including the Windows XP Professional WordPad and Notepad utilities. Here are the steps to create a file with Notepad:

1. Select Start ➢ All Programs ➢ Accessories ➢ Windows Explorer to open Windows Explorer (another option you could use is to right-click the Start menu and select Explore).

2. Expand My Computer and select the drive and folder where the file will be created.

3. Select File ➢ New ➢ Text Document.

4. A new file icon appears in the Windows Explorer window. Type in the name of the new file under the file icon.

5. Double-click the new file to open it in Notepad. Add text to the file, as shown in Figure 9.2.

FIGURE 9.2 Editing a text document with Notepad

6. Save the file by selecting File ➢ Save, the File ➢ Exit to close the Notepad utility.

In Exercise 9.1, you will create a simple directory structure and add files and folders. This structure will be used in the other exercises in this chapter.

EXERCISE 9.1

Creating a Directory and File Structure

1. Create a shortcut to Windows Explorer by right-clicking an empty space on the Desktop and selecting New ➢ Shortcut. The Create Shortcut Wizard will start. Type in **Explorer** and click the Next button. Type in the name of the shortcut as **Explorer**, then click the Finish button.

2. Double-click the Explorer shortcut to open Windows Explorer.

3. Expand My Computer, then Local Disk (D:). Select File ➢ New ➢ Folder.

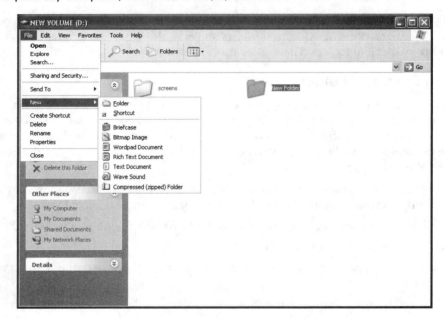

4. Name the new folder **DATA,** and double-click it to open it. Select File ➢ New ➢ Folder again, and name this new folder **WP DOCS**.

5. Confirm that you are in the DATA folder. Select File ➢ New ➢ Folder, and name this new folder **SS DOCS**.

6. Confirm that you are still in the DATA folder. Then select File ➢ New ➢ Text Document. Name the file **DOC1.TXT**.

7. Click the WP DOCS folder. Select File ➢ New ➢ Text Document. Name the file **DOC2.TXT**.

8. Navigate to the SS DOCS folder. Select File ≻ New ≻ Text Document and name the file **DOC3.TXT**. Your structure should look like the one shown below.

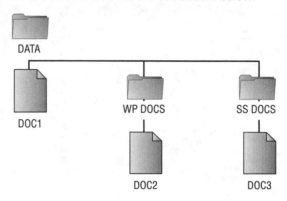

Renaming and Deleting Files and Folders

If you need to rename a file or a folder, right-click the file or folder that you want to rename and select Rename from the pop-up menu. The name will be selected and boxed. Start typing to replace the existing name with your entry, or position the cursor and edit the existing folder name or filename.

To delete a file or folder, right-click the file or folder that you want to remove and select Delete from the pop-up menu. When prompted, click the Yes button to confirm the deletion.

Deleted files or folders are moved to the Recycle Bin, which you can clear periodically to delete files or folders permanently. If you delete a file or folder by accident, you can usually restore the folder or file from the Recycle Bin (unless you do a Shift-Delete when deleting a file or folder).

Copying and Moving Files and Folders

You can easily reorganize your directory structure by copying and moving files and folders. When you move a file or folder from its original location (called the source) to a new location (called the destination), it no longer exists in the source location. When you copy a file or folder, it will exist in both the source and destination locations.

To copy or move a file or folder, right-click the file or folder that you want to copy or move, and drag and drop it into its destination location. When you release the mouse, you will see a pop-up menu that includes the options Copy Here and Move Here, as shown in Figure 9.3. Make the appropriate selection.

FIGURE 9.3 Moving a folder

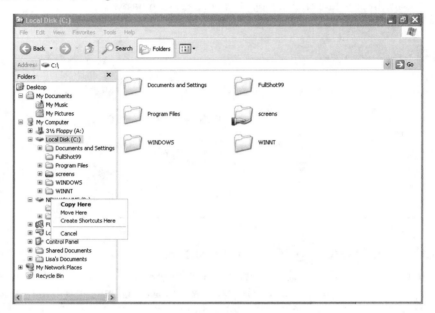

Managing Folder Options

Through the Folder Options dialog box, you can configure options such as the Desktop view and what you see when you open folders. To open the Folder Options dialog box, start Windows Explorer and select Tools ➢ Folder Options. You can also access Folder Options through its icon in Control Panel ➢ Appearance and Themes ➢ Folder Options. The Folder Options dialog box has four tabs: General, View, File Types, and Offline Files. The options on each of these tabs are described in the following sections.

General Folder Options

The General tab of the Folder Options dialog box, shown in Figure 9.4, includes the following options:

- A choice of showing common tasks in folders and if you want to use the Windows classic view for displaying folders.

- Whether folders are opened all in the same window when a user is browsing folders, or each folder is opened in a separate window.

- Whether a user opens items with a single mouse click or a double-click.

FIGURE 9.4   The General tab of the Folder Options dialog box

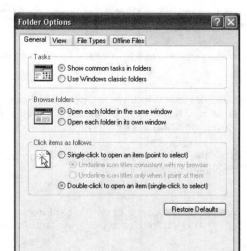

Folder View Options

The options on the View tab of the Folder Options dialog box, shown in Figure 9.5, are used to configure what users see when they open files and folders. For example, you can change the default setting so that hidden files and folders are shown in Windows Explorer and other file lists. The View tab options are described in Table 9.1.

FIGURE 9.5   The View tab of the Folder Options dialog box

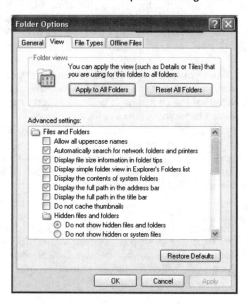

TABLE 9.1 Folder View Options

Option	Description	Default Value
Allow all uppercase names	Allows you to save files will all uppercase names.	Not selected
Automatically search for network folders and printers	Specifies that Windows will periodically search for all shared folders and printers and list all shared folders and printers in My Network Places.	Enabled
Display file size information in folder tips	Specifies whether the file size is automatically displayed in folder views.	Enabled
Display simple folder view in Explorer's Folders list	When you click a folder within Explorer, causes all other open folders to be closed automatically.	Enabled
Display the contents of system folders	Specifies whether you see the contents of system folders by default.	Not selected
Display the full path in the address bar	Specifies whether the address bar in the Windows Explorer window shows an abbreviated path of your location, such as Chapter 9 (from the Word Documents folder). Enabling this option displays the full path, such as C:\Word Documents\Sybex\XP Book\Chapter 9 as opposed to showing an abbreviated path such as Chapter 9.	Enabled
Display the full path in the title bar	By default, the title bar at the top of the Windows Explorer window shows an abbreviated path of your location. Enabling this option displays the full path.	Not selected
Do not cache thumbnails	When you open a folder, thumbnails are shown for the files in the folder. This option specifies whether the thumbnails will be cached or re-created every time you open a folder.	Not selected
Do not show hidden files and folders, Do not show hidden or system files, or Show hidden files and folders	By default, Do Not Show Hidden Files and Folders is selected, so files and folders with the Hidden attribute are not listed. Choosing Show Hidden Files and Folders displays these items.	Enabled
Hide extensions for known file types	By default, filename extensions, which identify the file type (for example, .DOC for Word files and .XLS for Excel files), are not shown. Disabling this option displays all filename extensions.	Enabled

TABLE 9.1 Folder View Options *(continued)*

Option	Description	Default Value
Hide protected operating system files (Recommended)	By default, operating system files are not shown, which protects operating system files from being modified or deleted by a user. Disabling this option displays the operating system files.	Enabled
Launch folder windows in a separate process	By default, when you open a folder, it shares memory with the previous folders that were opened. Enabling this option opens folders in separate parts of memory, which increases the stability of Windows XP but can slightly decrease the performance of the computer.	Not selected
Remember each folder's view settings	By default, any folder display settings you make are retained each time the folder is reopened. Disabling this option resets the folder display settings to their defaults each time the folder is opened.	Enabled
Restore previous folder windows at logon	Specifies that if you leave folders open at logoff, they will be automatically reopened when you log on again.	Not selected
Show Control Panel in My Computer	Specifies that Control Panel be listed in My Computer.	Not selected
Show encrypted or compressed NTFS files in color	Displays encrypted or compressed files in an alternate color when they are displayed in a folder window.	Enabled
Show pop-up description for folder and desktop items	By default, any summary information configured through file properties (such as title, subject, and author) appears when you click a file. Disabling this option suppresses the display of the summary information.	Enabled
Use simple file sharing (Recommended)	This option allows you to share folders with everyone in your workgroup or network, but is not used if you want to set folder permissions for specific users and groups.	Not selected
Hide icons when desktop is viewed as a Web page	If the desktop is configured to be viewed as a Web page, hides all icons on the desktop.	Not selected
Show window contents while dragging	Specifies that you want to display the window contents while dragging objects.	Enabled
Smooth edges of screen fonts	Used to smooth the edges of screen fonts.	Not selected

File Type Options

The File Types tab of the Folder Options dialog box, shown in Figure 9.6, is used to associate filename extensions with application file types. When an extension is associated with a file type, users can double-click the filename in Windows Explorer to open the file in its application. For example, if you have associated .PDF with Adobe Acrobat Reader and you double-click the Presentation.PDF file, Acrobat Reader will start and that file will be opened in it.

Through the File Types tab, you can add, delete, and change file-type associations. New filename extensions also may be added automatically when you install new applications on your computer.

FIGURE 9.6 The File Types tab of the Folder Options dialog box

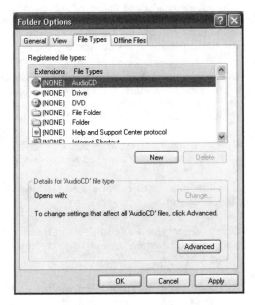

Offline Folder Options

Through the Offline Files tab of the Folder Options dialog box (Figure 9.7), you can configure the computer to use *offline files and folders*. This Windows XP Professional feature allows network files and folders to be stored on Windows XP clients. Then if the network location is not available, users can still access network files. In earlier versions of Windows, users who tried to access a network folder would receive an error message. With offline folders, users can still access the network folder even when they are not attached to the network.

Offline files and folders are particularly useful for mobile users who use the same set of files when they are attached to the network and when they are traveling. Offline files and folders are also useful on networks where users require specific files to perform their jobs, because they will be able to access those files even if the network server goes down (for scheduled maintenance or because of a power outage or another problem). Offline files and folders also improve performance even when the network is available, because users can use the local copy of the file instead of accessing files over the network.

FIGURE 9.7   The Offline Files tab of the Folder Options dialog box

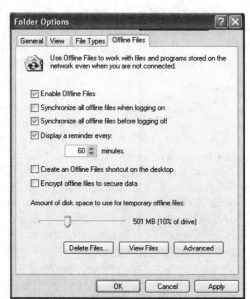

Configuring offline files and folders requires a minimum of two computers:

- The network computer that contains the network version of the files and folders
- The Windows XP client computer that will access the network files while they are online or offline

The network computer does not have to be running Windows XP, but it must use the file- and print-sharing protocol SMB (Server Message Blocks). All Microsoft operating systems use SMB, but some other operating systems do not. For example, if you were connected to a Novell NetWare 5 share, you would not be able to use offline files and folders, because NetWare uses a protocol called NCP (NetWare Core Protocol) for file and print sharing.

To use offline files and folders, you must complete the following tasks:

1. Attach to the shared file or folder that you want to access offline.

2. Configure your computer to use offline files and folders.

3. Make files and folders available for offline access.

4. Specify how offline files and folders will respond to network disconnection.

These tasks are covered in the following sections, as well as how to prevent confidential files from being accessed offline.

Offline files are not available when Windows 2000 Server or Windows Server 2003 is running Terminal Services, except in single-user mode.

Attaching to the Share

To use a file or folder offline, the file or folder must first be made available online. Someone at the server must share the folder, and the user must have proper permissions to access the file or folder. Then the user can attach to the shared file or folder. The procedure for sharing files and folders is described in the "Managing Network Access" section later in this chapter.

Configuring Your Computer

You configure your computer to use offline files and folders through the Offline Files tab of the Folder Options dialog box (see Figure 9.7). In this tab, verify that the Enable Offline Files box is checked (this option is enabled by default). To configure automatic synchronization between the offline and online files, make sure that the Synchronize All Offline Files before Logging Off option is checked (this option is also enabled by default). To use this option, you must disable the Fast User Switching option in Control Panel under User Accounts.

On the Offline Files tab, you can also configure several other options. These include the reminder balloon options that are associated with offline files, the amount of disk space that can be used by offline files, whether a shortcut is created for offline files on the Desktop, and whether you want to encrypt the offline files local cache.

If you don't configure offline files and folders to be synchronized automatically when you log on to or log off from your computer, you will need to perform the synchronization manually. To manually synchronize a file or folder, right-click the file or folder that has been configured for offline use and select Synchronize from the pop-up menu, as shown in Figure 9.8.

FIGURE 9.8 Manually synchronizing an offline folder

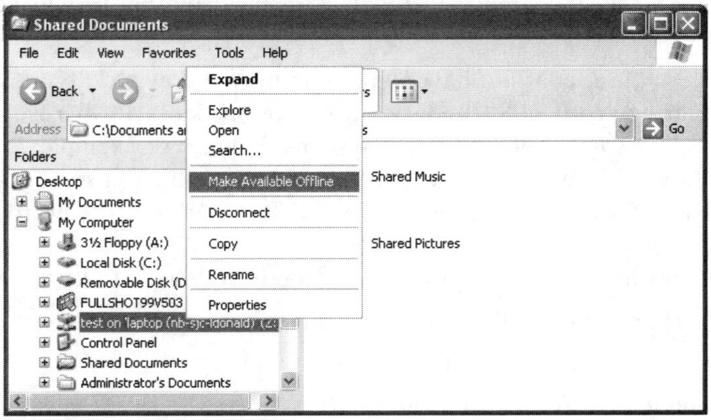

Making Files or Folders Available

To make a file or folder available for offline access, take the following steps:

1. Access the shared file or folder that you wish to use offline. Right-click the file or folder and select Make Available Offline from the pop-up menu (see Figure 9.8).

2. The Welcome to the Offline Files Wizard starts (this wizard will run only the first time you create an offline file or folder). Click the Next button.

3. As shown in Figure 9.9, a dialog box asks how to synchronize offline files. By default, the option to Automatically Synchronize the Offline Files When I Log On and Log Off My Computer is selected. If you would prefer to manually synchronize files, deselect this option. Click the Next button to continue.

FIGURE 9.9 Configuring the synchronization of offline files and folders

4. The next dialog box, shown in Figure 9.10, allows you to configure reminders and to create a shortcut to the Offline Files folder. Reminders periodically prompt you that you are not connected to the network and are working offline. The Offline Files shortcut is an easy way to access folders that have been configured for offline use. If you are online when you access this folder, you are working online. You can select or deselect either of these options. Then click the Finish button.

FIGURE 9.10 Configuring reminders and the Offline Files shortcut

5. If the folder you have selected contains subfolders, you will see the Confirm Offline Subfolders dialog box, shown in Figure 9.11. This dialog box allows you to choose

whether the subfolders should also be made available offline. Make your selection and click the OK button.

FIGURE 9.11 Configuring offline subfolder availability

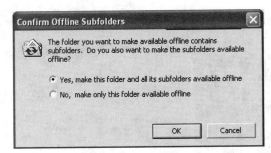

The offline files will be copied (synchronized) to the local computer. You can tell that a folder has been configured for offline access by the icon that appears under the folder, as shown in Figure 9.12.

FIGURE 9.12 The icon for offline folders

test

Preventing a Folder from Being Accessed Offline

Once a computer has been configured to support offline files and folders, you can access any share that has been configured with default properties. If you create a share and you do *not* want the files to be accessible offline, you can configure the share properties for offline access through the share's cacheing properties. Shares are discussed in greater detail later in this chapter.

Files are manually cached when a computer makes a request to a file or folder on the network that has been made available for offline access. By default, the Manual Caching for Documents setting is enabled. The default cache size for automatically cached files is 10 percent of the total disk space of the hard disk. If files are marked as manually cached, they are automatically marked as Always Available Offline In The Offline Files folder.

To configure the offline folder's cacheing, access the share's Properties dialog box, as shown in Figure 9.13. Click the Caching button. In the Caching Settings dialog box (Figure 9.14), uncheck the option Allow Caching of Files in This Shared Folder. With this option disabled, users can access the data while they are on the network, but they can't use the share offline.

 By default, `*.sim`, `*.mdb`, `*.ldb`, `*.mdw`, `*.mde`, `*.pst`, and `*.db?` are not cached. You can override this setting or specify which files will not be cached through Group Policy.

FIGURE 9.13 Sharing properties for a shared folder

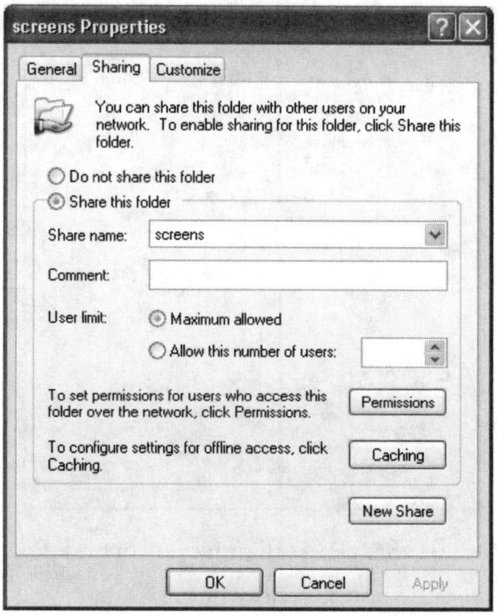

FIGURE 9.14 Caching Settings for a shared folder

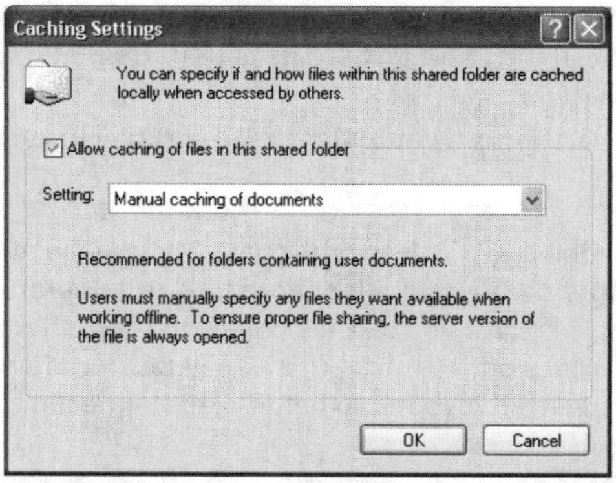

Configuring Your Computer's Behavior after Losing the Network Connection

Through the Offline Files tab of the Folder Options dialog box, you can specify whether your computer will begin working offline when a network connection is lost. To make this setting, click the Advanced button in the bottom-right corner of the dialog box. This brings up the Offline Files—Advanced Settings dialog box, as shown in Figure 9.15. Here, you can specify Notify Me and Begin Working Offline (the default selection) or you can select Never Allow My Computer to Go Offline. If you have created offline files and folders for multiple servers, you can use the Exception List portion of the dialog box to specify different behavior for each server.

FIGURE 9.15 The Offline Files—Advanced Settings dialog box

To reconnect to a network share after using offline files, all of the following conditions must be met:

- The network connection must not be a slow link.
- No offline files from the network share can contain changes that require synchronization.
- No offline files from the network share can be open on the user's local computer.

If any of these conditions are not met, the user will continue to work offline even though a network connection is available, and any changes that are made to local files will require synchronization with the network share.

In Exercise 9.2, you will set up your computer to use and synchronize offline files and folders.

 Your Windows XP Professional computer may be attached to a network that has another computer with shared files or folders. Just as described in the preceding sections, you can also attach to these shared files or folders that you want to access offline, make them available for offline access, and configure how the files will respond to network disconnection.

EXERCISE 9.2

Configuring Offline Files and Folders

1. Double-click the Explorer shortcut you created in Exercise 9.1.

2. In Windows Explorer, select Tools ➤ Folder Options and click the Offline Files tab.

3. In the Offline Files tab of the Folder Options dialog box, make sure that the following options are selected:

   - Enable Offline Files

- Synchronize All Offline Files before Logging Off

- Display a Reminder Every 60 Minutes

- Create an Offline Files Shortcut on the Desktop

4. Click the OK button to close the dialog box.

The Offline Files Database

When you enable offline files, the local computer stores information that is related to offline files in the Offline Files Database. By default, this database is stored in the *systemroot*\\CSC folder on the client computer. CSC stands for Client Side Cache and is a term associated with files that are cached with offline folders. When a user requests a file that is offline, the database mimics the network resource. All file system permissions are maintained by the database. The Offline Files folder is used to display all files stored within the database. Only members of the Administrator group are able to directly access the CSC folder. Files should not be directly deleted through the CSC folder.

> The CSC folder can be moved through the Cachemov command-line utility. If you move the CSC folder, you must ensure that the location that the cached files will be moved to has adequate disk space and that the user who is using offline files has appropriate permissions to the new location. This utility can be found on the Windows 2000 Resource Kit.

Encrypting Offline Files

Windows XP Professional offers support for encrypting offline files. In order to support this option, the Offline Files Database must be stored on an NTFS partition. If you refer back to the Offline Files tab of the Folder Options dialog box shown in Figure 9.7, you will notice that the option for Encrypt Offline Files to Secure Data is shaded out. This indicates that the CSC folder is on a FAT or FAT32 partition. In order to set this option, you must be a member of the Administrators group. This option can also be configured through the Group Policy MMC snap-in for a set of users or groups. If this option is set through the Group Policy tool, then it cannot be overridden by the Offline Files tab setting.

Troubleshooting Offline Files

If you are configuring offline files and folders, and you don't see the Make Available Offline option available as a folder property, check the following:

- Are you connected to a network share on a computer that uses SMB? Offline files and folders won't work from a network computer that does not use SMB.

- Have you configured your computer to use offline files and folders? Before you can make a file or folder available offline, this feature must be enabled through the Offline Files tab of the Folder Options dialog box (select Tools ➤ Folder Options in Windows Explorer).

- Has the folder that you want to access been shared, and do you have proper permissions to access the folder? If you don't see a folder that you want to configure for offline use, it may not be shared or you may not have proper share (and NTFS) permissions to the folder.

- Are files using the extensions .mdb, .1db, .mdw, .mde, or .db, which are not synchronized by default?

- If you are a member of the Active Directory, is group policy configured to specify that file extensions you are using are not to be synchronized?

- Do you have network errors that are preventing synchronization?

- Is there sufficient disk space on the client computer to support synchronization?

- Does the user have Read or Write permissions to the files they want to synchronize?

Searching for Files and Folders

Windows XP Professional offers more powerful search capabilities than Windows 2000 Professional. You can look for a file or folder based on the filename or folder name and also by searching for text that is contained in the file. This is an extremely useful feature when you know that you have saved a particular file on your computer but you can't find it. You can perform a search by selecting Start ➤ Search. Through the Search dialog box, shown in Figure 9.16, you can specify the following options for your search:

- Pictures, music, or video

- Documents (word processing, spreadsheet, etc.)

- All files and folders

- Computers or people

- Information in Help and Support Center

 If you use the search option from the Start menu on a computer that is a part of the Active Directory, you can also search for printers.

Depending on what you want to find—for example, a file or folder—you might specify the filename or folder name and/or the text that you are looking for. Only one of these fields must be filled in for a search. You must indicate the location that you want to look in; this can be as broad as My Computer or as specific as a particular drive or folder.

Once you have designated your search criteria, click the Search button to start the search. The results are displayed in the right side of the window, as shown in Figure 9.17.

FIGURE 9.16   The Search dialog box

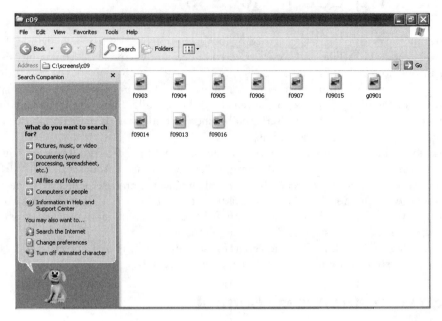

FIGURE 9.17   Search results

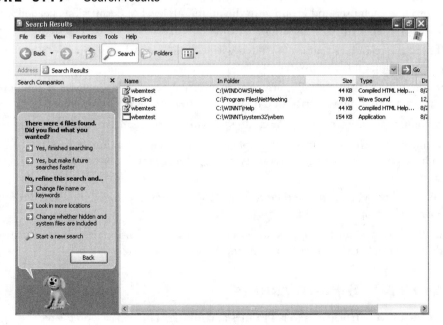

Managing Local Access

The two common types of file systems used by local partitions are FAT (which includes FAT16 and FAT32) and NTFS. (File systems are covered in detail in Chapter 8, "Managing Disks.") FAT partitions do not support local security; NTFS partitions do. This means that if the file system on the partition that users access is configured as a FAT partition, you cannot specify any security for the file system once a user has logged on locally. However, if the partition is NTFS, you can specify the access each user has to specific folders on the partition, based on the user's logon name and group associations.

Access control consists of rights and permissions. A right (also referred to as a privilege) is an authorization to perform a specific action. Permissions are authorizations to perform specific operations on specific objects. The *owner* of an object or any user who has the necessary rights to modify permissions can apply permissions to NTFS objects. If permissions are not explicitly granted within NTFS, then they are implicitly denied. Permissions can also be explicitly denied, which then overrides explicitly granted permissions.

The following sections describe design goals for access control, as well as how to apply NTFS permissions and some techniques for optimizing local access.

Design Goals for Access Control

Before you start applying NTFS permissions to resources, you should develop design goals for access control as a part of your overall security strategy. Basic security strategy suggests that you provide each user and group with the minimum level of permissions needed for job functionality. Some of the considerations when planning access control include:

- Defining the resources that are included within your network—in this case, the files and folders residing on the file system

- Defining which resources will put your organization at risk; this includes defining the resources and defining the risk of damage if the resource was compromised

- Developing security strategies that address possible threats and minimize security risks

- Defining groups that security can be applied to based on users within the group membership who have common access requirements, and applying permissions to groups, as opposed to users

- Applying additional security settings through Group Policy, if your Windows XP Professional clients are part of an Active Directory network

- Using additional security features, such as EFS to provide additional levels of security or file auditing to track access to critical files and folders

Applying NTFS Permissions

NTFS permissions control access to NTFS files and folders. This is based on the technology that was originally developed for Windows NT. Ultimately, the person who owns the object has complete control over the object. You configure access by allowing or denying NTFS permissions to users and groups. Normally, NTFS permissions are cumulative, based on group memberships if the user has been allowed access. However, if the user had been denied access through user or group membership, those permissions override the allowed permissions. Windows XP Professional offers five levels of NTFS permissions:

Full Control   This permission allows the following rights:

- Traverse folders and execute files (programs) in the folders. The ability to traverse folders allows you to access files and folders in lower subdirectories, even if you do not have permissions to access specific portions of the directory path.
- List the contents of a folder and read the data in a folder's files.
- See a folder's or file's attributes.
- Change a folder's or file's attributes.
- Create new files and write data to the files.
- Create new folders and append data to files.
- Delete subfolders and files.
- Delete files.
- Compress files.
- Change permissions for files and folders.
- Take ownership of files and folders.

If you select the Full Control permission, all permissions will be checked by default, and can't be unchecked.

Modify   This permission allows the following rights:

- Traverse folders and execute files in the folders.
- List the contents of a folder and read the data in a folder's files.
- See a file's or folder's attributes.
- Change a file's or folder's attributes.
- Create new files and write data to the files.
- Create new folders and append data to files.
- Delete files.

If you select the Modify permission, the Read & Execute, List Folder Contents, Read, and Write permissions will be checked by default, and can't be unchecked.

Read & Execute   This permission allows the following rights:

- Traverse folders and execute files in the folders.
- List the contents of a folder and read the data in a folder's files.
- See a file's or folder's attributes.

If you select the Read & Execute permission, the List Folder Contents and Read permissions will be checked by default, and can't be unchecked.

List Folder Contents   This permission allows the following rights:

- Traverse folders.
- List the contents of a folder.
- See a file's or folder's attributes.

Read   This permission allows the following rights:

- List the contents of a folder and read the data in a folder's files.
- See a file's or folder's attributes.
- View ownership.

Write   This permission allows the following rights:

- Overwrite a file.
- View file ownership and permissions.
- Change a file's or folder's attributes.
- Create new files and write data to the files.
- Create new folders and append data to files.

Any user with Full Control access can manage the security of a folder. By default, the Everyone group has Full Control permission for the entire NTFS partition. However, to access folders, a user must have physical access to the computer as well as a valid logon name and password. By default, regular users can't access folders over the network unless the folders have been shared. Sharing folders is covered in the "Managing Network Access" section later in this chapter.

You apply NTFS permissions through Windows Explorer. Right-click the file or folder to which you want to control access, and select Properties from the pop-up menu. This brings up the file's or folder's Properties dialog box. Figure 9.18 shows a folder Properties dialog box.

The process for configuring NTFS permissions for files and folders is the same. The examples in this chapter use a folder, since NTFS permissions are most commonly applied at the folder level.

The tabs in the file or folder Properties dialog box depend on the options that have been configured for your computer. For files and folders on NTFS partitions, the dialog box will contain a Security tab, which is where you configure NTFS permissions. (The Security tab is not present in the Properties dialog box for files or folders on FAT partitions, because FAT partitions do not support local security.) The Security tab lists the users and groups that have been assigned permissions to the file or folder. When you click a user or group in the top half of the dialog box, you see the permissions that have been allowed or denied for that user or group in the bottom half of the dialog box, as shown in Figure 9.19.

FIGURE 9.18   The Properties dialog box for a folder

FIGURE 9.19   The Security tab of the folder Properties dialog box

If the Security tab does not appear for your NTFS partition, and you are not a part of a domain, then Simple File Sharing is probably enabled, which will keep this option from appearing. To disable Simple File Sharing, select My Computer ➢ Tools ➢ Folder Options. In Advanced Settings, clear the box for Use Simple File Sharing (Recommended).

In the following subsections you will learn how to implement NTFS permissions and how to control permission inheritance.

Adding and Removing User and Group NTFS Permissions

To manage NTFS permissions, take the following steps:

1. In Windows Explorer, right-click the file or folder to which you want to control access, select Properties from the pop-up menu, and click the Security tab of the Properties dialog box.

2. Click the Add button to open the Select Users or Groups dialog box, as shown in Figure 9.20. You can select users from the computer's local database or from the domain you are in (or trusted domains) by typing in the user or group name in the Enter the object name to select portion of the dialog box and click the Add button.

FIGURE 9.20 The Select Users or Groups dialog box

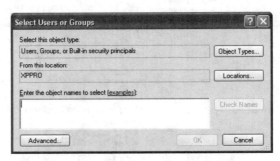

3. You return to the Security tab of the folder Properties dialog box. Highlight each user, computer, or group in the top list box individually, and in the Permissions list specify the NTFS permissions to be allowed or denied. When you are finished, click the OK button.

> Through the Advanced button of the Security tab, you can configure more granular NTFS permissions, such as Traverse Folder, Execute File, and Read Attributes permissions.

To remove the NTFS permissions for a user, computer, or group, highlight that entity in the Security tab and click the Remove button.

> Be careful when you remove NTFS permissions. You won't be asked to confirm their removal, as you are when deleting most other types of items in Windows XP Professional.

Controlling Permission Inheritance

Normally, the directory structure is organized in a hierarchical manner. This means you are likely to have subfolders in the folders to which you apply permissions. In Windows XP Professional, by default, the parent folder's permissions are applied to any files or subfolders in that folder, as well as any subsequently created objects. These are called *inherited permissions*.

In Windows NT 4, by default, files in a folder do inherit permissions from the parent folder, but subfolders do not inherit parent permissions. In Windows 2000 and XP Professional, the default is for the permissions to be inherited by subfolders.

You can specify how permissions are inherited by subfolders and files through the Advanced options from the Security tab of the folder Properties dialog box, by checking the Advanced button. This calls up the Permissions tab of the Advanced Security Settings dialog box, as shown in Figure 9.21. The options that can be selected include:

- Inherit from parent the permission entries that apply to child objects. Include these with entries explicitly defined here.

- Replace permission entries on all child objects with entries shown here that apply to child objects.

FIGURE 9.21   The Permissions tab of the Advanced Security Settings dialog box

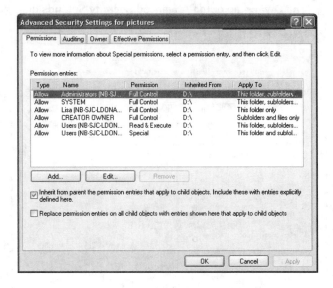

If an Allow or a Deny check box in the Permissions list in the Security tab has a shaded check mark, this indicates that the permission was inherited from an upper-level folder. If the check mark is not shaded, it means the permission was applied at the selected folder. This is known as an explicitly assigned permission. Knowing which permissions are inherited and which are explicitly assigned is useful when you need to troubleshoot permissions.

If you are within a domain with Active Directory and you need to apply a file permissions change to a large number of users, the most efficient way to manage the change is to use security templates as a way of modifying the file permissions. Then use a Group Policy Object to import and apply the security template to the users within the domain who require the new file permission settings. See Chapter 7 for more information.

Understanding Ownership and Security Descriptors

When an object is initially created on an NTFS partition, an associated security descriptor is created. A security descriptor contains the following information:

- The user or group that owns the object
- The users and groups that are allowed or denied access to the object
- The users and groups whose access to the object will be audited

After an object is created, the *owner* of the object has full permissions to change the information in the security descriptor, even for members of the Administrators group. You can view the owner of an object from the Security tab of the specified folder's Properties (as shown in Figure 9.19) and clicking the Advanced button (shown in Figure 9.20). Then click the Owner tab to see who the owner of the object is, as shown in Figure 9.22. From this dialog box you can change the owner of the object.

FIGURE 9.22   The Owner tab of the Advanced Security Settings dialog box

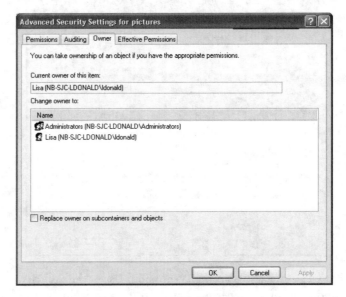

While the owner of an object can set the permissions of an object so that the Administrator can't access the object, the Administrator or any member of the Administrators group can take ownership of an object, and thus manage the object's permissions. When you take ownership of an object, you can specify whether you want to replace the owner on subdirectories and objects of the object.

From a command prompt, you can see who the owner of a directory is by typing **dir /q**.

Determining Effective Permissions

To determine a user's *effective rights* (the rights the user actually has to a file or folder), add all of the permissions that have been allowed through the user's assignments based on that user's username and group associations. After you determine what the user is allowed, you subtract any permissions that have been denied the user through the username or group associations.

As an example, suppose that user Marilyn is a member of both the Accounting and Execs groups. The following assignments have been made to the Accounting Group permissions:

Permission	Allow	Deny
Full Control		
Modify	X	
Read & Execute	X	
List Folder Contents		
Read		
Write		

The following assignments have been made to the Execs Group permissions:

Permission	Allow	Deny
Full Control		
Modify		
Read & Execute		
List Folder Contents		
Read	X	
Write		

To determine Marilyn's effective rights, you combine the permissions that have been assigned. The result is that Marilyn's effective rights are Modify, Read & Execute, and Read.

As another example, suppose that user Dan is a member of both the Sales and Temps groups. The following assignments have been made to the Sales Group permissions:

Permission	Allow	Deny
Full Control		
Modify	X	
Read & Execute	X	
List Folder Contents	X	
Read	X	
Write	X	

The following assignments have been made to the Temps Group permissions:

Permission	Allow	Deny
Full Control		
Modify		X
Read & Execute		
List Folder Contents		
Read		
Write		X

To determine Dan's effective rights, you start by seeing what Dan has been allowed: Modify, Read & Execute, List Folder Contents, Read, and Write permissions. You then remove anything that he is denied: Modify and Write permissions. In this case, Dan's effective rights are Read & Execute, List Folder Contents, and Read.

In Exercise 9.3, you will configure NTFS permissions based on the preceding examples. This exercise assumes that you have completed Exercise 9.1.

EXERCISE 9.3

Configuring NTFS Permissions

1. Using the Local Users and Groups utility, create two users: **Marilyn** and **Dan**. (See Chapter 6, "Managing Users and Groups," for details on creating user accounts.) Deselect the User Must Change Password at Next Logon option.

2. Using the Local Users and Groups utility, create four groups: **Accounting**, **Execs**, **Sales**, and **Temps**. (See Chapter 6 for details on creating groups.) Add Marilyn to the Accounting and Execs groups. Add Dan to the Sales and Temps groups.

3. Double-click the Explorer shortcut created in Exercise 9.1. Expand the DATA folder (on drive D:) that you created in Exercise 9.1.

4. Select Tools, then Folder Options.

5. Click the View tab and uncheck the Use Simple File Sharing (Recommended) option, then click the Apply button. Click OK.

6. Right-click DATA, select Properties, and click the Security tab.

7. In the Security tab of the DATA Properties dialog box, highlight the Everyone group and click the Remove button. You see a dialog box telling you that you cannot remove Everyone because this group is inheriting permissions from a higher level. Click the OK button.

8. Configure NTFS permissions for the Accounting, Execs, Sales, and Temps groups by clicking the Add button. In the Select Users and Groups dialog box, type in **Accounting;Execs;Sales; Temps** (you can add multiple users and groups by separating each entry with a semicolon) and click the Add button. Then click OK.

9. In the Security tab, highlight each group and check the Allow or Deny check boxes to add permissions as follows:

   - For Accounting, allow Read & Execute (List Folder Contents and Read will automatically be allowed) and Write.

   - For Execs, allow Read.

   - For Sales, allow Modify (Read & Execute, List Folder Contents, Read, and Write will automatically be allowed).

   - For Temps, deny Write.

10. Click the OK button to close the DATA Properties dialog box. Because you set a Deny permission, you will see a Security dialog box. Click the OK button to continue.

11. Log off as Administrator and log on as Marilyn. Access the D:\DATA\DOC1 file, make changes, and then save the changes. Marilyn's permissions should allow these actions.

12. Log off as Marilyn and log on as Dan. Access the D:\DATA\DOC1 file, make changes, and then save the changes. Dan's permissions should allow you to open the file but not to save any changes.

13. Log off as Dan and log on as Administrator.

Viewing Effective Permissions

If permissions have been applied at the user and group levels, and inheritance is involved, it can sometimes be confusing to determine what effective permissions are. To help identify which effective permissions will actually be applied, you can view them from the Effective Permissions tab of Advanced Security Settings, or you can use the CACLS command-line utility.

The Effective Permissions tab of Advanced Security Settings, shown in Figure 9.23, is a new feature in Windows XP Professional.

FIGURE 9.23 The Effective Permissions tab of the Advanced Security Settings dialog box

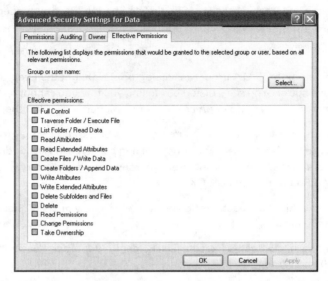

To see what the effective permissions are for a user or group, you click the Select button, then type in the user or group. Then click the OK button. If a box is checked and not shaded, then explicit permissions have been applied at that level. If the box is shaded, then the permissions to that object were inherited.

The CACLS command-line utility can also be used to display or modify user access rights. The options associated with the CACLS command are as follows:

- /g– grants permissions
- /r– revokes permissions
- /p– replaces permissions
- /d– denies permissions

Determining NTFS Permissions for Copied or Moved Files

When you copy or move NTFS files, the permissions that have been set for those files might change. The following guidelines can be used to predict what will happen:

- If you move a file from one folder to another folder on the same volume, the file will retain the original NTFS permissions.
- If you move a file from one folder to another folder between different NTFS volumes, the file is treated as a copy and will have the same permissions as the destination folder.
- If you copy a file from one folder to another folder on the same volume or on a different volume, the file will have the same permissions as the destination folder.
- If you copy or move a file or folder to a FAT partition, it will not retain any NTFS permissions.

Managing Network Access

Sharing is the process of allowing network users to access a folder located on a Windows XP Professional computer. A network share provides a single location to manage shared data used by many users. Sharing also allows an administrator to install an application once, as opposed to installing it locally at each computer, and to manage the application from a single location.

The following sections describe how to create and manage *shared folders*, configure *share permissions*, and provide access to shared resources.

Creating Shared Folders

To share a folder, you must be logged on as a member of the Administrators or Power Users group (or Server Operators if you are a part of a domain). You enable and configure sharing through the Sharing tab of the folder Properties dialog box, as shown in Figure 9.24.

FIGURE 9.24   The Sharing tab of the folder Properties dialog box

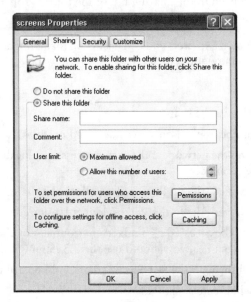

When you share a folder, you can configure the options listed in Table 9.2.

TABLE 9.2   Share Folder Options

Option	Description
Do Not Share This Folder	Makes the folder available only through local access
Share This Folder	Makes the folder available through local access and network access

TABLE 9.2   Share Folder Options *(continued)*

Option	Description
Share Name	A descriptive name by which users will access the folder
Comment	Additional descriptive information about the share (optional)
User Limit	The maximum number of connections to the share at any one time (default is to allow up to 10 users access to a share on a Windows XP Professional computer)
Permissions	How users will access the folder over the network
Caching	How folders are cached when the folder is offline

If you share a folder and then decide that you do not want to share it, just select the Do Not Share This Folder radio button in the Sharing tab of the folder Properties dialog box.

 In Windows Explorer, you can easily tell that a folder has been shared by the hand icon under the folder.

In addition:

- Only folders, not files, can be shared.

- Share permissions can be applied only to folders and not files.

- If a folder is shared over the network and a user is accessing it locally, then share permissions will not apply to the local user.

- If a shared folder is copied, the original folder will still be shared, but not the copy.

- If a shared folder is moved, the folder will no longer be shared.

- If the shared folder will be accessed by a mixed environment of clients including some that do not support long filenames, you should use the 8.3 naming format for files.

- Folders can be shared through the **Net Share** command-line utility.

In Exercise 9.4, you will create a shared folder.

EXERCISE 9.4

Creating a Shared Folder

1. Double-click the Explorer shortcut you created in Exercise 9.1. Expand My Computer, then expand Local Disk (D:).

2. Select File ➢ New ➢ Folder and name the new folder **Share Me**.

3. Right-click the Share Me folder, select Properties, and click the Sharing tab.

4. In the Sharing tab of the Share Me Properties dialog box, click the Share This Folder radio button.

5. Type **Test Shared Folder** in the Share Name text box.

6. Type **This is a comment for a shared folder** in the Comment text box.

7. Under User Limit, click the Allow radio button and specify **5** users.

8. Click the OK button to close the dialog box.

Configuring Share Permissions

You can control users' access to shared folders by assigning share permissions. Share permissions are less complex than NTFS permissions and can be applied only to folders (unlike NTFS permissions, which can be applied to files and folders).

To assign share permissions, click the Permissions button in the Sharing tab of the folder Properties dialog box. This brings up the Share Permissions dialog box, as shown in Figure 9.25.

FIGURE 9.25   The Share Permissions dialog box

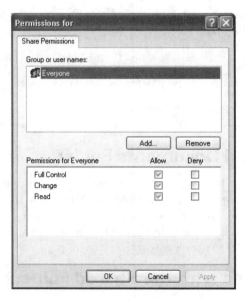

You can assign three types of share permissions:

Full Control   Allows full access to the shared folder.

Change Allows users to change data within a file or to delete files.

Read Allows a user to view and execute files in the shared folder.

Full Control is the default permission on shared folders for the Everyone group.

 Shared folders do not use the same concept of inheritance as NTFS folders. If you share a folder, there is no way to block access to lower-level resources through share permissions.

In Exercise 9.5, you will apply share permissions to a folder. This exercise assumes that you have completed Exercises 9.3 and 9.4.

EXERCISE 9.5

Applying Share Permissions

1. Double-click the Explorer shortcut you created in Exercise 9.1. Expand My Computer, then expand Local Disk (D:).

2. Right-click the Share Me folder, select Sharing and Security, and from the Sharing tab click the Permissions button.

3. In the Share Permissions dialog box, highlight the Everyone group and click the Remove button. Then click the Add button.

4. In the Select Users and Groups dialog box, type in users Dan; Marilyn, click the OK button, and then click the OK button.

5. Click user Marilyn and check the Allow box for the Full Control permission.

6. Click user Dan and check the Allow box for the Read permission.

7. Click the OK button to close the dialog box.

Using the Shared Documents Folder

One of the new features in Windows XP Professional is that if two or more user accounts are created on the local computer, then the Shared Documents folder is created under the My Documents folder. Files within this folder can be shared among multiple users of the local computer. The folder is also automatically shared and made accessible to other users if the computer is within a networked environment.

Managing Shares with the Shared Folders Utility

Shared Folders is a Computer Management utility for creating and managing shared folders on the computer. The Shared Folders window displays all of the shares that have been created on the computer, the user sessions that are open on each share, and the files that are currently open, listed by user.

To access Shared Folders, right-click My Computer from the Start menu and select Manage from the pop-up menu. In Computer Management, expand System Tools and then expand Shared Folders.

> You can add the Shared Folders utility as an MMC snap-in. See Chapter 4, "Configuring the Windows XP Environment," for information about adding snap-ins to the MMC.

Viewing Shares

When you select Shares in the Shared Folders utility, you see all of the shares that have been configured on the computer. Figure 9.26 shows an example of a Shares listing.

FIGURE 9.26   The Shares listing in the Shared Folders utility

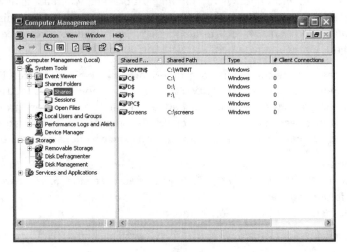

Along with the shares that you have specifically configured, you will also see the Windows XP special shares, which are created by the system automatically to facilitate system administration. Some of the administrative shares can't be configured and access is limited to administrators. A share that is followed by a dollar sign ($) indicates that the share is hidden from view when users access utilities such as My Network Places and browse network resources. The following special shares may appear on your Windows XP Professional computer, depending on how the computer is configured:

drive_letter$ Is the share for the root of the drive. By default, the root of every drive is shared. For example, the C: drive is shared as C$.

> On Windows XP Professional computers and Windows XP member servers, only members of the Administrators and Backup Operators groups can access the *drive_letter*$ share. On Windows 2000 or Windows 2003 domain controllers, members of the Administrators, Backup Operators, and Server Operators groups can access this share.

ADMIN$ Points to the Windows XP system root (for example, C:*Windows*).

IPC$ Allows remote administration of a computer and is used to view a computer's shared resources. (IPC stands for interprocess communication.)

PRINT$ Is used for remote printer administration if a printer has been defined.

FAX$ Is used by fax clients to cache fax cover sheets and documents that are in the process of being faxed if the fax service has been configured.

 Real World Scenario

Managing Remote Computers

Within your organization, you are responsible for managing hundreds of Windows XP computers. All of them are installed into Windows XP domains. At present, when users have problems accessing a local resource or want to create a share on their computer, an administrator is sent to the local computer. You want to be able to support remote management from a central location, but without adding remote management software to your network.

You can easily access remote computers' local drives through the hidden shares. For example, assume that user Peter has a computer called WS1. When this computer was added to the domain, the Domain Admins group was automatically added to the Administrators group on WS1. Currently no shares have been manually created on Peter's computer, and he wants to create a share on his C:\Test folder. Peter can't share his own folder because he does not have enough rights.

As a member of the Administrators group, you can remotely access Peter's C: drive through the following command: NET USE *x:* \\WS1\C$. Once you've accessed the network drive, you can access the Test folder and create the share remotely. This connection would also allow you to manipulate NTFS permissions on remote computers.

Creating New Shares

In Shared Folders, you can create new shares through the following steps:

1. Right-click the Shares folder and select New File Share from the pop-up menu.

2. The Create Shared Folder Wizard starts, as shown in Figure 9.27. Specify the folder that will be shared (you can use the Browse button to select the folder) and provide a share name and description. Click the Next button.

3. The Create Shared Folder Wizard dialog box for assigning share permissions appears next (Figure 9.28). You can select from one of the predefined permissions assignments or you can customize the share permissions. After you specify the permissions that will be assigned, click the Finish button.

4. The Create Shared Folder dialog box appears, to verify that the folder has been shared successfully. Click the Yes button to create another shared folder, or the No button if you are finished creating shared folders.

FIGURE 9.27   The Create Shared Folder Wizard dialog box

FIGURE 9.28   Assigning share permissions

You can stop sharing a folder by right-clicking the share and selecting Stop Sharing from the pop-up menu. You will be asked to confirm that you want to stop sharing the folder.

Viewing Share Sessions

When you select Sessions in the Shared Folders utility, you see all the users who are currently accessing shared folders on the computer. Figure 9.29 shows an example. The Sessions listing includes the following information:

- The username that has connected to the share
- The computer name from which the user has connected
- The client operating system that is used by the connecting computer
- The number of files that the user has open
- The amount of time for which the user has been connected
- The amount of idle time for the connection
- Whether the user has connected through Guest access

FIGURE 9.29 The Sessions listing in the Shared Folders window

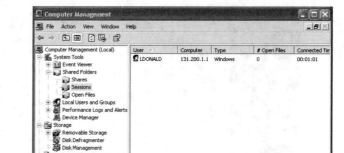

Viewing Open Files in Shared Folders

When you select Open Files in the Shared Folders utility, you see all the files that are currently open from shared folders. Figure 9.30 shows an example. The Open Files listing includes the following information:

- The path and files that are currently open
- The username that is accessing the file
- The operating system of the user who is accessing the file
- Whether any file locks have been applied (file locks are used to prevent two users from opening the same file and editing it at the same time)
- The open mode that is being used (such as read or write)

FIGURE 9.30 The Open Files listing in the Shared Folders window

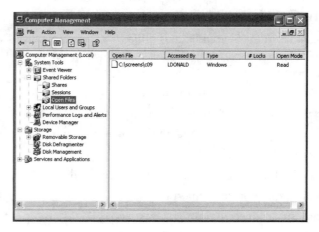

Providing Access to Shared Resources

There are many ways in which a user can access a shared resource. Here, we will look at three common methods:

- Through My Network Places
- By mapping a network drive in Windows Explorer
- Through the NET USE command-line utility

Accessing a Shared Resource through My Network Places

The advantage of mapping a network location through *My Network Places* is that you do not use a drive letter. This is useful if you have already exceeded the limit of 26 drive letters.

To access a shared resource through My Network Places, take the following steps:

1. Select Start ➤ My Computer and under Other Places, click My Network Places.

2. Under Network tasks, click Add Network Place.

3. When the Add Network Place Wizard starts, click the Next button. Type in the location of the Network Place. This can be a UNC path to a shared network folder, an HTTP path to a web folder, or an FTP path to an FTP site. If you are unsure of the path, you can use the Browse button to search for it. After specifying the path, click the Next button.

4. Enter the name that you want to use for the network location. This name will appear in the computer's My Network Places listing.

Network Places are unique for each user and are part of the user's profile. User profiles are covered in Chapter 6.

Mapping a Network Drive through Windows Explorer

Through Windows Explorer, you can map a network drive to a drive letter that appears to the user as a local connection on their computer. Once you create a *mapped drive*, it can be accessed through a drive letter using My Computer.

Here are the steps to map a network drive:

1. Open Windows Explorer.

2. Select Tools ➤ Map Network Drive.

3. The Map Network Drive dialog box appears, as shown in Figure 9.31. Choose the drive letter that will be associated with the network drive.

4. From the Folder drop-down list, choose the shared network folder to which you will map the drive.

5. If you want this connection to be persistent (the connection will be saved and used every time you log on), make sure that the Reconnect at Logon check box is checked.

FIGURE 9.31   Mapping the network drive

6. If you will be connecting to the share using a different username, click the underlined part of Connect Using a Different User Name. This brings up the Connect As dialog box, shown in Figure 9.32. Fill in the User Name and Password text boxes, then click OK.

FIGURE 9.32   The Connect As dialog box

Using the *NET USE* Command-Line Utility

The *NET USE* command-line utility provides a quick and easy way to map a network drive. This command has the following syntax:

NET USE *x:* *computername**sharename*

For example, the following command maps drive G: to a share called AppData on a computer named AppServer:

NET USE G: \\AppServer\AppData

You can get more information about the NET USE command by typing **NET USE /?** from a command prompt.

If you map network drives, they will not appear in My Network Places. To view mapped drives, use My Computer or the Windows Explorer Address bar.

In Exercise 9.6, you will access shared resources through My Network Places and map a drive in Windows Explorer. This exercise assumes that you have completed Exercise 9.5.

Accessing Network Resources

1.   Log on as user Marilyn. Select Start My Computer, then click My Network Places.

2.   Select Tools, then Map Network Drive. In the Map Network Drive dialog box, click the Browse button.

3.   Select the workgroup or domain in which your computer is installed. Click your computer name. Select Test Shared folder and click the OK button. Click the Finish button.

4.   Log off as Marilyn and log on as Dan.

5.   Select Start My Computer, then click My Network Places. You will not see the Network Place that you created as user Marilyn.

6.   Log off as Dan and log back on as Administrator.

The Flow of Resource Access

Understanding the resource-flow process will help you to troubleshoot access problems. As you've learned, a user account must have appropriate permissions to access a resource. Resource access is determined through the following steps:

1.   At logon, an *access token* is created for the logon account.

2.   When a resource is accessed, Windows XP Professional checks the *discretionary access control list (DACL)* to see if the user should be granted access.

3.   If the user is on the list, the DACL checks the *access control entries (ACEs)* to see what type of access the user should be given.

Access tokens, DACLs, and ACEs are covered in the following sections.

Access Token Creation

Each time a user account logs on, an access token is created. The access token contains the *security identifier (SID)* of the currently logged-on user. It also contains the SIDs for any groups with which the user is associated. Any other information about the user's security context is also attached. The access token is then attached to every process that the user runs while logged into the current session. Once an access token is created, it is not updated until the next logon.

Let's assume that user Kevin needs to access the Sales database and that SALESDB is the name of the shared folder that contains the database. Kevin logs on, but he is not able to access the database. You do some detective work and find that Kevin has not been added to the Sales group, which is necessary in order for anyone to have proper access to SALESDB. You add Kevin to the Sales group and let him know that everything is working. Kevin tries again to access SALESDB but is still unable to do so. He logs off and logs on again, and after that he can access the database. This occurs because Kevin's access token is not updated to reflect his new group membership until he logs off and logs back on. When he logs on, a new access token is created, identifying Kevin as a member of the Sales group.

WARNING Access tokens are updated only during the logon sequence. They are not updated on-the-fly. So if you add a user to a group, that user needs to log off and log on again to have their access token updated.

DACLs and ACEs

Each object in Windows XP Professional has an discretionary access control list (DACL). An *object* is defined as a set of data that can be used by the system, or a set of actions that can be used to manipulate system data. Examples of objects include folders, files, network shares, and printers. The DACL is a list of user accounts and groups that are allowed to access the resource. Figure 9.33 shows how DACLs are associated with each object.

FIGURE 9.33 Discretionary access control lists (DACLs) for network shares

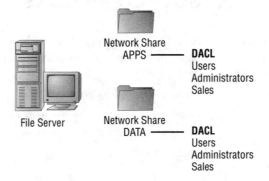

For each DACL, there is an access control entry (ACE) that defines what a user or a group can actually do at the resource. The steps that are taken when a resource is checked for access permissions are as follows:

1. The security subsystem checks to see if the object has an associated DACL.

2. If no DACL exists, then access is granted (for example, on FAT partitions). If a DACL exists, then the security subsystem traverses the DACL until it finds any ACEs that apply to the user and group SIDs that have been identified through the access token and any allow or deny access permissions that have been applied.

3. If any deny permissions are found for the user SID or group SIDs associated with the access token, then access is denied.

4. If no deny permissions are applied, then allow permissions for the combined user and group SIDs are applied.

5. If the security system finds a DACL and no explicit allow or deny permissions have been applied, then the security subsystem will deny access to the object.

Figure 9.34 illustrates the interaction between the DACL and the ACE.

FIGURE 9.34 Access control entries (ACEs) associated with a DACL

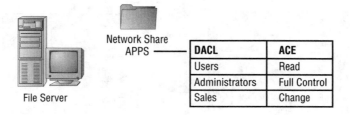

DACL	ACE
Users	Read
Administrators	Full Control
Sales	Change

You can see the DACL for a specific object when you access the Security tab of a folder's Properties dialog box.

Local and Network Resource Access

Local and network security work together. The most restrictive access will determine what a user can do. For example, if the local folder is NTFS and the default permissions have not been changed, the Everyone group has the Full Control permission. On the other hand, if that local folder is shared and the permissions are set so that only the Sales group had been assigned the Read permission, then only the Sales group can access that shared folder.

Conversely, if the local NTFS permissions allow only the Managers group the Read permission to a local folder, and that folder has been shared with default permissions allowing the Everyone group Full Control permission, only the Managers group can access the folder with Read permissions. This is because Read is the more restrictive permission.

For example, suppose that you have set up the NTFS and share permissions for the DATA folder as shown in Figure 9.35. Jose is a member of the Sales group and wants to access the DATA folder. If he accesses the folder locally, he will be governed by only the NTFS security, so he will have the Modify permission. However, if Jose accesses the folder from another workstation through the network share, he also will be governed by the more restrictive share permission, Read.

As another example, suppose that Chandler is a member of the Everyone group. He wants to access the DATA folder. If he accesses the folder locally, he will have Read permission. If he accesses the folder remotely via the network share, he will still have Read permission. Even though the share permission allows the Everyone group the Change permission to the folder, the more restrictive permission (in this case, the NTFS permission Read) will be applied.

FIGURE 9.35   Local and network security govern access

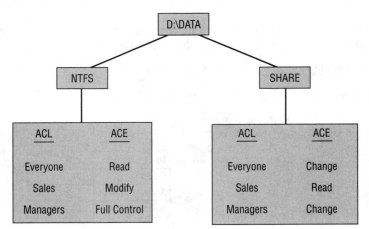

Summary

In this chapter, you learned about managing access to files and folders. We covered the following topics:

- Basic file management, which includes organizing files and folders, creating files and folders, managing folder options, and searching for files and folders

- Local access management, which includes assigning NTFS permissions and optimizing local access

- Network access management, which includes creating shared folders, assigning share permissions, and accessing network resources

- How resources are accessed when local NTFS permissions and network share permissions have been applied

- The flow of resource access, which includes creation of access tokens and controlling access to objects by checking the DACL and ACEs

Exam Essentials

Use offline folders.   Know what offline folders are and how they are used. Be able to configure network folders and Windows XP computers to use offline folders.

Be able to manage file and folder properties.   Understand what's needed to manage and configure file and folder properties, including setting overall folder options.

Know how to manage ownership of files and folders within NTFS.   You should understand how ownership is associated with NTFS objects and how to change ownership on NTFS objects if needed.

Be able to set folder and file security locally and for network shares.   Understand NTFS and share permissions and know how to apply permissions. You should also understand how the permissions work together and be able to troubleshoot permission problems. Also, know how to access network shares via Windows XP utilities.

Key Terms

Before you take the exam, be certain you are familiar with the following terms:

access control entries (ACEs)	NET USE
access token	NTFS permissions
discretionary access control list (DACL)	offline files and folders
effective rights	owner
inherited permissions	share permissions
mapped drive	shared folders
My Network Places	

Review Questions

1. Within your company, all users have Windows XP Professional laptop computers. The standard configuration is to use NTFS permissions because many users have confidential corporate information on their computers. Users have all received training so that they understand NTFS permissions and how they are applied. You want each user to be able to manage the permissions of their computer. Which of the following options would by default allow a user to manage NTFS permissions on NTFS folders? (Choose all that apply.)

   A. Administrators

   B. Power Users

   C. Any user with the Manage NTFS permission

   D. Any user with the Full Control NTFS permission

2. Sam is a member of the Sales group. Sam needs to be able to access the share \\SalesServer\Sales. The Sales group has Full Control permission for the Sales share. Sam also has individual permissions to the Sales share set to Read. However, when Sam tries to access the Sales share, he is denied access. Which of the following options would most likely solve Sam's problem?

   A. You should delete Sam's individual permissions.

   B. You should make sure that Sam is not a member of any groups that explicitly have Deny permissions.

   C. You should give Sam specific Full Control permission.

   D. You should delete the Sales group's permissions and reapply them.

3. Mary Jane runs Windows XP Professional on her laptop computer. She works in the Marketing department and is a part of the Marketing workgroup. One of her co-workers has requested access to some of the data files that Mary Jane has created and stored on her computer under C:\Data. Mary Jane wants to share folders on her Windows XP Professional computer. When she tries to create a share, she sees the following Properties dialog box. Which of the following options would allow Mary Jane to see the Sharing tab of this dialog box, containing options to create a share? (Choose all that apply.)

    A. Make her a member of the Administrators group.

    B. Make her a member of the Power Users group.

    C. Assign her Manage NTFS permission to the folders she wants to share.

    D. Assign her Full Control NTFS permission to the folders she wants to share.

4. You are the network administrator for a medium-sized company. You have just installed Windows XP Professional on the Accounting Manager's computer. His C: drive and D: drive have been formatted with NTFS because of his need for robust security. Occasionally this computer is accessed by other users and the files on the NTFS partitions need to be protected from access by anyone other than the Accounting Manager. If no changes are made to the default NTFS security permissions, what will the default NTFS permissions be for the users who occasionally access the computer?

    A. No permissions are assigned

    B. Read

    C. Read & Execute

    D. Full Control

5. Each user within your company uses Windows XP Professional and Windows 98 on laptop computers. Many of the users work partly at home or offsite and only occasionally come into the office. These users need a convenient way to manage their folders so that when they are online, their folders are automatically synchronized with the network. You decide to use offline folders. Which of the following options best describes which shares can be used for offline files and folders?

    A. You can use offline files and folders only from shares on Windows XP computers.

    B. You can use offline files and folders only from shares on Windows XP or Windows 98 clients.

    C. You can use offline files and folders from any share on a computer that uses the SMB protocol.

    D. You can use offline files and folders from any share that is local to your network.

6. You are the network administrator of a large company. You manage all of the Sales servers. Some of the folders that are shared on the Sales servers should be available for offline access, and other shared folders should only be available when users are directly attached to the network. How can you specify that a share can't be used in conjunction with offline folders?

    A. When you share the folder, uncheck the Make Available for Offline Access check box.

    B. In the Cache Settings properties for the shared folder, uncheck the Allow Caching of Shared Files in This Folder check box.

    C. In the Permissions Setting properties for the shared folder, specify that the Do Not Use Offline Folders option is disabled.

    D. By default, the shared folders can't be accessed as offline folders.

7. Brad, one of your users, wants to be able to use command-line utilities to access shared network folders instead of using GUI utilities. Which command-line utility can be used to map to shared network folders?

   A. MAP

   B. NET SHARE

   C. NET USE

   D. NET ACCESS

8. You have several users who want to access network shared folders. They want to know how they can access the shares. Which of the following options can be used to access shared network folders from a Windows XP Professional computer? (Choose all that apply.)

   A. Network Neighborhood

   B. My Network Places

   C. Map a drive in Windows Explorer

   D. Control Panel ➢ Network

9. You are the network administrator of a small network. One of your users is concerned that their computer is being accessed over the network. The computer has local C:, D:, and E: drives. You want to see a list of all folders that have been shared on all three local drives. Which utility can you use to quickly see a list of all shares that have been configured on your Windows XP Professional computer?

   A. Windows Explorer

   B. Shared Folders

   C. Share Manager

   D. Disk Management

10. Tom needs to create a shared folder to share with other managers. He does not want this share to appear within any browse lists. Which option can he add to the end of the share name to prevent a shared folder from being displayed in users' browse lists?

   A. $

   B. %

   C. *

   D. #

11. Linda has a folder that she would like to share on the network. This folder contains the `salesdata.txt` file. She wants to allow only one user at a time to edit the file, so that one user can't overwrite another user's changes if they open the file at the same time. How should Linda configure this share?

   A. She should set the user limit to allow one user.

   B. She should configure the file attribute on the `salesdata.txt` file as unshared.

   C. She should set a schedule so that users access the file at different times.

   D. In Windows Explorer, she should configure the shared folder so that users are not allowed offline access to the folder.

12. You have shared a folder on the network called Customer Contacts. You want this folder to be available to users who are connected to the network, but you don't want the folder to be accessed by users who are offline. What option should you configure to prevent offline access?

A. Within Windows Explorer, set the NTFS permissions of the folder so that it can't be accessed offline.

B. Within Windows Explorer, configure the share properties of the folder so that cacheing of the files in the folder is not allowed.

C. Within Windows Explorer, set the folder's property options so that offline files are not allowed.

D. Within Windows Explorer, uncheck the box to Allow Offline Access in the Sharing properties of the folder that you don't want accessed.

13. Rick has configured his D:\TEST folder so that the Everyone group has Read access to the folder. What will the Everyone group's permissions be for D:\TEST\DATA by default?

A. No permissions

B. Full Control permissions

C. Read permissions

D. Full Access permissions

14. You have a network folder that is also on an NTFS partition. NTFS permissions and share permissions have been applied. Which of the following statements best describes how share permissions and NTFS permissions work together if they have been applied to the same folder?

A. The NTFS permissions will always take precedence.

B. The share permissions will always take precedence.

C. The most restrictive permission within all the share and NTFS permissions will take precedence.

D. The system will look at the cumulative share permissions and the cumulative NTFS permissions. Whichever set is more restrictive will be applied.

15. Joe has his Windows XP Professional computer configured with a C: partition and a D: partition. The C: partition is configured with the FAT32 file system and the D: partition is configured with the NTFS. Joe uses a laptop computer and works in the office and also at home. To help support Joe's work at multiple locations, you have configured offline files for him. He had been successfully using offline files, but recently he reported that he was having problems due to the fact that his C: partition is running out of disk space. You check his D: partition and verify that there is plenty of available space, and that it will accommodate his offline file cacheing requirements. How do you move the Client Side Cache to the D: partition?

A. Use Windows Explorer to move the C:\CSC folder to D:\CSC.

B. Use the Offline Files Wizard to specify the new location of the Client Side Caching files.

C. Use the Cachemove command-line utility to move the CSC folder.

D. Specify the location of the CSC folder within the Offline Files—Advanced Settings dialog box.

16. You are the network administrator of a small company. You recently installed a new computer for Kaitlin, who is a new Account Representative for the Sales department. You installed her computer as a part of the Sales workgroup. When you installed Windows XP Professional, you created a single C: partition that was formatted with NTFS. Kaitlin sometimes needs to share her computer with other users and wants to ensure that her data is secure when someone other than herself logs in. When Kaitlin accesses the properties for C:\Data, she realizes that there is no security tab. What do you need to do to correct this problem?

    A. Add Kaitlin's account to the Administrators group.

    B. Ensure that Kaitlin has been assigned the Full Control NTFS permission to the C:\Data folder.

    C. Within My Computer, select Tools, then Folder Options, and ensure that the check box for Allow NTFS Permissions to Be Applied is checked.

    D. Within My Computer, select Tools, then Folder Options, and in Advanced Settings, clear the check box for Use Simple File Sharing (Recommended).

17. You are the network administrator for a large company. You are responsible for supporting all of the Finance users. Wendy is the manager of the Finance department. Because of the large number of confidential files that she manages, she configured her file systems with NTFS and applied NTFS permissions, as well as EFS to her C:\Data folder. Wendy is on vacation and not reachable for the next two weeks. While she is gone, the Vice President asks you to access some of the files in Wendy's C:\Data folder that are urgently needed to complete a presentation he is doing. You log on to Wendy's computer as the Administrator, and can see the C:\Data folder, but when you try to access any of the data files you receive an "Access Denied" error message. What course of action should you take?

    A. Rename Wendy's account to your name and then access the files with your logon name.

    B. Grant the Administrator account Full Control to the C:\Data files.

    C. Grant the Administrator account Change permission to the C:\Data files.

    D. As Administrator, take ownership of the C:\Data folder, then assign yourself rights to the folder.

Answers to Review Questions

1. **A, D.** Only members of the Administrators group and users with Full Control NTFS permissions can manage NTFS permissions on NTFS folders. Members of the Power Users group do not have any special access to NTFS folders. There is no "Manage NTFS" permission.

2. **B.** If a user has been denied permissions through any group membership or user assignment, it doesn't matter what permissions they are allowed because Deny permissions supersede allow permissions. You can determine what a user's effective rights are through the CACLS command-line utility to see if any Deny permissions have been applied.

3. **A, B.** Only members of the Administrators and Power Users (or Server Operators if you are in a domain environment) groups can create network shares. NTFS permissions have no impact on being able to create network shares.

4. **D.** By default, the Everyone group is assigned Full Control permission for NTFS volumes. For security purposes, it is recommended that you modify the default security permissions on sensitive directories.

5. **C.** You can use offline files and folders from any share on a computer that uses the SMB protocol, which is essentially any Microsoft computer with a share. The server that contains the share that will be used with offline files must also be configured for offline file support.

6. **B.** By default, any folder that has been shared on an SMB server can be accessed by computers that support offline folders. You can disable this feature through the Cache Settings properties for the shared folder, by unchecking the Allow Caching of Shared Files in This Folder check box.

7. **C.** Common ways of mapping shared network folders through GUI utilities are My Network Places and Windows Explorer. The NET USE command is used to map shared network folders.

8. **B, C.** You can access network shares through My Network Places or by mapping a drive in Windows Explorer. Network Neighborhood was in Windows NT 4, but is not in Windows XP. The Network icon in Control Panel is used to configure network settings, not map network drives.

9. **B.** The quickest way to see all of the folders that have been shared on a Windows XP Professional computer is to open the Shared Folders utility and select the Shares folder. All shares, including hidden shares, will be listed.

10. **A.** If you do not want a folder to be displayed in users' browse lists, you can hide the share by placing a $ at the end of the share name. Administrative shares are also hidden with the $ following the administrative share.

11. **A.** When you configure a share, you can specify a user limit. The Sharing tab of the folder Properties dialog box includes a User Limit option, which you can set to limit access to the folder to one user at a time.

12. **B.** When you create a share in Windows XP Professional, you see a Caching button in the share's Properties dialog box. If you click this button, you can specify that cacheing of the files in the folder is not allowed. This option is specifically for offline files and folders.

13. C. In Windows XP Professional, the default is for the permissions to be inherited by subfolders. This is different from the default in Windows NT 4, where files in a folder inherit permissions from the parent folder, but subfolders do not inherit parent permissions.

14. D. When both NTFS and share permissions have been applied, the system looks at the effective rights for NTFS and share permissions and then applies the most restrictive of the cumulative permissions. If a resource has been shared, and you access it from the local computer where the resource resides, then you will only be governed by the NTFS permissions.

15. C. The CSC folder can be moved through the Cachemove command-line utility. If you move the CSC folder, you must ensure that the location that the cached files will be moved to has adequate disk space and that the user who is using offline files has appropriate permissions to the new location.

16. D. If the Security tab does not appear for your NTFS partition, and you are not a part of a domain, then Simple File Sharing is probably enabled, which will keep this option from appearing. To disable Simple File Sharing, from My Computer, select Tools, then Folder Options. In Advanced Settings clear the box for Use Simple File Sharing (Recommended).

17. D. As an administrator you can take ownership of a folder, even if you have no permissions to the folder. Once you take ownership of the folder, as owner you have full permissions to the folder, and can then even assign permissions to other users.

Chapter

10

Managing Network Connections

MICROSOFT EXAM OBJECTIVES COVERED IN THIS CHAPTER:

✓ Implement, manage, and troubleshoot input and output (I/O) devices.

  ▪ Install, configure, and manage network adapters.

✓ Configure and troubleshoot the TCP/IP protocol.

For successful network connection management, you must have a properly installed and configured network adapter and network protocol. The first step is physically installing and configuring the network adapter you will use. The second step is installing and configuring the network protocol used by your network. The two protocols supported by Windows XP Professional are TCP/IP and NWLink IPX/SPX/NetBIOS.

In this chapter, you will first learn how to install and configure network adapters. Then you will learn about the network protocols supported by Windows XP Professional and how the protocols are configured. Finally, you will learn about network connectivity troubleshooting.

Installing and Configuring Network Adapters

Network adapters are hardware used to connect computers (or other devices) to the network. Network adapters are responsible for providing the physical connection to the network and the physical address of the computer. These adapters (and all other hardware devices) need a *driver* to communicate with the Windows XP operating system.

In the following sections, you will learn how to install and configure network adapters, as well as how to configure authentication, including advanced settings, and how to manage network bindings for your adapters. Finally, you will learn how to troubleshoot network adapters that are not working.

Installing a Network Adapter

Before you physically install your network adapter, it's important to read the instructions that came with the hardware. If your network adapter is new, it should be self-configuring, with Plug and Play capabilities. After you install a network adapter that supports Plug and Play, it should work the next time you start up the computer.

New devices will auto-detect settings and be self-configuring. Older devices rely on hardware setup programs to configure hardware. Really old devices require you to manually configure the adapter through switches or jumpers.

When you install a network adapter that is not Plug and Play, the operating system should detect that you have a new piece of hardware and start a wizard that leads you through the process of loading the adapter's driver.

Configuring a Network Adapter

Once the network adapter has been installed, you can configure it through its Properties dialog box. To access this dialog box, select Start ➤ Control Panel ➤ Network and Internet Connections. From the Network and Internet Connections dialog box, click the Network Connections option. You will see your Local Area Connection as an icon. Right-click Local Area Connection and select Properties. From within the General tab (shown in Figure 10.1), you will see your network adapter; click the Configure button to access the network adapter Properties dialog box, shown in Figure 10.2. The other tabs on the Local Area Connection Properties dialog box are defined at the end of this section.

FIGURE 10.1   Local Area Connection Properties dialog box

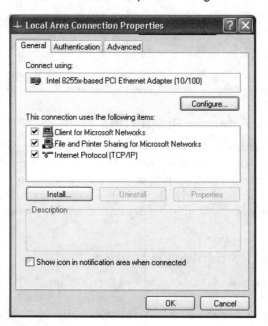

In the network adapter Properties dialog box, the properties are grouped on four tabs: General, Advanced, Driver, and Resources. These properties are explained in the following sections.

If you are using a laptop computer with ACPI features, you will also see a tab for Power Management.

FIGURE 10.2   The network adapter Properties dialog box

General Network Adapter Properties

The General tab of the network adapter Properties dialog box, shown in Figure 10.2, shows the name of the adapter, the device type, the manufacturer, and the location. The Device Status box reports whether the device is working properly. If the device is not working properly, you can click the Troubleshoot button to have Windows XP display some general troubleshooting tips. You can also enable or disable the device through the Device Usage drop-down list options.

Advanced Network Adapter Properties

The contents of the Advanced tab of the network adapter Properties dialog box vary depending on the network adapter and driver that you are using. Figure 10.3 shows an example of the Advanced tab for a Fast Ethernet adapter. To configure options in this dialog box, choose the property you want to modify in the Property list box on the left and specify the value for the property in the Value box on the right.

You should not need to change the settings on the Advanced tab of the network adapter Properties dialog box unless you have been instructed to do so by the manufacturer.

FIGURE 10.3   The Advanced tab of the network adapter Properties dialog box

Driver Properties

The Driver tab of the network adapter Properties dialog box, shown in Figure 10.4, provides the following information about your driver:

- The driver provider, which is usually Microsoft or the network adapter manufacturer.

- The date that the driver was released.

- The driver version, which is useful in determining whether you have the latest driver installed.

- The digital signer, which is the company that provides the digital signature for driver signing. (Driver signing is covered in Chapter 4, "Configuring the Windows XP Environment.")

Clicking the Driver Details button on the Driver tab brings up the Driver File Details dialog box, as shown in Figure 10.5. This dialog box lists the following details about the driver:

- The location of the driver file, which is useful for troubleshooting

- The original provider of the driver, which is usually the manufacturer

- The file version, which is useful for troubleshooting

- Copyright information about the driver

- The Digital Signer for the driver

FIGURE 10.4   The Driver tab of the network adapter Properties dialog box

FIGURE 10.5   The Driver File Details dialog box

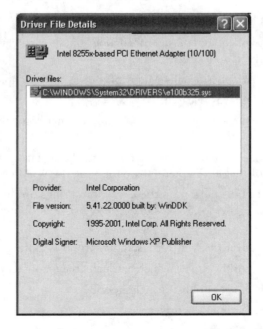

To update a driver, click the Update Driver button in the Driver tab. This starts the
Hardware Update Wizard, which steps you through upgrading the driver for an existing device.

The Roll Back Driver feature is new to Windows XP Professional. This button allows you to roll back to the previously installed driver if you update your network driver and encounter problems.

The Uninstall button at the bottom of the Driver tab removes the driver from your computer. You would uninstall the driver if you were going to replace it with a completely new one. Normally, you update the driver rather than uninstalling it.

If you cannot find the driver for your network card or the configuration instructions, check the vendor's website. Usually, you will be able to find the latest drivers. You also should be able to locate a list of Frequently Asked Questions (FAQs) about your hardware.

Resource Properties

Each device installed on a computer uses computer resources. Resources include interrupt request (IRQ), memory, and I/O (input/output) resources. The Resources tab of the network adapter Properties dialog box lists the resource settings for your network adapter, as shown in Figure 10.6. This information is important for troubleshooting, because if other devices are trying to use the same resource settings, your devices will not work properly. The Conflicting Device List box at the bottom of the Resources tab shows whether any conflicts exist.

FIGURE 10.6   The Resources tab of the network adapter Properties dialog box

In Exercise 10.1, you will view the properties of your network adapter. This exercise assumes that you have a network adapter installed in your computer.

EXERCISE 10.1

Viewing Network Adapter Properties

1. Select Start ➤ Control Panel ➤ Network and Internet Connections. From the Network and Internet Connections dialog box, click the Network Connections option. You will see your Local Area Connection as an icon. Right-click Local Area Connection, and select Properties. Click the Configure button.

2. In the General tab of the network adapter Properties dialog box, verify that the Device Status box shows "This device is working properly."

3. Click the Advanced tab. Note the properties that are available for your driver.

4. Click the Driver tab. Notice the driver date and version information. Click the Driver Details button to see the location of your network adapter's driver file. Click OK to close the Driver File Details dialog box.

5. Click the Resources tab. Note the resources that are being used by your network adapter. Verify that the Conflicting Device List box shows "No conflicts." Close any open dialog boxes.

Managing Authentication

In the Local Area Connection Properties dialog box, Authentication tab, shown in Figure 10.7, you can select the authentication configuration that will be used for network access. These are new options for Windows XP Professional. The options you can select include the following:

- Network access control using IEEE 802.1X
- Authenticate as computer when computer information is available
- Authenticate as guest when user or computer information is unavailable

When you select to enable network access control with the IEEE 802.1X port-based network access control, you can specify that network authentication methods such as smart cards, certificates, and passwords be used for authentication.

Authenticate as Computer when Computer Information Is Available means that the computer will attempt to authenticate to the network even when a user is not logged on. Authenticate as Guest when User or Computer Information Is Unavailable means that the computer will attempt to authenticate to the network as a guest even if no user or computer information is available.

FIGURE 10.7 The Authentication tab of the Local Area Connection Properties dialog box

Managing Advanced Configuration Properties

In the Local Area Connections Properties dialog box, Advanced Tab, shown in Figure 10.8, you can configure the Internet Connection Firewall and Internet Connection Sharing. The Internet Connection Firewall allows you to protect your computer by limiting or preventing access to the computer from the Internet. Internet Connection Sharing is used to share a single Internet connection among multiple users, and is associated with home networking. The Internet Connection Firewall is a new feature for Windows XP Professional.

FIGURE 10.8 The Advanced tab of the Local Area Connection Properties dialog box

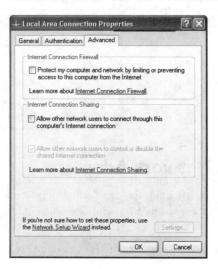

The Internet Connection Firewall and Internet Connection Sharing are covered in greater detail in Chapter 12, "Dial-Up Networking and Internet Connectivity."

Managing Network Bindings

Bindings are used to enable communication between your network adapter and the network protocols that are installed. If you have multiple network protocols installed on your computer, you can improve performance by binding the most commonly used protocols higher in the binding order.

To configure network bindings, access the Network Connections window and then select Advanced ➢ Advanced Settings from the main menu bar. The Adapters and Bindings tab of the Advanced Settings dialog box appears, as shown in Figure 10.9. For each local area connection, if multiple protocols are listed, you can use the arrow buttons on the right side of the dialog box to move the protocols up or down in the binding order.

FIGURE 10.9 The Adapters and Bindings tab of the Advanced Settings dialog box

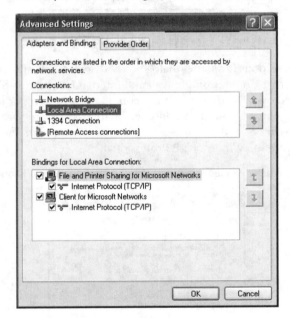

Troubleshooting Network Adapters

If your network adapter is not working, the problem may be with the hardware, the driver software, or the network protocols. The following are some common causes for network adapter problems:

Network adapter not on the HCL If the device is not on the HCL, contact the adapter vendor for advice.

Outdated driver   Make sure that you have the most up-to-date driver for your adapter. You can check for the latest driver on your hardware vendor's website.

Network adapter not recognized by Windows XP   Check Device Manager to see if Windows XP recognizes your device. If you do not see your adapter, you will have to manually install it (see "Installing a Network Adapter" earlier in the chapter). You should also verify that the adapter's resource settings do not conflict with the resource settings of other devices (check the Resources tab of the network adapter Properties dialog box).

Hardware that is not working properly   Verify that your hardware is working properly. Run any diagnostics that came with the adapter. If everything seems to work as it should, make sure that the cable is good and that all of the applicable network hardware is installed correctly and is working. This is where it pays off to have spare hardware (such as cables and extra network adapters) that you know works properly.

Improperly configured network protocols   Make sure that your network protocols have been configured properly. Network protocols are covered in detail in the next section of this chapter.

Improperly configured network card   Verify that all settings for the network card are correct.

Bad cable   Make sure that all network cables are good. This can be tricky if you connect to the network through a patch panel.

Bad network connection device   Verify that all network connectivity hardware is properly working. For example, on an Ethernet network, make sure the hub and port that you are using are functioning properly.

Check Event Viewer for any messages that give you a hint about what is causing a network adapter error. See Chapter 14, "Performing System Recovery Functions," for details on using Event Viewer.

 Real World Scenario

Are Ethernet Cards Properly Configured?

You are the network administrator of an Ethernet network. When you purchase Ethernet cards, they are special combo cards that support 10Mbps Ethernet and 100Mbps Ethernet. In addition, the cards have an RJ-45 connector for using unshielded twisted pair (UTP) cables, and a BNC connector for using coaxial cable. Your network is configured to use 100Mbps Ethernet over UTP cabling. Sometimes when you install the new Ethernet cards, they are not able to connect to the network.

A common problem is experienced with the combo Ethernet cards. Even when the hardware configuration for IRQ and base memory is correctly configured and you have the right driver, the correct configuration for speed and cable type may not be detected. Within an Ethernet network, all of the Ethernet cards must transmit at the same speed and be connected to a hub that supports the speed of the cards you are using. The cards must also be configured to support the cable type being used. You can verify these settings through the network adapter Properties dialog box. You can check the activity and speed of the connection in the Network Connections dialog box.

If the configuration is correct and you still can't connect to the network, you should check your network cables. It is estimated that between 70 and 80 percent of all network problems are related to cabling.

Overview of Network Protocols

Network protocols function at the Network and Transport layers of the OSI model. They are responsible for transporting data across an internetwork. You can mix and match the network protocols you use with Windows XP Professional, which supports two protocols: TCP/IP and NWLink IPX/SPX/NetBIOS.

 Previous versions of Windows also supported a protocol called NetBEUI. NetBEUI is a very easy protocol to install and requires no configuration. However, it does not offer as many networking features as TCP/IP and NWLink IPX/SPX/NetBIOS. Even though Microsoft discontinued support of NetBEUI with Windows XP, you can still install NetBEUI from the \ValueAdd folder located on the Windows XP Professional CD. Full instructions for installing the protocol can be found on the Microsoft Support website.

The following sections describe the basic features of each protocol, how to install and configure these protocols, and basic troubleshooting steps related to each protocol.

Overview of TCP/IP Protocol

Transmission Control Protocol/Internet Protocol (TCP/IP) is one of the most commonly used network protocols. It is a suite of interconnected protocols, which have evolved as the industry standard for network, internetwork, and Internet connectivity. The main protocols that provide basic TCP/IP services include Internet Protocol (IP), Transmission Control Protocol (TCP), User Datagram Protocol (UDP), Address Resolution Protocol (ARP), Internet Control Message Protocol (ICMP), and Internet Group Management Protocol (IGMP).

The following sections describe the benefits and features of the TCP/IP protocol, as well as the basics of TCP/IP addressing.

Benefits of Using TCP/IP

On a clean installation of Windows XP Professional, TCP/IP is installed by default. TCP/IP has the following benefits:

- TCP/IP is the most common protocol and is supported by almost all network operating systems. It is the required protocol for Internet access.

- TCP/IP is dependable and scalable for use in small and large networks.

- Support is provided for connectivity across interconnected networks, independent of the operating systems being used. TCP/IP provides connectivity for operating systems such as IBM mainframes, Apple Macintosh, Unix systems, and Open Virtual Memory Systems (VMS).

- TCP/IP provides standard routing services for moving packets over interconnected network segments. Dividing networks into multiple subnets optimizes network traffic and facilitates network management.

- TCP/IP is designed to be fault tolerant. It is able to dynamically reroute packets if network links become unavailable (assuming alternate paths exist).

- Protocol companions such as *Dynamic Host Configuration Protocol (DHCP)* and Domain Name System (DNS) offer advanced functionality.

- Support for *Automatic Private IP Addressing (APIPA)*, which is used by small networks without a DHCP server to automatically assign themselves IP addresses.

- Support for *NetBIOS* over TCP/IP (NetBT) is included. NetBIOS is used for identifying computer resources by name as opposed to IP address.

- Performance enhancements include a larger TCP receive window for more efficient communication.

- The inclusion of *Alternate IP Configuration*, a feature in Windows XP Professional, allows users to have a static and a DHCP-assigned IP address mapped to a single network adapter, which is used to support mobile users who roam between different network segments.

Features of TCP/IP

One of the main features of TCP/IP is that it allows a common structure for network communications across a wide variety of diverse hardware and operating systems. For example, the underlying hardware could be 10Mbps Ethernet, 100Mbps Ethernet, or Token Ring. The computer operating systems that commonly use TCP/IP are Windows operating systems, Unix, and NetWare. TCP/IP provides a common network access method independent of the hardware and operating systems used.

The features of TCP/IP included with Windows XP Professional are as listed:

- Logical and physical multihoming, which allows you to have multiple IP addresses on a single computer for single or multiple network adapters. Multiple network adapters installed on a single computer are normally associated with routing for internetwork connectivity.

- Support for internal IP routing, which allows a Windows XP Professional computer to route packets between multiple network adapters that have been installed.

- The ability to support multiple default network gateways, which are associated with network routing.

- Support for Virtual Private Networks, which allow you to transmit data securely across a public network via encapsulated and encrypted packets.

- My Network Places, which allows you to browse network resources even if they are located on a remote subnet.

- Use of a NetBIOS interface, which supports NetBIOS sessions, datagrams, and name management via the TCP/IP protocol.

- Inclusion of a Simple Network Management Protocol (SNMP) agent that can be used to monitor performance and resource use of a TCP/IP host.

- TCP/IP connectivity tools added for allowing access to heterogeneous hosts across a TCP/IP network. Connectivity tools include `ftp`, `tftp`, `rcp`, `rexec`, `telnet`, and `finger`.

- TCP/IP management and diagnostic tools included for providing maintenance and diagnostic support. TCP/IP management and diagnostic tools include `ipconfig`, `arp`, `ping`, `nbtstat`, `netsh`, `route`, `nslookup`, `tracert`, and `pathping`.

- Support for TCP/IP network printing, which allows you to print to other non-Microsoft TCP/IP print devices, such as Unix printers.

Basics of IP Addressing and Configuration

Before you can configure TCP/IP, you must have a basic understanding of TCP/IP configuration and addressing. To configure a TCP/IP client, you must specify an IP address and subnet mask. Depending on your network, optional settings might include the default gateway, DNS server settings, and WINS server settings.

In the following subsections, you will learn about these TCP/IP addressing and configuration options:

- IP address
- Subnet mask
- Default gateway
- Dynamic Host Configuration Protocol (DHCP)
- Domain Name System (DNS) servers
- Windows Internet Name Service (WINS) servers

In the next section, "Options for Deploying TCP/IP Configurations," you will learn about the four methods that can be used to implement TCP/IP addressing and configuration.

IP Address

The *IP address* uniquely identifies your computer on the network. The IP address is a four-field, 32-bit address, separated by periods (an example would be 165.76.21.22). Part of the address is used to identify your network address, and part is used to identify the host (or local) computer's address.

If you use the Internet, then you should register your IP addresses with one of the Internet registration sites. There are three main classes of IP addresses. Depending on the class you use, different parts of the address show the network portion of the address and the host address, as illustrated in Figure 10.10.

You can find more information about Internet registration at InterNIC's website, www.internic.net.

FIGURE 10.10   IP class network and host addresses

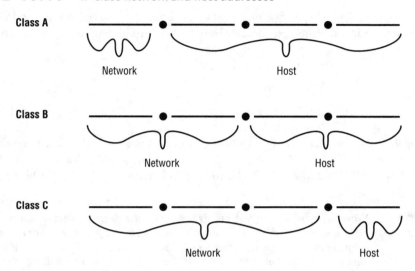

Table 10.1 shows the three classes of network addresses and the number of networks and hosts that are available for each network class.

TABLE 10.1   IP Class Assignments

Network Class	Address Range of First Field	Number of Networks Available	Number of Host Nodes Supported
A	1–126	126	16,777,214
B	128–191	16,384	65,534
C	192–223	2,097,152	254

Windows XP Professional supports IP version 4 (IPv4) and IP version 6 (IPv6). The primary differences between IPv4 and IPv6 is that IPv6 has improvements over IPv4 including the support of 128-bit addresses, as compared to the 32-bit addressing scheme used by IPv4. Other improvements include more simplified support for installation and configuration of wireless devices and more support for smart network–enabled devices. IPv6 is designed to coexist with IPv4, and most of the Internet traffic generated by IPv6 actually tunnels over existing IPv4 Internet infrastructure.

Subnet Mask

The *subnet mask* is used to specify which part of the IP address is the network address and which part of the address is the host address. By default, the following subnet masks are applied:

Class A   255.0.0.0

Class B   255.255.0.0

Class C   255.255.255.0

By using 255, you are selecting the octet or octets (or, in some cases, the piece of an octet) used to identify the network address. For example, in the Class B network address 191.200.2.1, if the subnet mask is 255.255.0.0, then 191.200 is the network address and 2.1 is the host address.

When a network administrator is designing the network infrastructure, the creation and administration of subnet masks can be a difficult task. For more detailed information on subnet masks, see *MCSE: Windows 2000 Network Infrastructure Study Guide*, 2nd edition, by Paul Robichaux with James Chellis (Sybex, 2001).

Default Gateway

You configure a *default gateway* if the network contains routers. A *router* is a device that connects two or more network segments together. Routers function at the Network layer of the OSI model.

You can configure a Windows XP Professional computer or a Windows Server 2003 computer to act as a router by installing two or more network cards in the server, attaching each network card to a different network segment, and then configuring each network card for the segment to which it will attach. You can also use third-party routers, which typically offer more features than Windows XP Professional computers or Windows Server 2003 computers configured as routers.

As an example, suppose that your network is configured as shown in Figure 10.11. Network A uses the IP network address 131.1.0.0. Network B uses the IP network address 131.2.0.0. In this case, each network card in the router should be configured with an IP address from the segment to which the network card is addressed.

FIGURE 10.11   Configuring default gateways

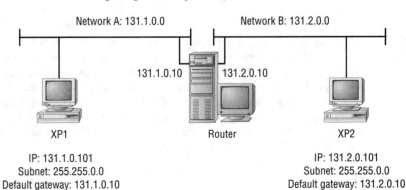

You configure the computers on each segment to point to the IP address of the network card on the router that is attached to their network segment. For example, in Figure 10.11, the computer XP1 is attached to Network A. The default gateway that would be configured for this computer is 131.1.0.10. The computer XP2 is attached to Network B. The default gateway that would be configured for this computer is 131.2.0.10.

DHCP

Each device that will use TCP/IP on your network must have a valid, unique IP address. This address can be manually configured or can be automated through *Dynamic Host Configuration Protocol (DHCP)*. DHCP is implemented as a DHCP server and a DHCP client as shown in Figure 10.12. The server is configured with a pool of IP addresses and their associated IP configurations. The client is configured to automatically access the DHCP server to obtain its IP configuration.

FIGURE 10.12   The DHCP lease-generation process

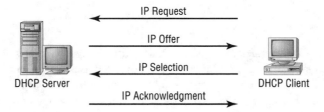

DHCP works in the following manner, all through the use of network broadcasts:

1. When the client computer starts up, it sends a broadcast DHCPDISCOVER message, requesting a DHCP server. The request includes the hardware address of the client computer.

2. Any DHCP server receiving the broadcast that has available IP addresses will send a DHCPOFFER message to the client. This message offers an IP address for a set period of time (called a *lease*), a subnet mask, and a server identifier (the IP address of the DHCP server). The address that is offered by the server is marked as unavailable and will not be offered to any other clients during the DHCP negotiation period.

3. The client selects one of the offers and broadcasts a DHCPREQUEST message, indicating its selection. This allows any DHCP offers that were not accepted to be returned to the pool of available IP addresses.

4. The DHCP server that was selected sends back a DHCPACK message as an acknowledgment, indicating the IP address, subnet mask, and duration of the lease that the client computer will use. It may also send additional configuration information, such as the address of the default gateway or the DNS server address.

If you want to use DHCP and there is no DHCP server on your network segment, you can use a DHCP server on another network segment—provided that the DHCP server is configured to support your network segment and a DHCP Relay Agent has been installed on your network router.

If you are not able to access a DHCP server installed on a Windows 2000 Server or Windows Server 2003 within Active Directory, make sure that the DHCP server has been authorized.

DNS Servers

Domain Name System (DNS) servers are used to resolve hostnames to IP addresses. This makes it easier for people to access domain hosts. For example, do you know what the IP address is for the White House? No? Do you know the domain hostname of the White House? You probably guessed that it's www.whitehouse.gov. You can understand why many people might not know the IP address but would know the domain hostname.

When you access the Internet and type in www.whitehouse.gov, there are DNS servers within the infrastructure of the Internet that resolve the hostname to the proper IP address. If you did not have access to a properly configured DNS server, you could configure a HOSTS file for your computer that contains the mappings of IP addresses to the domain hosts that you need to access.

WINS Servers

Windows Internet Name Service (WINS) servers are used to resolve NetBIOS (Network Basic Input/Output System) names to IP addresses. Windows XP uses NetBIOS names in addition to hostnames to identify network computers. This is mainly for backward compatibility with Windows NT 4, which used this addressing scheme extensively. When you attempt to access a computer using the NetBIOS name, the computer must be able to resolve the NetBIOS name to an IP address. This address resolution can be accomplished by using one of the following methods:

- Through a broadcast (if the computer you are trying to reach is on the same network segment)

- Through a WINS server

- Through an LMHOSTS file, which is a static mapping of IP addresses to NetBIOS computer names

Name resolution is covered in greater detail in the "Understanding TCP/IP Name Resolution" section of this chapter.

Options for Deploying TCP/IP Configurations

Windows XP Professional offers four methods for configuring the TCP/IP protocol. You can use Dynamic Host Configuration Protocol (DHCP), Automatic Private IP Addressing (APIPA), Static IP Addressing, or Alternate IP Configuration. The following sections include a description of each option, as well as instructions for configuring each option.

Using DHCP

Dynamic IP configuration assumes that you have a DHCP server on your network. DHCP servers are configured to automatically provide DHCP clients with all their IP configuration information. For large networks, DHCP is the easiest and most reliable way of managing IP configurations. By default, when TCP/IP is installed on a Windows XP Professional computer, the computer is configured for dynamic IP configuration.

If your computer is configured for manual IP configuration and you want to use dynamic IP configuration, take the following steps:

1. Select Start ➤ Control Panel ➤ Network and Internet Connections.

2. From the Network and Internet Connections dialog box, click the Network Connections option. You will see your Local Area Connection as an icon.

3. Right-click Local Area Connection, and select Properties.

4. In the Local Area Connection Properties dialog box, highlight Internet Protocol (TCP/IP) and click the Properties button.

5. The Internet Protocol (TCP/IP) Properties dialog box appears. Select the Obtain an IP Address Automatically radio button. Then click the OK button.

If your network adapter is a part of a network bridge, you will not be able to configure TCP/IP properties.

Using APIPA

Automatic Private IP Addressing (APIPA) is used to automatically assign private IP addresses for home or small business networks that contain a single subnet, have no DHCP server, and are not using static IP addressing. If APIPA is being used, then clients will only be able to communicate with other clients on the same subnet that are also using APIPA. The benefit of using APIPA in small networks is that it is less tedious and has less chance of configuration errors than statically assigning IP addresses and configuration.

APIPA is used with Windows XP Professional under the following conditions:

- The client is configured as a DHCP client, but no DHCP server is available to service the DHCP request.

- The client originally obtained a DHCP lease from a DHCP server, but when the client tried to renew the DHCP lease, the DHCP server was unavailable.

In the next sections you will learn how APIPA works, be able to determine if your computer is using APIPA, and how to disable APIPA.

How APIPA Works

By default, a range of Class B network addresses, 169.254.0.1 – 169.254.255.254, has been set aside as private Class B network addresses. Windows XP Professional uses this range of addresses to automatically assign IP addresses if APIPA is used.

The steps used by APIPA are as follows:

1. The client will select an address from the range of private Class B addresses that have been allocated, using the subnet mask of 255.255.0.0.

2. The client will use duplicate-address detection to verify that the address that was selected in not already in use.

3. If the address is already in use, the client will repeat steps 1 and 2, for a total of up to 10 retries. If the address is not already in use, the client will configure its interface with the address that was selected.

4. As a background process, the client will continue to search for a DHCP server every five minutes. If a DHCP server replies to the request, the APIPA configuration will be dropped and the client will receive new IP configuration settings from the DHCP server.

Determining if Your Computer Is Using APIPA

To determine if your computer is configured using APIPA, you would use the following command:

`Ipconfig /all`

The `Ipconfig /all` command will produce verbose text. If you see "Autoconfiguration Enabled" within the text and the IP address for your computer is within the 169.254.0.1 – 169.254.255.254 range, then APIPA is being used by your computer.

Disabling APIPA

If you want to disable APIPA for your computer, you can use one of the two following options:

- Confirm that a DHCP server has been properly configured to support requests from your computer.

- Disable APIPA (but not DHCP) for the computer by adding the **IPAutoconfiguration-Enabled** Registry entry with a value of 0 (REG_DWORD data type) to the following Registry subkey: HKEY_LOCAL_MACHINE\SYSTEM\CurrentControlSet\Services\Tcpip\Parameters\Interfaces*interface-name*.

  You will then need to restart the computer.

WARNING You edit the Registry with the `regedit` command-line utility. Improper editing of the Registry can cause the computer to fail to load Windows XP Professional. You should use this utility with great care.

Using Static IP Addressing

You can manually configure IP if you know your IP address and subnet mask. If you are using optional components such as a default gateway or a DNS server, you need to know the IP addresses of the computers that host these services as well. This option is not typically used in large networks because it is time-consuming and prone to user errors.

In Exercise 10.2, you will manually configure IP. This exercise assumes that you have a network adapter installed in your computer.

WARNING If you are on a "live" network, check with your network administrator before you make any changes to your IP configuration.

EXERCISE 10.2

Manually Configuring IP

1. Select Start ➤ Control Panel ➤ Network and Internet Connections.

2. From the Network and Internet Connections dialog box, click the Network Connections option. You will see your Local Area Connection as an icon.

3. Right-click Local Area Connection, and select Properties.

4. In the Local Area Connection Properties dialog box, highlight Internet Protocol (TCP/IP) and click the Properties button.

5. The Internet Protocol (TCP/IP) Properties dialog box appears, as shown below. Choose the Use the Following IP Address radio button.

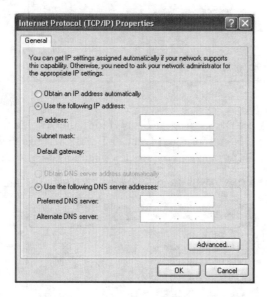

6. In the appropriate text boxes, specify the IP address 131.200.1.1 and subnet mask 255.255.0.0. Do not specify the default gateway option.

7. Click the OK button to save your settings and close the dialog box.

Advanced Configuration

Clicking the Advanced button in the Internet Protocol (TCP/IP) dialog box opens the Advanced TCP/IP Settings dialog box, shown in Figure 10.13. In this dialog box, you can configure advanced DNS, WINS, and other Options settings. The other options that can be configured include:

▪   The IP address that will be used. You can add, edit, or remove IP addresses.

▪   The default gateways that will be used and the metric associated with each gateway. Metrics are used to calculate the path that should be used through a network.

FIGURE 10.13 The Advanced TCP/IP Settings dialog box

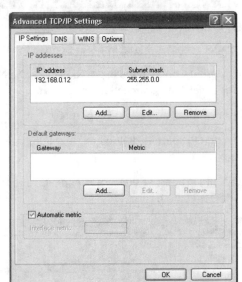

ADVANCED DNS SETTINGS

You can configure additional DNS servers to be used for name resolution and other advanced DNS settings through the DNS tab of the Advanced TCP/IP Settings dialog box, shown in Figure 10.14. The options in this dialog box are described in Table 10.2.

FIGURE 10.14 The DNS tab of the Advanced TCP/IP Settings dialog box

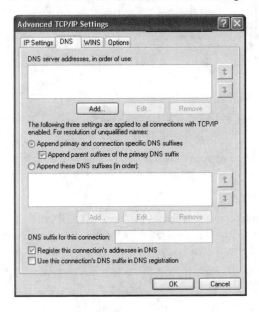

TABLE 10.2   Advanced DNS TCP/IP Settings Options

Option	Description
DNS server addresses, in order of use	Specifies the DNS servers that are used to resolve DNS queries. Use the arrow buttons on the right side of the list box to move a server up or down in the list.
Append primary and connection-specific DNS suffixes	Specifies how unqualified domain names are resolved by DNS. For example, if your primary DNS suffix is TestCorp.com and you type ping lala, DNS will try to resolve the address as lala.TestCorp.com.
Append parent suffixes of the primary DNS suffix	Specifies whether name resolution includes the parent suffix for the primary domain DNS suffix, up to the second level of the domain name. For example, if your primary DNS suffix is SanJose.TestCorp.com and you type ping lala, DNS will try to resolve the address as lala.SanJose.TestCorp.com. If this doesn't work, DNS will try to resolve the address as lala.TestCorp.com.
Append these DNS suffixes (in order)	Specifies the DNS suffixes that will be used to attempt to resolve unqualified name resolution. For example, if your primary DNS suffix is TestCorp.com and you type ping lala, DNS will try to resolve the address as lala.TestCorp.com. If you append the additional DNS suffix MyCorp.com and type ping lala, DNS will try to resolve the address as lala.TestCorp.com and lala.MyCorp.com.
DNS suffix for this connection	Specifies the DNS suffix for the computer. If this value is configured by a DHCP server and you specify a DNS suffix, it will override the value set by DHCP.
Register this connection's addresses in DNS	Specifies that the connection will try to register its addresses dynamically using the computer name that was specified through the Network Identification tab of the System Properties dialog box (accessed through the System icon in Control Panel).
Use this connection's DNS suffix in DNS registration	Specifies that when the computer registers automatically with the DNS server, it should use the combination of the computer name and the DNS suffix.

ADVANCED WINS SETTINGS

You can configure advanced WINS options through the WINS tab of the Advanced TCP/IP Settings dialog box, shown in Figure 10.15. The options in this dialog box are described in Table 10.3.

FIGURE 10.15 The WINS tab of the Advanced TCP/IP Settings dialog box

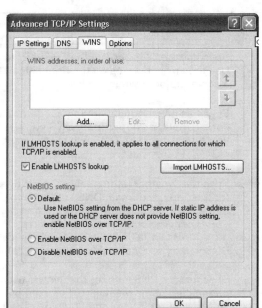

TABLE 10.3 Advanced WINS TCP/IP Settings Options

Option	Description
WINS addresses, in order of use	Specifies the WINS servers that are used to resolve WINS queries. You can use the arrow buttons on the right side of the list box to move a server up or down in the list.
Enable LMHOSTS lookup	Specifies whether an LMHOSTS file can be used for name resolution. If you configure this option, you can use the Import LMHOSTS button to import an LMHOSTS file to the computer.
Use NetBIOS setting from the DHCP server	Specifies that the computer should obtain its NetBIOS-over-TCP/IP and WINS settings from the DHCP server.
Enable NetBIOS over TCP/IP	Allows you to use statically configured IP addresses so that the computer is able to communicate with pre–Windows XP computers.
Disable NetBIOS over TCP/IP	Allows you to disable NetBIOS over TCP/IP. Use this option only if your network includes only Windows XP clients or DNS-enabled clients.

OPTIONS

The Options tab, shown in Figure 10.16, allows you to configure TCP/IP filtering options. By clicking the Properties button, you access the TCP/IP Filtering dialog box shown in Figure 10.17.

FIGURE 10.16   The Options tab of the Advanced TCP/IP Settings dialog box

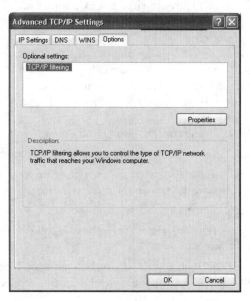

FIGURE 10.17   The TCP/IP Filtering dialog box

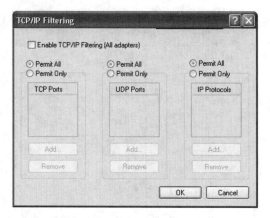

Through TCP/IP filtering, you can specify the following:

- Which TCP ports are permitted for your computer
- Which UDP ports are permitted for your computer
- Which IP protocols are permitted for your computer

Using Alternate IP Configuration

Windows XP Professional includes a new feature called Alternate IP Configuration. This feature is designed to be used by laptops and other mobile computers to manage IP configurations when the computer is used in multiple locations and one location requires a static IP address and the other location(s) require dynamic IP addressing. For example, a user with a laptop might need a static IP address to connect to their broadband ISP at home and then use DHCP when connected to the corporate network.

Alternate IP Configuration works by allowing the user to configure the computer so that it will initially try to connect to a network using DHCP; if the DHCP attempt fails (for example, when the user is at home), the alternate static IP configuration is used. The alternate static IP address can be an automatic private IP address (which would use APIPA) or a specifically configured IP address.

To configure Alternate IP Configuration, you would take the following steps:

1. Select Start ➢ Control Panel ➢ Network and Internet Connections.

2. From the Network and Internet Connections dialog box, click the Network Connection option. You will see your Local Area Connection as an icon.

3. Right-click Local Area Connection, and select Properties.

4. In the Local Area Connection Properties dialog box, highlight Internet Protocol (TCP/IP) and click the Properties button.

5. The Internet Protocol (TCP/IP) Properties dialog box appears. From the General tab, verify that the Obtain an IP Address Automatically radio button is selected. Click the Alternate Configuration tab as shown in Figure 10.18.

FIGURE 10.18   The Alternate Configuration tab of the Internet Protocol (TCP/IP) Properties dialog box

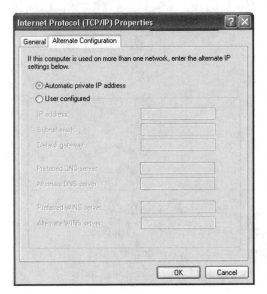

6. If you want to use APIPA to assign the alternate address, select the Automatic Private IP Address option. If you want to manually configure a static address, you would select the User Configured option. You would then need to supply the IP address, subnet mask—and, if needed, default gateway, preferred and alternate DNS servers and preferred and alternate WINS servers. Then click the OK button.

Additional TCP/IP Features and Options

The TCP/IP protocol is complex and offers many features. In addition to having a basic understanding of the TCP/IP protocol and being able to configure and manage basic IP configurations on a Windows XP Professional computer, you should be aware of some other key features and options of TCP/IP. The TCP/IP features and options that will be covered in greater detail in the following subsections include:

- Understanding TCP/IP name resolution
- Using multiple IP addresses
- Testing and verifying TCP/IP connectivity

Understanding TCP/IP Name Resolution

When users try to access a network resource, it is unusual for them to access the resource via an IP address. In Windows environments, users typically access resources using a hostname or a NetBIOS name. The methods used to manage TCP/IP name resolution are:

- DNS
- NetBIOS over TCP/IP (NetBT)
- WINS
- HOSTS or LMHOSTS files
- Subnet broadcasts

Domain Name System (DNS) is a global, distributed database that is based on a hierarchical naming system. DNS name resolution is used to name DNS-based names (friendly usernames such as Sybex.com) to IP addresses and vice versa. Windows 2000 and Windows 2003 domains inherently use DNS services, and DNS is the default name resolution method used.

Microsoft clients that are using Windows 9*x*, Windows Me, or other early implementations of Windows operating systems rely on NetBIOS names to identify computers on the network. Windows 2000 Server and Windows Server 2003 use a service called Windows Internet Name Service (WINS) for compatibility with applications and services that use NetBIOS services to map the NetBIOS name to an IP address.

HOSTS and LMHOSTS files are local files that must be maintained manually, to provide hostname-to-IP address resolution. This is not a common method of resolving IP addresses, as it is administrator intensive and prone to configuration errors.

If no name resolution method is configured for NetBIOS, the final way that address resolution is attempted is through the use of subnet broadcasts. You typically want to avoid these broadcasts since they are directed to all computers on the subnet as opposed to being sent only to the specified computer as a unicast transmission.

Using Multiple IP Addresses

Windows XP Professional allows you to configure more than one network adapter in a single computer, which is referred to as multihoming. Windows XP Professional also supports logical multihoming, which is when multiple IP addresses are configured for a single network adapter. You would use logical multihoming if you had a single physical network that was logically divided into subnets and you wanted your computer to logically be associated with more than one subnet.

To configure multiple IP addresses for a single network adapter, you would take the following steps:

1. Select Start ➢ Control Panel ➢ Network and Internet Connections.

2. From the Network and Internet Connections dialog box, click the Network Connections option. You will see your Local Area Connection as an icon.

3. Right-click Local Area Connection and select Properties.

4. In the Local Area Connection Properties dialog box, highlight Internet Protocol (TCP/IP) and click the Properties button.

5. From the Internet Protocol (TCP/IP) Properties dialog box, verify that Use the Following IP Address is selected and configured for the first configuration you want to use.

6. From the Internet Protocol (TCP/IP) Properties dialog box, click the Advanced button to access the Advanced TCP/IP Settings dialog box. From the IP Settings tab (shown in Figure 10.13), under IP Addresses, click the Add button. You will then be able to assign multiple IP addresses and subnet mask settings. Click the Add button again to add any additional addresses.

7. If you need to assign more than one default gateway to your IP configuration, use the Default Gateways section of Advanced IP Settings.

Testing IP Configuration

After you have installed and configured the TCP/IP settings, you can test the IP configuration using the IPCONFIG, PING, and NBTSTAT command-line utilities. These commands are also very useful in troubleshooting IP configuration errors. You can also graphically view connection details through Local Area Connection Status. Each command is covered in detail in the following subsections.

The *IPCONFIG* Command

The *IPCONFIG* command displays your IP configuration. Table 10.4 lists the command switches that can be used with the IPCONFIG command.

TABLE 10.4   IPCONFIG Switches

Switch	Description
/?	Shows all of the help options for IPCONFIG
/all	Shows verbose information about your IP configuration, including your computer's physical address, the DNS server you are using, and whether you are using DHCP
/release	Releases an address that has been assigned through DHCP
/renew	Renews an address through DHCP
/flushdns	Purges the DNS Resolver cache
/registerdns	Shows the contents of the DNS Resolver cache
/showclassid	Lists the DHCP class IDs allowed by the computer
/setclassID	Allows you to modify the DHCP class ID

In Exercise 10.3, you will verify your configuration with the IPCONFIG command. This exercise assumes that you have a network adapter installed in your computer and have completed Exercise 10.2.

EXERCISE 10.3

Using the IPCONFIG Command

1. Select Start ➤ All Programs ➤ Accessories ➤ Command Prompt.

2. In the Command Prompt dialog box, type **IPCONFIG** and press Enter. Note the IP address, which should be the address that you configured in Exercise 10.2.

3. In the Command Prompt dialog box, type **IPCONFIG /all** and press Enter. You now see more information.

The *PING* Command

The *PING* command is used to send an ICMP (Internet Control Message Protocol) echo request and echo reply to verify whether the remote computer is available. You can PING a computer based on the computer's IP address or the DNS name. If you were using an IP address, the PING command has the following syntax:

PING *IP address*

For example, if your IP address is 131.200.2.30, you would type the following command:

PING 131.200.2.30

If you were using an DNS name, the PING command has the following syntax:

PING *DNS name*

For example, if your DNS name was Example.Sybex.com, you would type the following command:

PING Example.Sybex.com

PING is useful for verifying connectivity between two hosts. For example, if you were having trouble connecting to a host on another network, PING would help you verify that a valid communication path existed. You would ping the following addresses:

- The loopback address, 127.0.0.1
- The local computer's IP address (you can verify this with IPCONFIG)
- The local router's (default gateway's) IP address
- The remote computer's IP address

If PING failed to get a reply from any of these addresses, you would have a starting point for troubleshooting the connection error. The error messages that can be returned from a PING request include:

- TTL Expired in Transit, which means that the packet exceeded the number of hops specified to reach the destination host computer. Each time a packet passes through a router, the Time To Live (TTL) counter reflects the pass through the router as a hop. You can use the ping -i parameter to increase TTL. This error can also be due to a routing configuration error, which has resulted in a routing loop. The tracert command can be used to identify routing loops.

- Destination Host Unreachable, which is generated when a local or remote route path does not exist between the sending host and the specified destination computer. This error could occur because the router is misconfigured or the target computer is not available.

- Request Timed Out, which means that the echo reply message was not received from the destination computer within the time allotted. By default, destination computers have four seconds to respond. You can increase the timeout value with the ping -w parameter.

- Ping Request Could Not Find Host, which indicates that the destination hostname couldn't be resolved. Verify that the destination hostname was properly specified, that all DNS and WINS settings are correct, and that the DNS and WINS servers are available.

The *NBTSTAT* Command

NBT is NetBIOS over TCP/IP, and the NBTSTAT command is used to display TCP/IP connection protocol statistics over NBT. Table 10.5 lists the command-line options that can be used.

TABLE 10.5   NBTSTAT Command-Line Options

Switch	Option	Description
/?	Help	Shows all of the help options for NBTSTAT
-a	Adapter Status	Shows adapter status and lists the remote computer's name, based on the hostname you specify
-A	Adapter Status	Shows adapter status and lists the remote computer's name, based on the IP address you specify
-c	Cache	Displays the NBT's cache of remote computers through their names and IP addresses
-n	Names	Shows a list of the local computer's NetBIOS names
-r	Resolved	Shows a list of computer names that have been resolved either through broadcast or WINS
-R	Reload	Causes the remote cache name table to be purged and reloaded
-S	Sessions	Shows the current sessions table with the destination IP addresses
-s	Sessions	Shows the current sessions table and the converted destination IP address to the computer's NetBIOS name
-RR	ReleaseRefresh	Sends a Name Release packet to the WINS server, then starts a refresh

Local Area Connection Status

To use a graphical interface to access local area connection status, you access the main windows of Network Connections (from Control Panel ➢ Network and Internet Connections), then right-click Local Area Connection and select Status.

From the Local Area Connection Status dialog box, shown in Figure 10.19, you can view connection information including status, duration, and the speed at which you connected. You can also see the activity that has been generated for the current session through all packets that have been sent and received through the network adapter.

If you click the Support tab on the Local Area Connection dialog box, you will see the support status, as shown in Figure 10.20. This will display the general configuration for your connection. If you click the Details button on the Status tab of the dialog box, you will see even more detailed configuration information on your connection on the Network Connection Details dialog box (Figure 10.21).

FIGURE 10.19 The Local Area Connection Status dialog box

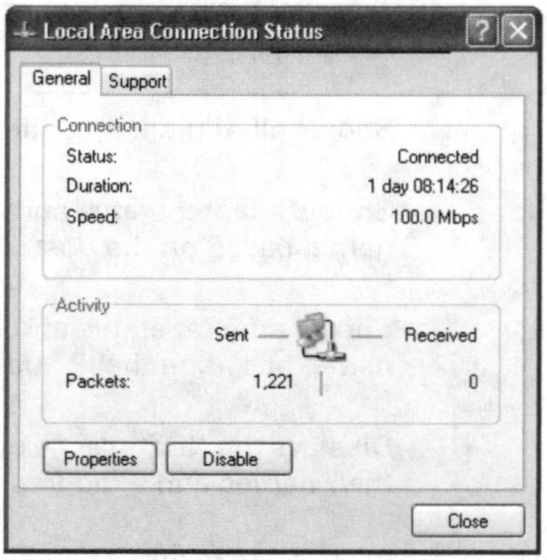

FIGURE 10.20 The Support tab of the Local Area Connection Status dialog box

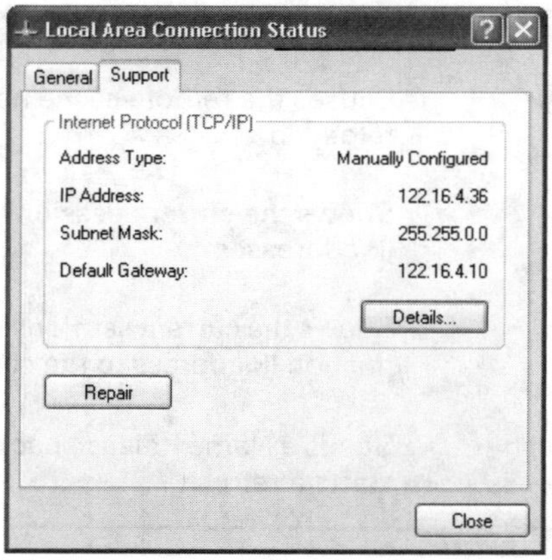

FIGURE 10.21 The Network Connection Details dialog box

Using NWLink IPX/SPX/NetBIOS

NWLink IPX/SPX/NetBIOS Compatible Transport is Microsoft's implementation of the Novell IPX/SPX (Internetwork Packet Exchange/Sequenced Packet Exchange) protocol stack. The Windows XP implementation of the IPX/SPX protocol stack adds NetBIOS support.

The main function of NWLink is to act as a transport protocol to route packets through internetworks. By itself, the NWLink protocol does not allow you to access NetWare File and Print Services. However, it does provide a method of transporting the data across the network. If you want to access NetWare File and Print Services, you must install NWLink and Client Services for NetWare (software that works at the upper layers of the OSI model to allow access to File and Print Services).

One advantage of using NWLink is that it is easy to install and configure. The following sections describe how to install and configure this protocol.

In Exercise 10.4, you will install the NWLink IPX/SPX protocol. This exercise assumes that you have a network adapter installed in your computer.

EXERCISE 10.4

Installing NWLink IPX/SPX Protocol

1. Select Start and right-click My Network Places, then select Properties. Right-click Local Area Connection and select Properties.

2. In the Local Area Connection Properties dialog box, click the Install button.

3. The Select Network Component Type dialog box appears. Highlight Protocol and click the Add button.

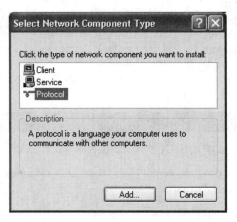

4. The Select Network Protocol dialog box appears. Select NWLink IPX/SPX/NetBIOS Compatible Transport Protocol from the list. Then click the OK button.

EXERCISE 10.4 *(continued)*

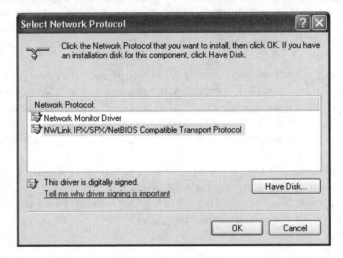

Configuring NWLink IPX/SPX

The only options that are configured for NWLink are the *internal network number* and the *frame type*. Normally, you leave both settings at their default values.

The internal network number is commonly used to identify NetWare file servers. It is also used when you are running File and Print Services for NetWare or using IPX routing.

The frame type specifies how the data is packaged for transmission over the network. If the computers that are using NWLink use different frame types, they are not able to communicate with each other. The default setting for frame type is Auto Detect, which will attempt to automatically choose a compatible frame type for your network. If you need to connect to servers that use various frame types, you should configure Manual Frame Type Detection, which will allow you to use a different frame type for each network.

In Exercise 10.5, you will configure the NWLink IPX/SPX protocol.

EXERCISE 10.5

Configuring the NWLink IPX/SPX Protocol

1. Select Start and right-click My Network Places, then select Properties. Right-click Local Area Connection and select Properties.

2. In the Local Area Connection Properties dialog box, highlight NWLink IPX/SPX/NetBIOS Compatible Transport Protocol and click the Properties button.

EXERCISE 10.5 *(continued)*

3. The NWLink IPX/SPX/NetBIOS Compatible Transport Protocol Properties dialog box appears. In this dialog box, you can configure your internal network number and frame type.

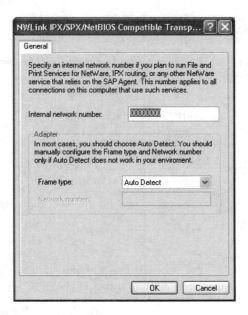

Summary

This chapter described how to manage network connections. We covered the following topics:

- Installing, configuring, and troubleshooting network adapters. You configure a network adapter through its Properties dialog box.

- Installing, configuring, and testing network protocols. TCP/IP is the default protocol installed with Windows XP Professional. You can also install the NWLink IPX/SPX/NetBIOS Compatible Transport protocol.

Exam Essentials

Be able to install, configure, and troubleshoot network adapters.   Know how to configure network adapters. Know how to troubleshoot network adapter problems that keep a client from attaching to the network.

Be able to configure and troubleshoot TCP/IP. Know the primary purpose and configuration options for TCP/IP, DHCP, WINS, and DNS. Know how to troubleshoot protocol-related network problems.

Key Terms

Before you take the exam, be certain you are familiar with the following terms:

Alternate IP Configuration	IPCONFIG
Automatic Private IP Addressing (APIPA)	NetBIOS
default gateway	network adapters
Domain Name System (DNS) servers	NWLink IPX/SPX/NetBIOS Compatible Transport
driver	PING
Dynamic Host Configuration Protocol (DHCP)	subnet mask
frame type	Transmission Control Protocol/Internet Protocol (TCP/IP)
internal network number	Windows Internet Name Service (WINS) servers
IP address	

Review Questions

1. You are the network administrator for a network that contains multiple subnets. You recently installed a computer on Subnet 2 called Client2. The user of computer Client2 requires access to a legacy application on a Windows NT Server 4 server called \AppServer that is located on Subnet 1 as shown in the following exhibit:

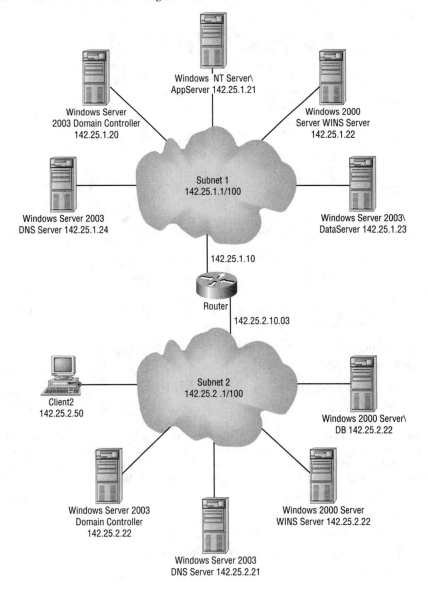

Windows NT Server\
AppServer 142.25.1.21

Windows Server
2003 Domain Controller
142.25.1.20

Windows 2000
Server WINS Server
142.25.1.22

Subnet 1
142.25.1.1/100

Windows Server 2003
DNS Server 142.25.1.24

Windows Server 2003\
DataServer 142.25.1.23

142.25.1.10

Router
142.25.2.10.03

Client2
142.25.2.50

Subnet 2
142.25.2 .1/100

Windows 2000 Server\
DB 142.25.2.22

Windows Server 2003
Domain Controller
142.25.2.22

Windows 2000 Server
WINS Server 142.25.2.22

Windows Server 2003
DNS Server 142.25.2.21

When the user who sits at Client2 tries to access \AppServer, they get the following error message:

"Network path not found."

When the user accesses the \DataServer on Subnet 1, they can successfully access shared resources. When the user accesses the \DB server on Subnet 2, they can successfully access shared resources. When you view the connection details for Client2, you see the following dialog box:

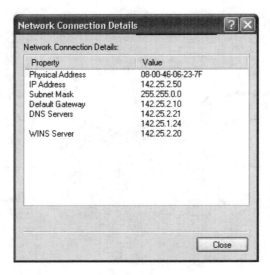

Based on the previous information, what course of action should you take so the user at Client2 can access the application on the \AppServer?

A. You should switch the order that the DNS servers are queried in.

B. The WINS server should be configured with the address 142.25.1.22.

C. The Default Gateway should be configured as 142.25.1.10.

D. You should configure Client2 to use an available IP address from Subnet 1.

2. You are the network administrator for a large company. It's Monday morning and you have just plugged your laptop into the corporate network. When you try to access network resources, you are unable to access anything. Your network uses the TCP/IP protocol with a DHCP server. On Friday, you had no problem accessing network resources. What is the first action you should take to determine the problem?

A. Replace your network cable.

B. Replace your network card.

C. Use IPCONFIG to make sure your IP configuration is valid.

D. Use TCPCONFIG to make sure your IP configuration is valid.

3. You are the network administrator of a medium-sized company. You are trying to attach a network share to a computer whose IP address is 131.200.1.16. You are not sure of the computer's NetBIOS name. Which of the following command-line utilities can you use to determine the NetBIOS name?

A. IPCONFIG

B. PING

C. NBTSTAT

D. GROPE

4. You have a network adapter that is not able to correctly attach to the network. You discover that the driver you are using is outdated and there is an updated driver that will likely solve your problem. In the network adapter's Properties dialog box, shown here, what tab will you work in to update the network adapter's driver?

A. General

B. Advanced

C. Driver

D. Resources

5. Your computer is called WS1. You are not able to access any network resources. You know that WS2 can access the network, and you want to test communication between WS1 and WS2. Which command would you use to test communications with another computer based on its IP address?

A. IPCONFIG

B. TESTIP

C. PING

D. GROPE

6. Your network uses the TCP/IP protocol. Julie configures her computer to use TCP/IP. When Julie tries to access network resources, she can't. She checks with you, the network administrator, and you discover that her subnet mask is incorrectly configured. When Julie asks you why the subnet mask is important, what do you tell her is its function?

A. To specify which part of the IP address is the network address and which part of the IP address is the host or client address

B. To specify how packets should be routed through an internetwork

C. To determine the preferred DNS and WINS servers that exist on a network

D. To specify whether you are using a dynamic or static configuration

7. When you try to access the SALES server, which is a Windows NT Server 4, you are able to access it via the IP address but not by its Windows NetBIOS name. In the following exhibit, what IP configuration should you check into?

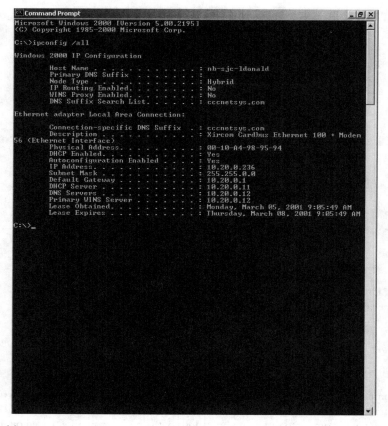

A. IP address

B. Default gateway

C. DNS server

D. Primary WINS server

8. Suzanne is sitting at computer XPPRO1. She wants to be able to access resources on XPPRO2. Based on the following diagram, how should Suzanne configure her default gateway?

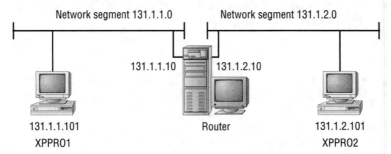

Network segment 131.1.1.0   Network segment 131.1.2.0

131.1.1.10   131.1.2.10

131.1.1.101   Router   131.1.2.101
XPPRO1   XPPRO2

   A. 131.1.1.0

   B. 131.1.1.10

   C. 131.1.2.0

   D. 131.1.2.10

9. Your primary DNS suffix is configured as `acmetest.com`. You want to access resources on the `acmecorp.com` domain without using fully qualified domain names. Which option should you use?

   A. Append Primary and Connection Specific DNS Suffixes

   B. Append These DNS Suffixes (in Order)

   C. Configure This as a HOSTS File

   D. Configure This as an LMHOSTS File

10. When you try to access the `sales.acmecorp.com` server, you can access the server using the server's IP address, but not the fully qualified domain name. Which configuration file can you use to alleviate this problem?

   A. HOSTS

   B. LMHOSTS

   C. dns.txt

   D. wins.txt

11. Your domain suffix is configured as `sanjose.acmecorp.com`. Normally, you access resources from within your domain. Occasionally, you access resources in the `acmecorp.com` domain. You want to be able to access resources in either domain without specifying a fully qualified domain name. Which option should you use?

   A. Append Parent Suffixes of the Primary DNS Suffix

   B. Append Secondary DNS Suffix

   C. Append Child Suffixes of the Primary DNS Suffix

   D. Append Upstream Suffixes of the Primary DNS Suffix

12. Your network consists of Windows XP Professional computers and Windows NT 4 Workstation computers. You want to be able to access the Windows NT 4 Workstation computers by using their NetBIOS names. Your network does not have WINS servers configured. Which file should you configure and use?

A. HOSTS

B. LMHOSTS

C. wins.cfg

D. wins.txt

13. Your network consists of many different versions of NetWare servers. You have configured your Windows XP Professional computer with the NWLink IPX/SPX/NetBIOS Compatible Transport protocol and Client Services for NetWare. You see only some of the NetWare servers, but not the servers you need to access. In the following exhibit, which item is most likely not configured properly?

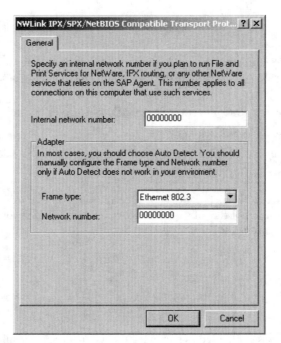

A. Internal network number.

B. Frame type.

C. Network number.

D. Everything is properly configured.

14. You have two DHCP servers on your network. Your computer accidentally received the wrong IP configuration from a DHCP server that was misconfigured. The DHCP server with the incorrect configuration has been disabled. What command would you use to release and renew your computer's DHCP configuration?

   A. IPCONFIG

   B. DHCPRECON

   C. RELEASE

   D. IPADJUST

15. Your Windows XP Professional computer is configured with TCP/IP, NWLink IPX/SPX/NetBIOS Compatible Transport, and NetBEUI. TCP/IP is your most commonly used network protocol. You want to configure your network bindings so that the TCP/IP protocol is listed first. How do you configure network bindings in Windows XP?

   A. In the Network and Dial-up Connections window, select Advanced, then Advanced Settings.

   B. In the network adapter Properties dialog box, click the Bindings tab.

   C. In the network adapter Properties dialog box, click the Advanced tab, then click the Bindings button.

   D. This is configurable only through the Registry.

Answers to Review Questions

1. B. Since the \AppServer is running Windows NT Server 4, you will need to have some sort of NetBIOS name resolution configured. In this case, the WINS Server can be used for NetBIOS-to-IP name resolution over the subnet. The configuration of the WINS Server on Client2 should be configured as 142.25.1.22.

2. C. If everything worked properly on Friday, then your hardware is most likely in good order. The first thing you should check is your IP configuration, making sure that it was properly set by the DHCP server. You can verify the configuration with the IPCONFIG command. If the IP configuration appears to be correct, use the PING command to verify that you can communicate with other computers using the TCP/IP protocol.

3. C. The NBTSTAT command with the –A switch will display the NetBIOS name of the computer. In this case, you would type **NBTSTAT –A 131.200.1.16**.

4. C. You use the settings in the Driver tab to uninstall or update a device driver. If the new driver does not work, you can use the Rollback Driver option to return to the previous driver that was working.

5. C. The PING command is used to send an ICMP echo request and echo reply between two IP hosts to test whether a valid communication path exits. If no valid path exists, the PING command can be used to trace where in the communications path the error exists.

6. A. The subnet mask is used to specify which part of the address is the network address and which part of the address is the host or client address. Improperly configured subnet masks can cause the computer not to communicate properly with the rest of the network.

7. D. You use WINS servers to resolve NetBIOS computer names to IP addresses. DHCP servers are used to dynamically assign the IP configuration. DNS servers are used to resolve domain names to IP addresses.

8. B. Suzanne needs to configure the default gateway with the IP address of the router connection that is attached to her subnet, 131.1.1.10. If her default gateway is not properly configured, she will only be able to communicate with other computers on her subnet.

9. B. The option to Append These DNS Suffixes (in Order), in the DNS tab of the Advanced TCP/IP Settings dialog box, specifies the DNS suffixes that will be used for unqualified name resolution. For example, if your primary DNS suffix is TestCorp.com and you type ping lala, DNS will try to resolve the address as lala.TestCorp.com. If you append the additional DNS suffix MyCorp.com and type ping lala, DNS will try to resolve the address as lala.TestCorp .com and lala.MyCorp.com.

10. A. If you do not have access to a properly configured DNS server, you can use a HOSTS file to map IP addresses to domain hostnames. This option is not commonly used, as it is administrator intensive and is prone to user errors.

11. A. If you use the option to Append Primary and Connection Specific DNS Suffixes (in the DNS tab of the Advanced TCP/IP Settings dialog box), you can also configure the Append Parent Suffixes of the Primary DNS Suffix option. This option specifies whether name resolution includes the parent suffix for the primary domain DNS suffix, up to the second level of the domain name.

12. B.   If your network does not use a WINS server, you can configure an LMHOSTS file to map IP addresses to NetBIOS computer names. This option is not commonly used, as it is administrator intensive and is prone to user errors.

13. B.   The NetWare server you need to connect to may be configured with a different frame type. You should find out what frame type the server is using and configure the Windows XP computer with the same frame type.

14. A.   You can release your DHCP configuration with the IPCONFIG /release command, and renew your DHCP configuration with the IPCONFIG /renew command. Then your IP configuration will be provided by the correct DHCP server.

15. A.   To configure network bindings, you open the Network and Dial-up Connections window and select Advanced ➢ Advanced Settings. You can specify the binding order in the Adapters and Bindings tab of the Advanced Settings dialog box.

Chapter
11

Managing Printing

MICROSOFT EXAM OBJECTIVES COVERED IN THIS CHAPTER:

✓ **Connect to local and network print devices.**

- Manage printers and print jobs.
- Control access to printers by using permissions.
- Connect to a local print device.

One common network management task is setting up and using printers. To manage printing, you need an understanding of the printing process and the terminology associated with the process.

The process of creating, managing, and deleting printers is fairly easy. When you create printers, you use a wizard, which leads you through each step of the configuration. Anything that is not configured through the Add Printer Wizard can be configured through the printer's properties. You can also manage printing options such as pausing and deleting print jobs for the entire printer or for specific print documents.

In this chapter, you will learn the basics of Windows XP Professional printing, how to set up and configure printers, and how to manage printers and print jobs. You will also learn how to troubleshoot printing problems.

The printing processes used by Windows XP Professional and Windows Server 2003 are the same.

Printing Basics

Before you learn about the specifics of Windows XP printing, you should have an understanding of basic network printing principles. Table 11.1 defines the terms that relate to network printing, and the following sections describe the printing process and the roles of print devices and printers.

TABLE 11.1   Windows XP Printing Terminology

Term	Definition
Printer	The software interface between the *physical printer* (the print device) and the operating system. This is also referred to as a *logical printer*. You can create printers through the Printers folder.
Print device	The actual physical printer or hardware device that produces the printed output.

TABLE 11.1   Windows XP Printing Terminology *(continued)*

Term	Definition
Print server	The computer on which the printer has been defined. When you send a job to a network printer, you are actually sending it to the print server first.
Print spooler	A directory or folder on the print server that stores the print jobs until they can be printed. This is also referred to as a *print queue*. Your print server and print spooler must have enough hard disk space to hold all the print jobs that could be pending at any given time.
Print processor	The process that determines whether a print job needs further processing once that job has been sent to the spooler. The processing (also called *rendering*) is used to format the print job so that it can print correctly at the print device.
Printer pool	A configuration that allows you to use one printer for multiple print devices. A printer pool is useful when you have multiple printer devices that use the same print driver and are in the same location. By using printer pools, users can send their print jobs to the first available printer device.
Print driver	The specific software that understands your print device. Each print device has its own command set, and each print device has an associated print driver.
Physical port	The port through which a printer is directly connected to a computer, either a serial (COM), parallel (LPT) port, or Universal Serial Bus (USB) port.
Logical port	The port through which a printer with a network card is attached to a network. A logical port is much faster than a *physical port*. It also is not restricted by parallel and serial cable distance limitations, which apply to printers connected to a PC's parallel or serial port.
Local printer	A printer that uses a physical port and that has not been shared. If a printer is defined as local, the only users who can use it are the local users of the computer to which the printer is attached.
Network printer	A printer that is available to local and network users. Network printers can use either a physical or logical port.

The Windows XP Printing Process

Printing is a common area of difficulty in many networks. To troubleshoot the problems related to the Windows XP printing process, you need to understand the steps involved in the process. A simple overview of the printing process is illustrated in Figure 11.1.

FIGURE 11.1   An overview of the Windows XP printing process

1. Client creates document.
2. Client connects to network printer (downloads print driver).
3. Print job is sent to spooler.
4. Job is sent to print device.

The following steps are involved in the printing process:

1. From the client, the user chooses to print. On any Windows platform, the print request is passed to the *Graphics Device Interface (GDI)*. The GDI calls the *print driver*. If the user is accessing the printer for the first time, the print driver is loaded into the client's memory from the *print server*. The print driver will stay in memory until the computer is turned off or a newer print driver is detected on the print server. The GDI is also responsible for processing print jobs for the appropriate print device.

2. The print job is sent to the computer's local *print spooler*, which in turn sends the job over the network to the print server.

3. The router at the print server receives the print job.

4. The router passes the print job to the print spooler on the print server, which spools the print job to a disk.

5. The *print processor* on the spooler analyzes the print job. If the job needs any further processing, the print processor does this so that the job will print correctly.

6. If specified, the separator page processor adds a *separator page* to the front of the print job.

7. The print job is passed to the Print Manager, which determines when the job should print and directs it to the correct port.

8. The print job goes to the print device, and the job prints.

To print to a printer, you must have that printer's driver in place to tell the application how to send the print job. Windows XP Professional clients automatically download the print driver from the print server each time they send a print job. If the print driver is updated on the print server, the next time the user sends a job to the printer, the driver is automatically updated.

With Windows XP Professional, you can also specify drivers for automatic download for other Windows NT, 2000, and XP clients. See the "Configuring Sharing Properties" section later in this chapter for details.

The Roles of Print Devices and Printers

A print device is the actual physical printer or hardware device that does the printing. In Windows XP terminology, a *printer* is the software interface between the print device and the operating system.

When you set up your computer or your network, you can determine the number of print devices by simply counting the devices you can see and touch. Printers are a bit trickier to enumerate, because you can configure them in several ways:

- One printer per print device
- One printer for multiple print devices, called *printer pooling*
- Multiple printers for a single print device, a configuration usually set up to allow print scheduling

You'll learn how to configure printer pools and set up print scheduling (by configuring the printer's availability) in the "Managing Printer Properties" section later in this chapter.

Setting Up Printers

Before you can access your physical print device under Windows XP Professional, you must first create a logical printer. To create a printer, you follow the steps in the Add Printer Wizard. To create a new printer in Windows XP Professional, you must be logged on as a member of the Administrators or Power Users group.

The computer on which you run the Add Printer Wizard and create the printer automatically becomes the print server for that printer. As the print server, the computer must have enough processing power to support incoming print jobs and enough disk space to hold all of the print jobs that will be queued.

In Exercise 11.1, you will create printers using the Add Printer Wizard.

EXERCISE 11.1

Creating Printers

In this exercise, you will create two local printers—one to share, and one that will not be shared. You will manually specify their print device configurations.

Adding the First Printer

1. Select Start ➤ Printers and Faxes, then under Printer Tasks, click Add a Printer.

EXERCISE 11.1 *(continued)*

2. The Add Printer Wizard starts. Click the Next button to continue.

3. In the Local or Network Printer dialog box, select the Local printer attached to this computer radio button. Make sure that the check box for "Automatically detect and install my Plug and Play printer" is not checked (unless you have a print device attached to your computer). If no printer is attached, you will see a message that no Plug and Play printer can be found. Click Next to continue.

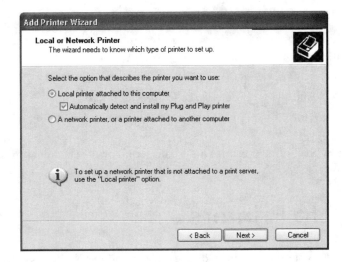

4. In the Select a Printer Port dialog box, select the Use the Following Port radio button, select LPT1 in the list box, and click the Next button.

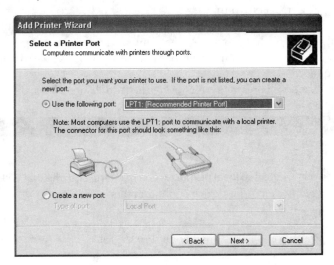

5. Next up is a dialog box that lists printer manufacturers and models. Select the print device manufacturer and model. In this example, choose HP in the Manufacturer list box and HP DeskJet 970Cse in the Printers list box. Then click the Next button.

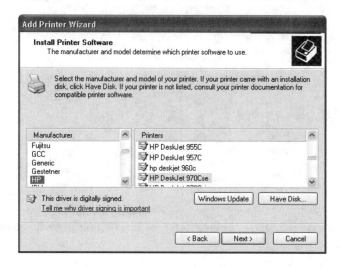

If you have already installed this driver on your computer, this dialog box will also include a Windows Update button next to the Have Disk button.

6. In the Name Your Printer dialog box, leave the default name of HP DeskJet 970Cse and click the Next button.

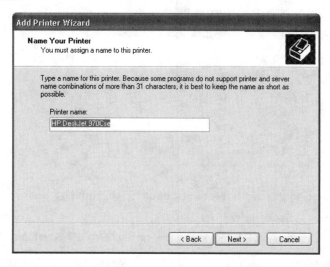

7. In the Printer Sharing dialog box, select the Share name radio button and type **HPDJ970** in the text box. Then click the Next button.

EXERCISE 11.1 *(continued)*

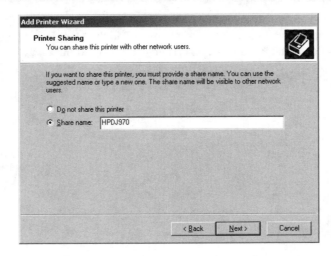

8. In the Location and Comment dialog box, type **Building 6, Room 765** into the Location text box, and **HP DeskJet 970Cse - Color Printer for the Technical Writers Group** into the Comment text box. Click the Next button.

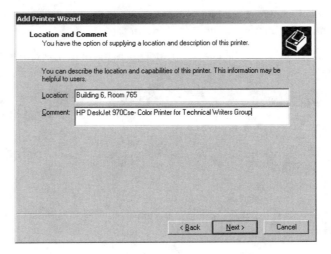

9. In the next dialog box, select the No radio button to skip printing a test page, and click Next to continue.

10. In the Completing the Add Printer Wizard dialog box, click the Finish button.

To complete the printer setup process, the Add Printer Wizard will copy files (if necessary) and create your printer. An icon for your new printer will appear in the Printers and Faxes folder.

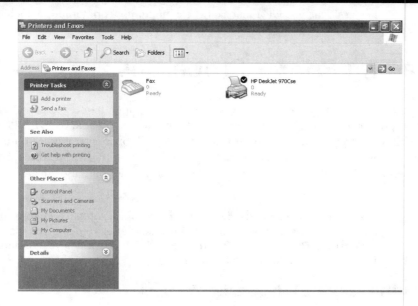

Adding the Second Printer

11. Select Start ➤ Printers and Faxes, then under Printer Tasks click Add a Printer. When the Add Printer Wizard starts, click the Next button to continue.

12. In the Local or Network Printer dialog box, select the Local printer attached to this computer radio button. Make sure the check box for "Automatically detect and install my Plug and Play printer" is not checked (unless you have a print device attached to your computer), and click Next to continue.

13. In the Select a Printer Port dialog box, select the Use the Following Port radio button, select LPT2 in the list box, and click the Next button.

14. In next dialog box, choose HP in the Manufacturer list box and HP LaserJet 4 in the Printers list box. Click the Next button.

15. In the Name Your Printer dialog box, leave the default name of HP LaserJet 4 and click the Next button.

16. In the Printer Sharing dialog box, select the Do Not Share This Printer radio button and click the Next button.

17. In the Print Test Page dialog box, select No to skip printing a test page and click the Next button.

18. In the Completing the Add Printer Wizard dialog box, click the Finish button.

If you are creating a printer that is attached to a computer running Windows XP Professional, you will most likely be configuring a printer for personal use or limited network access.

Managing Printer Properties

Printer properties allow you to configure options such as the printer name, whether the printer is shared, and printer security. To access the printer Properties dialog box, open the Printers folder, right-click the printer you want to manage, and choose Properties from the pop-up menu.

The printer Properties dialog box has six tabs: General, Sharing, Ports, Advanced, Security, and Device Settings. The following sections describe the properties on these tabs.

The Properties dialog boxes for some printers will contain additional tabs to allow advanced configuration of the printer. For example, if you install an HP DeskJet 970Cse printer, its Properties dialog box will have additional tabs for Color Management and Services.

Configuring General Properties

The General tab of the printer Properties dialog box, shown in Figure 11.2, contains information about the printer. It also lets you set printing preferences and print test pages. The information here (name of the printer, its location, and comments about it) reflects your entries when you set the printer up (as described in the preceding section). You can add or change this information in the text boxes.

FIGURE 11.2   The General tab of the printer Properties dialog box

Beneath the Comment box, you see the model of the printer. The items listed in the Features section depend on the model and driver you are using, and may include the following:

- Color printing support

- Double-sided printing support
- Stapling support
- The maximum number of pages that can be printed per minute (ppm)
- The maximum resolution for the printer, in dots per inch (dpi)

At the bottom of the dialog box, you see the Printing Preferences and Print Test Page buttons. Their functions are described in the following sections.

Setting Printing Preferences

Clicking the Printing Preferences button brings up the Printing Preferences dialog box, which allows you to specify the layout of the paper, page order, and paper source. In addition to the Layout and Paper Quality tabs, an Advanced button allows you to configure more printer options.

Layout Settings

The Layout tab of the Printing Preferences dialog box, shown in Figure 11.3, allows you to specify the orientation and page order. Your choices for the Orientation setting are Portrait (vertical) and Landscape (horizontal).

FIGURE 11.3   The Layout tab of the Printing Preferences dialog box

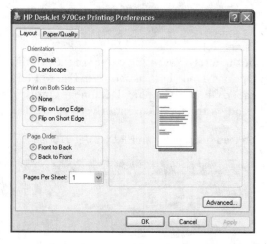

The Page Order setting specifies whether you want page 1 of the document to be on the top of the stack (Front to Back) or on the bottom of the stack (Back to Front).

 In Windows NT 4, your documents always print back to front, meaning page 1 prints first. At the end of the print job, you have to reorder your pages.

The Pages Per Sheet setting determines how many pages should be printed on a single page. You might use this feature if you were printing a book and wanted two pages to be printed side by side on a single page.

Paper/Quality Settings

The Paper/Quality tab allows you to configure properties that relate to the paper and quality of a print job. Available options depend on the features of your printer. For example, a printer may have only one option, such as Paper Source. For an HP DeskJet 970Cse printer, on the other hand, you can configure Paper Source, Media, Quality Settings, and Color options, as shown in Figure 11.4.

FIGURE 11.4 The Paper/Quality tab of the Printing Preferences dialog box

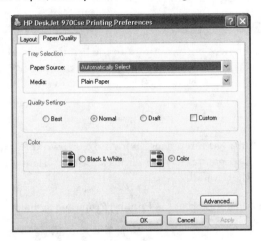

Advanced Settings

Clicking the Advanced button in the lower-right corner of the Printing Preferences dialog box brings up the Advanced Options dialog box, as shown in Figure 11.5. Here, you can configure printer options such as Paper/Output, Graphic, Document Options, and Printer Features. The options available depend on the specific print driver you are using.

FIGURE 11.5 Advanced options for an HP DeskJet 970Cse

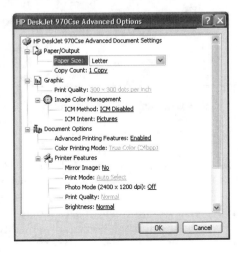

Printing a Test Page

The Print Test Page button at the bottom of the General tab of the printer Properties tab allows you to print a test page. This option is especially useful in troubleshooting printing problems. For example, you might use the Print Test Page option in a situation where no print driver is available for a print device and you want to try to use a compatible print driver. If the print job doesn't print or doesn't print correctly (it might print just one character per page, for example), you will know that the print driver isn't compatible.

Configuring Sharing Properties

The Sharing tab of the printer Properties dialog box, shown in Figure 11.6, allows you to specify whether the computer will be configured as a *local printer* (do not share) or as a shared *network printer* (share this printer). If you choose to share the printer, you also need to specify a share name, which will be seen by the network users. By default Windows XP will suggest a share name that is eight characters or less, so that the printer will be accessible by MS-DOS workstations. However, if you are in an environment that does not have MS-DOS workstations that will attach to your printer share, you can create longer share names.

FIGURE 11.6   The Sharing tab of the printer Properties dialog box

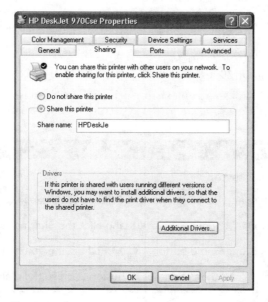

Also available in the Sharing tab is an option for driver support of print clients other than Windows XP clients. This is a significant feature of Windows XP Professional print support, because you can specify print drivers for other clients to automatically download. The only driver that is loaded by default is the Intel driver for Windows 2000 and XP. To provide the additional drivers for the clients, click the Additional Drivers button at the bottom of the Sharing tab. This brings up the Additional Drivers dialog box (Figure 11.7).

FIGURE 11.7 The Additional Drivers dialog box

Windows XP Professional supports adding print drivers for the following platforms:

- Alpha Windows NT 4
- IA64 Windows XP
- Intel Windows 2000 or XP
- Intel Windows 95, 98, or Me
- Intel Windows NT 4 or 2000

In Exercise 11.2, you will share an existing printer. This exercise assumes that you have completed Exercise 11.1.

EXERCISE 11.2

Sharing an Existing Printer

1. Select Start ➤ Printers and Faxes to open the Printers and Faxes utility.

2. Right-click HP LaserJet 4, choose Properties, and click the Sharing tab.

3. Click the Share This Printer radio button. Type **HPLJ4** in the text box.

4. Click the Apply button, and then click the OK button to close the dialog box.

Configuring Port Properties

Windows XP Professional supports local ports (physical ports) and standard *TCP/IP ports* (logical ports). A *port* is defined as the interface that allows the computer to communicate with the print device. Local ports are used when the printer attaches directly to the computer. In the case where you are running Windows XP Professional in a small workgroup, you would likely run printers attached to the local port LPT1. Standard TCP/IP ports are used when the printer is attached to the network by installing a network card in the printer. The advantage of network printers is that they are faster than local printers and can be located anywhere on the network. When you specify a TCP/IP port, you must know the IP address of the network printer.

In the Ports tab, shown in Figure 11.8, you configure all the ports that have been defined for printer use. Along with deleting and configuring existing ports, you can also set up printer pooling and redirect print jobs to another printer, as described in the next sections.

FIGURE 11.8 The Ports tab of the printer Properties dialog box

The Enable Bidirectional Support option on the Ports tab will be available if your printer supports this feature. It allows the printer to communicate with the computer. For example, your printer may be able to send more informative printer errors.

Printer Pooling

Printer pools are used to associate multiple physical print devices with a single logical printer, as illustrated in Figure 11.9. You would use a printer pool if you had multiple physical printers in the same location that were the same type and could use a single print driver. The advantage of using a printer pool is that the first available print device will print your job. This is useful in situations where a group of print devices is shared by a group of users, such as a secretarial pool.

To configure a printer pool, click the Enable Printer Pooling check box at the bottom of the Ports tab, and then check all the ports to which the print devices in the printer pool will attach. If you do not select the Enable Printer Pooling option, you can select only one port per printer.

 All of the print devices in a printer pool must be able to use the same print driver.

FIGURE 11.9   Printer pooling

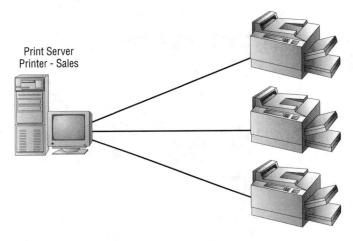

Print Server
Printer - Sales

Redirecting Print Jobs to Another Printer

If your print device fails, you can redirect all the jobs scheduled to be printed at that print device, to another print device that has been configured as a printer. For this redirection to work, the second print device must be able to use the same print driver as the first print device.

To redirect print jobs, click the Add Port button in the Ports tab, click the New Port button. In the Port Name dialog box, type the UNC name of the printer that you want to redirect the jobs to, in the format *computername**printer*.

Configuring Advanced Properties

The Advanced tab of the printer Properties dialog box, shown in Figure 11.10, allows you to control many characteristics of the printer. You can configure the following options:

- The availability of the printer
- The priority of the printer
- The driver the printer will use
- Spooling properties
- How documents are printed
- Printing defaults

- The print processor that will be used
- The separator page

FIGURE 11.10 The Advanced tab of the printer Properties dialog box

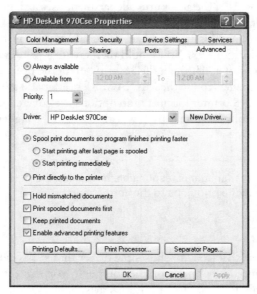

These options are covered in the following sections.

Printer Availability

Availability, or scheduling, specifies when a printer will service jobs. Usually, you control availability when you have multiple printers that use a single print device. For example, you might use this option if you have large jobs that tie up the print device for extended periods of time. You could schedule the large jobs to print only during a specified time, say between 10:00 P.M. and 4:00 A.M.

To set this up, you could create two printers on the same port, perhaps printers named LASER and REPORTS on the LPT1 port. (Both printers are on the same port since the same physical print device services them.) You would configure LASER to always be available, and REPORTS to be available only from 10:00 P.M. to 4:00 A.M. You would then instruct your users to send short jobs to LASER and long jobs to REPORTS, with the understanding that print jobs sent to REPORTS would print only during the specified hours.

By default, the Always Available radio button in the Advanced tab is selected, so users can use the printer 24 hours a day. To limit the printer's availability, select the Available From radio button and specify the range of time when the printer should be available.

Printer Priority

Priority is another option that you might configure if you have multiple printers that use a single print device. When you set priority, you specify how jobs are directed to the print device.

For example, you might use this option when two groups share a printer and you need to control the priority by which the device prints incoming jobs. In the Advanced tab of the printer Properties dialog box, you can set the Priority value to a number from 1 to 99, with 1 as the lowest priority and 99 as the highest priority.

As an example, suppose that the accounting department uses a single print device. The managers there want their print jobs always to print before jobs created by the other accounting department staff. To configure this arrangement, you could create a printer called MANAGERS on port LPT1 with a priority of 99. You would then create a printer on port LPT1 called WORKERS with a priority of 1. Through the Security tab of the printer Properties dialog box, you would allow only managers to use the MANAGERS printer and allow the other accounting users to use the WORKERS printer (Security tab options are covered later in this chapter). When the print manager polls for print jobs, it will always poll the higher-priority printer before the lower-priority printer.

The print manager is responsible for polling the print queue for print jobs and directing the print jobs to the correct port.

Print Driver

The Driver setting in the Advanced tab shows the driver that is associated with your printer. If you have configured multiple printers on the computer, you can choose to use any of the installed drivers. Clicking the New Driver button starts the Add Printer Driver Wizard, which allows you to update or add new print drivers.

Spooling

When you configure spooling options, you specify whether print jobs are spooled or sent directly to the printer. Spooling means that print jobs are saved to disk in a queue before they are sent to the printer. Consider spooling as the traffic controller of printing—it keeps all the print jobs from trying to print at the same time.

By default, spooling is enabled, with printing beginning immediately. Your other option is to wait until the last page is spooled before printing. An analogy for these choices is the actions you can take in a grocery store's cashier line. Let's say you have an entire cart full of groceries and the guy behind you has only a few things. Even if you've started loading your groceries onto the belt, as long as the cashier hasn't started with your items, you can choose to let the person with fewer items go before you, or you can make him wait. If the cashier has already started totaling your groceries, then you don't have that choice. Windows XP Professional spooling options allow you to configure your print environment similarly.

In the Advanced tab, you can leave the Start Printing Immediately option selected, or you can choose the Start Printing After Last Page Is Spooled option. If you choose the latter option, a smaller print job that finishes spooling first will print before your print job, even if your job started spooling before it did. If you specify Start Printing Immediately, the smaller job will have to wait until your print job is complete.

The other spooling option is Print Directly to the Printer, which bypasses spooling altogether. This option doesn't work well in a multiuser environment where multiple print jobs are sent to the same device. However, it is useful in troubleshooting printer problems. If you can print to a print device directly, but you can't print through the spooler, then you know that your spooler is corrupt or has other problems.

 Real World Scenario

Your Print Spooler Runs Out of Room

You have installed a printer on your Windows XP Professional computer. Four other users share another printer available to your computer.

Your computer has a C: drive and a D: drive, and the C: drive is running out of space. Spooler errors are occurring because of the large print jobs being sent to the printer. You would like to move the location of the spooler files to the computer's drive D:.

In Windows XP, you can change the location of your spooler file by accessing the Printers utility (Start ➤ Printers and Faxes) and then clicking File ➤ Server Properties. Then select the Advanced tab, and on the top of the dialog box you can select the location of your spool file. (The default location of the spool file is *windir*\system32\spool\printers.) Be aware that this will change the location of the spooler folders for all printers that are located on the computer. You could selectively change spool folder locations per printer, but that can only be done by directly editing the Registry.

Print Options

The Advanced tab of a printer's properties contains check boxes for four print options:

Hold Mismatched Documents   Is useful when you're using multiple forms with a printer. By default, this feature is disabled and jobs are printed on a first-in-first-out (FIFO) basis. You might enable this option if you need to print on both plain paper and certificate forms. Then all the jobs with the same form will print first.

Print Spooled Documents First   Specifies that the spooler will print jobs that have finished spooling before large jobs that are still spooling, even if that large print job has a higher priority. This option is enabled by default, which increases printer efficiency.

Keep Printed Documents   Specifies that print jobs should not be deleted from the print spooler (queue) when they are finished printing. By default, this option is disabled. You normally want to delete the print jobs as they print, because saving print jobs can take up substantial disk space.

Enable Advanced Printing Features   Specifies that any advanced features supported by your printer, such as Page Order and Pages Per Sheet, should be enabled. By default, this option is turned on. You would disable it if compatibility problems occurred. For example, if you are using the driver for a similar print device that does not support all the features of the print device the driver was written for, you should disable the advanced printing features.

Turning on the Keep Printed Documents option can be useful if you need to identify the source or other attributes of a finished print job. In one situation, this option helped track down a person who had been sending nasty notes to a coworker. The staff knew that the notes were being printed on the company laser printer. Since the print queue was on an NTFS volume, the administrator enabled the Keep Printed Documents option and was able to identify the offender through the owner attribute of the file.

Printing Defaults

The Printing Defaults button in the lower-left corner of the Advanced tab (see Figure 11.10) calls up the Printing Preferences dialog box. This is the same dialog box that appears when you click the Printing Preferences button in the General tab of the printer Properties dialog box, and its options were covered in the "Configuring General Properties" section earlier in this chapter.

Print Processor

Print processors are used to specify whether Windows XP Professional needs to do additional processing to print jobs. The five print processors supported by Windows XP Professional are listed in Table 11.2.

TABLE 11.2   Print Processors Supported by Windows XP

Print Processor	Description
RAW	Makes no changes to the print document
RAW (FF appended)	Makes no changes to the print document except to always add a formfeed character
RAW (FF Auto)	Makes no changes to the print document except to try to detect if a formfeed character needs to be added
NT EMF	Generally spools documents that are sent from other Windows XP clients; there are several versions of this support
TEXT	Interprets all the data as plain text, and the printer will print the data using standard text commands

To modify your Print Processor settings, click the Print Processor button at the bottom of the Advanced tab to open the Print Processor dialog box, shown in Figure 11.11. You will generally leave the default settings as is unless otherwise directed by the print device manufacturer.

FIGURE 11.11   The Print Processor dialog box

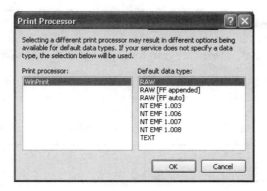

Separator Pages

Separator pages are used at the beginning of each document to identify the user who submitted the print job. If your printer is not shared, a separator page is generally a waste of paper. If the printer is shared by many users, the separator page can be useful for distributing finished print jobs.

To add a separator page, click the Separator Page button in the lower-right corner of the Advanced tab of the printer Properties dialog box. This brings up the Separator Page dialog box (Figure 11.12). Click the Browse button to locate and select the separator page file that you want to use. Windows XP Professional supplies the Separator files listed in Table 11.3, which are stored in *Windir*\System32.

FIGURE 11.12   The Separator Page dialog box

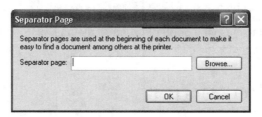

TABLE 11.3   Separator Page Files

Separator Page File	Description
pcl.sep	Used to send a separator page on a dual-language HP printer after switching the printer to PCL (Printer Control Language), which is a common printing standard

TABLE 11.3 Separator Page Files *(continued)*

Separator Page File	Description
pscript.sep	Does not send a separator page, but switches the computer to PostScript printing mode
sysprint.sep	Used by PostScript printers to send a separator page
sysprintj.sep	Same as sysprint.sep, but with support for Japanese characters

In Exercise 11.3, you will configure some advanced printer properties. This exercise assumes you have completed Exercise 11.2.

EXERCISE 11.3

Managing Advanced Printer Properties

1. Select Start ➢ Printers and Faxes to open the Printers and Faxes utility.

2. Right-click HP LaserJet 4, choose Properties, and click the Advanced tab.

3. Click the Available From radio button, and specify that the printer is available from 12:00 A.M. to 6:00 A.M.

4. Click the Start Printing After Last Page Is Spooled radio button.

5. Click the Separator Page button. In the Separator Page dialog box, click the Browse button and choose the sysprint.sep file. Click the Open button, then click the OK button in the Separator Page dialog box.

6. Click the OK button to close the printer Properties dialog box.

Security Properties

You can control which users and groups can access Windows XP printers by configuring the print permissions. In Windows XP Professional, you can allow or deny access to a printer. If you deny access, the user or group will not be able to use the printer, even if their user or group permissions allow such access.

You assign print permissions to users and groups through the Security tab of the printer Properties dialog box, as shown in Figure 11.13. Table 11.4 defines the print permissions that can be assigned.

FIGURE 11.13 The Security tab of the printer Properties dialog box

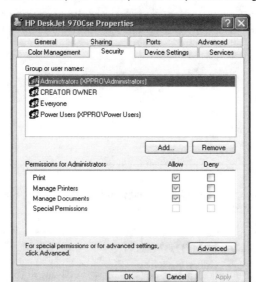

TABLE 11.4 Print Permissions

Print Permission	Description
Print	A user or group can connect to a printer and can send print jobs to the printer.
Manage Printers	Allows administrative control of the printer. With this permission, a user or group can pause and restart the printer, change the spooler settings, share or unshare a printer, change print permissions, and manage printer properties.
Manage Documents	Allows users to manage documents by pausing, restarting, resuming, and deleting queued documents. Users cannot control the status of the printer.
Special Permissions	Special Permissions are used to customize the print options with allow or deny access of the following permissions: Print, Manage Printers, Manage Documents, Read Permissions, Change Permissions, and Take Ownership.

By default, whenever a printer is created, default print permissions are assigned. The default permissions are normally appropriate for most network environments. Table 11.5 shows the default print permissions that are assigned.

TABLE 11.5 Default Print Permissions

Group	Print	Manage Printers	Manage Documents
Administrators	X	X	X
Power Users	X	X	X
Creator Owner	X		X
Everyone	X		

In the next sections, you will learn about assigning print permissions, advanced settings, and driver setting properties in detail.

Print Permission Assignment

Usually, you can accept the default print permissions, but you might need to modify them for special situations. For example, if your company bought an expensive color laser printer for the marketing department, you probably wouldn't want to allow general access to that printer. In this case, you would deselect the Allow check box for the Everyone group, add the Marketing group to the Security tab list, and then allow the Marketing group the Print permission.

To add print permissions, take the following steps:

1. In the Security tab of the printer Properties dialog box, click the Add button.

2. The Select Users or Groups dialog box appears. In the Enter the object names to select section, type in the user or group name that you want to add. After you specify all the users and groups you want to assign permissions to, click the OK button.

3. Highlight the user or group you want to manage permissions for. Select Allow or Deny access for the Print, Manage Printers, and Manage Documents permissions. Click the OK button when you are finished assigning permissions.

To remove an existing group from the permissions list, highlight the group and click the Remove button. That group will no longer be listed in the Security tab and cannot be assigned permissions.

In Exercise 11.4, you will assign print permissions. This exercise assumes that you have completed Exercise 11.1.

EXERCISE 11.4

Assigning Print Permissions

1. Using the Local Users and Groups utility, create two users, Kim and Jennifer. (See Chapter 6, "Managing Users and Groups," for details on creating user accounts.) Deselect the User Must Change Password at Next Logon option.

2. Using the Local Users and Groups utility, create a new group named Execs. (See Chapter 6 for details on creating groups.) Place Kim in the Execs group.

3. Select Start ➤ Printers and Faxes to open the Printers and Faxes utility.

4. Right-click HP LaserJet 4, select Properties, and click the Security tab. Click the Add button.

5. In the Select Users or Groups dialog box, under Enter the object names to select, type in **Execs** and click the Add button. Click the OK button to continue. If you are unsure of the group name, you can click the Advanced button and click the Find Now button. You can then pick the group name from the list that appears.

6. In the Security tab, highlight the Execs group. By default, the Allow check box should be selected for the Print permission. Leave the default setting. Highlight the Everyone group and click the Remove button. Click OK to close the Printer Properties dialog box.

7. Log off as Administrator and log on as Kim.

8. Open the Printers folder and select HP LaserJet 4. Kim should be able to connect to this printer based on her membership in the Execs group.

9. Log off as Kim and log on as Jennifer.

10. Open the Printers folder and select HP LaserJet 4. At the top of the dialog box, you should see the message "HP LaserJet 4 Access denied, unable to connect."

11. Log off as Jennifer and log on as Administrator.

Advanced Settings

The advanced settings accessed from the Security tab allow you to configure permissions, auditing, and owner properties. Clicking the Advanced button in the lower-right corner of the Security tab brings up the Access Control Settings dialog box, shown in Figure 11.14. This dialog box has four tabs that you can use to add, remove, or edit print permissions:

Permissions Lists all the users, computers, and groups that have been given permission to the printer, the permission granted, and whether the permission applies to documents or to the printer.

Auditing Tracks who is using the printer and what type of access is being used. You can track the success or failure of six events: Print, Manage Printers, Manage Documents, Read Permissions, Change Permissions, and Take Ownership.

Owner Shows the owner of the printer (the user or group who created the printer), which you can change if you have the proper permissions. For example, if the print permissions excluded the Administrator from using or managing the printer, and the print permissions needed to be reassigned, an Administrator could take ownership of the printer and then reapply print permissions.

Effective Permissions Lists the effective permissions a user has to a printer.

FIGURE 11.14 The Advanced Security Settings dialog box

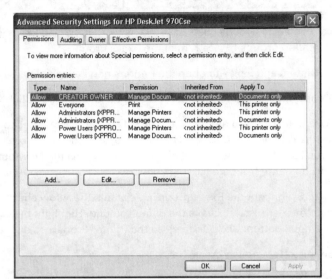

Device Settings Properties

The properties that you see on the Device Settings tab of the printer Properties dialog box depend on the printer and print driver that you have installed. You might configure these properties if you want to manage the associations of forms to tray assignments. For example, you could configure the upper tray to use letterhead and the lower tray to use regular paper. An example of the Device Settings tab for an HP DeskJet 970Cse printer is shown in Figure 11.15.

FIGURE 11.15 The Device Settings tab of the printer Properties dialog box

Managing Printers and Print Documents

Administrators or users with the Manage Printers permission can manage the printer's servicing of print jobs and of the print documents in a print queue. When you manage a printer, you manage all the documents in a queue. When you manage print documents, you manage specific documents.

As you would expect, you manage printers and print documents from the Printers and Faxes utility (select Start ➢ Printers and Faxes). The following sections describe the printer management and print document management options.

Managing Printers

To manage a printer, right-click the printer you want to manage. From the pop-up menu (Figure 11.16), select the appropriate option for the area you want to manage. Table 11.6 describes these options. Printer Properties were covered in the previous section, "Managing Printer Properties."

FIGURE 11.16   The printer management options

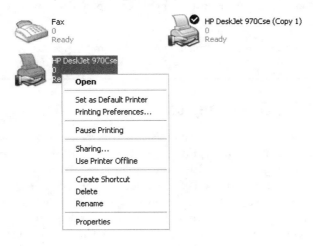

TABLE 11.6   Printer Management Options

Option	Description
Set as Default Printer	Specifies the default printer that will be used when the user does not send a job to an explicit printer (if the computer is configured to access multiple printers).
Printing Preferences	Brings up the Printing Preferences dialog box (see Figures 11.3 and 11.4), which allows you to configure printer settings for page layout and paper quality. You can also access this dialog box through the General tab of the printer Properties dialog box, as described earlier in this chapter.

TABLE 11.6 Printer Management Options *(continued)*

Option	Description
Pause Printing	While a printer is paused, print jobs can be submitted to the printer, but they will not be forwarded to the print device until you resume printing (by unchecking this option). You might use Pause Printing when you need to troubleshoot the printer or maintain the print device.
Sharing	Allows the printer to be shared or not shared.
Use Printer Offline	Pauses the printer. Print documents will remain in the print queue, even if you restart the computer.
Create Shortcut	Allows you to create a shortcut for the printer, which would typically be placed on the desktop.
Delete	Removes the printer. You might use this option if you no longer need the printer, if you want to move the printer to another print server, or if you suspect the printer is corrupt and you want to delete and re-create it.
Rename	Allows you to rename the printer. You might use this option to give a printer a more descriptive name or a name that follows naming conventions.

Managing Print Documents

As an Administrator or a user with the Manage Printers or Manage Documents permission, you can manage print documents within a print queue. For example, if a user has sent the same job multiple times, you might need to delete the duplicate print jobs.

To manage print documents, in the Printers folder double-click the printer that contains the documents. This opens a dialog box with information about the documents in its print queue. Select Document from the menu bar to access the pull-down menu of options that you can use to manage documents, as shown in Figure 11.17. These menu options are described in Table 11.7.

FIGURE 11.17 The Document menu options

TABLE 11.7 Document Management Options

Option	Description
Pause	Places the printing of this document on hold
Resume	Allows the document to print normally (after it has been paused)
Restart	Resends the job from the beginning, even if it has already been partially printed
Cancel	Deletes the job from the print spooler
Properties	Brings up the document Properties dialog box, containing options such as user notification when a print job is complete, document priority, document printing time, page layout, and paper quality

In Exercise 11.5, you will manage printers and print documents.

EXERCISE 11.5

Managing Printers and Print Documents

1. Select Start ➤ Printers and Faxes to open the Printers and Faxes utility.

2. Right-click HP LaserJet 4 and select Pause Printing.

3. Select Start ➤ All Programs ➤ Accessories ➤ Notepad.

4. Create a new text file and then select File ➤ Save As. In the Save As dialog box, save the file in the default location, My Documents, as `PrintMe.txt`. Click the Save button.

5. While still in Notepad, select File ➤ Print. Select HP LaserJet 4 and click the Print button. Repeat this step two more times so that you have sent a total of three print jobs. Close Notepad.

6. Return to the Printers and Faxes utility and double-click HP LaserJet 4. At the top of the window, you will see that the status of the printer is Paused.

7. Right-click one of the print jobs in the print queue, select Cancel, and click Yes. The print job will be deleted.

8. Right-click one of the print jobs in the print queue and select Properties. The print job Properties dialog box appears. Change Notify from Administrator to Emily. Change Priority from 1 to 99. For Schedule, select Only from 12:00 A.M. to 4:00 A.M. Then click the OK button.

9. Close all of the dialog boxes.

Connecting to Printers

Users can access a local printer or a shared printer. Once a printer has been shared, users with the Print permission can connect to the network printer through their network connection.

To connect to a network printer, access My Computer from the Start menu and from Other Places, click My Network Places, expand Entire Network, and click View Entire Contents. Expand Microsoft Windows Network, then Workgroup, then *computername*. Finally, double-click the printer to connect to it.

In Exercise 11.6, you will connect to a shared network printer.

EXERCISE 11.6

Connecting to a Shared Network Printer

1. Select Start then Printers and Faxes.

2. Select Add a Printer.

3. The Add Printer Wizard will start. Click the Next button.

4. In the Local or Network Printer dialog box, select a network printer, or a printer attached to another computer, and click the Next button.

5. In the Specify a Printer dialog box, verify that Browse for a Printer is selected and click the Next button.

6. Double-click Workgroup and then double-click your computer's name. You should see HPDJ970 and HPLJ4. These are the share names for the printers you created in earlier exercises in this chapter. Select one of the shared printers.

7. In the Default Printer dialog box select No for printing a test page and click the Next button.

8. In the Completing the Add Printer Wizard dialog box, click the Finish button.

Troubleshooting Printing

In the event you experience printing problems, the following list is designed to help you troubleshoot and resolve the problems:

Print output is garbled.   If you send a print job to the printer and it outputs garbled pages, you probably have a bad print driver. Ensure that the correct print driver is loaded and verify that it is working by printing a test page. If other users have connected to your printer, they will need to disconnect from the printer and reconnect to load the new print driver.

Can't install a plug and play printer.   If you have a print device that does not have a driver included with Windows XP Professional, then your computer will not automatically install your printer. This is especially common if you have a new print device that was released after Windows XP Professional was released. In this case, you will need to manually create the printer, and click Have Disk (in the Install Printer Software section of the Add Printer Wizard) to provide the Windows XP driver from the print device manufacturer.

Power Users in previous versions of Windows can't manage printers after you upgrade to Windows XP Professional.   In order to manage Windows XP Professional printers, users must now have the Load and Unload Device Drivers user right. Assign this user right to the Power Users group.

Pages only partially print.   If you encounter this error, verify that the printer has sufficient toner. Check that there is sufficient memory to print the document. If only specific text is missing, make sure that the printer can print the font that is being used for the missing text. Make sure that the page size in the document is not set larger than the print device is configured to support.

Print jobs go to the print queue, but do not print.   If you are using a multifunctional peripheral (MFP), then IEEE 1284.4 might not properly detect the device as a print device. In this case, turn off your computer and print device. Turn on the print device first, then the computer. IEEE 1284.4 should then recognize all features of your MFP.

Some users can properly print, but not others.   Verify that the print permissions have been properly configured for the users who are unable to print. If some users can print and not others, the most likely problem is security settings.

You are experiencing very slow printing.   If your printing is slowing down, verify that the print server has adequate space on the hard drive to support the temporary files created by print jobs. You may need to defragment the print server's hard disk. If you are using printer pooling and jobs are slow due to heavy printing load, consider adding more print devices to the printer pool.

You have a PostScript printer and you get "Out of Memory" error messages.   If the PostScript printer reports this message, you must allocate more memory to the printer, or break larger printer jobs into smaller jobs.

Graphic images do not print properly.   You may need to disable enhanced metafile spooling (EMF). To disable EMF, right-click the printer in Printers and Faxes, the select Properties. On the Advanced tab, clear the Enable Advanced Printing Features option.

Summary

This chapter explained how to manage printing with Windows XP Professional. We covered the following topics:

- Basic printing principles, which included printing terminology, an overview of the Windows XP Professional printing process, and how printers and print devices work together
- How to create local and network printers

- Printer properties, including general properties, sharing properties, port properties, advanced properties, security properties, and device settings
- Print management tasks, such as setting default printers and canceling all print documents
- Document management tasks, such as pausing, resuming, and canceling print documents
- Connecting to shared printers

Exam Essentials

Know how to create local and network printers.   Understand what rights are required to create local and network printers, and the process used to create Windows XP printers.

Manage network printers.   Know all the options that can be used to manage network printers, including all the printer properties and when they would be used. Be able to set printer priorities and scheduling. Know how to change the location of the spooler file. Set separator files to print or not print based on user preference.

Understand how print permissions are used.   Be able to determine how print permissions are applied based on network requirements.

Be able to connect to print devices as a user.   Know how to connect to and use local and network printers as a user. Be able to manage your own print jobs as a user.

Key Terms

Before you take the exam, be certain you are familiar with the following terms:

Graphics Device Interface (GDI)	print queue
local printer	print server
logical port	print spooler
logical printer	Printer
network printer	printer pooling
physical port	Rendering
print device	separator page
print driver	TCP/IP ports
print processor	

Review Questions

1. You are the network administrator for a medium-sized company. You support the Engineering department, which has over 50 printers. You hire Kevin to help you manage network printing maintenance and errors. You want Kevin to be able to manage and create network printers. You do not want him to have administrative rights if they are not required for his printing-related tasks. To which of the following group memberships should you add Kevin?

   A. The Print Operators group

   B. The Power Users group

   C. The Administrators group

   D. The Print Managers group

2. You are the network administrator for a small company. Your network consists of three workgroups. The Sales workgroup consists of a variety of Microsoft client operating systems. You want to make printing as easy as possible. You have shared a network printer on a Windows XP Professional computer. For which of the following clients can you support drivers on the print server? (Choose all that apply.)

   A. Windows 3.1

   B. Windows 95

   C. Windows 98

   D. Windows NT 4

3. You have just created a network printer called LASER for a print device that is physically attached to your Windows XP Professional computer. You are wondering what print permissions should be applied so that network users can access the new printer. Which of the following print permissions are applied to the Everyone group by default on shared Windows XP printers?

   A. No permissions are granted.

   B. Print.

   C. Manage Printers.

   D. Manage Documents.

4. You are the network administrator in charge of a medium-sized company. You manage a group of printers, including an expensive laser printer used by the Accounting department. The printer is called ACCTLASER. Meredith needs to access the ACCTLASER printer. Meredith is a member of Everyone, Print Managers, Power Users, and Accounting. The following print permissions have been applied to the ACCTLASER printer:

Group	Print	Manage Printers	Manage Documents
Everyone	Allow		
Print Managers		Allow	Allow
Accounting	Allow		Deny
Power Users	Allow	Allow	Allow

Based on these assignments, which of the following are Meredith's effective rights?

A. Print

B. Print and Manage Printers

C. Print and Manage Documents

D. Print, Manage Printers, and Manage Documents

5. You are the network administrator and support all of the executives for your corporation. Each executive has their own administrative assistant and they are all located on the top floor of the campus headquarters building. You have five print devices that are all used by a pool of administrative assistants. You want to configure the printing environment so that print jobs are sent to the first print device that is available. What requirement must be met if you want to use a printer pool?

A. You must use the same print manufacturer and model for all print devices within the printer pool.

B. All of your print devices must be network printers.

C. All of your print devices must be configured to use the same port.

D. All of your print devices must be able to use the same print driver.

6. You are the network administrator for a small company. Your company has two regional offices, one in New York and one in San Jose. You are based in San Jose. The Accounting printer is in the New York office, and occasionally experiences paper jams. Dan works in the New York office and is capable of managing the printer, but is unable to manage it due to his current print permissions. You want to configure the print permissions so Dan can help you manage the Accounting printer. Which of the following options can be managed by Dan if you give him the Manage Documents permission to the printer?

A. Connect and send jobs to a printer.

B. Pause a printer.

C. Pause a print job.

D. Manage the status of a printer.

7. You have an Acme laser printer called Acme1, used by 20 network Sales users. The printer has failed and has been sent out for servicing. It is estimated that the printer will be out of service for one week. In the meantime, you want the users to have all their print jobs connected to another Acme laser printer called Acme2, which is used by the Marketing staff. What is the easiest way to have the Sales users send their jobs to Acme2 until the Acme1 printer is back in service?

A. Have the Sales users create a printer for Acme2 and set this printer as their default printer. When Acme1 is back in service, have them reconfigure their default printer as Acme1.

B. Create a new port that will take all the print jobs sent to Acme1 and redirect them to Acme2. After the print device comes back into service, disable the redirection.

C. Rename the Acme2 printer to Acme1.

D. Rename the Acme1 printer to Acme2.

8. You have 10 users who send their print jobs to a Windows XP printer called MISLaser. You want to have a custom separator page that identifies the user and the date and time when the job is printed. You have a separator page created called `custom.sep`. Where should this file be stored?

A. `\Windir\Printers`

B. `\Windir\Queues`

C. `\Windir\System32`

D. `\Windir\System32\Printers`

9. You have a Windows XP printer called ABCLaser that is associated with the ABC laser device. This printer keeps jamming. Tim sits close to the print device and is able to unjam the printer. To perform this maintenance, he needs to be able to pause and restart the printer. What is the minimum permission that Jim needs to perform this task?

A. Grant Jim the Manage Documents print permission for the ABCLaser printer.

B. Grant Jim the Manage Printers print permission for the ABCLaser printer.

C. Grant Jim the Full Control print permission for the ABCLaser printer.

D. Make Jim a Printer Operator.

10. Your Windows XP Professional computer has an ABC laser printer attached. Five other users in your workgroup want to use your printer. These clients are also running the Windows XP Professional operating system. You create a printer called ABCLP and share it. All of the users can attach to the share and use the printer. Six months later, you update the print driver. What do the other users in your group need to do to update the print driver on their computers?

A. Use the Upgrade Driver Wizard to update the driver on their computers.

B. Upgrade the print driver through the Printers utility.

C. Use the Device Manager Wizard to update the driver on their computers.

D. Do nothing; the next time they attach to the printer, the new print driver will be loaded automatically.

11. You work in a small Windows XP Professional workgroup. You recently purchased a new laser printer and attached it to your Windows XP Professional computer. You want the printer to be accessed by other users in your workgroup. You configured your printer to be shared. When you configured the printer, you specified that it uses a Windows XP print driver. Which of the following clients can use the printer?

A. Only Windows XP and Windows 2000 clients

B. Windows NT 4 clients and Windows XP clients

C. Windows 98 clients, Windows NT 4 clients, and Windows XP clients

D. Windows 95 clients, Windows 98 clients, Windows NT 4 clients, and Windows XP clients

12. You are the network administrator for a medium-sized network. You recently purchased a network printer. Your network uses Ethernet, so you purchased a printer that had an Ethernet card installed. Your network uses TCP/IP. Based on this configuration, what port options do you need to configure for this printer?

A. A local port

B. A network port

C. A TCP/IP port

D. A URL port

13. You have set up the Accounting and Sales groups to share the same printer device. You want the Sales group's documents to print first. You create an Accounting printer and a Sales printer and assign the respective groups' permissions to their printers. Both printers point to the shared print device. How should you configure the printer priority? (Choose two answers.)

A. Configure Accounting priority 1.

B. Configure Accounting priority 99.

C. Configure Sales priority 1.

D. Configure Sales priority 99.

14. You have been having problems with the HR printer. You are not sure if the problem is with the print device or with the shared printer configuration. Which of the following steps can you take to bypass network spooling?

A. In the Advanced tab of the printer Properties dialog box, configure the Print Directly to the Printer option.

B. In the General tab of the printer Properties dialog box, configure the Print Directly to the Printer option.

C. In the Advanced tab of the printer Properties dialog box, configure the Bypass Network Printing option.

D. In the General tab of the printer Properties dialog box, configure the Bypass Network Printing option.

15. You have created two printers that both point to the same print device. One of the printers has been named Accounting and the other printer has been named Reports. You want the Accounting printer to be able to service jobs 24 hours a day. You want the Reports printer to only service jobs between 8:00 P.M. to 5:00 A.M. You will then instruct users that print jobs of over 100 pages should be sent to the Reports printer. In the Properties dialog box shown here, which tab should you click to configure the printer?

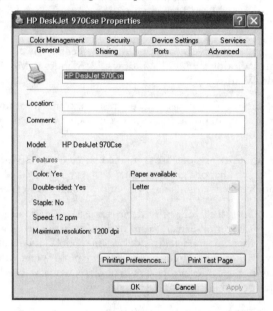

- **A.** Sharing
- **B.** Services
- **C.** Device Settings
- **D.** Advanced

Answers to Review Questions

1. **B.** To create a new printer on a Windows XP Professional computer, you must be logged on as a member of the Power Users or Administrators group. Because you want Kevin to have the least amount of administrative rights, however, you should choose the Power Users group for him. Print Operators and Print Managers groups do not exist by default on Windows XP Professional computers.

2. **B, C, D.** You can't provide drivers for Windows 3.1 clients. You can provide drivers for the following clients: Windows 95 and Windows 98, Windows Me, Windows NT 4, Windows 2000, and Windows XP.

3. **B.** By default, the Everyone group has Print permission to shared printers. Users also have the Manage Documents permission if they are the Creator Owner of a document, but they can't manage other users' documents.

4. **B.** Normally, your print permissions are combined based on group membership. In this case, however, Meredith is a member of a group that has been explicitly denied the Manage Documents permission. Meredith's effective rights are Print and Manage Printers.

5. **D.** To use a printer pool, all of your print devices must be able to use the same print driver. When they can use the same print driver, the print devices do not necessarily have to be from the same manufacturer or the same model. Print devices in a pool can be a mixture of local and network printers. They are not configured to use the same port. When you enable printer pooling through the Ports tab of the printer Properties dialog box, you can check multiple ports. You would check each port to which a print device was attached.

6. **C.** The Manage Documents permission allows a user to manage print documents, including pausing, resuming, and deleting queued documents. A user must have Print permission to connect and send jobs to a printer. To pause a printer or manage its status, a user must have the Manage Printers permission.

7. **B.** If your print device fails, you can redirect all its scheduled print jobs to another print device that has been configured as a printer. For this redirection to work, the new print device must be able to use the same print driver as the old print device. To redirect print jobs, click the Add Port button in the Ports tab. In the Port Name dialog box, type the UNC name of the printer to which you want to redirect the jobs, in the format *computername**printer*.

8. **C.** By default, Windows XP separator page files are stored in the *Windir*\System32 folder. You can specify what separator pages are used from the Advanced tab of a printer's properties by clicking the Separator Page button in the lower right-hand corner of the dialog box.

9. **B.** A person or group with the Manage Printers print permission has administrative control of the printer. With this permission, a user or group can pause and restart the printer, change the spooler settings, share and unshare the printer, change print permissions, and manage printer properties.

10. **D.** Windows XP clients automatically download the print driver for a print device when they connect to a network printer. If the print driver is updated on the print server, the driver is automatically updated on the clients the next time they send a print job.

11. A.   If you load only Windows XP drivers, only Windows XP and 2000 clients are supported, the other client platforms will not be able to use the printer. In Windows XP, you can also specify (and provide) print drivers for Windows 95/98 clients, Windows NT 3.1 clients (Alpha, Intel, or MIPS), Windows NT 3.5 and 3.51 clients (Alpha, Intel, MIPS, or PowerPC), and Windows NT 4 clients (Alpha, Intel, MIPS, or PowerPC).

12. C.   If you have a print device that attaches to the network with a network card using the TCP/IP protocol, you must configure a TCP/IP port for the printer's use. Network printers are more commonly used than local printers within medium- to large-sized networks.

13. A, D.   You can set printer priority from 1 to 99, with 1 as the lowest priority and 99 as the highest priority. This option is used in conjunction with multiple groups using the same print device. Each group is associated with a printer that has been configured with the appropriate priority. Print jobs are always processed first from the printer with the highest priority.

14. A.   The Print Directly to the Printer option, in the Advanced tab of the printer Properties dialog box, bypasses spooling altogether. You can use this setting to troubleshoot printer problems. If you can print to a print device directly, but you can't print through the spooler, then you know that your spooler is corrupt or has other problems.

15. D.   The Advanced tab of the printer Properties dialog box includes options for configuring a printer's availability. This option can be used to associate multiple printers with a single print device. By limiting when a printer can service print jobs, you can manage when large documents are processed.

Chapter

12

Dial-Up Networking and Internet Connectivity

MICROSOFT EXAM OBJECTIVES COVERED IN THIS CHAPTER:

- ✓ **Manage and troubleshoot access to shared folders.**
  - ▪ Manage and troubleshoot Web server resources.
- ✓ **Connect to local and network print devices.**
  - ▪ Connect to an Internet printer.
- ✓ **Implement, manage, and troubleshoot input and output (I/O) devices.**
  - ▪ Install, configure, and manage modems.
- ✓ **Connect to computers by using dial-up networking.**
  - ▪ Connect to computers by using a virtual private network (VPN) connection.
  - ▪ Create a dial-up connection to connect to a remote access server.
  - ▪ Connect to the Internet by using dial-up networking.
  - ▪ Configure and troubleshoot Internet Connection Sharing (ICS).
- ✓ **Connect to resources by using Internet Explorer.**
- ✓ **Configure, manage, and implement Internet Information Services (IIS).**
- ✓ **Configure, manage, and troubleshoot an Internet Connection Firewall (ICF).**
- ✓ **Configure, manage, and troubleshoot Internet Explorer security settings.**

When remote users want to access private networks or the Internet, they are faced with a variety of remote access options. You must first have a basic understanding of how remote access works, the connection options associated with remote access, and the security that is used by remote access.

Once you understand the theory behind remote access, you can implement remote access through Windows XP Professional. To use *dial-up networking*, you need a modem and connections to the remote server or the Internet. You can dial into a Remote Access Service (RAS) server or the Internet, or you can access a virtual private network (VPN) server on your network via a connection (for example, through the Internet).

With Windows XP Professional, you can also configure a feature called Internet Connection Sharing (ICS). It allows you to connect a single computer to the network. Then you can enable other users on the same small network to share the Internet connection.

Windows XP Professional also ships with a service called Internet Connection Firewall (ICF). ICF is used to provide firewall services to a Windows XP Professional computer that is directly attached to the Internet to protect the computer from outside threats.

Windows XP Professional uses Internet Explorer (IE) to access Internet and intranet resources. You will learn advanced configuration options for IE. You can also configure printers to be used through the Internet, or to be accessed by local clients through a web browser.

Finally, you will learn about Internet Information Services (IIS). Windows XP ships with a scaled down version of the IIS that ships with Windows 2000 Server and Windows Server 2003.

The server side of dial-up networking is covered in *MCSE: Windows 2000 Server Study Guide*, 2nd edition, by Lisa Donald with James Chellis (Sybex, 2001).

Overview of Dial-Up Networking

Windows XP Professional can be used within a local network or act as a remote client accessing another computer, a private network, or the Internet. There are several options for creating the connection that include:

- Choose the hardware and network infrastructure for connection
- Define the authentication that will be used
- Define whether data encryption will be used

The following example shows how a dial-up connection would be used to establish remote connectivity.

1. The remote user chooses to use dial-up networking with a standard modem and has access to the Public Switched Telephone Network, or PSTN (regular phone service).

2. The remote user knows the phone number that will be used to access the remote server.

3. The remote user must be able to negotiate a common authentication protocol with the server they will access. For example, with dial-up networking you can use Challenge Handshake Authentication Protocol (CHAP), Microsoft Challenge Handshake Authentication Protocol (MS-CHAP), or MS-CHAPv2.

4. The remote user and the server they will access may or may not use data encryption, based on settings that are configured on the server.

5. The remote client requests network protocol information and configuration settings from the server they will access. For example, the server would assign the remote connection a unique IP address, which is then used to access remote network resources, such as shares.

In the following sections, you will learn more about connection options, remote access security, how to setup a modem, and instructions for installing and configuring various dial-out connectivity options.

Understanding Connection Options

There are many different options that can be used for network connectivity. The connection option you choose is based on the connection requirement; for example, Local Area Network (LAN) connection options differ from wide area network (WAN) connection options.

Windows XP Professional supports the ability to initiate remote connections through a variety of options. Examples of outgoing connections include:

- Dialing into the Internet through an analog modem, Integrated Service Digital Network (ISDN), or X.25

- Connecting to the Internet through a broadband connection that uses Digital Subscriber Line (DSL), cable modem, Point-to-Point Protocol over Ethernet (PPPoE), or a leased line

- Dialing into a private network through an analog modem, ISDN, or X.25

- Connecting to a private network through a broadband connection that uses DSL, cable modem, PPPoE, or a leased line

- Accessing the Internet and using a virtual private network (VPN) connection to access a private network

The following sections will cover a broad overview of LAN connectivity, remote access connectivity, VPN connectivity, WAN connectivity, direct connection connectivity, and incoming connectivity. You will also learn about the communication methods used by each option.

Local Area Network Connections

Local Area Network (LAN) access is used to provide connectivity in a local corporate or home environment. The connection methods supported by Windows XP Professional for LAN access include:

Ethernet   *Ethernet* is the most common method for LAN access. Ethernet is based on the Institute of Electrical and Electronic Engineers (IEEE) 802.3 specification. There are several Ethernet standards, which include 10Mbps (megabits per second) Ethernet, 100Mbps Ethernet, and 1Gbps (gigabit per second) Ethernet. Ethernet uses a logical bus topology to transmit data via Carrier Sense Multiple Access with Collision Detection (CSMA/CD).

Token Ring   *Token Ring* is a LAN technology that was developed by IBM in the 1970s, and is defined by the IEEE 802.5 specification. In a Token Ring network, all nodes are wired into a physical ring. A token is used to manage communications. Token Ring is more difficult to install and configure and is more expensive than Ethernet. It is rarely used in corporate or home environments. Token Ring is most typically used in networks that use IBM equipment and require IBM connectivity.

Fiber Distributed Data Interface   *Fiber Distributed Data Interface (FDDI)* is a 100Mbps token-passing protocol that is designed for use with fiber-optic cabling. FDDI uses a dual-counter rotating ring technology. By default, only the primary ring is used. The secondary ring is used for fault tolerance in the event the primary ring fails.

Home Phoneline Network Adapter   *Home Phoneline Network Adapter (HPNA)* is used with existing telephone wiring, typically in home networks, to connect network devices without interrupting the standard telephone service.

802.11x Wireless LANs   *802.11x wireless LAN* in Windows XP Professional improves the support for wireless networks compared to the support that was available with Windows 2000. The key features of support include automatic wireless configuration (for zero client configuration), auto-detection of wireless networks, automatic switching between different access points (APs) when a client is roaming, and wireless device authentication support for Windows Remote Authentication Dial-In User Service (RADIUS) Server and Internet Authentication Service (IAS).

Infrared Data Association   *Infrared Data Association (IrDA)* defines a set of infrared protocols that are used by wireless devices for communication. IrDA uses short-range, high speed, bi-directional communication. Examples of devices that can use IrDA for communication include laptops, desktop computers, cameras, printers, and Personal Digital Assistants (PDAs).

LAN Emulation   *LAN Emulation (LANE)* is used to support Asynchronous Transfer Mode (ATM) over Ethernet or Token Ring networks and to access LAN-aware applications without any additional modifications.

IP over ATM   *IP over ATM* is used to provide IP services over ATM. IP over ATM maps IP requests to ATM and ATM requests to IP using an ATM Address Resolution Protocol (ATMARP) server, which is implemented through Windows 2000 Server or Windows Server 2003, on each IP subnet that will provide IP and ATM addressing and emulation services.

Remote Access Connections

A remote client can connect to a private network or the Internet via *remote access connections*. The connection methods used by Windows XP Professional for remote access include:

Dial-up modem   *Dial-up modems*, or slow links, use an analog dial-up connection over the *Public Switched Telephone Network (PSTN)*, which is regular phone service, for remote connectivity. It is the least expensive and most commonly used method for creating remote connections.

Integrated Services Digital Network   *Integrated Services Digital Network (ISDN)* provides digital telephone service. In order to use ISDN, an ISDN line must be installed and configured by the remote client and the server site. Basic rate ISDN lines can support transmissions of up to 128Kbps (kilobits per second) and use two 64Kbps channels. ISDN normally uses a dial-up connection, rather than a permanent connection.

X.25   *X.25* is used to provide connections between terminal and packet-switching networks, which was a common network structure prior to the introduction of ISDN and Frame Relay connection methods. Because of its early widespread use, it is still sometimes used in tandem with newer technologies.

Point-to-Point Protocol over Ethernet   *Point-to-Point Protocol over Ethernet (PPPoE)* uses the *Point-to-Point Protocol (PPP)* to provide remote connectivity services via Ethernet. PPP is a set of remote authentication protocols used by Windows remote access for interoperability with third-party remote access software. To use PPPoE, each PPP session uses a discovery protocol to learn the Ethernet address of the remote peer and establishes a unique session identifier.

PPPoE is typically associated with broadband ISPs. If your broadband ISP requires a username and password, it is most likely using PPPoE services. You can use the native support of Windows XP for PPPoE or you can use software that the ISP has provided, and no additional support for PPPoE is required.

Microsoft Ethernet PVC   *Microsoft Ethernet PVC* is used to support Ethernet and IP data encapsulation services over an ATM permanent virtual connection. Ethernet PVC is typically used to provide remote connectivity services for home networks that use Asymmetric Digital Subscriber Line (ADSL) modems. ADSL is a technology that allows you to use existing copper telephone lines to support data rate transmissions of 1.5Mbps to 9Mbps for receiving data and from 16Kbps to 640Kbps for sending data. The ADSL modem would connect to the PSTN. At the PSTN service provider, a Digital Subscriber Line Access Multiplexer (DSLAM) would act as a bridge to an ATM switch located at the host network that will be accessed by the remote client.

Virtual Private Network Connections

A *virtual private network (VPN)* is used to provide a remote user with a secure connection to a corporate network via the Internet. Within the VPN, all data to and from the remote access client is encapsulated and encrypted. VPNs are considered a very affordable option for providing high security access between home or small offices over any public network infrastructure that can transport IP packets. The connection methods supported by Windows XP Professional for use with VPNs include:

Point-to-Point Tunneling Protocol   The *Point-to-Point Tunneling Protocol (PPTP)* was developed as an open industry-standard by Microsoft and other industry leaders to provide support for tunneling of Point-to-Point Protocol (PPP) frames through an IP network. PPP provides authentication, compression, and encryption services. Used in conjunction with Microsoft Challenge Handshake Authentication Protocol Version 2 (MS-CHAPv2) and strong passwords, PPTP can provide secure access via a VPN for remote users who use dial-up connectivity to access an Internet service provider (ISP) and from there, the corporate network. This protocol is not considered as secure as L2TP, but it is easier to set up.

Layer Two Tunneling Protocol   The *Layer Two Tunneling Protocol (L2TP)* is an industry-standard VPN protocol that is used in conjunction with IP security (IPSec) to provide a high level of security when sending IP packets over the Internet or other public IP network. L2TP and IPSec provide data authentication, data encryption, and data integrity services that strengthen security when data is sent over an unsecured network. In order to use L2TP and IPSec for encryption, User Datagram Protocol (UDP) Ports 500 and 1701 must be opened on the corporate network that will be accessed by the remote user.

Wide Area Network Connections

A *wide area network (WAN)* is used to connect two geographically dispersed areas together via a persistent connection. The connection methods used with WANs include:

T-Carried leased lines   Before the introduction of current high-speed remote access network options, *leased lines* were used to provide a faster, permanent link as an alternative to dial-up networking. Leased lines are typically implemented as a T-carrier line—for example, a T1 or fraction T1 line. This legacy technology is still used and supported by Windows XP Professional, but is quickly being replaced by more cost-effective networking options.

Cable modem   *Cable modems* are used to provide two-way, high-speed connectivity to the Internet (or private networks using a VPN) through existing coaxial cabling that is used for transmitting cable television. Cable modems support a maximum throughput of 2.8Mbps, but because cable modems use a shared network contention topology, bandwidth availability will impact actual network throughput.

Digital Subscriber Line   *Digital Subscriber Line (DSL)* uses standard copper telephone lines to provide dedicated, high-speed access to the Internet.

Frame Relay   *Frame Relay* is a virtual circuit-based switching protocol used to connect devices on a WAN. Frame Relay is commonly implemented with a permanent virtual circuit.

Direct Cable Connections

Direct cable access, also referred to as *Direct Cable Connection (DCC)*, is used to directly connect two devices without the use of a network for the purpose of transferring data. When DCC is installed and configured on a Windows XP Professional computer, all of the computer's serial ports are listed as available for DCC use. The connection methods supported by Windows XP Professional that can be used with direct cable include:

Universal Serial Bus   *Universal Serial Bus (USB)* is a serial bus standard that defines device-to-device connectivity through direct cable access. The main purpose of USB is to allow peripherals (up to 127) to be attached to a PC using serial bandwidth of 1.5Mbps. Devices can attach to a computer and be recognized without having to restart the computer. Examples of USB devices include CD-ROM drives, cameras, printers, modems, and PDAs.

Serial cable   *Serial cables* are a type of cable used for data transmission. Serial cables transmit data one bit at a time, as opposed to parallel cables, which transmit data eight bits at a time. However, serial cables support longer distances between devices than parallel cables. There is a special form of serial cable, called a null-modem cable, which is used to emulate modem connectivity. A null modem cable is a serial cable that has been modified to support direct asynchronous communication between two computers over a short distance. This option is sometimes used to troubleshoot remote access server problems in a local setting.

Direct parallel cable   *Direct parallel cable* can be used to support file transfers between two computers. Parallel cables transmit data faster than serial cables. Windows XP Professional supports standard or basic 4-bit parallel cables, Enhanced Capabilities Port (ECP) cables, and Universal Cable Module cables for parallel DCC.

IEEE 1394 (Firewire)   *IEEE 1394 (Firewire)* is a standard that was defined by the IEEE to connect digital devices together at transmission speeds of 98Mbps to 393Mbps (for IEEE 1394a) or 400 to 800 Mbps (for IEEE 1394b), which is considerably faster than USB transmissions. Examples of devices that can use IEEE 1394 include high-speed digital video cameras and audio/video editing equipment.

Incoming Connection

Incoming connections allow connections to be established with the remote computer. The connection methods used with incoming connections include dial-up, VPN, and direct connections, all of which have been previously defined.

Understanding Remote Access Security

If you use dial-up networking, a VPN, or direct connections with Windows XP Professional, additional layers of security—beyond the standard security that is already applied at a local level—can be implemented. In the following sections, you will learn about password authentication and data encryption options that can be used with remote access.

Authentication Methods

When you access a network through a dial-up connection, VPN, or direct connection, Windows XP Professional uses a two-step authentication process. The two-step authentication process consists of an interactive logon process and network authorization. The interactive logon process confirms a user's identity based on the user account (local or domain) and password or smart card credentials. Network access control is used to confirm the user's identity to the network service or resource that the user is attempting to access.

To ensure that the interactive logon process is secure over a remote connection, remote authentication protocols can be used. The remote client and the remote network must be configured to negotiate a common remote authentication protocol.

The remote authentication protocols that are supported by Windows XP Professional are:

Password Authentication Protocol   *Password Authentication Protocol (PAP)* is the simplest authentication method. It uses unencrypted, plain text passwords. You would use PAP if the server you were connecting to didn't support secure validations or you were troubleshooting remote access and wanted to use the most basic authentication option.

Shiva Password Authentication Protocol   *Shiva Password Authentication Protocol (SPAP)* encrypts passwords with a two-way encryption scheme. With this option Windows XP Professional, Windows 2000 Servers, and Windows Server 2003 are able to dial into Shiva network access servers. Conversely Shiva clients can remotely access Windows XP Professional, Windows 2000 Servers, and Windows Server 2003 computers using SPAP.

Challenge Handshake Authentication Protocol   *Challenge Handshake Authentication Protocol (CHAP)* is used to negotiate secure authentication by using encryption that is based on the industry standard hashing scheme specified by Message Digest 5 (MD5). Hashing schemes are used to transform data into a scrambled format. CHAP uses a challenge-response process that sends the client a request with the hash scheme that will be used. The client then responds to the server with an MD5 hashed response. This method allows the server to authenticate a client without the client actually sending their password over the remote connection. Almost all third-party PPP servers support CHAP authentication.

Microsoft Challenge Handshake Authentication Protocol   *Microsoft Challenge Handshake Authentication Protocol (MS-CHAP)* is Microsoft's extension to CHAP and is designed to work with computers and networks that are using Windows 98, Windows Me, Windows NT 4 (all versions), Windows 2000 (all versions), Windows XP (all versions), and Windows Server 2003. Windows 95 computers are also supported, but require you to use the Windows Dial-up Networking 1.3 Performance and Security Upgrade for Windows 95.

Microsoft Challenge Handshake Authentication Protocol Version 2   *Microsoft Challenge Handshake Authentication Protocol Version 2 (MS-CHAPv2)* adds to the services provided by CHAP by providing mutual authentication, different encryption keys for sending and receiving, and stronger data encryption keys. Windows 2000 (all versions), Windows XP (all versions), and Windows Server 2003 can use MS-CHAPv2 with dial-up and VPN connections. If you are using Windows NT 4 (all versions) or Windows 95/98 computers, you can only use MS-CHAPv2 authentication with VPN connections.

Extensible Authentication Protocol   *Extensible Authentication Protocol (EAP)* extends the services of PPP by providing more updated and secure authentication services than were previously available with PPP. EAP was designed to provide secure authentication services for third-party (non-Microsoft) devices.

Certificate Authentication *Certificate authentication* uses a special authentication credential, called a certificate. A certificate is a digital signature that is issued by a certification authority. When a client and server are configured to use certificate authentication, they must both present a valid certificate for mutual authentication.

Smart cards are small credit-card-sized devices that are used with a smart card reader to provide an additional level of hardware security.

Remote Data Encryption Options

Data encryption adds an additional layer of security by encrypting all of the data that is sent through a remote connection in addition to adding security to the logon authentication process. If you are using Windows XP Professional to create a remote connection with dial-up, VPN, or remote connections, there are two options for using data encryption (both options support multiple key strengths that can be applied to data encryption):

Microsoft Point-to-Point Encryption *Microsoft Point-to-Point Encryption (MPPE)* is a PPP data encryption option that uses Rivest-Shamir-Adleman (RSA) RC4 encryption. MPPE supports strong (128-bit key) or standard (40-bit key) encryption. In order to use MPPE data encryption over a dial-up or VPN connection, the remote client and server that will be accessed must use the MS-CHAP, MS-CHAPv2, or EAP authentication protocols.

IPSec *Internet Protocol Security (IPSec)* uses Data Encryption Standard (DES) encryption, which is a suite of cryptography-based security protocols. IPSec uses computer-level authentication and provides data encryption services for L2TP and VPN connections. IPSec services include packet data authentication, data integrity, replay protection, and data confidentiality services. PPTP provides only packet data confidentiality services.

If the remote client and remote network use PAP, SPAP, or CHAP for authentication, you will not have the option to use data encryption for dial-up and PPTP connections.

Now that you have an understanding of remote connectivity options and security, you will learn how remote connectivity can be implemented in Windows XP Professional. You will start by configuring a modem for remote access use, then learn how to create remote connections to Remote Access Servers, the Internet, and VPNs.

Setting Up a Modem

Dial-up networking allows remote users (for example, a person working from home or someone with a laptop on a business trip) to dial into a corporate network or the Internet. The most common method for remote network access is using a modem. This section will cover how to install and configure modems for use with Windows XP Professional.

If you install a Plug and Play modem on your Windows XP computer, it should be recognized automatically, and an appropriate driver should be loaded. Some modems are not automatically recognized with Windows XP Professional. In this case, you would manually install the modem through the Add/Remove Hardware Wizard and supply the device driver for Windows XP Professional that was provided through the modem manufacturer.

You can configure and manage the modems installed on your computer through Device Manager. To access Device Manager, select Start, then right-click My Computer and select Manage from the pop-up menu. Select System Tools, then Device Manager. In the Device Manager window, select Modems and then double-click the modem you want to manage. This brings up the modem's Properties dialog box, as shown in Figure 12.1. Most modems' Properties dialog boxes have six tabs: General, Modem, Diagnostics, Advanced, Driver, and Resources. The options on these tabs are covered in the following sections.

FIGURE 12.1   The modem Properties dialog box

 Avoid changing the default modem properties unless advised to by your modem manufacturer or the entity you are connecting to (for example, your Internet service provider). If you make incorrect alterations to the modem configuration, your modem may not work.

Configuring General Modem Properties

The General tab of the modem Properties dialog box (see Figure 12.1) displays the device type, the manufacturer of the modem, and location (slot within the PC where the modem is installed).

The General tab also displays the current status of the modem. Typically the status should be The Device Is Working Properly. If the modem is not working properly, you can click the Troubleshoot button to start a Troubleshooting Wizard that will help you determine the cause of the problem. See Chapter 4, "Configuring the Windows XP Environment" for more information about troubleshooting devices.

Configuring Modem Properties

The Modem tab, shown in Figure 12.2, shows the port to which the modem is attached. From this tab, you can set the following options:

- The speaker volume for the modem, which would typically be turned down if everything was working properly, but might be turned up if you were trying to troubleshoot a modem that was not working properly

- The maximum port speed (specified in bits per second), which should be left at the default value

- Dial control, to wait for a dial tone before dialing, so that dialing is not initiated prior to confirming that a valid dial tone exists

FIGURE 12.2   The Modem tab of the modem Properties dialog box

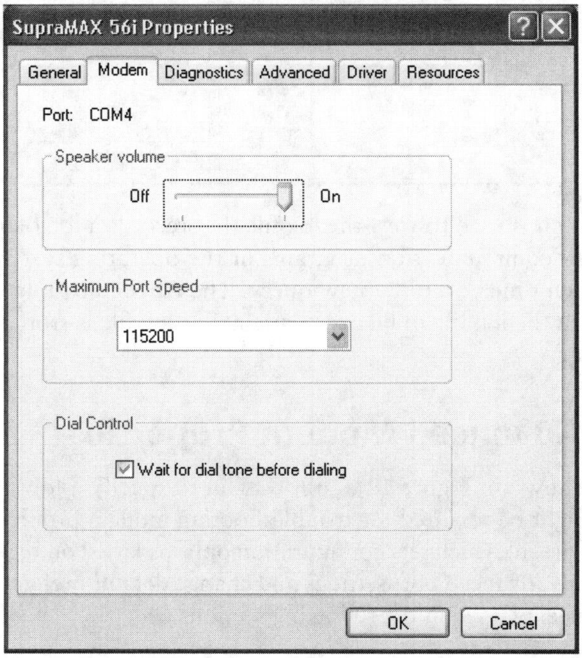

Running Modem Diagnostics

Through the Diagnostics tab, shown in Figure 12.3, you can query the modem. This process can be used in troubleshooting to ensure that the modem is properly responding to requests. Click the Query Modem button, and Device Manager will test the modem by issuing a series of modem commands. These commands and the responses sent back from the modem are listed in the Command/Response dialog box.

FIGURE 12.3 The Diagnostics tab of the modem Properties dialog box

The View Log button is used to view the log file that records a log of all of the commands sent to the modem by communication programs or the operating system. By default, this log is overwritten each time you run a new query. The Append to Log option can be specified if you don't want the log file to be overwritten. The log file is stored as *systemroot*\ *yourmodemmodel*.txt.

Configuring Advanced Modem Properties

The Advanced tab, shown in Figure 12.4, allows you to specify additional initialization commands, which might be required for troubleshooting modem problems, and the default Country/Region you are in, which sets configuration options based on regional phone systems. You can also configure advanced port settings and change default preferences by clicking their associated buttons, as explained in the following sections.

FIGURE 12.4   The Advanced tab of the modem Properties dialog box

Advanced Port Settings

Clicking the Advanced Port Settings button brings up the Advanced Settings dialog box for your communications (COM) port, as shown in Figure 12.5. Through this dialog box, you can specify whether the port will use FIFO (first in, first out) buffers, as well as the settings that will be used for the receive and transmit buffers. Lower settings can be used to correct connection problems. Higher settings can increase performance. You typically leave these values at default settings.

FIGURE 12.5   The Advanced Settings dialog box

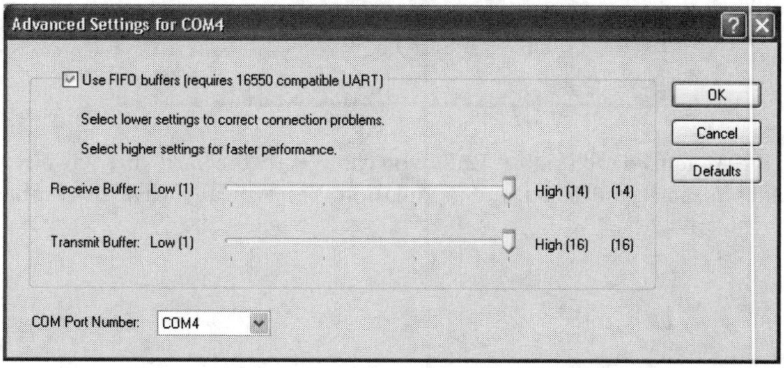

Default Preferences

Clicking the Change Default Preferences button (shown in Figure 12.4) brings up the modem's Default Preferences dialog box.

In the General tab (Figure 12.6), you can set preferences for calls and data connections. The Call Preferences options include settings for disconnecting a call if the connection is idle for more than the specified time, and how long to wait for a connection before canceling a call. The Data Connection Preferences include settings for the port speed, the data protocol, compression (enabled or disabled), and flow control (hardware or software). You typically leave these values at default settings.

FIGURE 12.6   The General tab of Default Preferences dialog box

Through the Advanced tab (Figure 12.7), you can specify the hardware settings for the port, including data bits, parity, stop bits, and modulation. You typically leave these values at default settings.

FIGURE 12.7   The Advanced tab of the Default Preferences dialog box

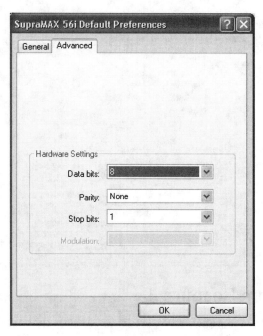

Viewing Driver Details and Updating Drivers

The Driver tab of the modem Properties dialog box, shown in Figure 12.8, displays information about the modem driver that is currently loaded. In the top half of the dialog box you can see:

- Driver Provider (which will be Microsoft if the driver was installed from the Windows XP Professional CD)

- Driver Date

- Driver Version

- Driver Signer

This information can be very useful in determining whether you have the most current driver for your modem. In addition, there are buttons for Driver Details, Update Driver, Roll Back Driver, and Uninstall.

Clicking the Driver Details button brings up a dialog box with additional information about the modem driver, including the location where the driver file has been installed. To update the driver, click the Update Driver button; this will initiate the Hardware Update Wizard, which will walk you through the process of updating your driver. The Roll Back Driver option is new for Windows XP Professional and allows you to roll back to a previously used driver in the event that you update a driver and it does not work properly. If the modem is removed from the computer, you can uninstall the driver, by clicking the Uninstall button.

FIGURE 12.8   The Driver tab of the modem Properties tab dialog box

Viewing Modem Resources

The Resources tab, shown in Figure 12.9, lists the resources that are used by your modem. Resources include memory, I/O memory, and interrupt request (IRQ) settings. You can use this information to detect resource conflicts, which may arise if you have non–Plug and Play hardware installed on your computer. The bottom of the dialog box will list any conflicts that have been detected with other devices that are installed on the computer.

FIGURE 12.9   The Resources tab of the modem Properties dialog box

Once your modem (or other connectivity option) is configured, you can create remote connections through the New Connection Wizard, which is covered in the following section.

Using the New Connection Wizard

The New Connection Wizard is used to guide you through the process of implementing all of the remote connections that can be used with Windows XP Professional. You access the New Connection Wizard through Start ➢ Control Panel ➢ Network and Internet Connections ➢ Network Connections. In the Network Connections dialog box, under Network Tasks, click Create a New Connection. The New Connection Wizard will start. From the Welcome screen, click the Next button to continue, and you will see the Network Connection Type dialog box, as shown in Figure 12.10.

FIGURE 12.10   The Network Connection Type dialog box

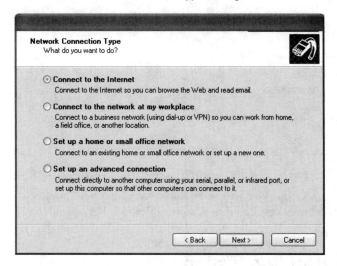

The options that can be configured through the Network Connection Wizard include:

- Internet connections
- Dial-up connections to private networks
- VPN connections to private networks
- Network for small office or home networks
- Direct connections to other computers through serial, parallel, or infrared connections

You will learn how to create a dial-up connection to a private network, create a connection to the Internet, and how to configure a VPN connection later in this chapter.

Creating a Connection to a Remote Access Server

One of the most common ways that remote users can access a private network is through the use of a *Remote Access Service (RAS)* server. The RAS server is used to respond to and provide services for remote clients. Methods for accessing a RAS server include analog modem and phone system, ISDN adapters and ISDN phone lines, Frame Relay, and leased T lines. The RAS server and the RAS client must use the same connectivity option. They must also use the same protocols as well as compatible security protocols. Figure 12.11 illustrates how you would access a RAS server through analog dial-in service.

FIGURE 12.11   Dial-in Connection to a Remote Access Service (RAS) server

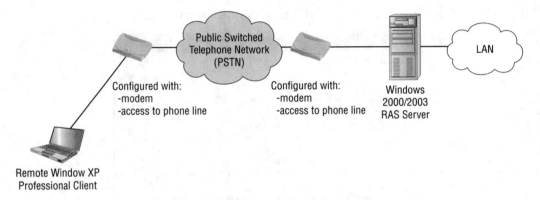

In the following sections you will learn how to create a RAS connection, configure the properties of a RAS connection, and how to troubleshoot RAS problems.

Creating a RAS Connection

To configure a RAS client, take the following steps:

1. Select Start ≻ Control Panel ≻ Network and Internet Connections, then select the option Create a Connection to the Network at Your Workplace.

2. The Network Connection dialog box appears next, as shown in Figure 12.12. Select the Dial-up Connection option and click the Next button.

3. The Connection Name dialog box will appear. Type in the name that you want to use for the connection, which will be the descriptive name that will be used when you access the connection, and click the Next button.

FIGURE 12.12   Network Connection dialog box

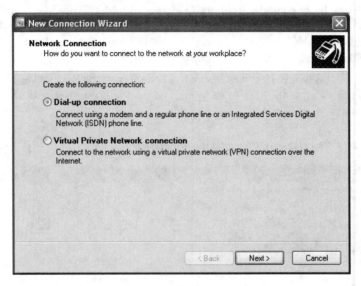

4. Next up is the Phone Number to Dial dialog box, as shown in Figure 12.13. Enter the telephone number you wish to dial. If the telephone number is in a different country, enter the associated country code in the Country/Region Code field (for example, the Czech Republic's country code is 420 when you are calling internationally). After you enter the information, click the Next button.

FIGURE 12.13   Phone Number to Dial dialog box

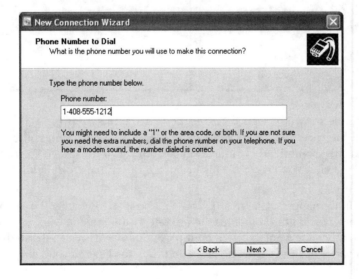

5. The Completing the New Connection Wizard dialog box will appear. By default, the connection will be saved in the Network Connections folder. From the Completing the New Connection Wizard, you can also specify that a shortcut will be added for the connection on the Desktop. Verify the new connection information, and click the Finish button. The Connect Dialup dialog box will automatically launch.

6. If you have access to a RAS server, you would connect to the RAS server through Control Panel ➢ Network and Internet Connections, and then selecting Network Connections. You will see a window similar to the one in Figure 12.14.

FIGURE 12.14 Network Connections window

7. In the example shown in Figure 12.14, there are connections for dial-up, LAN or high-speed Internet, and a network bridge. The RAS connection will be listed under Dial-up. In this example, the connection is Connection to Testco Corp. Click the dial-up connection you created. This brings up the connection dialog box shown in Figure 12.15.

8. Type in your username and password. You can also specify whether the username and password will be saved on the computer for you only or for anyone who uses the computer. Select the number you want to dial (if multiple options have been configured—for example, if the RAS server has five incoming lines) and click the Dial button.

FIGURE 12.15   The Connect Connection dialog box

Managing the Properties of a RAS Connection

To manage the properties of a RAS connection, click the Properties button shown in Figure 12.15. This brings up the Connection Properties dialog box shown in Figure 12.16. This dialog box has five tabs: General, Options, Security, Networking, and Advanced. The options on these tabs are covered in the following sections.

FIGURE 12.16   The Connection Properties dialog box

Configuring General RAS Connection Properties

The General tab (see Figure 12.16) includes options for configuring the connection you will use and the telephone number you are dialing. You can also specify whether an icon will be displayed on the Taskbar when a connection is in use.

The Connect Using option specifies the device that will be used to create the connection (for example, a modem or an ISDN adapter). To configure specific properties of the connection device, click the Configure button. In the example shown in Figure 12.17, you can configure the maximum speed of the modem and set hardware features for the modem. If you were troubleshooting connectivity, you might use this dialog box to reduce your connection speed.

FIGURE 12.17   The Modem Configuration dialog box

Within the General tab, the Phone Number section has text boxes for the area code and telephone number of the connection. To specify alternate telephone numbers to make a connection, if a RAS server has multiple phone lines that are supported, click the Alternates button. If you choose to use dialing rules, you can click the Dialing Rules button, which brings up the Dialing Rules dialog box. To modify dialing rules for an existing location, you select the location and click the Edit button. The Edit Location dialog box, as shown in Figure 12.18, allows you to configure General, Area Code Rules, or Calling Card information for the location. Examples of general properties include specifying a number that must be dialed before accessing an outside line or the number that must be specified for dialing a long distance number. Area code rules specify how numbers will be dialed based on the area code you are dialing from. Calling card is used to specify dialing rules if you access the remote connection using a calling card.

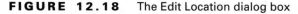

FIGURE 12.18   The Edit Location dialog box

The options for Area Code and Country/Region Code are grayed out unless you have checked the Use Dialing Rules check box on the General tab of the Connection Properties dialog box.

Configuring RAS Connection Options

The Options tab, shown in Figure 12.19, contains dialing options and redialing options. You can configure the following options for dialing:

- The Display Progress while Connecting option displays the progress of the connection attempt.

- The Prompt for Name and Password, Certificate, Etc. option specifies that before a connection is attempted, the user will be prompted for a username, password, or (if *smart card* authentication is being used) a certificate.

Smart cards are hardware devices used to provide additional security. They store public and private keys, passwords, and other personal information securely.

- The Include Windows Logon Domain option works in conjunction with the Prompt for Name and Password, Certificate, Etc. option. This option specifies that Windows logon-domain information should be requested prior to initiating a connection.

- The Prompt for Phone Number option allows the telephone number to be viewed, selected, or modified prior to initiating a connection.

FIGURE 12.19 The Options tab of the Connection Properties dialog box

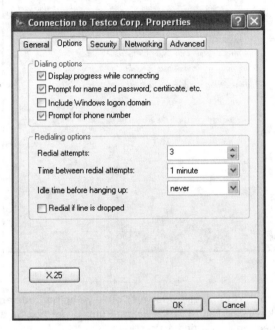

The options for redialing let you specify the number of redial attempts if the connection is not established, and the time between the redial attempts. You can also designate how long a connection will remain idle before the computer hangs up. If you want the computer to redial the connection number should the connection be dropped, check the Redial if Line Is Dropped check box.

The X.25 button at the bottom of this dialog box can be used to configure an X.25 connection. This requires you to know which X.25 provider you are using and the X.121 address of the remote server you wish to connect to.

Configuring RAS Connection Security

Security settings are among the most important options to be configured for dial-up connections. You can set typical or advanced (custom settings) security options in the Security tab of the Connection Properties dialog box, as shown in Figure 12.20. This tab also has options for interactive logon and scripting.

FIGURE 12.20   The Security tab of the Connection Properties dialog box

 Connections that are more secure require more overhead and are usually slower. Less-secure connections require less overhead and are typically faster.

Typical Security Settings

You generally will configure typical security settings unless you need to use specific security protocols. When you select the Typical radio button, you can then choose to validate the user's identity, to automatically use the Windows logon name and password (and domain, if specified), and whether data encryption is required. For validating the user's identity, you can select from the following options:

Allow Unsecured Password   Specifies that the password can be transmitted without any encryption.

Require Secured Password   Specifies that the password must be encrypted prior to transmission.

Use Smart Card   Specifies that you must use a smart card.

The options for configuring Automatically Use My Windows Logon Name and Password (and Domain if Any) and Require Data Encryption (Disconnect if None) are enabled based on the validation method you select, and whether the options are supported by the selected validation option.

Advanced Security Settings

If you need to configure specific security protocols, select the Advanced (Custom Settings) radio button in the Security tab and then click the Settings button. This brings up the Advanced Security Settings dialog box, as shown in Figure 12.21.

FIGURE 12.21 Connection Properties, Security tab, Advanced Settings dialog box

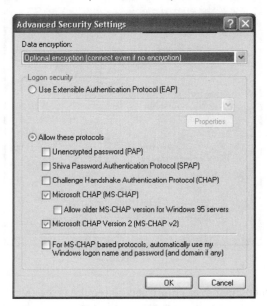

This dialog box allows you to configure the type of data encryption that will be employed. You also specify whether logon security will use the Extensible Authentication Protocol (EAP), which is used in conjunction with other security devices, including smart cards and certificates. You can select from the following protocols for logon security:

- Unencrypted Password (PAP)
- Shiva Password Authentication Protocol (SPAP)
- Challenge Handshake Authentication Protocol (CHAP)
- Microsoft CHAP (MS-CHAP), if you select this option, additionally you can specify that you want to support older MS-CHAP for Windows 95 servers
- Microsoft CHAP Version 2 (MS-CHAPv2)

If you are using MS-CHAP-based protocols, you can also specify that you want to automatically use your Windows logon name and password (and domain, if any).

The authentication security protocols were covered in the "Understanding Remote Access Security" section earlier in this chapter.

Interactive Logon and Scripting

The Interactive Logon and Scripting options on the Security tab are provided for users who use terminal services for remote access. These options allow you to display a terminal window after dialing, and run a script after dialing.

 Scripting features are supported only for serial modems. These features are not available for ISDN devices.

Configuring Networking Options for RAS Connections

The Networking tab, shown in Figure 12.22, contains networking options for the dial-up connection. You can configure the wide area network (WAN) protocol you will use and the network components that will be employed by the network connection.

FIGURE 12.22   The Networking tab of the Connection Properties dialog box

Your choices for the WAN protocol are the *Point-to-Point Protocol (PPP)* or *Serial Line Internet Protocol (SLIP)*. PPP offers more features and is the WAN protocol used by Windows *9x*, Windows NT (all versions), Windows 2000 (all versions), Windows XP, Windows Server 2003, and most Internet servers. SLIP is an older protocol that is used with some Unix servers. If you click the Settings button for PPP, you can configure options for Enable LCP Extensions, Enable Software Compression, and Negotiate Multi-link for Single Link Connections. You typically leave PPP settings at default values.

The network components used by the connection might include the protocols (such as Internet Protocol (IP) and NWLink IPX/SPX/NetBIOS Compatible Transport Protocol) and the client software (such as File and Printer Sharing for Microsoft Networks and Client for Microsoft Networks). By clicking the Install button, you can install additional connections. The Properties button allows you to configure the properties of whatever connection you have highlighted.

Configuring Advanced Options

The Advanced tab, shown in Figure 12.23, is used to configure an Internet Connection Firewall and Internet Connection Sharing. The Internet Connection Firewall is used to limit access to your computer through the Internet and is implemented as a security feature. Internet Connection Sharing is used to allow more than one Internet connection through a single computer. Both of these topics are covered in greater detail in the "Using Internet Connection Sharing" and "Using an Internet Connection Firewall" sections of the chapter.

FIGURE 12.23   The Advanced tab of the Connection Properties dialog box

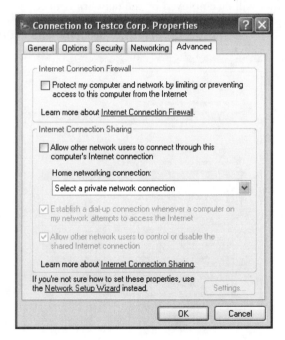

Troubleshooting Remote Access Connections

If your remote access connection is not working properly, there are many possible causes. The following list categorizes common problems and the options that can be used to troubleshoot, identify, and resolve configuration errors:

If you suspect the problem is with your modem:

- Verify that the modem you are using is on the Hardware Compatibility List (HCL) and that you have the most current driver.

- If you are using an external modem, verify that it is turned on and connected to the proper port, and that the modem cable is not defective. If you require a 9-to-25-pin serial connector, do not use one that came with a mouse, as most are not manufactured to support modem signals.

- Use modem logging and modem diagnostics to test the modem.

If you suspect the problem is with your access line:

- If you are using an unknown line type (for example, in a hotel), verify the line type you are using. Analog modems only use analog phone lines, and digital modems only use digital lines. The remote client and the server that is being accessed must also use a common access method, analog or digital.

- Verify that you dialed the correct number for the remote server. If you need to dial an external line-access number (usually 9), verify that it is properly configured.

- If the modem is having problems connecting, there may be excessive static on the phone line that is preventing the modem from connecting at the configured speed. Attempt to connect using lower speed and call the phone company to have the quality of the line checked.

If you suspect the problem is with the RAS server:

- Verify that you are using a valid user account and password. Make sure the user account has been granted remote access permission on the RAS server.

- Make sure the RAS server is properly configured and is running. If no remote clients can connect, the problem is most likely the RAS server. If other remote clients can connect, the RAS server is most likely properly configured.

If connections to the RAS server are being dropped:

- Verify that the connection is not being dropped due to inactivity. Check with the RAS server administrator to find out what the inactivity settings are.

- If your phone line uses call waiting, an incoming call may be disrupting your connection; verify that call waiting has been disabled.

Creating a Connection to the Internet

The most common option for remote access to the Internet is through a valid *Internet service provider (ISP)*. There are many ISPs to choose from, and they usually supply software to facilitate your Internet connection through their service. If you do not have software from your ISP, you can set up an Internet connection the first time you access Internet Explorer or through New Connection Wizard. Common options for accessing the Internet include analog modem and phone line, ISDN adapter and ISDN phone line, cable modem, and DSL.

In Exercise 12.1, you will create a dial-up Internet connection for a new Internet account.

EXERCISE 12.1

Creating a Dial-Up Connection to the Internet

1. Select Start ➤ Control Panel ➤ Network and Internet Connections ➤ Set Up or Change Your Internet Connection.

2. Click the Setup button on the Connections tab.

3. In the Welcome to the New Connection Wizard dialog box, click the Next button.

4. The Network Connection Type dialog box will appear. Select Connect to the Internet and click the Next button.

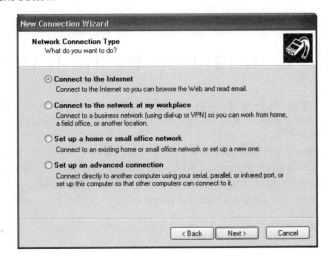

5. In the Getting Ready dialog box, you can choose from the following options:

    ▪ The Choose from a List of Internet Service Providers (ISPs) option guides you through selecting an ISP and setting up a new account. You can use this option if you do not already have an ISP.

    ▪ The Set Up My Connection Manually option is used for dial-up connections where you know the account name, password, and phone number for your ISP.

    ▪ The Use the CD I Got from an ISP is probably the most common option and includes all the software to connect to your ISP.

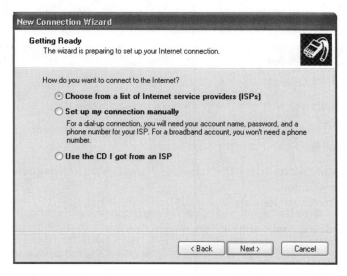

6. Select the option you will use to connect to your ISP and follow the remaining prompts.

Using Virtual Private Network Connections

A VPN is a private network that uses links across private or public networks (such as the Internet). When data is sent over the remote link, it is encapsulated and encrypted and requires authentication services. You must use Point-to-Point Tunneling Protocol (PPTP) or Layer Two Tunneling Protocol (L2TP) to support a VPN connection, both of which are automatically installed on Windows XP Professional computers. To have a VPN, you must also have a Windows 2000 Server or a Windows Server 2003 computer that has been configured as a VPN server. Figure 12.24 illustrates a VPN.

FIGURE 12.24 Making a virtual private network (VPN) connection

The main advantage of using a VPN rather than a RAS connection is that with a RAS connection, a long-distance call might be required to dial into the RAS server. With a VPN connection, all you need is access to a network such as the Internet.

In Exercise 12.2, you will configure the client for a VPN connection. This exercise assumes you already have a valid connection to the Internet.

EXERCISE 12.2

Configuring a VPN Client

1. Select Start ➤ Control Panel ➤ Network and Internet Connections.

2. In the Network Connection Type dialog box, click the Create a Connection to the Network at My Workplace option and click the Next button.

3. In the Network Connection dialog box, select the Virtual Private Network connection option and click the Next button.

4. The Connection Name dialog box will appear. Type in the name of the connection you will use and the company name, and click the Next button.

5. In the Public Network dialog box, select the Do Not Dial the Initial Connection option and click the Next button.

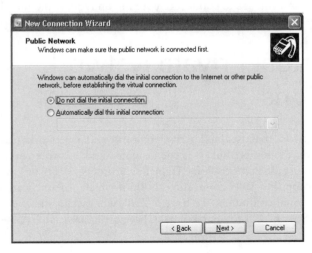

6. In the VPN Server Selection dialog box, enter the hostname or the IP address of the computer that you will connect to. Then click the Next button.

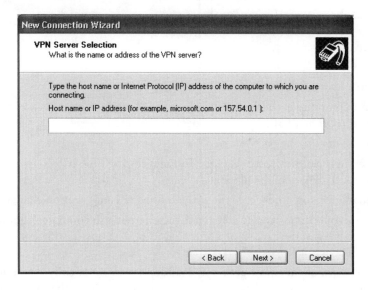

7. The Completing the New Connection Wizard will appear. Click the option Add a Shortcut to This Connection to My Desktop and click the Finish button.

8. Click the shortcut that is created on the Desktop to connect to the VPN. Type in your username and password and click the Connect button.

Using Internet Connection Sharing

Internet Connection Sharing (ICS) allows you to connect a small network (typically a home network) to the Internet through a single connection, as illustrated in Figure 12.25. The computer that provides ICS services is usually the one with the fastest outgoing connection—for example, using DSL.

The ICS host computer must have two connections. One of the connections is used to connect the computer to the LAN. The second connection—for example, a modem, ISDN adapter, DSL, or cable modem—is used to connect the computer to the Internet.

The ICS computer that accesses the Internet provides network address translation, IP addressing, and DNS name resolution services for all the computers on the network. Through Internet connection sharing, the other computers on the network can use Internet applications such as Internet Explorer and Outlook Express, as well as access Internet resources.

FIGURE 12.25 Internet Connection Sharing

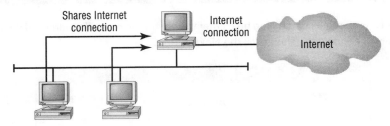

There are three main steps for using ICS:

1. The ICS host computer is configured to access the Internet through whatever connection method is appropriate (dial-up, cable modem, ISDN, etc.).

2. The ICS host computer has ICS enabled.

3. The client computers that will access the Internet through the ICS connection must be configured to use dynamic IP addressing.

When you enable ICS on a host computer, the following configuration changes will occur:

-   When Internet connection sharing is enabled, the Internet host computer's address becomes 192.168.0.1 with a subnet mask of 255.255.255.0. The host also becomes the DHCP allocator, which acts as a "baby" DHCP server.

-   All of the network clients must get their IP addresses automatically through the DHCP allocator, which gives out addresses randomly to the clients, in the range 192.168.0.2 through 192.168.0.254 with a subnet mask of 255.255.255.0.

-   The autodial feature is enabled on the ICS host computer.

-   DNS Proxy is enabled on the ICS host computer.

 To configure Internet connection sharing, you must be a member of the Administrators group.

 Real World Scenario

Using Internet Connection Sharing

You have Windows XP Professional on your home computer, which has Internet access. You also have three other computers running Windows 98, Windows Me, and Windows 2000 Professional. These computers, used as part of a home lab for testing and training preparation, are connected through an Ethernet LAN using TCP/IP. They do not have Internet access, and you want to change this so you can access the Internet from any of your computers.

This alteration is easily accomplished through Internet connection sharing. You will need to enable the Internet Connection Sharing service on the Windows XP Professional computer, and configure your client computers to use Internet connection sharing through their Internet browser software.

Configuring Internet Connection Sharing on the Host Computer

The computer that will act as the host computer for Internet connection sharing must be configured to support this option. Following are the options that can be configured:

Whether Internet connection sharing is enabled.   If it is, watch out—local network access may be momentarily disrupted because the IP address will automatically be reassigned to the computers that use Internet connection sharing.

Whether on-demand dialing is enabled.   When it is, if you do not have a permanent connection on the computer that hosts Internet connection sharing, the host computer will automatically dial out whenever a client tries to access the Internet. Enabling Internet Connection Sharing automatically enables on-demand dialing.

Which applications and services can be used through the shared connection.   For example, you could specify that only FTP requests on port 21, Telnet requests on port 23, and HTTP requests on port 80 can be passed through the shared Internet connection.

To configure Internet connection sharing on the host computer, take the following steps:

1. Create an Internet connection or a VPN connection.

2. Verify that the host computer is configured as a DHCP client and that each client (Internet Sharing) computer is also configured as a DHCP client. If the host has a static address, it will be changed to 192.168.0.1 automatically.

3. Select Start ➤ Control Panel ➤ Network and Internet Connections, then select Network Connections.

4. Right-click the connection you want to share, and select Properties from the pop-up menu.

5. The Properties dialog box for the selected connection appears. Click the Advanced tab and under Internet Connection Sharing, check the option for Allow Other Network Users to Connect through This Computer's Internet Connection, which was shown in Figure 12.23.

   Enabling Internet Connection Sharing automatically enables on-demand dialing. When on-demand dialing is enabled, if the Internet connection is not active and another computer tries to access Internet resources, a connection will be automatically established.

6. Click the Settings button to access the Advanced Settings dialog box (Figure 12.26). This dialog box allows you to specify which applications and services can be serviced through the shared Internet connection. If you leave the blank default settings as is, then all applications and services are supported. However, you may want to limit access to one application—for example, HTTP. If so, you could configure HTTP requests to only be serviced by limited access to HTTP on port 80 (which is the default port that is used by HTTP requests). When you are done, click the OK button twice to close both open dialog boxes.

FIGURE 12.26 Advanced Settings, Advanced tab, Internet Connection Sharing Settings dialog box

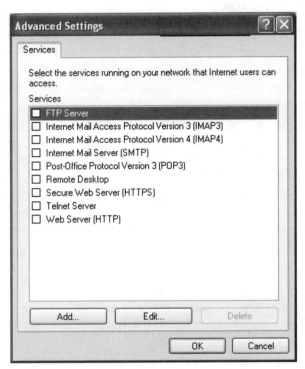

Configuring Internet Connection Sharing on the Network Computers

To configure Internet connection sharing on the network computers, take the following steps:

1. Right-click the Internet Explorer icon on the Desktop and select Properties from the pop-up menu.

2. In the Internet Properties dialog box, click the Connections tab (Figure 12.27) and click the Never Dial a Connection option.

3. Click the LAN Settings button, and in Automatic Configuration (Figure 12.28), clear the Automatically Detect Settings and Use Automatic Configuration Script boxes. In Proxy Server, clear the Use a Proxy Server check box.

FIGURE 12.27   The Connections tab of the Internet Properties dialog box

FIGURE 12.28   The Local Area Network (LAN) Settings dialog box

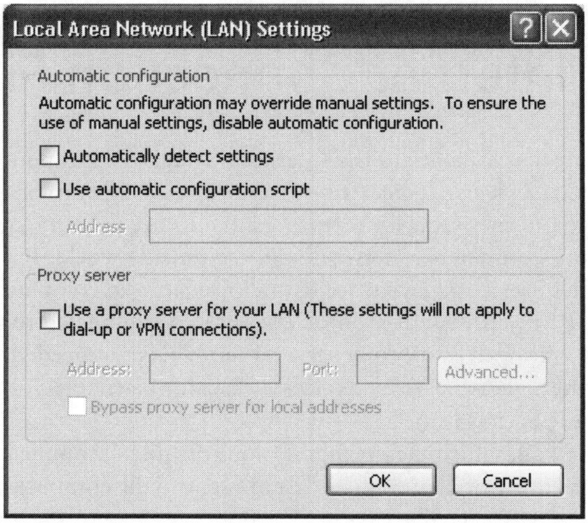

> Do not configure Internet connection sharing on corporate networks with domain controllers, DNS servers, WINS servers, DHCP servers, routers, or other computers that use static IP addresses. When Internet connection sharing is configured, it causes computers that use the shared Internet connection to lose their IP configuration and generates a new IP configuration. Normal network connections then have to be manually reset to access local network resources.

In Exercise 12.3, you will configure the VPN connection you created in Exercise 12.2 to support Internet connection sharing.

EXERCISE 12.3

Configuring Internet Connection Sharing

1. Select Start ≻ Control Panel and click Network and Internet Connections. Click Network Connections, then right-click the Dial-Up connection you created in Exercise 12.2 and select Properties.

2. In the Dial-Up Properties dialog box, select the Advanced tab. Under Internet Connection Sharing, click the Allow Other Network Users to Connect through This Computer's Internet Connection option. If you have not saved your username and password for the computer, you will see a dialog box warning you that Internet Connection Sharing will only dial the connection when you are logged in. If you want to enable automatic dialing, you will need to save your username and password in the Connect dialog box. Click the OK button.

3. In the Advanced tab, click the OK button to close the Dial-up Properties dialog box.

Using an Internet Connection Firewall

If you have a computer that attaches to the Internet through a dial-up modem, cable modem, or DSL connection, you can use *Internet Connection Firewall (ICF)* to protect your connection from passive or active Internet security threats. *Firewalls* are security systems that act as a boundary between your computer or network and the outside world. ICF works by acting as a protective mechanism by restricting what access is allowed to your computer through the Internet.

You would use ICF only if your computer was directly connected to the Internet. If your network already uses a firewall or a proxy server, then ICF is not needed. ICF should also not be installed on computers that use VPN services. ICF can't be enabled on private connections for host computers of ICS.

ICF is a stateful firewall, which means that it monitors all communications by defining the source and destination traffic of all messages that are sent to the computer. ICF works by using a flow table, which defines protected networks. The only incoming traffic that is allowed is traffic that can be validated through an entry in the flow table. If unauthorized traffic is detected, ICF automatically discards the unauthorized packets. If you originate traffic from an ICF computer, then that traffic is logged in a table, so that if you receive inbound traffic from a site you have contacted, that traffic is allowed to pass through.

To configure and manage ICF, you take the following steps:

1. Select Start ➢ Control Panel and click Network and Internet Connections. Click Network Connections and right-click the dial-up connection you want to enable ICF on. Select Properties.

2. Click the Advanced tab. Check the Protect My Computer and Network by Limiting or Preventing Access to This Computer from the Internet option.

3. To configure ICF logging, click the Settings button. In the Advanced Settings dialog box, click the Security Logging tab (Figure 12.29). This allows you to configure ICF logging options such as whether dropped packets are logged and whether successful connections are logged. You can also specify the log file that will be used and the maximum log file size.

FIGURE 12.29   The Security Logging tab of the Advanced Settings dialog box

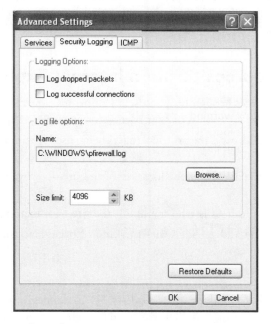

In Exercise 12.4, you will configure Internet Connection Firewall.

EXERCISE 12.4

Configuring Internet Connection Firewall

1. Select Start ➢ Control Panel and click Network and Internet Connections. Click Network Connections and right-click the dial-up connection you created in Exercise 12.2. Select Properties.

2. In the Dial-Up Properties dialog box, select the Advanced tab. Click the option Protect My Computer and Network by Limiting or Preventing Access to This Computer from the Internet.

EXERCISE 12.4 *(continued)*

3. Click the Settings button. In the Advanced Settings dialog box, select the Security Logging tab. Click the Log Dropped Packets option and the Log Successful Connections option. Click the OK button.

Configuring and Managing Internet Explorer

Internet Explorer (IE) is a web browser used to search and view information on the World Wide Web (WWW) via the Internet, or information that is stored on local intranets. You can access resources by typing in the address of the web page you wish to access or by selecting an address from your Favorites list. In this section you will learn about accessing resources through IE and how to configure IE.

Accessing Resources through Internet Explorer

When you access a resource through IE, you use a Uniform Resource Locator (URL) address. A URL address is typically composed of four parts—for example: `http://www.sybex.com`.

-   The first part of the address is the protocol that is being used. Examples of protocols include HTTP and FTP.

-   The second part of the address is the location of the site—for example, the World Wide Web (www).

-   The third part of the address is who maintains the site—for example, Sybex.

-   The fourth part of the address identifies the kind of organization. Examples of defined suffixes include .com, .gov, .org, and .edu.

Using HTTP

HTTP is the main protocol for making www requests. HTTP defines how messages are formatted and transmitted and the actions that will be executed by web servers and browsers based on the requests you make. The main standard that is used with HTTP is Hypertext Markup Language (HTML), which defines how web pages are formatted and displayed.

 If the web server you are trying to access is using Secure Sockets Layer (SSL) services, then instead of using http:// requests, you use secure HTTP, and the request would use https://.

Using FTP

FTP is mainly used to transfer files between computers on the Internet. Access to FTP servers is based on permissions that have been set on the FTP server you are trying to access. Access can be granted to anonymous users or users can be required to have a valid username and password.

Once you access a FTP site, you can:

- Work with files and folders in the same manner that would be used on a local computer

- View, download, upload, rename, and delete files and folders (based on your permissions)

When you use FTP for file transfer with IE, the syntax looks different than a typical HTTP request. FTP requests are made through the address bar on IE. For example, if you were trying to access Microsoft's FTP site, you would type:

`ftp://ftp.microsoft.com`

If the FTP site required user and password authentication services, you could use the File menu and select the Login As option.

If you need to provide logon credentials as a part of the FTP request, then the syntax you would use would be:

`ftp://username:password@ftp.microsoft.com`

Configuring Internet Explorer

Several options can be configured for Internet Explorer. You access Internet Properties by right-clicking Internet Explorer from the Start menu and selecting Internet Properties. This brings up the dialog box shown in Figure 12.30.

FIGURE 12.30   The Internet Properties dialog box

The options that can be configured are General, Security, Privacy, Content, Connections, Programs, and Advanced.

Configuring General Options

General properties are used to configure home page, temporary Internet files, and history information. Home Page is used to configure the default home page that is displayed when you launch Internet Explorer. You can specify that you want to use the current home page for whatever is currently loaded, use the default home page that was pre-configured, or leave the option blank.

The Temporary Internet Files options are used to manage cookies, files, and settings. Cookies are special files that are created by websites and store information, such as preferences used when you visited the website. By deleting files, you delete any temporary Internet files that have been stored on your computer. This option is useful when you are low on disk space. Settings is used to configure options such as how your computer checks for newer versions of stored files and the location and amount of space that can be used by temporary Internet files.

History saves all of the links to pages you have visited. By default, a history of all of the links you have accessed is kept for 20 days. You can customize how many days the history is stored or manually clear the history.

You can also set other options from the General tab that affect how Internet Explorer is customized, such as colors, fonts, languages, and accessibility options.

Configuring Security Options

The Security tab, as shown in Figure 12.31, allows you to configure the following options:

- The Internet content zones that can be used by the computer
- The local intranet zones that can be used by the computer
- The trusted sites that are allowed for the computer
- The restricted sites that are in effect for the computer

FIGURE 12.31 The Security tab of the Internet Properties dialog box

You set security zones by selecting the web content zone you want to configure, then clicking the Sites button. Custom Settings allow you to configure options such as whether you enable the downloading or use of signed or unsigned ActiveX controls. If you have configured your computer for security options and have specified security restrictions, you will receive an error message anytime you access a zone or site that is not configured for use with your computer.

Configuring Privacy Options

The Privacy tab, as shown in Figure 12.32, is used to configure privacy settings that relate to how third-party cookies are allowed to store information on your computer. You can select from different levels of security that range from blocking all cookies to allowing all cookies. When you click the Import button, you can import saved privacy settings from a predefined file. The Advanced button allows you to customize privacy settings. At the bottom of the screen, the Edit button for Web Sites allows you to customize privacy settings for specific websites.

FIGURE 12.32   Internet Properties, Privacy tab dialog box

Configuring Content-Related Options

The Content tab, as shown in Figure 12.33, is used to configure the options for Content Advisor, Certificates, and Personal Information.

FIGURE 12.33 The Content tab of the Internet Properties dialog box

Content Advisor

When you click the Enable button for Content Advisor, shown in Figure 12.34, you can set ratings of what can be viewed on the computer. This allows you to set flags to limit what is accessed based on language, nudity, sex, and violence on a sliding scale of acceptability. This option assumes that the website has been rated appropriately through the website configuration. The Approved Sites tab allows you to specifically define what sites are allowed or disallowed regardless of their content rating. The General tab allows you to configure options to allow a Supervisor to override content settings. The Advanced tab allows you to configure access for the ratings bureau you want to use for content ratings.

Certificates

Certificates are used to identify who you are based on a certificate that has been issued to you from a certification authority or certificate publisher. Through the Certificates section on the Content tab, you can Clear SSL State, configure Certificates, and configure Publishers.

With Secure Sockets Layer (SSL), any certificates that are used are automatically saved in SSL cache. The certificates are stored in SSL cache until the computer is restarted. If you need to use a new certificate, the Clear SSL Start button can be used to manually clear the SSL cache, so the new certificate can be used without restarting the computer.

The Certificates option is used to require a trusted website to provide you, the client, with a valid certificate. This option is used to verify that the website that is being accessed can be authenticated through certificate services.

FIGURE 12.34   The Content Advisor dialog box

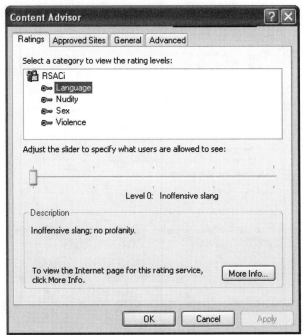

The Publishers button is used to configure all of the trusted publishers for the computer. You import a certificate from trusted publishers through the Import button in the Certificates dialog box.

Personal Information

Personal information allows you to configure AutoComplete and use the Microsoft Profile Assistant. With AutoComplete, the entries you make are stored, and when you type in a few keystrokes of a new entry, AutoComplete will compare the new entry to the previous entries and try and make a match for you. Profile Assistant is used to store personal information about you.

Configuring Connections

The Connections tab, as shown in Figure 12.35, is used to configure what connection is used to access the Internet. This can be any connection you have created or a connection that is using Internet Connection Sharing. You can also configure proxy server settings and the LAN settings that are used by the Internet connection.

FIGURE 12.35 The Connections tab of the Internet Properties dialog box

Dial-up settings include:

- Never Dial a Connection
- Dial Whenever a Network Connection Is Not Present
- Always Dial My Default Connection

LAN settings are used to define automatic configuration settings and proxy server settings (what the IP address for the proxy server is and the port that should be used). Proxy settings defined for the LAN do not apply to dial-up or VPN connections.

Configuring Program Options

The Programs tab, as shown in Figure 12.36, is used to configure what programs are associated with different Internet services. You can specify what programs are used for:

- HTML editor
- E-mail
- Newsgroups
- Internet call
- Calendar
- Contact list

When you click the Reset Web Settings button, Internet Explorer will default back to all of the default home and search page settings.

FIGURE 12.36   The Programs tab of the Internet Properties dialog box

Configuring Advanced Options

The Advanced tab, as shown in Figure 12.37, is used to configure Internet Explorer options for accessibility, browsing, how links are underlined, HTTP settings, multimedia, printing, and security settings.

FIGURE 12.37   The Advanced tab of the Internet Properties dialog box

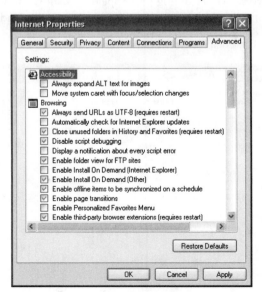

Managing Internet Printers

Windows XP automatically supports Internet printing when Internet Information Services (IIS) is installed on a Windows Server 2003 or a Windows XP Professional client. IIS is covered in greater detail at the end of this chapter. Any printers that are shared on the Windows XP Server are then automatically made accessible to Internet users through a protocol called *Internet Printing Protocol (IPP)*. Windows XP clients automatically include IPP print support, and the users can browse and print to Internet printers through Internet Explorer 4.01 or higher.

> This chapter covers the material related to Internet printing for the "Connect to local and network print devices" objective. The other subobjectives for this objective are covered in Chapter 11, "Managing Printing."

To install a printer from the Internet or an intranet, use the printer's URL as the name of the printer. To support all browsers, an administrator must choose basic authentication. Internet Explorer supports LAN Manager Challenge/Response and Kerberos version 5 authentication.

Adding an Internet Printer

To install an Internet printer on a Windows Server 2003 or Windows XP Professional client, you must first install IIS. Then you can create a shared printer (see Chapter 11 for details on setting up a shared printer). Once you have created a shared printer complete the following steps:

1. Select Start ➢ Printers and Faxes.
2. In the Printers folder, click the Add a Printer option.
3. The Welcome to the Add Printer Wizard starts. Click the Next button.
4. The Local or Network Printer dialog box appears, as shown in Figure 12.38. Select A Network Printer, or a Printer Attached to Another Computer, and click the Next button.

FIGURE 12.38   The Local or Network Printer dialog box

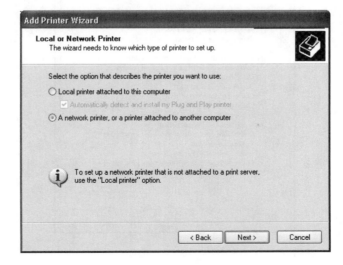

5. The Specify a Printer dialog box appears, as shown in Figure 12.39. Click the Connect to a Printer on the Internet or on a Home or Office Network option. In the URL box, type **http://*computername*/printers/*share_name*/.printer** and click the Next button.

FIGURE 12.39 The Specify a Printer dialog box

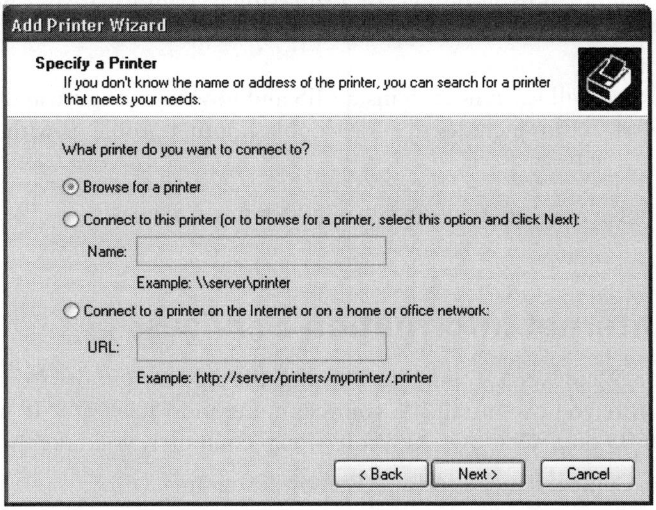

Connecting to an Internet Printer Using a Web Browser

You can manage printers from any browser, but you must use Internet Explorer 4.01 or later to connect to a printer using a browser (the browser must support frames).

To connect to an Internet printer using a web browser, take the following steps:

1. Open the web browser, type **http://print_server/printers** in the address bar, and press Enter. If prompted, type your username, domain name, and password.

2. Click the link for the printer you want to connect to.

3. Under Printer Actions, click Connect.

Overview of Internet Information Services

Windows XP Professional comes with *Internet Information Services (IIS)*, which allows you to create and manage websites. This software provides a wide range of options for configuring the content, performance, and access controls for your websites. IIS can be used to publish resources on the Internet or a private intranet.

The IIS software that is included with Windows XP Professional is designed for small-scale use, mainly for users who are developing web services for home or office use. IIS Professional version edition can support only 10 incoming client connections. IIS Professional version also does not support all of the features of IIS that are included with the server versions of IIS. In previous versions of Windows client operating systems, the scaled-down version of IIS was called Peer Web Services (PWS). Windows XP Professional does not ship with PWS, and if you upgraded to Windows XP Professional, then PWS can't be upgraded. The IIS Professional version software is included with Windows XP Professional, but is not installed by default.

In this section, you will learn how to install IIS and how to configure and manage website properties. The final section includes tips for troubleshooting problems with website access.

 IIS is not included with Windows XP Home Edition.

Installing Internet Information Services

IIS is installed on a Windows XP computer through the Add or Remove Programs option in Control Panel. Before you can install IIS, your computer must have TCP/IP installed and configured. To install IIS on a Windows XP Professional computer, you take the following steps:

1. Select Start ≻ Control Panel ≻ Add or Remove Programs.

2. In the Add or Remove Programs dialog box, click Add/Remove Windows Components.

3. In the Windows Components dialog box, shown in Figure 12.40, check the Internet Information Services box and click the Next button.

FIGURE 12.40 Windows Components dialog box

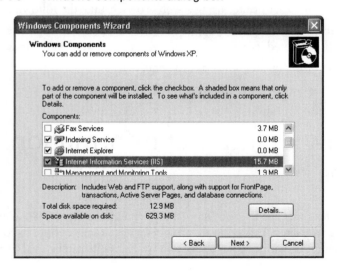

4. Configuration changes will be made to your computer and files will be copied. You may be prompted to provide the Windows XP Professional CD.

5. The Completing the Windows Components Wizard dialog box will appear. Click the Finish button.

 If you do not see an option for Administrative Tools from the Start menu, edit your Start menu to show Administrative Tools. Editing the Start menu was covered in Chapter 5, "Managing the Windows XP Professional Desktop."

Managing a Website

To access Internet Information Services, select Start ➢ Administrative Tools ➢ Internet Information Services. When you start Internet Information Services, you will see that items are defined by default for Web Sites and Default SMTP Virtual Server, as shown in Figure 12.41.

FIGURE 12.41   Internet Information Services dialog box

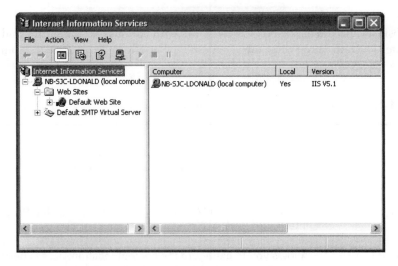

Through Internet Information Services, you can configure many options for your website, such as website identification and connection settings, performance settings, and access controls. To access a website's properties, right-click the website you want to manage in the Internet Information Services window and select Properties from the pop-up menu. This brings up the website Properties dialog box, as shown in Figure 12.42.

FIGURE 12.42 The website Properties dialog box

The website Properties dialog box has eight tabs with options for configuring and managing your website. The options on these tabs are described briefly in Table 12.1 and in more detail in the following sections.

TABLE 12.1 The Website Properties Dialog Box Tabs

Tab	Description
Web Site	Allows you to configure website identification, connections, and logging
ISAPI Filters	Allows you to set ISAPI (Internet Server Application Programming Interface) filters
Home Directory	Allows you to configure the content location, access permissions, content control, and application settings
Documents	Allows you to specify the default document that users will see if they access your website without specifying a specific document
Directory Security	Allows you to configure anonymous access and authentication control, IP address and domain name restrictions, and secure communications

TABLE 12.1   The Website Properties Dialog Box Tabs *(continued)*

Tab	Description
HTTP Headers	Allows you to configure values that will be returned to web browsers in the Hypertext Markup Language (HTML) headers of the web pages
Custom Errors	Allows you to present a customized error message that will appear when there is a web browser error
Server Extensions	Allows you to configure publishing controls for FrontPage options

Setting Website Properties

The Web Site tab (see Figure 12.42) includes options for identifying the website, controlling connections, and enabling logging.

Website Identification

The description of the website appears in the Internet Information Services window. By default, the website description is the same as the name of the website. You can enter another description in the Description text box.

You also configure the IP address that is associated with the site. The IP address must already be configured for the computer. If you leave the IP address at the default setting of All Unassigned, all of the IP addresses that are assigned to the computer and that have not been assigned to other websites will be used.

The TCP port specifies the port that will be used to respond to HTTP requests by default. The default TCP port that is used is TCP port 80. If you change this value, clients attempting to connect to the website must specify the correct port value. This option can be used for additional security.

Common ports that are used by IIS and can be modified for additional security include FTP on port 21, Telnet on port 23, and HTTP on port 80.

Connections

The Connection Timeout is used to specify how long an inactive user can remain connected to the website before the connection is automatically terminated.

If you select the HTTP Keep-Alives Enabled option, the client will maintain an open connection with the server, as opposed to opening a new connection for each client request. This enhances client performance, but may degrade server performance.

Logging

Logging is used to enable logging features, which record details of website access. If logging is enabled, you can select from several log formats that collect information in a specified format. If you want to log user access to the website, the Log Visits check box on the Home Directory tab must also be checked (which is the default setting).

Setting ISAPI Filters

Internet Server Application Programming Interface (ISAPI) filters direct web browser requests for specific URLs to specific ISAPI applications, which are then run. ISAPI filters are commonly used to manage customized logon authentication. These filters work by monitoring HTTP requests and responding to specific events that are defined through the filter. The filters are loaded into the website's memory.

Through the ISAPI Filters tab, shown in Figure 12.43, you can add ISAPI filters for your website. The filters are applied in the order they are listed in the list box. You can use the up and down arrow buttons to the left of the list box to change the order of the filters.

FIGURE 12.43 The ISAPI Filters tab of the website Properties dialog box

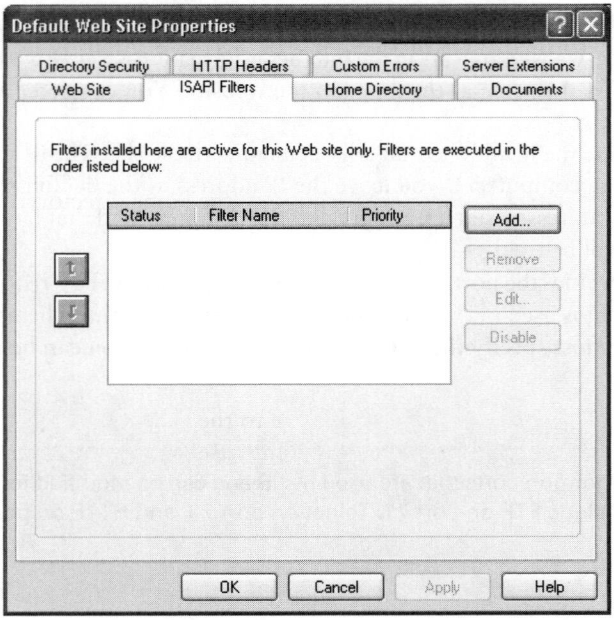

Configuring Home Directory Options

The Home Directory tab, shown in Figure 12.44, includes options for the content location, access permissions, content control, and application settings.

FIGURE 12.44   The Home Directory tab of the website Properties dialog box

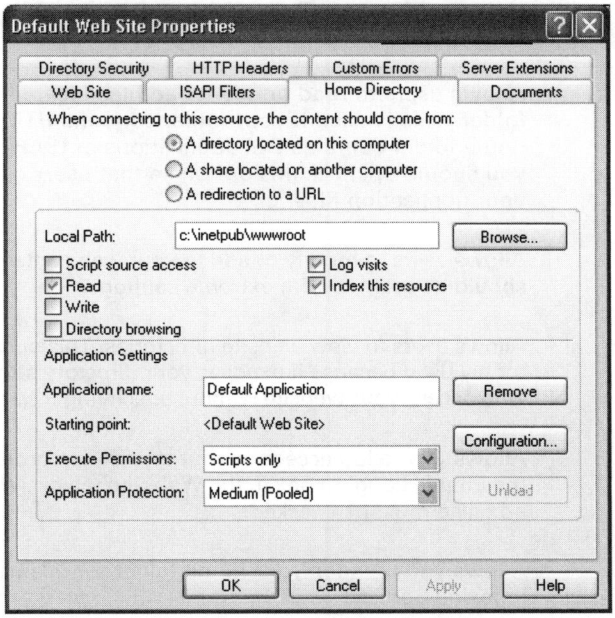

Content Location

The home directory is used to provide web content. The default directory is called inetpub\
wwwroot. You have three choices for the location of the home directory:

- A directory on the local computer
- A share on another computer (stored on the local network and identified by a UNC name)
- A redirection to a resource using a URL

Access Permissions and Content Control

Access permissions define what access users have to the website. Content control specifies
whether logging and indexing are enabled. By default, users have only Read access, and logging
and indexing are enabled. The access permissions and content control options are described in
Table 12.2.

TABLE 12.2   Access Permissions and Content Control Options

Option	Description
Script Source Access	Allows users to access source code for scripts, such as ASP (Active Server Pages) applications, if the user has either Read or Write permissions.

TABLE 12.2 Access Permissions and Content Control Options *(continued)*

Option	Description
Read	Allows users to read or download files located in your home folder. This is used if your folder contains HTML files. If your home folder contains CGI applications or ISAPI applications, you should uncheck this option so that users can't download your application files.
Write	Allows users to modify or add to your web content. This access should be granted with extreme caution.
Directory Browsing	Allows users to view website directories. This option is not commonly used because it exposes your directory structure to users who access your website without specifying a specific HTML file.
Log Visits	Allows you to log access to your website. In order to log access, the Enable Logging box in the Web Site tab of the Properties dialog box also must be checked.
Index This Resource	Allows you to index your home folder for use with the Microsoft Indexing Service.

Web service access permissions and NTFS permissions work together. The more restrictive of the two permissions will be the effective permission.

Application Settings

Application, in this context, is defined as the starting point of a specific folder (and its sub-folder and files) that has been defined as an application. For example, if you specify that your home folder is an application, every folder in your content location can participate in the application.

The Execute Permissions setting specifies how applications can be accessed within this folder. If you select None, no applications or scripts can be executed from this folder. The Scripts Only setting allows you to run script engines, even if no execute permissions have been set. This permission is used for folders that contain ASP scripts. The other option is Scripts and Executables, which allows all file types (including binary files with .exe and .dll extensions) to be executed.

The Application Protection setting specifies how applications will be run. There are three choices:

- Low (IIS Process) means that the application runs in the same process as the web service.

- Medium (Pooled) means that the application is run in an isolated pooled process with other applications.

- High (Isolated) means that each application runs as a separate isolated application.

Setting a Default Document

The Documents tab, shown in Figure 12.45, allows you to specify the default document users will see if they access your website without specifying a specific document. You normally set your default document as your website's home page.

FIGURE 12.45   The Documents tab of the website Properties dialog box

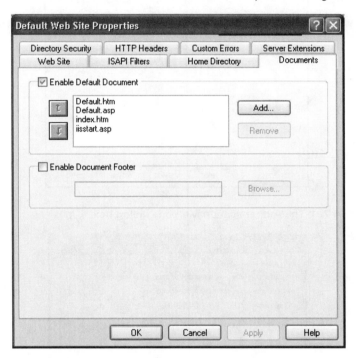

You can specify multiple documents in the order you prefer. This way, if a document is unavailable, the web server will access the next default document that has been defined.

You can also specify document footers. A document footer is an HTML document that will appear at the bottom of each web page that is sent to web clients.

Setting Directory Security

The Directory Security tab, shown in Figure 12.46, includes options for anonymous access and authentication control, IP address and domain name restrictions, and secure communications.

Anonymous Access and Authentication Control

To enable anonymous access and specify authentication control methods, click the Edit button in the Anonymous Access and Authentication Control section of the dialog box. This brings up the Authentication Methods dialog box, as shown in Figure 12.47.

FIGURE 12.46 The Directory Security tab of website Properties dialog box

FIGURE 12.47 The Authentication Methods dialog box

If your website is available for public use, you will most likely allow anonymous access.
If you enable anonymous access, by default, your computer will use the IUSR_*computername*
user account. You can limit the access the Anonymous user account has by applying NTFS
permissions to your web content.

There are three choices in the Authenticated Access section of the Authentication Methods dialog box:

- The Digest Authentication for Windows Domain Servers option works only for Windows 2000 and Windows Server 2003 domain accounts. This method requires accounts to store passwords as encrypted clear text.

- The Basic Authentication option requires a Windows 2000 or Windows 2003 domain user account. If anonymous access is disabled or the anonymous account tries to access data that the account does not have permission to access, the system will prompt the user for a valid Windows 2000 or Windows 2003 domain user account. With this method, all passwords are sent as clear text. You should use this option with caution since it poses a security risk.

- The Integrated Windows Authentication option uses secure authentication to transmit the Windows 2000 or Windows Server 2003 username and password.

IP Address and Domain Name Restrictions

This feature is not accessible and is only available with server versions of IIS.

Secure Communications

You can increase the security of your website by using secure communications. With secure communications, you are able to create and manage key requests and key certificates. These options are used in conjunction with Certificate Server. This allows you to specify that you will require secure channel services (using certificates) when accessing your website.

Configuring HTTP Headers

The HTTP Headers tab, shown in Figure 12.48, allows you to configure values that will be returned to web browsers in the HTML headers of the web pages.

FIGURE 12.48   The HTTP Headers tab of the website Properties dialog box

You can configure four options:

- If your website contains information that is time-sensitive, you can specify that you want to use content expiration. You can set content to expire immediately, after a specified number of minutes, or on a specific date. This helps the web browser determine whether it should use a cached copy of a requested page or it should request an updated copy of the web page from the website.

- Custom HTTP headers are used to replace the default HTTP headers that are normally used with customized HTTP headers from your web server to the client browser. For example, you may want to specify a custom HTTP header to send instructions that may not be supported by the HTML specification that is currently in use.

- Content ratings allow you to specify appropriate restrictions if a site contains violence, sex, nudity, or adult language. Most web browsers can then be configured to block objectionable material based on how the content rating has been defined.

- MIME (Multipurpose Internet Mail Extensions) maps are used to configure web browsers so that they can view files that have been configured with different formats.

Specifying Custom Error Messages

If the web browser encounters an error, it will display an error message. By default, predefined error messages are displayed. Through the Custom Errors tab, shown in Figure 12.49, you can customize the error message that the user will see. To generate a custom error message, you create an .htm file, which can then be mapped to a specific HTML error.

FIGURE 12.49   The Custom Errors tab of the website Properties dialog box

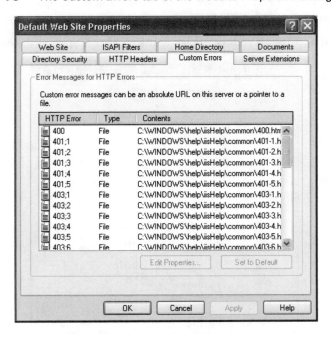

Setting Server Extensions

By default, Server Extensions are not enabled on IIS Professional version. You can enable Server Extensions by right-clicking your website and selecting All Tasks, then Configure Server Extensions, which will run the Server Extensions Wizard. Before you enable this option, you should have a good understanding of IIS security. Enabling Server Extensions can create security risks for IIS.

Once Server Extensions are enabled, the Server Extensions tab, shown in Figure 12.50, allows you to configure publishing controls for FrontPage options. FrontPage is used to create and edit HTML pages for your website through a What You See Is What You Get (WYSIWYG) editor.

FIGURE 12.50   The Server Extensions tab of the website Properties dialog box

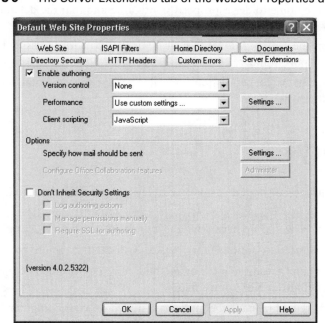

This tab includes the following options:

- The Enable Authoring option specifies whether authors can modify the content of the website. If this option is selected, you can specify version control, performance based on how many pages the website hosts, and the client scripting method that will be used.

- The Options section includes Settings and Administer buttons, which allow you to specify how mail should be sent and Office Collaboration features (this option is enabled only if Microsoft Office is configured).

- The Don't Inherit Security Settings option overrides the global security settings for the website.

Troubleshooting Website Access

If users are unable to access your website, the problem may be caused by improper access permissions, an improperly configured home folder or default document, or use of the wrong TCP port. Here are some tips for troubleshooting website access problems:

- Determine whether anonymous access is allowed. If so, verify that the username and password that have been configured through Internet Information Services match the name of the user account and password that are in the Windows XP, Windows 2000 domain, or Windows 2003 domain user database.

- Confirm that access has not been denied based on the IP address or domain name.

- Make sure that the proper access permissions have been configured.

- Confirm that the home folder is properly configured and that the default document has been properly configured.

- Make sure that the TCP port is set to port 80 or that you are accessing the website using the proper TCP port number.

- Make sure that the NTFS permissions have not been set on the home folder so that they deny access to website users.

Summary

In this chapter, you learned about dial-up networking and Internet connectivity. We covered the following topics:

- An overview of how dial-up networking is implemented.

- The different connection options that are used by local and remote connections.

- Remote security and the authentication methods and remote data encryption options that are used with Windows XP Professional.

- How to configure and manage the modems installed on your computer through Device Manager.

- Using dial-up networking, including creating dial-up connections to RAS servers and to the Internet. You also learned how to configure a VPN connection.

- The use and configuration of ICC.

- How to secure a Windows XP Professional computer that is directly connected to the Internet through ICF.

- Options for configuring and managing Internet Explorer.

- How to install and configure IIS Professional edition.

- The support for Internet printing through IPP.

Exam Essentials

Understand the different options that can be used for remote connectivity. Have a basic understanding of connectivity options. You should also know the security options that can be used for authentication and data encryption.

Be able to install a modem. Be able to install a modem and troubleshoot any configuration errors.

Be able to configure and support dial-up networking. Understand the purpose of RAS and VPN connections. Know how to install RAS and VPN clients. Understand the security issues and configure security based on network requirements. Be ready to troubleshoot any connectivity issues. Know how to connect to the Internet, to configure Internet connection sharing, and to define all the options that can be set for Internet connection sharing.

Provide support for Internet connection sharing. Specify the server requirements for supporting Internet connection sharing. Be able to access and submit print jobs to Internet printers.

Provide support for Internet Connection Firewall. Understand the purpose of an Internet Connection Firewall and how this option is configured.

Know the options that can be configured for Internet Explorer. Know how to use IE to make HTTP and FTP requests. Know how to configure IE, especially managing security settings.

Be able to install and configure IIS. Know how to install and configure IIS for Windows XP Professional.

Key Terms

Before you take the exam, be certain you are familiar with the following terms:

802.11x wireless LAN	Direct Cable Connection (DCC)
cable modems	direct parallel cable
certificate authentication	Ethernet
Challenge Handshake Authentication Protocol (CHAP)	Extensible Authentication Protocol (EAP)
data encryption	Fiber Distributed Data Interface (FDDI)
dial-up modems	firewalls
dial-up networking	Frame Relay
Digital Subscriber Line (DSL)	Home Phoneline Network Adapter (HPNA)

IEEE 1394

incoming connections

Infrared Data Association (IrDA)

Integrated Services Digital Network (ISDN)

Internet Connection Firewall (ICF)

Internet Connection Sharing (ICS)

Internet Explorer (IE)

Internet Information Services (IIS)

Internet Printing Protocol (IPP)

Internet Protocol Security (IPSec)

Internet service provider (ISP)

IP over ATM

LAN Emulation (LANE)

Layer Two Tunneling Protocol (L2TP)

leased lines

Local Area Network (LAN)

Microsoft Challenge Handshake Authentication Protocol (MS-CHAP)

Microsoft Challenge Handshake Authentication Protocol Version 2 (MS-CHAPv2)

Microsoft Ethernet PVC

Microsoft Point-to-Point Encryption (MPPE)

null-modem cables

Password Authentication Protocol (PAP)

Point-to-Point Protocol (PPP)

Point-to-Point Protocol over Ethernet (PPPoE)

Point-to-Point Tunneling Protocol (PPTP)

Public Switched Telephone Network (PSTN)

remote access connections

Remote Access Service (RAS)

serial cables

Serial Line Internet Protocol (SLIP)

Shiva Password Authentication Protocol (SPAP)

smart card

Token Ring

Universal Serial Bus (USB)

virtual private network (VPN)

wide area network (WAN)

X.25

Review Questions

1. You are a Help Desk technician for the Top Secret Stuff Foundation. Your company maintains an internal intranet that provides secure website internal resources for employee use only. The secure website is accessed through IE using the following URL:

    `http://intranet.tssf.com`

    A user named Aaron calls you to report that when he uses the specified URL, he gets an error message that the digital certificate is not from a trusted source. You confirm that you can access the URL. You also confirm that the company Certificate Authority, which is stored on a local server called `certserver.tssf.com`, is properly functioning.

    What configuration change needs to be made to Aaron's computer so that he can access the internal intranet?

    A. Import a certificate from the web server to the Trusted certificates store on Aaron's computer.

    B. Since Aaron is not an administrator, verify that the IIS properties for `intranet.tssf.com` are configured for SSL to use port 548.

    C. Through Internet Explorer, Security Properties, configure Aaron's computer so that `intranet.tssf.com` is a trusted site.

    D. Since Aaron is not an administrator, verify that the IIS properties for `intranet.tssf.com` are configured for SSL to use port 845.

2. Your computer is a part of a very small network. The network administrator recently configured your computer to use Internet Connection Sharing. After ICS was configured, you tested the connection and were able to access the Internet. When you then attempted to access a local resource, you were not able to. What is the most likely problem?

    A. Your IP address was reset through ICS.

    B. You need to disconnect any open Internet connections.

    C. Your computer name was reset through ICS and needs to be reestablished.

    D. You need to make an entry in the DNS server to reflect the changes made to your computer, to reflect the ICS support that was added.

3. You have a small network at home. Your computer connects to the Internet via a DSL connection. In addition, your computer connects to a LAN that contains four other computers that are all running Windows XP Professional or Windows 2000 Professional. The other computers in the LAN do not have Internet access. You decide to implement Internet Connection Sharing so that all of your computers can connect to the Internet via a single DSL connection. Which of the following requirements must be met in order to use ICS?

    A. You must have a VPN connection.

    B. The network clients must be configured to use WINS.

    C. The network clients must be configured to obtain an IP address automatically.

    D. The network clients must have the ICS service installed.

4. You are the network administrator for Wacky Widgets Inc. Dietrich is a user in the Finance department and requires access to an FTP site so that he can download financial analysis reports that have been created by a third-party vendor called Finance Data Gurus.

    When Dietrich attempts to access the FTP server with the URL

    `ftp://ftp.financedatagurus.com`

    Internet Explorer returns the following error message:

    "The password was rejected."

    Dietrich informs you that he has a username and password from Finance Data Gurus, but he can't figure out how to provide the username and password. What URL should Dietrich use to access the FTP site?

    A. `ftp://ftps.financedatagurus.com@Dietrich:`*`password`*

    B. `ftp://ftp.financedatagurus.com/Dietrich:`*`password`*

    C. `ftp://Dietrich:`*`password`*`@ftp.financedatagurus.com`

    D. `ftps://ftp.financedatagurus.com/Dietrich:`*`password`*

5. You are the network administrator for a small company. You have a DSL modem attached to your computer for Internet access. The users in your workgroup do not require Internet access, except to download and upload files to a FTP server. You decide to implement Internet Connection Sharing to provide the other users with Internet access. Which port should you configure through ICS so that FTP is the only service supported?

    A. Port 21

    B. Port 23

    C. Port 80

    D. Port 91

6. You are in the process of configuring Internet Connection Sharing. How do you set this up on the computer that will act as the host connection?

    A. On the computer that will act as the host, install the ICS service.

    B. On the computer that will act as the host, install the ISC service.

    C. Access the Internet Connections Properties dialog box, click the Advanced tab, and check the Enable Internet Connection Sharing option.

    D. Access the Internet Connections Properties dialog box, click the Sharing tab, and select the option to Enable Internet Connection Sharing.

7. You are using a modem to dial into a VPN server. When you attempt to dial into the VPN server, the connection can't be established. Listening to the connection, you don't hear anything—not even a dial tone. What option should you set so that you can hear what is happening when you try to establish the connection?

   A. In the Modem tab of the modem's Properties dialog box, set the Speaker Volume option using the High setting.

   B. In the Advanced tab of the modem's Properties dialog box, set the speaker volume to high.

   C. In the modem adapter Properties dialog box, select the Audible Connection option.

   D. Use the `volume` command-line utility to adjust the volume.

8. You are having trouble connecting to the Internet and are not sure if the problem is with your modem or with your configuration. How can you determine whether the modem is working properly?

   A. Use the `moddiag` command-line utility to run a series of modem diagnostics.

   B. Check the modem diagnostics log that is created in \Windir\System32\Moddiag.

   C. Use the `testcomm` command-line utility to run a series of modem diagnostics.

   D. In the Diagnostics tab of the modem Properties dialog box, click the Query Modem button.

9. You are configuring a dial-up connection on your Windows XP Professional computer. You want the connection to be available only for the user Martha. What should you configure?

   A. Log on as Administrator and create the connection. Then grant to Martha Full Control permission to the dial-up connection.

   B. In the user profile, configure the dial-up connection as nonshared. Specify that only Martha can use the dial-up connection.

   C. Log on as Martha and create the connection. For Connection Availability, specify that the connection is only available for the current user.

   D. In the user profile, configure the dial-up connection as private. Specify that only Martha can use the dial-up connection.

10. You are using a dial-up connection to connect to your company's RAS server. You want to use your company calling card for the connection. How do you configure this?

   A. In the Dial-up Connection Properties dialog box, General tab, select Dialing Rules to configure the calling card.

   B. In the modem's Properties dialog box, General tab, select Dialing Properties to configure the calling card.

   C. In the modem's Properties dialog box, use the Configure Calling Cards tab to configure the calling card.

   D. This option can't be configured.

11. Your company has a RAS server set up so that remote salespeople can dial in as necessary. Because of the sensitive information that your company stores on the server, security is a primary concern, so you require remote users to dial in with a smart card. Which protocol for dial-up connection security should you configure if your laptop will use a security device such as a smart card?

   A. EAP

   B. CHAP

   C. PAP

   D. RAP

12. You work for the Help Desk at Goofy Gidgets Corporation. One of the remote users, Gigi, asks you to help her configure her laptop so that she can access the corporate LAN through a RAS server that has been installed on a Windows Server 2003 computer. The RAS server hosts eight analog modems that connect to the PSTN. Because of the secure nature of information that is stored on the corporate LAN, corporate policy has defined that any user who will access the RAS server must have their logon credentials encrypted and use the highest level of security that is available.

   You need to help Gigi configure a dial-up connection to dial into your company's RAS server. Which of the following dial-in security protocols should you help her configure?

   A. PAP

   B. CHAP

   C. MS-CHAP

   D. MS-CHAPv2

13. You are a Help Desk technician for the Lucky Ducky Company. One of your users, Wendy, has a laptop at home that she wants to use for dialing into the corporate network via a RAS server. The laptop does not have a built-in modem connection, but does have an open PCMCIA slot. Wendy has installed the PCMCIA modem, but when she goes to the Network Connection Manager, the modem is not listed. You have Wendy restart the computer, and the modem is still not listed. What course of action should you take next?

   A. Make sure that all of the serial ports for the laptop are disabled.

   B. Use the Add/Remove Hardware wizard to manually install the modem.

   C. Verify that the PCMCIA slot has been enabled through the laptop's BIOS.

   D. Verify that the driver for the modem has been digitally signed and restart the computer again.

14. You are considering using a VPN network connection. Which of the following features are offered through VPN connections? (Choose all that apply.)

   A. The data will be encapsulated.

   B. The data will be encrypted.

   C. A username and password will be required.

   D. The data will require certificate services.

15. You have a workgroup with five computers, but you have only one telephone line that is dedicated to remote communications. All five users require Internet access to send and receive e-mail. Which option should you configure to support this environment?

   A. Dial-up Connection Sharing

   B. Internet Connection Sharing

   C. SLIP Connection Sharing

   D. PPP Connection Sharing

Answers to Review Questions

1. A. If the computer reports an error message that the digital certificate is not from a trusted source, then it indicates that the computer has been configured to accept certificates only from trusted sources. You need to configure the computer to accept a certificate from the local Certificate Authority by importing a certificate from the web server into Aaron's Trusted certificate store.

2. A. When you use Internet Connection Sharing, it causes computers that use ICS to lose their IP configuration. This must be reset so the computer can access local resources.

3. C. To use Internet Connection Sharing, the network clients must be able to get their IP addresses automatically (through DHCP). The host computer and the client computers must be configured to use ICS.

4. C. If you need to provide logon credentials as a part of the FTP request, then the syntax you would use would be:

    `ftp://username:password@company.com`

5. A. You can control the services available to a user by specifying which ports will be serviced. By default, FTP uses port 21, Telnet uses port 23, and HTTP uses port 80.

6. D. To configure Internet Connection Sharing on the computer that will act as the host connection, you create an Internet connection. Then access the Internet connection's Properties dialog box, click the Sharing tab, and select the option to Enable Internet Connection Sharing.

7. A. In the Modem tab of the modem Properties dialog box, you can set the speaker volume by adjusting a slider between Off and High.

8. D. The Diagnostics tab of the modem Properties dialog box contains a Query Modem button. Click this button to run a series of modem commands and see how the modem responds.

9. C. To create a dial-up connection, you use the Network Connection Wizard. One of the Wizard's dialog boxes asks you to specify the connection's availability. You can specify that the connection is to be used for all users or only for the current user.

10. A. To configure a connection to use a calling card, access the Connection Properties dialog box, General tab, and click the Dialing Rules button. Then click the Edit button and select the Calling Card tab.

11. A. The Extensible Authentication Protocol (EAP) is used in conjunction with security devices such as smart cards and certificates. This provides a very high level of security.

12. D. The MS-CHAPv2 protocol is the most secure form of the Challenge Handshake Authentication Protocol. The PAP protocol uses an unencrypted password.

13. B. Some modems are not automatically recognized with Windows XP Professional. In this case, you would manually install the modem through the Add/Remove Hardware wizard and supply the device driver for Windows XP Professional that was provided through the modem manufacturer.

14. A, B, C.   When you use virtual private network (VPN) connections, data is encapsulated, is encrypted, and requires authentication services. This allows you to have secure network communications over public networks, such as the Internet.

15. B.   Internet Connection Sharing allows you to connect a small network to the Internet through a single connection. A host computer must be configured to provide Internet Connection Firewall (ICF) services.

Chapter

13

Optimizing Windows XP

MICROSOFT EXAM OBJECTIVES COVERED IN THIS CHAPTER:

✓ **Monitor, optimize, and troubleshoot performance of the Windows XP Professional desktop.**

- Optimize and troubleshoot memory performance.
- Optimize and troubleshoot processor utilization.
- Optimize and troubleshoot disk performance.
- Optimize and troubleshoot application performance.
- Configure, manage, and troubleshoot Scheduled Tasks.

To have an optimized system, you must monitor its performance. The two tools for monitoring Windows XP Professional are System Monitor and Performance Logs and Alerts. With these tools, you can track memory, processor activity, the disk subsystem, the network subsystem, and other computer subsystems.

In this chapter, you will learn how to monitor and optimize Windows XP Professional using the System Monitor, Performance Logs and Alerts, the System Tool, and Task Manager utilities. You will also learn how to optimize application performance. Finally, you will learn how to make your administrative tasks easier by automating some of them. You can schedule system tasks by using the Task Scheduler utility.

Overview of System Monitoring Tools

Before you can optimize the performance of Windows XP Professional, you must monitor critical subsystems to determine how your system is currently performing and what (if anything) is causing system bottlenecks. Windows XP Professional ships with two tools that you can use to track and monitor system performance: the System Monitor utility and the Performance Logs and Alerts utility.

Each of these utilities is covered in greater detail within this chapter. In addition, you will install and configure each utility for performance monitoring.

The monitoring tools allow you to assess your server's current health and determine what it requires to improve its present condition. With System Monitor and Performance Logs and Alerts, you can perform the following tasks:

- Create baselines
- Identify system bottlenecks
- Determine trends
- Test configuration changes or tuning efforts
- Create alert thresholds

Each of these tasks is discussed in the following sections.

Creating Baselines

A *baseline* is a snapshot of how your system is currently performing. Suppose that your computer's hardware has not changed over the last six months, but the computer seems to be performing more slowly now than it did six months ago. If you have been using the Performance Logs and Alerts utility and taking baseline logs, as well as noting the changes in your workload, you can more easily determine what resources are causing the system to slow down.

You should create baselines at the following times:

- When the system is first configured, without any load
- At regular intervals of typical usage
- Whenever any changes are made to the system's hardware or software configuration

Baselines are particularly useful for determining the effect of changes that you make to your computer. For example, if you are adding more memory to your computer, you should take baselines before and after you install the memory to determine the effect of the change. Along with hardware changes, system configuration modifications also can affect your computer's performance, so you should create baselines before and after you make any changes to your Windows XP Professional configuration.

For the most part, Windows XP Professional is a self-tuning operating system. If you decide to tweak the operating system, you should take baselines before and after each change. If you do not notice a performance gain after the tweak, you should consider returning the computer to its original configuration, because some tweaks may cause more problems than they solve.

Identifying System Bottlenecks

A *bottleneck* is a system resource that is inefficient compared with the rest of the computer system as a whole. The bottleneck can cause the rest of the system to run slowly.

You need to pinpoint the cause of a bottleneck to correct it. Consider a system that has a Pentium 166 processor with 64MB of RAM. If your applications are memory-intensive and lack of memory is your bottleneck, then upgrading your processor will not eliminate the bottleneck.

By using System Monitor, you can measure the performance of the various parts of your system, which allows you to identify system bottlenecks in a scientific manner. You will learn how to set counters to monitor your network and spot bottlenecks in the "Using System Monitor" section later in this chapter.

Determining Trends

Many of us tend to manage situations reactively instead of proactively. With reactive management, you focus on a problem when it occurs. With proactive management, you take steps to avoid the problem before it happens. In a perfect world, all management would be proactive.

System Monitor and Performance Logs and Alerts are great tools for proactive network management. If you are creating baselines on a regular basis, you can identify system trends. For example, if you notice average CPU utilization increasing 5 percent every month, you can assume that within the next six months, you're going to have a problem. Before performance becomes so slow that your system is not responding, you can upgrade the hardware.

Testing Configuration Changes or Tuning Efforts

When you make configuration changes or tune your computer, you may want to measure the effects of those changes. When making configuration changes, the following recommendations apply:

- Only make one change at a time. If you are making configuration changes for tuning, and you make multiple changes at one time, it is difficult to quantify the effect of each individual change. In addition, some changes may have a negative impact that, if you have made multiple changes, may be difficult to identify.

- Repeat monitoring with each individual change you make. This will help you determine whether additional tuning is required.

- As you make changes, check the Event Viewer event log files. Some performance changes will generate events within Event Viewer that should be reviewed. Event Viewer is covered in more detail in Chapter 14, "Performing System Recovery Functions."

- If you suspect that network components are affecting performance, compare the performance of the network version with a version that runs locally.

Using Alerts for Problem Notification

The Performance Logs and Alerts utility provides another tool for proactive management in the form of *alerts*. Through Performance Logs and Alerts, you can specify alert thresholds (when a counter reaches a specified value) and have the utility notify you when these thresholds are reached.

For example, you could specify that if your logical disk has less than 10 percent of free space, you want to be notified. Once alerted, you can add more disk space or delete unneeded files before you run out of disk space. You will learn how to create alerts in the "Using Performance Logs and Alerts" section later in this chapter.

Using System Monitor

The *System Monitor* utility is used to measure the performance of a local or remote computer on the network. System Monitor enables you to do the following:

- Collect data from your local computer or remote computers on the network. You can collect data from a single computer or multiple computers concurrently.

- View data as it is being collected in real-time, or historically from collected data.

- Have full control over the selection of what data will be collected, by selecting which specific objects and counters will be collected.

- Choose the sampling parameters that will be used, meaning the time interval that you want to use for collecting data points and the time period that will be used for data collection.

- Determine the format in which data will be viewed, in either graph, histogram, or report views.
- Create HTML pages for viewing data.
- Create specific configurations for monitoring data that can then be exported to other computers for performance monitoring.

In order to view data on remote computers, you need to have administrative rights to the remote computer.

Through System Monitor, you can view current data or data from a log file. When you view current data, you are monitoring real-time activity. When you view data from a log file, you are importing a log file from a previous session.

You can access System Monitor through Start ➤ All Programs ➤ Administrative Tools ➤ Performance or as an MMC snap-in. The System Monitor snap-in is added as an ActiveX control. Figure 13.1 shows the main System Monitor window when it is initially opened without configuration.

FIGURE 13.1 The main System Monitor window

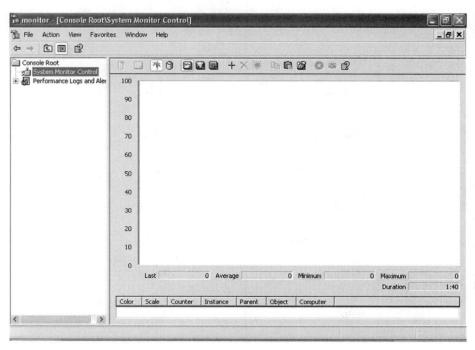

The main functionality of System Monitor is provided through the toolbar at the top of the main dialog window, or through keystroke combinations. The buttons for the toolbar, each associated function, and the keystroke alternatives are defined in Table 13.1.

TABLE 13.1 System Monitor Toolbar Functions Defined

Button	Function	Associated Keystrokes
	New Counter Set	Ctrl+E
	Clear Display	Ctrl+D
	View Current Activity	Ctrl+T
	View Log Data	Ctrl+L
	View Graph	Ctrl+G
	View Histogram	Ctrl+B
	View Report	Ctrl+R
	Add	Ctrl+I
	Delete	Delete
	Highlight	Ctrl+H
	Copy Properties	Ctrl+C
	Paste Counter List	Ctrl+V
	Properties	Ctrl+Q
	Freeze Display	Ctrl+F
	Update Data	Ctrl+U
	Help	F1

When you first start System Monitor, you will notice that nothing is tracked by default. For System Monitor to be useful, you must configure it to track some type of system activity, which is done by adding counters, as described shortly. After you've added counters, they will be listed at the bottom of the System Monitor window. The fields just above the counter list will contain data based on the counter that is highlighted in the list, as follows:

Last   Displays the most current data.

Average   Shows the average of the counter.

Minimum   Shows the lowest value that has been recorded for the counter.

Maximum   Shows the highest value that has been recorded for the counter.

Duration   Shows how long the counter has been tracking data.

The following sections describe the three System Monitor views, how to add counters to track data, and how to configure System Monitor properties.

Selecting the Appropriate View

By clicking the appropriate button on the System Monitor toolbar, you can see your data in one of three views:

Chart view   The chart view, shown in Figure 13.2, is System Monitor's default view. It's useful for viewing a small number of counters in a graphical format. The main advantage of chart view is that you can see how the data has been tracked during the defined time period. This view can be difficult to interpret, however, when you start to track a large number of counters.

FIGURE 13.2   The chart view of System Monitor

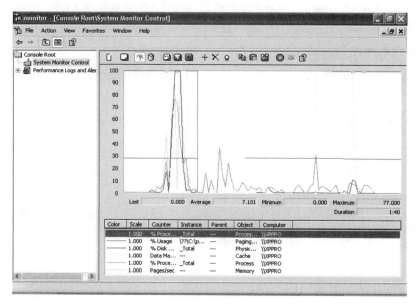

Histogram view   The histogram view, shown in Figure 13.3, shows the System Monitor data in a bar graph. This view is useful for examining large amounts of data. However, it only shows performance for the current period. You do not see a record of performance over time, as you do with the chart view.

FIGURE 13.3 The histogram view of System Monitor

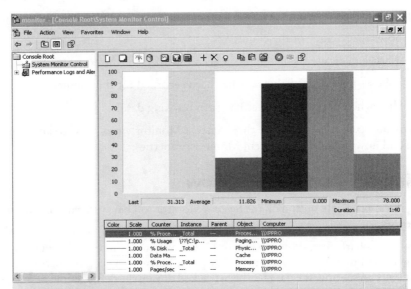

Report view   The report view, shown in Figure 13.4, offers a logical report of all the counters that are being tracked through System Monitor. Only the current session's data is displayed. The advantage of report view is that it allows you to easily track large numbers of counters in real time.

FIGURE 13.4 The report view of System Monitor

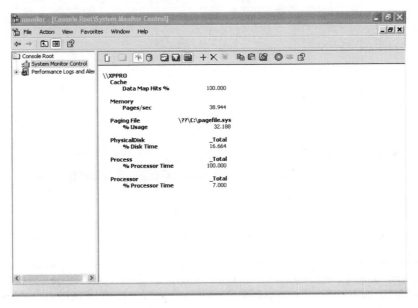

It is important to note that when you view data in real-time format, the data can appear skewed as applications and processes are started. It is typically more useful to view data as an average over a specified interval.

Adding Counters

As mentioned earlier, you must add *counters* to System Monitor to track data. To add counters, use the following steps:

1. In System Monitor, click the Add button on the toolbar. This brings up the Add Counters dialog box (Figure 13.5).

FIGURE 13.5   The Add Counters dialog box

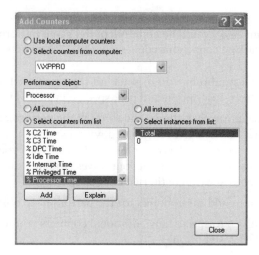

To see information about a specific counter, in the Add Counters dialog box select the counter from the list and click the Explain button beneath the list. System Monitor will display text regarding the highlighted counter.

2. In the Add Counters dialog box, select the Use Local Computer Counters (the default) radio button to monitor the local computer. Alternatively, to select counters from a specific computer, choose Select Counters from Computer and pick a computer from the drop-down list.

    You can monitor remote computers if you have administrative permissions. This option is useful when you do not want the overhead of System Monitor running on the computer you are trying to monitor.

3. Select a performance object from the drop-down list. All Windows XP system resources are tracked as performance objects, such as Cache, Memory, Paging File, Process, and Processor.

All the objects together represent your total system. Some performance objects exist on all Windows XP computers; other objects appear only if specific processes or services are running. For example, if you want to track the physical disk's level of activity, choose the PhysicalDisk performance object.

4. Select the All Counters radio button to track all the associated counters, or choose Select Counters from List and pick specific counters from the list box below.

   Each performance object has an associated set of counters. Counters are used to track specific information regarding a performance object. For example, the PhysicalDisk performance object has a %Disk Time counter, which will tell you how busy a disk has been in servicing read and write requests. PhysicalDisk also has %Disk Read Time and %Disk Write Time counters, which show you what percentage of disk requests are read requests and what percentage are write requests, respectively.

 You can select multiple counters of the same performance object by Shift+clicking contiguous counters or Ctrl+clicking noncontiguous counters.

5. Select the All Instances radio button to track all the associated instances, or choose the Select Instances from List option and pick specific instances from the list box below.

   An instance is a mechanism that allows you to track the performance of a specific object when you have more than one item associated with a specific performance object. For example, suppose your computer has two physical drives. When you track the PhysicalDisk performance object, you can track both of your drives (within a single counter), or you can track drive 0 and drive 1 separately (in two counters).

6. Click the Add button to add the counters for the performance object.

7. Repeat steps 2 through 6 to specify any additional counters you want to track. When you are finished, click the Close button.

After you've added counters, you can select a specific counter by highlighting it in System Monitor. To highlight a counter, click it and then click the Highlight button on the System Monitor toolbar, or select the counter and press Ctrl+H.

To remove a counter, highlight it in System Monitor and click the Delete button on the toolbar.

Managing System Monitor Properties

To configure the System Monitor properties, click the Properties button on the System Monitor toolbar. The System Monitor Properties dialog box has five tabs: General, Source, Data, Graph, and Appearance. The properties you can configure on each of these tabs are described in the following sections.

General Properties

The General tab of the System Monitor Properties dialog box (Figure 13.6) contains the following options:

- The view that will be displayed: graph, histogram, or report

- The display elements that will be used: legend, value bar, and/or toolbar
- The data that will be displayed: default (for reports or histograms, this is current data; for logs, this is average data), current, minimum, maximum, or average
- The appearance, either flat or 3D
- The border, either none or fixed single
- How often the data is updated, in seconds
- Whether duplicate counter instances are allowed

FIGURE 13.6   The General tab of System Monitor Properties

Source Properties

The Source tab, shown in Figure 13.7, allows you to specify the data source. This can be current activity, or it can be data that has been collected in a log file. If you import data from a log file, you can specify the time range that you wish to view.

Data Properties

The Data tab, shown in Figure 13.8, lets you specify the counters that you wish to track. You can add and remove counters by clicking the Add and Remove buttons. You can also select a specific counter and define the color, scale, width, and style that are used to represent the counter in the graph.

FIGURE 13.7 The Source tab of the System Monitor Properties dialog box

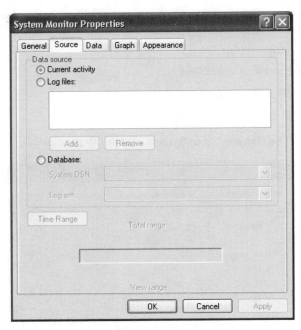

FIGURE 13.8 The Data tab of the System Monitor Properties dialog box

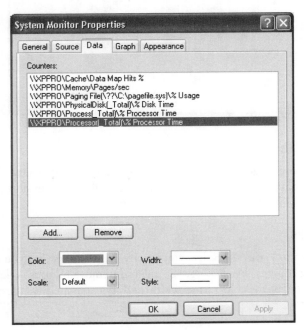

Graph Properties

The Graph tab, shown in Figure 13.9, contains the following options, which can be applied to the chart or histogram view:

- A title

- A vertical axis label

- Whether you will show a vertical grid, a horizontal grid, and/or vertical scale numbers

- The minimum and maximum numbers for the vertical scale

FIGURE 13.9   The Graph tab of the System Monitor Properties dialog box

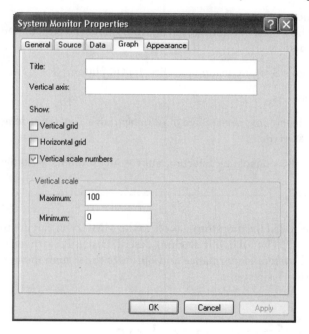

Appearance Properties

The Appearance tab of the System Monitor Properties dialog box has options for customizing the colors and fonts used in the System Monitor display.

In Exercise 13.1, you will create a management console for monitoring system performance. This console will be used for subsequent exercises in this chapter.

EXERCISE 13.1

Creating a Management Console for Monitoring System Performance

1.   Select Start ➢ Run, type **MMC** in the Run dialog box, and click the OK button.

2.   Select File ➢ Add/Remove Snap-in.

EXERCISE 13.1 *(continued)*

3. In the Add/Remove Snap-in dialog box, click the Add button. In the Add Available Standalone Snap-in dialog box, select ActiveX Control and click the Add button.

4. In the Insert ActiveX Control dialog box, click the Next button.

5. In the Insert ActiveX Control dialog box, select System Monitor Control and click the Next button. Click the Finish button.

6. In the Add Standalone Snap-in dialog box, click the Close button.

7. In the Add/Remove Snap-in dialog box, click the Add button. In the Add Standalone Snap-in dialog box, select Performance Logs and Alerts and click the Add button, then click the Close button.

8. In the Add/Remove Snap-in dialog box, click the OK button.

9. Select File ➢ Save As.

10. In the Save As dialog box, select Save in Administrative Tools (the default selection) and save the file as **Monitor**.

You can now access this console by selecting Start ➢ All Programs ➢ Administrative Tools ➢ Monitor.

Now that you've added the monitoring tools to the MMC, you can use them to monitor and optimize Windows XP. The following sections describe using Performance Logs and Alerts and how to manage system performance and optimize the system memory, processor, disk subsystem, and network subsystem.

Using Performance Logs and Alerts

The *Performance Logs and Alerts* snap-in to the MMC is shown expanded in Figure 13.10. With it, you can create counter logs and trace logs, and you can define alerts. You can view the log files with the System Monitor, as described in the previous section. After you've added the Performance Logs and Alerts snap-in (see Exercise 13.1), open it by selecting Start ➢ All Programs ➢ Administrative Tools ➢ Monitor and clicking Performance Logs and Alerts.

The following sections describe how to define new counter logs, trace logs, and alerts.

FIGURE 13.10   The expanded Performance Logs and Alerts snap-in

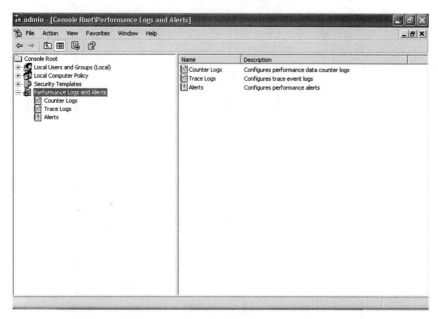

Creating a Counter Log

Counter logs record data about hardware usage and the activity of system services. You can configure logging to occur manually or on a predefined schedule.

To create a counter log, take the following steps:

1. Expand Performance Logs and Alerts, right-click Counter Logs, and select New Log Settings from the pop-up menu.

2. In the New Log Settings dialog box that appears, type a name for the log file. For example, you might give the log a name that indicates its type and the date, such as Counter*mmddyy*. Then click the OK button.

3. The counter log file's Properties dialog box appears. You can configure counter log properties as follows:

   - In the General tab, shown in Figure 13.11, specify the counters you want to track in the log and the interval for sampling data. Click the Add button to add counters.

   - In the Log Files tab, shown in Figure 13.12, configure the log file's location, filename, type, and size.

   - In the Schedule tab, shown in Figure 13.13, specify when the log file will start, when it will stop, and what action should be taken, if any, when the log file is closed.

4. When you are finished configuring the counter log file properties, click the OK button. The log will be created and will record the activity for the counters you specified.

FIGURE 13.11   General properties of the counter log file

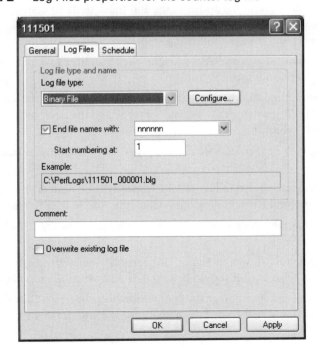

FIGURE 13.12   Log Files properties for the counter log file

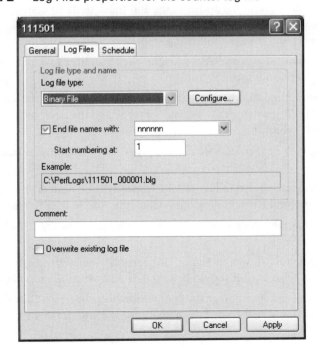

FIGURE 13.13   Schedule properties for the counter log file

Creating a Trace Log

Trace logs measure data continually as opposed to measuring data through periodic samples. Trace logs are also used to track data that is collected by the operating system or programs. For example, you could specify that you want to trace the creation or deletion of processes and threads.

To create a trace log, take the following steps:

1. Expand Performance Logs and Alerts, right-click Trace Logs, and select New Log Settings from the pop-up menu.

2. In the New Log Settings dialog box, type in a name for the log file and click the OK button. For example, you might use the type of log and the date (Trace*mmddyy*).

3. The trace log file's Properties dialog box appears. You can configure trace log properties as follows:

   - In the General tab, select the check boxes for the system events you want to track—for example, Process Creations/Deletions and Thread Creations/Deletions. You can also specify which system nonproviders you want to track, such as the Active Directory NetLogon process or the Local Security Authority (LSA).

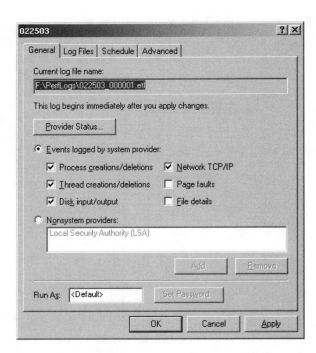

- In the Log Files tab, configure the log file's location, filename, type, and size.

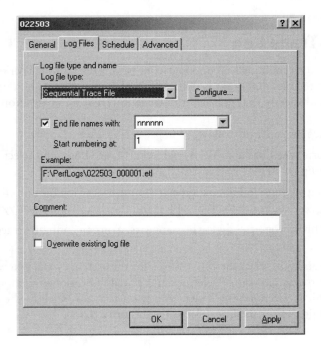

- In the Schedule tab, configure when the log file will start, when it will stop, and what action should be taken, if any, when the log file is closed.

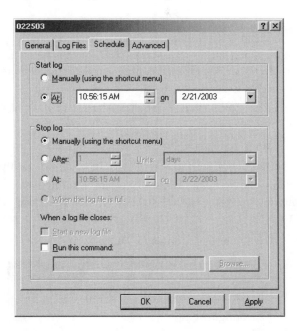

- In the Advanced tab, configure the buffer settings for the log file. By default, the log service will save the trace log file to memory and then transfer the data to the log file.

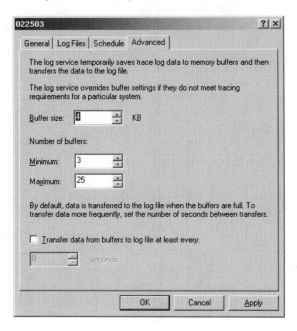

4. When you are finished configuring the trace log file properties, click the OK button. The log will be created and will record the activity for the system events you specified.

Creating an Alert

Alerts can be generated when a specific counter exceeds or falls below a specified value. You can configure alerts so that a message is sent, a program is run, or a more detailed log file is generated. Here are the steps to create an alert:

1. Expand Performance Logs and Alerts, right-click Alerts, and select New Alert Settings from the pop-up menu.

2. In the New Alert Settings dialog box, type a name for the alert file and click the OK button.

3. The alert file Properties dialog box appears. You can configure alert properties as follows:

   - In the General tab, shown in Figure 13.14, select the counters you want to track. When you add a counter, you must specify that the alert be generated when the counter is under or over a certain value. You can also set the interval for sampling data.

FIGURE 13.14   The General properties for an alert

   - In the Action tab, shown in Figure 13.15, specify what action should be taken if an alert is triggered. This can be logging an entry in the application event log, sending a network message, starting another performance data log, and/or running a specific program.

   - In the Schedule tab, shown in Figure 13.16, configure the start and stop dates/times for scans of the counters you have defined.

4. When you are finished configuring the alert properties, click the OK button.

FIGURE 13.15   The Action properties for an alert

FIGURE 13.16   The Schedule properties for an alert

Managing System Performance

By analyzing data, you can determine whether any resources are placing an excessive load on your computer that is resulting in a system slowdown. Some of the causes of poor system performance include:

- A resource is insufficient to handle the load that is being placed upon it, and the component may need to be upgraded, or additional components may be required.

- If a resource has multiple instances, the resources may not be evenly balancing the workload, and the workload may need to be balanced over the multiple instances more effectively.

- A resource might be malfunctioning. In this case, the resource should be repaired or replaced.

- A specific program might be allocated resources improperly or inefficiently, in which case the program needs to be rewritten or another application should be used.

- A resource might be configured improperly and causing excessive resource usage, and needs to be reconfigured.

  The four main subsystems that should be monitored are:

- The memory subsystem

- The processor subsystem

- The disk subsystem

- The network subsystem

  Each of these subsystems is examined in greater detail in the following sections.

Monitoring and Optimizing Memory

When the operating system needs a program or process, the first place it looks is in physical memory. If the required program or process is not in physical memory, the system looks in logical memory (the *page file*). If the program or process is not in logical memory, the system then must retrieve the program or process from the hard disk. It can take thousands of times longer to access information from the hard disk than to get it from physical RAM. If your computer is using excessive paging, that is an indication that your computer does not have enough physical memory.

Insufficient memory is the most likely cause of system bottlenecks. If you have no idea what is causing a system bottleneck, memory is usually a good place to start checking. To determine how memory is being used, you need to examine two areas:

Physical memory   The physical RAM you have installed on your computer. You can't have too much memory. It's actually a good idea to have more memory than you think you will need just to be on the safe side. As you've probably noticed, each time you add or upgrade applications, you require more system memory.

Page file Logical memory that exists on the hard drive. If you are using excessive paging (swapping between the page file and physical RAM), it's a clear sign that you need to add more memory.

The first step in memory management is determining how much memory your computer has installed and what the appropriate memory requirements are based on the operating system requirements and the applications and services you are running on your computer.

 In this book, we use the following format for describing performance object counters: *performance object > counter*. For example, Memory > Available MBytes denotes the Memory performance object and the Available MBytes counter.

Key Counters to Track for Memory Management

Following are the three most important counters for monitoring memory:

Memory > Available MBytes Measures the amount of physical memory that is available to run processes on the computer. If this number is less than 4MB, it indicates that you have an overall shortage of physical memory for your computer, or you possibly have an application that is not releasing memory properly. You should consider adding more memory or evaluating application memory usage.

Memory > Pages/Sec Shows the number of times the requested information was not in memory and had to be retrieved from disk. This counter's value should be below 20; for optimal performance, it should be 4 or 5. If the number is above 20, you should add memory or research paging file use more thoroughly. Sometimes a high Pages/Sec counter is indicative of a program that is using a memory-mapped file.

Paging File > % Usage Indicates the percentage of the allocated page file that is currently in use. If this number is consistently over 70%, you may need to add more memory or increase the size of the page file.

These counters work together to show what is happening on your system. Use the Paging File > % Usage counter value in conjunction with the Memory > Available MBytes and Memory > Pages/Sec counters to determine how much paging is occurring on your computer.

If you suspect that one of your applications has a memory leak, you should monitor the following counters:

- Memory > Available Bytes
- Memory > Committed Bytes
- Process > Private Bytes (for the application you suspect is leaking memory)
- Process > Working Set (for the application you suspect is leaking memory)
- Process > Handle Count (for the application you suspect is leaking memory)
- Memory > Pool Nonpaged Bytes
- Memory > Pool Nonpaged Allocs

Managing the Windows XP Page File

Typically, if your computer is experiencing excessive paging, the best way to optimize memory is to add more physical memory. However, there are some other options for managing the paging file for better performance. They include:

- Spreading the page file across multiple hard disks, which allows the disk I/O associated with paging to be spread over multiple disk I/O channels, for faster access.

- If you have sufficient disk space, increasing the size of the page file. By default, Windows XP Professional creates a page file (`pagefile.sys`) that is 1.5 times the amount of physical memory that has been installed on your computer. You would want to consider increasing the page file size if the Paging File > %Usage counter was near 100%.

The main counters for tracking page file usage are:

- Paging File > %Usage
- Paging File > %Usage Peak (bytes)

 If a paging file reaches the maximum size, the user will see a warning displayed, and the system might halt. This is another reason to monitor the page file and increase the size.

 You will learn how to view and manage the page file later in this chapter in the "Using the System Tool in Control Panel" section. Only Administrators can manage this option.

Tuning and Upgrading Memory

If you suspect that you have a memory bottleneck, the following options can be used to tune or upgrade memory:

- Increase the amount of physical memory that is installed on the computer.
- If your computer has multiple disk channels, create multiple page files across the disk channels.
- Verify that your paging file is sized correctly.
- Try to run less memory-intensive applications.
- Try to avoid having your paging file on the same partition as the system files.

 **Real World Scenario**

Using System Monitor to Identify Bottlenecks

You are the system administrator of a large network. The accounting department has just started using a new accounting application that runs on the department manager's local computer. The manager is complaining about the slowness of this application and says she needs a new computer.

You decide to use System Monitor to find out why her computer is responding so slowly. You see that the processor utilization is at 10% (low). You also can tell that the system is using excessive paging based on the Memory > Pages/Sec counter, currently showing at 25. Considering this information, you determine that for the accounting manager's computer to work efficiently with the application, the computer needs a memory upgrade.

System Monitor helps you measure the performance of various parts of your system, allowing you to identify system bottlenecks scientifically.

In Exercise 13.2, you will monitor your computer's memory subsystem. This exercise assumes that you have completed Exercise 13.1.

EXERCISE 13.2

Monitoring System Memory

1. Select Start ➤ All Programs ➤ Administrative Tools ➤ Monitor.

2. In the System Monitor window, click the Add button on the toolbar.

3. In the Add Counters dialog box, specify the following performance objects and counters:

    ▪ Select Memory from the performance object drop-down list, choose Available MBytes in the counter list box, and click the Add button.

    ▪ Select Memory from the performance object drop-down list, choose Pages/Sec in the counter list box, and click the Add button.

    ▪ Select Paging File from the performance object drop-down list, choose %Usage in the counter list box, and click the Add button.

4. Click the Close button. You should see a chart showing how your computer's memory is being used.

5. To generate some activity, select Start ➤ Help. Close Help. Open Help again and then close it. The first time you opened Help, you should have seen a spike in the Memory > Pages/Sec counter, and a much lower spike the second time you accessed Help. This occurs because the Help program must be retrieved from disk the first time you accessed it; the second time you accessed it, it was already in memory.

6. Note the Paging > %Usage counter. If this counter is below 70%, your system is not using excessive paging.

7. Note the Memory > Available MBytes counter. If this counter is above 4MB, you should have sufficient RAM.

Leave System Monitor open, for use again in Exercise 13.3.

Monitoring and Optimizing the Processor

Processor bottlenecks can develop when the threads of a process require more processing cycles than are currently available. In this case, the process will wait in a processor queue and system responsiveness will be slower than if process requests could be immediately served. The most common causes of processor bottlenecks are processor-intensive applications and other subsystem components that generate excessive processor interrupts (for example, disk or network subsystems).

In a workstation environment, processors are usually not the source of bottlenecks. You should still monitor this subsystem to make sure that processor utilization is at an efficient level.

Key Counters to Track for Processor

You can track processor utilization through the Processor and System objects to determine whether a processor bottleneck exists. The following are the two most important counters for monitoring the system processor:

Processor > %Processor Time   Measures the time that the processor spends responding to system requests. If this value is consistently above an average of 85%, you may have a processor bottleneck. The Processor > %User Time and Processor > %Privileged Time counters combine to show the total %Processor Time counter. You can monitor these counters individually for more detail.

Processor > Interrupts/Sec   Shows the average number of hardware interrupts received by the processor each second. If this value is more than 1,000 on a Pentium computer, you might have a problem with a program or hardware that is generating spurious interrupts.

System > Processor Queue Length   Used to determine whether a processor bottleneck is due to high levels of demand for processor time. If a queue of two or more items exists, a processor bottleneck may be indicated.

If you suspect that a processor bottleneck is due to excessive hardware I/O requests, or improperly configured IRQs, then you should also monitor the System > File Control Bytes/Sec counter.

Tuning and Upgrading the Processor

If you suspect that you have a processor bottleneck, you can try the following solutions:

- Use applications that are less processor-intensive.
- Upgrade your processor.
- If your computer supports multiple processors, add one. Windows XP Professional can support up to two processors, which will help if you use multithreaded applications. You can also use processor affinity to help manage processor intensive applications.

Beware of running three-dimensional screensavers on your computer. As you will see in Exercise 13.3, they can use quite a bit of the processor's time.

In Exercise 13.3, you will monitor your computer's processor. This exercise assumes that you have completed the other exercises in this chapter.

EXERCISE 13.3

Monitoring the System Processor

1. If System Monitor is not already open, select Start ➤ All Programs ➤ Administrative Tools ➤ Monitor.

2. In the System Monitor window, click the Add button on the toolbar.

3. In the Add Counters dialog box, specify the following performance objects and counters:

   - Select Processor from the performance object drop-down list, select %Processor Time in the counter list box, and click the Add button.

   - Select Processor from the performance object drop-down list, select Interrupts/Sec in the counter list box, and click the Add button.

4. Click the Close button. You should see these counters added to your chart.

5. To generate some activity, select Start ➤ Control Panel ➤ Appearance and Themes ➤ Display. Click the Screen Saver tab. Select 3D FlowerBox and click the Preview button. Let this process run for about 5 seconds, and close all of the dialog boxes you opened in this step. You should see that the %Processor Time counter spiked during this process.

6. Note the Processor > %Processor Time counter. If this counter's average is below 85%, you do not have a processor bottleneck.

7. Note the Processor > Interrupts/Sec counter. If this counter is below 1,000 on a Pentium computer, you do not have any processes or hardware that are generating excessive interrupts.

Leave System Monitor open, for use again in Exercise 13.4.

Monitoring and Optimizing the Disk Subsystem

Disk access is the amount of time your disk subsystem takes to retrieve data that is requested by the operating system. The two factors that determine how quickly your disk subsystem will respond to system requests are the average disk access time on your hard drive and the speed of your disk controller.

Key Counters to Track for the Disk Subsystem

You can monitor the PhysicalDisk object, which is the sum of all logical drives on a single physical drive, or you can monitor the LogicalDisk object, which represents a specific logical disk. Following are the most important counters for monitoring the disk subsystem. These counters can be tracked for both the PhysicalDisk object and the LogicalDisk object.

PhysicalDisk > %Disk Time   Shows the amount of time the physical disk is busy because it is servicing read or write requests. If the disk is busy more than 90% of the time, you will improve performance by adding another disk channel and splitting the disk I/O requests between the channels.

PhysicalDisk > %Current Disk Queue Length   Indicates the number of outstanding disk requests that are waiting to be processed. This value should be less than 2.

Tuning and Upgrading the Disk Subsystem

When you suspect that you have a disk subsystem bottleneck, the first thing you should check is your memory subsystem. Insufficient physical memory can cause excessive paging, which in turn affects the disk subsystem. If you do not have a memory problem, you can try the following solutions to improve disk performance:

- Use faster disks and controllers.

- Confirm that you have the latest drivers for your disk host adapters.

- Use Disk Manager to use disk striping to take advantage of multiple I/O channels.

- Balance heavily used files on multiple I/O channels.

- Add another disk controller for load balancing.

- Use Disk Defragmenter to consolidate files so that disk space and data access are optimized.

- If you are on a network, distribute applications that have high disk I/O through the Distributed File System (DFS) to balance workload.

In Windows NT 4, you enabled all disk counters through the DISKPERF -Y command. Physical and logical disk counters are automatically enabled in Windows XP Professional.

In Exercise 13.4, you will monitor your disk subsystem. This exercise assumes that you have completed the other exercises in this chapter.

EXERCISE 13.4

Monitoring the Disk Subsystem

1. If System Monitor is not already open, select Start ➤ All Programs ➤ Administrative Tools ➤ Monitor.

2. In the System Monitor window, click the Add button on the toolbar.

3. In the Add Counters dialog box, specify the following performance objects and counters:

   - Select PhysicalDisk from the performance object drop-down list, select %Disk Time from the counter list box, and click the Add button.

   - Select PhysicalDisk from the performance object drop-down list, select Current Disk Queue Length from the counter list box, and click the Add button.

- ▪ Select LogicalDisk from the performance object drop-down list, select %Idle Time from the counter list box, and click the Add button.

4. Click the Close button. You should see these counters added to your chart.

5. To generate some activity, open and close some applications and copy some files between the C: drive and D: drive.

6. Note the PhysicalDisk > %Disk Time counter. If this counter's average is below 90%, you are not generating excessive requests to this disk.

7. Note the PhysicalDisk > %Current Disk Queue Length counter. If this counter's average is below 2, you are not generating excessive requests to this disk.

Leave System Monitor open; you will use this utility again in Exercise 13.5.

You can monitor the amount of free disk space on your logical disk through the LogicalDisk > %Free Space counter. This counter can also be used as an alert. For example, you might set an alert to notify you when LogicalDisk > %Free Space on drive C: is under 10%.

Monitoring and Optimizing the Network Subsystem

Windows XP Professional does not have a built-in mechanism for monitoring the entire network. However, you can monitor and optimize the traffic that is generated on the specific Windows XP computer. You can monitor the network interface (your network card), and you can monitor the network protocols that have been installed on your computer.

Network bottlenecks are indicated when network traffic exceeds the capacity that can be supported by the Local Area Network (LAN). Typically, you would monitor this activity on a network-wide basis—for example, with the Network Monitor utility that is shipped with Windows Server 2003.

Key Counters to Track for the Network Subsystem

If you are using the System Monitor utility to monitor local network traffic, the following two counters are useful for monitoring the network subsystem:

Network Interface > Bytes Total/Sec   Measures the total number of bytes sent or received from the network interface and includes all network protocols.

TCP > Segments/Sec   Measures the number of bytes sent or received from the network interface and includes only the TCP protocol.

Normally, you monitor and optimize the network subsystem from a network perspective rather than from a single computer. For example, you can use a network protocol analyzer to monitor all traffic on the network to determine whether the network bandwidth is acceptable for your requirements and that network bandwidth is saturated.

Tuning and Upgrading the Network Subsystem

The following suggestions can help to optimize and minimize network traffic:

- Use only the network protocols you need. For example, use TCP/IP and don't use NWLink.
- If you need to use multiple network protocols, place the most commonly used protocols higher in the binding order.
- Use network cards that take full advantage of your bus width—for example, 32-bit cards instead of 16-bit cards.
- Use faster network cards—for example, 100Mbps Ethernet instead of 10Mbps Ethernet.

In Exercise 13.5, you will monitor your network subsystem. This exercise assumes that you have completed the other exercises in this chapter.

EXERCISE 13.5

Monitoring the Network Subsystem

1. If System Monitor is not already open, select Start ➤ All Programs ➤ Administrative Tools ➤ Monitor.

2. In the System Monitor window, click the Add button on the toolbar.

3. In the Add Counters dialog box, specify the following performance objects and counters:

   - Select Network Interface from the performance object drop-down list, select Bytes Total/Sec in the counter list box, and click the Add button.

   - Select TCP from the performance object drop-down list, select Segments/Sec from the counter list box, and click the Add button.

4. Click the Close button. You should see these counters added to your chart.

5. To generate some activity, copy some files between your C: drive and D: drive.

6. Note the two counters Network Interface > Bytes Total/Sec and TCP > Segments/Sec. These numbers are cumulative. Use them in your baselines to determine network activity.

Leave your Monitor console open, for use again in Exercise 13.6.

Creating Baseline Reports

As explained earlier in this chapter, baselines show how your server is performing at a certain time. By taking baselines at regular intervals and also whenever you make changes to the system's configuration, you can monitor your server's performance over time.

You can create baselines by setting up a counter log file in the Performance Logs and Alerts utility. After you've created the baseline log file, you can view it in System Monitor, as shown in Figure 13.17.

FIGURE 13.17 Viewing a performance baseline in System Monitor

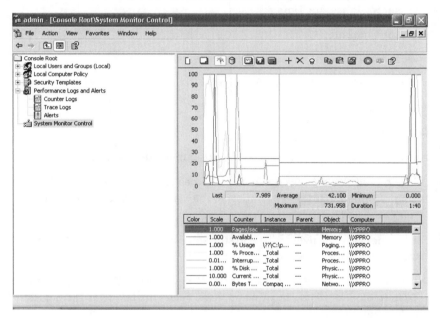

In Exercise 13.6, you will create a baseline report for your computer.

EXERCISE 13.6

Creating a Baseline Report

1. If the Monitor console is not already open, select Start ➢ All Programs ➢ Administrative Tools ➢ Monitor.

2. Double-click Performance Logs and Alerts.

3. Right-click Counter Logs and select New Log Settings.

4. In the New Log Settings dialog box, type **Counter***mmddyy* (replace *mmddyy* with the current month, date, and year) as the log name. The log file will be stored in the C:\PerfLogs folder by default. Click the OK button.

5. In the General tab of the counter log Properties dialog box, click the Add Counters button and add the following counters:

  ▪ Memory > Available MBytes

  ▪ Memory > Pages/Sec

  ▪ Paging File > %Usage

  ▪ Processor > %Processor Time

  ▪ Processor > Interrupts/Sec

  ▪ PhysicalDisk > %Disk Time

  ▪ PhysicalDisk > Current Disk Queue Length

  ▪ Network Interface > Bytes Total/Sec

  ▪ TCP > Segments/Sec

6. Click the Close button, and set the interval for sampling data to 5 seconds.

7. Click the Log Files tab. Uncheck the End File Names With check box. This will prevent the appending of *mmddhh* (month/day/hour) to the filename. Click the OK button to close the Properties dialog box and start the log file.

8. Generate some system activity: Start and stop some applications, copy a few files, and run a screensaver for 1 or 2 minutes.

9. To view your log file, open System Monitor. Click the View Log Data button on the toolbar. In the System Monitor dialog box that appears, select the Log Files radio button and click the Add button.

10. In the Select File dialog box, select C:\PerfLogs\Counter*mmddyy* and click the Open button.

11. Add the counters from the log file you created to see the data that was collected in your log.

Using the System Tool in Control Panel

The System Tool in Control Panel can be used to manage performance options for your computer. The performance-related options that can be configured through the System Tool include how visual settings affect performance, processor scheduling, memory usage, and how the paging file is configured.

To access these options, select Start ➢ Control Panel ➢ Performance and Maintenance ➢ System. Select the Advanced tab, and then for Performance, click the Settings button. You will see two tabs, Visual Effects and Advanced.

From the Visual Effects tab (see Figure 13.18), you can specify how performance is tuned based on the visual effects you choose to use with your user interface. The selections for visual effect settings include:

- Let Windows choose what's best for my computer

- Adjust for best appearance

- Adjust for best performance

- Custom

FIGURE 13.18   The Visual Effects tab of the Performance Options dialog box

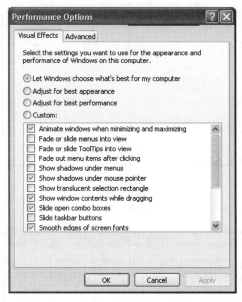

If you click the Advanced tab, you will see the dialog box shown in Figure 13.19. From the Advanced tab, you can configure:

- Processor scheduling, which allows you to optimize the processor time for running programs or background services

- Memory usage, which allows you to optimize memory for programs or system cache

- Virtual memory, which is used to configure the paging file

If you click on the Change button within the Virtual Memory section of the Advanced tab, you can manage the page file, as shown in Figure 13.20.

When Windows is initially installed, the page file, pagefile.sys, is set to 1.5 times the amount of physical memory. You can optimize the page file by moving it from the drive that contains the system partition or by splitting the it over multiple disk I/O channels.

In order to make changes to the System Tool, you must be logged onto the local computer with administrative rights.

FIGURE 13.19 The Advanced Tab of the System Tool

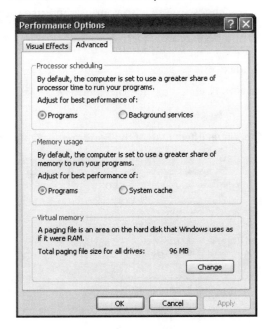

FIGURE 13.20 Virtual Memory dialog box

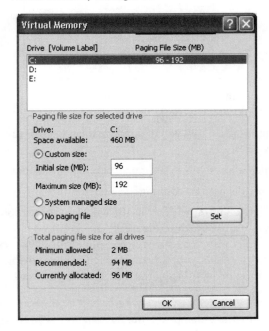

Using Task Manager

The *Task Manager* utility shows the applications and processes that are currently running on your computer, as well as CPU and memory usage information. To access Task Manager, press Ctrl+Alt+Delete and click the Task Manager button. Alternatively, right-click an empty area in the Taskbar and select Task Manager from the pop-up menu.

The Task Manager dialog box has four main tabs, Applications, Processes, Performance, and Networking. These options are covered in the following subsections.

Managing Application Tasks

The Applications tab of the Task Manager dialog box, shown in Figure 13.21, lists all of the applications that are currently running on the computer. For each task, you will see the name of the task and the current status (running, not responding, or stopped).

FIGURE 13.21   The Applications tab of the Task Manager dialog box

To close an application, select it and click the End Task button at the bottom of the dialog box. To make the application window active, select it and click the Switch To button. If you want to start an application that isn't running, click the New Task button and specify the location and name of the program you wish to start.

Managing Process Tasks

The Processes tab of the Task Manager dialog box, shown in Figure 13.22, lists all the processes that are currently running on the computer. This is a convenient way to get a quick look at how your system is performing. Unlike System Monitor, Task Manager doesn't require that you first configure the collection of this data; it's gathered automatically.

FIGURE 13.22   The Processes tab of the Task Manager dialog box

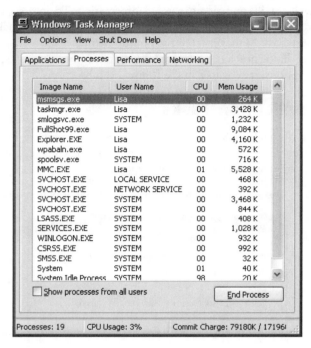

For each process, you will see the image name (the name of the process), the user name (the user account that is running the process), CPU (the amount of CPU utilization for the process), and Mem Usage (the amount of memory that is being used by the process).

From the Processes tab, you can organize the listing and control processes as follows:

- To organize the processes based on usage, click the column headings. For example, if you click the CPU column, the listing will start with the processes that use the most CPU resources. If you click the CPU column a second time, the listing will be reversed.

- To manage a process, right-click it and choose an option from the pop-up menu. You can choose to end the process, end the process tree, or set the priority of the process (to realtime, high, abovenormal, normal, belownormal, or low). If your computer has multiple processors installed, you can also set processor affinity (the process of associating a specific process with a specific processor) for a process. See Chapter 4, "Configuring the Windows XP Environment," for details on setting processor affinity.

- To customize the counters that are listed, select View ➢ Select Columns. This brings up the Select Columns dialog box, shown in Figure 13.23, where you can select the information that you want to see listed on the Processes tab.

FIGURE 13.23   Selecting information for the Task Manager's Processes tab

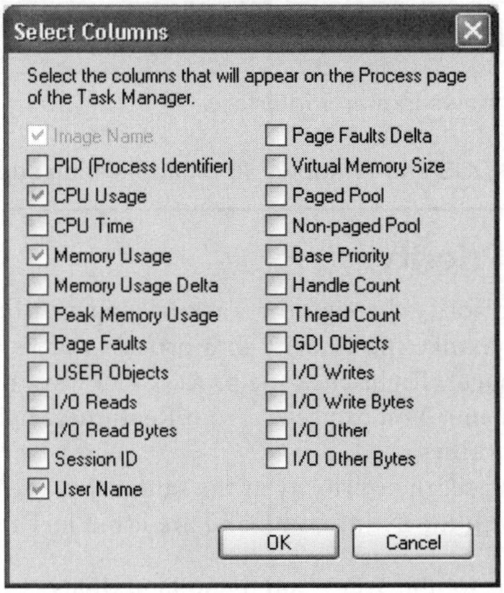

In the following subsections you will learn how to stop processes and manage process priority.

Stopping Processes

You may need to stop a process that isn't executing properly. To stop a specific process, select the process you want to stop in the Task Manager's Processes tab and click the End Process button. Task Manager displays a Warning dialog box. Click the Yes button to terminate the process.

If you right-click a process, you can end the specific process or you can use the option End Process Tree. The End Process Tree option ends all processes that have been created either directly or indirectly by the process.

Some of the common processes that can be managed through Task Manager are listed in Table 13.2.

TABLE 13.2   Common Processes

Process	Description
System Idle Process	A process that runs when the processor is not executing any other threads
smss.exe	Session Manager subsystem
csrss.exe	Client-server runtime server service
mmc.exe	Microsoft Management Console program (used to track resources used by MMC snap-ins such as System Monitor)

TABLE 13.2 Common Processes *(continued)*

Process	Description
explorer.exe	Windows Explorer interface
Ntvdm.exe	MS-DOS and Windows 16-bit application support

Managing Process Priority

You can manage process priority through the Task Manager utility or through the start command-line utility. To change the priority of a process that is already running, use the Processes tab of Task Manager. Right-click the process you want to manage and select Set Priority from the pop-up menu. You can select from Realtime, High, Abovenormal, Normal, Belownormal, and Low priorities.

To start applications and set their priority at the same time, use the start command. The options that can be used with the start command are listed in Table 13.3.

TABLE 13.3 Options for the start Command-Line Utility

Option	Description
/low	Starts an application in the idle priority class.
/normal	Starts an application in the Normal priority class.
/high	Starts an application in the High priority class.
/realtime	Starts an application in the Realtime priority class.
/abovenormal	Starts an application in the Abovenormal priority class.
/belownormal	Starts an application in the Belownormal priority class.
/min	Starts the application in a minimized window.
/max	Starts the application in a maximized window.
/separate	Starts a Windows 16-bit application in a separate memory space. By default Windows 16-bit applications run in a shared memory space, NTVDM, or NT Virtual DOS Machine.
/shared	Starts a DOS or Windows 16-bit application in a shared memory space.

Running a process-intensive application in the Realtime priority class can significantly impact Windows XP Professional performance.

In Exercise 13.7, you will set the priority for a process.

EXERCISE 13.7

Setting a Process Priority

1. Right-click an empty space on your taskbar and select Task Manager from the pop-up menu.

2. In the Applications tab, click the New Task button.

3. In the Create a New Task dialog box, type **CALC** and click the OK button.

4. Click the Processes tab. Right-click calc.exe and select Set Priority, then Low. In the Task Manager Warning dialog box, click the Yes button to continue.

5. Right-click calc.exe and select End Process. In the Task Manager Warning dialog box, click the Yes button.

Managing Performance Tasks

The Performance tab of the Task Manager dialog box, shown in Figure 13.24, provides an overview of your computer's CPU and memory usage. This is similar to the information tracked by System Monitor, and you don't have to configure it first as you do with System Monitor.

FIGURE 13.24   The Performance tab of the Task Manager dialog box

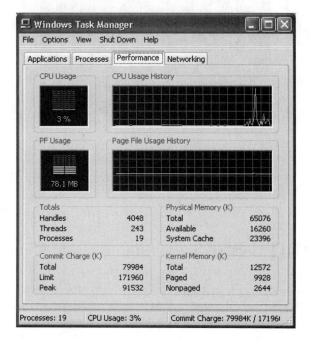

The Performance tab shows the following information:

- CPU usage, in real time and in a history graph
- Page file usage, in real time and in a history graph
- Totals for handles, threads, and processes
- Physical memory statistics
- Commit charge memory statistics
- Kernel memory statistics

Managing Networking Tasks

The Networking tab of the Task Manager dialog box, shown in Figure 13.25, provides an overview of your networking usage. This is similar to the information tracked by System Monitor, and you don't have to configure it first as you do with System Monitor.

FIGURE 13.25   The Networking tab of the Task Manager dialog box

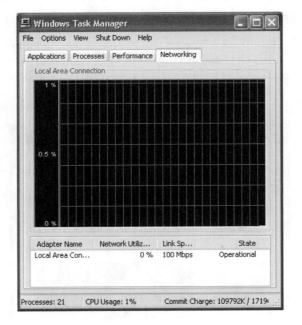

Scheduling Tasks

Windows XP Professional includes a *Task Scheduler* utility that allows you to schedule tasks to occur at specified intervals. You can set any of your Windows programs to run automatically at a specific time and at a set interval, such as daily, weekly, or monthly. For example, you might schedule your Windows Backup program to run daily at 2:00 A.M.

In Exercise 13.8, we will create a new scheduled task.

EXERCISE 13.8

Creating a New Scheduled Task

1. Select Start ➤ Control Panel ➤ Performance and Maintenance, and select Scheduled Tasks.

2. In the Scheduled Tasks window, double-click the Add Scheduled Task icon.

3. When the first page of the Scheduled Task Wizard appears, click the Next button to continue.

4. The first Scheduled Task Wizard dialog box lists applications you can run. You can select an application from the list or click the Browse button to locate any application or program to which your computer has access. After you select an application, click the Next button.

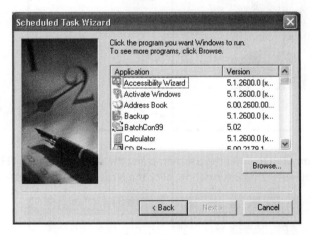

5. The next wizard dialog box prompts you to select a name for the task and specify when it will be performed. Make your selection and click the Next button.

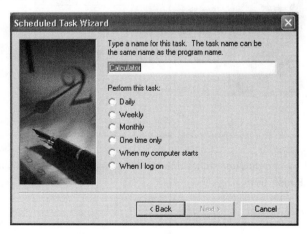

6. Depending on the selection you made for the task's schedule, you may see another dialog box for setting the specific schedule. For example, if you chose to run the task weekly, the next dialog box lets you select the start time for the task, choose to run the task every *x* weeks, and pick the day of the week that the task should be run. Make your selection and click the Next button.

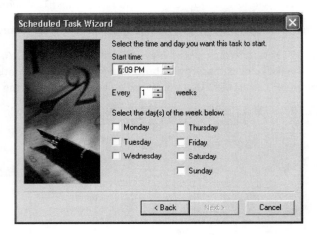

7. Next, you are prompted to enter the username and the password that will be used to start the task. After you enter this information, click the Next button.

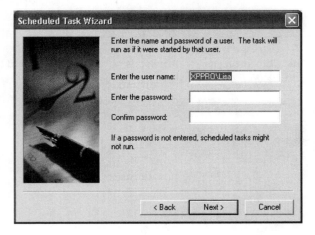

8. The final dialog box shows your selections for the scheduled task. If this information is correct, click the Finish button.

Managing Scheduled Task Properties

You can manage a scheduled task through its properties dialog box; Figure 13.26 shows the properties for the Calculator job. To access this dialog box, open the Scheduled Tasks window (Start ➢ Control Panel ➢ Performance and Maintenance, and then select Scheduled Tasks). Right-click the task you wish to manage, and choose Properties from the pop-up menu.

FIGURE 13.26   The Task properties for the scheduled task

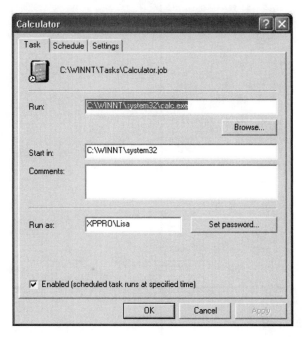

The scheduled task properties dialog box has three tabs, Task, Schedule, and Settings, with options for managing how and when the task is run and who can manage it. These options are described in the following sections.

Task Properties

Through the Task tab (see Figure 13.26), you can configure the following options:

- The command-line program that is used to run the task
- The folders containing related files that might be required to run the specified task (this is the Start In information)
- Any comments that you want to include for informational purposes
- The username and password to be used to run the specified task (this is the Run As information)
- Whether the scheduled task is enabled

Schedule Properties

The Schedule tab, shown in Figure 13.27, shows the schedule configured for the task. You can change any of these options to reschedule the task.

FIGURE 13.27 The Schedule properties for the scheduled task

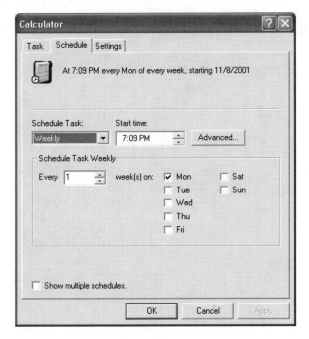

Settings Properties

The Settings tab (Figure 13.28) offers several configuration settings for the scheduled task:

- The options in the Scheduled Task Completed section allow you to delete the task if it will not be run again and specify how long the task should be allowed to run before it is stopped.

- The options in the Idle Time section are useful if the computer must be idle when the task is run. You can specify how long the computer must be idle before the task begins and whether the task should be stopped if the computer ceases to be idle.

- The options in the Power Management section are applicable when the computer on which the task runs may be battery powered. You can specify that the task should not start if the computer is running from batteries and choose to stop the task if battery mode begins.

If you are using Task Scheduler and your jobs are not running properly, make sure that the Task Scheduler service is running and is configured to start automatically. You should also ensure that the user who is configured to run the scheduled task has sufficient permissions to run the task.

FIGURE 13.28   The Settings tab of the scheduled task dialog box

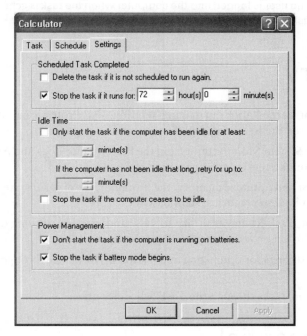

Troubleshooting Scheduled Tasks

If you are trying to use Scheduled Tasks and the tasks are not properly being executed, one of the following troubleshooting options may resolve the problem.

- If a scheduled task does not run as expected, right-click the task and select Properties. From the Task tab, verify that the Enabled check box is selected. From the Schedule tab, verify the schedule that has been defined for the task to run.

- If the scheduled task is a command-line utility, make sure that you have properly defined the command-line utility, including any options that are required for the utility to run properly.

- Verify that the user who is configured to run the scheduled task has the necessary permissions to the task that will be run.

- Within the Scheduled Tasks window, check the task status within the Status column. The status types are defined as:
  - Blank, which indicates that the task is not running, or that it was run successfully
  - Running, which means that the task is currently being run
  - Missed, which specifies that one or more attempts to run the task were missed
  - Could not start, which indicates that the most recent attempt to start the task failed

- Verify that the Scheduled Tasks service has been enabled on the computer if no tasks can be run on the computer.

If no user is logged into the computer when the task is scheduled to be run, the task will still run, but it will not be visible.

Summary

In this chapter, you learned about managing Windows XP Professional optimization and reliability. We covered the following topics:

- How to use the System Monitor utility and the Performance Logs and Alerts utility to track and monitor your system's performance

- How to monitor and optimize memory, the processor, the disk subsystem, and the network subsystem, and how to create a system baseline

- How to use the Task Manager utility to view and manage running applications and processes, and to get an overview of CPU and memory usage

- How to access settings for optimizing application performance through the System icon in Control Panel

- How to automate tasks through the Task Scheduler utility

Exam Essentials

Be able to monitor and troubleshoot Windows XP Professional performance. Know which utilities can be used to track Windows XP performance events and issues. Know how to track and identify performance problems related to memory, the processor, the disk subsystem, and the network subsystem. Be able to correct system bottlenecks when they are identified.

Know how to use the Task Scheduler to automate system tasks. Understand the purpose of Task Scheduler. Be able to configure Task Scheduler and identify problems that would keep it from running properly.

Key Terms

Before you take the exam, be certain you are familiar with the following terms:

alerts	Performance Logs and Alerts
baseline	System Monitor
bottleneck	Task Manager
counters	Task Scheduler
page file	

Review Questions

1. You are the network administrator of a medium-sized company. Tim is a user in the Finance department. He notices that his computer's performance is slow at times. You decide to monitor the computer's performance through Performance Logs and Alerts. You monitor counters related to memory, processor, the disk subsystem, and the network subsystem. For memory, you are monitoring the Memory > Available Mbytes counter. When you analyze the data from Tim's computer, the value for the Memory > Available Mbytes counter averages 12MB over a typical sampling period. Based on this data, what course of action should you take?

    A. Add RAM.

    B. Increase the size of the page file.

    C. Split the page file over two physical disk channels.

    D. Take no action.

2. Your accounting department runs a processor-intensive application and you are trying to determine whether their current computers need to have the processors upgraded. You load a test computer with a configuration identical to the production computers' and run a program that simulates a typical user's workload. You monitor the Processor > %Processor Time counter. What average value for this counter would indicate a processor bottleneck?

    A. Over 5%

    B. Over 50%

    C. Over 60%

    D. Over 85%

3. You are the network administrator for the XYZ Corporation. Users in the Sales department have been complaining that the Sales application is slow to load. Using Performance Logs and Alerts, you create a baseline report for one of the computers, monitoring memory, the processor, the disk subsystem, and the network subsystem. You notice that the disk subsystem has a high load of activity. What other subsystem should you monitor before you can know for sure whether you have a disk subsystem bottleneck?

    A. Memory

    B. Processor

    C. Network

    D. Application

4. You are the network administrator for a network that consists of Windows XP Professional computers configured as a workgroup. One of your users, Curtis, recently installed Visio on his computer for creating engineering diagrams. When Curtis runs this application, it takes between 5 and 10 seconds to load. He uses the Task Manager utility to try to determine if he has a resource bottleneck. Which two of the following subsystems should he monitor through Task Manager to help determine what the bottleneck is?

   A. Memory

   B. Processor

   C. Network

   D. Disk

5. You are the network administrator for a large corporation. The accounting department requires that a specific application, ABC.EXE, be run every day to create daily reports on accounting activity. The application needs to be run at 6 P.M. on Monday through Friday. The Accounting Manager has asked you to automate the process so that reports are generated on the specified schedule without any user interaction. Which Windows XP utility allows you to configure automated tasks?

   A. Scheduled Tasks

   B. Automated Scheduler

   C. Task Manager

   D. Task Automater

6. You are the network administrator for a large company. The payroll manager has Windows XP Professional installed on her desktop computer. The computer has the following configuration:

   - Dual Pentium III Processors
   - 128MB of RAM
   - Two physical SCSI disks
   - Disk 0 has Partition C: and D
   - Disk 1 has Partition E:
   - 192MB page file on C:
   - 100Mbps Ethernet NIC

   The payroll manager requires the use of a database application. She has come to you to report that when the database application is running, the computer slows down very significantly, and she is unable to run any other applications. You run System Monitor on her computer and record the following information when the database application is running:

   - Sustained processor utilization is at 100% for both processors
   - There are a significant number of hard page faults

When you record the data for the computer when the database application is not running, you record the following information:

- Average processor utilization is at 30%
- There are a significant number of hard page faults

The database application is critical to the finance manager's job. In order to be able to better manage her productivity, which of the two following actions will have the greatest impact on optimizing her computer's performance?

A. Upgrade the processors in her computer.

B. Add memory to the computer.

C. Split the page file over D: and E:.

D. Increase the page file to 256MB.

7. You are the network administrator, responsible for managing the computers used by the Engineering department. Each user has a dual processor computer. The engineers all run CAD, Visio, and some other specialized engineering applications. You are testing how performance can be improved for these computers and want to test what will happen if you use processor affinity to associate specific applications with specific processors. Which of the following options should you use to configure processor affinity?

A. Through Control Panel, System

B. Task Manager

C. Performance Monitor

D. System Logs and Alerts

8. You are the network administrator for a large company. The payroll manager has Windows XP Professional installed on her desktop computer. The computer has the following configuration:

- Dual Pentium III Processors
- 128MB of RAM
- Two physical SCSI disks 20GB each
- Disk 0 has Partition C: (10GB, 8GB free, and the system partition) and D (10GB, 4GB free)
- Disk 1 has Partition E: (20GB, 12GB free)
- 192MB page file on E:
- 100Mbps Ethernet NIC

The payroll manager uses a specialized payroll application. She reports that when she initially starts her computer, everything works well, but after using the payroll application for two hours, her computer starts to get slower and slower. After about two hours and 15 minutes, she gets an error message stating that her system is low on virtual memory. You have ordered additional memory for her computer, but it is out of stock. In the meantime you want to optimize her computer as much as possible. What course of action should you take?

A. Increase the size of the paging file to 256MB.

B. Move the paging file to the C: drive.

C. Edit the `config.sys` file so that buffers = 128.

D. In Control Panel, System, Advanced Options, configure memory for Allow Best Performance for System Cache.

9. You are the Help Desk manager of a large corporation. You want to make some changes to your computer and would like to create a baseline report that will be used to measure your computer's performance before and after each change is made to the computer's configuration. When you open System Monitor, which of the following counters are active by default?

A. Memory > Pages/Sec

B. Processor > %Processor Time

C. Paging File > %Usage

D. None

10. You are the network administrator for a large company. One of the computers that you are monitoring is a Pentium computer. You suspect that you have a bottleneck, possibly due to a malfunctioning piece of hardware. When you monitor the computer through System Monitor, one of the counters you track is Processor > Interrupts/Sec. Which of the following values would first indicate that a piece of hardware is malfunctioning due to spurious interrupts?

A. 250

B. 500

C. 750

D. 1,000

11. You are the network administrator for a medium-sized company. One of your responsibilities is to monitor performance for the computers in the accounting department. You create a baseline report that tracks counters for memory, processor, the disk subsystem, and the network subsystem. One of the counters you track through System Monitor is the PhysicalDisk > Current Disk Queue Length counter. You might have a disk subsystem bottleneck when this counter is initially over which of the following values?

A. 1

B. 2

C. 10

D. 12

12. You are the network administrator for the XYZ Corporation. Your accounting manager uses a financial application that requires several hours a day to create reports that are required by the accounting department. While the application is running, the accounting manager finds that his computer is very slow when running other accounting applications. You have been asked to configure his computer so that the other accounting applications that are being run are more responsive. Which of the following configuration changes should you make?

   A. Configure the accounting applications to run at high priority.

   B. Configure the accounting applications to run at realtime priority.

   C. Configure the financial application to run at below normal priority.

   D. Configure the financial application to run at above normal priority.

13. When you schedule a task to be run, which of the following task properties *cannot* be configured?

   A. The username and password of the user who will run the task

   B. Power management, so that if the computer is a laptop and is running from the battery, the task will not run

   C. Whether the task will be run once or repeatedly

   D. Whether another task will be run if specific conditions trigger the secondary task

14. You want to track system performance for a baseline over a period of two days. You want the data to be collected every 5 minutes. What type of log would you create for this monitoring, through Performance Logs and Alerts?

   A. Counter log

   B. Trace log

   C. Monitoring log

   D. Baseline log

15. You are monitoring the Memory > Pages/Sec counter through System Monitor. Which of the following statements reflects what is considered optimal performance for this counter?

   A. This counter's value should be around 4 to 5.

   B. This counter's value should be around 30 to 40.

   C. This counter's value should be around 40 to 50.

   D. This counter's value should be around 50 to 60.

Answers to Review Questions

1. D. As long as the counter for Memory > Available MBytes shows more than 4MB of memory, no bottleneck is indicated and no intervention is needed. If the number is below 4MB, then you should add more physical memory to the computer.

2. D. If the average Processor > %Processor Time counter is consistently above 85%, a processor bottleneck may be indicated. (Normally this number will spike up and down over time. If it spikes over 85%, it is not necessarily alarming. If the average is over 85%, then a bottleneck is indicated.)

3. A. You should check the memory counters. If your computer does not have enough memory, it can cause excessive paging, which may be perceived as a disk subsystem bottleneck.

4. A, B. Through the Performance tab of Task Manager, you can easily monitor your computer's current processor activity and memory utilization. Task Manager does not track disk statistics and based on his local use of the application, a network bottleneck is not indicated. If you used the System Monitor utility, you would need to configure it before any data could be collected or analyzed.

5. A. To automate scheduled tasks, you use the Scheduled Tasks utility. You can schedule tasks to be run based on the schedule you specify and the username and password that will be used to run the task.

6. A, B. The greatest improvement in performance for this computer can be obtained by upgrading the processors and adding more physical RAM. Because the database application is using 100% processor utilization over a sustained period, you need to upgrade the processors. The hard page faults indicate that you also have a memory bottleneck. While moving or increasing the page file might have an impact on performance, neither would have as large an impact as adding more physical memory will.

7. B. You can configure processor affinity through the Task Manager utility. This is one option for optimizing processor performance.

8. A. Creating a larger initial paging file will help alleviate the current problem. You need to add additional RAM to the computer, but to prevent the error message from occurring, you can help minimize the problem until more memory is installed by increasing the initial size of the paging file.

9. D. None of System Monitor's counters are on by default. If you want to see how your processor and memory are being utilized without setting any configuration options, you should use Task Manager.

10. D. The Processor > Interrupts/Sec counter shows the average number of hardware interrupts the processor receives each second. If this value is more than 1,000 on a Pentium computer, you might have a problem with a program or hardware that is generating spurious interrupts.

11. B. The PhysicalDisk > Current Disk Queue Length counter indicates the number of outstanding disk requests waiting to be processed. This counter value should be less than 2.

12. C.   You should configure the financial application to run at below normal priority. This will cause the running of the financial application to have less of a performance impact on the accounting applications as they are processed.

13. D.   There are no options to trigger secondary conditional tasks. You can configure the user who will be used to run the task, the schedule for running the task, and how the task will be executed in conjunction with a laptop's power state.

14. A.   Counter logs record data about hardware usage and the activity of system services. You can configure logging to occur manually or on a predefined schedule.

15. A.   The Memory > Pages/Sec counter shows the number of times that the requested information was not in memory and had to be retrieved from disk. This counter's value should be below 20. For optimal performance, it should be 4 to 5.

Chapter

14

Performing System Recovery Functions

MICROSOFT EXAM OBJECTIVES COVERED IN THIS CHAPTER:

✓ **Restore and back up the operating system, System State data, and user data.**

- Recover System State data and user data by using Windows Backup.

- Troubleshoot system restoration by starting in safe mode.

- Recover System State data and user data by using the Recovery console.

✓ **Configure, manage, and troubleshoot Remote Desktop and Remote Assistance.**

System recovery is the process of making your computer work again in the event of failure. In this chapter, you will learn how to safeguard your computer and how to recover from a disaster. The benefit of having a disaster recovery plan is that when you expect the worst to happen and are prepared for it, you can easily recover from most system failures.

One utility that you can use to diagnose system problems is Event Viewer. Through the Event Viewer utility, you can see logs that list events related to your operating system and applications.

If your computer will not boot, an understanding of the Window XP boot process will help you identify the area of failure and correct the problem. You should know the steps in each stage of the boot process, the function of each boot file, and how to edit the `BOOT.INI` file.

When you have problems starting Windows XP, you can press F8 when prompted during the boot sequence. This calls up the Windows XP Advanced Options menu. This menu includes several special boot options, such as Safe Mode and Last Known Good Configuration, that are useful for getting your system started so you can track down and correct problems.

One of the new features of system recovery in Windows XP Professional is driver rollback, which allows you to easily roll back to a previously used driver.

The Startup and Recovery options are used to specify how the operating system will react in the event of system failure. For example, you can specify whether the system should automatically reboot and whether administrative alerts should be sent.

You can use the Dr. Watson utility, which ships with Windows XP Professional, to diagnose application errors. When an application error occurs, Dr. Watson starts automatically, displaying information about the error.

Backups are the best protection you can have against system failure. You can create backups through the Backup utility, which offers options to run the Backup and Restore Wizard and the Automated System Recovery Wizard.

System Restore allows you to create and use restore points to return your operating system to a previous configuration.

Another option that experienced administrators can use to recover from a system failure is the Recovery Console. The Recovery Console boots your computer so that you have limited access to FAT16, FAT32, and NTFS volumes.

In this chapter, you will learn how to use all these system recovery functions of Windows XP Professional. We'll begin with an overview of techniques to protect your computer and recover from disasters. In addition, we'll also look at two new options in Windows XP: Remote

Desktop and Remote Assistance. Remote Desktop is used to access a Windows XP Professional computer remotely. Remote Assistance is used to request assistance from another Windows XP user.

Safeguarding Your Computer and Recovering from Disaster

One of the worst events you will experience is a computer that won't boot. An even worse experience is discovering that there is no recent backup for that computer.

The first step in preparing for disaster recovery is to expect that a disaster will happen at some point, and take proactive steps to plan your recovery before the failure occurs. Following are some of the preparations you can make:

- Perform regular system backups.
- Use virus-scanning software.
- Perform regular administrative functions, such as monitoring the logs in the Event Viewer utility.

If you can't start Windows XP Professional, there are several options and utilities that can be used to identify and resolve Windows errors. The following is a broad list of troubleshooting options:

- If you have recently made a change to your computer's configuration by installing a new device driver or application and Windows XP Professional will not load properly, you can use the Last Known Good Configuration, roll back the driver, or use System Restore to restore a previous system configuration.
- If you can boot your computer to Safe Mode, and you suspect that you have a system conflict, you can temporarily disable an application or processes, services, or uninstall software.
- If your computer will not boot to Safe Mode, you can use the Recovery Console to replace corrupted files or perform other recovery options manually. For example, on an $x86$-based system, you should verify that the BOOT.INI settings are correct. On an Itanium-based computer, you would verify that the NVRAM startup settings were correct.
- If necessary, you can use the Backup utility to restore operating and data files from backup media. You can also use Automated System Recovery Wizard in conjunction with the Backup utility to reformat the system partition and restore operating system files from backup media you previously created.

Table 14.1 summarizes all of the Windows XP utilities and options that can be used to assist in performing system recovery.

TABLE 14.1   Windows XP Professional Recovery Techniques

Recovery Technique	When to Use
Event Viewer	If the Windows XP operating system can be loaded through Normal or Safe Mode, one of the first places to look for hints about the problem is Event Viewer. Event Viewer displays System, Security, and Application logs.
Safe Mode	This is generally your starting point for system recovery. Safe Mode loads the absolute minimum of services and drivers that are needed to boot Windows XP. If you can load Safe Mode, you may be able to troubleshoot devices or services that keep Windows XP from loading normally.
Last Known Good Configuration	This option can help if you made changes to your computer and are now having problems. Last Known Good Configuration is an Advanced Options menu item that you can select during startup. It loads the configuration that was used the last time the computer booted successfully. This option will not help if you have hardware errors.
Driver Rollback	Driver rollback is used to restore a driver to a previous version that has been saved. This option is used when you update a driver and it is not functioning properly.
Dr. Watson	This utility helps when you are experiencing problems with an application. Dr. Watson is used to diagnose and troubleshoot application errors.
Backup Utility	You should use this utility to safeguard your computer. Through the Backup utility, you can back up the system or parts of the system and restore data from backups that you have made.
System Restore	System Restore is used to create known checkpoints of your system's configuration. In the event that your system becomes misconfigured, you can restore the system configuration to one of the known good checkpoints.
Recovery Console	You can use this option if none of the other options or utilities works. The Recovery Console starts Windows XP without the graphical interface and allows the administrator limited capabilities, such as adding or replacing files and enabling/disabling services.

All these Windows XP Professional recovery techniques are covered in detail in this chapter.

Using Event Viewer

You can use the *Event Viewer* utility to track information about your computer's hardware and software, as well as to monitor security events. All of the traced information is stored in three types of log files:

System log   Tracks events related to the Windows XP operating system.

Security log   Tracks events related to Windows XP auditing.

Application log   Tracks events related to applications that are running on your computer.

You can access Event Viewer by selecting Start ➢ Control Panel ➢ Performance and Maintenance ➢ Administrative Tools ➢ Event Viewer. Alternatively, you can right-click My Computer, choose Manage from the pop-up menu, and open Event Viewer under System Tools. From Event Viewer, select the log you want to view. Figure 14.1 shows Event Viewer with the System log displayed.

FIGURE 14.1   A System log in Event Viewer

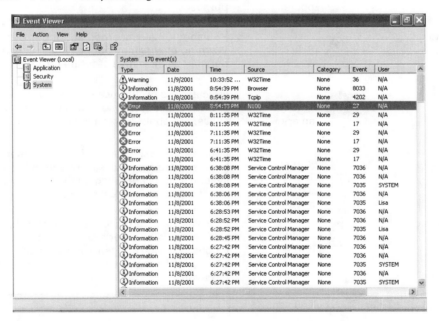

You can also add Event Viewer as a Microsoft Management Console (MMC) snap-in. Adding MMC snap-ins is covered in Chapter 4, "Configuring the Windows XP Environment."

In the log files, you will see all the events that have been recorded. By default, the oldest events are at the bottom of the window and the newest events are at the top. This arrangement can be misleading in troubleshooting, since one error can precipitate other errors. You should always resolve the oldest errors first. To change the default listing order and put the oldest events at the top, click one of the three logs and select View ➤ Oldest First.

The following sections describe how to view events and manage logs.

Reviewing Event Types

The Event Viewer logs display five event types, denoted by their icons. Table 14.2 describes each event type.

TABLE 14.2 Event Viewer Log Events

Event Type	Icon	Description
Information		Informs you of the occurrence of a specific action, such as the startup or shutdown of a system. *Information events* are logged for informative purposes.
Warning		You should be concerned about this event. *Warning events* may not be critical in nature but may be indicative of future errors.
Error		Indicates the occurrence of an error, such as a driver's failing to load. You should be very concerned about *Error events*.
Success Audit		Indicates the occurrence of an event that has been audited for success. For example, when system logons are being audited, a *Success Audit event* is a successful logon.
Failure Audit		Indicates the occurrence of an event that has been audited for failure. For example, when system logons are being audited, a *Failure Audit event* is a failed logon due to an invalid username and/or password.

Getting Event Details

Double-clicking an event in an Event Viewer log file brings up the Event Properties dialog box, which shows details about the event. An example of the Event Properties dialog box for an Information event is shown in Figure 14.2. Table 14.3 describes the information that appears in this dialog box.

FIGURE 14.2   The Event Properties dialog box

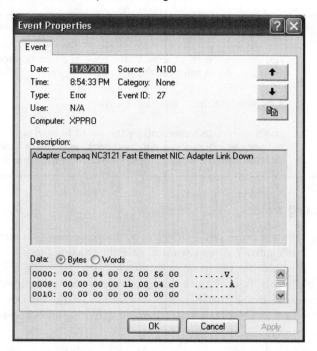

TABLE 14.3   Event Properties Dialog Box Items

Item	Description
Date	The date on which the event was generated.
Time	The time at which the event was generated.
Type	The type of event that was generated: Information, Warning, Error, Success Audit, or Failure Audit.
User	The name of the user to whom the event is attributed, if applicable (not all events are attributed to a user).
Computer	The name of the computer on which the event occurred.
Source	The software that generated the event (e.g., operating system components or drivers).
Category	The source that logged the event (this field will say "None" until this feature has been fully implemented in Windows XP).

TABLE 14.3 Event Properties Dialog Box Items *(continued)*

Item	Description
Event ID	The event number specific to the type of event generated (e.g., a print error event has the event ID 45).
Description	A detailed description of the event.
Data	The binary data generated by the event (if any; some events do not generate binary data) in hexadecimal bytes or DWORD format (programmers can use this information to interpret the event).

Managing Log Files

Over time, your log files will grow, and you will need to decide how to manage them. You can clear a log file for a fresh start. You may want to save the existing log file before you clear it, to keep that log file available for reference or future analysis.

To clear all log file events, right-click the log you wish to clear and choose Clear All Events from the pop-up menu. Then specify whether you want to save the log before it is cleared.

If you just want to save an existing log file, right-click that log and choose Save Log File As. Then specify the location and name of the file.

To open an existing log file, right-click the log you wish to open and choose Open Log File. Then specify the name and location of the log file and click the Open button.

Setting Log File Properties

Each Event Viewer log has two sets of properties associated with it:

General properties   Control items such as the log filename, its maximum size, and the action to take when the log file reaches its maximum size.

Filter properties   Specify which events are displayed.

To access the log Properties dialog box, right-click the log you want to manage and select Properties from the pop-up menu. The following sections describe the properties available on the General and Filter tabs of this dialog box.

General Properties

The General tab of the log Properties dialog box, shown in Figure 14.3, displays information about the log file and includes options to control its size. Table 14.4 describes the properties on the General tab.

 The Clear Log button in the General tab of the log Properties dialog box clears all log events.

FIGURE 14.3   The General properties for an Application log

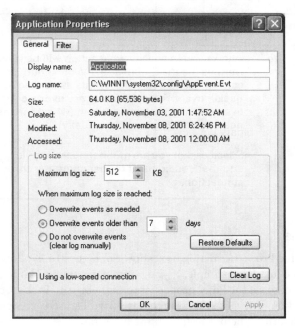

TABLE 14.4   General Log Properties

Property	Description
Display Name	Allows you to change the name of the log file. For example, if you are managing multiple computers and want to distinguish the logs for each computer, you can make the names more descriptive (e.g., SalesServer-App Log and MarketingServer-Security Log).
Log Name	Path and filename of the log file.
Size	Current size of the log file.
Created	Date and time when the log file was created.
Modified	Date and time when the log file was last modified.
Accessed	Date and time when the log file was last accessed.
Maximum Log Size	Allows you to specify the maximum size for the log file. You can use this option to prevent the log file from growing too large and taking up excessive disk space.

TABLE 14.4 General Log Properties *(continued)*

Property	Description
When Maximum Log Size Is Reached	Allows you to specify what action will be taken when the log file reaches the maximum size (if a maximum size is specified). You can choose to overwrite events as needed (on a first-in-first-out basis), overwrite events that are over a certain age, or prevent events from being overwritten (which means that you would need to clear log events manually).
Using a Low-Speed Connection	Specifies that you are monitoring the log file of a remote computer and that you connect to that computer through a low-speed connection.

Filter Properties

The Filter tab of the log Properties dialog box, shown in Figure 14.4, allows you to control the listing of events in the log. For example, if your system generates a large number of logged events, you might want to set the Filter properties so that you can track specific events. You can filter log events based on the event type, source, category, ID, users, computer, or specific time period. Table 14.5 describes the properties on the Filter tab.

FIGURE 14.4 The Filter properties for an Application log

TABLE 14.5   Filter Properties for Logs

Property	Description
Event Type	Allows you to list only the specified event types (Information, Warning, Error, Success Audit, or Failure Audit). By default, all event types are listed.
Event Source	Filters events based on the source of the event. The drop-down box lists the software that might generate events, such as Application Popup and DHCP. By default, events triggered by all sources are listed.
Category	Filters events based on the category that generated the event, such as Privilege Use. The drop-down box lists the event categories. By default, events in all categories are listed.
Event ID	Filters events based on a specific event number.
User	Filters events based on the user who caused the event to be triggered.
Computer	Filters events based on the name of the computer that generated the event.
From-To	Filters events based on the date and time when the events were generated. By default, events are listed from the first event to the last event. To specify specific dates and times, select Events On from the drop-down list and select dates and times.

In Exercise 14.1, you will view events in Event Viewer and set log properties.

EXERCISE 14.1

Using the Event Viewer Utility

1. Select Start ➢ Control Panel ➢ Performance and Maintenance ➢ Administrative Tools ➢ Event Viewer.

2. Click System Log in the left pane of the Event Viewer window to display the System log events.

3. Double-click the first event in the right pane of the Event Viewer window to see its Event Properties dialog box. Click the Cancel button to close the dialog box.

4. Right-click System Log in the left pane of the Event Viewer window and select Properties.

EXERCISE 14.1 *(continued)*

5. Click the Filter tab. Clear all the check marks under Event Types except those in the Warning and Error check boxes; then click the OK button. You should see only Warning and Error events listed in the System log.

6. To remove the filter, return to the Filter tab of the System Properties dialog box, click the Restore Defaults button at the bottom, and click the OK button. You should see all of the event types listed again.

7. Right-click System Log and select Clear All Events.

8. You see a dialog box asking if you want to save the System log before clearing it. Click the Yes button. Specify the path and filename for the log file, then click the Save button. All the events should be cleared from the System log.

 Real World Scenario

Using Event Viewer Logs for Problem Resolution

You are a senior network engineer for a company using specialized hardware and software that is run on Windows XP Professional computers in the field. One of your junior network engineers is on site in another state. She is reporting errors with your software and hardware but is not able to diagnose the problem.

You want to be able to troubleshoot the problem remotely if possible. One way that you can view a complete history of any informational, warning, or error messages is to have the on-site engineer send the log files to you or to another senior engineer. To do this for both the Application log and System log, the on-site engineer right-clicks on the log, selects Save Log File As, and saves the log file to a file that will automatically be given an .evt extension. These .EVT files can then be e-mailed to the more experienced engineer for problem resolution.

The Event Viewer is a handy utility because it lets you track information about your computer's hardware and software. You can also use it to monitor security events.

Understanding the Windows XP Professional Boot Process

When you are diagnosing a computer error, you first need to determine if the error is occurring when Windows XP Professional is loading, when Windows XP Professional is running, or when Windows XP Professional is shutting down. Some of the problems that cause system failure are related to the Windows XP Professional boot process. The boot process starts when you turn on your computer and ends when you log onto Windows XP Professional. The boot process your computer uses will depend on if your computer is *x*86-based or Itanium-based. If your computer is Itanium-based, then you will need to install the 64-bit version of Windows XP Professional.

There are many reasons why you might have startup failures. Some errors can be easily corrected, while others might require you to reinstall Windows XP Professional. Some of the errors that occur during the startup process are related to:

- User error in configuration
- Application errors
- Hardware failures—for example, the hard drive is failing
- Virus activity, which could damage or delete files or corrupt the Master Boot Record (MBR), partition table, or boot sector
- Incompatible or improperly configured hardware
- Corrupt or missing system files

Depending on whether your computer is using an *x*86-based or an Itanium-based processor, the boot process for will be slightly different. The following sections review the boot process for each platform.

Reviewing the *x*86-Based Boot Process

If you are running Windows XP Professional on an *x*86-based platform, which is the most common platform, the boot process consists of six major stages:

1. The pre-boot sequence
2. The boot sequence
3. Kernel load
4. Kernel initialization
5. Logon
6. Plug and Play device detection

Many files are used during these stages of the boot process. The following sections describe the steps in each boot process stage, the files used, and the errors that might occur.

The Pre-Boot Sequence

A normal boot process begins with the pre-boot sequence, in which your computer starts up and prepares for booting the operating system. In the following sections you will learn about the pre-boot sequence in greater detail.

File Accessed in the Pre-Boot Sequence

The computer will search for a boot device based on the boot order that was configured in the computer's CMOS settings. If the boot device is defined as the hard drive with the Windows XP

Professional system partition, then during the pre-boot sequence your computer accesses the *NTLDR* file. This file is used to control the Windows XP Professional boot process until control is passed to the NTOSKRNL file for the boot sequence. The NTLDR file is located in the root of the system partition. It has the file attributes of System, Hidden, and Read-only.

Steps in the Pre-Boot Sequence

The pre-boot sequence consists of the following steps:

1. When the computer is powered on, it runs a *Power-On Self-Test (POST)* routine. The POST detects the processor you are using, how much memory is present, what hardware is recognized, and whether the BIOS (Basic Input/Output System) is standard or has Plug-and-Play capabilities. The system also enumerates and configures hardware devices at this point.

2. The BIOS points to the boot device, and the *Master Boot Record (MBR)* is loaded.

3. The MBR points to the active partition. The active partition is used to specify the partition that should be used to boot the operating system. This is normally the C: drive. Once the MBR locates the active partition, the boot sector is loaded into memory and executed.

4. As part of the Windows XP Professional installation process, the NTLDR file is copied to the active partition. The boot sector points to the NTLDR file, and this file executes. The NTLDR file is used to initialize and start the Windows XP Professional boot process.

Possible Errors during the Pre-Boot Sequence

If you see errors during the pre-boot sequence, they are probably not related to Windows XP Professional, since the operating system has not yet been loaded. Table 14.6 lists symptoms and causes for pre-boot sequence errors.

TABLE 14.6   Pre-Boot Errors and Causes

Symptom	Possible Cause
Improperly configured hardware	If the POST cannot recognize your hard drive, the pre-boot stage will fail. This error is most likely to occur in a computer that is still being initially configured. If everything has been working properly and you have not made any changes to your configuration, a hardware error is unlikely.
Corrupt MBR	Viruses that are specifically designed to infect the MBR can corrupt it. You can protect your system from this type of error by using virus-scanning software. Also, most virus-scanning programs can correct an infected MBR.
No partition is marked as active	This can happen if you used the FDISK utility and did not create a partition using all of the free space. If the partition is FAT16 or FAT32 and on a basic disk, you can boot the computer to DOS or Windows 9x with a boot disk, run FDISK, and mark a partition as active. If you created your partitions as a part of the Windows XP Professional installation and have dynamic disks, marking an active partition is done for you during installation.

TABLE 14.6   Pre-Boot Errors and Causes *(continued)*

Symptom	Possible Cause
Corrupt or missing NTLDR file	If the NTLDR file does not execute, it may have been corrupted or deleted (by a virus or malicious intent).
SYS program run from DOS or Windows 9*x* after Windows XP Professional installation	The NTLDR file may not execute because the SYS program was run from DOS or Windows 9*x* after Windows XP Professional was installed. If you have done this, you should run the Repair option from the Windows XP Professional CD.

The Boot Sequence

When the pre-boot sequence is completed, the boot sequence begins. NTLDR switches the CPU to Protected Mode, which is used by Windows XP Professional, and starts the appropriate file systems. The contents of the BOOT.INI file are read and the information is used to build the initial boot menu selections. Then NTDETECT.COM file gathers the computer's basic hardware configuration data and passes the collected information back to NTLDR. The system also checks to see if more than one hardware profile is detected; if so, the hardware profile selection menu will be displayed as a part of the startup process. As a part of the boot sequence, your computer's firmware will also be checked for ACPI compatibility. If your computer is ACPI compatible, then ACPI features will be loaded onto the computer. In the following sections, you will learn about the boot sequence in greater detail.

Files Accessed in the Boot Sequence

Along with the NTLDR file, the following files are used during the boot sequence:

- *BOOT.INI* is used to build the operating system menu choices that are displayed during the boot process. It is also used to specify the location of the boot partition. This file is located in the root of the system partition. It has the file attributes of System and Hidden.

- *BOOTSECT.DOS* is an optional file that is loaded if you choose to load an operating system other than Windows XP Professional. It is only used in dual-boot or multi-boot computers. This file is located in the root of the system partition. It has the file attributes of System and Hidden.

- *NTDETECT.COM* is used to detect any hardware that is installed and add information about the hardware to the Registry. This file is located in the root of the system partition. It has the file attributes of System, Hidden, and Read-only.

- *NTBOOTDD.SYS* is an optional file that is used when you have a Small Computer Standard Interface (SCSI) adapter with the onboard BIOS disabled. (This option is not commonly implemented.) This file is located in the root of the system partition. It has the file attributes of System and Hidden.

- *NTOSKRNL.EXE* is used to load the Windows XP Professional operating system. This file is located in *Windir*\System32 and has no file attributes.

Steps in the Boot Sequence

The boot sequence consists of the following steps:

1. For the initial boot loader phase, NTLDR switches the processor from real mode to 32-bit flat memory mode and starts the appropriate mini file system drivers. Mini file system drivers are used to support your computer's file systems and include FAT16, FAT32, and NTFS.

2. For the operating system selection phase, the computer reads the BOOT.INI file. If you have configured your computer to dual-boot or multi-boot and Windows XP Professional recognizes that you have choices, a menu of operating systems that can be loaded is built. If you choose an operating system other than Windows XP Professional, the BOOTSECT.DOS file is used to load the alternate operating system, and the Windows XP Professional boot process terminates. If you choose a Windows XP Professional operating system, the Windows XP Professional boot process continues.

3. If you choose a Windows XP Professional operating system, the NTDETECT.COM file is used to perform hardware detection. Any hardware that is detected is added to the Registry, in the HKEY_LOCAL_MACHINE key. Some of the hardware that NTDETECT.COM will recognize includes communication and parallel ports, the keyboard, the floppy disk drive, the mouse, the SCSI adapter, and the video adapter.

4. Control is passed to NTOSKRNL.EXE to start the kernel load process.

Possible Errors during the Boot Sequence

Table 14.7 lists some common causes for errors during the boot stage:

TABLE 14.7 Boot Sequence Error Symptoms and Causes

Symptom	Possible Cause
Missing or corrupt boot files	If NTLDR, BOOT.INI, BOOTSECT.DOS, NTDETECT.COM, or NTOSKRNL.EXE is corrupt or missing (by a virus or malicious intent), the boot sequence will fail. You will see an error message that indicates which file is missing or corrupt.
Improperly configured BOOT.INI file	If you have made any changes to your disk configuration and your computer will not restart, chances are your BOOT.INI file is configured incorrectly. The BOOT.INI file is covered after the next sections about the boot process stages.
Unrecognizable or improperly configured hardware	If you have serious errors that cause NTDETECT.COM to fail, you should resolve the hardware problems. If your computer has a lot of hardware, remove all of the hardware that is not required to boot the computer. Add back the hardware one piece at a time, booting the computer after each piece is added. This will help you identify which piece of hardware is bad or is in conflict over a resource with another device.

The Kernel Load Sequence

All of the information that is collected by NTDETECT.com is passed to the NTOSKRNL.EXE file. In the kernel load sequence, the Hardware Abstraction Layer (HAL), computer control set, Registry information, and low-level device drivers are loaded. The NTOSKRNL.EXE file, which was described in the previous section, is used during this stage.

The kernel load sequence consists of the following steps:

1. The NTOSKRNL.EXE file is loaded and initialized.
2. The HAL is loaded.
3. The control set that the operating system will use is loaded. The control set is used to control system configuration information, such as a list of device drivers that should be loaded.
4. Low-level device drivers, such as disk drivers, are loaded.

If you have problems loading the Windows XP Professional kernel, you will most likely need to reinstall the operating system.

 The user will see a progress indicator at the bottom of the screen during the kernel load sequence.

The Kernel Initialization Sequence

In the kernel initialization sequence, the HKEY_LOCAL_MACHINE\HARDWARE Registry hive and Clone Control set are created, device drivers are initialized, and high-order subsystems and services are loaded.

The kernel initialization sequence consists of the following steps:

1. Once the kernel has been successfully loaded, the Registry key HKEY_LOCAL_MACHINE\HARDWARE is created. This Registry key is used to specify the hardware configuration of hardware components when the computer is started.
2. The Clone Control set is created. The Clone Control set is an exact copy of the data that is used to configure the computer and does not include changes made by the startup process.
3. The device drivers that were loaded during the kernel load phase are initialized.
4. Higher-order subsystems and services are loaded.

If you have problems during the kernel initialization sequence, you might try to boot to the Last Known Good Configuration, which is covered in the "Using Advanced Startup Options" section later in this chapter.

The Logon Sequence

In the logon sequence, the user logs on to Windows XP Professional and any remaining drivers and services are loaded.

The logon sequence consists of the following steps:

1. After the kernel initialization is complete, the Log On to Windows dialog box appears. At this point, you type in a valid Windows XP Professional username and password (or Active Directory name and password if the computer is a part of the domain and a domain user account has been created).

2. The service controller executes and performs a final scan of `HKEY_LOCAL_MACHINE\SYSTEM\CurrentControlSet\Services` to see if there are any remaining services that need to be loaded.

If logon errors occur, they are usually due to an incorrect username or password or to the unavailability of a domain controller to authenticate the request (if the computer is a part of a domain). See Chapter 6, "Managing Users and Groups," for more information about troubleshooting user authentication problems.

Errors can also occur if a service cannot be loaded. If a service fails to load, you will see a message in the System log of Event Viewer. Using the Event Viewer utility was covered earlier in this chapter.

Plug and Play Device Detection Phase

If Windows XP Professional has detected any new devices during the startup process, they will automatically be assigned system resources. If the device is Plug and Play and the needed driver can be obtained from the `DRIVER.CAB` file, they are extracted. If the needed driver files are not found, the user will be prompted to provide them. Device detection occurs asynchronously with the initial user logon process when the system is started.

Configuring the *BOOT.INI* File

If you are using an *x*86-based system, it is critical that the `BOOT.INI` file be configured properly. This file is created during the Windows XP Professional installation and is stored in the system root partition. The `BOOT.INI` file contains the information required by `NTLDR` to create and display the boot startup menu. The information that is contained in the `BOOT.INI` file includes:

- The path to the boot partition
- Descriptive text that should be displayed on the boot startup menu
- Optional parameters for managing computer startup
- Optional support for multiple boot configurations if other Microsoft operating systems have been installed in separate partitions

The `BOOT.INI` file contains two main sections for configuration: the Boot Loader and Operating Systems. Options that are configured in the Boot Loader section are applied to all Windows installations on the computer. Settings in the Operating Systems section are applied only to the specific Windows installation that is referenced within the Operating Systems section.

The following is an example of text that you might see in a `BOOT.INI` file.

```
[boot loader]
timeout=30
```

```
default=multi(0)disk(0)rdisk(0)partition(1) \Windows
[operating systems]
multi(0)disk(0)rdisk(0)partition(1) \Windows="Microsoft Windows XP
    Professional" /fastdetect
```

If you have only one operating system installed, and one entry under the Operating Systems section, then that option will be installed by default and you will not see a Boot Loader menu presented when the operating system is started.

In the following sections, you will learn about Boot Loader configuration options, ARC naming conventions, BOOT.INI operating system parameters, options for editing the BOOT.INI file, and how to replace a damaged BOOT.INI file.

Boot Loader Configuration Options

The parameters that can be configured within Boot Loader include Timeout and Default settings. The Timeout setting is used when the startup menu contains more than one option. In the event that more than one option exists, Timeout specifies how long the boot startup menu will be displayed. The Default setting specifies the default operating system that will be loaded in the event that no selection is made.

If you set Timeout=0, NTLDR will automatically load the default operating system selection, and no boot startup menu will be displayed. If you set Timeout=-1, NTLDR will display the Boot Loader menu indefinitely until the user makes an operating system selection manually.

ARC Naming Conventions

In the BOOT.INI file, the ARC path is used to specify the location of the boot partition within the disk channel. ARC names are made up of the information shown in Table 14.8.

TABLE 14.8   ARC Naming Conventions

ARC Path Option	Description
Multi (w) or scsi (w)	Identifies the type of disk controller that is being used by the system. The multi option is used by IDE controllers and SCSI adapters that use the SCSI BIOS. The scsi option is used by SCSI adapters that do not use the SCSI BIOS. The number (w) represents the number of the hardware adapter you are booting from.

TABLE 14.8   ARC Naming Conventions *(continued)*

ARC Path Option	Description
disk (x)	Indicates which SCSI adapter you are booting from if you use the scsi option. If you use multi, this setting is always 0.
Rdisk (y)	Specifies the number of the physical disk to be used. In an IDE environment, it is the ordinal of the disk attached to the controller and will always be a 0 or a 1. On a SCSI system, this is the ordinal number of the SCSI drive.
partition (z)	Specifies the partition number that contains the operating system files. The first partition is always 1.

As an example, the BOOT.INI file shown in the following text contains the following line:

multi(0)disk(0)rdisk(0)partition(1)\WINDOWS= "Microsoft Windows XP Professional"

This indicates that the boot partition is in the following location:

- multi(0) is an IDE controller or a SCSI controller with the BIOS enabled.
- disk(0) is 0 since the multi option was used.
- rdisk(0) specifies that the first disk on the controller is being used.
- partition(1) specifies that the system partition is on the first partition.
- \WINDOWS indicates the folder that is used to store the system files.
- "Microsoft Windows XP Professional" is what the user sees in the boot menu.

If you use the SCSI or Signature syntax with a disk controller with disabled firmware, you will be required to use NTBOOTDD.SYS. NTBOOTDD.SYS is a storage controller device driver and resides on the startup partition at the root.

You might also see the Signature syntax. Signature is similar to SCSI and is implemented when you have added drive controllers to your computer through Plug and Play associated with ATA or SCSI hard disks. The Signature syntax also indicates that the NTBOOTDD.SYS file is required to access the boot partition and one or both of the following conditions exist: In the first case, Windows XP Professional was installed on a disk partition that was greater than 7.8GB and the ending cylinder was higher than 1024 for the partition. In the second case, the system firmware or the BIOS for the startup controller can't gain access to the partition by using extended Interrupt 13 calls and/or the hard disk controller's BIOS has Interrupt 13 calls disabled. Because Windows XP uses Interrupt 13 calls for the startup process, the NTBOOTDD.SYS file is then required for boot partition access. Depending on the controllers you are using, the Signature option may increase the time it takes Windows XP Professional to boot.

BOOT.INI Operating System Parameters

When you edit your BOOT.INI file, you can add switches or options that allow you to control how the operating system is loaded. Table 14.9 defines the BOOT.INI switches.

TABLE 14.9 BOOT.INI Switches

Switch	Description
/3GB	Used for *x*86-based system to specify that the operating system can allocate up to 3GB of virtual address space for applications and 1GB for the kernel and executive components. The application must be designed to take advantage of the additional memory allocation.
/basevideo	Boots the computer using a standard VGA video driver (640×480 resolution with 16 colors). This option is used when you change your video driver and then cannot use the new driver. You can then remove, update, or roll back the video driver to proper settings.
/baudrate	Used in conjunction with kernel debugging. Specifies the baud rate that can be used, and must be used in conjunction with the /debug parameter. Settings can range from 9600Kbps (for modems) to 115,200Kbps for null modem cables.
/bootlog	Used to enable boot logging. The file that is created is called *systemroot*\Ntbtlog.txt.
/burnmemory=*number*	Specifies the amount of memory in megabytes that Windows XP Professional can't use. This parameter is used to confirm performance problems that are related to RAM depletion.
/crashdebug	Used to load the Kernel Debugger when the Windows XP Professional operating system is loaded. However, the kernel debugger will remain active until a Stop error occurs. This parameter is used to debug random stop kernel errors.
/debug	Specifies that the Kernel Debugger should be loaded with Windows XP Professional.
/debugport={*com1, com2,* or *1394*}	Used with the Kernel Debugger and specifies what communication port will be used for kernel debugging.
/fastdetect=com*x*	Keeps the computer from auto-detecting a serial mouse attached to a serial port with NTDETECT.COM.
/maxmem:*number*	Specifies the maximum amount of RAM that is recognized. This option is sometimes used in test environments where you want to analyze performance using different amounts of memory or if you are trying to identify a faulty memory component.

TABLE 14.9   BOOT.INI Switches *(continued)*

Switch	Description
/noguiboot	Boots Windows XP Professional without loading the GUI. With this option, a command prompt appears after the boot process ends.
/nodebug	Disables the Kernel Debugger.
/numproc=*number*	If your computer is using multiple processors, allows you to specify how many processors will be used.
/pciclock	Applies to *x*86-based systems and prevents the operating system from dynamically assigning hardware I/O and IRQs to PCI devices.
/safeboot:*parameter*	Forces a start in Safe Mode using one of the safeboot parameters such as Safe Mode with Networking or Safe Mode with Command Prompt. Safe Mode options are covered in greater detail later in this chapter.
/sos	Displays the name of each device driver as it is loaded. This is useful in troubleshooting if a driver is failing to load.

Editing the *BOOT.INI* File

By default, the BOOT.INI file is hidden. The following options can be used to edit the BOOT.INI file:

- BOOTCFG.EXE
- System Configuration Utility
- Control Panel
- Text editor (such as Notepad.exe)

 You should always make a copy of the BOOT.INI file before editing it. Improper edits can cause the operating system to not load.

Editing the *BOOT.INI* File with *BOOTCFG.EXE*

The BOOTCFG.EXE is a new command-line tool for viewing and editing the BOOT.INI file with Windows XP Professional and Windows Server 2003. The following command-line switches can be used in conjunction with the Bootcfg utility:

- /query is used to view the contents of the BOOT.INI file
- /copy makes a copy of existing boot entries for the Operating Systems section of the BOOT.INI file

- /delete is used to delete an entry from an existing boot entry in the Operating Systems section of the BOOT.INI file

Editing the *BOOT.INI* File with the System Configuration Utility

One of the easiest ways to edit the BOOT.INI file is with the System Configuration Utility. To access the System Configuration Utility, you select the Run dialog box and type **Msconfig**, then click the BOOT.INI tab to show the dialog box shown in Figure 14.5. Only administrators can make changes to configuration files through **Msconfig**.

FIGURE 14.5 The BOOT.INI tab of the System Configuration Utility dialog box

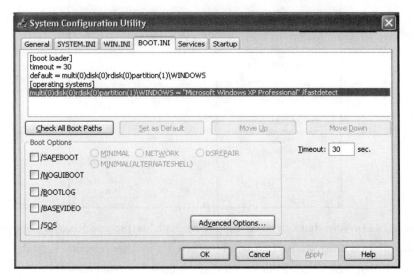

 When editing the BOOT.INI file with the System Configuration Utility, there is an option called Check All Boot Paths that will check all lines in your BOOT.INI file to see if anything has been misconfigured.

 The System Configuration Utility is covered in greater detail in the "Using the System Configuration Utility" section at the end of this chapter.

Editing the *BOOT.INI* File with Control Panel

Some of the options within the BOOT.INI file can be edited through the System applet in Control Panel. To access these settings, go to Start ➤ Control Panel ➤ Performance and Maintenance, then select System. From System, select the Advanced tab, then select Settings under Startup and Recovery to see the dialog box shown in Figure 14.6.

FIGURE 14.6   The Startup and Recovery dialog box

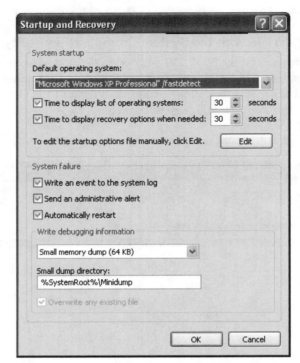

The BOOT.INI options that can be configured through Startup and Recovery options include:

- The default operating system that will be selected if no user selection is made
- The number of seconds (timeout value) that the boot loader menu will be displayed when the system is started
- The option to edit the BOOT.INI file in a Notepad text editor (enabled by clicking the Edit button)

Editing the *BOOT.INI* File with a Text Editor

Because the BOOT.INI file is marked with the System and Hidden attributes, it is not normally seen through Windows Explorer or the DOS DIR command. It is located at the root of the system partition, usually the C: drive. Once you modify the file attributes through Windows Explorer or the DOS Attrib command, you can edit the BOOT.INI file with a text editor. The System Configuration Utility is a much easier option for editing the BOOT.INI file than changing file attributes and using a text editor.

Replacing a Damaged *BOOT.INI* File

If you can't start Windows XP Professional on an *x*86-based system because the BOOT.INI file is damaged or missing, you can try to use the Automatic Recovery utility, or manually recover it. Each is discussed in the following sections.

Automatic Recovery

To use the Automatic Recovery utility, follow these steps:

1. Start the Recovery Console.
2. At the Recovery Console prompt, type **bootcfg /rebuild**.

Windows XP Professional will then scan the hard disk on your computer and rebuild the BOOT.INI file.

 The Bootcfg command that is used within Recovery Console is not the same as the Bootcfg command-line utility. The Automatic Recovery Utility is covered in greater detail later in this chapter.

Manual Recovery

To use the Recovery Console to create a new BOOT.INI file manually, you would take the following steps:

1. Start the Recovery Console.
2. At the Recovery Console prompt, type **map**.

A list will appear containing all of the hard disk and partition information for Windows XP Professional and any other Windows operating systems that are detected. This information can be used to correct or build a BOOT.INI file using a text editor, such as Notepad. You will not be able to edit the file with Recovery Console, since Recovery Console does not support text editing. You could edit the file on another computer, then replace it through Recovery Console.

Reviewing the Itanium Boot Process

If you are using an Itanium-based computer for Windows XP Professional, then the following boot process would apply:

1. Power-On Self-Test phase
2. Initial startup and the boot manager phase
3. Kernel load phase
4. Device drivers and service initialization phase
5. Logon phase
6. Plug and Play device detection phase

Each of the Itanium boot process phases (that are different than $x86$-based systems') are covered in greater detail in the following sections.

Power-On Self-Test Phase

Itanium-based computers use a POST process that is similar to $x86$-based systems. However, instead of using BIOS, Itanium-based systems use the Extensible Firmware Interface (EFI), which is a new model for defining the interface between the operating system and the platform firmware. The EFI performs rudimentary hardware checks and specifies and verifies which devices will be used to start the computer.

Initial Startup and the Boot Manager Phase

When the POST is complete, the boot manager, which is a part of the EFI, specifies which EFI drivers should be used, the EFI tool set that will be available to the user, and the EFI startup options that should be displayed. Depending on your Itanium-based system, the boot manager features will vary, and you should check the manufacturer's documentation for managing options such as performing system recovery tasks, restoring the boot manager startup window, and updating system firmware.

When Windows XP Professional is started, the boot manager will perform the following tasks:

- Read the EFI configuration settings, which specify the boot order sequence, which is specified in non-volatile memory (NVRAM). Settings in NVRAM are saved, even when the computer is turned off; this is the equivalent of CMOS settings on *x*86-based systems.

- Initialize the drivers that are needed to start Windows XP Professional. The configuration for storage devices, and any other required devices, is also stored in NVRAM. Device detection is also performed. Some of the devices that might be detected at this stage include:

  - Drive controllers (ATA or SCSI)
  - Storage devices
  - Keyboard
  - Video adapters
  - Network adapters

- Determine where the EFI system partition image has been stored. The EFI system partition holds the files required to start Windows XP Professional. The EFI system partition must be a minimum of 100MB and a maximum of 1000MB. The remaining system files for the *windir* folder (the \\Windows folder by default) must be stored on another partition.

- Locate the *windir* folder and the directories that contain the Windows XP Professional files.

- Locate and start the loader file, which is called IA64ldr.efi. The IA64ldr.efi file is responsible for starting the 64-bit Windows kernel.

 The BOOT.INI, NTDETECT.COM, and NTLDR files are not used on Itanium-based systems.

Kernel Load Phase

Instead of using the NTLDR file to load the kernel, Itanium-based systems use the IA64ldr.efi file to load the kernel (NTOSKRNL.EXE) and the HAL into memory.

Device Drivers and Service Initialization Phase

The process for loading device drivers and service initialization is similar to the process used by x86-based systems.

The Logon Sequence

The process for the logon sequence is similar to the process used by x86-based systems.

Plug and Play Device Detection Phase

The process for Plug and Play device detection is similar to the process used by x86-based systems.

Managing NVRAM Startup Settings

As noted previously, x86-based computers use the BOOT.INI file to track ARC paths for Windows startup. Itanium-based systems use NVRAM settings and the EFI boot manager to build the Windows XP Professional boot options. These settings can be managed through the BOOTCFG.EXE and NVRBOOT.EFI utilities.

BOOTCFG.EXE is used to change the startup parameters in NVRAM. NVRBOOT.EFI is a menu-driven utility and is used to restore boot manager setup options.

 Most Windows XP computers use x86-based computers. If you are using an Itanium-based computer, check the Microsoft website for detailed startup procedures.

Creating the Windows XP Boot Disk

To create a *Windows XP boot disk* for an x86-based computer, you would use the following process:

1. Format a floppy disk through the Windows XP Professional operating system.
2. Copy the following files from the Windows XP Professional system partition:

    NTLDR

    NTDETECT.COM

    NTBOOTDD.SYS (if you use SCSI controllers with the BIOS disabled)

    BOOT.INI

3. Test the boot disk by using it to boot to Windows XP Professional.

   After you create a Windows XP boot disk, you can use it to boot to the Windows XP Professional operating system in the event of a Windows XP Professional boot failure. If the BOOT.INI file for the computer has been edited, you will need to update the BOOT.INI file on your Windows XP boot disk.

WARNING The BOOT.INI file on the Windows XP Professional boot disk contains a specific configuration that points to the computer's boot partition. This might keep a Windows XP boot disk that was made on one computer from working on another computer.

In Exercise 14.2, you will create a Windows XP boot disk for an *x*86-based computer.

EXERCISE 14.2

Creating a Windows XP Boot Disk

1. Put a blank floppy disk in your floppy drive.

2. Select Start ➤ All Programs ➤ Accessories ➤ Windows Explorer.

3. In Windows Explorer, expand My Computer, right-click 3 1/2 Floppy (A:), and select Format. Accept all of the default options and click the Start button.

4. You see a dialog box warning you that all the data will be lost. Click the OK button.

5. When you see the Format Complete dialog box, click the OK button, and click the Close button to close the Format dialog box.

6. Select Start ➤ All Programs ➤ Accessories ➤ Command Prompt.

7. In the Command Prompt dialog box, type **ATTRIB** and press Enter. You see all of the files at the root of the C: drive. Note the file attributes of the NTLDR, NTDETECT.COM, and BOOT.INI files.

8. Type **ATTRIB NTLDR –S –H –R** and press Enter.

9. Type **COPY NTLDR A:** and press Enter.

10. Type **ATTRIB NTLDR +S +H +R** and press Enter.

11. Repeat steps 8 through 10 for the NTDETECT.COM and BOOT.INI files, to remove the file attributes, copy the file, and replace the file attributes. If you have a SCSI adapter with the BIOS disabled, you will also need to copy the NTBOOTDD.SYS file.

12. Verify that all of the files are on the boot disk by typing **DIR A:**.

13. Type **EXIT** to close the Command Prompt dialog box.

14. To test your Windows XP boot disk, select Start ➤ Shut Down ➤ Restart and click the OK button.

15. Label your Windows XP boot disk and put it in a safe place.

Using Advanced Startup Options

The Windows XP advanced startup options can be used to troubleshoot errors that keep Windows XP Professional from successfully booting.

 To access the Windows XP advanced startup options, press the F8 key when prompted during the beginning of the Windows XP Professional boot process. This will bring up the Windows XP Advanced Options menu, which offers numerous options for booting Windows XP. If Windows XP Professional starts without displaying the Boot Loader menu, you should press F8 after the firmware POST process, before Windows XP Professional displays graphical output, to access the Advanced Options menu.

These advanced startup options are covered in the following three sections.

Starting in Safe Mode

When your computer will not start, one of the fundamental troubleshooting techniques is to simplify the configuration as much as possible. This is especially important when you do not know the cause of your problem and you have a complex configuration. After you have simplified the configuration, you can determine whether the problem is in the basic configuration or is a result of your complex configuration. If the problem is in the basic configuration, you have a starting point for troubleshooting. If the problem is not in the basic configuration, you should proceed to restore each configuration option you removed, one at a time. This helps you to identify what is causing the error.

If Windows XP Professional will not load, you can attempt to load the operating system through *Safe Mode*. When you run Windows XP in Safe Mode, you are simplifying your Windows configuration as much as possible. Safe Mode loads only the drivers needed to get the computer up and running. The drivers that are loaded with Safe Mode include basic files and drivers for the mouse (unless you have a serial mouse), monitor, keyboard, hard drive, standard video driver, and default system services. Safe Mode is considered a diagnostic mode, so you do not have access to all of the features and devices in Windows XP Professional that you have access to when you boot normally, including networking capabilities.

A computer booted to Safe Mode will show "Safe Mode" in the four corners of your Desktop, as shown in Figure 14.7.

If you boot to Safe Mode, check all of your computer's hardware and software settings in Device Manager (which is covered in Chapter 4) and try to determine why Windows XP Professional will not boot properly. After you take steps to fix the problem, try to boot to Windows XP Professional as you normally would.

FIGURE 14.7 A computer running in Safe Mode

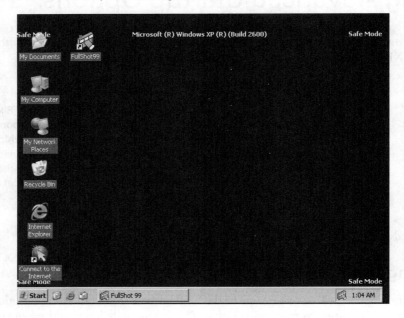

When you start your computer in Safe Mode, the following Registry hive is loaded: HKEY_LOCAL_MACHINE\SYSTEM\CurrentControlSet\Control\SafeBoot\ Minimal. When you start your computer in Safe Mode with networking, the following Registry hive is loaded: HKEY_LOCAL_MACHINE\SYSTEM\CurrentControlSet\ Control\SafeBoot\Network.

In Exercise 14.3, you will boot your computer to Safe Mode.

EXERCISE 14.3

Booting Your Computer to Safe Mode

1. If your computer is currently running, select Start ➤ Shutdown ➤ Restart.

2. During the boot process, press the F8 key to access the Windows XP Advanced Options menu. If you do not see the Boot Loader menu, which displays the operating system selections, press F8 after the firmware POST process and before Windows XP Professional displays graphical output, in order to access the Advanced Options menu.

3. Highlight Safe Mode and press Enter. Then log on as Administrator.

4. When you see the Desktop dialog box letting you know that Windows XP is running in Safe Mode, click the OK button.

EXERCISE 14.3 *(continued)*

5. Try accessing network resources in Windows Explorer. You should get an error message stating that you are unable to browse the network (because you are in Safe Mode). Click OK to close the error dialog box.
6. Select Start, then right-click My Computer and select Manage. The Computer Management window will open. Look in Device Manager to see if any devices are not working properly.
7. Don't restart your computer yet; you will do this as a part of the next exercise.

Enabling Boot Logging

Boot logging creates a log file that tracks the loading of drivers and services. When you choose the *Enable Boot Logging* option from the Advanced Options menu, Windows XP Professional loads normally, not in Safe Mode. This allows you to log all of the processes that take place during a normal boot sequence.

This log file can be used to troubleshoot the boot process. When logging is enabled, the log file is written to `\`*`Windir`*`\Ntbtlog.txt`. A sample of the `Ntbtlog.txt` file is shown in Figure 14.8.

FIGURE 14.8 The Windows XP boot log file

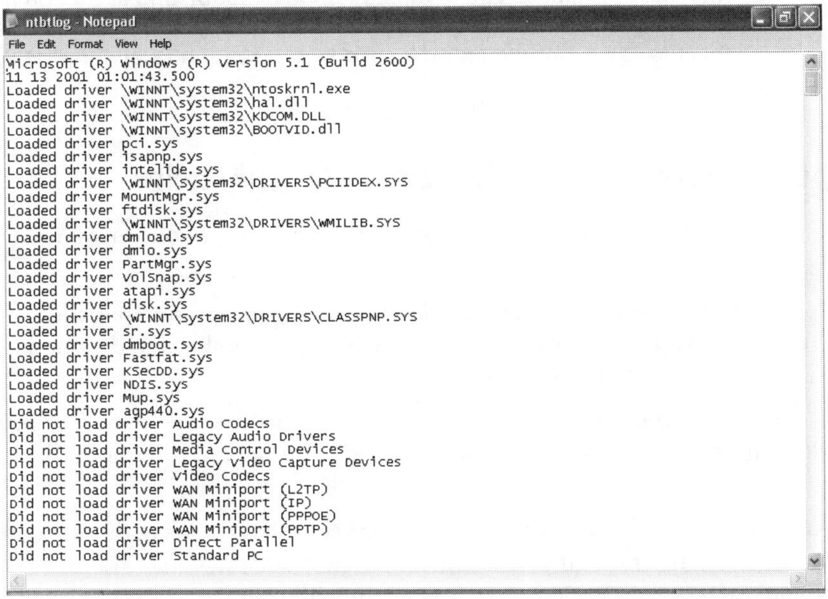


```
Microsoft (R) Windows (R) Version 5.1 (Build 2600)
11 13 2001 01:01:43.500
Loaded driver \WINNT\system32\ntoskrnl.exe
Loaded driver \WINNT\system32\hal.dll
Loaded driver \WINNT\system32\KDCOM.DLL
Loaded driver \WINNT\system32\BOOTVID.dll
Loaded driver pci.sys
Loaded driver isapnp.sys
Loaded driver intelide.sys
Loaded driver \WINNT\System32\DRIVERS\PCIIDEX.SYS
Loaded driver MountMgr.sys
Loaded driver ftdisk.sys
Loaded driver \WINNT\System32\DRIVERS\WMILIB.SYS
Loaded driver dmload.sys
Loaded driver dmio.sys
Loaded driver PartMgr.sys
Loaded driver VolSnap.sys
Loaded driver atapi.sys
Loaded driver disk.sys
Loaded driver \WINNT\System32\DRIVERS\CLASSPNP.SYS
Loaded driver sr.sys
Loaded driver dmboot.sys
Loaded driver Fastfat.sys
Loaded driver KSecDD.sys
Loaded driver NDIS.sys
Loaded driver Mup.sys
Loaded driver agp440.sys
Did not load driver Audio Codecs
Did not load driver Legacy Audio Drivers
Did not load driver Media Control Devices
Did not load driver Legacy Video Capture Devices
Did not load driver Video Codecs
Did not load driver WAN Miniport (L2TP)
Did not load driver WAN Miniport (IP)
Did not load driver WAN Miniport (PPPOE)
Did not load driver WAN Miniport (PPTP)
Did not load driver Direct Parallel
Did not load driver Standard PC
```

In Exercise 14.4, you will create and access a boot log file.

EXERCISE 14.4

Using Boot Logging

1.   Start your computer. If it is already running, select Start ➤ Shutdown ➤ Restart.

2.   During the boot process, press the F8 key to access the Windows XP Advanced Options menu. If you do not see the Boot Loader menu screen, press F8 after the firmware POST process, before Windows XP Professional displays graphical output, to access the Advanced Options menu.

3.   Highlight Enable Boot Logging and press Enter. Then log on as Administrator.

4.   Select Start ➤ All Programs ➤ Accessories ➤ Windows Explorer.

5.   In Windows Explorer, expand My Computer, then C:. Open the WINDOWS folder and double-click Ntbtlog.txt.

6.   Examine the contents of your boot log file.

7.   Shut down your computer and restart it without using Advanced Options.

The boot log file is cumulative. Each time you boot to any Advanced Options menu mode (except Last Known Good Configuration), you are writing to this file. This allows you to make changes, reboot, and see if you have fixed any problems. If you want to start from scratch, you should manually delete this file and reboot to an Advanced Options menu selection that supports logging.

Using Other Advanced Options Menu Modes

In this section, you will learn about the additional Advanced Options menu modes. These include:

Safe Mode with Networking   This is the same as the Safe Mode option but adds networking features. You might use this mode if you need networking capabilities to download drivers or service packs from a network location.

Safe Mode with Command Prompt   This starts the computer in Safe Mode, but instead of loading the Windows XP graphical interface, it loads a command prompt. Experienced troubleshooters use this mode.

Enable VGA Mode   This loads a standard VGA driver without starting the computer in Safe Mode. You might use this mode if you changed your video driver, did not test it, and tried to boot to Windows XP with a bad driver that would not allow you to access video. The Enable VGA Mode bails you out by loading a default driver, providing access to video so that you can properly install (and test!) the correct driver for your computer.

When you boot to any Safe Mode, you automatically use VGA mode.

Last Known Good Configuration   This boots Windows XP using the Registry information that was saved the last time the computer was successfully booted. You would use this option to restore configuration information if you have improperly configured the computer and have not successfully rebooted the computer. When you use the Last Known Good Configuration option, you lose any system configuration changes that were made since the computer last successfully booted.

Debugging Mode   This runs the Kernel Debugger, if it is installed. The Kernel Debugger is an advanced troubleshooting utility.

Boot Normally   This boots to Windows XP in the default manner, which means you are not using any of the Advanced Startup options. This option is on the Advanced Options menu in case you accidentally hit F8 during the boot process, but really wanted to boot Windows XP normally.

Windows 2000 and Windows XP handle startup options slightly differently from Windows NT 4. In Windows NT 4, the boot loader menu shows an option to load VGA Mode, which appears each time you restart the computer. In Windows XP, this has been moved to the Advanced Options menu to present the user with a cleaner boot process. Also, in Windows NT 4, you need to press the spacebar as a part of the boot process to access the Last Known Good Configuration option.

Using Driver Rollback

Windows XP Professional and Windows Server 2003 offer a new feature call *driver rollback*. You would use driver rollback if you installed or upgraded a driver and you encountered problems that you did not have with the previous driver. Some of the problems with drivers relate to the following errors:

- Use of unsigned drivers
- Resource conflicts
- Badly written drivers

The following steps would be used to roll back a driver:

1. Select Start ➤ Control Panel ➤ Performance and Maintenance ➤ System.
2. From the System Properties dialog box, select the Hardware tab, then select Device Manager.
3. Expand the category for the device driver you want to roll back—for example, a network card—then double-click the device and select the Driver tab, as shown in Figure 14.9. From the Driver tab, click the Roll Back Driver option.

FIGURE 14.9   Driver tab of a device's Properties in Device Manager

4. You will be prompted to confirm that you want to overwrite the current driver. Click the Yes button. The rollback process will proceed or you will be notified that an older driver was not available for rollback.

> The System Properties dialog box can be opened from the Start menu by selecting Run and then typing in **sysdm.cpl**.

Using Startup and Recovery Options

The Startup and Recovery options (see Table 14.10) are used to specify the default operating system that is loaded and to specify which action should be taken in the event of system failure. You can access the Startup and Recovery options from the Start menu, then right-click My Computer and choose Properties. Click the Advanced tab; under Startup and Recovery, click the Settings button. Alternatively, select Start ➢ Control Panel ➢ Performance and Maintenance ➢ See Basic Information About Your Computer ➢ Advanced tab ➢ Startup and Recovery ➢ Settings. You will see the dialog box shown in Figure 14.10.

FIGURE 14.10   The Startup and Recovery dialog box

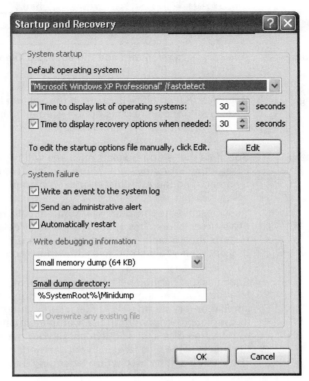

TABLE 14.10   Startup and Recovery Options

Option	Description
Default Operating System	Specifies the operating system that is loaded by default if no selection is made from the operating system selection menu (if your computer dual-boots or multi-boots and an operating system selection menu appears during bootup). The default setting for this option is Microsoft Windows XP Professional.
Time to Display List of Operating Systems	Specifies how long the operating system selection menu is available before the default selection is loaded (if your computer dual-boots or multi-boots and an operating system selection menu appears during bootup). The default setting for this option is 30 seconds.
Time to Display Recovery Options When Needed	Specifies how long the advanced recovery options selection menu will be displayed if the computer cannot start properly. The default setting for this option is 30 seconds.

TABLE 14.10 Startup and Recovery Options *(continued)*

Option	Description
Edit the Startup Options File Manually	Allows you to open and edit the BOOT.INI file via a text editor.
Write an Event to the System Log	Specifies that an entry is made in the System log any time a system failure occurs. This option is enabled by default, which allows you to track system failures.
Send an Administrative Alert	Specifies that a pop-up alert message will be sent to the Administrator any time a system failure occurs. This option is enabled by default, so the Administrator is notified of system failures.
Automatically Restart	Specifies that the computer will automatically reboot in the event of a system failure. This option is enabled by default, so the system restarts after a failure without intervention. You would disable this option if you wanted to see the blue screen for analysis.
Write Debugging Information	Specifies that debugging information (a memory dump) is written to a file. You can choose not to create a dump file or to create a small memory dump (64KB) file, a kernel memory dump file, or a complete memory dump file. Complete memory dump files require free disk space equivalent to your memory, and a page file that is at least as large as your memory with an extra 2MB. The default setting is to write debugging information to a small memory dump file.
Overwrite Any Existing File	If you create dump files, this option allows you to create a new dump file that overwrites the old dump file, or to keep all dump files each time a system failure occurs.

In Exercise 14.5, you will access the Startup and Recovery options and make changes to the settings.

EXERCISE 14.5

Using Startup and Recovery Options

1. Select Start, then right-click My Computer and choose Properties. Click the Advanced tab, then under Startup and Recovery, click the Settings button.

2. Change the setting for Display List of Operating Systems from 30 seconds to 10 seconds.

3. In the Write Debugging Information section, choose (None) from the drop-down list.

4. Click the OK button to close the Startup and Recovery dialog box.

Using the Dr. Watson Utility

The *Dr. Watson* utility detects and displays information about system and program failures. When an application error occurs, Dr. Watson will run automatically and you will see a pop-up message letting you know that an application error has occurred. (You can also access Dr. Watson by invoking the *DRWTSN32* command.) Application developers can use the Dr. Watson utility to debug their programs. When an application encounters an error or crashes, Dr. Watson can display the application error and dump the contents of memory into a file.

Although average users will not be able to determine what is wrong with an application by looking at a memory dump file, they might be asked to configure a memory dump so that it can be sent to an application developer for analysis. The information collected by Dr. Watson is stored in a log file that can be viewed at any time.

To access Dr. Watson, select Start ➤ Run and type **Drwtsn32**. The main dialog box for Dr. Watson is shown in Figure 14.11. The Application Errors box at the bottom of the dialog box displays any program errors that Dr. Watson encountered. Above this section are the options that can be configured through Dr. Watson, which are described in Table 14.11.

FIGURE 14.11   The Dr. Watson for Windows dialog box

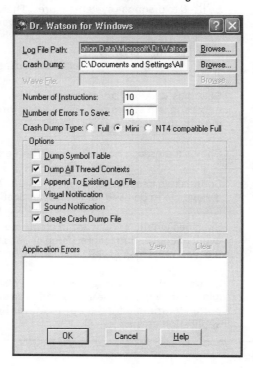

T A B L E   1 4 . 1 1   Dr. Watson Configuration Options

Option	Description
Log File Path	Location of the log file that contains application error information.
Crash Dump	Location of the memory dump file that is created when an application crashes (if you choose to create a crash dump file).
Wave File	WAV sound file to execute when an error occurs.
Number of Instructions	Maximum number of instructions, or threads, that Dr. Watson can track.
Number of Errors to Save	Maximum number of errors that Dr. Watson can store within the dump file.
Crash Dump Type	Specifies the format that Dr. Watson will use to create the dump file. Options include Full and Mini dumps and NT 4 compatible Full, which allows you to use older, Windows NT 4 debugging tools.
Dump Symbol Table	Specifies that the symbol table should be included in the dump file. Symbol files provide more verbose information, which can be used to diagnose system failures. The drawback of this option is that it can cause the log file to grow very quickly.
Dump All Thread Contexts	Specifies whether Dr. Watson will dump all threads to the memory dump, or dump only the thread that caused the application failure.
Append to Existing Log File	Specifies whether Dr. Watson will create a new log file for new program errors or append log information to the existing log file.
Visual Notification	Shows a message box with a program error notification.
Sound Notification	Sounds two beeps when an error occurs. You can also configure a wave file to be used for sound notification.
Create Crash Dump File	Specifies whether you want to create a crash dump file in the event of application failure. If you choose to create a crash dump file, you must also specify a crash dump location.
Application Errors	Lists all of the program errors that Dr. Watson has logged for the computer. You can click an application error and then click the View button for more information. The Clear button clears all saved application errors.

The difference between setting Startup and Recovery options and running the Dr. Watson utility is that Startup and Recovery options are used to diagnose operating system problems. The Dr. Watson utility, on the other hand, is used to diagnose application errors.

Using the Backup Utility

The *Windows XP Backup* utility allows you to create and restore backups. Backups protect your data in the event of system failure by storing the data on another medium, such as another hard disk or a tape. If your original data is lost due to corruption, deletion, or media failure, you can restore the data using your backup. *System State data* includes the Registry, the COM+ registration database, and the system boot files.

To access the Backup utility, select Start ➤ All Programs ➤ Accessories ➤ System Tools ➤ Backup. In the Welcome to the Backup or Restore Wizard dialog box, select the Advanced Mode option. This brings up the Backup Utility window, as shown in Figure 14.12.

FIGURE 14.12   The Advanced Mode window of the Backup Utility

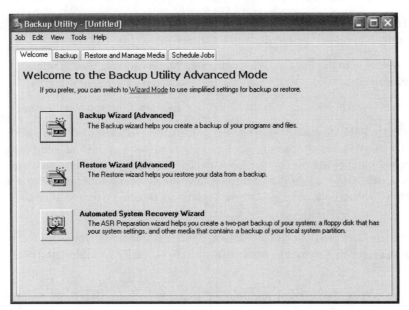

From this window, you can start the Backup Wizard, the Restore Wizard, or the Automated System Recovery Wizard. These options, as well as some additional backup options, are all covered in the following sections.

External tape drives, which attach to your parallel port, are not supported by the Windows XP Professional operating system when using the Backup utility. However, you can use third-party backup software to support this configuration.

Using the Backup Wizard

The *Backup Wizard* takes you through all the steps that are required for a successful backup. Before you start the Backup Wizard, be sure you are logged on as an Administrator or a member of the Backup Operators group.

In Exercise 14.6, you will use the Backup Wizard to make a sample backup of files. You will need a blank formatted, high-density floppy disk for this exercise.

EXERCISE 14.6

Using the Backup Wizard

1. Create a folder on your D: drive called DATA. Create some small text files in this folder. The size of all the files combined should not exceed 1MB.

2. Select Start ➢ All Programs ➢ Accessories ➢ System Tools ➢ Backup. Click the Advanced Mode option to open the main Backup Utility screen.

3. In the Welcome to the Backup Utility Advanced Mode window, click the Backup Wizard (Advanced) button.

4. The Welcome to the Backup Wizard dialog box appears. Click the Next button.

5. The What to Back Up dialog box appears. This dialog box allows you to select what you will back up. You can choose to back up everything; back up just selected files, drives, or network data; or back up only the System State data. System State data includes the Registry, the COM+ registration database, and the system boot files. For this example, select the Back Up Selected Files, Drives, or Network Data radio button, then click the Next button.

6. The Items to Back Up dialog box appears. Check the items that you want to back up (in this case, select My Computer, expand D:, and check the DATA folder) and click the Next button.

7. The Backup Type, Destination, and Name dialog box appears. Select the destination for your backup in the Choose a place to save your backup. You can select from drop-down selections or click the Browse button to locate it.

8. Click the Browse button, which brings up the Open dialog box. Select the drive (in this case, your floppy drive), give your backup a filename (for example, you might use the date as the filename), and click the Save button.

9. When you return to the wizard's Backup Type, Destination, and Name page, make sure your backup media or filename path is correct, and click the Next button. In the Completing the Backup Wizard page, make sure all the information is correct and click the Finish button. (Clicking the Advanced button in the Completing the Backup Wizard dialog box brings up a dialog box that allows you to specify the type of backup: Normal, Copy, Incremental, Differential, or Daily. These are discussed in detail in the section "Selecting a Backup Type" below.)

10. During the backup process, the wizard displays the Backup Progress dialog box. Once the backup process is complete, you can click the Report button in this dialog box to see details of the backup session.

Configuring Backup Options

You can configure specific backup configurations by selecting backup options. To access these options, start the Backup utility and select Tools ➢ Options. In the Options dialog box that appears, you'll have five tabs: General, Restore, Backup Type, Backup Log, and Exclude Files. The following sections describe the options on these tabs, used for controlling the backup and restore processes.

Configuring General Backup Options

The General tab, as seen in Figure 14.13, contains options for configuring backup sessions. Table 14.12 describes these options.

FIGURE 14.13 The General tab of the Backup utility's Options dialog box

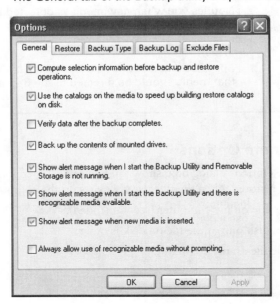

TABLE 14.12 General Backup Options

Option	Description
Compute selection information before backup and restore operations.	Estimates the number of files and bytes that will be backed up or restored during the current operation and displays this information prior to the backup or restore operation.
Use the catalogs on the media to speed up building restore catalogs on disk.	Specifies that you want to use an on-media catalog to build an on-disk catalog, which can be used to select the folders and files to be restored during a restore operation.
Verify data after the backup completes.	Makes sure that all data has been backed up properly.
Back up the contents of mounted drives.	Specifies that the data should be backed up on mounted drives; otherwise, only path information on mounted drives is backed up.
Show alert message when I start the Backup utility and Removable Storage is not running.	Notifies you if Removable Storage is not running (when you are backing up to tape or other removable media).
Show alert message when I start the Backup utility and there is recognizable media available.	Notifies you when you start Backup if new media has been added to the Removable Storage import pool.
Show alert message when new media is inserted.	Notifies you when new media is detected by Removable Storage.
Always allow use of recognizable media without prompting.	Specifies that if new media is detected by Removable Storage, that media should be directed to the Backup media pool.

Configuring Restore Options

The Restore tab of the Options dialog box, shown in Figure 14.14, contains three options that relate to how files are restored when the file already exists on the computer:

- Do not replace the file on my computer (recommended).
- Replace the file on disk only if the file on disk is older.
- Always replace the file on my computer.

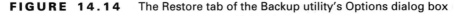

FIGURE 14.14   The Restore tab of the Backup utility's Options dialog box

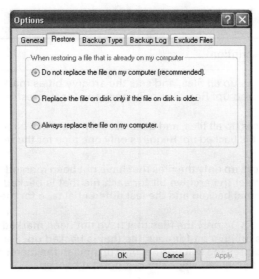

Selecting a Backup Type

In the Backup Type tab (Figure 14.15), you can specify the default backup type that will be used. You should select this default backup type based on the following criteria:

- How much data you are backing up
- How quickly you want to be able to perform the backup
- The number of tapes you are willing to use should you need to perform a restore operation

FIGURE 14.15   The Backup Type tab of the Backup utility's Options dialog box

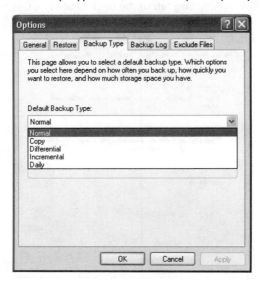

Table 14.13 describes the backup type options.

TABLE 14.13 Backup Type Options

Option	Description
Normal	Backs up all files, and sets the archive bit as marked for each file that is backed up. Requires only one tape for the restore process.
Copy	Backs up all files, and does not set the archive bit as marked for each file that is backed up. Requires only one tape for the restore process.
Differential	Backs up only the files that have not been marked as archived, and does not set the archive bit for each file that is backed up. Requires the last normal backup and the last differential tape for the restore process.
Incremental	Backs up only the files that have not been marked as archived, and sets the archive bit for each file that is backed up. For the restore process, requires the last normal backup and all the incremental tapes that have been created since the last normal backup.
Daily	Backs up only the files that have been changed today and does not set the archive bit for each file that is backed up. Requires each daily backup and the last normal backup for the restore process.

Setting Backup Log Options

The Backup Log tab (Figure 14.16) allows you to specify the amount of information that is logged during the backup process. Table 14.14 describes the backup log options.

FIGURE 14.16 The Backup Log tab of the Backup utility's Options dialog box

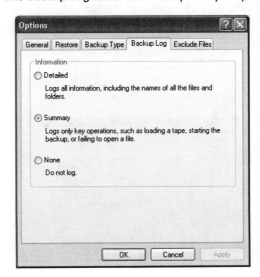

TABLE 14.14   Backup Log Options

Option	Description
Detailed	Logs all information, including the names of the folders and files that are backed up.
Summary	Logs only key backup operations, such as starting the backup.
None	Specifies that a log file will not be created.

Excluding Files

Use the Exclude Files tab of the Options dialog box (Figure 14.17) to explicitly exclude specific files during the backup process. For example, you might choose to exclude the page file or application files by clicking the Add New button and selecting the files you want to be excluded. The top of the dialog box allows you to specify the files that will be excluded for all users of the computer. The bottom of the dialog box allows you to exclude files that will not be backed up for the current user.

FIGURE 14.17   The Exclude Files tab of the Backup utility's Options dialog box

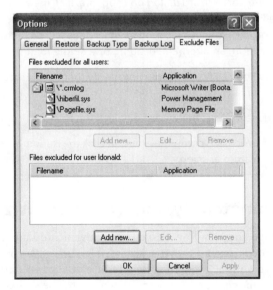

Using the Restore Wizard

Having a complete backup won't help you if your system should fail, unless you can successfully restore that backup. To be sure that you can restore your data, you should test the restoration process before anything goes wrong. You can use the *Restore Wizard* for testing purposes, as well as when you actually need to restore your backup.

In Exercise 14.7, you will use the Restore Wizard.

EXERCISE 14.7

Using the Restore Wizard

1. Select Start ➢ All Programs ➢ Accessories ➢ System Tools ➢ Backup. Click the Advanced Mode option to open the main Backup utility screen.

2. In the Welcome to the Backup Utility Advanced Mode window, click the Restore Wizard (Advanced) button.

3. The Welcome to the Restore Wizard dialog box appears. Click the Next button.

4. The What to Restore dialog box appears next. Click the filename of the backup session that you want to restore (in this case, the file backup session you created in Exercise 14.6). Click the Next button. After you select the backup you want to restore, you can choose to restore the entire session, or you can selectively restore drives, folders, or files from the backup session.

5. The Completing the Restore Wizard dialog box appears. If all the configuration information is correct, click the Finish button. (Clicking the Advanced button here brings up another dialog box where you can choose a location to which files will be restored. You can choose from the original location, an alternate location, or a single folder.)

6. Next, in the Enter Backup File Name dialog box, verify that the correct filename is specified and click the OK button.

7. During the restoration process, the wizard displays the Restore Progress dialog box.

8. Once the restoration process is complete, you can click the Report button in this dialog box to see details of the restore session.

Using the Automated System Recovery Wizard

Windows XP Professional and Windows Server 2003 now include a new feature of the Backup utility called the Automated System Recovery Wizard. The *Automated System Recovery Wizard* is used for system recovery in the event of system failure. It is a two-part system recovery that consists of a backup component and a restore component. The system information that is backed up by ASR includes System State data, system services, and disk configuration information (information about basic and dynamic disks and the file signature associated with each disk).

This utility is only used to back up system data and does not back up folders and files.

WARNING   You should only use the Automated System Recovery Wizard for system recovery after you have tried to boot the computer to Safe Mode and used the Last Known Good Configuration option. You should always try the easiest and less invasive methods of recovery before trying more complex recovery options.

In Exercise 14.8, you will create an Automated System Recovery backup. You will need some form of backup media, a 1.44MB floppy disk, and a Windows XP Professional distribution CD.

EXERCISE 14.8

Using the Automated System Recovery Wizard

Create an Automated System Recovery backup

1. Select Start ➢ All Programs ➢ Accessories ➢ System Tools ➢ Backup. Click the Advanced Mode option to open the main Backup utility screen.

2. Select Tools ➢ ASR Wizard.

3. The Automated System Recovery Preparation Wizard will start. Click the Next button to continue.

4. The Backup Destination dialog box will appear. Specify the location of your backup media and click the Next button.

Perform an Automated System Recovery restore

5. Boot your computer using the Windows XP Professional CD. During the boot process, you may need to press a specified key (based on your computer's BIOS) to boot the computer from CD.

6. Press F2 when prompted during the text-mode portion of the Windows XP Setup process to initiate the recovery process. You will be prompted to insert the ASR floppy disk. Insert the disk and press any key.

7. You have only a few seconds to cancel the recovery by hitting the Esc key. Otherwise, the system reformats the C drive automatically. After the format is complete, the Automated System Recovery Wizard begins an installation process very similar to the initial Windows XP installation.

8. After the XP files are copied to the hard drive and the computer reboots, the Windows XP setup procedure continues. During the procedure, the Automated System Recovery Wizard appears automatically and prompts you for the backup location. Select the correct backup location to complete the wizard and continue with the normal setup process. At the end of the Automated System Recovery process, the Backup utility will open automatically and restore the system.

Using System Restore

Windows XP Professional offers a new feature called System Restore. The System Restore utility monitors a computer for changes and creates restore points that can be used to restore the computer to a previous configuration. Restore points are automatically created on a daily basis and any time significant changes are made to your computer.

System Restore is used for the following:

- To restore your computer to a previous state
- To restore your computer without losing personal files
- To store one to three weeks of past restore points
- To keep dates associated with restore points
- To make restorations possible
- To offer several types of restore points

By default, System Restore is enabled. You can manage the settings through Control Panel ≻ Performance and Maintenance. Under See Also, select System Restore, or alternatively through Start ≻ All Programs ≻ Accessories ≻ System Tools ≻ System Restore. This brings up the dialog box shown in Figure 14.18.

FIGURE 14.18 The System Restore dialog box

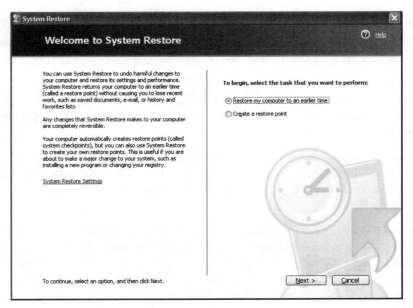

In Exercise 14.9, you will use the System Restore Wizard to create a restore point and to restore your computer's configuration to an earlier time. Before you start, you should close any programs that are currently open on the computer.

EXERCISE 14.9

Using the System Restore Wizard

1. Select Start ➤ All Programs ➤ Accessories ➤ System Tools ➤ System Restore.

2. The Welcome to the System Restore dialog box appears. Click the Create a Restore Point radio button and click the Next button.

3. The Create a Restore Point dialog box will appear. Type in the name you want to use for the restore point. The date and time will automatically be added to the restore point. Click the Create button.

4. The Restore Point Created dialog box will appear. Click the Home button.

5. On the Welcome to System Restore dialog box, click the Restore My Computer To an Earlier Time radio button and click the Next button.

6. The Select a Restore Point dialog box will appear. Select the restore point that you will restore to and click the Next button.

7. The Confirm a Restore Point Selection screen will appear. If the restore point is correct, click the Next button. Your computer will restart. After restarting you will see a confirmation screen that the restoration is complete. Click the OK button, and the computer is rolled back to the restore point.

Using the Recovery Console

If your computer will not start, and you have tried unsuccessfully to boot to Safe Mode, there's one more option you can try. The *Recovery Console* is designed for administrators and advanced users. It allows you limited access to FAT16, FAT32, and NTFS volumes without starting the Windows XP Professional graphical interface.

Through the Recovery Console, you can perform the following tasks:

- Copy, replace, or rename operating system files and folders. You might have to do this if your boot failure is caused by missing or corrupt files.

- Enable or disable the loading of services when the computer is restarted. If a particular service may be keeping the operating system from booting, you could disable the service. If a particular service is required for successful booting, you want to make sure that the service is configured to start automatically.

- Repair the file system boot sector or the MBR. You might use this option if a virus may have damaged the system boot sector or the MBR.

- Create and format partitions on the drives. You might use this option if your disk utilities will not delete or create Windows XP partitions. Normally, you use a disk-partitioning utility for these functions.

In the following sections, you will learn how to access and use the Recovery Console.

Starting the Recovery Console

You can add the Recovery Console to your computer from the Windows XP Professional CD or as a startup option. These options are covered in the following sections.

Starting the Recovery Console with the Windows XP CD

To use the Recovery Console from the Windows XP CD, follow these steps:

1. Restart your computer using the Windows XP Professional distribution CD.
2. When prompted, press any key to boot from the CD.
3. In the Welcome to Setup dialog box, press the **R** key to repair a Windows XP installation.
4. From the Windows XP Repair Options menu, press 1 to repair Windows XP using the Recovery Console. You will then be prompted to supply the Administrator password. The Windows XP Recovery Console will start.

 See the section "Working with the Recovery Console," coming up, for details on using the Recovery Console.

Adding the Recovery Console to Windows XP Startup

You can add the Recovery Console to the Windows XP Professional startup options so it will be available in the event of a system failure. This configuration takes about 7MB of disk space to hold the CMDCONS folder and files. To set up this configuration, follow these steps:

1. Insert the Windows XP Professional CD into your CD-ROM drive. You can disable auto-play by pressing the Shift key as the CD is read. From the command prompt, type **cd I386** and press Enter. Then type **WINNT32 /CMDCONS**.
2. The Windows XP Setup dialog box appears, asking you to confirm that you want to install the Recovery Console. Click the Yes button.
3. The installation files will be copied to your computer. Then you will see a dialog box letting you know that the Recovery Console has been successfully installed. Click the OK button to continue.

The next time you restart your computer, you will see an option for the Microsoft Windows XP Recovery Console. You will learn how to use the Recovery Console in the next section.

In Exercise 14.10, you will add the Recovery Console to the Windows XP startup options. You will need the Windows XP Professional distribution CD for this exercise.

EXERCISE 14.10

Adding Recovery Console to Windows XP Startup

1. Insert the Windows XP Professional distribution CD in your CD-ROM drive. Hold down the Shift key as the CD is read, to prevent auto-play.

2. Select Start ➤ All Programs ➤ Accessories ➤ Command Prompt.

3. Change the drive letter to your CD-ROM drive.

4. From the CD drive letter prompt (*x:\\>*), type **CD I386** and press Enter.

5. From *x:\I386>*, type **WINNT32 /CMDCONS**.

6. In the Windows XP Setup dialog box, click the Yes button to confirm that you want to install the Recovery Console.

7. After the installation files are copied to your computer, a dialog box appears to let you know that the Recovery Console has been successfully installed. Click the OK button.

8. Shut down and restart your computer. In the Startup selection screen, select the option for Microsoft Windows XP Recovery Console.

9. At the command prompt, type **EXIT** to close the Recovery Console. You will return to the Windows Desktop.

Working with the Recovery Console

After you add the Recovery Console, you can access it by restarting your computer. In the Boot Loader menu, you will see an option for Microsoft Windows XP Recovery Console. Select this option to start the Recovery Console.

WARNING
Use the Recovery Console with extreme caution. Improper use may cause even more damage than the problems you are trying to fix—such as the computer not booting, requiring a complete reinstallation of the Windows XP Professional operating system.

The Recovery Console presents you with a command prompt and very limited access to system resources. This keeps unauthorized users from using the Recovery Console to access sensitive data. The following are the only folders you can access through the Recovery Console:

- The root folder
- The *Windir* folder and the subfolders of the Windows XP Professional installation
- The CMDCONS folder
- Removable media drives such as CD-ROM drives

If you try to access any other folders besides the ones listed above, you will receive an "access denied" error message.

In the Recovery Console, you cannot copy files from a local hard disk to a floppy disk. You can only copy files from a floppy disk or CD to a hard disk, or from one hard disk to another hard disk. This is for security purposes.

The first option you must specify is which Windows XP operating system you will log onto. Next, you must specify the Administrator password for the system you are logging onto. When the Recovery Console starts, you can use the commands defined in Table 14.15 (you can see a full list of supported commands by typing Help at the console prompt):

TABLE 14.15   Commands Available with the Recovery Console

Command	Description
ATTRIB	Used to set file attributes. You can set file attributes for Read-only (R), System (S), Hidden (H), or Compressed (C).
BATCH	Used to execute commands in a specified input file.
BOOTCFG	Used to view or configure BOOT.INI settings.
CHDIR (or you can use CD)	Used to navigate the directory structure. If executed without a directory name, the current directory is displayed. (CHDIR and CD work the same way.)
CLS	Used to clear any text that is currently displayed on the console.
CHKDSK	Used to check the disk and display a disk status report.
COPY	Used to copy a single file from one location to another. COPY does not support wildcards and does not copy files to removable media (such as floppy disks).
DELETE (DEL)	Used to delete a single file. Wildcards are not supported. (DELETE and DEL work the same way.)
DIR	Used to display lists of files and subdirectories in the current directory.
DISABLE	Used to disable Windows XP Professional system services and drivers.
DISKPART	Used to manage disk partitions. If executed without a command-line argument, a user interface is displayed.
ENABLE	Used to enable Windows XP Professional system services and drivers.
EXIT	Used to quit the Recovery Console and restart the computer.
EXPAND	Used to expand compressed files.

TABLE 14.15   Commands Available with the Recovery Console *(continued)*

Command	Description
FIXBOOT	Used to write a new boot sector onto the computer's system partition.
FIXMBR	Used to repair the MBR of the computer's boot partition.
FORMAT	Used to prepare a disk for use with Windows XP Professional by formatting the disk as FAT16, FAT32, or NTFS.
HELP	Used to display help information for Recovery Console commands.
LISTSVC	Used to list all available services and drivers on the computer, as well as the current status of each service and driver.
LOGON	If the computer is configured for dual-booting or multi-booting, used to log onto other installations as the local administrator.
MAP	Used to display the current drive letter mappings.
MKDIR (MD)	Used to create new directories. (MKDIR and MD work the same way.)
MORE	Used to display a text file on the console screen. (Same as TYPE.)
NET	Used to access Net services command, for example Net Use or Net Share.
RENAME (REN)	Used to rename a single file. (RENAME and REN work the same way.)
RMDIR (RD)	Used to delete directories. (RMDIR and RD work the same way.)
SYSTEMROOT	Used to specify that the current directory is the system root.
TYPE	Used to display a text file on the console screen. (Same as MORE.)

In Exercise 14.11, you will use the Recovery Console. This exercise assumes that you completed Exercise 14.10 to add the Recovery Console to the Windows XP Professional startup options.

EXERCISE 14.11

Using the Recovery Console

1. Restart the computer. In the operating system selection menu, select the Microsoft Windows XP Professional Recovery Console option.

EXERCISE 14.11 *(continued)*

2. Select the Windows XP Professional installation you want to manage and press Enter. (If the computer has been configured as specified in this book, this will be option 1.)

3. Enter the Administrator password and press Enter. You see the `C:\Windows>` prompt.

4. Type **DIR** and press Enter to see a current listing of available files and folders. In the listing, you can press Enter to scroll down line by line or the spacebar to scroll continuously.

5. Type **CD ..** and press Enter to move to the root of the C: drive. You see the `C:\>` prompt.

6. Type **DIR BOOT.INI** and press Enter to see the file attributes of the `BOOT.INI` file.

7. Type **MORE BOOT.INI** and press Enter to see the contents of the `BOOT.INI` file.

8. Type **LISTSVC** and press Enter to see a list of all the services and drivers.

9. Type **EXIT** to exit the Recovery Console and restart your computer.

 Real World Scenario

Recovery Console to the Rescue

Windows XP Professional is currently installed on your home computer. On that computer you want also to work with software that does not run properly on Windows XP, but runs fine on Windows 98. You decide to install Windows 98 on your computer and dual-boot between the two operating systems. After you've set this up, installing Windows 98 with Windows XP already installed, Windows 98 rewrites the Master Boot Record and you no longer see an option to boot Windows XP.

All is not lost: The Recovery Console can be used to recover in the event of this type of failure, by allowing you to run the FIXMBR command to rewrite the master boot record to support Windows XP again.

Using Remote Desktop and Remote Assistance

Remote Desktop and Remote Assistance are new features of Windows XP Professional. *Remote Desktop* is a service that allows you to remotely take control of your computer from another location. For example, you could access your work computer from home or while traveling on business. *Remote Assistance* is used to request assistance from another Windows XP user.

You will learn more about Remote Desktop and Remote Assistance in the following sections.

Using Remote Desktop

Remote Desktop is a new tool of Windows XP Professional that allows you to take control of a remote computer's keyboard, video, and mouse. This tool does not require that someone collaborate with you on the remote computer. While the remote computer is being accessed, it remains locked and any actions that are performed remotely will not be visible to the monitor that is attached to the remote computer. Remote Desktop was designed to be used in the following situations:

- For troubleshooting computers within an organization that may be in a remote location, but are connected to the central network through a direct network connection, secure Virtual Private Network (VPN), or remote access

- To allow Help Desk administrators within a network to remotely troubleshoot organizational computers

- To allow remote access to organizational computers without security concerns that unauthorized users are viewing the remote computer's monitor and watching what actions are being performed remotely

In the following sections you will learn:

- The Remote Desktop restrictions

- The minimum set of requirements for Remote Desktop

- How to configure the computer that will be accessed remotely

- How to configure the computer that will be used to access the remote computer

- How to start a remote Desktop session

- How to customize a remote Desktop session

- How to end a remote Desktop session

Remote Desktop Restrictions

Remote Desktop uses all of the inherent security features of Windows XP Professional. In addition, Remote Desktop imposes the additional security features:

- Remote Desktop is designed to be used for accessing internal domain computers. If the computer that you want to access is outside your organization's firewall, then you will need to use Internet proxy software or Microsoft Internet Security and Acceleration Server client software.

- If you want to establish a session from a computer via the Internet to your company's internal network, you must first establish a secure VPN connection to the internal network you wish to access.

- Remote Desktop can't be used to create a connection between two computers directly connected to the Internet.

- There is no option for simultaneous remote and local access to the Windows XP Professional Desktop. If a computer will be accessed remotely, Windows XP will prompt the local user that they need to be logged off before the computer can be accessed remotely.

Remote Desktop Requirements

To use Remote Desktop, the following requirements must be met:

- Windows XP Professional must be running on the computer that will be accessed remotely.
- The computer that will access the remote computer must be running Windows 95 or higher and have Remote Desktop client software installed and configured.
- There must be an IP connection between the two computers that will be used to establish a Remote Desktop session.

Configuring a Computer for Remote Access

You enable a computer to be accessed remotely through Control Panel. To enable remote access, select Start ➤ Control Panel ➤ Performance and Maintenance ➤ System. Click the Remote tab. Within the Remote tab of System Properties, check Allow Users to Connect Remotely to This Computer, as shown in Figure 14.19. To enable Remote Desktop, you must be logged onto the computer as an administrator or a member of the Administrators group.

FIGURE 14.19   The Remote tab of the System Properties dialog box

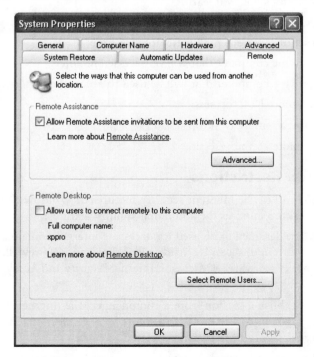

By default, only members of the Administrators group can access a computer that has been configured to use Remote Desktop. To enable other users to access the computer remotely, click the Select Remote Users button shown in Figure 14.19. This brings up the Remote Desktop Users dialog box, as shown in Figure 14.20, and allows you to specify which users can access the remote computer by selecting users through the Add or Remove buttons.

FIGURE 14.20 The Remote Desktop Users dialog box

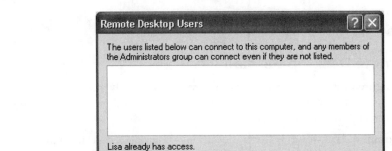

 When you enable remote access to a computer, the changes will take effect immediately. By default, members of the local or domain Administrators group will have Remote Desktop permissions. Members of the Administrators groups can end a local user's session without permission. Non-administrative users who are granted Remote Desktop permissions can't end a local user's session if the local user refuses the session.

Installing the Remote Desktop Client Software

The Remote Desktop Connection client software is used to control a Windows XP Professional computer remotely. This software is installed by default on computers running Windows XP Home Edition and Windows XP Professional. The Remote Desktop Communications client software is used for remote desktop support on pre-Windows XP clients, which are listed within this section.

To install the Remote Desktop Connection client software on a Windows XP computer, take the following steps:

1. Insert the Windows XP Professional CD in the computer that will be used for remote access.

2. The Welcome Page will appear. Select Perform Additional Tasks, then click the Setup Remote Desktop option.

3. Follow the prompts that appear.

You can also install the Remote Desktop Communications client software on the following computers:

- Windows 95
- Windows 98

- Windows Me
- Windows NT 4
- Windows 2000

Starting a Remote Desktop Session

Once you have configured the computer that will be accessed remotely and have installed the Remote Desktop Connection client software, you are ready to start a Remote Desktop session. You start a session through the following steps:

1. Start ➤ All Programs ➤ Accessories ➤ Communications ➤ Remote Desktop Connection. You could also use the command-line utility MSTSC to start the Remote Desktop connection. This will bring up the dialog box shown in Figure 14.21.

FIGURE 14.21 The Remote Desktop Connection dialog box

2. In the Computer name field, type in the name of the computer you wish to access. Remote Desktop must be enabled on this computer and you must have permissions to access the computer remotely.

3. Click the Connect button.

4. The Logon to Windows dialog box will appear. Type in your username, password, and domain name, and click OK.

5. The Remote Desktop Connection window will open, and you will now have remote access.

Once a computer has been accessed remotely, it will be locked. No one at the local site will be able to use the local computer without a password. In addition, no one at the local site will be able to see the work that is being done on the computer remotely.

Customizing a Remote Desktop Connection

You can manage your Remote Desktop connection settings by clicking the Options button that was shown in Figure 14.21. This brings up the dialog box shown in Figure 14.22. Through this dialog box you can configure the following:

General Contains logon settings.

Display Is used to set the size of the remote Desktop and the colors used by the remote Desktop.

FIGURE 14.22   The Remote Desktop Connection options

Local Resources   Are used to specify whether you hear remote computer sounds, the Windows keyboard combinations that will be applied, and which local devices you will automatically connect to on the local computer.

Programs   Allows you to start a program on connection.

Experience   Is used to select your connection speed, so performance can be optimized based on your connection speed.

The General tab contains a Connection Settings button. This allows you to save your settings. By default, settings are saved in the My Documents\Remote Desktop folder. The default extension for Remote Desktop files is .rdp.

Ending a Remote Desktop Session

To end a Remote Desktop Session, take the following steps:

1. In the Remote Desktop Connection window, select Start ➢ Shutdown.

2. The Shut Down Windows dialog box appears. In the drop-down menu, select Log Off and click the OK button.

Using Remote Assistance

Remote Assistance provides a mechanism for requesting help for $x86$-based computers through Windows Messenger and e-mail, or by sending a file. To use Remote Assistance, the computer requesting help and the computer providing help must be using Windows XP Professional and both computers must have interconnectivity. Common examples of when you would use Remote Assistance include:

- When you are diagnosing problems that are difficult to explain or reproduce. By using Remote Assistance, you can remotely view the computer and the remote user can show you what the error is or step you through the processes that are used to cause the error to occur.

- When you need an inexperienced user to perform a complex set of instructions. Instead of asking the inexperienced user to complete the task, you can use Remote Assistance to take control of the computer and complete the tasks yourself.

In the following sections you will learn more about:

- Differences between Remote Desktop and Remote Assistance
- Options for establishing remote connections
- Enabling Remote Assistance
- How users request remote assistance
- How administrators respond to remote assistance requests
- Administrator-initiated remote assistance
- Limitations of Remote Assistance invitations
- Security and Remote Assistance

Differences Between Remote Desktop and Remote Assistance

The key differences between the Remote Desktop utility and the Remote Assistance utility are:

- With Remote Desktop, there is only one connection at a time. With Remote Assistance, the expert is able to establish a concurrent session with the user at the remote computer.

- Remote Assistance requires the user at the remote computer to authorize access. Remote Desktop does not require administrators to seek permission before they establish a remote session.

- With Remote Assistance, both computers have to be running Windows XP Professional.

Options for Establishing Remote Assistance

The following options can be used to establish remote connections:

- A Local Area Network connection between the expert's computer and the novice's computer
- An Internet connection between the expert's computer and the novice's computer
- Connection via the Internet when the expert computer is behind a firewall and the novice computer is just connected to the Internet
- Connection via the Internet when the expert computer is behind a firewall and the novice computer is also behind a firewall

 If the Remote Assistance connections are made through a firewall, the firewall may need to be configured to open TCP Port 3389.

Enabling Remote Assistance

You can enable Remote Assistance through the following steps:

1. Select Start ➢ Control Panel ➢ Performance and Maintenance ➢ System.

2. Click the Remote tab and select the Allow Remote Assistance Invitations to Be Sent from This Computer check box, as shown in Figure 14.23.

FIGURE 14.23   The Remote Tab of the System Properties dialog box

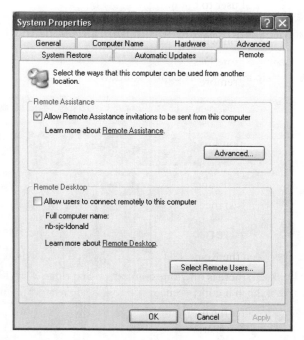

If you click the Advanced button from the Remote tab, you can set configuration options for the maximum number of days that invitations will remain open, as shown in Figure 14.24.

FIGURE 14.24   The Remote Assistance Settings dialog box

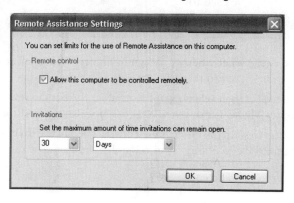

Requesting Remote Assistance

If a user requires remote assistance, they send an invitation. The following steps are used to request remote assistance:

1. Notify the person providing assistance that you will be sending a Remote Assistance invitation. Notification methods might include e-mail, instant messaging, or a telephone call. Give the person providing assistance the password that will be used for the Remote Assistance session.

2. Select Start ➢ Help and Support.

3. From the Help and Support Center widow, under Ask for Assistance, click the Invite a Friend to Connect to Your Computer with Remote Assistance option, as shown in Figure 14.25.

FIGURE 14.25   Help and Support Center window

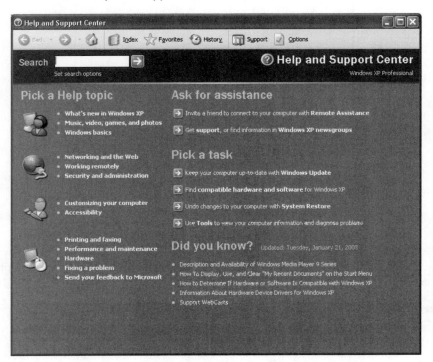

4. From the Remote Assistance window, shown in Figure 14.26, select Invite Someone to Help You.

5. You will be asked to specify how you want to contact the person providing assistance. You can specify Windows Messenger or e-mail (for example using Outlook or Outlook Express).

6. Click Send Invitation to send the invitation. You can specify the invitation delivery method, the length of time until the invitation expires, and whether to use the optional password protection feature.

FIGURE 14.26 Remote Assistance window

FIGURE 14.26 Remote Assistance window

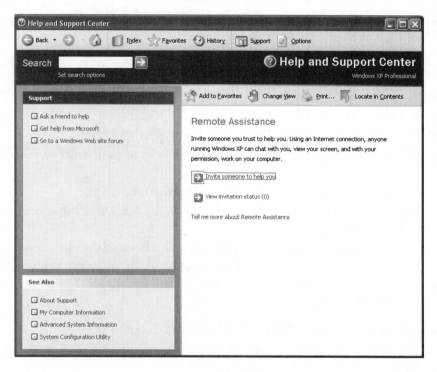

Responding to Remote Assistance Requests

When you receive a Remote Assistance invitation, you would use the following steps to respond:

1. Receive the Remote Assistance invitation via e-mail or Instant Messenger.

2. Open the invitation and double-click the attachment that is used to start the session. If a password has been configured, provide the appropriate password.

3. The user seeking assistance will see an acceptance message on their screen and be prompted to verify that you be allowed to view the remote screen and chat with them.

4. The user seeking assistance should confirm the acceptance message and a terminal window will appear on the your monitor, displaying the user's computer Desktop.

5. You will then be able to manipulate remotely the user's computer by using the Take Control option, after the user approves the interaction by clicking the Allow Expert Interaction button that they see in the Remote Assistance window.

The person who requested remote assistance can terminate the session at any time by clicking the Stop Control button in the Remote Assistance window.

Initiating a Remote Assistance Session

Administrators can also initiate a remote assistance session through the Offer Remote Assistance feature. By default, this option is disabled, but can be enabled through Group Policy by taking the following actions:

1. Select Start ➤ Run and in the Run dialog box, type **gpedit.msc**.
2. Expand Local Computer Policy ➤ Computer Configuration ➤ Administrative Templates.
3. Expand System, then Remote Assistance.
4. In the details pane, double-click Offer Remote Assistance, click Enabled, then the OK button.

Once Offer Remote Assistance is enabled, you can offer remote assistance to a user through the following steps:

1. Inform the user that you will be offering remote assistance.
2. From the Help and Support Center dialog box, under the Pick a Task list, select Tools, then Offer Remote Assistance.
3. Follow the instructions for providing the name or IP address of the user's computer.
4. The user will see a prompt that you—the network administrator—would like to view the screen, chat with them in real time, and work on their computer. The user then accepts your assistance request.

Re-Use of Remote Assistance Invitations

If both of the following conditions are met, a Remote Assistance ticket can be used more than once:

- The invitation ticket can't be expired.
- The IP address of the computer cannot have changed since the ticket was issued. Such a change can occur if a user connects to the Internet through an ISP that assigns dynamic IP addresses each time the user connects to the Internet.

Security and Remote Assistance

A security concern and security configuration concern when using Remote Assistance include:

- If a user clicks the Allow Expert Interaction button, then the person providing expert assistance will have all of the security privileges that the local user has.
- If you allow a user outside of your organization to access your computer, you should have them connect via a VPN account. If they connect through the network firewall, then TCP Port 3389 must be opened.

Summary

In this chapter, you learned about Windows XP Professional's system recovery options and utilities. We covered the following topics:

- Basic techniques that you can use to safeguard your computer and plan for disaster recovery

- The Event Viewer utility, including how to view the details of an event and manage log files

- The Windows XP boot process, including the steps in a normal boot; the BOOT.INI file; and how to create a Windows XP boot disk

- Advanced startup options, including Safe Mode, Enable Boot Logging, Last Known Good Configuration, and other options for booting in special modes

- The driver rollback feature, which allows you to roll back to a previously used driver in the event you update a driver and the new driver does not function properly

- Startup and Recovery options for specifying what action Windows XP should take in the event of system failure

- The Dr. Watson utility, which diagnoses application errors

- The Backup utility, which includes a Backup Wizard, a Restore Wizard, and an Automated System Recovery Wizard

- The System Restore utility, which is used to create checkpoints of your system configuration, so that you can restore previous configurations in the event you need to restore a previously known good configuration

- The Recovery Console, a special boot process that gives you limited access to your file system for replacement of files, or to specify the services that should be started the next time the computer is booted

- How to use Remote Desktop, which is used to access a local computer remotely; and Remote Assistance, which is used to request help remotely

Exam Essentials

Understand the different options for managing system recovery and when it is appropriate to use each option. Know how to use Event Viewer, advanced startup options, Startup and Recovery options, and Dr. Watson for troubleshooting system errors.

Be able to perform system recovery with the Backup utility. Understand the options that are supported through the Backup utility and how to use backup and restore procedures. Understand System State data and how it can be backed up.

Know how to manage system recovery through Safe Mode. Be able to list the options that can be accessed through Safe Mode, and know when it is appropriate to use each option.

Know how to use the Recovery Console. Be familiar with the features and purpose of the Recovery Console. Be able to access and use the Recovery Console to facilitate system recovery.

Know how to use the Remote Desktop and Remote Assistance. Be familiar with how Remote Desktop and Remote Assistance work and how they are configured and accessed.

Key Terms

Before you take the exam, be certain you are familiar with the following terms:

Application log	NTDETECT.COM
Automated System Recovery Wizard	NTLDR
Backup Wizard	NTOSKRNL.EXE
Boot Normally	Power-On Self-Test (POST)
BOOT.INI	Recovery Console
BOOTSECT.DOS	Remote Assistance
Debugging Mode	Remote Desktop
Dr. Watson	Restore Wizard
driver rollback	Safe Mode
DRWTSN32	Safe Mode with Command Prompt
Enable Boot Logging	Safe Mode with Networking
Enable VGA Mode	Security log
Error events	Success Audit event
Event Viewer	System log
Failure Audit event	System State data
Information events	Warning events
Last Known Good Configuration	Windows XP Backup
Master Boot Record (MBR)	Windows XP boot disk
NTBOOTDD.SYS	

Review Questions

1. You are the network administrator for a small company. You manage the computers for the Marketing department, all of which are running the Windows XP Professional operating system. You are making several configuration changes to the manager's computer to enhance performance. Before you make any changes, you want to create a restore point that can be used if any problems arise. How do you create a restore point?

    A. By using System Restore Wizard in Device Manager

    B. By using System Restore Wizard in the System Tools program group

    C. By using the Recovery Console in Control Panel

    D. By using the System File Recovery utility in Control Panel

2. Your computer uses a SCSI adapter that supports a SCSI drive, which contains your Windows XP system and boot partitions. After updating the SCSI driver, you restart your computer, but Windows XP will not load. You need to get this computer up and running as quickly as possible. Which of the following repair strategies should you try first to correct your problem?

    A. Restore your computer's configuration with your last backup.

    B. Boot your computer with the Last Known Good Configuration.

    C. Boot your computer with the Safe Mode option.

    D. Boot your computer to the Recovery Console and manually copy the old driver back to the computer.

3. You recently updated your video driver. When you restart the computer, the video display isn't working properly. You now want to load a generic video driver so that you can correct the video problem. Which configuration file includes an option that allows you to load a standard VGA video driver?

    A. `BOOT.INI`

    B. `BOOT.VID`

    C. `VIDEO.INI`

    D. `CONFIG.SYS`

4. You are the network administrator for a medium-sized company. You support all of the users in the Accounting and Finance departments. The manager of the Accounting department, Catherine, recently installed the XYZ application on her Windows XP Professional computer. Sometimes when she runs the XYZ application, she reports that the application is generating errors. Which utility is used within Windows XP to help diagnose application errors?

    A. Dr. Watson

    B. Sherlock

    C. Application Manager

    D. Application Event Viewer

5. You are about to install a new driver for your CD-ROM drive, but you are not 100 percent sure that you are using the correct driver. Which of the following options will allow you to most easily and quickly save your current configuration and then return your computer to the previous state if the new driver is not correct?

    A. Safe Mode

    B. Driver rollback

    C. System Restore utility

    D. System File Recovery utility

6. You work on the Help Desk for the ABC Corporation. One of your users who works remotely is having trouble getting an application you manage to work. You would like to use Remote Assistance to troubleshoot and correct the problem. The user connects to the Internet through a standard ISP connection. You connect to the Internet via a corporate network that is protected by a firewall. The firewall is not configured to use Network Address Translation (NAT). The remote user sends you a Remote Assistance invitation. When you attempt to accept the invitation, you can't connect to the remote computer. When you ping the remote user's computer, you verify that you have TCP/IP connectivity. Which of the following options should you take next?

    A. Ask the system administrator to open Port 3389 on the firewall.

    B. Ask the system administrator to open Port 2671 on the firewall.

    C. Verify that the remote user has your computer added the Remote Desktop Users list on the Remote tab of System Properties.

    D. Have the remote user resend the invitation and verify that the time has not expired.

7. After you updated Stuart's computer, his boot files became corrupt due to a virus and now need to be restored. Which of the following processes will allow you to start the computer the most quickly?

    A. Boot with the ERD.

    B. Use the Backup utility.

    C. Use the Windows XP boot disk.

    D. Use the Windows XP Professional Setup Disks.

8. Your Engineering department uses Windows XP as the primary operating system on their development computers. Because these computers are mission critical, you want to facilitate any recovery process that may be required. You decide to install the Recovery Console on each computer. Which of the following commands should you use to install the Recovery Console?

    A. RECCON

    B. RECCON32

    C. WINNT32 /RC

    D. WINNT32 /CMDCONS

9. You are the network administrator for a large company. You have several remote locations that are connected via a wide area network. One of your users, Emily, calls you with an application error she is encountering. Her computer is running Windows XP Professional. You want to see exactly what is happening so you can help her resolve the problem. Your computer is also running Windows XP Professional. Which of the following options can be used to start a Remote Assistance session? (Choose all that apply.)

    A. Emily can request Remote Assistance through Windows Messenger.

    B. As an Administrator, you can start a Remote Assistance session through the Remote Assistance Manager.

    C. Emily can request Remote Assistance by sending an e-mail asking for assistance.

    D. The Administrator can initiate the session by sending a file to Emily offering remote assistance.

10. When you booted Windows XP Professional, you noticed that an error appeared during the startup sequence. You need the exact error code that was generated, but you can't remember what the error code was. Where can you find this information?

    A. *Windir*\\error.log file

    B. *Windir*\System32\error.log file

    C. *Windir*\System32\startup.log file

    D. Event Viewer System log

11. You are unable to boot your Windows XP Professional computer, so you decide to boot the computer to Safe Mode. Which of the following statements regarding Safe Mode is false?

    A. When the computer is booted to Safe Mode, there is no network access.

    B. Safe Mode loads all the drivers for the hardware that is installed on the computer.

    C. When you run Safe Mode, boot logging is automatically enabled.

    D. When you run Safe Mode, the Enable VGA Mode is automatically enabled.

12. You have been having problems with your Windows XP Professional computer. You decide to start the computer using the Enable Boot Logging option on the Advanced Options menu. Where can you find the log file that is created?

    A. *Windir*\ntbtlog.txt

    B. *Windir*\System32\ntbtlog.txt

    C. *Windir*\ntboot.log

    D. *Windir*\System32\ntboot.log

13. Which Advanced Options menu item can you use during the system boot to enable and run the Kernel Debugger utility if it's installed on your computer?

    A. Run Kernel Debugger

    B. Run Advanced Troubleshooting

    C. Use the Debugging Mode

    D. Boot to Troubleshooting Mode

14. Your computer is configured to dual-boot between Windows 98 and Windows XP. How would you configure the computer so that Windows 98 would be the default selection if the user did not make a choice within the specified amount of time?

    A. Through the STARTUP.INI file

    B. Through the SYSTEM.INI file

    C. Through Control Panel ➢ Startup Options

    D. Through Control Panel ➢ Performance and Maintenance ➢ System ➢ Advanced tab ➢ Startup and Recovery Settings

15. You are using the Windows XP Backup utility and have decided to back up the System State data. Which of the following items is not backed up when you choose this option?

    A. Registry

    B. COM+ registration database

    C. Windows XP OLE database

    D. System boot files

Answers to Review Questions

1. B.   To manually create a restore point or to restore your computer to a previous restore point, you use the System Restore Wizard. This is accessed through Start ➢ All Programs ➢ Accessories ➢ System Tools ➢ System Restore.

2. B.   If you need to get a stalled computer up and running as quickly as possible, you should start with the Last Known Good Configuration option. This option is used when you've made changes to your computer's hardware configuration and are having problems restarting. The Last Known Good Configuration will revert to the configuration used the last time the computer was successfully booted. (Although this option helps overcome configuration errors, it will not help for hardware errors.)

3. A.   The BOOT.INI file specifies the location of the boot partition, the boot menu, and the default operating system that should be loaded. This file can also be configured with switches that specify how the operating system should load (for example, with a standard VGA video driver).

4. A.   The Dr. Watson utility is used to diagnose application errors. Windows XP Professional does not ship with utilities called Sherlock, Application Manager, or Application Event Viewer.

5. B.   The Roll Back Driver option is the easiest way to roll back to a known good driver. You could also use the System Restore utility to roll back your computer to a known restore point if you make harmful changes to your computer, but driver rollback is easier and faster.

6. A.   If you want to have access between a user from the Internet and a user who is behind a corporate firewall, then TCP Port 3389 must be opened. If you do not want to open this port, then you should connect the session through VPN.

7. C.   To quickly boot the computer, you can use a Windows XP boot disk. You can restore the missing files through the Backup utility (specifically by using its Automated System Recovery Wizard), but the boot disk is faster.

8. D.   The commands in the first three options do not exist. You use WINNT32 /CMDCONS to install the Recovery Console.

9. A, C.   Remote Assistance provides a mechanism for requesting help through Windows Messenger, through e-mail, or by sending a file. To use Remote Assistance, both the computer requesting help and the computer providing help must be using Windows XP Professional and both computers must be connected to the Internet. There is no such thing as Remote Assistance Manager. The Administrator sends a direct request, not a file, although the user can request assistance by sending a file via e-mail.

10. D.   The Event Viewer utility is used to track information about your computer's hardware and software. The System log includes any error messages that have been generated.

11. B.   When you run your computer in Safe Mode, you simplify your Windows XP configuration. Only the drivers that are needed to get the computer up and running are loaded.

12. A.   When you enable boot logging, the file created is *Windir*\ntbtlog.txt. This log file is used to troubleshoot the boot process.

13. C. If you select Debugging Mode and have the Kernel Debugger installed, the Kernel Debugger can be used for advanced troubleshooting. There are several BOOT.INI boot options associated with the Kernel Debugger.

14. D. You can make Windows 98 the default selection through Control Panel ➢ Performance and Maintenance ➢ System ➢ Advanced tab ➢ Startup and Recovery Settings. The Default Operating System option lets you specify which operating system will load if no user selection is made. You could also specify this option through the BOOT.INI file.

15. C. When you back up System State data, you back up the Registry, the COM+ registration database, and the system boot files. This data can all be backed up through the Backup utility.

Glossary

802.11 wireless LAN   802.11 is a wireless standard for LAN support that includes automatic wireless configuration (for zero client configuration), auto-detection of wireless networks, automatic switching between different access points (APs) when a client is roaming, and wireless device authentication support for Windows Remote Authentication Dial-In User Service (RADIUS) Server and Internet Authentication Service (IAS).

A

access control entry (ACE)   An item used by the operating system to determine *resource* access. Each *discretionary access control list (DACL)* has an associated ACE that lists the permissions that have been granted or denied to the users and groups listed in the DACL.

access token   An object containing the *security identifier (SID)* of a running *process*. A process started by another process inherits the starting process's access token. The access token is checked against each object's *discretionary access control list (DACL)* to determine whether appropriate permissions are granted to perform any requested service.

Accessibility Options   Windows XP Professional features used to support users with limited sight, hearing, or mobility. Accessibility Options include special keyboard, sound, display, and mouse configurations.

Accessibility Wizard   A Windows XP Professional Wizard used to configure a computer based on the user's vision, hearing, and mobility needs.

account lockout policy   A Windows XP policy used to specify how many invalid *logon* attempts should be tolerated before a user account is locked out. Account lockout policies are set through *account policies*.

account policies   Windows XP policies used to determine password and *logon* requirements. Account policies are set through the *Microsoft Management Console (MMC) Local Computer Policy snap-in*.

ACE   See *access control entry*.

ACPI   See *Advanced Configuration and Power Interface*.

Active Directory   A directory service available with the Windows 2000 Server and Windows Server 2003 platforms. The Active Directory stores information in a central database and allows users to have a single user account (called a *domain user account* or *Active Directory user account*) for the network.

Active Directory user account   A user account that is stored in the Windows 2000 or Windows 2003 *Active Directory*'s central database. An Active Directory user account can provide a user with a single user account for a network. Also called a *domain user account*.

adapter   Any hardware device that allows communications to occur through physically dissimilar systems. This term usually refers to peripheral cards that are permanently mounted inside computers and provide an interface from the computer's bus to another medium such as a hard disk or a network.

Administrator account   A Windows XP special account that has the ultimate set of security permissions and can assign any permission to any user or group.

Administrators group   A Windows XP local built-in group that consists of *Administrator accounts*.

Advanced Configuration and Power Interface (ACPI)   A specification that controls the amount of power given to each device attached to the computer. With ACPI, the operating system can turn off peripheral devices when they are not in use.

Accelerated Graphics Port (AGP)   A type of expansion slot supported by Windows XP. AGP is used by video cards and supports very high-quality video and graphics performance.

AGP   See *Accelerated Graphics Port*.

alert   A system-monitoring feature that is generated when a specific *counter* exceeds or falls below a specified value. Through the *Performance Logs and Alerts* utility, administrators can configure alerts so that a message is sent, a program is run, or a more detailed log file is generated.

Alternate IP Configuration   A feature that allows users to have a static and a *DHCP*-assigned IP address mapped to a single network adapter, which is used to support mobile users who roam between different network segments.

Anonymous Logon group   A Windows XP *special group* that includes users who access the computer through anonymous logons. Anonymous logons occur when users gain access through special accounts, such as the IUSR_*computername* and TsInternetUser user accounts. Normally, a password is not required, so that anyone can log on.

answer file   An automated installation script used to respond to configuration prompts that normally occur in a Windows XP Professional installation. Administrators can create Windows XP answer files with the *Setup Manager* utility.

APIPA   See *Automatic Private IP Addressing*.

Application log   A log that tracks events that are related to applications that are running on the computer. The Application log can be viewed in the *Event Viewer* utility.

ASR   See *Automated System Recovery*.

assigned applications   Applications installed with *Windows Installer packages*. Assigned applications are automatically installed when the user selects the application on the All Programs menu or by document invocation (by the document extension).

Asynchronous Transfer Mode (ATM)   A network technology used with *wide area networks (WANs)* for data transfer. ATM transmits data using small packets of a fixed size and can be used to transmit computer data, audio, or video over the same network.

ATM   See *Asynchronous Transfer Mode*.

audit policy   A Windows XP policy that tracks the success or failure of specified security events. Audit policies are set through *Local Computer Policy snap-in*.

Authenticated Users group   A Windows XP *special group* that includes users who access the Windows XP operating system through a valid username and password.

authentication   The process required to log onto a computer locally. Authentication requires a valid username and a password that exists in the local accounts database. An *access token* will be created if the information presented matches the account in the database.

Authentication is also used when you access a network through a dial-up connection, *virtual private network (VPN)*, or direct connection. Windows XP Professional uses a two-step authentication process, which consists of an interactive logon process and network authorization. The interactive logon process confirms a user's identity based on the user account (local or domain) and password or *smart card* credentials. Network access control is used to confirm the user's identity to the network service or resource that the user is attempting to access.

automated installation   The process of installing Windows XP using an unattended setup method such as *Remote Installation Services (RIS)*, *unattended installation*, or *RIPrep disk images*.

Automated System Recovery (ASR)   A process used for system recovery in the event of system failure. It is a two-part system recovery that consists of a backup and restore component. The system information that is backed up by ASR includes *System State data*, system services, and disk configuration information (information about basic and dynamic disks and the file signature associated with each disk).

Automatic Private IP Addressing (APIPA)   A service that is used to automatically assign private IP addresses for home or small business networks that contain a single subnet, have no DHCP server, and are not using static IP addressing. If APIPA is being used, then clients will only be able to communicate with other clients on the same subnet that are also using APIPA. The benefit of using APIPA in small networks is that it is less tedious and has less chance of configuration errors than statically assigned IP addresses and configuration.

B

backup   The process of writing all the data contained in online mass-storage devices to offline mass-storage devices for the purpose of safekeeping. Backups are usually performed from hard disk drives to tape drives. Also referred to as archiving.

Backup Operators group   A Windows XP built-in group that includes users who can back up and restore the *file system*, even if the file system is *NTFS* and they have not been assigned permissions to the file system. The members of the Backup Operators group can access the file system only through the *Backup utility*. To be able to directly access the file system, the user must have explicit permissions assigned.

backup type   A *backup* choice that determines which files are backed up during a backup process. Backup types include *normal backup*, *copy backup*, *incremental backup*, *differential backup*, and *daily backup*.

Backup utility   The Windows XP utility used to run the Backup Wizard, the *Restore Wizard*, and the *Automated System Recovery Wizard*.

Backup Wizard   A wizard that is used to perform backup operations. The Backup Wizard is accessed through the Backup utility.

baseline   A snapshot record of a computer's current performance statistics that can be used for performance analysis and planning purposes.

Basic Input/Output System (BIOS)   A set of routines in firmware that provides the most basic software interface drivers for hardware attached to the computer. The BIOS contains the boot routine.

basic storage   A disk-storage system supported by Windows XP that consists of *primary partitions* and *extended partitions*.

Batch group   A Windows XP *special group* that includes users who log on as a user account that is only used to run a batch job.

binding   The process of linking together software components, such as network *protocols* and *network adapters*.

BINL   See *Boot Information Negotiation Layer*.

BIOS   See *Basic Input/Output System*.

boot   The process of loading a computer's operating system. Booting usually occurs in multiple phases, each successively more complex until the entire operating system and all its services are running. Also called bootstrap. The computer's *BIOS* must contain the first level of booting.

Boot Information Negotiation Layer (BINL)   The Boot Information Negotiation Layer (BINL) service responds to client requests for files from the *Remote Installation Services (RIS)* server. It is responsible for management of the RIS environment.

BOOT.INI   A file accessed during the Windows XP *boot* sequence. The BOOT.INI file is used to build the operating system menu choices that are displayed during the boot process. It is also used to specify the location of the *boot partition*.

Boot Normally option   A Windows XP Advanced Options menu item used to boot Windows XP normally.

boot partition   The *partition* that contains the system files. The system files are located in C:\Windows by default.

BOOTSECT.DOS   An optional file that is loaded if the user chooses to load an operating system other than Windows XP. This file is used only in *dual-booting* or *multi-booting* computers.

bootstrap image   The bootstrap image is the fundamental network software that allows a remote client to get access to the *Remote Installation Services (RIS)* server via the *Trivial File Transfer Protocol (TFTP)* protocol.

bottleneck   A system *resource* that is inefficient compared with the rest of the computer system as a whole. The bottleneck can cause the rest of the system to run slowly.

C

cable modem   Hardware that is used to provide two-way, high-speed connectivity to the Internet (or private networks using a *virtual private network*, or *VPN*) through existing coaxial cabling that is used for transmitting cable television. Cable modems support a maximum throughput of 2.8Mbps, but because cable modems use a shared network contention topology, bandwidth availability will impact actual network throughput.

caching   A speed-optimization technique that keeps a copy of the most recently used data in a fast, high-cost, low-capacity storage device rather than in the device on which the actual data resides. Caching assumes that recently used data is likely to be used again. Fetching data from the cache is faster than fetching data from the slower, larger storage device. Most caching algorithms also copy data that is most likely to be used next and perform *write-back caching* to further increase speed gains.

CD-based image   A type of image configured on a *Remote Installation Services (RIS)* server. A CD-based image contains only the Windows XP Professional operating system.

CDFS   See *Compact Disk File System*.

central processing unit (CPU)   The main *processor* in a computer.

certificate authentication   A security authentication process that uses a special authentication credential, called a certificate. A certificate is a digital signature that is issued by a certificate authority. When a client and server are configured to use certificate authentication, they must both present a valid certificate for mutual authentication.

Challenge Handshake Authentication Protocol (CHAP)   A security protocol used to negotiate secure authentication by using encryption that is based on the industry standard hashing scheme specified by Message Digest 5 (MD5). Hashing schemes are used to transform data into a scrambled format. CHAP uses a challenge-response process that sends the client a request with the hash scheme that will be used. The client then responds to the server with an MD5 hashed response. This method allows the server to authenticate a client without the client actually sending their password over the remote connection. Almost all third-party *Point-to-Point Protocol (PPP)* servers support CHAP authentication.

CHAP   See *Challenge Handshake Authentication Protocol*.

Check Disk utility   A Windows XP utility that checks a hard disk for errors. Check Disk (chkdsk) attempts to fix file-system errors and scans for and attempts to recover bad sectors.

CIPHER   A command-line utility that can be used to encrypt and decrypt files on NTFS volumes.

cipher text   Encrypted data. Encryption is the process of translating data into code that is not easily accessible. Once data has been encrypted, a user must have a password or key to decrypt the data. Unencrypted data is known as plain text.

clean install   A method of Windows XP Professional installation that puts the operating system into a new folder and uses its default settings the first time the operating system is loaded.

client   A computer on a network that subscribes to the services provided by a server.

COM port   Communications port. A serial hardware interface conforming to the RS-232C standard for low-speed, serial communications.

Compact Disk File System (CDFS)   A *file system* used by Windows XP to read the file system on a CD-ROM.

compression   The process of storing data in a form using special algorithms that takes less space than the uncompressed data.

Computer Management   A consolidated tool for performing common Windows XP management tasks. The interface is organized into three main areas of management: *System Tools*, Storage, and Services and Applications.

computer name   A *NetBIOS* name used to uniquely identify a computer on the network. A computer name can be from 1 to 15 characters long.

Control Panel   A Windows XP utility that allows users to change default settings for operating system services to match their preferences. The *Registry* contains the Control Panel settings.

CONVERT   A command-line utility used to convert a *partition* or *volume* from *FAT16* or *FAT32* to the *NTFS* file system.

copy backup   A *backup type* that backs up selected folders and files but does not set the archive bit.

counter   A performance-measuring tool used to track specific information regarding a system resource, called a performance object. All Windows XP system resources are tracked as performance objects, such as Cache, Memory, Paging File, Process, and Processor. Each performance object has an associated set of counters. Counters are set through the *System Monitor* utility.

CPU   See *central processing unit*.

Creator Group   The Windows XP *special group* that created or took ownership of the object (rather than an individual user). When a regular user creates an object or takes ownership of an object, the username becomes the *Creator Owner group*. When a member of the *Administrators group* creates or takes ownership of an object, the Administrators group becomes the Creator Group.

Creator Owner group   The Windows XP *special group* that includes the account that created or took ownership of an object. The account, usually a user account, has the right to modify the object, but cannot modify any other objects that were not created by the user account.

D

DACL   See *discretionary access control list*.

daily backup   A *backup type* that backs up all of the files that have been modified on the day that the daily backup is performed. The archive attribute is not set on the files that have been backed up.

data compression   The process of storing data in a form using special algorithms that takes less space than the uncompressed data.

data encryption   The process of translating data into code that is not easily accessible to increase security. Once data has been encrypted, a user must have a password or key to decrypt the data. Data encryption adds an additional layer of security in remote communications, by encrypting all of the data that is sent and adding security to the logon authentication process.

DCC   See *Direct Cable Connection.*

Debugging mode   A Windows XP Advanced Option menu item that runs the Kernel Debugger, if that utility is installed. The Kernel Debugger is an advanced troubleshooting utility.

default gateway   A *TCP/IP* configuration option that specifies the gateway that will be used if the network contains routers.

Desktop   A directory that the background of the Windows Explorer shell represents. By default, the Desktop includes objects that contain the local storage devices and available network *shares.* Also a key operating part of the Windows XP graphical interface.

device driver   Software that allows a specific piece of hardware to communicate with the Windows XP operating system.

Device Manager   A Windows XP utility used to view information about the computer's configuration and set configuration options.

DHCP   See *Dynamic Host Configuration Protocol.*

DHCP server   A server configured to provide *DHCP* clients with all of their *IP* configuration information automatically.

dial-up modem   Hardware used for remote communication which uses slow links and uses an analog dial-up connection over the *Public Switched Telephone Network (PSTN)*, which is regular phone service, for remote connectivity. It is the least expensive and most commonly used method for creating remote connections.

dial-up networking   A service that allows remote users to dial into the network or the Internet (such as through a telephone or an *ISDN* connection).

Dialup group   A Windows XP *special group* that includes users who log onto the network from a dial-up connection.

differential backup   A *backup type* that copies only the files that have been changed since the last *normal backup* (full backup) or *incremental backup*, and does not reset the archive bit.

Digital Subscriber Line (DSL)   Used for remote communications and uses standard copper telephone lines to provide dedicated, high-speed access to the Internet.

Digital Video Disc (DVD)   A disk standard that supports 4.7GB of data per disk. One of DVD's strongest features is backward compatibility with CD-ROM technology, so that a DVD drive can play CD-ROMs. Formerly known as Digital Video Disk.

Direct Cable Connection (DCC)   An option for directly connecting two devices without the use of a network for the purpose of transferring data.

direct parallel cable   An option for supporting file transfers between two computers. Parallel cables transmit data faster than *serial cables*. Windows XP Professional supports standard or basic 4-bit parallel cables, Enhanced Capabilities Port (ECP) cables, and Universal Cable Module cables for parallel *DCC*.

directory replication   The process of copying a directory structure from an export computer to an import computer or computers. Any time changes are made to the export computer, the import computers are automatically updated with the changes.

discretionary access control list (DACL)   An item used by the operating system to determine *resource* access. Each object (such as a folder, network share, or printer) in Windows XP has a DACL. The DACL lists the *security identifiers (SIDs)* contained by objects. Only the users or groups identified in the list as having the appropriate permission can activate the services of that object.

Disk Cleanup   A Windows XP utility used to identify files that can be deleted to free additional hard disk space. Disk Cleanup works by identifying temporary files, Internet cache files, and unnecessary program files.

disk defragmentation   The process of rearranging the existing files on a disk so that they are stored contiguously, which optimizes access to those files.

Disk Defragmenter utility   A Windows XP utility that performs *disk defragmentation*.

disk duplicator   A special piece of hardware, used to copy the image of one hard drive to another hard drive.

disk image (disk imaging)   An exact duplicate of a hard disk, used for *automated installation*. Using third-party software, the disk image is copied from a reference computer that is configured in the same manner as the computers on which Windows XP Professional will be installed.

Disk Management utility   A Windows XP graphical tool for managing disks, *partitions*, and *volumes*.

disk partitioning   The process of creating logical *partitions* on the physical hard drive.

disk quotas   A Windows XP feature used to specify how much disk space a user is allowed to use on specific *NTFS volumes*. Disk quotas can be applied to all users or to specific users.

distribution server   A network server that contains the Windows XP distribution files that have been copied from the distribution CD. Clients can connect to the distribution server and install Windows XP over the network.

DNS   See *Domain Name System*.

domain   In Microsoft networks, an arrangement of client and server computers referenced by a specific name that shares a single security permissions database. On the Internet, a domain is a named collection of hosts and subdomains, registered with a unique name by the InterNIC.

domain name   A name that identifies one or more *IP addresses*, such as `sybex.com`. Domain names are used in *URLs* to identify particular web hosts.

Domain Name System (DNS)   The *TCP/IP* network service that translates fully qualified domain names (or host names) into *IP addresses*.

Domain Name System (DNS) server   An Internet host dedicated to the function of translating fully qualified domain names into *IP addresses*.

domain user account   A user account that is stored in the Windows 2000 Server or Windows Server 2003 *Active Directory*'s central database. A domain user account can provide a user with a single user account for a network. Also called an Active Directory user account.

drive letter   A single letter assigned as an abbreviation to a mass-storage *volume* available to a computer.

driver   A program that provides a software interface to a hardware device. Drivers are written for the specific devices they control, but they present a common software interface to the computer's operating system, allowing all devices of a similar type to be controlled as if they were the same.

driver rollback   An option that allows you to restore a previously used driver after a driver has been upgraded. This option provides an easy mechanism for restoring a driver if the upgraded driver does not work properly.

driver signing   A digital imprint that is Microsoft's way of guaranteeing that a driver has been tested and will work with the computer.

Dr. Watson   A Windows XP utility used to identify and troubleshoot application errors.

DRWTSN32   The command used to access the *Dr. Watson* utility.

DSL   See *Digital Subscriber Line*.

dual-booting   The process of allowing a computer to *boot* more than one operating system.

DVD   See *Digital Video Disc*.

dynamic disk   A Windows XP disk-storage technique. A dynamic disk is divided into dynamic *volumes*. Dynamic volumes cannot contain *partitions* or *logical drives*, and they are not accessible through DOS. You can size or resize a dynamic disk without restarting Windows XP. Dynamic disks are accessible only to Windows, Windows XP, and Windows Server 2003 computers.

Dynamic Host Configuration Protocol (DHCP)   A method of automatically assigning *IP addresses* to client computers on a network.

dynamic storage   A Windows XP disk-storage system that is configured as *volumes*. Windows XP Professional dynamic storage supports *simple volumes*, *spanned volumes*, and *striped volumes*.

E

EAP   See *Extensible Authentication Protocol.*

EB   See *exabyte.*

effective rights   The rights that a user actually has to a file or folder. To determine a user's effective rights, add all of the permissions that have been allowed through the user's assignments based on that user's username and group associations. Then subtract any permissions that have been denied the user through the username or group associations.

EFS   See *Encrypting File System.*

Enable Boot Logging option   A Windows XP Professional Advanced Options menu item that is used to create a log file that tracks the loading of *drivers* and *services*.

Enable VGA Mode option   A Windows XP Professional Advanced Options menu item that loads a standard VGA driver without starting the computer in *Safe Mode*.

Encrypting File System (EFS)   The Windows XP technology used to store encrypted files on *NTFS partitions*. Encrypted files add an extra layer of security to the *file system*.

encryption   The process of translating data into code that is not easily accessible to increase security. Once data has been encrypted, a user must have a password or key to decrypt the data.

Error event   An *Event Viewer* event type that indicates the occurrence of an error, such as a driver failing to load.

Ethernet   The most popular Data Link layer standard for local area networking. Ethernet implements the Carrier Sense Multiple Access with Collision Detection (CSMA/CD) method of arbitrating multiple computer access to the same network. This standard supports the use of Ethernet over any type of media, including wireless broadcast. Standard Ethernet operates at 10Mbps. Fast Ethernet operates at 100Mbps.

Event Viewer   A Windows XP utility that tracks information about the computer's hardware and software, as well as security events. This information is stored in three log files: the *Application log*, the *Security log*, and the *System log*.

Everyone   A Windows XP *special group* that includes anyone who could possibly access the computer. The Everyone group includes all of the users (including *Guests*) who have been defined on the computer.

exabyte   A computer storage measurement equal to 1,024 *petabytes*.

extended partition   In *basic storage*, a *logical drive* that allows you to allocate the logical partitions however you wish. Extended partitions are created after the *primary partition* has been created.

Extensible Authentication Protocol (EAP)   A remote access protocol used for logon authentication. EAP extends the services of *Point-to-Point Protocol (PPP)* by providing more updated and secure authentication services than were previously available with PPP. EAP was designed to provide secure authentication services for third-party (non-Microsoft) devices.

F

Failure Audit event   An *Event Viewer* entry that indicates the occurrence of an event that has been audited for failure, such as a failed logon when someone presents an invalid username and/or password.

FAT16   The 16-bit version of the *File Allocation Table (FAT)* system, which was widely used by DOS and Windows 3.*x*. The file system is used to track where files are stored on a disk. Most operating systems support FAT16.

FAT32   The 32-bit version of the *File Allocation Table (FAT)* system, which is more efficient and provides more safeguards than *FAT16*. Windows 95 OSR2, Windows 98, and Windows XP all support FAT32. Windows NT does not support FAT32.

fault tolerance   Any method that prevents system failure by tolerating single faults, usually through hardware redundancy.

fax modem   A special modem that includes hardware to allow the transmission and reception of facsimiles.

FDDI   See *Fiber Distributed Data Interface.*

Fiber Distributed Data Interface (FDDI)   A 100Mbps token-passing protocol that is designed for use with fiber-optic cabling. FDDI uses a dual-counter rotating ring technology. By default, only the primary ring is used. The secondary ring is used for fault tolerance in the event the primary ring fails.

File Allocation Table (FAT)   The *file system* used by *MS-DOS* and available to other operating systems such as Windows (all versions) and OS/2. FAT, now known as *FAT16*, has become something of a mass-storage compatibility standard because of its simplicity and wide availability. FAT has fewer fault-tolerance features than the *NTFS* file system and can become corrupted through normal use over time.

File and Settings Transfer Wizard   A utility used by administrators to migrate files and settings from one computer to another computer. This option is used when you purchase a new computer with Windows XP Professional already installed, and you want to migrate files and settings from an existing computer that is running a previous version of Windows.

file attributes   Information stored along with the name and location of a file in a directory entry. File attributes show the status of a file, such as archived, hidden, and read-only. Different operating systems use different file attributes to implement services such as sharing, *compression*, and *security*.

file system   A software component that manages the storage of files on a mass-storage device by providing services that can create, read, write, and delete files. File systems impose an ordered database of files on the mass-storage device. Storage is arranged in *volumes*. File systems use hierarchies of directories to organize files.

File Transfer Protocol (FTP)   A simple Internet protocol that transfers complete files from an FTP server to a client running the FTP client. FTP provides a simple, low-overhead method of transferring files between computers but cannot perform browsing functions. Users must know the *URL* of the FTP server to which they wish to attach.

Firewall   Combination of hardware and software that is used to provide security between an internal network or intranet or a remote client and the Internet. The use of a firewall prevents unauthorized access by preventing direct communication between a computer behind the firewall and the Internet via a proxy server.

fragmentation   A process that naturally occurs as users create, delete, and modify files. The access of noncontiguous data is transparent to the user; however, when data is stored in this manner, the operating system must search through the disk to access all the pieces of a file. This slows down data access.

frame   A data structure that network hardware devices use to transmit data between computers. Frames consist of the addresses of the sending and receiving computers, size information, and a checksum. Frames are envelopes around packets of data that allow the packets to be addressed to specific computers on a shared media network.

frame type   An option that specifies how data is packaged for transmission over the network. This option must be configured to run the *NWLink IPX/SPX/NetBIOS Compatible Transport* protocol on a Windows XP computer. By default, the frame type is set to Auto Detect, which will attempt to automatically choose a compatible frame type for the network.

Frame Relay   A technology that uses a virtual circuit-based switching protocol to connect devices on a WAN. Frame Relay is commonly implemented with a permanent virtual circuit.

FTP   See *File Transfer Protocol.*

G

GB   See *gigabyte.*

GDI   See *Graphic Device Interface.*

gigabyte   A computer storage measurement equal to 1,024 *megabytes.*

GPO See *Group Policy Object.*

Graphical User Interface (GUI) A computer shell program that represents mass-storage devices, directories, and files as graphical objects on a screen. A cursor driven by a pointing device such as a mouse manipulates the objects.

Graphic Device Interface (GDI) The programming interface and graphical services provided to *Win32* for programs to interact with graphical devices such as the screen and printer.

Group Policy Object (GPO) An option for managing configuration settings that comprises Windows XP configuration settings, administered through the use of Group Policy Objects (GPOs). GPOs are data structures that are attached in a specific hierarchy to selected Active Directory Objects. You can apply GPOs to sites, domains, or organizational units.

Group Policy Result tool A tool used to help determine which policies will actually be applied. This tool is accessed through the GPResult.exe command line utility. The GPResult.exe command displays the resulting set of policies that were enforced on the computer and the specified user during the logon process.

groups Security entities to which users can be assigned membership for the purpose of applying a broad set of group permissions to the user. By managing permissions for groups and assigning users to groups, rather than assigning permissions to users, administrators can more easily manage security.

Guest account A Windows XP user account created to provide a mechanism to allow users to access the computer even if they do not have a unique username and password. This account normally has very limited privileges on the computer. This account is disabled by default.

Guests group A Windows XP built-in group that has limited access to the computer. This group can access only specific areas. Most administrators do not allow Guest account access because it poses a potential security risk.

GUI See *Graphical User Interface.*

H

HAL See *Hardware Abstraction Layer.*

hard disk drive A mass-storage device that reads and writes digital information magnetically on discs that spin under moving heads. Hard disk drives are precisely aligned and cannot normally be removed, except for maintenance. Hard disk drives are an inexpensive way to store *gigabytes* of computer data permanently. Hard disk drives also store the software installed on a computer.

Hardware Abstraction Layer (HAL) A Windows XP service that provides basic input/output services such as timers, interrupts, and multiprocessor management for computer hardware.

The HAL is a *device driver* for the motherboard circuitry that allows different families of computers to be treated the same by the Windows XP operating system.

Hardware Compatibility List (HCL)   A list of all of the hardware devices supported by Windows XP. Hardware on the HCL has been tested and verified as being compatible with Windows XP.

hardware profile   A file that stores a hardware configuration for a computer. Hardware profiles are useful when a single computer (a laptop that can be docked or undocked) has multiple hardware configurations.

HCL   See *Hardware Compatibility List*.

HelpAssistant   The *HelpAssistant* account is used in conjunction with the Remote Desktop Help Assistance feature.

HelpServices group   The *HelpServices group* has special permissions needed to support the computer through Microsoft Help Services.

hibernation   The process of storing anything that is in memory on the computer's hard disk. Hibernation ensures that none of the information stored in memory is lost when the computer is put in low-power mode. When the computer is taken out of hibernation, it is returned to its previous state.

home folder   A folder where users normally store their personal files and information. A home folder can be a local folder or a network folder.

Home Phoneline Network Adapter (HPNA)   A method used for remote communications, which is used with existing telephone wiring, typically in home networks, to connect network devices without interrupting the standard telephone service.

host   An Internet server. A host is a node that is connected to the Internet.

hot swapping   The ability of a device to be plugged into or removed from a computer while the computer's power is on.

HPNA   See *Home Phoneline Network Adaptor*.

HTML   See *Hypertext Markup Language*.

HTTP   See *Hypertext Transfer Protocol*.

hyperlink   A link within text or graphics that has a web address embedded in it. By clicking the link, a user can jump to another web address.

Hypertext Markup Language (HTML)   A textual data format that identifies sections of a document such as headers, lists, hypertext links, and so on. HTML is the data format used on the World Wide Web for the publication of web pages.

Hypertext Transfer Protocol (HTTP)   An Internet protocol that transfers HTML documents over the Internet and responds to context changes that happen when a user clicks a *hyperlink*.

I

ICF   See *Internet Connection Firewall.*

ICS   See *Internet Connection Sharing.*

IE   See *Internet Explorer.*

IEEE   See *Institute of Electrical and Electronic Engineers.*

IIS   See *Internet Information Services.*

incoming connection   A process used to allow connections to be established with the remote computer. The connection methods used with incoming connections include dial-up modem, *virtual private network (VPN)*, and direct connections.

incremental backup   A *backup type* that backs up only the files that have changed since the last normal or incremental backup. It sets the archive attribute on the files that are backed up.

Indexing Service   A Windows XP *service* that creates an index based on the contents and properties of files stored on the computer's local hard drive. A user can then use the Windows XP Search function to search or query through the index for specific keywords.

Information event   An *Event Viewer* entry that informs you that a specific action has occurred, such as when a system shuts down or starts.

Infrared Data Association (IrDA)   A set of infrared protocols that are used by wireless devices for communication. IrDA uses short-range, high speed, bi-directional communication. Examples of devices that can use IrDA for communication include laptops, desktop computers, cameras, printers, and Personal Digital Assistants (PDAs).

inherited permissions   Parent folder permissions that are applied to (or inherited by) files and subfolders of the parent folder. In Windows XP Professional, the default is for parent folder permissions to be applied to any files or subfolders in that folder.

initial user account   The account that uses the name of the registered user and is created only if the computer is installed as a member of a workgroup (not into the *Active Directory*). By default, the initial user is a member of the *Administrators group.*

Institute of Electrical and Electronic Engineers (IEEE)   A professional organization that defines standards related to networks, communications, and other areas.

Institute of Electrical and Electronic Engineers (IEEE) 1394 standard   A standard that supports data transfer at speeds up to 400Mbps. Some of the trademark names for this standard are FireWire, I-link, and Lynx.

Integrated Services Digital Network (ISDN)   Provides digital telephone service. In order to use ISDN, an ISDN line must be installed and configured by the remote client and the server site. Basic-rate ISDN lines can support transmissions of up to 128Kbps (kilobits per second) and use two 64Kbps channels. ISDN normally uses a dial-up connection, rather than a permanent connection.

Intel architecture   A family of microprocessors descended from the Intel 8086, itself descended from the first microprocessor, the Intel 4004. The Intel architecture is the dominant microprocessor family. It was used in the original IBM PC microcomputer adopted by the business market and later adapted for home use.

Interactive group   A Windows XP *special group* that includes all the users who use the computer's resources locally.

interactive logon   A *logon* when the user logs on from the computer where the user account is stored on the computer's local database. Also called a *local logon*.

interactive user   A user who physically logs onto the computer where the user account resides (rather than logging on over the network).

internal network number   An identification for *NetWare* file servers. An internal network number is also used if the network is running File and Print Services for NetWare or is using IPX routing. This option must be configured to run the *NWLink IPX/SPX/NetBIOS Compatible Transport* protocol on a Windows XP computer. Normally, the internal network number should be left at its default setting.

Internet Connection Firewall (ICF)   A service used by Windows XP to protect a computer that is connected to the Internet from unauthorized Internet access.

Internet Connection Sharing (ICS)   A Windows XP feature that allows a small network to be connected to the Internet through a single connection. The computer that dials into the Internet provides network address translation, addressing, and name resolution services for all of the computers on the network. Through Internet connection sharing, the other computers on the network can access Internet resources and use Internet applications, such as Internet Explorer and Outlook Express.

Internet Explorer (IE)   A World Wide Web browser produced by Microsoft and included with Windows 9*x*, Windows Me, Windows NT 4, Windows 2000, and now Windows XP.

Internet Information Services (IIS)   Software that serves Internet higher-level protocols such as *HTTP* and *FTP* to clients using web browsers. The IIS software that is installed on a Windows Server 2003 computer is a fully functional web server and is designed to support heavy Internet usage. A scaled-down version of IIS server is included with Windows XP Professional.

Internet Printing Protocol (IPP)   A Windows XP protocol that allows users to print directly to a *URL*. Printer- and job-related information are generated in *HTML* format.

Internet printer   A Windows XP feature that allows users to send documents to be printed through the Internet.

Internet Protocol (IP)   The Network layer protocol upon which the Internet is based. IP provides a simple connectionless packet exchange. Other protocols such as TCP use IP to perform their connection-oriented (or guaranteed delivery) services.

Internet Protocol Security (IPSec)   A remote data encryption standard that uses Data Encryption Standard (DES) encryption, which is a suite of cryptography-based security protocols. IPSec uses computer-level authentication and provides data encryption services for *Layer Two Tunneling Protocol (L2TP)* and *virtual private network (VPN)* connections. IPSec services include packet data *authentication*, data integrity, replay protection, and data confidentiality services. *Point-to-Point Tunneling Protocol (PPTP)* only provides packet data confidentiality services.

Internet service provider (ISP)   A company that provides dial-up connections to the Internet.

Internet Services Manager   A Windows XP utility used to configure the protocols that are used by *Internet Information Services (IIS)*.

internetwork   A network made up of multiple network segments that are connected with some device, such as a router. Each network segment is assigned a network address. Network layer protocols build routing tables that are used to route packets through the network in the most efficient manner.

InterNIC   The agency that is responsible for assigning *IP addresses*.

interprocess communications (IPC)   A generic term describing any manner of client/server communication protocol. IPC mechanisms provide a method for the client and server to trade information.

interrupt request (IRQ)   A hardware signal from a peripheral device to the microcomputer indicating that it has input/output (I/O) traffic to send. If the microprocessor is not running a more important service, it will interrupt its current activity and handle the interrupt request. IBM PCs have 16 levels of interrupt request lines. Under Windows XP, each device must have a unique interrupt request line.

intranet   A privately owned network based on the *TCP/IP* protocol suite.

IP   See *Internet Protocol*.

IP address   A four-byte number that uniquely identifies a computer on an IP *internetwork*.

IP over ATM   Used to provide IP services over *ATM*. IP over ATM maps IP requests to ATM and ATM requests to IP using an ATM Address Resolution Protocol (ATMARP) server, which is implemented through Windows 2000 Server or Windows Server 2003, on each IP subnet that will provide IP and ATM addressing and emulation services.

IPC   See *interprocess communications*.

IPCONFIG   A command used to display the computer's *IP* configuration.

IPSec   See *Internet Protocol Security*.

IPP   See *Internet Printing Protocol*.

IrDA   See *Infrared Data Association*.

IRQ   See *interrupt request*.

ISA See *Industry Standard Architecture.*

ISDN See *Integrated Services Digital Network.*

ISP See *Internet service provider.*

K

kernel The core process of a preemptive operating system, consisting of a multitasking scheduler and the basic security services. Depending on the operating system, other services such as virtual memory drivers may be built into the kernel. The kernel is responsible for managing the scheduling of *threads* and *processes.*

L

L2TP See *Layer Two Tunneling Protocol.*

LAN See *Local Area Network.*

LANE See *LAN Emulation.*

LAN Emulation (LANE) Used to support *Asynchronous Transfer Mode (ATM)* over Ethernet or *Token Ring* networks and to access LAN-aware applications without any additional modifications.

Last Known Good Configuration option A Windows XP Advanced Options menu item used to load the control set that was used the last time the computer was successfully booted.

Layer Two Tunneling Protocol (L2TP) An industry-standard VPN protocol that is used in conjunction with IP *security (IPSec)* to provide a high level of security when sending *IP* packets over the Internet or other public IP network. L2TP and IPSec provide data *authentication*, data *encryption*, and data integrity services that strengthen security when data is sent over an unsecured network.

LGPO See *Local Group Policy Object.*

Local Area Network (LAN) An access standard that is used to provide connectivity in a local corporate or home environment. The connection methods supported by Windows XP Professional for LAN access include *Ethernet, Token Ring, FDDI, HPNA, 802.11 wireless LANs, IrDA, LANE,* and *IP* over *ATM.*

Local Computer Policy snap-in A *Microsoft Management Console (MMC) snap-in* used to implement local group policies, which include computer configuration policies and user configuration policies.

local group A group that is stored on the local computer's accounts database. These are the groups that administrators can add users to and manage directly on a Windows XP Professional computer.

local group policies   A combination of security settings that are used to specify the levels of security defined on a Windows XP computer.

Local Group Policy Object (LGPO)   A set of security configuration settings that are applied to users and computers. LGPOs are created and stored on the Windows XP Professional computer.

Local Group Policy snap-in   The utility that is used to create and manage *local group policies*.

local logon   A *logon* when the user logs on from the computer where the user account is stored on the computer's local database. Also called an interactive logon.

local policies   Policies that allow administrators to control what a user can do after logging on. Local policies include *audit policies*, *security option policies*, and *user right policies*. These policies are set through *Local Computer Policy snap-in*.

local printer   A printer that uses a *physical port* and that has not been shared. If a printer is defined as local, the only users who can use the printer are the local users of the computer that the printer is attached to.

local security   Security that governs a local or interactive user's ability to access locally stored files. Local security can be set through *NTFS permissions*.

local user account   A user account stored locally in the user accounts database of a computer that is running Windows XP Professional.

local user profile   A profile created the first time a user logs on, stored in the Documents and Settings folder. The default user profile folder's name matches the user's logon name. This folder contains a file called NTUSER.DAT and subfolders with directory links to the user's *Desktop* items.

Local Users and Groups   A utility that is used to create and manage local user and group accounts on Windows XP Professional computers and Windows Server 2003 member servers.

locale settings   Settings for regional items, including numbers, currency, time, date, and input locales.

logical drive   An allocation of disk space on a hard drive, using a *drive letter*. For example, a 50GB logical drive could be partitioned into two logical drives: a C: drive, which might be 20GB, and a D: drive, which might be 30GB.

logical port   A port that connects a device directly to the network. Logical ports are used with printers by installing a network card in the printers.

logical printer   The software interface between the physical printer (the *print device*) and the operating system. Also referred to as just a *printer* in Windows XP terminology.

logoff   The process of closing an open session with a Windows XP computer or Windows domain.

logon   The process of opening a session with a Windows XP computer or a network by providing a valid authentication consisting of a user account name and a password. After logon, network resources are available to the user according to the user's assigned *permissions*.

logon script   A command file that automates the *logon* process by performing utility functions such as attaching to additional server resources or automatically running different programs based on the user account that established the logon.

M

Magnifier   A Windows XP utility used to create a separate window to magnify a portion of the screen. This option is designed for users who have poor vision.

mandatory profile   A *user profile* created by an administrator and saved with a special extension (.man) so that the user cannot modify the profile in any way. Mandatory profiles can be assigned to a single user or a group of users.

mapped drive   A shared network folder associated with a drive letter. Mapped drives appear to users as local connections on their computers and can be accessed through a drive letter using My Computer.

Master Boot Record (MBR)   A record used in the Windows XP *boot* sequence to point to the active partition, which is the partition used to boot the operating system. This is normally the C: drive. Once the MBR locates the active partition, the boot sector is loaded into memory and executed.

MB   See *megabyte*.

MBR   See *Master Boot Record*.

megabyte   A computer storage measurement equal to 1,024 kilobytes.

megahertz   One million cycles per second. The internal clock speed of a microprocessor is expressed in megahertz (MHz).

member server   A Windows Server 2003 or Windows 2000 Server that has been installed as a non-domain controller. This allows the server to operate as a file, print, and application server without the overhead of account administration.

memory   Any device capable of storing information. This term is usually used to indicate volatile *random-access memory (RAM)* capable of high-speed access to any portion of the memory space, but incapable of storing information without power.

MHz   See *megahertz*.

Microsoft Challenge Handshake Authentication Protocol (MS-CHAP)   A remote access authentication protocol and is Microsoft's extension to *CHAP*. It is designed to work with computers and networks that are using Windows 98, Windows Me, Windows NT 4 (all versions),

Windows 2000 (all versions), Windows XP (all versions), and Windows Server 2003. Windows 95 computers are also supported, but require you to use the Windows Dial-up Networking 1.3 Performance and Security Upgrade for Windows 95.

Microsoft Challenge Handshake Authentication Protocol Version 2 (MS-CHAPv2) A remote access authentication protocol that adds to the services provided by *CHAP* by providing mutual *authentication*, different *encryption* keys for sending and receiving, and stronger data encryption keys. Windows 2000 (all versions), Windows XP (all versions), and Windows Server 2003 can use MS-CHAPv2 with dial-up and *virtual private network (VPN)* connections. If you are using Windows NT 4 (all versions) or Windows 95/98 computers, you can only use MS-CHAPv2 authentication with VPN connections.

Microsoft Disk Operating System (MS-DOS) A 16-bit operating system designed for the 8086 chip that was used in the original IBM PC. MS-DOS is a simple program loader and *file system* that turns over complete control of the computer to the running program and provides very little service beyond file system support and that provided by the *BIOS*.

Microsoft Ethernet PVC Used to support *Ethernet* and *IP* data encapsulation services over an *Asynchronous Transfer Mode (ATM)* permanent virtual connection. Ethernet PVC is typically used to provide remote connectivity services for home networks that use Asymmetric Digital Subscriber Line (ADSL) modems. ADSL is a technology that allows you to use existing copper telephone lines to support data rate transmissions of 1.5Mbps to 9Mbps for receiving data and from 16Kbps to 640Kbps for sending data. The ADSL modem would connect to the *Public Switched Telephone Network (PSTN)*. At the PSTN service provider, a Digital Subscriber Line Access Multiplexer (DSLAM) would act as a bridge to an ATM switch located at the host network that will be accessed by the remote client.

Microsoft Installer (MSI) A standard that is used to automatically deploy applications with *Windows Installer packages*.

Microsoft Management Console (MMC) A console framework for management applications. The MMC provides a common environment for *snap-ins*.

Microsoft Point-to-Point Encryption (MPPE) A remote data encryption standard that is a *Point-to-Point Protocol (PPP)* data encryption option that uses Rivest-Shamir-Adleman (RSA) RC4 encryption. MPPE supports strong (128-bit key) or standard (40-bit key) encryption. In order to use MPPE data encryption over a dial-up or *virtual private network (VPN)* connection, the remote client and server that will be accessed must use the *MS-CHAP, MS-CHAPv2,* or *EAP authentication* protocols.

MMC See *Microsoft Management Console.*

modem Modulator/demodulator. A device used to create an analog signal suitable for transmission over telephone lines from a digital data stream. Modern modems also include a command set for negotiating connections and data rates with remote modems and for setting their default behavior.

MPPE See *Microsoft Point-to-Point Encryption.*

MS-CHAP   See *Microsoft Challenge Handshake Authentication Protocol*.

MS-CHAPv2   See *Microsoft Challenge Handshake Authentication Protocol Version 2*.

MS-DOS   See *Microsoft Disk Operating System*.

MSI   See *Microsoft Installer*.

multi-booting   The process of allowing a computer to *boot* multiple operating systems.

My Computer   The folder used to view and manage a computer. My Computer provides access to all local and network drives, as well as *Control Panel*.

My Documents   The default storage location for documents that are created. Each user has a unique My Documents folder.

My Network Places   The folder that provides access to shared resources, such as local network resources and web resources.

N

Narrator   A Windows XP utility used to read aloud on-screen text, dialog boxes, menus, and buttons. This utility requires some type of sound output device.

NetBEUI   See *NetBIOS Extended User Interface*.

NetBIOS   See *Network Basic Input/Output System*.

NetBIOS Extended User Interface (NetBEUI)   A simple Network layer transport protocol developed to support *NetBIOS* installations. NetBEUI is not routable, and so it is not appropriate for larger networks. NetBEUI is the fastest transport protocol available for Windows XP.

Net PC/PC 98   A standard for PCs using industry-standard components for the PC, including *processor*, *memory*, *hard disk drive*, video, audio, and an integrated *network adapter* and *modem*, in a locked case with limited expandability capabilities. Net PCs cost less to purchase and to manage.

NET USE   A command-line utility used to map network drives.

NetWare   A popular network operating system developed by Novell in the early 1980s. NetWare is a cooperative, multitasking, highly optimized, dedicated-server network operating system that has client support for most major operating systems. Recent versions of NetWare include graphical client tools for management from client stations. At one time, NetWare accounted for more than 70 percent of the network operating system market.

network adapter   The hardware used to connect computers (or other devices) to the network.

Network Basic Input/Output System (NetBIOS)   A client/server *interprocess communications (IPC)* service developed by IBM in the early 1980s. NetBIOS presents a relatively primitive mechanism for communication in client/server applications, but its widespread acceptance and availability across most operating systems make it a logical choice for simple network applications. Many of the network IPC mechanisms in Windows XP are implemented over NetBIOS.

Network Configuration Operators group   Members of the *Network Configuration Operators group* have some administrative rights to manage the computer's network configuration.

Network group   A Windows XP *special group* that includes the users who access a computer's resources over a network connection.

network printer   A *printer* that is available to local and network users. A network printer can use a *physical port* or a *logical port*.

New Technology File System (NTFS)   A secure, transaction-oriented file system developed for Windows NT and used by Windows 2000, Windows XP, and Windows Server 2003. NTFS offers features such as *local security* on files and folders, *data compression*, *disk quotas*, and *data encryption*.

normal backup   A *backup type* that backs up all selected folders and files and then marks each file that has been backed up as archived.

NTBOOTDD.SYS   A file accessed in the Windows XP *boot* sequence. NTBOOTDD.SYS is an optional file (the *SCSI* driver) that is used when the computer has a SCSI adapter with the on-board *BIOS* disabled.

NTDETECT.COM   A file accessed in the Windows XP *boot* sequence. NTDETECT.COM is used to detect any hardware that is installed and add information about the hardware to the *Registry*.

NTFS   See *New Technology File System*.

NTFS permissions   Permissions used to control access to *NTFS* folders and files. Access is configured by allowing or denying NTFS permissions to users and groups.

NTLDR   A file used to control the Windows XP *boot* process until control is passed to the NTOSKRNL.EXE file.

NTOSKRNL.EXE   A file accessed in the Windows XP *boot* sequence. NTOSKRNL.EXE is used to load the *kernel*.

NTUSER.DAT   The file that is created for a *user profile*.

NTUSER.MAN   The file that is created for a *mandatory profile*.

NWLink IPX/SPX/NetBIOS Compatible Transport   Microsoft's implementation of the Novell IPX/SPX protocol stack.

O

offline files and folders   A Windows XP feature that allows network folders and files to be stored on Windows XP clients. Users can access network files even if the network location is not available.

On-Screen Keyboard   A Windows XP utility that displays a keyboard on the screen and allows users to enter keyboard input by using a mouse or other input device.

optimization   Any effort to reduce the workload on a hardware component by eliminating, obviating, or reducing the amount of work required of the hardware component through any means. For instance, file *caching* is an optimization that reduces the workload of a hard disk drive by reducing the number of requests sent to the hard disk drive.

organizational unit (OU)   In *Active Directory*, an organizational unit is a generic folder used to create a collection of objects. An OU can represent a department, division, location, or project group. Used to ease administration of AD objects and as a unit to which group policy can be deployed.

OU   See *organizational unit*.

owner   The user associated with an *NTFS* file or folder who is able to control access and grant permissions to other users.

P

page file   Logical memory that exists on the hard drive. If a system is experiencing excessive paging (swapping between the page file and physical RAM), it needs more memory.

PAP   See *Password Authentication Protocol*.

partition   A section of a hard disk that can contain an independent *file system* volume. Partitions can be used to keep multiple operating systems and file systems on the same hard disk.

Password Authentication Protocol (PAP)   A remote access authentication protocol. It is the simplest authentication method. It uses unencrypted, plain text passwords. You would use PAP if the server you were connecting to didn't support secure validations or you were trouble-shooting remote access and wanted to use the most basic authentication option.

password policies   Windows XP policies used to enforce security requirements on the computer. Password policies are set on a per-computer basis, and they cannot be configured for specific users. Password policies are set through *account policies*.

PB   See *petabyte*.

PC Card   A special credit-card-sized device used to add devices to a laptop computer. Also called a *Personal Computer Memory Card International Association (PCMCIA) card*.

PCI   See *Peripheral Component Interconnect*.

PCMCIA card   See *Personal Computer Memory Card International Association (PCMCIA) card*.

Performance Logs and Alerts   A Windows XP utility used to log performance-related data and generate *alerts* based on performance-related data.

Peripheral Component Interconnect (PCI)   A high-speed, 32/64-bit bus interface developed by Intel and widely accepted as the successor to the 16-bit Industry Standard Architecture (ISA) interface. PCI devices support input/output (I/O) throughput about 40 times faster than the ISA bus.

permissions   Security constructs used to regulate access to resources by username or group affiliation. Permissions can be assigned by administrators to allow any level of access, such as read-only, read/write, or delete, by controlling the ability of users to initiate object services. Security is implemented by checking the user's *security identifier (SID)* against each object's *discretionary access control list (DACL)*.

Personal Computer Memory Card International Association (PCMCIA) card   A special credit-card-sized device used to add devices to a laptop computer. Also called a *PC Card*.

petabyte   A computer storage measurement that is equal to 1,024 *terabytes*.

physical port   A serial (COM) or parallel (LPT) port that connects a device, such as a printer, directly to a computer.

PING   A command used to send an Internet Control Message Protocol (ICMP) echo request and echo reply to verify that a remote computer is available.

Plug and Play   A technology that uses a combination of hardware and software to allow the operating system to automatically recognize and configure new hardware without any user intervention.

Point-to-Point Protocol (PPP)   A set of remote authentication protocols used by Windows during remote access for interoperability with third-party remote access software.

Point-to-Point Protocol over Ethernet (PPPoE)   A protocol that uses *PPP* to provide remote connectivity services via *Ethernet*. PPP is a set of remote authentication protocols used by Windows during remote access for interoperability with third-party remote access software. To use PPPoE, each PPP session uses a discovery protocol to learn the Ethernet address of the remote peer and establishes a unique session identifier.

Point-to-Point Tunneling Protocol   An open industry-standard developed by Microsoft and other industry leaders to provide support for tunneling of *Point-to-Point Protocol (PPP)* frames through an *Internet Protocol (IP)* network. PPP provides *authentication*, *compression*, and *encryption* services.

policies   General controls that enhance the *security* of an operating environment. In Windows XP, policies affect restrictions on password use and rights assignments, and determine which events will be recorded in the *Security log*.

POST   See *Power-On Self-Test*.

Power-On Self-Test (POST)   A part of the Windows XP *boot* sequence. The POST detects the computer's *processor*, how much memory is present, what hardware is recognized, and whether the *BIOS* is standard or has *Plug and Play* capabilities.

Power Users group   A Windows XP built-in group that has fewer rights than the *Administrators group*, but more rights than the *Users group*. Members of the Power Users group can perform tasks such as creating local users and groups and modifying the users and groups that they have created.

PPP   See *Point-to-Point Protocol*.

PPPoE   See *Point-to-Point Protocol over Ethernet*.

PPTP   See *Point-to-Point Tunneling Protocol*.

Pre-boot eXecution Environment (PXE)   A technology that allows a client computer to remotely boot and connect to a *Remote Installation Services (RIS)* server.

primary partition   A part of *basic storage* on a disk. The primary partition is the first partition created on a hard drive. The primary partition uses all of the space that is allocated to the partition. This partition is usually marked as active and is the partition that is used to *boot* the computer.

print device   The actual physical printer or hardware device that generates printed output.

print driver   The specific software that understands a *print device*. Each print device has an associated print driver.

print processor   The process that determines whether a print job needs further processing once that job has been sent to the *print spooler*. The processing (also called *rendering*) is used to format the print job so that it can print correctly at the *print device*.

print queue   A directory or folder on the *print server* that stores the print jobs until they can be printed. Also called a print spooler.

print server   The computer on which the printer has been defined. When a user sends a print job to a *network printer*, it goes to the print server first.

print spooler   A directory or folder on the *print server* that stores the print jobs until they can be printed. Also called a print queue.

printer   In Windows XP terminology, the software interface between the physical printer (see *print device*) and the operating system.

printer pool   A configuration that allows one printer to be used for multiple *print devices*. Printer pooling can be used when multiple printers use the same *print driver* (and are normally in the same location). With a printer pool, users can send their print jobs to the first available printer.

priority   A level of execution importance assigned to a *thread*. In combination with other factors, the priority level determines how often that thread will get computer time according to a scheduling algorithm.

process   A running program containing one or more *threads*. A process encapsulates the protected memory and environment for its threads.

processor   A circuit designed to automatically perform lists of logical and arithmetic operations. Unlike microprocessors, processors may be designed from discrete components rather than be a monolithic integrated circuit.

processor affinity   The association of a *processor* with specific *processes* that are running on the computer. Processor affinity is used to configure multiple processors.

protocol   An established rule of communication adhered to by the parties operating under it. Protocols provide a context in which to interpret communicated information. Computer protocols are rules used by communicating devices and software services to format data in a way that all participants understand.

PSTN   See *Public Switched Telephone Network.*

Public Switched Telephone Network (PSTN)   The network that provides regular, analog phone service.

published applications   Applications installed with *Windows Installer packages.* Users can choose whether they will install published applications through the Control Panel Add or Remove Programs icon. Administrators can choose to have published applications installed when the applications are invoked.

PXE   See *Pre-boot eXecution Environment.*

R

RAM   See *random-access memory.*

random-access memory (RAM)   Integrated circuits that store digital bits in massive arrays of logical gates or capacitors. RAM is the primary memory store for modern computers, storing all running software processes and contextual data.

RAS   See *Remote Access Service.*

RBFG   See *Remote Boot Floppy Generator.*

real-time application   A *process* that must respond to external events at least as fast as those events can occur. Real-time *threads* must run at very high priorities to ensure their ability to respond in real time.

Recovery Console   A Windows XP option for recovering from a failed system. The Recovery Console starts Windows XP without the graphical interface and allows the administrator limited capabilities, such as adding or replacing files and enabling and disabling services.

Recycle Bin   A folder that holds files and folders that have been deleted. Files can be retrieved or cleared (for permanent deletion) from the Recycle Bin.

REGEDIT   A Windows program, the *Registry Editor*, which is used to edit the *Registry.*

Regional Options   A *Control Panel* utility used to enable and configure multilingual editing and viewing on a localized version of Windows XP Professional.

Registry   A database of settings required and maintained by Windows XP and its components. The Registry contains all of the configuration information used by the computer. It is stored as a hierarchical structure and is made up of keys, hives, and value entries.

Registry Editor   The utility used to edit the Windows XP registry. You can use *REGEDIT* or REGEDT32.

remote access connections   A method for allowing remote clients connectivity to a private network or the Internet.

Remote Access Service (RAS)   A service that allows network connections to be established over a modem connection, an *Integrated Services Digital Network (ISDN)* connection, or a null-modem cable. The computer initiating the connection is called the RAS client; the answering computer is called the RAS server.

Remote Assistance   A mechanism for requesting help for x86-based computers through Windows Messenger and e-mail, or by sending a file requesting help. To use Remote Assistance, the computer requesting help and the computer providing help must be using Windows XP Professional and must have some sort of interconnectivity.

Remote Boot Floppy Generator (RBFG)   If you are using *Remote Installation Services* and the RIS client computer is not using a *Pre-boot eXecution Environment (PXE)*-based boot ROM, then you can use this utility to create a RIS-boot disk.

Remote Desktop   A new tool for Windows XP Professional that allows you to take control of a remote computer's keyboard, video, and mouse. This tool does not require that someone collaborate with you on the remote computer. While the remote computer is being accessed, it remains locked and any actions that are performed remotely will not be visible to the monitor that is attached to the remote computer.

Remote Desktop Users group   A special group automatically created on Windows XP Professional computers that is used in conjunction with the Remote Desktop service.

remote installation   Installation of Windows XP Professional performed remotely through *Remote Installation Services (RIS)*.

Remote Installation Preparation (RIPrep) image   A type of image configured on a *Remote Installation Services (RIS)* server. A RIPrep image can contain the Windows XP operating system and applications. This type of image is based on a preconfigured computer.

Remote Installation Preparation (RIPrep) Tool   A utility used to prepare a pre-installed and configured Windows XP Professional computer for disk imaging and then to replicate the *disk image* to a *Remote Installation Services (RIS)* server.

Remote Installation Services (RIS)   A Windows XP technology that allows the remote installation of Windows XP Professional. A RIS server installs Windows XP Professional on RIS clients. The RIS server can be configured with a *CD-based image* or a *Remote Installation Preparation (RIPrep) image*.

Removable Storage   A Windows XP utility used to track information on removable storage media, which include CDs, DVDs, tapes, and jukeboxes containing optical discs.

rendering   The process that determines whether a print job needs further processing once that job has been sent to the spooler. The processing is used to format the print job so that it can print correctly at the *print device*.

Replicator group   A Windows XP built-in group that supports *directory replication*, which is a feature used by domain servers. Only *domain user accounts* that will be used to start the replication service should be assigned to this group.

Requests for Comments (RFCs)   The set of standards defining the Internet protocols as determined by the Internet Engineering Task Force and available in the public domain on the Internet. RFCs define the functions and services provided by each of the many Internet protocols. Compliance with the RFCs guarantees cross-vendor compatibility.

resource   Any useful service, such as a *shared folder* or a *printer*.

Restore Wizard   A Wizard used to restore data. The Restore Wizard is accessed through the *Backup utility*.

RFC   See *Requests for Comments*.

RIPrep image   See *Remote Installation Preparation image*.

RIS   See *Remote Installation Services*.

roaming profile   A *user profile* that is stored and configured to be downloaded from a server. Roaming profiles allow users to access their profiles from any location on the network.

router   A Network layer device that moves packets between networks. Routers provide *internetwork* connectivity.

S

Safe Mode   A Windows XP Advanced Options menu item that loads the absolute minimum of *services* and *drivers* that are needed to start Windows XP. The drivers that are loaded with Safe Mode include basic files and drivers for the mouse (unless a serial mouse is attached to the computer), monitor, keyboard, hard drive, standard video driver, and default system services. Safe Mode is considered a diagnostic mode. It does not include networking capabilities.

Safe Mode with Command Prompt   A Windows XP Advanced Options menu item that starts Windows XP in *Safe Mode*, but instead of loading the graphical interface, it loads a command prompt.

Safe Mode with Networking   A Windows XP Advanced Options menu item that starts Windows XP in *Safe Mode*, but adds networking features.

SCP   See *Service Control Point.*

SCSI   See *Small Computer Systems Interface.*

security   The measures taken to secure a system against accidental or intentional loss, usually in the form of accountability procedures and use restriction—for example, through *NTFS permissions* and *share permissions.*

Security Configuration and Analysis Tool   A utility that is used to analyze and help configure the computer's local security settings. This utility works by comparing your actual security configuration to a security template configured with your desired settings.

security identifier (SID)   A unique code that identifies a specific user or group to the Windows XP security system. SIDs contain a complete set of *permissions* for that user or group.

Security log   A log that tracks events that are related to Windows XP auditing. The Security log can be viewed through the *Event Viewer* utility.

security option policies   Policies used to configure security for the computer. Security option policies apply to computers rather than to users or groups. These policies are set through *Local Computer Policy snap-in.*

separator page   A page used at the beginning of each document to identify the user who submitted the print job. When users share a printer, separator pages can be useful for distributing print jobs.

serial   A method of communication that transfers data across a medium one bit at a time, usually adding stop, start, and check bits.

serial cable   A type of cable used for data transmission. Serial cables transmit data one bit at a time, as opposed to parallel cables, which transmit data eight bits at a time. However, serial cables support longer distances between devices than parallel cables. There is a special form of serial cable, called a null-modem cables, which is used to emulate modem connectivity through the use of a special serial cable that has been modified to support direct asynchronous communication between two computers over a short distance. This option is sometimes used to troubleshoot remote access server problems in a local setting.

Serial Line Internet Protocol (SLIP)   An older *wide area network (WAN)* protocol that is used with some Unix servers. The *Point-to-Point Protocol (PPP)* protocol is used for incoming remote connections within a Microsoft environment.

service   A *process* dedicated to implementing a specific function for another process. Most Windows XP components are services used by user-level applications.

Service Control Point (SCP)   An object access entry point within the *Active Directory* that is used in conjunction with *Remote Installation Services.*

Service group   A Windows XP *special group* that includes users who log on as a user account that is only used to run a *service*.

service pack   An update to the Windows XP operating system that includes bug fixes and enhancements.

Services utility   A Windows XP utility used to manage the *services* installed on the computer.

Setup Manager (SETUPMGR)   A Windows XP utility used to create automated installation scripts or unattended *answer files*.

SETUPMGR   See *Setup Manager*.

share   A *resource* such as a folder or printer shared over a network.

share permissions   Permissions used to control access to shared folders. Share permissions can only be applied to folders, as opposed to *NTFS permissions*, which are more complex and can be applied to folders and files.

shared folder   A folder on a Windows XP computer that network users can access.

Shared Folders   A Windows XP utility for managing *shared folders* on the computer.

Shiva Password Authentication Protocol (SPAP)   A remote access authentication method that encrypts passwords with a two-way encryption scheme. With this option, Windows XP Professional, Windows 2000 Server, and Windows Server 2003 are able to dial into Shiva network access servers. Conversely, Shiva clients can remotely access Windows XP Professional, Windows 2000 Servers, and Windows Server 2003 computers using SPAP.

shortcut   A quick link to an item that is accessible from a computer or network, such as a file, program, folder, printer, or computer. Shortcuts can exist in various locations including the *Desktop* and the *Start menu*, or within folders.

SID   See *security identifier*.

Simple Mail Transfer Protocol (SMTP)   An Internet protocol for transferring mail between Internet hosts. SMTP is often used to upload mail directly from the client to an intermediate host, but can only be used to receive mail by computers constantly connected to the Internet.

simple volume   A *dynamic disk* volume that contains space from a single disk. The space from the single disk can be contiguous or noncontiguous. Simple volumes are used when the computer has enough disk space on a single drive to hold an entire volume.

SIS   See *Single Instance Store*.

SIS Groveler service   This service works in conjunction with files used for automated installation when using *disk images*. The *SIS* Groveler service scans the SIS volume for files that are identical. If identical files are found, this service creates a link to the duplicate files instead of storing duplicate files.

Single Instance Store (SIS)   The Single Instance Store (SIS) manages duplicate copies of disk images by replacing duplicates with a link to the original files. This service works in conjunction with *disk images* used for Windows XP automated installations.

SLIP   See *Serial Line Internet Protocol.*

slipstream technology   A Windows XP technology for *service packs.* With slipstream technology, service packs are applied once, and they are not overwritten as new services are added to the computer.

Small Computer Systems Interface (SCSI)   A high-speed, parallel-bus interface that connects hard disk drives, CD-ROM drives, tape drives, and many other peripherals to a computer. SCSI is the mass-storage connection standard among all computers except IBM compatibles, which use SCSI or IDE.

smart card   A special piece of hardware with a microchip, used to store public and private keys, passwords, and other personal information securely. Can be used for other purposes, such as telephone calling and electronic cash payments.

SMTP   See *Simple Mail Transfer Protocol.*

snap-in   An administrative tool developed by Microsoft or a third-party vendor that can be added to the *Microsoft Management Console (MMC)* in Windows XP.

SPAP   See *Shiva Password Authentication Protocol.*

spanned volume   A *dynamic disk* volume that consists of disk space on 2 to 32 dynamic drives. Spanned volume sets are used to dynamically increase the size of a dynamic volume. With spanned volumes, the data is written sequentially, filling space on one physical drive before writing to space on the next physical drive in the spanned volume set.

special group   A group used by the Windows XP, in which membership is automatic if certain criteria are met. Administrators cannot manage special groups.

spooler   A service that buffers output to a low-speed device such as a printer, so the software outputting to the device is not tied up waiting for the device to be ready.

Standby   A power management option. Standby does not save data automatically as *hibernation* does. With Standby you can access your computer more quickly than a computer that is in hibernation, usually through a mouse click or keystroke, and the Desktop appears as it was prior to the standby. The response time depends on the level of your computer's standby state. On an *Advanced Configuration and Power Interface (ACPI)*–compliant computer, there are three levels of standby, each level putting the computer into a deeper sleep. The first level turns off power to the monitor and hard drives. The second level turns off power to the CPU and cache. The third level supplies power to RAM only and preserves the Desktop in memory.

Start menu   A Windows XP *Desktop* item, located on the *Taskbar.* The Start menu contains a list of options and programs that can be run.

stripe set   A single *volume* created across multiple hard disk drives and accessed in parallel for the purpose of optimizing disk-access time. *NTFS* can create stripe sets.

striped volume   A *dynamic disk* volume that stores data in equal stripes between 2 to 32 dynamic drives. Typically, administrators use striped volumes when they want to combine the space of several physical drives into a single logical volume and increase disk performance.

subnet mask   A number mathematically applied to *IP addresses* to determine which IP addresses are a part of the same subnetwork as the computer applying the subnet mask.

Success Audit event   An *Event Viewer* entry that indicates the occurrence of an event that has been audited for success, such as a successful logon.

Support_*xxxxxxx*   Microsoft uses the Support_*xxxxxxx* account for the Help and Support Service. This account is disabled by default.

Sysprep   See *System Preparation Tool.*

System Configuration Utility   A utility that allows the administrator to see and edit configuration information about the computer. You access this utility through the `Msconfig` command-line utility.

System group   A Windows XP *special group* that contains system processes that access specific functions as a user.

System Information   A Windows XP utility used to collect and display information about the computer's current configuration.

System log   A log that tracks events that relate to the Windows XP operating system. The System log can be viewed through the *Event Viewer* utility.

System Monitor   A Windows XP utility used to monitor real-time system activity or view data from a log file.

system partition   The active *partition* on an *x*86–based computer that contains the hardware-specific files used to load the Windows XP operating system.

System Preparation Tool (Sysprep)   A Windows XP utility used to prepare a *disk image* for disk duplication.

System State data   A set of data that is critical to the operating system booting and includes the Registry, the COM+ registration database, and the system boot files.

System Tools   A Computer Management utility grouping that provides access to utilities for managing common system functions. The System Tools utility includes the *Event Viewer*, *System Information*, *Performance Logs and Alerts*, *Shared Folders*, *Device Manager*, and *Local Users and Groups* utilities.

T

T1 carried leased line   Before the introduction of current high-speed remote access network options, leased lines were used to provide a faster, permanent link as an alternative to dial-up networking. Leased lines are typically implemented as a T-carrier line—for example, a T1 or fractional T1 line. This legacy technology is still used and supported by Windows XP Professional, but is quickly being replaced by more cost-effective networking options.

Task Manager   A Windows XP utility that can be used to start, end, or prioritize applications. The Task Manager shows the applications and *processes* that are currently running on the computer, as well as *CPU* and *memory* usage information.

Task Scheduler   A Windows XP utility used to schedule tasks to occur at specified intervals.

Taskbar   A Windows XP *Desktop* item, which appears across the bottom of the screen by default. The Taskbar contains the *Start menu* and buttons for any programs, documents, or windows that are currently running on the computer. Users can switch between open items by clicking the item in the Taskbar.

TB   See *terabyte*.

TCP   See *Transmission Control Protocol*.

TCP/IP   See *Transmission Control Protocol/Internet Protocol*.

TCP/IP port   A *logical port* used when a printer is attached to the network by installing a network card in the printer. Configuring a TCP/IP port requires the IP address of the network printer to connect to.

terabyte (TB)   A computer storage measurement that equals 1,024 *gigabytes*.

Terminal Server User group   A Windows XP *special group* that includes users who log on through Terminal Services.

TFTP   See *Trivial File Transfer Protocol*.

thread   A list of instructions running in a computer to perform a certain task. Each thread runs in the context of a *process*, which embodies the protected memory space and the environment of the threads. Multithreaded processes can perform more than one task at the same time.

Token Ring   A LAN technology that was developed by IBM in the 1970s, and is defined by the *IEEE* 802.5 specification. In a Token Ring network, all nodes are wired into a physical ring. A token is used to manage communications. Token Ring is more difficult to install and configure and is more expensive than *Ethernet*. It is rarely used in corporate or home environments. Token Ring is most typically used in networks that use IBM equipment and require IBM connectivity.

Transmission Control Protocol (TCP)   A Transport layer protocol that implements guaranteed packet delivery using the *IP* protocol.

Transmission Control Protocol/Internet Protocol (TCP/IP)   A suite of Internet protocols upon which the global Internet is based. TCP/IP is a general term that can refer either to the *TCP* and *IP* protocols used together or to the complete set of Internet protocols. TCP/IP is the default protocol for Windows XP.

Trivial File Transfer Protocol (TFTP)   A network application that is simpler than the *File Transfer Protocol (FTP)* but less capable. It is used where user *authentication* and directory visibility are not required. TFTP is used to download the Windows XP Client Installation Wizard from the *Remote Installation Services (RIS)* server to the RIS clients. TFTP uses the *User Datagram Protocol (UDP)*.

U

Unattend.txt   An *answer file* used in conjunction with *unattended installations* to provide answers to installation queries that would normally be supplied by an interactive user.

unattended installation   A method of installing Windows XP Professional remotely with little or no user intervention. Unattended installation uses a *distribution server* or the Windows XP Professional CD to install Windows XP Professional on a target computer.

UNC   See *Universal Naming Convention*.

Uniform Resource Locator (URL)   An Internet standard naming convention for identifying resources available via various *TCP/IP* application protocols. For example, `http://www`.`microsoft.com` is the URL for Microsoft's World Wide Web server site, and `ftp://gateway`.`dec.com` is a popular *FTP* site. A URL allows easy hypertext references to a particular resource from within a document or mail message. A URL always has the *domain* name on the right and the *host* name on the left.

uninterruptible power supply (UPS)   An emergency power source that can provide a limited amount of power to a computer in the event of a power outage.

Universal Naming Convention (UNC)   A multivendor, multiplatform convention for identifying shared resources on a network. UNC names follow the naming convention `\\`*`computername`*`\`*`sharename`*.

Universal Serial Bus (USB)   An external bus standard that allows USB devices to be connected through a USB port. USB supports transfer rates up to 12Mbps. A single USB port can support up to 127 devices.

upgrade   A method for installing Windows XP that preserves existing settings and preferences when converting to the newer operating system from Windows NT 4 Workstation or Windows 2000 Professional.

upgrade pack   Software in the form of a migration DLL (dynamic link library) used with applications that need to be upgraded to work with Windows XP.

Upgrade Report   A report generated by the Windows XP Professional Setup program when upgrading to Windows XP Professional from a previous operating system. The report summarizes any known compatibility issues that you might encounter during the upgrade. The Upgrade Report can be saved as a file or printed.

UPS   See *uninterruptible power supply*.

URL   See *Uniform Resource Locator*.

USB   See *Universal Serial Bus*.

user profile   A profile that stores a user's *Desktop* configuration and other preferences. A user profile can contain a user's Desktop arrangement, program items, personal program groups, network and printer connections, screen colors, mouse settings, and other personal preferences. Administrators can create *mandatory profiles*, which cannot be changed by the users, and *roaming profiles*, which users can access from any computer they log onto.

user right policies   Policies that control the rights that users and groups have to accomplish network tasks. User right policies are set through *Local Computer Policy snap-in*.

User State Migration Tool (USMT)   A utility used by administrators to migrate users from one computer to another via a command-line utility.

username   A user's account name in a logon authenticated system.

Users group   A Windows XP built-in group that includes end users who should have very limited system access. After a *clean install* of Windows XP Professional, the default settings for this group prohibit users from compromising the operating system or program files. By default, all users who have been created on the computer, except the *Guest account*, are members of the Users group.

USMT   See *User State Migration Tool*.

Utility Manager   A Windows XP utility used to manage the three accessibility utilities: *Magnifier*, *Narrator*, and *On-Screen Keyboard*.

V

video adapter   The hardware device that outputs the display to the monitor.

virtual memory   A *kernel* service that stores memory pages not currently in use on a mass-storage device to free the memory occupied for other uses. Virtual memory hides the memory-swapping process from applications and higher-level services.

virtual private network (VPN)   A private network that uses secure links across private or public networks (such as the Internet). When data is sent over the remote link, it is encapsulated, encrypted, and requires *authentication* services.

volume A storage area on a Windows XP *dynamic disk*. Dynamic volumes cannot contain *partitions* or *logical drives*. Windows XP Professional dynamic storage supports three dynamic volume types: *simple volumes*, *spanned volumes*, and *striped volumes*. Dynamic volumes are accessible only to Windows 2000, Windows XP, and Windows Server 2003. They are not accessible through DOS, Windows 9*x*, Windows Me, or Windows NT.

VPN See *virtual private network*.

W

WAN See *wide area network*.

Warning event An *Event Viewer* entry that indicates that you should be concerned with the event. The event may not be critical in nature, but it is significant and may be indicative of future errors.

web browser An application that makes *HTTP* requests and formats the resultant *HTML* documents for the users. Most web browsers understand all standard Internet protocols.

wide area network (WAN) Used to connect two geographically dispersed areas together via a persistent connection. Connection methods used with WANs include *T1 carried leased line*, *cable modem*, *DSL*, and *Frame Relay*.

Win16 The set of application services provided by the 16-bit versions of Microsoft Windows: Windows 3.1 and Windows for Workgroups 3.11.

Win32 The set of application services provided by the 32-bit versions of Microsoft Windows: Windows 95, Windows 98, Windows Me, Windows NT, Windows 2000, Windows XP, and Windows Server 2003.

Windows 9*x* The 32-bit Windows 95, Windows 98, and Windows Me versions of Microsoft Windows for medium-range, *x*86-based personal computers. This system includes peer networking services, Internet support, and strong support for older DOS applications and peripherals.

Windows Backup The utility used to access the *Backup Wizard*, the *Restore Wizard*, and *Automated System Recovery* options.

Windows Installer packages Special application distribution files used to automate the installation of applications. Windows Installer packages work with applications that are in *Microsoft Installer (MSI)* format or *ZAP file* format. The use of Windows Installer packages requires a Windows XP Server computer with *Active Directory* installed.

Windows Internet Name Service (WINS) A network service for Microsoft networks that provides Windows computers with the *IP address* for specified *NetBIOS* computer names, facilitating browsing and intercommunication over *TCP/IP* networks.

Windows NT The predecessor to Windows 2000 that is a 32-bit version of Microsoft Windows for powerful Intel, Alpha, PowerPC, or MIPS-based computers. These operating systems include Windows NT 3.1, Windows NT 3.5, Windows NT 3.51, and Windows NT 4 and include peer networking services, server networking services, Internet client and server services, and a broad range of utilities.

Windows Update   A utility that connects the computer to Microsoft's website and checks the files to make sure that they are the most up-to-date versions.

Windows XP boot disk   A disk that can be used to *boot* to the Windows XP Professional operating system in the event of a Windows XP Professional boot failure.

Windows XP Client Installation Wizard (CIW)   A program that is used with *Remote Installation Services (RIS)* to automate Windows XP Professional installation to provide clients with the list of available images that can be used with the *automated installation*.

Windows XP Deployment Tools   A set of management tools, which include the *Setup Manager* utility for creating unattended *answer files*, as well as the *System Preparation Tool* utility for creating disk images. The Deployment Tools are stored on the Windows XP Professional CD, in \Support\Tools, in the Deploy.cab file. You can extract these files by using the File ➤ Extract command in Windows Explorer.

Windows XP Multilanguage Version   The version of Windows XP that supports multiple-language user interfaces through a single copy of Windows XP.

Windows XP Professional   The current version of the Windows operating system for high-end desktop environments. Windows XP Professional integrates the best features of Windows 98, Windows Me, and Windows 2000 Professional, and supports a wide range of hardware, makes the operating system easier to use, and reduces the cost of ownership.

WINNT.EXE   A program used to install or upgrade to Windows XP Professional from computers that are running Windows 98, Windows Me, Windows NT 4 Workstation, Windows 2000 Professional, or Windows XP Home Edition. You would run WINNT.EXE from all other operating systems.

WINNT32.EXE   A program used to install Windows XP Professional on a computer that is not running Windows 98, Windows Me, Windows NT 4 Workstation, Windows 2000 Professional, or Windows XP Home Edition. You would run Winnt from all other operating systems.

WINS   See *Windows Internet Name Service*.

WINS server   The server that runs *WINS* and is used to resolve *NetBIOS* computer names to *IP addresses*.

WMI Control   A Windows XP utility that provides an interface for monitoring and controlling system resources. WMI stands for Windows Management Instrumentation.

workgroup   In Microsoft networks, a collection of related computers, such as those used in a department, that do not require the uniform security and coordination of a domain. Workgroups are characterized by decentralized management, as opposed to the centralized management that domains use.

write-back caching   A caching optimization wherein data written to the slow store is cached until the cache is full or until a subsequent write operation overwrites the cached data. Write-back caching can significantly reduce the write operations to a slow store because many write operations are subsequently obviated by new information. Data in the write-back cache is also available for subsequent reads. If something happens to prevent the cache from writing data to the slow store, the cache data will be lost.

write-through caching   A caching optimization wherein data written to a slow store is kept in a cache for subsequent rereading. Unlike *write-back caching*, write-through caching immediately writes the data to the slow store and is therefore less optimal but more secure.

X

X.25   A remote access technology that is used to provide connections between terminal- and packet-switching networks, which was a common network structure prior to the introduction of *ISDN* and *Frame Relay* connection methods. Because of its early widespread use, it is still sometimes used in tandem with newer technologies.

Z

ZAP files   Files that can be used with *Windows Installer packages* instead of *Microsoft Installer (MIS)* format files. ZAP files are used to install applications using their native Setup program.

Index

Note: **Bolded** page numbers refer to main discussions of a topic and to definitions. *Italicized* page numbers refer to illustrations and to tables.

X

Z

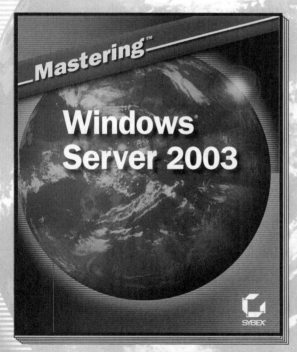

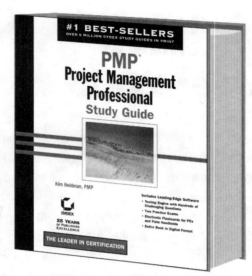

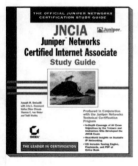

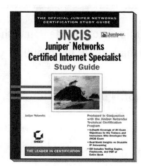
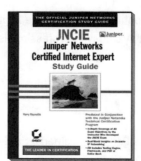

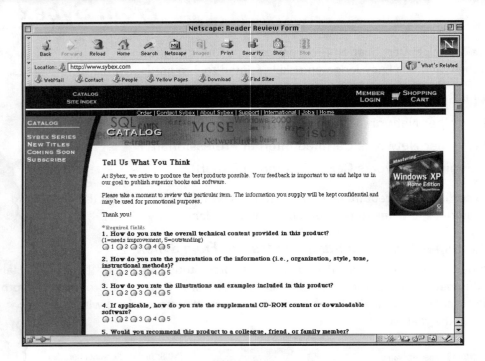

Sybex Offers the Complete Solution

MCSA/MCSE: Windows Server 2003 Environment Management and Maintenance Study Guide
ISBN 0-7821-4260-5 • $49.99

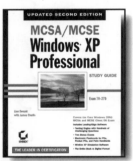

MCSA/MCSE: Windows XP Professional Study Guide, Second Edition
ISBN 0-7821-4241-9 • $49.99

MCSA: Windows 2003 Core Requirements
ISBN 0-7821-4264-8 • $119.99

The Microsoft Certified Systems Administrator (MCSA) will put you on the path to manage and maintain the computing environment of medium- to large-sized companies.

MCSA 2003 Track

Choose ONE Client OS Requirement	
Exam #	**Exam**
70-210	Installing, Configuring and Administering Microsoft Windows 2000 Professional
70-270	Installing, Configuring and Administering Windows XP Professional

2 Network Operating System Requirements	
Exam #	**Exam**
70-290	Managing and Maintaining a Microsoft Windows Server 2003 Environment
70-291	Implementing, Managing, and Maintaining a Microsoft Windows Server 2003 Network Infrastructure

Choose ONE Elective	
Exam #	**Exam**
70-086	Implementing and Supporting Microsoft Systems Management Server 2.0
70-227	Installing, Configuring, and Administering Microsoft Internet Security and Acceleration (ISA) 2000
70-228	Installing, Configuring and Administering SQL Server 2000
	CompTIA A+ and Network+ combo
	CompTIA A+ and Server+ combo

For a list of all Sybex products that will help prepare you for any of the MCSA exams, visit **www.sybex.com**.